Andy Beckett was born ten days ... studied Modern History at Oxfor... ... the University of California in Berke... ...rst, widely praised book, *Pinochet in Piccadilly: Britain and Chile's Hidden History* (2002), he was nominated as *Sunday Times* Young Writer of the Year. Since 1993, he has written for the *New York Times*, the *Economist*, the *Independent on Sunday* and the *London Review of Books*. For the last twelve years, he has been a feature writer at the *Guardian*. He lives in London.

Further praise for *When the Lights Went Out*:

'A triumph . . . fresh, stylish. . . brilliantly researched . . . Beckett seems to have interviewed almost every one of the Seventies' movers and shakers . . . When it is written as well as this, history can constantly take you by surprise . . . It's hard to imagine anyone writing a more lucid, revealing and enjoyable book about the decade.' David Robinson, *Scotsman*

'No one will ever write a better biography of the 1970s . . . The decade formed my politics and Andy Beckett captures it perfectly . . . I just couldn't put it down.' Ken Livingstone

'Thoughtful, balanced and illuminating.' Brian Groom, *Financial Times*

'As Britain once again lurches from boom to bust, as security alerts continue to punctuate our days, and a re-born Conservative Party threaten to take office, the 1970s have never seemed closer, and the legacy of that decade never more relevant. In an absorbing and compelling narrative, Andy Beckett vividly tells the history of that most complex of decades, destroying the old clichés and providing new insights.' David Peace

'Very entertaining.' Dominic Sandbrook, *Sunday Times*

'Fascinating . . . This revealing and honest look at the decade goes well beyond the clichés.' Simone Baird, *Time Out*

When the Lights Went Out

What Really Happened to Britain in the Seventies

ANDY BECKETT

faber and faber

by the same author

PINOCHET IN PICCADILLY

———————————

First published in 2009
by Faber and Faber Ltd
Bloomsbury House
74–77 Great Russell Street
London WC1B 3DA
This paperback edition first published in 2010

Typeset by Faber and Faber Limited
Printed in England by CPI Bookmarque, Croydon

Lyrics from 'Part of the Union' by John Ford and Richard Hudson (Strawbs),
reprinted with the permission of Fazz Music

A CIP record for this book
is available from the British Library

ISBN 978-0-571-22137-0

10 9 8 7 6 5 4 3 2 1

For my parents

Contents

List of Illustrations ix
Introduction: Our Weimar? 1

Part One: Optimism

1 Champagne and Rust 9
2 The Great White Ghost 19
3 Heathograd 33

Part Two: Shocks

4 Close the Gates! 53
5 Questions of Sovereignty 88
6 Lights Out 125
7 Waiting for the Collapse 157

Part Three: New Possibilities

8 The Great Black Hope 185
9 The Real Sixties 209
10 Get Out of the City 234
11 Margaret and the Austrians 260
12 A Relationship of Forces 289
13 Marxism at Lunchtime 307

Part Four: The Reckoning

14 William the Terrible 317
15 Brent vs the Cotswolds 358
16 Getting Away with It? 404
17 Pressures Building 434
18 The Peasants' Revolt 464
19 Last-ditch Days 498

CONTENTS

Conclusion: The Long Seventies 516
Acknowledgements 525
Chronology 526
Sources 529
Index 555

Illustrations

1 Edward Heath celebrates winning the June 1970 general election.

2 Heath's dream of the future: an early model of Maplin airport, planned by his government to be built on an artificial island off Southend-on-Sea.

3 Striking miners swamp the police cordon and close the Saltley coke depot in Birmingham in February 1972.

4 A Belfast street on a bad day in the seventies.

5 When the lights went out: Piccadilly Circus partly blacked-out during the three-day week, 1 February 1974.

6 Harold Wilson, a fading prime minister by 1975, in the custody of Jack Jones, General Secretary of the Transport and General Workers' Union, and Vic Feather, Secretary of the Trades Union Congress.

7 North Sea oil rigs under construction at Nigg in the Scottish Highlands, mid-seventies.

8 Members of the Gay Liberation Front protest on behalf of arrested members of the Women's Liberation Front outside Bow Street Magistrates Court, 4 February 1971.

9 Sid Rawle, hippy anarchist and organiser of the 1975 Watchfield free festival, arrives for a meeting at the Department of the Environment, 20 August 1975.

10 Waiting for the next Britain: the newly-built Civic Centre in Milton Keynes, May 1977.

11 Police shove back pickets so that a bus carrying Grunwick employees who are still working can get through, 11 July 1977.

12 Jayaben Desai, one of the leaders of the strike at the Grunwick plants between 1976 and 1978.

13 The limits of seventies union power: pickets stuck outside 'Fort Grunwick', as George Ward called his premises, summer 1977.

14 Prime Minister Jim Callaghan speaking in Tamworth during the 1979 general election.

15 Public Enemy Number One: Jamie Morris, ex-Tory, militant shop steward, and leader of the infamous strike at Westminster Hospital during the Winter of Discontent.

16 The shape of things to come: Margaret Thatcher speaking two months before becoming prime minister.

Introduction: Our Weimar?

The seventies. Two words that have won a million British political arguments. All countries have their difficult eras – periods of national embarrassment, of slipping confidence, of decline, of crisis, both real and imagined. We are in one now. But for Britain since the Second World War, by common consent for decades now, the worst of times came between the election of Edward Heath in 1970 and the election of Margaret Thatcher in 1979.

Here is Tony Blair, speaking at the 2005 Labour Party conference, shortly after the death of perhaps the most tainted seventies prime minister of all, James Callaghan:

When I listened on Sunday to the tributes to Jim Callaghan, I recalled the 90th birthday party we gave for him at Downing Street a few years back. Around the room: Denis Healey talking to Roy Jenkins; Tony Benn with Shirley Williams. Michael Foot, Jack Jones. What brilliance; and what a pity . . . They were great people. But they were not ready [before 1979] to see change was coming . . . And if they had been, how many fewer lives would have been destroyed? How much harsh and bitter medicine for some of the poorest in our society might have been avoided?

And here is David Cameron, barely a teenager when the seventies ended, still feeling he should include a passage about the decade in a speech to the think tank Demos in 2006:

Economic decline was embodied in inflation, stagnation and rising unemployment . . . deteriorating industrial relations: unions versus management, workers versus the bosses . . . In 1950 1,389,000 working days were lost to industrial action. By 1979, this had multiplied to 29,400,074 – the highest on record. Margaret Thatcher set out to deal not only with the problems of this British disease but also with its causes . . . With huge courage and perseverance, she turned Britain into a different country.

I was born in 1969. The politics of the seventies, even in their broadest sense, are in the blurriest margins of my childhood memories. In 1974, in retrospect around the high-water mark of radical hippiedom in provincial England, I remember mysterious hairy men coming and going between terrifying banks of nettles to a disused glasshouse they had turned into an 'arts centre' behind our back garden in the Hertfordshire suburbs. In the feverish summer of 1975, a boom time for plots and protests in Britain, I remember being frustrated on holiday in Suffolk by the first test-cricket match I had tried to follow. With England close to victory, the match, inexplicably to my mind, was called off. Saboteurs seeking the release from prison of an East End robber I had never heard of had poured oil on the wicket. Two years later, in the snowy, bad-tempered winter of 1977 – a dress rehearsal, it turned out, for the Winter of Discontent the year after – I remember my father, then a colonel in the Royal Engineers, working late and seeming slightly irritable. The firemen were on strike and he had suddenly become Kent's chief fire officer. And in the slow grey spring of 1979, with Margaret Thatcher moving seemingly unstoppably towards Downing Street, I remember watching the election build-up on television in my grandmother's bedroom. I remember feeling sorry for Callaghan, without knowing exactly why.

I can't recall much else. But I have been hearing what was wrong with Britain and British politics in the seventies all my adult life. No other political theme has been as unrelenting. The seventies were grim. The seventies were the hangover from the sixties. The seventies were violent. The seventies were a dead end. Above all: we don't want to go back to the seventies.

The decade of Watergate and Baader Meinhof, of world recession and the oil crisis, was a jarring period for most wealthy countries, just like the current one. Yet Britain's problems in the seventies were widely seen at the time – and since, by foreign as well as domestic commentators – as among the worst in the West. Since then, Britain has arguably changed more than any other rich nation. Part of this transformation is down to the power of British prime ministers with large parliamentary majorities to impose their domestic policies, which is greater than in most democracies, and to the effectiveness at this task of Margaret Thatcher in particular. But her eighties majorities and policies and ways of operating politically were, in a substantial sense, products of the previous decade. They were reactions against the 'failures' of the seventies, a counter-revolution against its consensuses, a determination not to repeat its 'mistakes'.

I grew up in the eighties and nineties basically believing the traditional story of the British seventies. After all, it was not just Thatcherites who told it: left-wing people would scorn or regret the Callaghan years; liberals would condemn the brutality towards Irish republicans under Edward Heath; almost no one had a good word for the Harold Wilson administration of 1974–6.

Yet occasionally this version of the seventies would seem too neat. First, there was the question of seventies popular culture. Almost as soon as that decade was over, people had started reviving its tastes. By 2000, as far as such things can be measured, the seventies had probably even overtaken the sixties as the British nostalgia market's favourite. How had the dead-end Britain of the seventies produced such a flowering of pop music, fashion and television? Some of it could be attributed to the stimulus of bad times – seventies Britain as a kind of Weimar Republic, a spooky parallel often invoked under Wilson and Callaghan – while some of the recurring appetite for seventies culture could be put down to simple generational nostalgia and love of kitsch.

But these explanations have a blind spot. If Britain was so sickly in the seventies, where did people get the money at the time to buy so many records and bold pairs of trousers? A poster campaign mounted by the Labour Party in 2005 inadvertently provided an answer. 'Lowest Unemployment for 29 Years', the posters read in fat pink seventies letters. For anyone who also knew about another, more famous political billboard concerning the Labour Party and unemployment – Saatchi and Saatchi's corrosive 'Labour Isn't Working' campaign for the Conservatives against the Callaghan government in 1978 – the 2005 posters came as an unexpected corrective. Unemployment in the seventies, taken at the time to be a great symptom of political failure, and notorious as such ever since, was actually low by modern standards, even during the long economic boom of the Blair years.

In 2004, the respected radical think tank the New Economics Foundation devised a new index of national economic, social and environmental well-being called the Measure of Domestic Progress (MDP). By this measure the best year in Britain since 1950 turned out to be, rather astonishingly, 1976 – the year of the IMF crisis, of Wilson's undignified resignation, of the disillusioned fury of the Sex Pistols and British punk rock. I read the British press reports about this finding with some scepticism. What pleasures had 1976 offered except for a famously hot summer? Then, later in 2004, I came across an interview with the Sex Pistols' singer Johnny Rotten in an old issue of the *New Musical Express* from the seventies. On his band's biggest and bleakest single, 1977's 'God Save the Queen', he had famously sung that England had 'no future'. Now it was late December 1978; the Sex Pistols had split up and the Winter of Discontent was starting to bite. Rotten, who had reverted to his sober actual surname Lydon but was living surrounded by half-drunk cans of lager, did the interview from bed. Yet the interviewer also noted some details that told of a different seventies:

John Lydon lives in the upper maisonette of the end terrace of a row of sturdily built Victorian houses on the Fulham/Chelsea border. He picked it up very cheaply indeed shortly before the beginning of the current property boom. It was, he says, one of the sharpest things he ever did . . .

This book is not a complete rewriting of the decade. Something profound and unsettling did happen to Britain in the seventies, and Britons have been living with the consequences ever since. At the very least, the British seventies showed that an old, stable, supposedly exemplary democracy can have a crisis of confidence. During the most turbulent middle years of the decade, the director general of the National Economic Development Council, or 'Neddy', one of those vanished seventies institutions where trade unions, government and business would attempt to collaborate for the greater good – or seem to collaborate for their own good – was a worldly and well-connected civil servant called Ronald McIntosh. He kept a diary. His entry, no grimmer in tone than those for many other dates, for 5 August 1975 read: 'Going to work I ran into Len Neal [another well-connected political fixer]. I asked him how he was, to which he replied, "Like everyone else, waiting for the collapse."'

Yet not all of the seventies was like this. In politics, things are never just moving in one direction, and especially not for an entire decade. For many political people in Britain in the seventies, the time was dominated not by Heath and Thatcher and Callaghan but by the rise of environmentalism, or feminism, or the Gay Liberation Front, or Rock Against Racism, and other new forms of politics with their own rhythms and preoccupations, only sometimes connected to those of the House of Commons. In the London listings magazine *Time Out* in the early seventies, between the sections for children's activities and exhibitions, there used to be a section called 'Revolution'. This is an entry from 1970:

COMMUNITY ACTION IN CABLE STREET Tenants in the Cable Street area have . . . a piece of previously derelict land that they seized and cleared. As soon as they did this, of course, the council suddenly discovered the land was theirs and that they needed it. But the tenants threatened to withdraw their kids from the local schools, and made contacts with local TV . . . who also made militant noises. The council gave in, so the tenants now have their own adventure playground.

British politics in the seventies, for all the gothic prose it usually prompts, was about moments of possibility as well as periods of entropy; about stretches of calm as well as sudden calamity. Politics was rawer and more honest – in the sense that conflicts between interests and ideologies were out in the open – than perhaps we are used to nowadays. It was also more obviously connected to everyday life – not just through the much higher turnouts at general elections, but through the disruptions wrought by the strikes and other shocks, by voters' living-room lights suddenly going out. And where all this was leading, finally, was much less fixed than we have tended to assume since. Right up until the last days of the 1979 general election, Margaret Thatcher was not the only possible answer to the questions the decade posed. Hindsight is a great simplifier, and the seventies as an era has been simplified more than most.

This book is not intended to be a traditional, encyclopedic history of a decade. It is the story of a search – my search – for the truth about an era, as much as the story of that era. This book tries to select and scrutinize – for in single, sometimes forgotten events the essence of a time quite often lies – rather than painstakingly list and summarize. It is mainly about the politics of the British seventies, broadly defined, rather than the country's wider culture during the period, which already has its own enormous and nearly exhaustive literature, and which has been dulled as a tool for understanding the mood and events of the period through overuse and carelessness. I have lost track of how many times I have read or heard that the punk revolt of 1976–7 was a 'reaction' to the Winter of Discontent of 1978–9. Of course, popular culture can tell us about an era's politics, intentionally and otherwise, but sometimes sifting it for such evidence, which anyway can be indistinct or ambiguous, leaves you studying political life at one remove. In the seventies, the heart of politics was often the picket line or the think-tank pamphlet – the clash of interest groups and ideas at its starkest. Much of what is most compelling and important about the period is right there, in its everyday political life.

Hopefully this book will restore some of the vivid complexity of the decade as it was actually experienced. Hopefully it will capture something of the seventies' political protagonists, many of whom have died since I interviewed them. And British politics in the seventies may come to seem both more fascinatingly alien and more like what has happened since.

Andy Beckett
London, January 2009

PART ONE
Optimism

1

Champagne and Rust

In British politics the seventies began as they would go on: with a shallow feeling of optimism followed by a jolt. The general election of 18 June 1970 seemed a predictable contest when campaigning started that spring. On one side was the Labour prime minister Harold Wilson, winner of the last two general elections, in this area of politics, if not all, famously shrewd and charming. On the other side was the Conservative leader Edward Heath, the loser of the last general election, a largely uninspiring head of the Opposition who was considered by his many critics to be naive and charmless. Heath had never won a general election. Wilson had never lost one. For most of the 1970 campaign, this did not appear likely to change.

The sun shone almost every day. Wilson dominated the Labour campaign with even less effort than usual. He smoked his pipe at press conferences. He sauntered through crowds in his raincoat. He mocked hecklers in his small, seductive voice. He carried himself like an American president with good ratings, like a much-loved northern entertainer of a certain age, like the personification of what was left of the confidence of the sixties. Wilson was fifty-four and had been an MP since the Second World War; he knew how to deploy his trademarks. And they were affectionately received: during the walkabouts he conducted all over Britain, so many women wanted to brush his raincoat that his wife Mary called them 'touchers'.

Heath campaigned less fluently. His morning press conferences, wrote his then aide Douglas Hurd in a candid account published much later, were 'uneasy and defensive'. In private, among 'serious people', Hurd continued, Heath was an excellent communicator. '[But] introduce a rostrum, a microphone, an interviewer . . . and the result could be disastrously different. The voice might change its quality. The vocabulary might become stilted . . . The thread of the argument might be lost in a mass of detail. Instead of trying to speak to people, Mr Heath would too often speak at them.'

His infrequent walkabouts had something of the same quality. His stride was a little too fast, his smile a little too fixed, his handshake a little too brisk. For a politician with a liking for consensus he had a striking ability to enrage. On the night of the election result, a Labour supporter infiltrated the crowd outside Conservative Central Office in London and stubbed out a cigarette on Heath's thick, tanned neck.

For much of the campaign Heath was protected from such gestures. After his morning press conference and his daily television engagements he would take off each lunchtime in a private plane with staff and journalists to travel to a rally outside London with a selected audience. Electioneering by air was intended to be efficient and to look modern – key Heath preoccupations. Wilson campaigned by train; Heath did not like trains. But his faith in technology, not for the last time, proved over-optimistic. 'The weather was hot,' recalled Heath's then parliamentary private secretary Jim Prior. 'The plane journey generally bumpy, the whole affair was extraordinarily tiring and likely to make anyone tense.' Hurd recalls: 'On 8 June we sat miserable in fierce sunshine on the tarmac at Heathrow [waiting] for the appearance from the airline's catering department of the packed lunches on which we and all the accompanying journalists had relied. Those cross, hot and hungry moments were a low point of the campaign.'

Electioneering always has its frictions, yet even the Conservatives' tiniest ones were taken as significant this time, because almost everyone thought Heath was losing badly. In Britain, the opinion polls had correctly predicted the outcome of every general election since the Second World War. For most of the Wilson government between 1966 and 1970, which had been punctuated by crises, the Conservatives had been comfortably in the lead despite Heath's shortcomings. In July 1969, with a general election due in less than two years, the Conservatives were ahead by an average of over 19 per cent: a crushing victory at the next election looked possible, a comfortable one better than probable. But then the government's difficulties started to abate, and the Conservative lead disappeared. By April 1970, Labour were ahead – the strongest sustained surge in the polls that had ever been recorded. In early May, the party gained hundreds of seats in local elections, a rare feat for a government in its latter stages. A few days later, Wilson announced the date of the general election, which was almost a year earlier than it needed to be – the sign of a confident prime minister. The same month, the pollsters Gallup put Wilson's personal ratings lead over Heath at 21 per cent.

Labour's advantage over the Conservatives was actually much slimmer – an average of 3 per cent in mid-May – but the momentum seemed to be with them. During the campaign, their lead in the polls held, and in some surveys grew. The bookmakers Ladbrokes lengthened their odds on a Conservative win from 11/10 in early June to 6/1 in mid-June. Then they stopped taking bets on a Labour victory altogether. The mood of the press was similar. 'It was unnerving', wrote Hurd, 'to travel through this campaign in the company of highly intelligent journalists who were convinced that we had already lost. They were polite, even sympathetic, but they knew the answer, and it was not ours. Two of them were already writing a book during the campaign to explain *how* we had lost.'

On 13 June, for its final issue before the election *The Economist* put a photograph of the prime minister and his chancellor Roy Jenkins on the cover. The accompanying headline – 'In Harold Wilson's Britain' – avoided direct predictions, but it suggested that the Labour leader was the British politician who mattered, not least by making no mention of Heath at all. And the photograph underlined the message. Wilson and Jenkins were pictured walking side by side in the sunshine along a spotless pavement, by the look of it somewhere in Whitehall, with elegant iron railings to their right and solid old buildings in the distance. Wilson was grey-haired and watchful, his head like a great silver cannonball; Jenkins, four years younger, a little less solid around the waist, had a hint of a smile playing across his broad, amused mouth. The two of them were walking perfectly in step, shoes gleaming, official papers in their hands, gaits unflustered but purposeful. With their matching dark suits and old-fashioned parted haircuts they still had a strong air – as did much of

Britain in 1970 – of the fifties or even the thirties. And they looked like members of a ruling establishment with quite a few years to run.

This sense of the government's impregnability infected many Conservatives. 'Most of us – including myself – thought that we would lose,' wrote Margaret Thatcher, then the shadow education secretary. 'The gloom steadily deepened during the campaign.' Hurd remembers: 'The opinion polls were hypnotic.' Six days before the election, he helplessly watched a journalist inform Heath of a new poll giving Labour a lead of 12.4 per cent and then ask the Conservative leader for his reaction. 'I cannot remember his reply, but I can remember the blank look on his face.'

In the run-up to the campaign and throughout it, there were murmurs in Conservative circles that Heath was about to be ousted. Even for the Conservatives, with their famous lack of squeamishness about replacing unsatisfactory leaders, this was a sign of panic. The coup never materialized, but on election day itself Heath was left in no doubt about how the party's feelings towards him were running. 'At lunchtime,' he remembers in his autobiography, 'there was an unexpected visit from Peter Carrington [the influential shadow defence secretary]. After congratulating me on the fight, he told me that, should we lose, I would be expected immediately to stand down.'

On 18 June, the polling stations closed as usual at 10 p.m. Wilson went with journalists and his retinue to the place he customarily received good news on general election night: the grand old Adelphi Hotel in Liverpool, a few miles from his constituency. The day before, the minister for technology Tony Benn, at this stage a Wilson ally and protégé, reflected the prevailing Labour view of the coming result in his diary: 'We should win by a large majority, certainly with a working majority.'

Heath was not even sure of getting a majority in his own constituency. At the last general election, his victory margin in Bexley in Kent, a semi-detached south London suburb with a Labour-voting past, had fallen to a vulnerable 2,333. This time, to make things worse, Heath faced a potentially damaging additional rival candidate: a campaigner against the European Common Market, which Heath wanted Britain to join, who had changed his name by deed poll to

Edward Heath. On election day in Bexley, Conservative activists had to stand outside polling stations with placards warning people against voting for the wrong Heath. That evening, the Conservative leader waited in the constituency for news of his local and national fate. 'I always remained confident,' he insists in his autobiography. But the star *Guardian* writer Terry Coleman, who spent the last two days of the campaign with him, gained a different impression:

He believed, even to the end, that he had lost. It was late at night [on 17 June] in the headmaster's study of a grammar school at Bexley . . . Mr Heath was alone, without his aides, and without his Central Office girls, who had all gone home. He poured himself half a tumbler full of whisky . . . and for the first time that day forgot to sit up straight, and for the first time let his suit sag around him . . . I asked some question about a biographer who had attributed to him . . . a belief that he was a man of destiny. Was he? . . . He mumbled something I couldn't catch, said after a while that the man who had talked about his feeling for destiny hadn't seen him for thirty-five years . . .

At the Adelphi, Wilson chatted happily to the reporters for half an hour or so after the polling stations closed. The usual election-day survey conducted by Labour Party headquarters in London of how the voting had gone had found nothing to disturb his confidence. But then came the first puzzling tremor. News arrived of a more independent and concrete survey, of people coming out of the polling booths in Gravesend in Kent, traditionally a revealing constituency. There appeared to have been a swing from Labour to the Conservatives of over 4 per cent. If this exit-poll figure proved correct and was repeated across Britain, all the pre-election polls may as well have been conducted on Mars. The Conservatives would win.

A few minutes later, at around 11 p.m., the first actual result came in. In Guildford there had been a swing to the Conservatives of 6 per cent. Wilson, who had retreated to his suite to see the results on television, like almost 20 million other Britons, reportedly said: 'I don't like the look of that swing.' Benn's reaction, as he watched in his Bristol constituency, was less understated: 'In a fraction of a second, one went from a pretty confident belief in victory to absolute certainty of defeat.'

His sudden pessimism was justified. By the time all the results were in, the Conservatives had a majority of thirty. In the early hours of 19 June, Heath was driven into London from Bexley, the results flowing like his favourite champagne from the car radio. He struggled deliciously through the cheering crowd of supporters and party workers outside Conservative Central Office, retired temporarily to his smart bachelor flat in Albany, an exclusive nineteenth-century enclave off Piccadilly, and there received a congratulatory phone call from the Conservative chief whip, his close ally Willie Whitelaw. Whitelaw told the London *Evening Standard* that Heath, who never usually showed his deeper feelings, was so emotional he could not speak. Later that day, after sleeping and accepting more calls, Heath set off from his flat for Central Office again. In his autobiography, published twenty-eight years later, he recalls what followed as if he still cannot quite believe it:

The [Albany] porter told me that there was a vast crowd waiting for me in Piccadilly. As soon as I appeared, the crowd surged across the road, stopping traffic and requiring a great deal of police activity to clear it away. Everyone looked remarkably pleased, cheerfully shouting congratulations and waving, without any sign of a hostile protester.

That evening, he was welcomed for the first time by the staff of 10 Downing Street. A photograph of the scene appears in the book. Heath's small eyes are tiny with delight. His big white smile looks genuine for once, almost sharkish with triumph. 'The experts, the know-alls, and the trend-setters had been confounded,' Hurd wrote of Heath's victory. Now Heath just had to confound them again – by reviving the country.

The notion of British decline had been around for over a century. In 1835, the British economic reformer Richard Cobden wrote after visiting the United States: 'Our only chance of national prosperity lies in the timely remodelling of our system, so as to put it as nearly as possible upon an equality with the improved management of the Americans.' At the time, Britain was the dominant economic, military and imperial power in the world – and would remain so for almost another fifty years. Cobden's worries could be dismissed as the sort you heard in any country with a degree of national self-consciousness and a past against which the present could be anxiously measured.

Yet his alarmism did contain an insight: the prospect of decline was built into Britain's nineteenth-century pre-eminence like the rust-prone metal on a battleship. Firstly, all superpowers lost their supremacy eventually; secondly, Britain had a modest population and resources; and thirdly, as the first country to have an industrial revolution, Britain was always going to see its lead slip economically when other countries enjoyed their own transformations. In the last three decades of the nineteenth century, America, Germany and other close competitors emerged, just as Cobden had feared. In the first five decades of the twentieth, Britain's position was further eroded by two costly world wars and too many overseas commitments. From 1945 onwards, the issue of Britain's decline changed from a matter for intermittent public debate into a major and growing preoccupation of political life.

The decline was seen as having diverse symptoms – not just military and territorial but moral, cultural, spiritual and physical. The centuries-old British empire was dismantled in a couple of decades. In the late forties, the 'brain drain' began, as promising scientists emigrated in search of better prospects. The national birth rate peaked in 1964 and then fell every year for the rest of the decade. Britain's cities, overcrowded to bursting in the Victorian boom years, emptied out. The population of Greater London dropped by 600,000 between 1961 and 1971. Many of the urban Britons who remained lived in landscapes spotted with decay: prematurely aged post-war housing estates, emptying docksides, bombsites unrepaired and lost to weeds, decades after the German air raids. The energy and colour of British popular culture during the sixties and early seventies – the peacock rock stars, the outrageous boutiques – could not disguise the fact that much of everyday life took place on streets of worn-out brown and grey.

Some of these symptoms of decline were deceptive, the products of social change – suburbanization, contraception – not social entropy. Other portents favoured by newspaper columnists and other professional declinists were ambiguous. Did the drug experiments of the Beatles or the unashamed randiness of *On the Buses* represent decadence or progress? It depended on your morals. There was one set of national symptoms, however, that seemed less subjective and more measurable, and which, as a result, was watched with a near-continuous intensity in post-war Britain. This was the state of the economy.

Between 1950 and 1970, the country's share of the world's manufacturing exports shrank from over a quarter to barely a tenth. Between 1950 and 1964, the British gross domestic product grew at an annual average of 3 per cent, while in Germany, France, Italy and Japan it grew at an average of at least 5 per cent. Between 1950 and 1976, British productivity grew at an annual average of 2.8 per cent, while in Germany it grew at 5.8 per cent and in Japan it grew at 7.5 per cent. There were other economic totems during these years: the value of the pound against the American dollar; the inflation and unemployment rates; the balance of payments. Such figures, in fact, can both distort and be distorted. Dates can be chosen to give a particular impression. Different national contexts – the contrasting economic positions of Britain and continental Europe at the end of the Second World War, for example – can be omitted from international comparisons. The precise definition of productivity, unemployment or inflation can be debated indefinitely. All economics is, to some degree, a construct, and the economic indicators given prominence in a particular era reflect that era's assumptions. Yet, despite these drawbacks, it is hard for such indicators to lie completely when considered together.

So it proved in Britain between the election of Clement Attlee in 1945 and the election of Heath in 1970. Over that period, Labour and Conservative governments were responsible for the economy to an almost equal degree, with Labour in office for twelve years, and the Conservatives for thirteen. Both parties had their successes. Labour rescued the economy from the damage and exhaustion of the Second World War. The Conservatives facilitated Britain's first mass consumer boom in the fifties. Both parties kept unemployment and poverty very low compared to the era between the First and Second World Wars – and compared to now. Britain in 1970, for all its economic anxieties, remained a rich country that was getting richer. *The British Household in the Seventies*, an authoritative marketing survey published in 1975, found 'a rising standard of living throughout the [post-war] period and, until 1973, no slowing down [in the rate of improvement] in spite of economic difficulties'.

But a country's material well-being, like a country's sense of its more cosmic trajectory, is partly relative. Between 1945 and 1970, many Britons were not doing as well economically as their counterparts in comparable countries, and neither of the main parties seemed able to do much about it. Booms lasting a year or two, often just before general elections, were followed by lingering recessions. At least once a decade, the pound fell disastrously on the international currency markets as foreign investors lost faith in Britain's prospects. Chancellors came and went, leaving office after a few years either having obviously failed or having deftly handed on their difficulties to their successor. With each stage of the whole jittery cycle, the more ominous indicators – inflation, unemployment – tended to edge a little higher.

Changes in the structure of the British economy made it seem more vulnerable. The post-war nationalization of large areas of heavy industry, itself partly an attempt to transform British business, made the success or failure of enterprises such as British Leyland a matter of patriotic importance. Meanwhile, the fashion in the private sector for joining companies together into large conglomerates created other economic virility symbols. In the protracted run-up to the 1964 general election, books such as Michael Shanks's *The Stagnant Society* and Arthur Koestler's *Suicide of a Nation?* caught the declinist mood. Wilson exploited it expertly. At the 1963 Labour conference, he described Britain as 'a nation of Gentlemen in a world of Players', with an economy enfeebled by 'restrictive practices' and 'outdated methods' that only a 'revolution' in government economic policy could sweep away. He won the election narrowly. In 1966, he called another and increased his majority to ninety-seven, big enough to be truly radical.

Over its two terms, the Wilson government of the sixties treated the economy as its central priority, creating a new Department of

Economic Affairs to augment the Treasury. In 1965, a national plan was devised, 'covering all aspects of the country's development for the next five years'. The plan set a target for Britain's economic growth: an increase of almost a third. Wilson himself was a trained economist; as his chancellor he had first Callaghan, a revered political operator, and then Jenkins, one of the ablest economic ministers since the war. The government had an unusual number of other significant talents, including the intense young Roundhead Tony Benn, Barbara Castle, the country's first potent female minister, and Tony Crosland, the leading British philosopher-politician of the post-war period.

Yet all this promise and initiative led not to economic salvation but to a succession of economic crises, climaxing in November 1967 with Callaghan's resignation and a forced devaluation of the pound, shocks from which the government never quite recovered. Over the next two and a half years, Jenkins restored a degree of calm and coherence to the Treasury. Some of the key economic statistics improved, and Labour revived in the polls. But when the general election came, for all Jenkins' and Wilson's reassurances, the state of the economy remained a potentially lethal issue for the government.

On 15 June, three days before the vote, the trade figures for the previous month were announced. Instead of an expected surplus, there was a small deficit of £31 million. More than half of the sum was something of a fluke: the one-off purchase of two jumbo jets from the US. Yet for the Conservatives, who had been trying, with mixed results, to make the weaknesses of the economy the focus of the election, the trade figures were just what they needed. 'On Monday 15 June the atmosphere began to lift,' Hurd writes. 'We handed [Heath] the unexpectedly bad trade figures in time for him to use them for the rest of the afternoon. There seemed then . . . a fleeting chance of success.' On the morning of polling day, a small-scale but thorough survey of voters by the Opinion Research Centre, conducted as the trade figures were being debated, gave the Conservatives an advantage of 1 per cent, their first lead for weeks. The poll was barely noticed or else dismissed as a freak. By the following evening, Heath was picking his Cabinet.

2

The Great White Ghost

In background and character, Heath was both the best and the worst kind of person to be a reforming prime minister. He had been born in 1916 in Broadstairs, a slightly prim clifftop resort in coastal Kent. His parents were like those of no previous Conservative leader. His mother Edith was in domestic service as a lady's maid until she had children. His father William was a carpenter who later became a small employer of other craftsmen. The Heaths lived in cramped, spotless houses, took in lodgers and looked to improve themselves. Edward, the eldest of two sons, serious, self-contained, precociously interested in adults, was quickly seen to have unusual potential. At eleven, he won a scholarship to the local grammar school, where he lobbied successfully to take the School Certificate exam a year early, and passed. In his final years, he became a school prefect with a reputation for strictness, and secretary of the debating society, making firm moralistic speeches. 'During the school holidays,' he remembered later, 'I particularly enjoyed sitting outside an ice-cream parlour in Broadstairs talking earnestly with my friends about the major issues of the day.'

Heath's upbringing was not overtly political. There were few family discussions about public affairs. But Broadstairs was a strongly Conservative seaside town, and the Heaths' modest upward mobility, typical of the place, exerted an influence. William switched from the Liberals to the Conservatives, while maintaining a fierce small businessman's dislike of the other alternative: 'I was never Labour,' he told the writer Anthony Sampson later. 'I had too much to do with labour to vote Labour.' In 1935, with a Conservative-dominated National Government in power in Westminster, Edward Heath stood as the National Government candidate in a mock school election. He won with the help of an endorsement he had solicited from the local Conservative MP.

As well as politics, Heath had a consuming interest in classical music. In 1934, he tried to win an organ scholarship to Cambridge. He failed, so he tried for an organ scholarship at Oxford. He failed, so he sought a scholarship to study politics, philosophy and economics there – and failed again. In the end, he had to accept an unfunded place at Oxford to take the combined degree. Kent County Council gave him a loan, and his parents, with difficulty and after some persuasion by his schoolteachers, paid the rest.

Heath arrived at Oxford in the autumn of 1935. Then, as now, it was a university made up of very different, semi-independent colleges. The one he had finally settled on was highly significant: Balliol. In the thirties, much of Oxford undergraduate life was flavoured, as it had long been, by smart social networks and a tendency not to take things too seriously. Yet, since the mid-nineteenth century, Balliol had self-consciously stood apart from such escapism and privilege. The college pioneered competitive entrance exams rather than entrance by wealth and connections; it actively sought students from less grand backgrounds and, with seemingly relentless efficiency, turned them into successful public men. Balliol produced senior civil servants and top colonial administrators, famous social reformers and chancellors, bishops and prime ministers, all in greater numbers than any comparable British institution. These 'Balliol men', as they sometimes called themselves with a degree of self-congratulation, were loyal members of the British Establishment, but also a distinct tribe within it: a little more driven and restless, more impatient with the traditional way of doing things, more liberal – in fact, often left-wing. Denis Healey, then a communist, was in the year below Heath at Balliol. Jenkins, whose father was a miner, was in the year below Healey. The master of the college was a Scottish socialist, A. D. Lindsay, who publicly supported the General Strike in 1926 and had Mahatma Gandhi to stay in his official lodgings for a fortnight during the Indian anti-imperialist's visit to Britain in 1931.

Broadstairs it was not. But Heath had chosen Balliol fully aware of its reputation. He quickly took to the college: 'No idea was too outrageous for examination,' he remembered. 'I revelled in the arguments.' At the end of his first term, he finally won a scholarship, which enabled him to be there for an extra year: 'This', he wrote, 'was a real privilege.'

Seven decades later, after studying at the college myself, I went to a reunion at Balliol for former undergraduates. It was the summer of 2000. Before dinner, we had drinks in the slow dusk in the main quadrangle. At the edge of the crowd, mostly casually dressed people in their twenties and thirties, I suddenly noticed Heath. He was then well into his eighties and was standing on his own, hugely stout, in a suit so pale it was almost luminous. There was an air of immense contentment about him. He came every year, someone told me afterwards, like a great white ghost.

At Oxford, Heath's politics matured. He joined the Oxford Union debating society and the Oxford University Conservative Association, both traditional training grounds for a young Tory with ambitions. But he was open to broader political experiences. He also joined Labour and Liberal undergraduate organizations, 'so that I could hear their main speakers', he wrote later. At Balliol, he listened attentively to Lindsay and the college's other socialists, and busily read books by a rising generation of left-wing or left-leaning authors. It was the mid-thirties, with the Depression dragging on and unemployment in Britain and elsewhere rising to unprecedented levels; it was hard for anyone political to avoid pondering the problems of contemporary capitalism. Even before Oxford, in Broadstairs, which like much of the south-east of England had escaped the worst, Heath's world view had been affected by the slump. 'I saw my father working hard in very difficult circumstances,' he told an interviewer later. Now, at Oxford, two books in particular further crystallized his thinking:

The first was John Maynard Keynes's *General Theory of Employment, Interest and Money*, published in 1936. Inspired by a world depression which had been caused by laissez-faire [free-market] policies, it put forward a wholly new view of economics . . . that full and stable levels of employment could be maintained if governments intervened counter-cyclically [subsidized economic growth during recessions] . . . Although his ideas were not put into practice in Britain until after the Second World War, they provided some intellectual basis for Roosevelt's 'New Deal', which was already successfully pulling America out of depression.

Heath was barely twenty when he read the *General Theory*, but it helped convince him 'once and for all' that 'neither socialism nor the pure free market could provide the answer'. What was needed was a kind of fusion of the two. Two years after the *General Theory*, another influential book offered a formula. *The Middle Way*, by Harold Macmillan, then a young Conservative MP, was the other work to have a decisive impact on Heath. It argued that capitalism needed to be reformed. To make it fairer, more efficient and more stable, capitalism should be rationalized through planning. And this planning was best done by the state. Yet unlike in the Soviet Union, in Macmillan's version of a planned economy free enterprise and the freedom of the individual would not be abolished but strengthened. Businessmen would be helped by government to think more about the long term. Wealth would be redistributed by government to the millions of Britons with little, who would live more comfortable and happier lives as a result. The country's 'latent productive possibilities' would be released.

If, however, British capitalism was not reformed, Macmillan warned, 'Anxious days . . . lie ahead': there would be increased 'class antagonism', revolutionary stirrings from the far left, authoritarian ones from the far right. Macmillan was writing about the thirties, yet he was unintentionally prophetic about the anxieties political moderates would feel in Britain in the seventies. *The Middle Way* also foresaw much of what the Heath government would do to try to remove these fears. What the book could not do was predict the consequences.

Apart from the Depression, there was another feature of the thirties that profoundly shaped Heath's ideas: the ominous political events on the Continent. He had been fascinated by Europe from boyhood, Broadstairs being one of the places in Britain closest to France. 'Every time I walked along the cliffs,' Heath wrote in his 1977 memoir *Travels*, 'I looked across the Channel . . . Sometimes [the coast of France] stood out white and clear . . . at others it was just a dark grey smudge.' In 1931, partly as a reward for passing his School Certificate early, his parents scraped together the money for him to cross the Channel for the first time, on a school trip to Paris. The experience, he judged later, was 'the most exciting event of my life so far'. He walked and watched, sat outside cafes, deciphered menus, bought gateaux, wondered at landmarks and persuaded car-showroom staff to let him look at their catalogues. He was fourteen; for the next six years, he had too little money and too much study-ing to do to visit the Continent again. Then, in the summer of 1937, during his university holidays, his parents fixed up an exchange with a German student from Düsseldorf.

Heath spoke no German – his French accent was also atrocious – but he was undeterred: he loved the German composers and he want-ed to learn about Hitler. At Oxford, Heath had already made a noted speech at the Union criticizing the National Government's appease-ment of the dictator. So, in 1937, after a few days in Düsseldorf, he set off alone on a political exploration of Germany. In Munich, he found the beer cellar where the Nazi party had first met. In the Bavarian Alps, he watched children march in formation to school every morning beneath his bedroom window. And in Nuremberg, he attended a Nazi rally:

An intense silence spread over the whole auditorium. I suddenly realized that Hitler himself was entering from the back of the hall and striding up the centre gangway to the stage . . . My seat was on the inside [of the] gangway and I remember thinking at the time how narrow the aisle was . . . Sure enough, Hitler came alongside me, almost brushing my shoulder . . . His face had little colour . . . When he mounted the platform the response became hysterical.

Heath returned to England, 'utterly convinced now that a conflict was inevitable'. The following year, he went to the part of Europe where the war with fascism had already started. In Spain, the elected Republican government, an undisciplined coalition of left-wing and liberal parties, had been struggling since 1936 against a right-wing insurrection led by General Franco and supported by Hitler and Mussolini. In Britain, the National Government and many Conservatives, following the logic of appeasement and disliking the Republicans' politics, refused to take sides. Yet Heath took a different view: 'I was rather fond of quoting Gladstone's dictum', he writes in *Travels*, 'that when in doubt about foreign policy England should always lean towards those supporting the cause of liberty.' In the early summer of 1938, still at Oxford but now chairman of the Federation of University Conservative and Unionist Associations, another shrewd move up the party ladder, Heath was invited by the Republicans to join a delegation of British students and see what was happening in Spain for himself.

As in France and Germany, Heath was seduced by the good things of Continental living that he glimpsed. Even a civil war could not dull, in his description, 'the deep ultramarine of the Mediterranean'. But his ten days in Spain were raw as well as inspiring. By this stage, the Republicans were losing the war. Heath found their Barcelona stronghold blacked-out and short of food, yet impressively functional. 'Law and order are very well maintained,' he wrote afterwards in an article for the Broadstairs *Advertiser & Echo*. 'At night . . . it is perfectly safe to go anywhere . . . All the cinemas and theatres are open.'

Heath and the rest of the student delegation were driven out to the battlefront west of the city. On a small stony plateau they were introduced to some Britons who were making a more profound contribution to the Republican cause: the British members of the International Brigade. 'They were tough, hardened soldiers, burned by the Spanish sun to a dark tan,' Heath wrote. 'One could not but admire these men, civilians at heart, who had to learn everything of a military nature as they went along.' The student delegation, in tweed jackets and with hair still neat enough for a debate at the Union, addressed the soldiers in their sweaty vests and open-necked shirts. Heath's speech was stiff and cautious: 'I confined myself to telling them that in Britain we closely followed their activities . . . and wanted to see them safely back.'

One of the soldiers was a young trade unionist from Liverpool called Jack Jones. He was small, slight and quietly spoken, but three years older than Heath; before Spain, he had already been a veteran of left-wing activism in the Mersey docks. Heath did not impress him. 'I was there to fight,' Jones said when I asked him about the encounter, 'and he was from Oxford.' Jones was almost as dismissive in his autobiography: 'Heath . . . was to the right of the five-man [student] delegation. I suppose he reflected a strand of Conservative thinking which had some sympathy with the Republic.' Yet a bond had been formed with significance for the future. By the time Heath became prime minister, Jones would be Britain's most powerful trade unionist.

After visiting the battlefront, Heath and the other students were driven south. On a main road near his intoxicating Mediterranean, their convoy was spotted by an enemy aircraft, which was flying low up and down the coast machine-gunning passing vehicles. The students had to hide in a ditch until the plane departed.

Within two years, Heath was a fighting soldier himself. At first, in 1940 and 1941, he had a relatively quiet war as an anti-aircraft gunner in the north of England. With the German bombers concentrating on the south, he had time, he writes, 'to arrive at a considered view of the prevailing social and environmental conditions of the north', which he had never visited before. 'I was astonished, indeed horrified, to see . . . the rows of tiny houses back to back . . . the litter and the dirt . . . the decaying remnants of industrial activity. I realised then how much needed to be done.' But such musings about national renewal had to be put on hold in 1944, when Heath's unit was sent to France. He fought there and in Belgium, Holland and Germany. He saw a recently liberated concentration camp and commanded a firing squad that executed a soldier for rape and murder.

The Heath who returned to civilian life in Britain in 1946 at the age of thirty was still a Conservative. But he had his doubts. The previous year, he had watched from Germany as the party fought a general-election campaign which claimed, tastelessly and exaggeratedly, that Labour plans to nationalize industries and decisively expand the welfare state would require 'some form of Gestapo'. Heath considered the claim 'objectionable' and, after Labour under Attlee went on to win the election by a huge majority, completely out of step with public attitudes which, like his, had been shifted leftwards by the Depression and the war against fascism. 'It was only if the [Conservative] party decided to acclimatise itself to the new Britain of the late 1940s', he writes in his autobiography, 'that I could foresee a political career for myself.'

The party moved in the direction he wanted. Between the late forties and the mid-sixties, first in opposition and then in government, the Conservatives accepted the main ideas of what became known as the post-war consensus: a larger welfare state funded by higher taxation; a Keynesian approach to the economy as set out in the *General Theory*; and an acceptance of strong trade unions. Heath rose through this new Conservative Party doggedly. In 1947, he put himself forward for four parliamentary constituencies, failed to be selected for three, and finally got Bexley. In 1950, he squeezed into the House of Commons with a majority of 133. In 1951, with promising speed, he was made an assistant whip, one of the Commons' junior prefects, helping to discipline his fellow Conservative MPs. In 1955, he was promoted to chief whip, holding the parliamentary party together during the Suez crisis. In 1959, he became minister of labour and defused a threatened strike by the National Union of Railwaymen. In 1960, he was put in charge of negotiating Britain's entry into the Common Market, failing with honour and for the first time becoming a national figure. In 1963, he became president of the Board of Trade and boldly abolished Resale Price Maintenance, the system regulating retail prices, in favour of a more market-driven free-for-all. In 1964, he became shadow chancellor and, finally, a Commons star, attacking the new Wilson government with contempt and fluency. In 1965, he was elected Conservative leader by a small margin.

The Heath who emerged in the sixties and became prime minister in 1970 was not an outstanding politician. The cool response to him during his five years as Opposition leader, from his party and more widely, reflected his obvious limitations. He was energetic and conscientious, but sometimes gratingly relentless; stubborn and a loner, but with a contradictory belief in consensus; inquisitive, but not a great communicator of new ideas; impatient with post-war Britain, but also full of its assumptions. Above all, he was famously difficult to get on with – a quality, unfortunate in a democratic politician, that did not diminish as he got older. In the summer of 2004, a few days after his eighty-eighth birthday, I arranged to see him.

Someone who knew Heath briefed me beforehand. Heath, he warned, would be 'brusque'. In retirement as during his political career, Heath was 'extraordinarily insular as a person'. He was 'still furious' at how his time as Conservative leader had culminated. And there was one more thing to be wary of: 'He falls asleep after lunch.' My interview was scheduled for straight after his nap.

It was a perfect July morning when I left London, but the clouds had closed over by the time the train reached Salisbury. The city where Heath had lived since 1985 was all traffic and tea rooms; with three hours to fill before the interview, I found a special issue of a music magazine on early seventies British glam rock in WHSmith and looked at the pictures of Heath-era male pop stars in their make-up and silver trousers. They seemed almost as ancient and alien as medieval jesters. Then I went to look at his house.

It was right next to the cathedral in a great, hushed half-square of old mansions. The three-storey house was broad, built of faded gold stone, with high gates and long windows like a French presidential residence. A single upstairs window was slightly open; otherwise, the house was symmetrical, immaculate, inscrutable. Heath's autobiography included a four-page section on the house, of which one detail was perhaps especially significant: 'Arundells is one of the few houses in the [Cathedral] Close which is well set back.'

When the time for my appointment came, a middle-aged policeman with a weary moustache and a machine gun materialized at the gates from somewhere in the depths of the garden. He put a single key in the lock, which was spotted with lichen, and at the other end of the long drive one of Heath's staff opened the front door. Inside the house there was silence. In the hallway and the rooms that led off it, the floors gleamed like a museum's and models of sailing vessels sat in glass cases – after music, sailing was Heath's other famous off-duty interest. On the walls, closely but very neatly hung, were hundreds of political cartoons. Above the cistern in the downstairs loo, perfectly positioned at eye level for visitors, was one showing Heath dragging Margaret Thatcher along the ground by the hair.

I was shown into a small sitting room. There were bookshelves ostentatiously free of serious political volumes, and a tabletop of bottles of whisky and other spirits in the corner. Heath, I was told, would be 'a few minutes'. I sat and waited. There was a thud from somewhere upstairs. Then an audible groan and a series of heavy steps across the ceiling. 'I think he's on his way downstairs,' said one of the housekeepers.

Heath came slowly into the room, supported by a walking stick and another of his staff. His clothes – a baggy cream short-sleeved shirt with half the buttons undone, and casual grey chinos – came as a small shock after watching hours of his pinstriped and uncomfortable early seventies political broadcasts. But his face was much the same: the small determined eyes, the proud mountain of a nose, the big plump cheeks barely lined despite his lingering yachtsman's tan – a usefully aspirational political signal back in the pre-easyJet Britain of his premiership. He acknowledged me fleetingly and sat down.

Then he realized that our chairs were side by side and that we could not face each other comfortably. He looked up at the housekeeper: 'Can we turn this around,' he said, a note of impatient command in his plummy, slightly studied voice, 'so we can talk properly?' She bent down and took one of his arms, and gestured that I should do the same. We lifted Heath a few inches towards the vertical, but then his weight told. The former prime minister landed back in his chair with a thump. We hauled him up again. This time our grip held. As we adjusted the furniture and then sat him down, Heath's glacial blue eyes showed not a trace of embarrassment. When I sat down, he looked at me properly for the first time. 'Right. What can I help you with?'

I asked him what he had wanted to do to Britain in 1970. 'Speak up,' he said, unsmiling. I asked the question again. His gaze warmed a fraction: 'Well, we thought the country was in a bad state. Particularly in its basic framework and structure. We set out a list of policies in 1970, and it covered a great field. And all too many commentators have never bothered to find out what that list was. And we moved on all of them. We moved on all of them. In housing we got tremendous movement . . . We got into Europe . . . And we freed large areas of the economy from being tied to the arrangements of twenty or thirty years before.' Heath looked at the bookshelves. 'Of course, we had struggles in some areas . . . we gave way to a certain extent. But not very much actually.'

The memories of retired politicians, even more than their memoirs, should be regarded with a degree of caution, yet an undeniable air of confidence and momentum did accompany the Heath government in the beginning. Anthony Sampson, a self-taught expert on British power structures, picked it up in his 1971 book *The New Anatomy of Britain*:

Power has already begun to change [Heath] . . . He is more relaxed, rather fatter; he wears very good and quite trendy clothes . . . His hair is much longer, coming down thickly at the back, and his sideburns are more evident; he might even be mistaken for a musician.

Peter York, the veteran observer of British fashions, remembered the vogue for Heath too: 'Among the *bien pensant*, among modernizers of all kinds,' he told me, 'the idea of Heath was quite a thing. Cleverer people than me were telling me that Heath was the new middle way.'

Heath had won power partly because Labour had underestimated him. He had won power after many on his own side and most commentators had written him off. The credit for victory went to him personally – and further Heath miracles were not considered out of the question. 'Mr Heath', commented *The Times*, '[is] in a position of great strength. He has no personal obligations to anybody . . . [His] commitments to policy . . . are of his own choosing . . . He will be a considerably more powerful Prime Minister . . . because he made his victory in such difficult circumstances.' During his first months in office, Heath himself boldly talked up his government's prospects. 'We were returned to office to change the course of history of this nation,' he told the Conservative Party conference in October 1970. 'Nothing less.'

Heath's plan for Britain had been drawn up with unusual thoroughness during his long, derided tenure as Opposition leader. 'We produced this huge path chart, the day every bit of legislation was going to be introduced,' remembers Brendon Sewill, director of the powerful Conservative Research Department during the period. 'We posted it through the letterbox at Number 10 on the morning after we won the election.' Heath relished this patient, preparatory side of politics – between leaving the army and becoming an MP he had briefly been a civil servant in the Long-Range Planning Department of the Ministry of Civil Aviation – and frequently dropped in on the Research Department's policy discussions. The press were less interested. The legislative ambitions of Opposition parties can often seem like castles in the sky, and the regular dramas of the Wilson government seemed more substantial material.

The one exception to this pattern came in January 1970. With a general election expected soon, Sewill organized a weekend retreat for Heath and his shadow cabinet. 'The idea was to try to pull together all the policies which had been developed by this incredible number of policy groups, and make the shadow cabinet consider them and say, "Are we trying to do too much? And do these policies conflict with each other?" And then we said to each other at the Research Department, "Well, it would be rather good publicity too."'

The retreat was held at the Selsdon Park Hotel, a baronial complex of long conference rooms and photogenic lawns near Croydon in south London. The shadow cabinet's discussions were energetic and thorough but not conclusive. Little was said that challenged Heath's central idea about how to revive Britain: that a Conservative administration could make the economy vastly more efficient through government chivvying and ingenuity, and that everything else would follow, which had been in his head since he had read Keynes and Macmillan in the thirties. Then, midway through the weekend, came a moment that would make the Selsdon conference infamous.

Peter Walker, a close ally of Heath then and since, described it to me. 'On the Saturday morning, at about a quarter to twelve, Michael Fraser [a senior Conservative party official] said to Ted, "Don't forget you've got the press at 12.15." "Press?" said Ted.

Michael said, "Yes, we agreed we'd have a press conference today to get in the Sunday papers." So Ted said, "What on earth am I going to say to them? We haven't decided anything." So Iain Macleod of all people [the liberal shadow chancellor] said, "It's quite easy, Ted, you just tell them we believe in law and order." So Ted went off and said at the press conference, "We're going to be very strong on law and order." And the next day every Sunday paper did enormous right-wing stuff.'

The press – and Wilson – claimed to have sighted a new, crueller species of British Conservative: 'Selsdon Man', tougher on crime and on immigration, harsher in his economic thinking, impatient, in fact, with the whole herbivorous post-war consensus. In reality, 'Selsdon Man' was somewhere between a breathless exaggeration and a malicious fiction, but in the seventies, more than in most decades, political spectres and misrepresentations had a habit of solidifying into flesh-and-blood political issues. Heath, grateful for the publicity and for a catchphrase to differentiate his policies from Wilson's, did not completely disown the label.

In the short term, it seemed a canny decision. With a general-election campaign coming, the Conservatives suddenly looked more focused and hungry. And in the election itself, they received more votes than usual from a group of growing social and political importance. One of the consequences of Britain's increasing suburbanization and prosperity in the fifties and sixties was the appearance of a wealthier, more individualistic skilled working class in the new towns and commuter settlements that increasingly ringed the run-down cities. Sociologists christened them C2s; later, this sort of person would be called Essex Man. In 1969, Rupert Murdoch relaunched the *Sun*, aimed at upwardly mobile 'pacesetters', partly to appeal to the C2s. At first the paper supported Labour, expecting its readers to do likewise, but there was an abrasiveness in the Selsdon message that appealed to the embryonic Essex Man.

The long-term consequences of Selsdon for Heath himself were less favourable. The conference awakened hopes in right-wing Conservatives which he, not being a genuine right-winger, would inevitably dash when he took power. This had a damaging effect on his reputation, and ultimately on his position as party leader. And 'Selsdon Man' allowed left-wing Britons to believe – or to pretend to believe – that Heath was a thuggish Tory who would turn the country upside down. They would prove much worse opponents as a result.

3
Heathograd

In the first purposeful months of Ted Heath's administration, Selsdon soon became only one political initiative among many. The government set up a new Department of Trade and Industry and a new Department of the Environment, covering housing, public works and transport. It established an official Whitehall 'Think Tank', then an untried concept, to work on long-term strategy. It hired businessmen to stir up the civil service. It despatched ministers to stir up businessmen. The personification of this approach, this hoped-for fusion of the public and private sectors into a vigorous new whole, was the confident young Peter Walker.

Like Heath, he came from a strikingly modest background. His father worked in an engineering factory, was unemployed for a year and a half during the Depression and later became a shop steward, a shop-floor trade-union official. But Walker's father and mother were both Tories, and, before he reached his teens, so was he. He first stood for Parliament, in 1955, at the age of twenty-three; by the early sixties, he was a noted Conservative MP; by 1965, he was running Heath's successful leadership campaign. Walker's politics were typical of the rising generation of post-war liberal Tories who were in favour of material advancement for the masses and a more efficient capitalism, but what gave his views an additional credibility was his own parallel career as an entrepreneur. He had begun reading the *Financial Times* at thirteen. In his twenties he became a well-known City of London player in property and insurance. In 1964, he joined up with a frustrated motor-industry executive called Jim Slater to form an investment company, Slater Walker. Between 1964 and 1970, when Walker became a minister and scaled back his business activities, the firm made huge and spiralling profits by buying shares in companies that were, in Walker's description, 'badly managed', taking them over and running them on a more realistic basis, or – as Slater Walker's critics saw it – stripping their assets and quickly getting out. The company grew with an aggression and raw ambition new to the relatively gentlemanly post-war City. Slater Walker would prove too jerry-built and controversial to survive the harsher economic climate of the seventies, but Walker would have too many other interests by then to be seriously damaged.

Between 1970 and 1972, Heath promoted him from minister for housing and local government to secretary of state for the environment to secretary of state for trade and industry. Walker was still in his thirties, with a slightly gauche smile and cocky long sideburns, at a time when most of the people who ran things in Britain, such as Heath and the rest of the Cabinet, were middle-aged or older. Yet Walker sometimes approached his duties as if he alone was a man of the world:

When I became the Secretary of State for Trade and Industry, my surprise was how bad top management was . . . The great one was at a shipbuilding yard. I had lunch with the board, and we had grouse and salmon, and you knew that the salmon had been caught by the board and the grouse had been shot by the board. They were all that sort of background. And when you started to discuss what was happening in worldwide shipping, they were lost. When I went down and had tea with the union, they were incredibly well-informed. When I left, I said, 'If in that shipyard the shop stewards would become the board and the board would become the shop stewards, you would have the ideal combination.'

Walker finished the anecdote with a jolly laugh. He was sitting, almost slouching, with one hand in a suit trouser pocket, on a pale green sofa with gold trim in his office in the City of London. It was 2004; he was seventy-two, still slim, and a director of the Anglo-German bank Dresdner Kleinwort Wasserstein. Through the glass walls of his corner office the tops of other skyscrapers steamed below us in the blue morning and the Thames was a silvery scribble. Walker's upward trajectory and air of self-assurance had comfortably survived the seventies – he had called his memoirs *Staying Power* – and the very different decades that came after.

So had his belief in the Heath government. On one of the walls of

Walker's office, among photographs of him meeting various dignitaries, there were pictures of Heath as prime minister, and Walker spoke about the time as if it had been one of almost unbroken government successes and timely initiatives. 'There was a united Cabinet,' he said in his brisk voice. 'There was no disunity. There was never a moment in the whole period of Ted's Cabinet where there was disunity in the Cabinet. Margaret [Thatcher, then education secretary], Keith [Joseph, then social services secretary] – none of them were voicing opinions against Ted.' Walker continued: 'The start of trade union reform was done by the Heath government. The basic reform of things like water cleanliness. A new approach to the environment was done by the Heath government. I think there are areas where if we had had more time . . . we were very busy during that government . . .' His voice turned quieter and more thoughtful: 'If we'd won that next term, then I think we would have been a very successful government.' His confident broad-brush tone returned: 'I think the government, when history gets it properly in perspective, will be seen as a very considerable one.'

One of the main ways the Heath administration sought to modernize Britain was through large building projects. Back in the thirties, Heath had noted the success of Roosevelt's New Deal in reviving the American economy. The New Deal included much state-funded construction work, creating jobs and economically beneficial new infrastructure. In the early seventies, with the British economy in trouble, the Heath government embarked on massive building schemes of its own. Undeterred by almost a century of false starts, it started digging a Channel Tunnel to France. As environment secretary, Walker commissioned the Thames Barrier in east London to avert the growing possibility of the capital flooding. 'The estimate of the cost was £60 million, and it turned out to be £600 million,' he remembered. He gave a satisfied look: 'And we got the go-ahead on it.'

But perhaps the most ambitious project of all, and the most revealing about how the British government still thought during this phase of the seventies – a phase which later in the decade would come to seem almost impossibly comfortable and remote – was begun about thirty miles to the east. It was a building scheme which assumed that state spending would remain relatively unconstrained, and that much of it should be directed towards the long term. The scheme was called Maplin.

The Maplin Sands are a great smooth maze of mudflats and grey-brown horizon the size of central London, gleaming dully as an old hubcap off the coast of Essex near Shoeburyness, the easternmost suburb of Southend. At low tide in the summer, parts of the sand bake hard enough in the sun for you to walk out on, and you can listen to the small noises of water trickling and poke dead jellyfish and cockle shells. In other places the quicksands go eighty feet down. Sudden North Sea fogs are also common. In February 1970, a Mr P. Arnold, a local explorer and authority on the area, noted eighty-eight people buried in the churchyard of St Mary the Virgin on Foulness, a marshy island north of Shoeburyness, 'whose bodies were found on the sands'.

Foulness has been farmed by a scattering of people since Saxon and possibly Roman times. In the Middle Ages sea walls were built, and the island began to be slowly extended. Maplin Sands to the east became favoured by cockle pickers. But until the mid-nineteenth century the island and the sands were best known for their great clouds of seagulls and Brent geese, Foulness meaning 'place of birds' in Old English. Then, in 1849, an official use was found for the area's emptiness, when the government opened an artillery range, allowing firing from the shore onto the mudflats. Over a century later, as Heath took power, military fences, warning flags and distant booms still dominated life on Foulness and Maplin Sands. But he had other plans for the area.

During his time at the Ministry of Civil Aviation in the late forties, Heath recalls, 'I sat on numerous committees, including one overseeing the building and development of the new airport at Heathrow. Every time I arrive at Heathrow,' he continues, 'I shudder to think that I was in any way, however slightly, involved in the creation of that monstrosity.' By 1960, the noise of Heathrow was considered enough of a political problem to merit investigation by a government committee, which concluded in 1963: 'The noise to which many people near Heathrow . . . are subjected is more than they can reasonably be expected to tolerate . . . Heathrow has proved to have been established in a much too densely populated area.' Yet there was no question of restricting the rapid post-war growth of British civil aviation. Governments from Attlee's onwards regarded airports as essential generators of economic growth and voters' pleasure, so other airports had to be built near London to relieve Heathrow. The first was Gatwick, commissioned in the mid-fifties after years of planning strife, financial headaches for the government and frenetic switching between possible sites. In the early sixties, Whitehall decided that London needed a third airport, and the same painful process started again.

In January 1971, after what was then the longest and most expensive public planning inquiry in British history, the Roskill Commission recommended that the airport be built at Cublington, a village in rural Buckinghamshire. The Commission conceded that the choice would be controversial, but asserted that if Britain's decline was to be reversed, such decisions were unavoidable: 'The nation's unsatisfactory economic performance in recent years can at least in part be attributed to a national tendency to forgo economic gains and to prefer other goals.' Yet Cublington quickly proved politically impractical. The village and its soft surrounding fields and hills was the kind of corner of England – conventionally pretty, pastoral-seeming, prosperous – that could organize a ferocious campaign against the government imposition of an airport. At the same time, the Cublington campaign was able to dignify and publicize its more parochial arguments by invoking a new political philosophy: environmentalism.

Britain at the beginning of the seventies was fertile ground for green politics. For decades, conservation and animal welfare had been more popular causes there than in most comparable countries. During the sixties, such thinking began to intertwine with the back-to-the-land strand of hippy idealism. In 1966, the first British environmentalist magazine, *Resurgence*, was set up. In 1970 came a second, *The Ecologist*, edited by Edward, or 'Teddy', Goldsmith, the well-connected brother of the millionaire businessman James Goldsmith. In 1971, a British wing was established of the pioneering American green pressure group Friends of the Earth. In 1972, a paperback spin-off from *The Ecologist* called *A Blueprint for Survival*, which warned that 'the industrial way of life' was 'not sustainable', became a best-seller in Britain.

Westminster politicians took note. Walker invited the *Blueprint* authors to come and brief him, while Heath established the Department of the Environment. For the first time, green concerns, for presentational reasons at the very least, became a regular factor in government decisions. When the Roskill Commission announced its decision to concrete over Cublington, one of its members, the famous town planner Colin Buchanan, publicly dissented. An airport at Cublington, he wrote, would be an 'environmental disaster'. Instead, the runways should be sited somewhere emptier and on the coast, where the damage would be much less. 'I believe the mood of the country is such', he continued, 'that some inconvenience of accessibility to a new airport would be willingly accepted as the price for conserving the environment.' And he had a site in mind: 'Foulness . . . would be a [choice] of great significance for the future of Britain. It would show that this country, in spite of economic difficulties, is prepared to take a stand.'

Buchanan made another potent argument. An airport on the Maplin Sands (for which 'Foulness' was the shorthand) would, through its eastern position and transport connections, 'assist the less prosperous eastern side of London' – the depopulating East End, with its soupy miles of derelict river wharves and disintegrating dockyard economy. Walker and his new Department of the Environment were persuaded – in *The Times* he praised the 'beautiful prose' of Buchanan's arguments – and Walker persuaded the Cabinet. In April 1971, the trade and industry secretary John Davies announced that the government would ignore the Roskill Commission's painstakingly formed preference for Cublington: 'On environmental and planning grounds the Foulness site is the best.' The response was unambiguous. 'For the first time in nearly thirty years,' wrote the journalist David McKie in a book on British airports published in 1973, 'a major decision in airport policy commanded general enthusiasm.'

The project got under way at unusual speed. In 1971, civil servants were ordered to make an immediate start on the paperwork for the airport and any transport links it needed. The following year, a special army unit, 71 Explosives Ordnance Disposal Squadron, was formed to clear decades' worth of old artillery shells from the sands. In 1973, the Maplin Development Act was passed, creating a government-appointed Maplin Development Authority (MDA) with powers to borrow up to £250 million, 'acquire land compulsorily for any purpose connected with its functions' and pay compensation to 'any person [who] . . . derived the whole or part of his means of livelihood from the taking of fish or shellfish or the gathering of white weed' on the sands.

That same year, the first construction work started. In the spring, when the North Sea storms were at their most testing, 155,000 cubic metres of gravel were deposited on the sands almost three miles from shore and piled up using pumps and bulldozers into a long, concave, artificial island, like the fuselage of some enormous passenger aircraft rising up from the shallows. This 'trial bank', 300 metres by 30 at high tide, was a tiny fragment of the planned airport, built at the same angle to the shore and intended to test if the complex could be protected by gravel-based, relatively economical sea walls. In April 1974, an MDA report on the trial bank's condition after a year found that it had been 'exposed to very severe conditions . . . with a large number of southerly gales and waves up to one and a half metres high', but that the damage had been minor. The MDA's logo, appropriately it seemed, was of a muscular letter 'M' standing impregnably above bobbing waves.

The confidence that Maplin could be built had several sources. There was the long history of land reclamation at Foulness; there was the fact that the Dutch had already constructed an offshore airport, Schipol, in similar North Sea conditions; and then there were the private plans for airports off Foulness that had been piling up for decades. The first scheme had been in the thirties. Another had been drawn up in the fifties. In the sixties, a consortium including major construction companies got as far as unveiling a model airport the size of several tennis courts, complete with simulated tides and winking miniature runway lights.

In a crowded coastal country like Britain, it was perhaps not surprising that people should dream of expanding their island a little. But with Maplin there were also more abstract and political preoccupations at work. Britain's airports and airlines, disproportionately large for a middle-ranking European country, were a legacy of the empire and its need for a far-flung transport network and one of the dwindling number of areas of economic activity where Britain remained a world power. Yet, by the early seventies, there was a growing fear that in civil aviation Holland and France, which was also rapidly expanding its airport capacity, would catch up. 'Maplin is necessary to maintain Britain's position as one of the world's great centres of international aviation,' Walker's successor as environment secretary, Geoffrey Rippon, told the Commons in early 1973.

Heath himself, with his deep-seated dislike of Heathrow and his belief in government planning to get the economy moving, was excited by Maplin. Later the same year, he told a meeting of Conservative MPs, 'As a nation, we should not falter in major projects which other countries take in their stride.' The airport scheme was also a literal manifestation of his desire to move Britain closer to the rest of Europe. In 1972, the year he signed the treaty marking Britain's entry into the Common Market, an outline of how Essex would be extended eastwards to accommodate the airport was produced.

I looked at the drawings on a sweltering May afternoon in the House of Lords record office thirty-two years later. A young woman in a sundress fetched the huge rolled-up sheets of paper with a slight air of puzzlement at my interest. Unrolled, they seemed pristine enough to have barely ever been touched. Across empty expanses of white representing the North Sea, bold lines were flung out to form a new lozenge-shaped peninsula, eight miles long and three miles wide. Part of one side was shielded by the eastern edge of Foulness; the rest was surrounded by water. A sea wall around the airport was indicated, with a height of between forty and fifty feet. Two runways were also marked, positioned so that the planes, as in many of the world's more shrewdly sited airports, came in to land over the sea and not over the roofs of Southend to the west.

These plans, however, were just a cautious early draft of the ambitions for Maplin. Once the first runway was completed, which it was initially anticipated would be in 1975 or 1976, and the second became operational, anticipated in 1980, work would begin on a further two runways, giving the airport twice as many as Heathrow. In addition, the Maplin complex would contain a new seaport that would receive container ships and supertankers. With oil being so cheap and very much in demand in the early seventies, it was believed the latter would soon be too big to sail up the Thames Estuary towards London. The seaport would replace the capital's dying docks and rival the much more modern Dutch port of Rotterdam, Europe's largest.

And then there would be a Maplin New Town. 'Maplin will create a need for large-scale urban development . . . built to the highest environmental standards,' announced the junior environment minister Eldon Griffiths in 1972. The following year, his department predicted that the New Town – or 'a brand new jet city', as it was sometimes more excitedly referred to in the Commons – would have an eventual population of over 300,000. This new settlement would extend from the airport and seaport in the east, across the flat windswept vastness of Foulness and its neighbouring islands and tidal creeks to Southend and the hills beyond, half a dozen miles to the west. The building work would continue 'to the turn of the century and beyond'. New industrial estates would serve the conurbation, and additional expansion out into the North Sea was anticipated. 'Further reclamation', said Griffiths in 1972, 'will be undertaken when needed.'

To link it all to London and the rest of Britain there would be a new eight-lane motorway and high-speed railway, racing through the towns, villages and marshes of south-east Essex. There was talk – and with Maplin it was sometimes difficult to separate the plans from hopes and rumours – of 'an Advanced Passenger Train system' carrying people at 125 miles per hour non-stop from the airport to a new station between King's Cross and St Pancras in central London; or of the same twenty-minute journey time being achieved by the use of passenger-carrying 'tracked hovercraft'. Around King's Cross, one of London's tattiest railway quarters, property speculators bought up streets of buildings in anticipation.

In Essex, the reaction to Maplin was more ambivalent. Southend was a place in a slight limbo in the early seventies. It was a British seaside resort in a dawning era of cheap flights to Spain – a problem that building Maplin was not going to diminish. And it was a potentially well-positioned dormitory town – but before mass commuting from Essex to London had really started. Local unemployment was notably high, even at a time when the national rate was rising rapidly. In 1973, the British Airports Authority predicted that building Maplin would create over 16,000 long-term construction jobs, 'approaching' 70,000 positions serving the airport and seaport, and over 15,000 additional vacancies in the enlarged Essex economy. People began moving to Southend to wait for them.

The borough council strongly supported Maplin. So did the local trade unions. In 1973, a Maplin Movement was formed which would claim 'several thousand' members. Yet others felt differently about living next door to what Rippon liked to call 'the world's first environmental airport'. The most prominent were the Defenders of Essex.

In Southend, people still nod knowingly when you mention them. The Defenders were strongest in Shoeburyness and the other parts of town closest to the Maplin site, but they had support from all over the county and from all three Southend MPs. The Defenders' campaigning was a mixture of church-hall politeness – coffee mornings, piano concerts, raffles – and something more abrasive and modern – mass rallies, lurid yellow posters of 'Jackboots Over Essex', a car convoy to London to dramatize the extra road traffic Maplin would generate. Local and national journalists loved the Defenders; Friends of the Earth, damagingly for the airport's green credentials, backed them too. One of the Defenders' most fruitful issues was the proposed demolition of properties that stood in the way of the Maplin motorway. When the government distributed a questionnaire to Essex libraries asking the public which of six nervously circuitous motorway routes they preferred, the libraries ran out of copies in twenty-four hours.

Other local objections to Maplin made equally good news stories. Foulness islanders claimed that noise carried unusually far across the sands: a conversation between two yachtsmen was said to have been overheard half a mile away. The quicksands would destroy the runways: they were said to have swallowed a ship carrying timber in a matter of minutes. In Leigh-on-Sea, a picturesque old part of Southend whose cocklers made a living from the sands, the Shellfish Merchants Association claimed that the national balance of payments would be damaged by cockle imports if Maplin was built. And then there were the Brent geese. A fifth of the world's population spent their winter on the sands. The birds were large and dark-bellied and hard to see in dim light; they might be sucked into jet engines over Maplin, with catastrophic results for all concerned. The possibility was exhaustively debated all the way to the House of Commons.

But for all the colour of the Essex protesters, they did not seem to be gathering decisive momentum. The minutes of a meeting of Southend anti-Maplin protesters in March 1973 note in exasperation that even 'At Shoebury . . . the apathy of people was appalling . . . Young people had accepted the government's assurances and adopted the attitude that if the airport comes, we can move. The old . . . took the view that they would be dead before the airport was built.'

It was in the Commons that the scheme began to encounter more formidable opposition. Crosland, now shadow environment secretary, was an eloquent and relentless critic. Maplin was a 'thoroughly bad site' for an airport, he argued in a debate in February 1973; rather than reviving east London, it would draw people and jobs away; and, above all, it was a reckless extravagance: 'We have . . . much experience now of the constantly escalating cost of these grandiose projects.' Labour's scepticism was shared by some Conservative MPs – not just the traditional foes of development in rural areas, but also a new kind of Tory.

Norman Tebbit was one. He was from a working-class background and represented one of the upwardly mobile working-class constituencies on the London–Essex borders – first Epping, then Chingford – that had recently acquired political significance. He was unashamedly right-wing and abrasive in his manner. In the debate on Maplin in February 1973, despite having been an MP for less than three years, he was openly contemptuous of his party's flagship infrastructure project. 'This will be the most expensive airport ever built,' he said, his prediction given credibility by the fact that he had been an airline pilot before becoming an MP. He went on to compare Maplin to one of post-war Britain's most disastrous government economic initiatives, the Attlee administration's abortive scheme to solve a shortage of cooking oil by growing peanuts in Tanganyika.

In Tebbit and Crosland's attacks on Maplin, the beginnings of broader misgivings about the high level of British state spending since the Second World War could be heard. In early 1973, the rising right-wing economist Alan Walters, who had been expressing doubts about the post-war consensus for years, turned his attention to the airport project in a letter to *The Times*. Building Maplin, he suggested, might contribute to Britain's worsening rate of inflation. By June 1973, when the airport was debated in the Commons again, additional worries had crystallized. It was noted that none of the airlines were keen on the site and might have to be compelled by the government to use it. The Labour MP Tam Dalyell, often full of foreboding but far-sighted with it, also raised the possibility that Maplin might be made redundant by future problems with the global supply of jet fuel. The government won the debate by only nine votes.

Crosland began mocking Maplin as 'Heathograd'. Like the best political insults, it had a strong core of truth. The prime minister remained determined to see the scheme built. He personally reprimanded Michael Heseltine, one of the more ambivalent members of the Cabinet, for failing to sell it to Tory MPs with sufficient enthusiasm. Heseltine recalls in his memoirs: 'The prime minister insisted categorically [that] anyone with doubts [be] put firmly in his place.'

Yet Heath, with stubborn confidence, as on other occasions during his government, increasingly ignored the way the situation was developing. The predicted cost of reclaiming the land for Maplin rose from £70 million in 1971 to £110 million in 1972 to £175 million in 1973. By the autumn of 1973, with a building boom in the south of England pushing up construction prices, the overall cost of Maplin was being talked about in Parliament as £1,000 million, or £2,000 million, or even higher.

In September, the government conceded that the airport would not open in 1980, as planned, but in 1982. The following week, the international oil crisis that Dalyell had half-predicted began, with seemingly disastrous implications for civil aviation and airport-building. In November, Maplin's opening date was put back again, to 1983. On 16 January 1974, with the Heath government now struggling with a whole host of oil-related problems, it was announced in the Commons that Maplin was to be subject to a 'wide-ranging and comprehensive' review. 'In view of the ornithological implications,' the Conservative MP and Maplin critic Robert Adley asked the environment secretary Geoffrey Rippon with typically heavy-handed Commons wit, 'may I ask whether my right honourable and learned friend is able to differentiate between a lame duck and a dead duck?'

One weekday morning three decades later, I took a train from London towards the Maplin Sands. The train was clean and modern, with air conditioning and a smooth gliding motion, but it took four times as long as the public transport the airport's planners had envisaged. Shoeburyness, six miles short of the sands, was the last stop. Half a dozen other passengers got off.

I started walking north-east towards the airport site. The centre of Shoeburyness – a few shops, a quiet seaside park – soon gave way to dusty cul-de-sacs and fenced-off old warehouses. Beyond them flat countryside opened out, windy and treeless, with empty roads and tidal creeks where the skeletons of ancient boats gleamed in the silence. All the way to the east, where the airport would have been, there was blue-grey sea and an empty horizon.

The Ministry of Defence was still using the sands as an artillery range. When I reached the southern boundary of the MOD land, there was a phone number pinned to the fence for inquiries about access. I rang it, and a security officer politely explained that access would be difficult. But when I mentioned my interest in the airport, he offered a consolation. 'The experiment', as he called the Maplin scheme, had left one trace: the trial bank built out to sea in 1973. 'People round here', he said, 'call it sand island.' Then he explained how to get the best view of it.

I took a taxi back to Shoeburyness, walked to the north end of the park and looked out to sea. The sun had come out and the waves were a deep blue; just below the horizon, too far out to be a sand-bank, there was a sliver of gold. The sun went in and it disappeared. Then the sea brightened again and the golden sliver returned. I put 20p in a seafront telescope and traced its profile, which was long and bare and gently sloping, like some fantastical sand dune marooned in an ocean or a story-book desert island that had lost its palm trees. Two container ships ghosted by behind it. A small passing cloud covered it in rippling shadow. Next to the telescope, a middle-aged man was sitting on a bench watching the sea. I asked him if I had been looking at sand island. 'I don't know what it is,' he said. 'But I do believe it was something to do with the airport at one time.'

When I got back to London, the jumbo jets were moaning overhead as usual, queueing for Heathrow. In Salisbury a few weeks later, near the end of our interview, I asked Heath if he wished Maplin had been built. 'Yes,' he said with emphasis. 'There would have been enormous benefit.' From the depths of his chair came a heavy mirthless laugh. 'Look what's happening over London at the moment – all that. And if we'd done Maplin in time the cost was bearable.'

The scheme – perhaps the most melancholy symbol of Heath's foiled ambitions for Britain – was never cancelled by his government. That decision was taken by the next administration. The idea was never quite killed off, however. During the late seventies, and again in the eighties, and into the present century, the idea of an airport built on an artificial island in the North Sea or the Thames Estuary has periodically bobbed to the surface. Besides Heath, its supporters have included the consumer guru Sir Terence Conran, the British National Party and, most vocally since his election in 2008, the mayor of London, Boris Johnson.

*

Many of the Heath government's other great hopes proved less enduring. The first of these was its ability to transform the economy smoothly. In July 1970, barely a month after the Conservatives' election triumph, the chancellor Iain Macleod died of a heart attack, and the new administration lost one of its best economic brains, most effective communicators and most popular figures. Almost immediately, the fragile recovery inherited from Wilson, far from strengthening into a boom under Heath as the Conservatives had planned, seemed to go into reverse.

Growth fell from a vigorous 3.3 per cent in the second half of 1970 to a sickly 0.3 per cent in the first half of 1971. Inflation, which had been steadily declining before the election, began to rise sharply afterwards. Most dramatically of all, the number of unemployed Britons, which had grown slowly in 1969 and 1970, suddenly surged by over a quarter in 1971. By the end of the year, the total was approaching a million, a level not seen since 1940.

In Britain, as in many Western democracies, the mass unemployment of the Depression years and the fear that it might return still chilled politicians, economists and voters. 'Full employment' – official code for a situation where only those who would not or could not work were jobless for long – 'had to be maintained,' says Brendon Sewill, who was a special adviser to Macleod's less able successor as chancellor, Anthony Barber. 'To suggest that you should . . . increase the level of unemployment so that [for example] trade unions became weaker was unthinkable.' Having grown up and formed many of his political ideas during the Depression, Heath, even more than most, regarded mass unemployment as a social evil. Yet within three months of his becoming prime minister, the Conservative Research Department announced that a 'seismic change' in the British job market was under way. The CRD saw only one parallel in recent British history: the years leading up to the thirties.

The government's response was jumpy. In the run-up to the 1970 election, and particularly at the Selsdon Park conference, the Conservatives had given contradictory signals about how they would treat the economy. As well as promoting Heath's rather convention-al, essentially Keynesian ideas about using state initiatives and new ministries to invigorate business, the party had talked another, tougher, in some respects new economic language: reduce the govern-ment's role, free up the market, let 'lame duck' enterprises fail. Some of this was just political point-scoring, an attempt to distinguish the Conservative approach from Wilson's Keynesian policies in the six-ties. But the Tories' new tone also reflected the influence of a genuinely anti-Keynesian school of economics that had been gather-ing momentum in Britain and the US since the Second World War.

In Britain by 1970, this movement had an effective propaganda and research centre, the Institute of Economic Affairs (IEA), several influential advocates in the media and a small but increasingly active minority of converts in the parliamentary Conservative party. Even Heath himself had offered them intermittent encouragement. His abolition of Resale Price Maintenance in 1964 had been a deregulat-ing, anti-government initiative, influenced by the arguments of an IEA pamphlet. In 1969, he appeared to promise further such reforms in his speech to the Conservative Party conference: 'We will banish the regulation and control of business activities,' he said. 'We will begin to introduce private ownership into nationalized industries.'

Yet Heath's bold undertakings soon turned out to be little more than rhetoric, one of his periodic – and often damaging – moments of overcompensation for his lack of charisma as a public speaker. In office, he made only a few early concessions to the new right-wing radicalism. He 'denationalized' (the word 'privatized' was still thought too raw and undignified even for use in IEA pamphlets) the pubs of Carlisle, a backwater of the state-owned economy left over from the First World War, and the travel agents Thomas Cook.

But as the broader economy began to ail he quickly switched back to traditional Keynesian remedies. In early 1971, when the aircraft division of Rolls-Royce was threatened with bankruptcy, the Conservatives effectively nationalized it, citing the size of its work-force in areas already short of jobs. In the summer, the government began to increase public spending on housing and public works. In the autumn, a secret Cabinet committee chaired by Sir William

Armstrong, Heath's most trusted civil-service adviser, began a review of the economic situation. Its conclusion that cutting unemployment should be an urgent priority would heavily colour the government's policies the following year: simultaneous tax cuts, increases in state benefits, and new subsidies for industry, the latter on an unprecedented scale for a Conservative administration, especially one elected promising to let 'lame ducks' fail. Heath's critics quickly came up with a memorable phrase for the direction of economic policy from 1971 onwards. They called it his 'U-turn'.

Democratic governments always betray some of their initial promise. Incompatible interest groups and electioneering's necessary half-truths see to that. But Heath's administration had started out with less political credit than most. It owed its existence to a shock election result, miscalculations by opponents and a vague feeling of national disillusionment rather than to any deep popular enthusiasm for Heath and his brand of Conservatism. As soon as the government's novelty wore off and it encountered the inevitable problems of office, public attitudes to Heath and the Tories simply reverted, in a sense, to what they had been for much of the sixties. At the end of 1970, after a strikingly brief post-election honeymoon, the Conservatives fell behind Labour in the polls – including the one poll that had correctly predicted their recent general-election victory – and remained behind almost continuously for the next three years.

Yet over this period their unpopularity also acquired new dimensions. Some of this would come from the right-wing radicals at the IEA and inside the party, and their reaction to the 'U-turn'; and some would come from the other strengthening political movement that Heath, for all his ponderous moderation and reasonable intentions, roused to fury and politically lethal plotting: the trade unions.

PART TWO
Shocks

4

Close the Gates!

The week before Heath took office, a junior official from the National Union of Mineworkers appeared on a local television discussion programme called *Yorkshire Matters*. Arthur Scargill was thirty-two. He wore a black suit which emphasized the paleness of his face. His hair, swept back in an old-fashioned fifties style, was already receding slightly, and he had the beginnings of a double chin. He spoke in a thin but piercing voice that leapt unevenly in tone at moments of emphasis, almost as if it were still breaking.

Yet there was an air of utter confidence about Scargill. Beside him sat two other junior officials from other unions, selected for the programme, as he had been, solely for being promising Yorkshire trade unionists. They were slightly older and talked at greater length, attempting, with some awkwardness, to sound simultaneously moderate and militant about the appropriate function of unions in modern Britain. Scargill watched them with his small bright eyes, making a show of listening carefully. But a faintly mocking smile kept sneaking across his face. Then he broke in: 'I'm completely convinced that victory is won by militancy,' he said, his smile gone in an instant, his eyes abruptly cold and fierce. 'I've never known the employer who gives you anything. You get as much as you are prepared to go out and take.'

The bare, overlit set of the programme was silent for a moment. When the discussion started again, the balance had shifted. The other union officials and even the presenter now deferred to Scargill as the show's main attraction. At the end, it was suggested he might become leader of the NUM one day. 'Well, I hope you're right, obviously,' said Scargill with utter composure, his long dagger nose completely still in the studio lights. Only a single impatient bob of a shiny black shoe betrayed other feelings.

*

In 1970, the unions were approaching their zenith. Ever since they had been pioneered in Britain in the nineteenth century, their potency had risen and fallen. As recently as the fifties, they had been widely written off, their memberships stagnating, their faith in class-based collective action considered out of step with the aspirational, more individualistic Britain emerging from the first post-war consumer boom. Yet such dips in influence had proved temporary. From their intimate involvement in the founding and functioning of the Labour Party, to the unique legal protections they had enjoyed since the Edwardian era, to the powerful economic position Keynesian thinking assumed they should naturally occupy, the trade unions' underlying trajectory was upward. Their total membership increased every year during the forties, fifties and sixties. During the late sixties and seventies, this growth accelerated: in 1968, 43 per cent of the British workforce were union members; by 1978, the figure was 54 per cent. Although this was not an especially high proportion by international standards – in Denmark and Sweden at the end of the seventies membership was around 70 per cent – the power of British trade unionists was magnified by their willingness to use it.

The reasons for this were as much social and economic as political. Britain in the sixties and seventies was a Western country particularly troubled by rising inflation, unemployment and taxation, yet the material expectations of its population were still growing. In this context, it made sense to join a union which, assuming politicians, employers and economists continued to accept such a role for them, would give you a degree of protection from the bad times and increase your ability to cash in when times were good. It also made sense, once you were in a union, to support at least periodically the exercise of union power. In his 1976 book *The New Barons: Union Power in the 1970s*, *The Economist*'s labour correspondent Stephen Milligan – a telling position for a magazine aimed at business executives – noted that successful strikes boosted the recruitment of new members and the profile of victorious unions, making further strikes and further gains for members more likely in the future.

From the early sixties, the apparent logic of acting militantly began to change how British unions functioned. Many of them were already vast, dispersed organizations: in 1964, the biggest, the Transport and General Workers' Union (TGWU), had over 1.5 million members, from Birmingham brewery staff to Scottish sewage workers. Previously, such unions had been steered by elected general secretaries, often autocratic in style and in the job for decades. But, during the sixties, this top-down, hierarchical way of doing things began to be challenged by a less deferential, more egalitarian form of industrial relations, a shift that went with the grain of social change in Britain as a whole. In rapidly increasing numbers shop stewards started representing small groups of people in individual workplaces. The stewards were unpaid, usually unelected, part-time and younger than regular union officials, yet increasingly they came to dominate the everyday dealings between workers and management. 'Down on the shopfloor or in the office,' the leading analyst of trade unions Robert Taylor could write by 1978, 'the wise or foolish words of a trade union general secretary do not enjoy a lasting impact in the course of industrial relations. The gulf between the settled world of the union leader sitting in head office (usually down in London suburbia a long way from Britain's industrial heartland) and the fluid, informal routine of union life in industry remains enormous.' During the seventies, the number of shop stewards in Britain quadrupled.

Most of them were not revolutionaries. In fact, Taylor found that many were as keen to avoid strikes and other frictions in industrial relations as their employers were. Acting as the valued link between the workers and the bosses brought its own satisfactions. However, one feature of the seventies was the frequency with which people who did not think of themselves as terribly political ended up in confrontational situations, through seeking to defend what they saw as their interests against an increasingly threatening outside world. Another feature of the decade was the spread of radical left-wing activism, which had revived in Britain in the fifties and sixties, into new and fruitful areas. Militant trade unionism was by far the most significant example. In 1987, a much less sympathetic time for unions, the left-wing historian Raphael Samuel looked back at seventies union activism for part of an essay called 'The Lost World of British Communism':

Trade unionism in the 1970s was not only a cause. For its most fervent defenders . . . it was also, in the absence of socialism or communism, something approaching a workers' faith . . . Beneath the militant rhetoric, and the seemingly narrow demands, it is possible to discern a quasi-religious impulse at work . . . a search for self-transcendence; the claim to collective dignity by reference to the past; the joy of a wider belonging. Strikes, for those who took part in them, took on something of the character of [religious] Revivals, such as those which swept the coalfields in the past: an occasion for mass conversion, a time when all things are made anew. The mass picket was a ceremonial demonstration of strength. Confrontations with the police, however unequal the contestants, were cathartic . . . The main enemy were characterized as 'scabs', a category of folk-devil which treated as pariahs any who flinched from the storm. The struggle to defend trade unionism, like the struggle for socialism in earlier years, was indivisible.

In Britain, starting in the late sixties, Samuel records,

The incidence of strikes increased dramatically; by the time of the 'pay explosion' of 1969–72, they were more frequent than at any time since 1919, and more successful in attaining their immediate objectives than any since the 'strike explosion' of 1871–73.

Many of these strikes were 'unofficial' – often initiated at very short notice, without the permission, or in open defiance of, the relevant union's chain of command. By 1968, the Wilson government was already sufficiently concerned to set up a Royal Commission to examine industrial relations in Britain, and then to task one of its most able ministers, Barbara Castle, with toughening the Commission's extremely cautious suggestions for restricting strikers' freedoms into something much more fundamental. The result was 1969's 'In Place of Strife', a White Paper proposing that the government should have the power to require a ballot of workers and a four-week 'cooling-off period' before a strike could begin. Within five months of publication, after opposition from the unions and their closest allies among Labour MPs and the Cabinet, in particular Jim Callaghan, the White Paper was abandoned.

*

To the Conservatives, what seemed the increasingly impregnable position of the unions was an even greater and more long-standing worry than it was to Labour industrial-relations reformers like Castle. 'Many of us on the right of the Party – and not just on the right – were becoming very concerned about the abuse of trade union power,' writes Margaret Thatcher of her first years as an MP in the late fifties and early sixties. The first post-war Conservative scheme for curbing the unions was a pamphlet entitled 'A Giant's Strength'. It was written by – Thatcher's description – 'a brilliant young Tory barrister called Geoffrey Howe' and published in 1958. The following year Heath became minister of labour.

However, his feelings about unions were, and remained, more complicated – you could say contradictory – than those of Tories like Howe and Thatcher. Unlike them, Heath had grown up in an era when unions were weak rather than domineering. He had had his encounter with Jack Jones, who became TGWU general secretary in 1968, in Spain decades earlier. In theory and sometimes in practice, Heath thought unions were a good thing. 'The unions were an estate of the realm with whom cooperation was both desirable and necessary, if the nation was to remain united,' is how he summarizes his philosophy as minister of labour in his autobiography. 'Most union leaders were ultimately responsible people who could be reasoned with.' His success in halting the threatened strike by the National Union of Railwaymen in 1959 through negotiation strengthened this conviction.

Heath's respect for unions was sometimes reciprocated. 'No Prime Minister, either before or since, could compare with Ted Heath in the efforts he made to establish a spirit of camaraderie with trade unions,' Jones wrote in his memoirs. 'Over the years he revealed the human face of Toryism, at least to the trade union leaders who met him frequently.' Taylor notes that while he was prime minister, 'Employers' leaders in the Confederation of British Industry often gained the impression Heath much preferred the social company of the TUC [Trades Union Congress] establishment to their own.'

Yet Heath's conciliatory attitude to unions depended on their remaining 'responsible' and 'reasonable' in his eyes. When they did not, he responded with the intemperance of a thin-skinned person whose strenuous patience has been exhausted. In Salisbury, I asked him about the behaviour of the NUM during his government. Heath's voice instantly clotted with distaste: 'Oh, they wanted to bust up the whole thing.' In the Conservatives' private policy discussions at Selsdon Park in 1970, he was already showing signs of impatience with British industrial relations. 'Up to 1939 the balance was on the side of the employer,' the minutes record him saying. 'After 1945 the balance was on the side of the unions and it is still on the side of the unions . . . Employers have to be free to . . . get rid of men . . . The trouble at the moment is they cannot.'

In 1971, the Heath government produced a characteristically ambitious blueprint for transforming industrial relations. The Industrial Relations Bill was a mixture of both the consensual and the confrontational Heath approaches to unions. On the one hand, it recognized the right of workers to what the employment secretary Robert Carr called 'strong trade union representation' and compelled employers by law to do the same. On the other, the bill attempted to regulate virtually every aspect of union conduct, with potentially heavy legal penalties for non-compliance. The whole legislative package was so long and fussily written that even Carr himself later admitted he did not fully understand its provisions. It quickly proved even more politically indigestible than 'In Place of Strife'.

Most unions were horrified at the prospect of their activities being tightly controlled by law. Many also felt a degree of discomfort at having damaged the Wilson government by opposing Castle's reforms, and were keen to make up for it by taking on the Conservatives. Labour, meanwhile, saw an opportunity to hurt the Tories – Wilson remained a master of such manoeuvres – and to exact revenge for the Conservatives' own, equally cynical refusal to support 'In Place of Strife'. In the late sixties and early seventies, the possibility that obstructing trade union reform for short-term political advantage might be storing up trouble for the long term was not a decisive consideration for either party.

For much of 1971, the Industrial Relations Bill met major resistance: in Parliament, where debates on it took up more time than those on any non-financial legislation since 1945; at the TUC, where unions devised the effective strategy of simply refusing to register with the legal bodies the bill intended to set up; and on the streets, where between 120,000 and 250,000 'Kill the Bill' protesters, said to constitute the largest ever British trade union demonstration, chanted their way through central London. Yet the bill survived. In August 1971, it became law. 'It felt like there were going to be big battles with the unions, but that the reforms and strong government would sort them out,' remembers Brendon Sewill. 'And if those battles were won, one would come out all right on the other side.' But he and the rest of the Heath government had not thought enough about the miners.

I met Charlie McLaren on a bright September weekday in 2004. He was a stout man of sixty-two, with a wheeze behind his easy laugh. He lived in a neat new bungalow in a suburb of Stoke-on-Trent, between a branch of the budget supermarket Lidl and a lumpy ex-industrial hillside. In the clear, unforgiving sunshine, there were a lot of middle-aged men about. They did not seem to be working. There was a sense of premature retirements being eked out.

It was midday but McLaren still had his slippers on. We sat in his living room while his grandchildren played outside the open windows. He told me he had not worked as a miner for over twenty years. 'I got sacked during the '84–5 strike,' he said. He looked at his slippers. 'They said I hit a scab. But I didn't.' He had had one job since, as a trade union lecturer in Wolverhampton, but his health had ended that: 'I couldn't run for a bus or anything.' He looked up again, eyebrows black and bristling but the gaze neutral beneath them. 'My chest,' he said matter-of-factly. 'From the pit.'

He had started as a miner in 1958, at the age of sixteen. His father had been a miner and NUM activist before him. The melancholy twentieth-century history of the British coal industry ran through their lives. The presence of coal in accessible locations had been central to the Industrial Revolution and Britain's rise to global pre-eminence. But by the Edwardian era, the mining business, like the national economy, faced unbeatable international competition and the beginnings of decline. British coal output peaked in 1913; subsequent innovations – rationalizing the number of pits, nationalizing them all in 1947, securing preferential financial treatment from the government – were often simply ways of postponing the industry's fate. In 1955, McLaren's father gave up on the shrinking Lanarkshire coalfields in Scotland and moved to England with his family to find more secure mining work. Three years later, the teenage McLaren joined a pit in Staffordshire. 'I was a face-worker,' he said. 'It was better paid but the hardest job. All bloody pick and shovel until mechanization in the late sixties.'

Because of the historic significance of their industry and the grim struggle of their working lives, miners continued to be revered, even romanticized, long after such feelings had dwindled, if they ever existed, for the rest of the industrial working class. 'The men who work in the coal industry rightly evoke our sympathy and admiration,' declared Heath's trade and industry secretary John Davies in the Commons in January 1972. The government's former adviser Brendon Sewill remembers: 'I went down a coal mine while I was studying economics at Cambridge. I reckoned it was part of my education. I was totally aware of what a bloody awful job it was.'

Another element of the miners' mid-twentieth-century mystique was their unusual politics: a mixture of militancy and reticence. From the earliest days of the industry in the eighteenth century, British miners had been the pioneers of strikes and other forms of workplace activism. 'Coalmining had a tradition,' wrote the mining historian William Ashworth in 1986, 'so old as to be apparently ineradicable, of quick resort to small-scale [industrial] action in cases of disagreement.' By the twentieth century, the importance of coal to the economy as a whole had established a widespread fear of miners' rebellions. Yet their militancy tended to follow an unusual cycle, with insurrectionary periods – for example, the succession of major strikes in 1912, 1920, 1921 and 1926 – followed by long stretches of relative inaction, when remembering past struggles seemed more of a priority than launching new ones. The miners were also strongly divided along political and regional lines. The Yorkshire NUM, for example, had a reputation between 1940 and 1970 for being right-wing by trade union standards and for acting virtually as a union within a union. When Heath took office, there had not been a national miners' strike for almost half a century.

In Staffordshire at the start of the seventies, McLaren's NUM activism involved no more than attending union branch meetings. 'It was a pretty moderate area. There had been only one short strike in the sixties.' But elsewhere the union's placidity was at best superficial. During the sixties, the chairman of the National Coal Board had been Lord Robens, an ex-miner, NUM member and *Guardian* reader. Despite these credentials, his memoirs are shrill with warnings about an upsurge in 'subversive' miners' behaviour. During a strike in Yorkshire in 1960, he records, 'Agitators toured the coalfield in flying columns.' In 1970, again in Yorkshire, Robens had an encounter with a 'yarling mob' of rebellious miners. He found them 'crude, vulgar and unfit to lead the decent men I know in the pits. How in heaven's name men like this can possibly be elected as leaders of good Yorkshire miners, I cannot understand . . . But for the presence of the police I believe they would cheerfully have murdered me.'

This return to militancy had many sources. The mechanization of the industry required changes in work practices, and the precise shape of the miner's working day had long led to disputes and tricky negotiations. In 1971, a new NUM president, Joe Gormley, had been elected. He was a self-styled 'realist' who sensed a more abrasive kind of leadership was required by his members. Miners' pay had fallen behind that of comparable workers during the sixties: 'We were looking at what other people were earning,' remembers McLaren, 'and even Staffordshire miners had begun to realize we weren't getting paid what we should.' There was also a sense that the time for militancy might be running out. In September 1971, oil overtook coal as the leading fuel consumed in Britain for the first time. The number of miners had already shrunk by more than half during the previous decade, and of those who remained twice as many were in their fifties as in their twenties. In addition, there was an ancient score for the NUM to settle. The miners' last national strike, in 1926, had not been won and had not been forgotten.

Finally, there was the Communist Party of Great Britain's involvement in the NUM. The CP's peak of popularity had been decades before, in the forties, when half a million Britons regularly voted Communist and the party could count its local councillors in the hundreds. Since then, the CP had faced growing difficulties. The Russian invasion of Hungary in 1956 and of Czechoslovakia in 1968 had cost it members and sympathy: while the CP strongly criticized the latter, it remained closely associated with the Soviet Union. Between 1957 and 1979, the British CP received a secret subsidy from the Russian embassy in London, dispensed in cash in large leather holdalls. Meanwhile, the CP's austere and disciplined political style left it ill-suited, in many ways, to the looser Britain of these years: the party was uncomfortable with the libertarian, hard-to-control character of many of the period's radical movements and campus rebellions. The CP was even sometimes uncomfortable with its members having long hair. Its Trotskyite rivals – the International Socialists, the International Marxist Group – took advantage.

The one area of British political life where the CP was still making progress was in the unions. Like the party, they were still full of middle-aged men who believed in the class struggle. From the late fifties, the party's highly effective 'industrial organizer' Baruch ('Bert') Ramelson, a Ukrainian immigrant of considerable charm, worked quietly to secure the election of party members as senior union officials. Ramelson astutely realized that CP men would only achieve influence in unions if they showed themselves to be good union men first. He encouraged them to be low-key, at least in public, about their involvement in the party, and discouraged the party from keeping them on too tight a rein. He also encouraged the CP to form alliances with left-wing union leaders such as the TGWU general secretary Jack Jones who were not communists but shared some of the party's broad goals.

Yet it was in the NUM that Ramelson's strategy paid the the most dramatic dividends. By the early seventies, one of the CP's ruling committee, Mick McGahey, was the leader of the Scottish miners. Five other members of the twenty-six-strong NUM executive were also communists. Even the once-conservative Yorkshire NUM had moved strongly leftwards. In the summer of 1971, the union embarked on a national campaign that would enter NUM mythology – and the collective memory of British politics.

In July, the union's annual conference voted unanimously that miners should receive an average pay increase of 25 per cent. In October, the union's national executive rejected a Coal Board offer of 7.5 per cent. The Heath government had imposed a ceiling of 8 per cent on pay increases across the economy in an attempt to control inflation. In November, miners throughout Britain stopped doing any overtime. The same month, a strike ballot was held, and 58.8 per cent voted in favour. On 9 January 1972, the strike began.

It was widely expected to fail. The vote for a stoppage had not been overwhelming; the NUM did not have enough money for strike pay; the winter had been mild so far, so coal stocks were high; and the government had made preparations. 'During the past months,' explained a secret memo written by a civil servant two days before the strike started, 'measures have been taken . . . to maximise the level of [coal] consumers' stocks and ensure that as far as possible these were reasonably distributed throughout the country.' In the Cabinet a day earlier, the mood was quietly confident: 'The Home Secretary', the minutes record, 'said that the general arrangements to deal with the initial effects of the strike appeared satisfactory.'

The media were less guarded in their assessments. 'Rarely have strikers advanced to the barricades with less enthusiasm or hope of success,' wrote the columnist Woodrow Wyatt in the *Daily Mirror*. 'It will hurt them more than it hurts us,' forecast the *Daily Mail*. 'Few believe that the miners will stay out long enough to inconvenience the public.' The *Financial Times* delivered a stern lecture to the miners about 'the futility of taking on a determined government', especially given 'the apparent inability of the unions to unite together in battle'. A Thames Television documentary about the build-up to the strike summed up the prevailing mood: it was titled *The Miners' Last Stand*.

Yet the NUM quickly upset all these predictions. The union made a virtue of its weaknesses. Lacking the funds and the support from his members for a drawn-out stoppage, Gormley and his strategists devised a brief, aggressive campaign. Instead of simply shutting down the pits and other coal-mining facilities in the traditional attritional NUM style, the union went for the 'pressure points' of the coal-dependent economy: power stations, coal depots, anywhere coal was consumed or distributed in significant quantities. Each regional NUM organization was assigned a non-mining area to cover as well as its own backyard. Kent miners watched the grey Thames Estuary for coal ships and patrolled its muddy inlets and wharves in motor boats provided by sympathizers. Yorkshire miners recruited students from the University of Essex in Colchester to act as auxiliary pickets and lookouts. Power stations everywhere were blockaded. Where they had adequate reserves of coal, out of reach behind their perimeter fences, the miners cut off other vital supplies instead: 'lighting-up oil', which kept the coal-combustion process stable – and which had not been stockpiled by the government – and even food for the power-station canteens. Power-station managers tried to counter by bringing in oil at night, or by helicopter, or by smuggling it in in containers disguised as engineering components. But by only the third week of the strike, sections of power stations were having to be shut down.

That a shrinking union with a membership of less than 300,000 was able to undertake such an effective campaign demonstrated something important about the NUM, and about striking unions generally, in Britain in the early seventies: their political and social clout extended far beyond their memberships. Striking miners could be deployed in small numbers because they would be supported or obeyed by other trade unionists and members of the public. The left-wing sociologist and NUM ally V. L. Allen later cited 'the case of the train driver [during the 1972 miners' strike] who stopped at a station to discharge his goods, looked back and saw a solitary picket standing on a bridge over the railway lines and, on realizing he had crossed a picket line, backed his train to the other side of the bridge'. On 18 January, a civil servant wrote in a briefing note to the new chairman of the Coal Board, Derek Ezra: 'The union are winning a lot of public sympathy. That has its roots in history. We are not going to be able to change that.' Three days later, NUM headquarters felt compelled to include a paragraph headed 'casual helpers' in its latest set of instructions for pickets. The paragraph read: 'In many areas, members of the public are offering help on picket lines. This help should be accepted but there must be at least one NUM member in charge of the line at all times.'

Much faster than the government had anticipated, the coal-fired economy became vulnerable. In November 1971, at the beginning of the miners' overtime ban, the power stations held 16,900,000 tons of coal, their highest-ever reserves. By the start of the strike the following January, the overtime ban had already reduced stocks to 12,300,000 tons. By the beginning of February, stocks were down to 7,600,000 tons, enough for less than four weeks' electricity in average winter weather. On cue, a cold snap began.

Sewill remembers the anxiety beginning to seep through Whitehall. 'I heard the Treasury Permanent Secretary talking about the possible need to activate the regional government centres, as in the case of nuclear war. Because if all the lights went out, there would be no way of governing the country from the centre. Some civil servants were . . . absolutely traumatized by the fact that the country was facing that sort of shutdown.' On 11 February, a secret official report on the effects of the strike recorded: 'The first unplanned power cuts occurred yesterday . . . The [planned] 9–10% power cuts which are being introduced today will have to be increased to about 20% in about a week's time; to about 30% after a further week; and to about 40% in about three weeks.'

On 21 February, the children's television programme *Blue Peter* opened with an item on how to cope. 'Power cuts are an especially difficult time for old people,' began the presenter Peter Purves. 'They get cold. But you can look out for the ones you know . . .' Behind him, in the optimistic white expanse of the *Blue Peter* studio, stood a narrow single bed made up with brown blankets. Purves walked over to the bed and was joined by his co-presenter John Noakes. Together they started vigorously pulling apart tabloid newspapers. 'Lay out sheets of newspaper,' said Purves. 'Place them fairly thickly between the blankets.' He and Noakes bent over the bed, sifting heavy wool and flimsy newspaper. 'And if you do that, the old folks will stay as warm as toast.' With his trademark Boy Scout smile, Noakes added: 'With all this newspaper, I shouldn't go to bed with a candle, though.'

For a prime minister who had promised 'to change the course of history of this nation' less than eighteen months earlier, it was not a glorious outcome. But the decisive, televised moment of the 1972 miners' strike did not happen on *Blue Peter*. It happened in the less controlled environment of a live news broadcast, from a type of political arena with which British viewers in the seventies would become very familiar.

Saltley was a dying industrial suburb a mile east of the centre of Birmingham. In the seventies, there were places like it in almost every town and city in the country. Tools and other metal goods had been manufactured in Saltley and neighbouring Nechells since the early sixteenth century, but by 1972 its dim reddish landscape of Victorian brick and low hills, terraced houses and canals, viaducts and cobbled factory yards was fast depopulating and had been officially earmarked as 'a demolition area'. There were a few neglected shops and too many pubs. The air smelled vaguely of gas on windless days. A dark dust constantly got into people's houses. 'We used to have a saying in Saltley,' says Arthur Harper, a union activist who lived there in the seventies, 'that you used to wake up to hear the birds coughing.'

The source of the smell and the dust was the coke depot. It occupied a large, roughly triangular site at the bottom of a hill and was operated by the West Midlands Gas Board, a local state-owned company that would soon be absorbed into British Gas. One of the Gas Board's businesses was the extraction of gas from coal – a common way of extending coal's usefulness – and the sale of the resulting husks, known as coke, as a smokeless fuel for hospitals, schools and other premises. At Saltley, the coke, which had lost the glossiness of coal and was a dry matt black instead, was heaped up into a great uneven ridge, like a range of small grim mountains, while awaiting sale. The coke pile was Saltley's landmark. 'For a hundred years the local urchins would go [to the depot] and buy a bucket of coke for their mum,' remembers a former West Midlands Gas Board manager. 'Otherwise it was three lorries a day at most on a normal day.'

But with the miners' strike this trade changed dramatically. The day before the stoppage started, the Birmingham *Sunday Mercury* found 'panic buying' of coal in the city. 'Merchants were reporting last night that the rush . . . would leave them out of stock in a matter of days.' Yet buried on an inside page, at the end of one of many strike-related reports, was the following:

A West Midlands Gas Board official confirmed last night that there are coke stocks of at least 100,000 tons at the board's Windsor Street depot in Saltley . . . 'The reason we have so much is because demand has been so low due to a mild winter,' he said. 'We would be willing to sell the coke to coal merchants, subject to loading facilities being available.'

Like other coke depots, at the start of the strike Saltley had been given 'guidelines', agreed between the government and the NUM, that it should continue to supply only 'priority customers' such as hospitals and the vulnerable. Yet the West Midlands Gas Board argued that the guidelines did not apply to Saltley: unlike other coke depots, it belonged to a gas company, which was not and should not become involved in a strike concerning a different industry. It was a legalistic, restrictive view of industrial disputes that was not – yet – widely shared in Britain. But the effects of the Gas Board's stance were undeniable. By the beginning of February, with the miners having steadily cut off the movement of coal and coke in the rest of the country, Saltley was receiving and filling several hundred trucks a day. They came from Wales, Cornwall, Lancashire, Yorkshire, Derbyshire, Wiltshire, queueing along the roads to the depot from early in the morning. Birmingham's rush hour was disrupted, at times by up to a mile of idling articulated lorries. On 3 February, the Birmingham *Evening Mail* ran a feature on the queues, with photographs. 'The coke drivers said today they feared that striking miners might start picketing the stockpile next week,' the paper reported. 'Bolton driver Mr Arthur Saxon said: "I'm amazed they haven't started picketing it already."'

The Midlands NUM had known about the activity at the depot for a fortnight, but it was a small, politically cautious part of the union and it had not had the manpower or the will to blockade the site. Instead, it had tried to negotiate with the Gas Board; when that tactic failed, it despatched two dozen pickets. They arrived outside the depot on 4 February, a Friday. Half a dozen policemen arrived too.

In Britain in 1972 the law regarding picketing, like much of the law regarding trade unions and industrial disputes, was at best vague and at worst contradictory. Strikers had the right to picket 'any place' except for people's homes, as long as their activities went no further than 'peaceful persuasion'. But as Heath's home secretary Reginald Maudling put it in a Commons debate that year, 'It is difficult to know in any particular set of circumstances when the right of people to persuade others not to go into a factory becomes intimidation.' The Labour MP Leslie Huckfield pointed out that the law could be equally unsatisfactory from a trade union perspective: 'If pickets just stand harmlessly and aimlessly by the roadside, that is called peaceful picketing. But if they are successful . . . that is intimidation.'

For the first few days at Saltley, the former of Huckfield's two scenarios seemed to be unfolding. The pickets stood either to the side or in front of the high metal gates used by the lorries to enter the depot. They indicated to the drivers that they should stop, declare whether the coke they were picking up was for a permitted 'priority customer', and if it was not, submit themselves to verbal 'persuasion' and agree to drive away empty-handed. Almost to a man, the drivers – who were not required by law to stop and talk to pickets – ignored the miners' wishes. 'We weren't stopping even half of the lorries,' remembers McLaren, who went to Saltley as part of the NUM contingent from the Midlands. 'And even the ones who we stopped and talked to, most of them said, "We sympathize, but I've got a family to support." A huge cheer would go up if a driver said, "All right then," and turned back. And we didn't get many bloody cheers.' Some of the truckers, when they got to the front of the queue of lorries, simply accelerated towards the gates and their flimsy cordon of pickets. The miners had to get out of the way as best they could.

Over the weekend, 200 more pickets arrived from pits in the Midlands. The police presence increased to fifty officers, and there were one or two arrests for scuffling and obstruction. A slightly greater proportion of lorries were persuaded to drive away empty, but the situation remained essentially the same. Then Arthur Scargill intervened.

Both his father and grandfather had been miners. At twelve, Scargill began going to political meetings with his father, who was an NUM activist and a Communist Party member. At fifteen, Scargill started at a pit near Barnsley in south Yorkshire. At sixteen, he joined the NUM; at seventeen, the Young Communist League. He quickly realized that politics appealed to him more than mining. Even when he worked above ground at the pit, he would later tell interviewers, he had to wash the caked dust from his lips before eating lunch.

By his early twenties, however, he had lost patience with the stifling orthodoxies of British communism. Instead, he favoured a loosely defined militant leftism that emphasized aggressive direct action – primarily the use of strikes – and the potency of trade unions as a crusading vanguard for socialism. In the cautious Yorkshire NUM of the late fifties, Scargill's thinking and methods encountered considerable resistance from union colleagues, as well as from the local Coal Board management, but he was shrewd and relentless. In 1960, aged twenty-two, he led a noisy and successful campaign over the seemingly minor issue of the timing of union branch meetings at his pit, which climaxed in a thousand-strong miners' march through Barnsley. Journalists and NUM officials across Yorkshire took note.

With his youth, his smart suits, his ease on television, his deliberately concise, quotable rhetoric and his ability to build broad left-wing alliances – he stayed friendly enough with the Communist Party to secure its backing at critical moments – Scargill was a new and formidable kind of trade unionist. In 1962, he set out to widen his understanding of the Britain beyond the pit and union branch meeting by beginning a part-time course in economics, industrial relations and social history at Leeds University. By the late sixties, he and a group of fellow left-wingers, working in public and in private as the anodyne-sounding Barnsley Miners' Forum, had effectively turned the Yorkshire NUM, the union's most powerful regional organization, from a byword for caution into a byword for radicalism. In 1969, and again in 1970, the Yorkshire miners went on unofficial strike. Neither campaign won the gains the miners wanted, but a pattern of self-perpetuating militancy had been established.

The 1969 dispute also featured the first widespread use of a potent new strike tactic, the flying picket. In a long admiring interview with Scargill published in the grandest British left-wing journal, the *New Left Review*, six years later and titled 'The New Unionism', he explained how flying pickets worked:

We launched from the coalfield here [in Yorkshire] squads of cars, minibuses and buses, all directed on to predetermined targets, with five, six hundred miners at a time. Of course, the police were going to come, but they couldn't cover forty points at a time, without bringing the British armed forces in.

In the 1972 miners' strike, this Yorkshire innovation went national. With no strike pay available, the NUM shrewdly agreed to give its members £2 a day in expenses, roughly half their normal daily wage, if they picketed premises away from their own area. Charlie McLaren was one of thousands who took up the offer:

For the first couple of weeks of the strike we had just picketed our own pit. A few people would turn up for work, see the pickets, turn around and go home . . . One day we got word from the union saying, 'Go to Saltley.' Two buses would be laid on the next day to take anyone that wants to go . . . I don't think I'd even heard of Saltley, but it was, 'Come on, let's go and cut the bloody boredom. Better than standing here talking to each other.'

Scargill was already busy in the weeks before Saltley. When the strike started, the Yorkshire NUM divided itself into four local strike committees, and he became spokesman for Barnsley. After it was decided that the Yorkshire miners should also picket in East Anglia, he helped devise a picketing strategy. At the time and afterwards he skilfully played up his role, telling the *Observer* magazine – he was beginning to win national media attention – that he deployed flying pickets from a military-style headquarters in Barnsley 'like shock troops'. In fact, he was a relatively junior member of the strike committee, but the effectiveness of the strategy was undeniable: large numbers of Yorkshire miners, despatched at short notice to form a succession of 'mass pickets' at significant locations, had shut down East Anglia's coal-related economy by the first week of February.

Hundreds of miles from home, the miners were put up by sympathetic university students and academics. Scargill was thrilled by the potential of the coalition he saw forming: 'I went on a tour of all the universities in East Anglia and spoke to enthusiastic audiences packed with university students *and* miners together,' he recalled in the *New Left Review*. 'The barriers were completely down . . . That was, I think, one of the most remarkable experiences that I have ever had.' The University of Essex, which was well known for its left-wing students and relatively tolerant authorities, became the miners' East Anglian headquarters. 'We showed to the university students a degree of discipline and organization which they had probably read about in their Marxist books . . . We had the International Marxist Group, the International Socialists, the Workers' Revolutionary Party and all the other [campus] organizations coming together . . . and agreeing with us they would have to sink their differences; that we would have to fight one common enemy and that we had no time to discuss whether Trotsky said X, Y or Z in 1873.'

Scargill also felt these heady campus weeks had an effect on the miners: 'Our people . . . in a matter of days, they were changing . . . not only listening to speeches, but actually getting on their feet and speaking themselves.' There were other benefits for some of the miners who stayed in the university's residential tower blocks, which were only lightly supervised by the campus staff. The tabloids began to report that the attraction between students and miners was sometimes more than political. As Scargill put it, 'Some of our boys were very comfortable there. We had difficulty in getting them home.'

After the success and triumphalism of the miners' campaign in East Anglia – and in most of the rest of the country by early February – the news that huge quantities of coke were still moving freely out of Saltley came as a shock to Scargill and his strike committee. Over the weekend of the 5th and 6th, he quickly set about turning it into an opportunity.

At teatime on the Saturday, Barnsley, like several other strike committees, had received a request from NUM national headquarters for help with the Saltley situation. In his autobiography Gormley remembers telling his NUM subordinates: 'Get some bloody pickets down there as soon as you can.' While the other committees hesitated, unsure how to mount and finance a mass picket in an inner-city suburb far from most mining areas, Scargill spent the late afternoon and evening arranging coaches, alerting Yorkshire miners and despatching 400 of them to Birmingham. Later that night, he drove down there himself.

He had allies in the city. The Communist Party district secretary Frank Watters had been an NUM activist in Yorkshire; more significantly, he had been a close friend of Scargill's for decades. In Birmingham the hub of the CP's activities was the Star Club, a plainly decorated but innovative venue that held political and cultural events attended by the whole broad church of socialist Birmingham. The resourceful, deceptively genial Watters oversaw proceedings. When Scargill phoned him from Barnsley on the afternoon of 5 February, Watters already knew about Saltley; in fact, he had been trying for several days to drum up local reinforcements for the struggling depot pickets, with limited success. Watters now put the Star Club and his Birmingham network at Scargill's disposal. Some of the arriving Yorkshire miners were bought a few pints in the club, then allowed to sleep on the floor between the plastic chairs. Blankets had been procured from the Salvation Army. Other miners were taken home and put up by the club's Saturday-night customers. Scargill himself arrived in Birmingham at 3 o'clock in the morning.

The next day, he and the miners went to have a look at the depot. 'I have never seen anything like it in my life,' he remembered in the *New Left Review*. 'It was like the most gigantic stack of any colliery that I'd ever seen . . . It was like a mountain . . . It was an Eldorado of coke . . . You can imagine the reaction of our boys.'

Some of the details of what followed have become blurred by myth-making and credit-seeking and by the opposing positions of many of the Saltley protagonists. Scargill and Watters, both of whose accounts have a romantic tinge, have claimed that the miners forced the depot to stop admitting trucks that Sunday. In 1985, British Gas, into which the West Midlands Gas Board had been absorbed, published an internal report, 'The "Saltley" Incident', which it described as 'inevitably subjective'. The report claimed that the depot was not open for business that Sunday at all.

However, the direction and significance of events at Saltley between 6 and 10 February can be established with more certainty. Although there were already hundreds of miners from the Midlands picketing the depot, under the command of the secretary of the Midlands NUM, the well-known moderate Jack Lally, the much more junior Scargill quickly took charge of the operation. He had swapped his television-studio suits for a more proletarian donkey jacket, with the collar turned up and trade union badges on the lapels, plus a baseball cap and a thick red scarf. He held a loudhailer, and his speech was even quicker and more staccato than usual. He sensed faster than many of those present that a historic moment might be at hand. Scargill described his mindset during the strike in the *New Left Review*: 'We were in a class war. We were not playing cricket on the village green . . . We were out to defeat Heath and Heath's policies . . . Anyone who thinks otherwise is living in cloud-cuckoo land.'

Not all the Midlands miners were delighted at the arrival of this faintly messianic Yorkshireman. 'We'd heard of him,' McLaren remembers. 'I'm a bit of a cynic, and I thought, "Here's another bloody union man come to make a name for himself. We haven't asked for help from any other area. We've got our own fucking union men. What the hell are you doing here?" I'm a big Arthur supporter now, but at the time I thought, "Just keep your bloody arse out."'

Scargill ignored such sensitivities. By Monday, he had between 500 and 2,000 pickets (the numbers went up and down during each day, and the estimates differ wildly) to deploy against the depot. He swiftly established a command post. Opposite the depot gates, on a small triangular traffic island, there stood a public toilet with a low, flat roof. He climbed up with his loudhailer. From there he could see every element of the crowd as it thickened in the thin February sunshine: the police, over 200 of them, drawn up in two parallel lines to make a corridor towards the gates for the incoming lorries; the miners, many of them men of a certain age with old-fashioned haircuts, massing either side of the police corridor like a restive seventies football crowd; and, on the fringes of the action, left-wing newspaper sellers, students who had come to support the picket, local schoolchildren and residents who had come to have a look, and the television cameras.

Each time a lorry came down the hill towards the depot, Scargill would try to get the pickets to surge forward. The miners would duck their heads and shove together like a giant rugby scrum. The police, standing with their backs to the pickets, would link arms, brace their legs and dig their heels into the cobbles. Extra officers would run to the points where the police lines threatened to give way. Strained shouts of 'Dig in, lads! Dig in!' reverberated off chipped Victorian walls. Then Scargill – or simply the group mind of the shoving miners – would decide to switch the picket's angle of attack. If the police reacted too slowly, the miners would break through and spill onto the road. The depot gates would be blocked.

If the incoming lorry was caught in the sudden crush of pickets, the encounter could be volatile. Few of the drivers were trade unionists: the TGWU, the main union for lorry drivers, had warned its members their union cards would be withdrawn and their companies blacklisted if they crossed the picket line. By the Monday, with the Saltley mass picket fully established and gaining notoriety, the truckers still driving and queueing for many hours to get into the depot were determined or desperate for work, or both, and often self-employed – effectively frustrated small businessmen sitting in very big vehicles. The pickets would lie down in the road in front of them or climb up to their cab windows and cling on. They would bang on the sides of the trucks. There would be shouting matches. If a lorry finally got into the depot and out again with a load of coke, it would sometimes be pursued. 'When they stopped at the traffic light at the top of the hill,' remembered McLaren, 'miners would knock out the two pegs that held up the loading flap at the back. The coal came back down the hill.' He smiled: 'It was a bit of sabotage.' Was he ever involved? He gave a slightly shifty look. 'No.'

The Birmingham *Evening Mail* reported on the Wednesday that one driver had been seen wearing a crash helmet. 'Two others had Alsatian dogs in their cabs.' Richard Webb worked as a police constable at Saltley throughout the mass picket. 'The drivers had got pickaxe handles,' he told me when I met him, still cropped and broad-shouldered, in a cafe in Birmingham. 'I remember one time a lorry stopped and a pickaxe fell out.' He unfurled a worldly smile: 'That got the pickets stirred up.'

The truckers were hard to get at, high up in their cabs, but the miners were ingenious. 'The Communist Party would come round with sandwiches and pies for us,' said McLaren. 'We all started chucking the fucking pies. And then after we did it, I said, "I'm fucking starving."' In his memoirs, Watters records with relish the sight of truckers driving into the depot with steak and kidney pie hanging off their faces. The pickets also threw pies at the police, and during the shoving matches the police responded with a needling violence of their own. 'They were up to their bloody tricks,' said McLaren. 'I remember one day you had the police in front of you, just sort of standing there with their backs to you. And they'd start kicking you in the legs. And if you turned to react, they'd drag you away and arrest you.' I asked Webb if there had been kicking by the police. He wrinkled his big forehead. 'There probably was.' Just inside the depot gates, a 'truce area' was set up for administering First Aid. 'I went in to have some treatment,' Webb remembered. 'Somebody [had] pulled my thumb back – strained it. It swelled up. Initially it was quite painful.'

The week before Saltley, a miner had been killed by a truck as it drove through a picket line outside a power station in Scunthorpe. There was an immediate and melodramatic debate in the Commons – 'This could be the start of another Ulster in the Yorkshire coalfield,' warned a Labour MP with a mining constituency – and so the Saltley confrontation built up in an atmosphere of heightened sensitivity to violence. By the Monday, the Birmingham *Evening Mail*, whose coverage was notably more restrained and factual than that of many national newspapers, was already referring to the 'Battle of Saltley'. That day, the paper reported 'bottles, bricks, [and] stones' being thrown, 'crush injuries', and 'one driver . . . almost dragged from his cab' before defending himself with an iron bar. The same day, even the mild NUM official Jack Lally warned of retaliation if the police kept 'putting the boot in'. Meanwhile, the nightly television news, with its footage of pickets chanting, police carrying away wounded colleagues and the grappling crowd at the depot gates surging this way and that, seemingly uncontrollably, appeared to confirm that an ominous, even apocalyptic political disorder was breaking out at Saltley.

On the Tuesday, there were 350 policemen outside the gates. On the Wednesday, there were 600. On the Thursday, 800. Officers arrived in coaches. Police vans waited in side streets to receive arrested pickets. Plainclothes officers tried to mingle with the miners to pick out troublemakers or – some pickets alleged – act as provocateurs. Alongside this small army of policemen was a unit of the Special Patrol Group. It had been founded in 1961 as a mobile police force for dealing with situations thought beyond the capabilities of local officers. By the early seventies, this increasingly meant problems of public order, for which the SPG's sometimes violent solutions would become increasingly notorious. Richard Webb was an SPG member. 'We did a lot of work at football matches,' he recalled, with a police veteran's easy deployment of euphemism. The SPG also began to appear at political demonstrations and industrial disputes. At Saltley, Webb remembered, 'I think the thing that got us was Arthur Scargill on top of the toilets egging them on.'

In fact, the confrontation outside the coke depot was less ferocious than much of the coverage suggested. The British Gas report on the mass picket found that until its climactic stages,

Notwithstanding the evidence of violence depicted in the media . . . relations between police and pickets on the whole remained friendly and low key. Only when either lorries and/or TV crews arrived did the atmosphere change . . . Once the lorries and TV cameras had left the scene, the atmosphere relaxed, and often cigarettes were exchanged between pickets and police. Gas Board personnel had free access through the pickets . . .

In 1978, in a doomy book called *Britain in Agony: The Growth of Political Violence*, a retired major general and self-styled expert on social turbulence called Richard Clutterbuck – the British seventies were a boom time for such people – published casualty and arrest figures for the Saltley mass picket. They were modest enough to inadvertently undermine his book's melodramatic argument. 'During the six days,' wrote Clutterbuck, 'thirty people had been injured, sixteen of them police. Seventy-six arrests had been made.' He categorized most of those arrested:

61 miners
3 drivers
2 motor workers
1 insurance agent
2 unemployed
5 students
1 academic

In 1985, in a more sober book called *Policing Industrial Disputes: 1893 to 1985*, the sociologist Roger Geary suggested that the early seventies were, in fact, a relatively peaceful period for picket-line behaviour. Until the early twentieth century, he wrote, the police had effectively acted 'as an employer's private army' during British strikes, with all the street battling that implies. But between the Edwardian and Heath eras a whole host of factors – stronger trade unions, closer government supervision of the police, the growth of civil-liberties groups and the emergence of a more consensual, less starkly divided country than in Victorian times – changed the nature of factory-gate confrontations. The 'mass pushing and shoving' of the early seventies, Geary wrote, 'can be seen as a solution to the problem of making picketing effective without resorting to violence'. On the police side, he noted the absence of riot shields, riot helmets and even truncheons for officers on picket-line duty. At Saltley, even the SPG were lightly equipped. 'We'd have been bloody bollocked if we'd used truncheons,' Webb recalled. 'It wasn't that sort of incident.'

Of course, the British police in the early seventies were hardly social workers in uniform. Many IRA suspects, ethnic-minority Britons and other members of the period's lower-status groups could testify to that. And Geary acknowledges that in 1972, arrested miners (his anonymous informant does not say where) received brutal treatment 'on at least one occasion' once they had been removed to the more private, lightly regulated world of the police station. Yet on picket lines members of powerful trade unions were often protected by the invisible shield of their social standing and connections. Webb summarized his feelings towards the miners at Saltley: 'I went to school in a mining area in Kent. There was a friend of mine whose dad was a miner. We [the police at Saltley] were on poor money too, so we had sympathy with the miners. My view was that . . . there were one or two hotheads. The rest were ordinary working blokes looking after their interests.'

The residents and businesses of Saltley, despite the disruption the mass picket brought, also basically accepted the miners' presence. The struggling pubs and shops eagerly sold them beer and sandwiches. At J. H. Richards, a long-established manufacturer of metal bearings immediately round the corner from the depot gates, the managing director Philip Bellingham watched the mass picket ebb and flow. 'It built up from about 8 o'clock in the morning. The police would arrive at the same time as the pickets. It became something for people here, to go and have a look. The scene was just like the road outside a football stadium just before kick-off. I found the pickets polite, friendly. You could certainly sort of pass the time of day.' The miners' manners were not impeccable, though: 'We had to shut our gates at the front because they were walking in and, frankly, peeing up our wall.'

As the picket grew, Bellingham remembered, someone painted 'THE MINERS WILL WIN' in big white letters on a wall just up the hill from the depot. Tactical mistakes by the police made this more likely. In 2006, when I belatedly met Scargill, by then in semi-retirement as honorary president of a much-reduced NUM and much less available for interviews, he recalled one of them. 'At Saltley,' he said, 'the police were either side of the gates at the bottom of the hill, and we were above them.' His tiny, slightly tired eyes suddenly flashed with triumph: 'They had to push uphill!' Webb, for one, found it hard work. 'I was knackered each night. Most policing is quite boring, and I found Saltley quite exhilarating. But I got back absolutely knackered.'

The fundamental weakness of the police's position at Saltley, and ultimately that of the Heath government, was their shared belief that the miners could not or should not be taken on too aggressively. In mid-February, a secret civil-service memo on the miners' strike included a section titled 'Police Views':

Chief officers of police . . . are naturally anxious to avoid exacerbating feeling by strenuous action which would both embitter relations with the community and . . . lead to still greater numbers turning out to support the pickets . . . The police have on the whole felt relieved when those having charge of fuel depots . . . have come to terms with the miners about arrangements for access to the premises, although recognising that these have in effect been victories for the miners.

The government was more supportive of those who defied the NUM – but only unofficially. On the Tuesday at Saltley, the British Gas report records, 'The Chairman of the [West Midlands Gas] Board received a message from a senior Government Minister: "Whatever happens, don't close the gates – but don't say I told you as I shall deny having said it."' Moreover, the Heath administration remained squeamish about what supporting the Saltley management might ultimately involve. As the home secretary Reginald Maudling put it in his memoirs six years later:

. . . the number of strikers involved was so great, and feelings were running so high, that any attempt by the relatively small body of police who could be assembled to keep the depot open by force could have led to very grave consequences. Some of my colleagues asked me afterwards why I had not sent in troops to support the police, and I remember asking them one simple question, 'If they had been sent in, should they have gone in with their rifles loaded or unloaded?'

All Scargill needed to win at Saltley was enough pickets. During the Tuesday and the Wednesday, more miners arrived from Yorkshire, Derbyshire, Scotland and Wales. A few dozen local students and car workers came to help out, but the flood of people required to swamp the depot completely did not materialize: pickets, like policemen, got tired, and by midweek many miners had been sleeping on floors and shoving and chanting in the cold for days. A hardcore of lorry drivers were still forcing their way into the depot by forming tight convoys of a dozen vehicles, grinding forward en masse and refusing to stop in any circumstances. The West Midlands Gas Board was still refusing to limit its coke sales as the government and NUM had requested. The Gas Board received a joint telegram from local MPs urging it to compromise with the pickets. In the Commons, Maudling was pressured by senior Labour figures from Wilson downwards to force the Gas Board to concede ground. Maudling replied that the distribution of coke was not a matter for the home secretary. And the Gas Board continued to insist that the miners' strike was nothing to do with them. This supposed neutrality, however, did not stop the canteen at the coke depot from supplying the policemen outside the gates with tea and sandwiches.

On the picket line, Charlie McLaren's morale was dipping. 'It didn't seem we were making any bloody progress. We felt we weren't going to shut it unless something bloody big happened. There were rumours going round that the other unions were going to come . . . And then nothing would happen . . . My own thought was, "It's just a rumour to keep our spirits up."'

But it was not just a rumour. Starting on the Tuesday evening, after his loudhailer duties were over for the day, Scargill set up meetings with representatives of the main Birmingham unions. 'I said they could come out on strike and write themselves into history,' he told me, 'or they could do nowt.' Arthur Harper was one of those who heard Scargill's appeal. Besides living a few hundred yards from the coke depot, Harper was strongly left-wing and active in the Amalgamated Union of Engineering Workers (AUEW) and the Birmingham Trades Council, both important local union bodies. He had his reservations about the miners: 'The NUM was a very insular union. It was never affiliated to the Trades Council. We were having collections for the miners every week in the factory. There were rows because the power was being knocked off thanks to the strike, and guys were losing money.' Yet, in the end, Scargill's rhetoric and feelings of collective union solidarity – and a long-standing local resentment of strike-breaking truckers – prevailed. On the Thursday, 10 February, it was arranged that sympathy strikes in support of the miners would take place across the city. Workers would be encouraged to converge on Saltley.

From 7 o'clock in the morning, miners and police began to gather outside the depot as usual. The weather was bright and crisp, but the imminent sympathy strikes gave the now-ritual deployments an additional charge. The chief constable of Birmingham, Sir Derrick Capper, had joined his officers. Richard Webb was slightly nervous: 'We'd heard that there were more pickets coming.' The previous day, the Cabinet had been warned by the Department of Trade and Industry, the section of Whitehall in closest touch with developments at Saltley, that if pickets arrived at the depot in overwhelming numbers the situation might 'oblige closure on public safety grounds'.

For the first part of the morning there was an uneasy lull. No trucks tried to get into the depot, and the pickets were quieter than normal. Nine o'clock came and went. No reinforcements came over the hill.

The Birmingham trade unionists wanting to picket Saltley had been instructed to assemble at their workplaces. Roger Harper had a surprise when he got to his factory: 'Even the guys who had been against it were expecting to take part. We got the old banner, and we walked down the hill. We had thought there might be some aggravation at the depot, but there was a body of us, 800 or 1,000 out of 5,000 in the factory, so we weren't concerned any more. And I remember the Lucas workers coming down the hill opposite. People coming down other hills, over the Saltley viaduct . . .'

Webb was outside the depot gates with the 800 policemen. 'We heard that some pickets were coming over the Saltley viaduct. The plan was to block off the bridge, steer them away. But' – he made a helpless, sweeping gesture across the cafe – 'I can still see it now, them coming over the hill . . .'

McLaren was outside the depot gates with the 2,000 miners. 'We heard someone playing the bagpipes first. I thought at first that one or two factories had come out. And then you saw more, and more behind them. I thought, "The whole of bloody Birmingham's out!"'

Scargill remembered the moment with a sudden wolfish smile: 'It was so big, you had to see it to believe it. I could see thousands of people. The five roads into Saltley were all filled with marchers. The police tried to tell them to carry on past the gates, but I said to the marchers through my megaphone, "No, stop here. Close the gates." And when the crowd got to the gates, it began to move forward six inches at a time. The police were hemmed in' – Scargill almost licked his lips – 'like the cream in a cake.'

Webb remembered: 'They just overwhelmed us. They were in front of us, behind us . . .'

Harper remembered, 'We filed in behind the coppers. We made no attempt to push the coppers. Then it sort of went quiet. All the traffic in the area had stopped. We thought, "What has happened to all the cars?" We didn't know that the people marching were blocking all the roads.'

By about ten-thirty, between 10,000 and 20,000 trade unionists and their supporters were standing on the pavements and in the road in front of the depot gates. There were men in their best clothes, with ties on under their work coats. There were women holding shopping bags. There were pensioners. There were people with small children. A bedlam of clashing chants – 'We shall not be moved!', 'Support the miners!', Heath out!', 'Tories out!' – echoed off the cobbles, and then settled into a single, incessant one: 'Close the gates! Close the gates! Close the gates!'

The line of police protecting the depot was four officers deep but obviously insufficient. Standing next to the gates, Capper looked at the crowd and then down at the ground. Beneath his chief constable's cap, his mouth was set and grim. He made his decision. Between 10.42 and 10.45 a.m. – accounts vary – the police by the gates waved the pickets nearest them back. The pickets grudgingly obeyed. Then a middle-aged man in a straining grey overcoat, an official of the West Midlands Gas Board, appeared from inside the depot. Behind him the coke mountain, lower and flat-topped now, loomed black in the low sun. A young policeman swung forward one of the heavy gates, eight feet high and topped with iron spikes, with visible haste. The end of the gate swung past where it was supposed to come to rest, and had to be swung back. Finally, the two gates were brought together with a heavy metallic clank, just audible above the whistles and chants. Two policemen approached and stood in front of where the gates met, facing the pickets. Then the man in the grey overcoat walked over with his hands in his pockets. His eyes were narrow, his face tight. He glanced at the pickets and then turned his back. He seemed to bare his teeth in something like disgust. He took a key from his pocket. Around the bars of both gates there was a thick chain and, attached to it, a padlock. The man turned the key in the lock.

From all sides there was a deep, lingering roar like the sound of a goal in a Cup Final. The mouths of the people in the crowd were gaping with joy, their heads tilted back, their eyes closed. Policemen were slapped on the back. People cried. Children were held up in the air to catch the moment. 'We were all bloody shouting,' McLaren recalled. 'I remember thinking, "Jesus Christ, what we could do if we stuck together."'

Capper asked Scargill to help him disperse the crowd. Scargill agreed, on the condition that he could make a speech first and that he could borrow a police loudhailer, as his had stopped working. Then he climbed back on to the roof of the public toilet. 'This will go down in trade union history,' he declared. 'It will also go down in history as the Battle of Saltley Gate. The working people have united in a mass stand.' When he had finished speaking, the crowd quickly dissolved. A small picket remained to ensure the depot stayed closed, while many more people headed for the local pubs. McLaren got the NUM coach back to his colliery. 'I never saw the gates closing. But I felt great. You felt that if need be, that can happen again.'

In London that morning, the Cabinet was meeting to consider the already bleak situation in the miners' strike. The topics for discussion included 'the deadlock in negotiations' between the Coal Board and NUM; 'the increasing difficulty of maintaining supplies of coal'; and the urgent need 'to introduce severe restrictions on the use of electricity'. Then Maudling was given the news from Saltley. He told his colleagues, and declared the depot closure 'a victory for violence'. He went on: 'This experience . . . provides disturbing evidence of the ease with which, by assembling large crowds, militants can flout the law with impunity because of the risk that attempts to enforce it would provoke disorder on a large scale.' The next day, Capper was quoted in the Birmingham *Post*. 'I understand the views of those who think I might have given the impression of bowing to a mob,' he conceded, 'but . . . when I saw the crowd, I said to myself: "Is it worth pushing forward a principle . . . when the result might be a serious danger to public safety?"'

Within hours of the closure of the Saltley gates, the Cabinet resolved that 'the Secretary of State for Employment, in consultation with the Attorney-General, should arrange for the law governing picketing to be reviewed'. The minutes do not record a contribution on the subject by Margaret Thatcher, but she wrote in her memoirs: 'For me, what happened at Saltley took on no less significance than it did for the Left.'

When I went there in 2004, it was hard at first to find much trace of the battle. Most of the old Saltley had made way for poky new houses and dual carriageways. When I eventually found the site of the coke depot, it was an expanse of rusty brown rubble. A solitary workman told me that the last of the depot's facilities, its gas holders, had been demolished a few months before. 'We're doing them all over the country,' he said. 'They don't need gas holders any more.'

In the pub just up the hill, where the landlord had once talked about getting a special afternoon licence to serve the picketing miners, the net curtains and corned beef in white rolls still suggested 1972, its provincial food and fussy social niceties. But there was a landlady now, and she and the lunchtime drinkers at the bar had not even heard of the coke depot. I went back to the pub later in the afternoon and found an older man who remembered the pie throwing. I asked him about Scargill standing on top of the public toilet. 'Best place for him,' the man said. 'He spoke a load of crap.' Everyone in the bar laughed.

The only reliable eyewitness I found was Philip Bellingham at J. H. Richards. He had been thirty-six in 1972; now he was semi-retired, with a lean, wise-looking face. We talked for an hour in one of the company's old-fashioned offices, all dark wood and frosted glass partitions. Then we walked across to where the Saltley gates had stood. There was nothing left of them. Instead, Bellingham told me about the graffiti which had promised 'THE MINERS WILL WIN'. It had stayed up for years after the mass picket, he said. 'To see that, decade after decade, knowing the history that they didn't win . . .' He paused. 'I remember going to power stations during the early days of the Thatcher government – we were supplying bearings to power stations then. The huge additional equipment they'd got, to be ready for the next miners' strike. The stores had become vast warehouses of materials. It must have cost millions . . .'

A few months later, I went to south Yorkshire for a day of commemorative events for former miners. It was held at Wortley Hall outside Sheffield, an old colliery owner's mansion that had been taken over by trade unions and other Labour-affiliated groups in the fifties. The house and gardens were still elegant, their careful stewardship as 'the workers' stately home' quite inspiring. A brilliant autumn sun shone. But there was something melancholy about the occasion. The main hallway of the house was dominated by stalls selling memorabilia from the defeated miners' strike of 1984. 'Superb Poster: A Badge for Every Pit We Had in 1984,' ran one neatly handwritten notice. 'There Are Now Only 10 Pits in the Whole of Britain.' The ex-miners I met were all still full of the injustices and lost possibilities of ''84', not the victory of 1972. I began to wonder slightly why I had come.

The answer arrived after lunch when the hallway suddenly emptied. I followed the stragglers through a maze of panelled corridors until we came to a large windowless back room. Beneath a low striplit ceiling rows of chairs had been laid out facing a small stage. Every chair was taken: by ex-miners, their wives, their children, their grandchildren, all of them quiet and expectant. The Banner Theatre company of Birmingham, a survivor of the seventies boom in left-wing stage troupes, was about to stage a section of its long-running *Saltley Gate* show.

Initially it was underwhelming. Three actors in plain T-shirts with acoustic guitars sang and chanted – 'I'd Rather Be a Picket than a Scab', 'We'll win through/Just like in '72' – between telling the story of the mass picket in the simplest political terms. People in the audience sang and clapped along or listened, apparently rapt, but to an outsider it felt like a slightly routine religious occasion. Then, almost imperceptibly, a more charged atmosphere started to build. The actors sang louder and louder. The hum of their guitars got bolder and harsher. By the time the narrative reached the march of the workers of Birmingham on the coke depot, the performers had lost themselves in the words: '. . . We are the engineers/Close the gates/Close the gates/You servants of the Crown/Close the gates/Close the gates/No power in the land/Can gain the upper hand/When we are united . . .' At the climax, some bleached-out old footage of the gates being shut flashed up on a screen above the stage. A woman standing next to me at the back of the room, who could not have been more than twenty-five, cheered and whooped and stomped her feet as if she was personally witnessing Sir Derrick Capper bow to the workers. A few minutes later, I shared a taxi back to Sheffield railway station with an ex-miner. Had he been at Saltley? 'No,' he said. 'But everyone says they were.'

In some ways, Saltley was a merely symbolic triumph. By the time the gates were closed, barely a third of the coke that had been in the depot at the start of the strike remained, and it can be convincingly argued that the miners were well on the way to a national victory before the Birmingham mass picket began. Yet the manner and visibility of the unions' success at Saltley gave it an immediate as well as a long-term importance. The day after the depot's closure, on 11 February, Heath's political secretary Douglas Hurd wrote in his diary that the government was 'now wandering vainly over [the] battlefield looking for someone to surrender to'. On 18 February, a hasty government-appointed Court of Inquiry led by Lord Wilberforce recommended that the miners receive an average pay increase approaching 20 per cent – less than the 25 per cent the NUM had originally demanded but more than double the previous highest offer, and more than double the maximum permitted by the government's national pay guidelines. The NUM's executive, sensing weakness, rejected the offer.

National coal stocks were now down to ten days' supply. After a brief stalemate, the bargaining resumed, this time in Downing Street, with Heath himself involved, as well as the Coal Board and the more emollient TUC president Vic Feather. While Joe Gormley and his negotiators worked into the night, the rest of the twenty-six-man NUM executive sat in an adjoining room consuming rounds of beer and sandwiches. The miners now presented a 'shopping list' – as Gormley put it in his memoirs – of additional demands, including free transport for miners to their collieries, free work clothes and increased overtime payments. 'At one point,' Scargill's biographer Paul Routledge records, 'the union's industrial relations officer . . . was scratching around in his files for conference demands that had been rejected by the Coal Board in previous years.' Every demand was conceded. When the NUM negotiators finally could not come up with anything more to ask for, the union's executive voted to recommend that the strike be called off. 'We left Downing Street at two o'clock in the morning,' Gormley recalled with satisfaction, 'and as we got into our taxis, Vic Feather said, "I don't know what the hell you did to Ted Heath, but you frightened me to bloody death!"'

Early on in my interview with Heath in Salisbury, I risked asking him about the way the strike had ended. 'The Wilberforce report did give the miners – well, not everything they were asking, but quite a lot of it,' he said. He paused. 'Most of it, in fact.'

And the miners, I suggested, had ended up with even more. Had that been difficult to swallow?

There was a much longer pause. From somewhere beyond the sitting-room door came the distant clatter and chatter of the ex-prime minister's staff. 'Yes,' Heath said finally, his voice even deeper and slower than usual. 'Yes.' Then he changed the subject back to his government's housing policy.

5

Questions of Sovereignty

In Salisbury, there were moments when Ted Heath brightened. Most of them came when we got onto the subject of Europe. His cold blue eyes would take on a slight glitter, his voice unclot a little, his answers grow more expansive. 'I knew that de Gaulle was favourable to me,' he said at one point, with evidently enduring pride. 'He told me in 1965 that if I came into office and did the European things which I'd proposed, then our application to join the Common Market would go through.' At another point, I asked a general question about his government's ambitions and achievements. With a hopeful lift to his voice, he replied: 'As far as Europe is concerned?'

The negotiations for Britain's entry into the Common Market, as the European Economic Community (EEC) was informally known, began in July 1970, the month after Heath won power. They concluded in January 1972, the month the miners' strike started. 'Everyone who worked closely with him', writes Douglas Hurd, 'knew that [taking Britain into Europe] was the first . . . of the two aims which he had set for his premiership.' Like the other goal, the transformation of the British economy, the issue of Europe preoccupied Heath in office and arguably distracted him from the less predictable challenges, such as the arrival of the Yorkshire miners at Saltley, that would undermine his government. But Europe and the economy had dominated Heath's political thoughts for so long before he became prime minister – and he was by nature such a ruminative rather than spontaneous politician – that even the shocks of the early seventies did not prompt him to adjust his priorities. Nor had he reconsidered them since. I asked him if, in retrospect, it had been too much for his government to cope simultaneously with EEC entry and the mounting difficulties at home. In an instant Heath switched to his prickly, contemptuous mode. 'Quite honestly, no.'

By 1970, he had been admiring and visiting continental Europe – undertaking his own personal version of cross-Channel integration – for almost forty years. The official British appetite for involving the country in a united Europe developed over the same period. But it was a much more halting process.

In 1930, the year before Heath had his first continental epiphany amid the gateaux and Citroën showrooms of Paris, Winston Churchill wrote a pioneering article for an American magazine, calling for a United States of Europe. By the Second World War, having moved from the margins to the centre of British politics, Churchill was able to set out his European vision more publicly and more concretely. In a 1943 prime-ministerial broadcast, he put before Britons the prospect of an 'integrated life of Europe that is possible . . . without destroying the individual characteristics and traditions of its many ancient and historic races'. Three years later, he made a high-profile speech in Zürich, addressed to the public and politicians right across the battered post-war continent. He urged the creation of a united Europe based, just as the future EEC would be, around a partnership between France and Germany. He concluded: 'We must begin now.'

Yet, as enthusiasts for British participation in Europe would soon discover, that 'we' was monumentally ambiguous. Post-war Britain still had substantial connections to its colonies and former colonies; a strong official desire to collaborate with the US; stubborn hopes of remaining a global rather than merely European power; and a centuries-old foreign-policy and public-opinion tradition of keeping 'the Continent' at arm's length. During the fifties, the EEC was put together without Britain. Only slowly did the humiliation of the Suez crisis and other evidence of post-war delusions and decline create a momentum in Britain for Common Market membership.

In the early sixties, while Heath was patiently leading the British negotiators through eighteen months of entry negotiations, British public support for joining the EEC peaked at a less than overwhelming 53 per cent, before falling back. In 1964, after de Gaulle had vetoed the British application anyway, Heath and the Conservatives were removed from power. It took until 1967 for the subsequent

Labour government to overcome its anti-Common Market faction and apply for membership again. Once more, de Gaulle said no. In 1969, he retired as French president and was replaced by the less obstructive Georges Pompidou, but a British wariness towards the Common Market endured. The following February, the Wilson government, which was still officially committed to trying to join, published a White Paper on the likely costs of being part of the EEC. Food prices, it predicted, could rise by between 18 and 26 per cent; the overall rate of inflation – already beginning to become a national anxiety – by 5 per cent. The document did not read like the work of a Europhile government. A few weeks later, in their 1970 election manifesto, Labour promised again to seek EEC membership. But, the manifesto went on: 'If satisfactory terms cannot be secured . . . Britain will be able to stand on her own feet outside the Community.'

It took Heath's shock election to change the British position fundamentally. In a typical moment of pro-EEC advocacy during a television broadcast in July 1971, he was direct and emotional where previous prime ministers had been vague or legalistic. 'For twenty-five years we've been looking for something to get us going again,' Heath said. 'Now here it is . . . We have the chance of new greatness. Now we must take it.' Douglas Hurd describes the care and eagerness with which Heath, the former civil servant, had prepared for the climax of the negotiations with the French two months earlier:

At Number Ten the briefing sessions were held in the garden, where for hours on end the Prime Minister sat under a tree, dunking biscuits in tea. Experts were produced . . . They each had their session under the tree, while ducks from the park waddled amorously across the lawn . . .

In his autobiography, Heath makes the talks with Pompidou that followed sound even more idyllic:

It was symbolic to me that all this should be happening in Paris, the city to which I had come as a boy . . . For two days there were just the two of us, each with an interpreter . . . It is difficult to think of more attractive surroundings in which to carry on talks of this kind. The elegance of the Elysée inspires a spirit of reasonableness . . . [On the second evening] we held our conference for the press . . . I had managed to convince President Pompidou

... that Britain was genuine in its desire to enter the European family ... The President and I looked across at each other with delight ... For me personally, it was a wildly exciting moment.

The actual terms secured for Britain's admission into the Common Market were less perfect. The British government's initial bargaining position, that it should contribute 3 per cent of the EEC budget in the first year of British membership – absurdly low for a large European state hoping to become one of only ten Common Market countries – was not well received. In the end, Britain had to agree to contribute almost 9 per cent, rising to almost 19 per cent by 1977, its fifth year of membership. Underlying the scale of the concession was the assumption that Britain would maintain its economic status relative to its Common Market collaborators during the seventies and therefore be justified in paying such a large share of the EEC budget. It was an assumption that would prove highly optimistic.

Compromises with consequences were also made in other politically charged areas. Compensating dairy farmers in New Zealand for the loss of their traditional British customers – as the Common Market removed the trade barriers between Britain and continental Europe, New Zealand butter would become expensive compared with European imports – cost the British government £100 million. Britain was also forced to accept the EEC's Common Fisheries Policy, which opened its waters to trawlers from countries with far less extensive and productive coastlines. Most notoriously of all, Britain had to sign up to the Common Agricultural Policy, which forced EEC countries to buy farm produce from each other, regardless of whether it was more expensive than produce from elsewhere, and which effectively paid Common Market countries with less efficient farmers, notably France, a subsidy.

Joining the EEC, in short, required Britain to give ground to ancient enemies, loosen ties with old imperial allies and make life harder for its fishermen and farmers, both interest groups with a privileged and historic role in the national consciousness. The move would mark a profound break with the British political consensus, not only of the post-war decades but of earlier decades, and earlier centuries. In return for this upheaval, Heath promised an undefined,

EEC-driven economic revival in Britain and, even vaguer, the country's participation in a new Europe free of its traditional rivalries and wars.

Unsurprisingly, not everyone was persuaded. Turning the deal made with Pompidou and during subsidiary negotiations into legislation required 104 separate votes in Parliament and took up much of 1971 and 1972. Enoch Powell, on the Conservative right, and Tony Benn, on the Labour left, both argued eloquently in the Commons – and to wider audiences – that joining the EEC would undermine British national sovereignty. Harold Wilson, with characteristic cunning and shamelessness, reversed his party's position on the Common Market, and opposed Heath's plan. Both Labour and the Conservatives experienced large-scale internal rebellions against their EEC policies. These splits would endure through the seventies and far beyond, with ultimately disastrous consequences for both parties. More immediately, the divisions and U-turns over the Common Market, like the factional, world-weary parliamentary manoeuvrings of the decade as a whole, helped feed the growing public disillusionment with the main parties, which was beginning to shrink their share of the vote at general elections, make such contests more volatile and render British politics as it had existed since 1945 less viable.

Yet, for all this, Heath got his way. Sometimes by the tiniest of margins, often by the crudest Commons arm-twisting, on one occasion by threatening rebel Conservative MPs with a general election if the government was defeated, at a time when the miners were on strike and his administration was deeply unpopular, he won every parliamentary vote on the Common Market. His agreement with the French was accepted by the other five EEC countries. Britain would become a member on 1 January 1973.

Like the 1970 election, it was a personal triumph for Heath. It showed his political strengths: doggedness, a degree of idealism, his tendency to be underestimated by opponents. But as in 1970, the success did not represent a lasting breakthrough in his wider political standing or an overwhelming public mandate for his policies. On the day Britain joined the Common Market, *The Times* published a

MORI poll on attitudes to entry. It found 38 per cent of Britons happy at the prospect, 39 per cent unhappy, and 23 per cent undecided. The same day, the pro-membership *Daily Mirror*, which described the EEC as 'the greatest trading bloc in the entire world' and headlined Britain's admission as 'A Day in History', revealed the results of its own more detailed survey. Despite the paper's prediction that 'today's child [who] leaves school in the 1980s . . . will have to be Anglo-European to survive', those polled showed a limited appetite for a more continental Britain. 'Would you like to see these "Common Market customs"?' the survey asked:

	YES	NO
regular wine with meals	23%	21%
more pavement cafes	11%	34%
more shops open on Sunday	5%	40%
coffee and a roll for breakfast, not bacon and eggs	13%	58%
pubs open all day	18%	44%

Two days later, on 3 January, *The Times* published a prominent article doubting one of the main potential economic impacts on Britain of EEC membership:

Our climate, both economic and meteorological, is unattractive to most European workers. There is no reason that many or even any will want to give up a job in, say, Holland, to earn less money in a country with shorter holidays and a higher unemployment rate, unfamiliar beer and a foreign language. Equally there is no reason to expect a large-scale migration of British workers in search of sun or fatter wage packets.

Within three decades at most, all of these working patterns and pleasures would be part of everyday life in Britain. But three decades can be an eternity in politics, and in 1973 Heath's long-standing enthusiasm for a closer Europe, like his concerns about the power of the unions and the impact of airports, was too far ahead of British public opinion – and at times too clumsily communicated. Between 3 and 14 January, both these political weaknesses were vividly demonstrated by Fanfare for Europe, an official national festival to mark Britain's admission to the EEC. With a perky trumpet as its logo, the festival was intended to be part celebration, part rallying call, part advertisement for the mutual benefits of EEC membership. Yet what ensued was considerably less inspiring than previous government-backed cultural events, such as Attlee's 1951 Festival of Britain. On 3 January, a football match at Wembley between a team drawn from the original six Common Market nations and one selected from the new member states – Britain, Denmark and Ireland – was played before a less than half-full stadium. 'The loudest cheer of the night', reported the *Guardian*, 'greeted the news on the information board that Norwich City had reached the final of the League Cup.'

At the Victoria and Albert Museum in London, there was a rather diffuse exhibition of 'Treasures from the European Community', including bronze-age trumpets from Denmark and a George Stubbs painting of a racehorse, each selected by a member government and displayed in their own isolated, high-security alcove. There was also a 'Dutch breakfast' and food festival at a London hotel; an exhibition of European sweets at the Whitechapel Art Gallery; a stage show in French and English for all the family at the Caricature Theatre in Cardiff; and, in Scotland, a coordinated demonstration of 'Continental cooking' in Gas and Electricity Board showrooms.

Press coverage varied from politely supportive to dismissive. The event that received the most publicity was the opening gala. Wilson, pointedly, did not attend, flying off instead to the Scilly Isles, his habitual holiday refuge and one of his favourite public stages for playing the plain Englishman against the cosmopolitan Heath. Meanwhile, the *Guardian* and other papers made the gala sound like an uncomfortable evening:

About 300 opponents [of the EEC] booed and chanted 'Sieg Heil', as the Queen, Prince Philip, and Mr Heath arrived at the Royal Opera House . . . the Queen and Prince Philip both seemed momentarily shaken by the size and noise of the demonstration – the largest involving members of the Royal Family seen in London.

In his autobiography, Heath makes no mention of any of this. Instead, he describes a blissful night, with legendary classical musicians and actors from many nations 'drawing widely upon our shared European heritage . . . Performers and audience then mingled

afterwards for a splendid dinner . . . My heart was full of joy . . .'
Given his years of work for EEC membership and the unappealing
tone, either hysterical or carping, of some of his opponents on the
issue, Heath's selective view of his European achievement was perhaps understandable. However, even he had to concede that entry
did not quickly invigorate the British economy as he had hoped.
'After . . . 1973–4 the Community lost its momentum,' he wrote.
'Each member state drifted back to seeking its own, unilateral solution to unemployment and inflation.'

In 1972, while the small print of Britain's admission was being
negotiated, ambitious EEC plans had been conceived for a continent-
wide industrial policy, with economic and monetary union to follow
by the end of the decade. But by the time Britain joined, the world
economy was entering an unstable phase that would soon render
these schemes impractical. One element of this instability was a surge
in the value of commodities: in Britain, the cost of food went up by
over a tenth during the first nine months of 1973. Although price
rises caused by the country's involvement in the Common
Agricultural Policy made up only a small fraction of this increase, the
Common Market was seen as the main villain. Blaming Brussels was
on its way to becoming one of the most entrenched British political
habits. Meanwhile, during the mid-seventies, trade between Britain
and the Common Market countries expanded beyond its pre-1973
levels steadily rather than spectacularly, slowed by the global recession: according to the Department of Trade, British exports to the
EEC rose from £4.1 billion in 1973 to £5.6 billion in 1974 to £6.5
billion in 1975. Heath had taken the country into Europe, yet other
British prime ministers, less Europhile but governing in more
favourable economic circumstances, would be the true beneficiaries.

During Heath's government, it was another controversy about the
relationship between Britain and its closest neighbours that had a
more immediate impact. It concerned Northern Ireland.

During my childhood in the seventies, although I was barely aware
of politics, Northern Ireland was always there in the background.
Part of it came from having a father in the army. For the middle years

of the decade he was stationed in Maidstone in Kent, an old military town half-buried under concrete and ring roads. One of its functions then wās as a staging post for British soldiers en route to Londonderry, South Armagh and Belfast. Among the army families we mixed with, even in conversations between army children, this was a prospect that was talked about with a quiet dread. When a squadron from the regiment my father commanded was sent to Northern Ireland, and he went out to visit them, a vague unease descended on my family that did not lift until he came back. When I asked him about his trip, he answered in euphemisms. He was never sent to Northern Ireland again, yet the possibility remained.

One day on the army housing estate where we lived, I remember soldiers in full battle dress, rifles cradled in very still hands, suddenly ghosting into position either side of the chainlink fence that surrounded the playpark. At the time, it seemed quite exciting, like a grown-up version of the war games I played with the other children. After a few minutes, the soldiers slipped away. It was only after visiting Derry thirty years later and seeing some old photographs of the Creggan, a local estate strongly associated in the seventies with IRA activity that had semis and low hedges just like the estate in Maidstone, that I realized what the soldiers in the playpark had been practising.

In 1978, my father was posted to Germany, but Northern Ireland followed us. A British officer my parents knew was shot by the IRA on his doorstep a short drive away. For a time, the army lent us a small mirror, attached at an angle to a long handle, so that we could check under our car for bombs each morning.

Yet in truth these incidents in Germany and Kent were exceptions. Most of the time in my family, as in many British families in the seventies, Northern Ireland was the great unspoken. My father's father was Irish, a Protestant from Limerick in the Republic, but he was dead, and my father would gently but firmly dissuade me and my sister whenever we suggested a holiday there. Family discussions about Northern Ireland would quickly peter out, with my mother saying she felt browbeaten by Ian Paisley and all the others, and my father muttering about 'impossible people'. The riots, bombings and shootings continued numbingly on the news. It seemed like it would never end. The army, meanwhile, gave my father clearer military situations to think about.

By the seventies, the British state had been trying to forget about Northern Ireland, and about Ireland in general, for almost half a century. In a sense this was understandable. Over the centuries prior to the partition of Ireland in 1921, Britain had invaded and colonized the island, and worried incessantly about rival powers doing likewise; suffered repeated military reverses there, and committed infamous atrocities; attempted to exploit and modernize the Irish economy with uneven results; and contributed to the growth of a ferocious local religious sectarianism. In the decades immediately before 1921, the 'Irish Question' had led to bombings in London, mutinous behaviour in the British army and the expression of open support by a leader of the Conservative and Unionist Party, Andrew Bonar Law, for an insurrection in Ulster against the elected government of the United Kingdom.

So from partition onwards Britain drew back. Northern Ireland was given its own government with a large degree of independence. In 1923, it was decided that 'matters of administration for a minister in Northern Ireland could not be discussed' in the Commons. Visits to the province by British ministers and prime ministers dwindled to almost nothing, and the British political parties began to operate there only sporadically. The Conservative and Unionist Party became simply the Conservative Party. Northern Ireland's representation in the Commons shrank to a mere dozen MPs, even fewer than that warranted by its small population, only a thirtieth of the United Kingdom's as a whole. At Balliol in the thirties, Denis Healey records in his autobiography, it was normal to talk about 'the insolubility' of 'Ulster's problems'. In the Commons, Winston Churchill famously characterized the province and its politics as 'the dreary steeples of Fermanagh'.

Successive British governments tried to keep Ulster relatively peaceful and prosperous through subsidies. Public spending there, calculated according to a formula that was not revealed to the Cabinet, was over a third higher per head than elsewhere. Less generous strategies were also employed to sedate Northern Ireland's politics: from 1937, the controller of the BBC was given the power to veto the transmission to the province of any Ulster-related programme deemed problematic. In Britain, Northern Ireland featured little in school textbooks, newspapers or university syllabuses. During the Second World War, the province served as an important airbase, but afterwards Ulster's strategic value to Britain declined, and Whitehall's remaining interest diminished accordingly. In December 1967, when Jim Callaghan became home secretary, he discovered that the supervision of Northern Ireland

was crammed into what was called the General Department . . . It covered such matters as ceremonial functions, British Summer Time, London taxicabs, liquor licensing . . . and the protection of animals and birds. One Division [of the department] also dealt with the Channel Islands, the Isle of Man, the Charity Commission and Northern Ireland, and this group of subjects was under the control of a staff of seven . . . There seemed to me at that time no reason to disturb the arrangement.

Briefing papers that Callaghan requested on the impending problems facing his ministry contained 'not a word about Northern Ireland'. Yet unknown to him and this token group of civil servants, events in Belfast had already begun to make British policy towards the province obsolete. Eleven months earlier, the Northern Ireland Civil Rights Association had been founded. Its aim was to end the anti-Catholic discrimination in housing, employment and the voting system that had been ubiquitous in Ulster since partition. The Civil Rights Association was broad in its membership, containing Protestants as well as Catholics, unionists as well as nationalists, and at first mild in its methods by the standards of the late sixties, relying on marches and small acts of civil disobedience. But its challenge to the status quo in Ulster was a fundamental one. Even worse for the Association's chances of securing reforms without a confrontation, many unionists regarded it as a Trojan horse for Irish nationalism, with the undeclared goal of undermining Ulster and uniting the province with the Republic.

The situation was further sharpened by the decay of Ulster's economy. During the nineteenth century, Belfast had been a model imperial boom town, noisy with shipbuilders and linen mills, its centre a handsome grid of domes and columns, its west Belfast suburbs packed with rural incomers. But, by the late sixties, the empire and the boom were over, and Belfast's empty factories and patchy government regeneration projects were a bleak vision in lumpy concrete and orphaned brick of what might await the rest of the UK. Unemployment in the province was three times the national average; in west Belfast, long divided into neighbouring sectarian ghettos such as the Catholic Falls Road and the Protestant Shankill, the rate was six times worse.

The first confrontation, however, came in Londonderry. Only a few miles from the Republic, Derry was much less Protestant than Belfast, and anti-Catholic discrimination there was even more blatant. Although Catholics of voting age outnumbered Protestants by two to one, restriction of the right to vote and manipulation of electoral boundaries kept the city council Protestant. In October 1968, a civil-rights march there was attacked by a unit of the Royal Ulster Constabulary, Northern Ireland's paramilitary, Protestant-dominated police force. In front of television cameras and three British Labour MPs taking part in the march – for decades a minority had vainly campaigned against discrimination in the province – demonstrators were viciously beaten with batons and battered with water cannon. That evening, Northern Ireland's minister of home affairs, William Craig, who had initially tried to ban the march, defended the RUC's conduct and denounced the civil-rights demonstrators as connected to 'the IRA and Communism'. But the pictures of the beatings went around the world. In Britain, almost overnight, it was no longer possible to believe – or to pretend to believe – that the province was a healthy democracy which could be left to its own devices.

Over the next ten months came ample further evidence. The Northern Irish prime minister Terence O'Neill, a relatively moderate unionist, was summoned to Downing Street and agreed to make concessions to the civil-rights movement. Yet while these were insufficient to satisfy the movement's radicals and the young disenfranchised Catholics who were now engaged in regular stone-throwing battles with the RUC and were erecting street barricades in Catholic areas, they were enough to convince some Protestants that a sell-out of Ulster unionism was imminent. In January 1969, another civil-rights march was attacked; the same month, the Bogside, a poor Catholic enclave downhill from the Creggan, declared itself 'Free Derry' and Catholic vigilante groups with clubs began patrolling its alleyways. In March and April, bombs planted by unionists but blamed on the IRA destroyed parts of Ulster's water and electricity network. In April, O'Neill was forced to resign by the escalating disorder. As spring became summer, traditionally the peak period for sectarian frictions, something approaching a civil war spread through Derry and Belfast and the pale country towns of Northern Ireland. There were petrol bombs and gunshots, house burnings and households fleeing, tear-gas clouds and panicking policemen, even rumours of an invasion by the Irish army. There was the sobering – or intoxicating – reality of the casualties: ten killed in the instantly mythologized 'battles' of July and August, and approaching a thousand wounded.

Back in London, the British government had dispersed for the summer recess regardless. But, by 14 August, Callaghan had decided that the disorder in Ulster required a radical solution. Harold Wilson was on holiday in the Scillies, so Callaghan flew to meet him nearby in Cornwall and they held a hasty discussion. 'We did not have a map of Northern Ireland with us,' Callaghan later recalled, 'so when at one point Wilson wanted to know how far somewhere was from somewhere else the Group Captain hurried off and came back with a small atlas which we all pored over.' Wilson agreed that British troops could be deployed on the streets of Ulster if required. Then he flew back to the Scillies. Callaghan got a plane back to London:

We had not been in the air for more than ten minutes when the navigator came into the cabin with a pencilled message scribbled on a signal pad . . . An official request for the use of troops had been made by the Northern Ireland Government. I immediately scribbled 'Permission granted' on the signal pad and handed it back to the navigator.

*

Northern Ireland can be a disorientating place, now as in the seventies, for inexperienced visitors from Britain, whether writers or soldiers or politicians. I went there for the first time in December 2005. From the plane, the Ulster countryside looked faintly claustrophobic and foreign, all dark lakes and tiny fields. I worried fleetingly about whether sons of British army officers should make research trips to the Bogside or the Falls Road. But then I read the front page of my copy of the *Irish News* – 'Troops cut to lowest level since early 70s' – and the opposite anxiety stirred. There might not be much of Heath and Callaghan's Northern Ireland left to look at.

I needn't have worried. The centre of Belfast was like Leeds, proud Victoriana and post-war concrete disappearing behind confident new office blocks. Yet it only took a few minutes walking westwards to leave it behind, for a tattier no man's land of cheap cafes and butcher's shops. Beyond them was a ring road. Beyond that, the Falls Road.

The first thing that struck me was the scale of it. The Falls rose steadily for miles towards an enclosing wall of bare hills, twisting and dipping and steepening, but everything either side of it seemed in miniature. Narrow side streets ran off at seemingly random angles, revealing the smallest Victorian terraces I had ever seen. Behind the houses were minuscule walled-in yards and tight back alleys full of dustbins and blind corners. There were no front gardens, no window boxes, no trees set in the mean, uneven pavements – nothing to conceal an outsider for a second as they passed the endless rows of net curtains.

Near the lower end of the Falls Road there was an IRA 'Garden of Remembrance'. It was immaculately kept, all buffed black stone and gold and not a quiver of graffiti. One of many plaques began, 'Roll of Honour D Coy 2nd Battalion Belfast Brigade . . .' A list of activists' names followed, when they died – '1971 1972 1972 1972 1972 1973 1973 1974 1974 1975 . . .' – and their ages – '26 17 21 24 18 17 27 17 54 20 . . .' At the centre of the garden a mural commemorated the local resistance to an official curfew in 1970. In it eager children shoved aside coils of barbed wire, and women held aloft dustbin lids, the area's traditional tool to warn of approaching soldiers and policemen. Everyone in the painting had an expression of utter happiness and defiance.

Even in 2005, there was still not much along the Falls to suggest other, less charged ways of living: just a few shops and small businesses, the smell of frying from the open doors of takeaways, and an extravagant new leisure centre. A few hundred yards behind it, oddly, there was another. I set off down a side street towards it. The terraced houses ended abruptly in a stretch of waste ground, all ancient buddleia and dumped mattresses and fire extinguishers; and then the terraces started again, but with conspicuously different murals: this leisure centre was in the Shankill.

'Ulster Will Always Remain British', said the walls; and 'No Surrender!'; and '1969 Volunteers Defend Shankill Community from Republican Attack'. There was another commemorative list of the fallen – the same sense as in the Falls of history slowing to a crawl. 'Beatties High Class Restaurant', said a sign over a cafe. 'Teas. Coffees. Bovril.'

The situation in Ulster at the end of the sixties, however much it was of the British government's own making, was, short of a world war, perhaps the most extreme test that could have been devised for politicians such as Callaghan, Wilson and Heath, with their limited knowledge of and inherited assumptions about the province, coupled with their dislike of confrontation and their belief in negotiation and compromise, even when undignified. Sectarianism based on centuries of history and dogma, fundamental conflicts of interest, terrorism, the possible collapse of law and order – such challenges can bring out the worst, as well as the best, in politicians who think of themselves as reasonable and moderate. Britain's actions in Northern Ireland during the seventies would demonstrate the former reflex more than the latter.

Then again, the unfamiliarity of the situation in Ulster could be overstated. Bitter animosity between Catholics and Protestants, expressed through riots and religious discrimination and at elections, had existed in northern England, notably in Liverpool, and Scotland since at least the nineteenth century. And British troops had been sent to pacify Northern Ireland before: in 1907, 1920 and 1935, for example. For anyone who cared to notice, the 1907 deployment contained ominous lessons about the suitability or otherwise of British soldiers for policing urban Ulster. During a riot in the lower Falls, the Belfast *News-Letter* reported, 'in one of the bye [side] streets a squadron of cavalry were subjected to a terrific storm of paviors [paving stones], which rained down on them from the upper windows, and the men to save their faces had to lie down on their saddles'. The *Northern Whig* recorded that the troops found the spidery layout of west Belfast bewildering, 'while the rioters knew every hole'.

Yet for all this the Ulster crisis of the late sixties and early seventies was something new. Unlike its predecessors, it came as a shock to the rest of the UK; it arrived during a period of wider national self-doubt; and it was broadcast on television. And by the time Heath became prime minister in 1970, it had got much worse.

After the troops' arrival the previous August, there had been a brief lull. Using simple streetcorner diplomacy – wearing berets rather than helmets, making a show of consulting all parties – and occasional force – when unionist demonstrators shot at soldiers, they shot more lethally back – the army restored a degree of order. Famously, soldiers were given tea and even fish and chips by grateful Catholics, who thought that the policing of Northern Ireland was now in neutral hands. In Britain, there was a sense of cautious satisfaction about how things were going. 'In Belfast the British army is once again in the old routine,' began a television documentary broadcast a month into the deployment. 'Men in the middle, keeping the peace between two warring factions. But this isn't Aden, or Cyprus. It is, incredibly, in Britain's own backyard.'

Yet citing Aden and Cyprus, and by implication the dozens of other civil wars and end-of-empire conflicts which Britain had been involved in since the Second World War, was more double-edged than the documentary-makers probably intended. The behaviour of the British army during these operations had not always been as benign as mainstream British opinion liked to maintain. And when the documentary-makers interviewed the soldiers as they tramped the Belfast pavements, their answers were not wholly reassuring. 'They change their minds by the hour,' said one crisp young officer of the local residents, with a slow smile and shake of his head. A skinny private was asked if he and his comrades understood what Ulster's sectarianism was really about. 'No. Not really,' he said. 'We're not really interested about the problem. We're just here to do a job.' And that job was about to change.

In December 1969, the Provisional IRA was founded. The armed struggle for a united Ireland was about to resume. In recent decades it had been less than glorious. Since its peak in the early twenties during the war of independence against the British and during the Irish civil war that followed, the Irish Republican Army had been steadily suppressed in the Republic and had lost momentum in Ulster. It mounted campaigns in the late thirties and early forties, and again in the late fifties and early sixties, but with diminishing returns: whereas the former included bomb attacks across Britain, from Coventry to King's Cross station, and prompted repressive British emergency legislation, the latter was confined to Ulster and was so fitful that it barely featured in British newspapers. By the late sixties, despite the political polarization in Ulster, and the frequency with which unionists invoked the spectre of armed republicanism, the IRA was, in reality, dwindling and divided. In Belfast, it was down to fewer than sixty members and a few guns. In Dublin, where the IRA leadership was based, there was a growing inclination to abandon violence in favour of a peaceful left-leaning nationalism. 'It seemed to me that if this went on much longer,' wrote the IRA's head of intelligence Seán Mac Stíofáin afterwards, 'the IRA would end up as a paper army.' When Protestants rampaged through Catholic areas of Belfast in August 1969, the IRA did little to stop them. Angry residents and local graffiti began to say that IRA stood for 'I Ran Away'.

Mac Stíofáin helped organize a breakaway by IRA members who still believed in military methods. He became chief of staff of the new group, which called itself the Provisional IRA. The Provisionals, or the Provos, or simply the IRA, as they soon became known, were even less of an army at first than the body from which they had seceded. But their timing was perfect. During early 1970, relations between the British troops and many Catholics began to fray. In the Catholic parts of Derry and Belfast, the army had effectively replaced the RUC as the local police. On isolated housing estates and in the mazes of inner-city terraces, soldiers with limited experience of and patience for policing, and sometimes with heads full of the age-old British prejudices against the Irish, met bored young men with few job prospects and their own deep-set enmities towards the forces of law and order, towards the British, and towards British soldiers on Irish soil in particular. At the same time, the events of 1968 and 1969 had created a new and lingering appetite for disorder, 'a sudden generation of kamikaze children', in the phrase of the civil-rights activist and author Eamonn McCann.

In March 1970, an RUC post in Londonderry used by British troops was attacked by a crowd, and twelve soldiers were injured. In April, troops trying to stop a sectarian confrontation on a Belfast estate used tear gas and dragged alleged ringleaders out of the melee. The soldiers were pelted with stones and bricks. The same month, the commander of the British forces in Ulster warned that petrol-bombers would be shot. In July, a patrol searching for weapons around the Falls Road was trapped by a hostile crowd, and other soldiers nearby were shot at by snipers from the Official IRA, as what was left of the original IRA now called itself. More troops were sent in to save the situation and conducted pointedly brutal house-to-house searches. Four civilians were killed by the soldiers, a visiting English photographer among them. The restraints and studied optimism of peacekeeping were being superseded by another military mode, of which Britain also had much recent experience: counter-insurgency, war waged against both guerrillas and the civilians who support them.

It was just what the Provisionals needed. 'The behaviour of the British army was quite stupid,' writes Gerry Adams, then a young but rising IRA activist in Belfast, in his memoirs. 'They acted as an oppressive occupying force . . . affecting everybody [on my estate] and uniting against them people who were already fairly coordinated . . . dealing with refugees and defending their area.' Some British officers came to share this view. 'The Lower Falls operation changed everything,' wrote Colonel Michael Dewar, who had extensive experience of commanding troops in Belfast, in his 1985 book *The British Army in Northern Ireland*. 'PIRA grew from fewer than 100 activists in May–June to roughly 800 in December 1970.'

And not all these recruits were stone-throwing teenagers. Many already had military skills which they had acquired – such are the black ironies of civil wars – in the British armed forces. Mac Stíofáin himself, who was born and grew up in London and claimed to have been politicized then by the anti-Irishness he encountered, had served in the Royal Air Force in the late forties: 'I would get what I realised by then was very useful to have, which was some military training.' The campaign he now intended to launch in Ulster had three elements: the IRA would aggressively defend Catholic areas; it would attack 'economic' targets, making Northern Ireland's place in the UK financially unsustainable; and it would kill British soldiers. Mac Stíofáin estimated that when the death toll reached forty, the British government would pull its troops out.

It was an ambitious, in some ways naive strategy. It ignored the ability of unionists to resist a British withdrawal, by peaceful means and otherwise; it did not consider Britain's capacity, demonstrated in recent decades from Cyprus to Malaya, for enduring long counter-insurgency campaigns that involved significant casualties; and it assumed that IRA members based in beleaguered Catholic areas of Northern Ireland would act exactly as the IRA leadership in distant, relatively peaceful Dublin instructed. But during 1970 and 1971, the IRA's new campaign developed a momentum regardless. From the early summer of 1970, snipers began firing sporadically at British soldiers. In January 1971, there were sixteen IRA bomb attacks in Ulster. In February, there were thirty-eight. On the 6th, a Royal Artillery patrol in a rioting section of Belfast met an IRA man with a sub-machine gun. Billy Reid had never fired such a weapon before, but he hit and killed Gunner Robert Curtis. Curtis was the first British soldier to be killed in Ireland for more than half a century. Reid himself was killed in a gun battle with the army three months later.

*

The response of the Heath government to the worsening Ulster crisis was, as its response to crises tended to be, erratic. Like many members of the Wilson administration, Heath disliked the discrimination that had come with unionist domination of Ulster and had a tentative degree of sympathy for Irish nationalism. 'I had no objection to reunification in principle,' he writes in his autobiography, 'with the consent of the majority of the people of Northern Ireland.' Yet, at first, the new Conservative government took a more authoritarian, more pro-unionist approach to Ulster, allowing the British army and the government of the province to participate in an escalating confrontation with militant Catholics. Partly this was due to circumstances: the IRA campaign, the growing bloodshed and Heath's small majority in the Commons. His party had its historic ties to Ulster unionism, and there were still twelve unionist MPs at Westminster. But in other ways the new Tory approach suggested a reversion to the old British impatience with Ireland.

In June 1970, after a weekend of rioting and gunfire in Belfast during which the army had partially lost control of events and had managed to antagonize both Protestants and Catholics, Reginald Maudling made his first visit to the province as home secretary. An officer at the army's headquarters in Lisburn, south of Belfast, later recalled: 'He sat in my office with his head in his hands and said, "Oh, these bloody people! How are you going to deal with them?"' The next day, Maudling flew back to London. 'For God's sake, bring me a large Scotch,' he was infamously reported to have said on the plane. 'What a bloody awful country.'

Even Heath's most able Ulster lieutenant, who from 1972 would pursue a much more subtle and even-handed policy, at first regarded the province as political purgatory. In Tory circles, William 'Willie' Whitelaw, a former Conservative chief whip, was revered for his air of calm and his ability to arm-twist discreetly and make deals that appeared to please everybody. Yet he took a while to acquire a worldliness about Ulster. 'I had been to Northern Ireland only twice in my life,' he confessed in his memoirs, 'the first time to attend a friend's twenty-first birthday just before the war and the second on a golf tour in the 1950s.' Two decades later, on hearing of his posting there as a minister, he told a Conservative Party meeting, 'I am undertaking the most terrifying, difficult and awesome task.' At the end of his first ministerial day in the province, he held a press conference for local journalists. 'Questions were fired at me like bullets from a machine-gun,' he wrote with slightly flustered indelicacy later, 'couched in the most aggressive, and usually personal, terms. Several questioners spoke at once, there was a general atmosphere of background noise and turbulence and few opportunities to complete an answer . . .'

Whitelaw's arrival in Ulster in March 1972 signalled the beginning of what was known as Direct Rule. The province's parliament and government were suspended and replaced by an outpost of Whitehall, the Northern Ireland Office, with Whitelaw as secretary of state. This new British bureaucracy – a world away from the half-dozen distracted civil servants of old – required a substantial headquarters. In Belfast, Ulster's biggest city and its capital, the British chose a location that scored highly for its practicality, although rather less so for its political sensitivity: Stormont.

On my second day in Belfast I took a bus there. It was an icy clear morning in the city centre, but as the bus moved into Protestant east Belfast it entered a thick mist. Union Jack bunting hung from houses in the gloom. Unionist murals guarded grimy cul-de-sacs. Then the road climbed, and gardens and larger houses began to materialize. We passed a private school, a rugby pitch, Mercedes estates parked in driveways. We could have been in Bath.

I got off the bus at a pair of enormous gates. Behind them a wide straight road, flanked by benches and lamp posts at stately intervals, disappeared into the trees and mist of the Stormont estate. The road led uphill past infinities of lawn to a large statue of a man standing with one leg thrust forward and a hand heroically clutching the air. 'Carson', said the plaque. 'Erected by the Loyalists of Ulster.' Edward Carson, Conservative minister, Ulster unionist leader, organizer in 1914 of armed Protestant resistance to Irish Home Rule (and therefore to the Liberal government in London whose policy it was), had personally supervised the unveiling of the statue in 1932. By then

Stormont had already housed the unionist-dominated Northern Ireland government and parliament for a decade, and would continue to do so until Direct Rule.

Behind the statue was the cream neo-classical bulk of the parliament building, like some enormous marooned Whitehall ministry or an English country house expanded to monstrous proportions. And to the right of the parliament, down in a dip and half-hidden by trees, were the faint grey towers and battlements of Stormont Castle. Until 1972, the castle was the administrative hub of the Ulster government. When Direct Rule was imposed, the British took over its cramped rooms with their spectacular Belfast views. Civil servants from London moved in to work alongside – and often exclude – their Northern Irish counterparts. With the legislature suspended, the Northern Ireland Office occupied the parliament building as well. Members of MI5, MI6 and Military Intelligence squeezed into the castle's attics and turrets. Whitelaw acquired an office with French windows. 'At no time during his spell in Northern Ireland', record his biographers Mark Garnett and Ian Aitken, 'could he look out over the city without expecting to see a plume of smoke; it was even possible to hear the larger detonations.'

Between the summer of 1971 and the autumn of 1972, the most violent phase of the conflict so far, there were four bomb explosions and approaching thirty shootings on an average day in Northern Ireland. Increased British military activity poured petrol on the flames. In August 1971, after months of lobbying from the struggling Northern Ireland government, the Heath administration agreed that terrorist suspects could be interned – detained indefinitely without charge – and interrogated. At 4 o'clock in the morning on Monday 9 August, thousands of British troops, equipped with lists of names and addresses by the RUC, began hammering on doors across the province and taking people away. The IRA had long been expecting such a move, and many of its members were sleeping elsewhere. No IRA leaders were apprehended; a third of those arrested had to be released within two days. 'Many of those arrested had not been active members of the IRA for years,' Heath wrote in frustration afterwards, 'some [not] since the 1920s.' More damagingly still, none of those arrested were Protestants, despite the growing number of attacks that loyalists were carrying out on British troops and Catholic civilians. Internment had been used before in Northern Ireland against the IRA, with a degree of success, in 1922, 1942 and the late fifties; yet this time it appeared little more than the clumsy harassment and collective punishment of Catholics.

Defenders of internment in the seventies would attribute its biases, not altogether convincingly, to a British blindness about the sectarianism of some of the RUC's intelligence-gathering. What would be harder to explain away was the fate of the internees who were not quickly released. Most of them were taken to an old army-vehicle depot outside Belfast known first as Long Kesh, and then as the Maze Prison. For the British governments of the seventies, with their Cabinets full of proud veterans of the Second World War and the fight against fascism, the 'cages' of Long Kesh, with their hastily strung barbed wire and converted Second World War Nissen huts, were shaming enough. But thirteen of the internees endured much worse. They were taken to other British military bases in Northern Ireland and held in secret interrogation centres. There, for a week or more, they were subjected to the 'Five Techniques'.

There was nothing about them in any British army directive or training manual. Their origins were highly problematic: they were derived from the methods of questioning used by North Korea against British prisoners during the Korean War. Yet the Five Techniques had been employed, refined and passed on by word of mouth in the British army for decades, as it fought its small, semi-clandestine post-colonial wars. The techniques included depriving prisoners of food; depriving them of sleep; putting hoods over their heads; forcing them to listen to continuous high-pitched noise; and making them stand spread-eagled for hours against walls. These methods were applied with such brutality in Ulster in the late summer and autumn of 1971 that five years later the European Commission of Human Rights found Britain guilty 'not only of inhuman and degrading treatment but also of torture'. In 1978, the European Court of Human Rights downgraded the offence to 'inhuman and degrading treatment'. The British government was delighted. Such were the diminished expectations of Northern Ireland policy by the late seventies.

In February 1972, Heath announced that the Five Techniques would no longer be used. But by then the international notoriety of Britain's behaviour in Ulster had been deepened by another, even more corrosive scandal.

In Salisbury, Heath brought up the subject of Bloody Sunday without my asking. 'What this group on Ireland' – he did not dignify the Saville inquiry which was re-examining Bloody Sunday by using its name – 'is going to produce in its report, I can't tell,' he said, trying to sound philosophical. But then he let out a bitter, exasperated laugh. 'I was the first prime minister who's been summoned by a fully established committee of inquiry – if you like to call them that. And I was kept there for three weeks . . .'

In Derry, a year later, I visited the half-dozen underheated rooms of the Bloody Sunday Centre. The steward that afternoon was a big man of about sixty with an air of studied restraint. I asked him if he thought it was a shame that Heath had died before the Saville inquiry reported. The steward gave a small smile. 'Well, he had to meet his maker.'

In the next room, the events of 30 January 1972 and what led up to them were set out in greying photographs: Catholic barricades standing in the Bogside, waist-high and rushed-looking, all rubble and wire and steel girders; the roof of the Rossville Flats, the tower block that used to dominate the area, with an orderly line of milk and lemonade bottles leaning against the low parapet, each one filled with petrol and a neat little fuse of rolled-up carpet; a scene from an anti-internment protest near Derry eight days before Bloody Sunday, with soldiers lunging at demonstrators on a wintry beach, one with his rifle held upside down and the butt raised; and a crowd standing over two inky bodies on Bloody Sunday itself.

Fourteen unarmed people were killed that day by the British army. One hundred and eight shots were fired by the soldiers. The next day, Heath summoned the Lord Chief Justice of England, Lord Widgery, a former brigadier, to lead an inquiry. As they talked in Downing

Street, Heath told Widgery that 'it had to be remembered that we are in Northern Ireland fighting not only a military war but a propaganda war'. Three months later, Widgery concluded that while some of the soldiers' shooting had 'bordered on the reckless', their actions had been essentially justified.

Most observers outside the British army and the Heath government disagreed. In the days following Bloody Sunday, there were protests across Northern Ireland. In Dublin, demonstrators burned down the British embassy. In the Commons, the independent Ulster MP Bernadette Devlin, a Catholic who had been in Derry on Bloody Sunday, got up from her seat and slapped Maudling in the face. In Australia, dockers boycotted British ships. In America, donations to Irish Northern Aid (NORAID), which raised funds for IRA weapons, increased threefold between January and July 1972. In Canada, there was still sufficient interest thirty years later for a commemorative television documentary called *Bloody Sunday: Massacre of the Innocents*. The steward in Derry put a tape of it on for me. When the film had finished, I went to have a look at where the shootings had happened.

The December afternoon was dimming when I got to the Bogside. The light went quickly down there, in the narrow flatlands beneath the Creggan on its hill to the west and the old city walls on the ridge to the east. Low blocks of flats in drab post-war pastels stood in the gloom. The Rossville Flats were gone, but little else seemed altered. 'You Are Now Entering Free Derry', said the famous murals. Fresh IRA graffiti was scrawled on other walls. Behind the buildings were the same alleys, cul-de-sacs and blind corners where terrible things had been done. In the bare courtyard between the maisonettes of Glenfada Park, four people were killed on Bloody Sunday. In 1997, a previously unheard account of the day, written shortly afterwards by one of the soldiers present, appeared in the Dublin *Sunday Business Post*. It would become one of the main reasons for the setting up of the Saville inquiry. As the shooting reached its climax on Bloody Sunday, the soldier wrote,

A group of some 40 civilians were there running in an effort to get away. [Another soldier] fired from the hip at a range of 20 yards. The bullet passed through one man and into another and they both fell . . . A Catholic priest ran across to the bodies shouting about giving the last rites. He was clubbed down with rifle butts . . . I remember thinking . . . that no one would ever know about it.

In 2005, the courtyard was still exposed and bleak, just kerbstones and grey tarmac, with the tiny back windows of the maisonettes looking blindly on. In one corner a shipping container had been turned into a beleaguered-looking newsagent's, like something you might imagine seeing in Baghdad or Kabul. Somewhere in the walls around the courtyard there were still two bullet holes, preserved by order of the Saville inquiry, but I couldn't find them in the dusk. The courtyard was deserted and I didn't feel like lingering. I started walking back towards the city centre and my bed-and-breakfast, where the owner had talked vividly, almost entertainingly, about the bomb shrapnel from the seventies embedded until recently in his living-room wallpaper and how the IRA used to roll car bombs down the steep hill outside his windows.

As I was crossing the last road of the Bogside, a man came up to me. He was middle-aged but very thin and held two creased carrier bags. He indicated my notebook. I said I was doing some research about Bloody Sunday. 'I was shot too,' the man said, eyes suddenly like lasers. 'I was in an active-service unit. Do you want to see the scar?' Despite the December air he started to untuck his red check shirt. I got a glimpse of rigid muscle, then he stopped. 'Can't show it to you here,' he said abruptly, tucking the shirt back in. I made an excuse about not being able to go with him, and he walked nervily off towards Glenfada Park.

Bloody Sunday was a nadir in the war in Northern Ireland, but it was also a turning point. Afterwards, few people in the British army or the Heath administration believed – if they ever had – that the Ulster crisis could be ended by military means alone. The first consequence of this was Direct Rule, which terminated the unionist government of the province, with its vulnerability to Protestant pressure for ever more draconian and disastrous anti-IRA clampdowns. The second consequence was a more nuanced use of force by the British. In truth, the behaviour of the army in Ulster had rarely been as brutal as in a classic counter-insurgency operation: the province's proximity to Britain, its population made up of UK citizens and the presence of so many reporters saw to that. Now, after Bloody Sunday, the British mounted more careful undercover operations of deliberately blurred official and legal status but growing effectiveness, and better-planned conventional manoeuvres such as Operation Motorman, the biggest deployment by the British since Suez, which captured Free Derry and other IRA-controlled 'no-go' areas in July 1972 with barely a shot fired.

The third consequence was a readiness to talk to the Provisionals. Alternating between confrontation and conciliation, or pursuing both approaches simultaneously, had long been a Heath trademark. It was also how the British state traditionally dealt with rebellions against its authority that could not be straightforwardly defeated. As Heath justifies the switch in his Ulster policy, a little testily, in his autobiography: 'British government representatives have been meeting terrorists in different parts of the world for years . . . It was Lloyd George's meetings in 1921 with de Valera and the leader of the IRA, Michael Collins, which had made an independent Ireland possible . . . the Mau Mau revolt in Kenya would [not] have been settled had it not been for meetings with the rebel leaders . . .'

By the summer of 1972, the Provisionals were also ready to talk. This was partly because they felt their position was strong. They believed that they were winning the war, and they wanted to see what concessions they could force the British to make. But the IRA's new stance also derived from the worry that their position might soon weaken. After nearly four years of increasingly indiscriminate bloodshed – the IRA's attacks on 'economic' targets were often hard to distinguish from crude sectarian warfare against Protestants – a disillusionment with the armed struggle was beginning to settle over even some militant Catholic areas. In May, the Official IRA killed a nineteen-year-old soldier from Derry who had never served in Ulster and was on leave at his family home in the Creggan. The local outcry was so strong that the Officials declared an indefinite ceasefire and renounced violence permanently.

On 7 July, a minibus with brown paper taped across its side windows containing a single British negotiator and an army officer in civilian clothes met a car containing Mac Stíofáin, Gerry Adams, Martin McGuinness and three other senior IRA negotiators close to the border with the Irish Republic. From a nearby field a British army helicopter took the seven negotiators to Aldergrove airport outside Belfast, where they were saluted by an official RAF greeter with a disbelieving expression and flown to England. 'We landed at Benson RAF airport in Oxfordshire', Adams recalled, 'and were transferred to two limousines. At Henley-on-Thames we stopped: Seamus Twomey [the commander of the IRA's Belfast Brigade] wanted to go to the toilet . . . Seamus was away for what seemed to be a very long time and this caused consternation amongst our minders . . . Eventually Seamus strolled back . . . remarking on how pleasant the place was.' The limousines drove on to London. They stopped outside a large house near the Thames in Chelsea. It belonged to one of Whitelaw's junior ministers. The IRA men were invited in.

The secret talks did not go well. Whitelaw was late. 'When he came in,' Adams writes, 'he struck me as florid and flustered; his hand was quite sweaty.' Mac Stíofáin began by reading out a list of essentially impossible demands: that Britain should allow the fate of Ulster to be decided by the whole population of Ireland; that Britain should publicly promise to withdraw all its forces from Northern Ireland by 1 January 1975; and that, before then, Britain should issue 'a general amnesty for all political prisoners . . . internees and detainees and . . . people on the wanted list'.

The meeting broke up not long afterwards. Whitelaw dismisses it in his memoirs as 'a non-event'. Yet in the fact of the meeting itself, in the many small indignities swallowed by both sides to make it happen and in some of those present – notably McGuinness and Adams, who said little while Mac Stíofáin declaimed and Twomey thumped the table – the distant outline of a more peaceful Northern Ireland could perhaps be glimpsed. For almost a fortnight before the meeting and two days afterwards, the IRA maintained a ceasefire: 'It was agreed that the IRA and the British army could both have the freedom of the streets,' records Adams, 'and the IRA could bear arms – openly displaying them in republican areas only.'

*

But there was a problem with placing too much hope in these developments. Ending the bloodshed in Northern Ireland was not just about tentative and perilous negotiations between the British and the Provisionals; there were the militant unionists to consider too. Their politics had had a violent edge for years; now, confronted with the rise of the Provisionals, the deaths of increasing numbers of Protestant civilians in IRA attacks and the threat by the British government to unionism's traditional hold on the province from Stormont, the Protestant vigilantes of the late sixties became paramilitaries.

In 1971, the Ulster Defence Association (UDA) was founded. It began barricading off its own 'no-go' areas and killing Catholics, sometimes in the belief that this would cut off support for the IRA, sometimes purely at random. Within a year, the UDA was murdering twice as many civilians as its republican counterpart. In February 1972, William Craig, the former Stormont home affairs minister and outspoken opponent of the civil-rights movement, set up another loyalist paramilitary organization, the Ulster Vanguard. 'We must build up a dossier of the men and women who are a menace to this country,' he told a rally of supporters in Belfast the following month, 'because if and when the politicians fail us, it may be our job to liquidate the enemy.' Craig arrived at the rally in a car with motorcycle outriders; ranks of men in leather jackets among the crowd of 70,000 gave the occasion an additional menace. Ten days later, when the imposition of Direct Rule was met by unionist rallies, strikes and power cuts, a rumour circulated that the Ulster Vanguard was about to mount a coup.

The rumour, like the Ulster Vanguard itself, quickly evaporated. The UDA's 'no-go' areas were, for now, easily dismantled by the army, but the killings of Catholic civilians continued, generating their own revenge killings of Protestant civilians by the IRA. And the threat of unionist militancy remained: both to any British deal with the IRA or more moderate republicans to secure peace, and to the more realistic prospect that the situation in Northern Ireland might at least become – or seem to become – more manageable and tolerable. During the seventies and long afterwards, the latter kind of 'progress' in Ulster was assessed according to the casualty figures and whether they constituted, in Maudling's infamous but coldly realistic phrase, 'an acceptable level of violence'. In 1970, 16 civilians were killed; in 1971, 61 civilians and 43 soldiers; in 1972, 223 and 103 respectively; in 1973, 128 and 58; in 1974, 145 and 28; in 1975, 196 and 14; in 1976, 223 and 14; in 1977, 59 and 15; in 1978, 43 and 14; in 1979, 48 and 38.

The trouble with following such statistics closely, apart from the false dawns, disappointments and sense of grim stasis they could prompt, was the political leverage it gave to successful acts of violence. Throughout the Heath government, the amount of time devoted by the House of Commons to Northern Ireland rose and fell almost precisely in proportion with the death rate in the conflict. Whatever non-violent strategies the armed protagonists in Ulster, including the British, developed during the seventies, the use of force remained a key tactic and became an increasingly entrenched habit. In 1972, after the failure of the talks with the British, Mac Stíofáin decided to 'intensify' the IRA campaign in the province. The following year, after a rash of arrests of IRA members, with the British making damaging use of disillusioned IRA members as informers, the Provisionals responded by reopening an old front in the armed struggle: taking the war to England.

In 1978, the University of Strathclyde in Glasgow published a study of attitudes in Britain, Ireland and Ulster since the late sixties to the conflict in the province. The study's most interesting and unpredictable results came from Britain. It found that during the first, supposedly momentous weeks of the British military intervention in Northern Ireland in 1969, the public at home had remained largely unmoved. That September, a survey by National Opinion Polls saw the Ulster crisis ranked last by voters when they were given a list of ten problems facing the Wilson government. Two years of bloodshed later, the profile of the crisis had risen sharply – a November 1971 Gallup poll ranked it Britain's second most serious problem – but it had not overtaken public anxieties about the economy. During 1972, as the violence reached a peak, Ulster began to recede as an issue in Gallup's monthly polls. 'March 1973', noted the University of Strathclyde study, 'was the last month in which as many as ten per cent of Britons thought it the country's most important problem.'

In Britain in the seventies, there was increasingly strong competition for that honour, but the studied indifference of the British public to the war in Ulster became a frustration, and then a motivation, for the IRA. In 1974, David O'Connell, a member of its ruling Army Council with a reputation for keen political thinking and for helping to invent the car bomb, gave an interview to the respected British current-affairs programme *Weekend World*. Interviews with IRA members were rare – after this one there would be no more on British television until 1983 – and it quickly became obvious why. With his side parting, smart jacket and striped tie, the middle-aged O'Connell looked like a country bank manager – eerily out of time, like the young IRA gunmen on the Creggan who still wore tight Mod suits and Chelsea boots in the era of flares and platforms. But he spoke from the start with a barely contained anger that was as compelling as it was almost unwatchable. Sweat shone on his bony forehead. One of his blue-grey eyes twitched. One of his hands made a fist.

'Let me make this point,' he said at the interview's climax. 'For five years the British government has had its forces waging a campaign of terror. For five years . . . [the counter-insurgency] theory of leaning on the people, of squeezing the people has been done in the north of Ireland. What have we got from the British public? Total indifference. They can wash their hands.' He jabbed a finger up and down: 'The British government and the British people must realize that . . . they will suffer the consequences.'

Four days after the interview was broadcast, two pubs in the centre of Birmingham were bombed by the IRA and twenty-one people were killed. It was the worst attack in a campaign by the IRA's 'England' department that would continue until the end of the decade and far beyond. During the mid-seventies alone, it included attacks on the Tower of London and an army recruiting centre in Whitehall; on the Old Bailey and Euston station; on a coach on the

M62 and pubs in Guildford; on restaurants in Mayfair and Westminster; on a hotel near Oxford Street and on the Park Lane Hilton; and on Heath's home in London, where a bomb thrown from a car onto a first-floor balcony in front of his favourite desk missed him by five minutes. He had stayed for tea with friends for slightly longer than planned after conducting his traditional Christmas carol concert in Broadstairs.

For over twelve months during 1974 and 1975, a four-man IRA unit, which would become notorious as the Balcombe Street Gang, averaged more than a shooting or a bombing a week in the capital. The effectiveness of these and other England department operations was as variable as their targets: sometimes property; sometimes military personnel; sometimes politicians, with or without Ulster connections; sometimes random civilians; and sometimes an indiscriminate mixture of several of these categories. The deadliness of these attacks depended partly on the IRA leadership's own shifting conception of the 'acceptable level of violence'. The warnings the Provisionals offered beforehand were equally unpredictable. Car bombs could be announced as much as an hour before detonation, with the locations of the devices given, right down to the registration numbers of the vehicles; or sometimes no warning was given at all.

Britain had not experienced political violence on anything approaching this scale since the IRA campaign during the Second World War. Since then, changes in the population had made Irish terrorism in Britain potentially more destabilizing. Post-war Britain had been built in large part with labour imported from a stagnating Ulster and an Irish Republic that was still an economic backwater. By the start of the seventies, there were over a million Irish-born people in Britain, with half a million in London and almost a thousand still arriving each week from the Republic. Unsurprisingly, some retained their old political convictions. In Kilburn in north London, then a poor, close-packed Irish quarter of republican pubs and after-hours rebel songs that was not utterly different in atmosphere from west Belfast, there were marches against internment involving demonstrators wearing Sinn Féin armbands and paramilitary berets. The Provisionals had a local branch. In 1971, an alarmed Catholic priest

in London told the BBC programme *Panorama*, 'Every Irishman is a potential IRA man.'

In Liverpool, the same programme found four councillors belonging to the city's Protestant Party who said they were 'prepared to go to Northern Ireland and fight'. In Scotland, where the connections to Ulster through geography, immigration and religion were even tighter, and where weapons and safe houses had been provided for Irish nationalists during the war against the British half a century earlier, IRA and UDA graffiti began to appear on housing estates in the most sectarian areas. The Protestant Orange Order, which had been declining in Scotland during the sixties, revived as the Ulster crisis deepened, and developed a militant fringe which favoured smuggling guns across to Belfast. The old republican channels between Glasgow and Derry were also quietly reopened.

And yet, for all the divisive potential of the Ulster issue in Britain in the seventies, and despite the IRA's 'mainland' campaign, most Britons were not affected by the conflict in the politically decisive way that O'Connell and his fellow IRA strategists had hoped. Only the Birmingham pub bombings reversed Northern Ireland's drift down Gallup's monthly rankings of the most pressing British political issues, and then only briefly. Two months after the killings, those surveyed considered Ulster even less of a priority than they had done before.

In fact, a minority of Britons, unacknowledged by O'Connell, had long opposed the presence of British soldiers in Northern Ireland. In 1969, the radical London newspaper *Red Mole* had passed on advice about how to cope with tear gas – 'breathe through a handkerchief soaked in vinegar . . . short even breaths . . . do not rub the eyes . . . do not drink for at least 3 hrs (if gassed)' – to Catholics confronting troops in Derry. By 1971, marches in London against the Ulster deployment were attracting support from an eclectic range of leftish political groups – 'Gay Liberation Front Supports Battle for Freedom in Ireland', read one placard – as well as traditional republican sources. John Lennon took part in one march, holding a copy of *Red Mole* with the headline 'For the IRA – Against British Imperialism'.

The following year, he wrote 'Sunday Bloody Sunday': '. . . The cries of thirteen martyrs/Filled the Free Derry air . . .' A few months later, Paul McCartney released a single titled 'Give Ireland Back to the Irish'. Banned by the BBC, it reached a respectable Number 16 in the charts.

In 1973, the Troops Out Movement was founded at a meeting of 400 self-described 'trade unionists, housewives, students and ex-soldiers' in Fulham Town Hall. It leafleted and petitioned, set up branches and sent delegations to Northern Ireland. Support arrived from left-wing Labour MPs, and there were melodramatic public meetings about the wider significance of events in Ulster, with themes such as 'The British Army in Ireland and its Projected Role in Britain'. In addition, Troops Out helped pioneer a new kind of eclectic, coalition-based, left-wing politics, which would become increasingly important in Britain from the mid-seventies onwards.

But Northern Ireland was not Vietnam. Without young Britons being conscripted to fight there, and with the period's profusion of other radical causes competing with it for attention, it was difficult for Troops Out to become a mass movement or acquire real leverage in Parliament. Instead, it won a paper victory. As Ulster lost its purchase in Britain as a major political issue from 1974 onwards, so the opinion polls began to show that the public wanted, as the Troops Out slogan put it, 'our boys to be brought home'. In 1969, support for the military intervention in Ulster had been recorded at 61 per cent, with 29 per cent against; by 1974, the position had been almost completely reversed: only 32 per cent favoured keeping the soldiers there, with 59 per cent favouring withdrawal. This balance of opinion remained roughly constant until well into the late seventies. Yet over the same period, and sometimes in the same polls, equally high levels of British support were recorded for an army crackdown in Ulster, and also for the notion that a military withdrawal would bring chaos and civil war.

In this fog of erratic and contradictory opinions the University of Strathclyde detected an exasperation – 'British public opinion appears to endorse a "tough" Ulster policy for its own sake, regardless of the consequences, good, bad, or nil' – and a deepening weariness – 'It appears that political killings in Northern Ireland, whether they involve British soldiers or Ulstermen, have become "boring".' The study cited one further set of poll figures in conclusion. Between 1969 and 1976, the proportion of Britons who supported a united Ireland fell from 43 per cent to 38 per cent, almost precisely matching the figure for 'don't know'.

For centuries, most Britons had managed not to think too much about events across the Irish Sea. The way the Ulster conflict was covered during the seventies often reinforced that reflex. Irish jokes were a British light-entertainment staple and Irish joke books were best-sellers, but Irish history rarely featured on British television, despite its growing relevance. At the BBC from 1971 onwards, proposed programmes about Ulster were, uniquely, always 'referred upwards' to senior management for approval. BBC chairmen received unsubtle advice from government ministers and right-wing newspapers about how Northern Ireland should be covered, although it is not clear whether that advice was always needed: 'Between the British army and the gunmen, the BBC is not and cannot be impartial,' wrote the corporation's chairman Lord Hill in 1971. Factual and fictional works alike were doctored or banned outright. The most notorious example of the latter was *Article 5*, a drama about British interrogations in Northern Ireland made for the prestigious 'Play for Today' series in 1975. The controller of BBC2 stopped its transmission on the distinctly contradictory grounds that 'The play would have caused such offence to viewers that its impact would have been dulled and its message negated.' *Article 5* has never been broadcast or even made available to researchers since.

In Northern Ireland, meanwhile, a large army information – and disinformation – office strongly influenced what was reported. 'Most journalists . . . are almost completely dependent on this information service,' wrote the *Guardian* correspondent Simon Hoggart, who had just finished his time in Ulster, in an article for *New Society* magazine in 1973. When something newsworthy happened, he went on, 'The first account [in the press] is always the unchecked word of the soldier on the spot.' The conscientious or truly independent journalist, and there were always some, would find the time to investigate further. But as the seventies went on, the focus of British Ulster coverage was increasingly the plume of smoke on the horizon: the act of violence – or in fact, even narrower than that, its aftermath – presented without context or causes or consequences.

In the tabloids, such reporting often had an apocalyptic tone. In 1971, the *Sun* reported that the IRA was sending into battle 'bomb-throwing eight-year-olds'. The following year, the *Daily Mirror* said the IRA had 'hired assassins from behind the Iron Curtain to gun down British troops'. In 1976, the *Daily Express* alleged that millions of pounds of British social-security benefits were being diverted to the IRA by Irish immigrants. In 1977, the *Mirror* warned:

IRA-linked Left-wing militants are planning a bomb war on English cities . . . British Trotskyists and Marxists have spent two months forging links with wildcat IRA bombers. They are believed to have offered help to the bombers in organising a blitz of shopping centres, railway stations . . .

None of these reports were true. Some of them came from army briefings. But such scare stories, and their regularity and prominence, did say something about how Northern Ireland affected British life and politics in the seventies. The Ulster crisis bored many people but it was in the air. In London, during the periods when bombs were going off, the shops in the West End were quieter than usual. Some people stopped travelling on the Tube because it seemed such an obvious target. Restaurants were emptier. Policemen were suddenly everywhere. Bomb scares brought hold-ups and evacuations; the real thing brought a new kind of legislation. Four days after the Birmingham pub bombings, the 1974 Prevention of Terrorism Act, which proposed that suspects could be held without charge for seven days or permanently expelled from Britain, began a rapid passage through Parliament. By today's standards, the Act was mild, but at the time the usually liberal home secretary Roy Jenkins considered it a highly regrettable necessity: 'These powers are draconian,' he told the Commons. 'In combination they are unprecedented in peacetime.'

The Ulster crisis never fully arrived on the mainland. Liverpool was not Londonderry and Glasgow was not Belfast. Sectarianism came in different, not necessarily compatible forms, and the armed struggle, republican or loyalist, soon got too bloody and attritional for many Britons to want to join it. And when the IRA took the struggle to the mainland, its effect was limited. In London and other English cities, in relatively recent memory, people had endured much worse than the Balcombe Street bombers. Yet the unravelling of Northern Ireland did help fray the wider post-war consensus in the UK – ignoring Ulster had been part of that, after all – and did help make Britain a harsher, more fragmented country. While most Irish immigrants in Britain went about their lives unmolested for most of the seventies, there were spasms of hostility against them. After the Birmingham pub bombings (in which nine of the twenty-one dead were Irish), for several weeks Irish people were assaulted, anonymously threatened, thrown off buses, refused service in shops, suspected, arrested or wrongfully imprisoned. Nowadays, terrorism and its consequences are part of the everyday landscape in Britain; in the seventies, their arrival seemed part of a more general darkening.

6

Lights Out

The crisis that did for Ted Heath was both more prosaic and more all-pervading than events in Ulster. And, like all crises, it had its beneficiaries. One of them was a former electrician from London called David Constable.

During the early sixties, he had moved to Germany to avoid national service. While he was there, he had an idea for a business. In the shops he noticed 'lovely coloured candles' of a sort that were not for sale in Britain. He moved back to England, and several years slipped by: 'We were hippy sort of types.' Then, in 1969, he and his girlfriend opened a small basement shop in west London selling kits for making your own candles. 'You got wicks, a couple of kilos of wax, a box of dye and a book on how to do it. You used yoghurt cartons, things around the house as moulds. We were the first to sell the kits,' Constable remembered. It was a bit like the new fashion for home brewing and all the other self-sufficiency fads that were seeding little bohemian businesses across Britain in the late sixties and early seventies. 'Our market was loonies, policemen, vicars, hippies.'

One morning during the 1972 miners' strike, Constable and his girlfriend woke up at home and found their lights wouldn't work. It was the first power cut of the Heath era in their part of London. But its significance was lost on them, so they drove to the shop as usual. 'When we got there, there was a queue round the block. We sold everything by lunchtime. We had no wax left, no wicks, nothing. I kept saying, "What's happening to our shop?"'

That morning was just the beginning. 'We had queues for weeks and weeks afterwards. There was a bit of a wax shortage in the early seventies. The wax was a byproduct of oil refining at Burmah and Shell and BP, and the oil price was going up. There were spivs on Oxford Street selling wax in yoghurt cartons with not even a wick in them.' By the time that the three-day week, with its accompanying blackouts and shoppers' panics, was imposed by the Heath government in 1973, 'We were having a ten-ton delivery of wax every morning,' Constable recalled. 'A lorry would wait outside, and we wouldn't even unload it before selling it. We had a friend who was a bit of a hard nut on guard. But we did lose a bit. People nicked a bit.'

Constable shrugged. With his angular rimless glasses and choppy grey haircut, even in 2005 he still did not quite look like a conventional businessman. Behind him his current shop, which had clung on in one of Kensington's few remaining tatty backstreets since 1976, was a great cavern of candles and seventies lettering. Then a sharper, deal-maker's look came into his eyes. 'We didn't put our prices up during the power cuts,' he said. 'Should've done. Now it's not anywhere near as busy as in those days. Chinese imports are hurting the industry here. There's only a few companies left now.' Then the look was gone, and he shrugged again. 'But we were hippies then, of course.'

The three-day week began at midnight on New Year's Eve in 1973, a Monday. The Heath administration decreed that until further notice all businesses except shops and those deemed essential to the life of the country would receive electricity only on Mondays, Tuesdays and Wednesdays, or on Thursdays, Fridays and Saturdays. Non-essential shops would only get power in the morning or the afternoon. Four days before the restrictions started, the archbishops of Canterbury and York suggested every British church congregation should pray that 'God may guide us in facing the present crisis with wisdom, justice and self-sacrifice.' Two days beforehand, the *Daily Mail* reported that 'Industry Minister Tom Boardman has said that a two-day week could not be ruled out.'

The national emergency that followed would last for two months, January and February 1974. Yet its roots went back much further than that winter. One of them was Heath's economic policy.

From the beginning, his government had impatiently sought to boost the performance of the British economy. But from 1971, frustrated by a general lack of progress and spooked by that year's sudden surge in unemployment, the Heath administration had sought this transformation by increasingly bold – you could say reckless – means. During late 1971 and early 1972, the government cut interest rates, greatly loosened the rules that governed lending by banks, increased public spending and cut taxes. 'No government has ever before taken so much action in the space of one year to expand demand,' declared the chancellor Anthony Barber on New Year's Day in 1972.

For a time the results were spectacular: the Gross National Product, which had grown by a feeble 1.4 per cent in 1971, grew by 3.5 per cent in 1972, and by a close to unprecedented 5.4 per cent in 1973 – the kind of rate usually achieved by Britain's economic superiors, such as Germany and Japan. The main FTSE share index leapt from 339 in January 1971 to 544 in May 1972. Between mid-1971 and mid-1973, house prices rose by almost three quarters. Margaret Drabble caught the feeling of the boom in her 1977 novel *The Ice Age*:

Go for growth, had been the slogan, and everybody had gone for it . . . When the I. D. Property Company's office block, Imperial House, had been completed . . . there had been champagne – for the foreman, the architect, the three partners in greed, and the borough planner, who had accepted his glass with a nervous laugh. The sun had beat down upon them, on the high roof. On top of their own building, on top of the world. It had been a curious thrill, an impious thrill. Whom had they celebrated up there? Themselves, or the mightier power which had permitted them to play for a while?

In fact, the boom was too reliant on speculation and one-off government initiatives, and too removed from the underlying realities of the British economy, to last long. Shortages of skilled labour and of modern, flexible industrial premises, the legacy of decades of underinvestment and poor training and management, meant that the increased appetite for goods and services awakened by the government soon could not be efficiently met. The result was higher inflation and a growing reliance on foreign goods, which were themselves inflationary, as the other rich countries were experiencing feverish booms and price spirals of their own. Britain's trade balance worsened drastically and the pound, which in 1972 had been freed to rise and fall in value against other currencies, began to fall much more than the Heath government had allowed for.

In May 1973, Barber started to rein in its 'dash for growth' by cutting public spending. In July, he raised interest rates to their highest level since 1914. Boom had not quite yet turned to bust: 'Britain is two-thirds of the way to an economic miracle,' judged *The Economist*, reflecting a still quite common view, at the start of September. But the British economy entered the autumn in a delicate condition, even more vulnerable than usual to unforeseen problems. Then, on 6 October, came the biggest shock for Western economies of the entire decade, and the second catalyst for the three-day week. In a surprise attack, Egyptian troops crossed the Suez Canal and invaded the Israeli-occupied Sinai Peninsula. The Yom Kippur War had started, and with it the 1973 oil crisis.

Cheap and plentiful oil from the Middle East had been one of the foundations of Western prosperity since before the Second World War. As early as 1914, the British government had recognized the commodity's importance by investing in the pioneering Anglo-Persian Oil Company (now BP) when it was still struggling to attract business backers. But it was after 1945 that the miracle of Middle Eastern oil began to change the world. Production doubled each decade. The oil price, allowing for inflation, steadily fell. For the first time most people in the West could acquire cars, plastic goods, electrical gadgets. A whole new world of mobility and consumerism opened up, directly or indirectly the product of this cheap fuel. In Highgate in north London during the late sixties and early seventies, the stepfather of a friend of mine, a City banker with a strong interest in architecture, helped design himself a Californian dream of a house, with a pool and infinities of windows. To heat it all against the un-Californian winds off Hampstead Heath, he chose what seemed the most modern solution: a great, elegantly concealed tank of oil.

Since 1973, the pool has gone unheated. Starting in the thirties, a reaction set in against the unequal oil relationship between the West and the Middle East. It began with a challenge by the Iranian government to the freedoms enjoyed in the Middle East by British oilmen, strengthened in 1960 with the formation of the Organization of Petroleum Exporting Countries (OPEC), and sharpened from 1970, with OPEC beginning to sense its power and securing the first significant oil-price increases of the post-war years. A few British and American observers spotted the trend and its implications before the oil crisis struck. Some of them worked for the Heath administration. Lord Rothschild, a free-thinking former oil executive, had been hired in 1970 to head the government's pioneering in-house 'Think Tank' and to anticipate and ponder Britain's long-term dilemmas. The Think Tank looked at oil and warned that the price of a barrel, which was under $2 in 1972, could rise to between $6 and $9 by the mid-eighties.

The Think Tank's prediction was dismissed by ministers as too pessimistic. In the event, it proved too optimistic. With the outbreak of the Yom Kippur War, OPEC's increasing impatience to secure a better deal for its members acquired an additional, more overtly political edge: the Arab oil-producing countries who made up much of the OPEC membership now wished to isolate Israel from its allies in the West. The result was a volatile four months of selective oil boycotts of Western countries, cuts in oil production and, above all, oil-price increases. By January 1974, a barrel cost well over $11 – more than a five-fold increase on two years earlier.

For every oil-hungry rich country this presented huge difficulties. For the foreseeable future, their businesses and consumers would be paying much more for oil and oil-derived products and would be left with much less to spend on everything else. Overall inflation would rise sharply, while the general demand for goods and services would fall (the oil-producing countries did not yet have the populations or the traditions of mass consumerism to make up for the Western public's sudden loss of spending power). The Western economies, therefore, would plunge together into a severe recession, while at the same time suffering the shortages and price hikes that usually came with an overripe boom. During the seventies an ugly new word, 'stagflation' – a crude welding of 'stagnation' and 'inflation' – would come into use to describe this grim new economic world. And of all the Western economies it was Britain's, which before the oil crisis already had unusually bad inflation, a deflating property bubble and other unique economic frailties, that was worst equipped to cope with it. On 12 December 1973, the minutes of the Heath Cabinet record: 'The Chancellor said that the country was now facing the gravest economic crisis since the second world war.'

To make matters even worse, the British crisis quickly acquired a potentially lethal political dimension. Four days after the start of the Yom Kippur War, the leadership of the National Union of Mineworkers rejected a pay offer from the National Coal Board. Behind their decision lay a number of predictable factors: some clumsy negotiating by the Coal Board, the success of the miners' confrontational tactics in 1971 and 1972, and the continuing rise of the NUM's militant left as personified by Arthur Scargill and Mick McGahey. But there was also a new aggression and confidence that derived directly from the oil crisis. In a BBC television interview on 13 December, the ever-pragmatic NUM president Joe Gormley gave voice to it.

'The supplies of cheap oil are finished for ever,' he began, slowly and gravely, his thin lips barely moving but expecting to be heard. 'They [the government] are going to need more and more of our own indigenous energy sources to fill the gap. And they won't have anybody to do that' – here his voice quickened and became more impatient – 'because men will not continue to work at the coalfaces of Britain for less than forty quid a week, which is what the [Coal Board] offer will bring them.' Gormley looked unblinkingly at the camera: 'If the country doesn't see the sense of our argument, then it's woe betide them for the future.'

The NUM's stance did not come as a complete surprise to the government. After the 1972 strike, writes Douglas Hurd in his memoirs, 'Most of us dreaded, beyond anything else, a further engagement with the miners.' To avert another dispute, Heath had been pulling rank on the Coal Board and personally holding meetings with Gormley and the NUM's other negotiators since the summer of

1973, well before the oil crisis. Yet, at best, these talks achieved nothing. The miners wanted an average pay increase of 31 per cent; Heath and the Coal Board, desperate to prevent British wages rocketing and sending inflation higher, were prepared to give them barely half that. At worst, the negotiations were counterproductive. The intimate, one-to-one nature of the meetings encouraged Heath to believe that, despite the NUM and the government's divergent and essentially immovable positions, a deal could somehow be put together by the two leaders. At the same time, his involvement in the talks encouraged the NUM to see their argument as being with his administration rather than with the Coal Board.

In early November, with winter not far off now, the union launched a ban on overtime working that cut coal production by close to a third. On 28 November, another meeting took place between Heath and the NUM. The union justified its demands by an indelicate but hard-to-fault logic: 'Why can't you pay us for coal what you are willing to pay the Arabs for oil?' one of the NUM executive asked Heath. 'The Prime Minister really had no answer,' recalled the head of the civil service Sir William Armstrong, who was also present, in an interview later. The other key moment of the meeting involved the Scottish miners' leader and communist Mick McGahey. Accounts of exactly what was said vary, but it seems fairly clear that when Heath asked him what he wanted, he answered without ambiguity. He said he wanted to get rid of the government.

The encounter left a lasting impression on Heath. In Salisbury, he still talked with a hiss of bitterness about 'the communist wing of the miners' in the seventies. 'They wanted to get control of the Labour Party, and everything else,' he said, suddenly glaring up at the sitting-room bookshelves from his chair. 'Gormley hadn't got the strength to say no to them.' During November and December 1973, as the second national coal strike of his government changed from a possibility into a probability, Heath's conviction that the miners' militancy was ideological – rather than, as it also was, opportunistic and materialistic – became entwined with his wish to avoid a repeat of the 1972 strike's unpredictable social and economic consequences, with the oil crisis, with his tendency to dig his heels in under pressure, and with his proclivity for state initiatives and economic planning. The result was the three-day week.

Its official aim was to get the country through the winter. With oil expensive and in short supply, and coal stocks not especially high – partly because the oil crisis had increased consumption – a reduction in energy use was essential, the trade and industry secretary Peter Walker told the Cabinet on 12 December, to avoid 'enforced electricity disconnections', 'essential services . . . in difficulty' and 'factories on the point of closing' by 'mid-January'.

But the three-day week was also the product of less openly voiced political calculations. Britain in the seventies was a country with potent recent memories of periods of national sacrifice and austerity, from the rationing of the Second World War and the Attlee era to the power cuts during the icy winter of 1963. Britons were thought to respond well to such emergencies, and to governments that dealt boldly with them. By 12 December, the Heath Cabinet was convinced that 'Many people in the country were now in the mood where, above all, they wish to try and make a personal contribution to the solution of the present crisis.' The government should therefore 'appeal to moderate opinion by seeking to enlist help in the national interest'. As for the miners and the other unions that might influence them, 'The best way to bring pressure to bear . . . was to shock them.'

The next day, Heath made a special prime-ministerial broadcast. Wearing a dark blue suit and a tie almost fit for a funeral, he looked less healthy than usual: pale pink rather than brown. He had a bag under one eye. He was increasingly suffering from an underactive thyroid – common symptoms include weight gain and a general sluggishness – that would not be diagnosed until 1975. With a long drawing in of breath that caused his heavy chest and shoulders to rise visibly, he began.

The country, he said, was facing a 'grave emergency'. In a formal, rather resigned tone, he listed the oil crisis, the miners' dispute, the problems with the economy – but without clearly explaining the relationship between them or how they had led to the broader emergency. Instead, he gave a summary of how the three-day week would work. 'I know', he went on, 'that the new restrictions will make life very much harder for all of us . . . We shall have a harder Christmas than we have had since the war . . . We shall have to postpone some of the hopes and aims we have set ourselves for expansion and for our standard of living.' Then a more defiant note entered his voice: 'The government is determined to ensure the survival of this nation at a reasonable level of life and industrial production . . . but in the end our ability to survive depends on our willingness as a nation to act together and to act responsibly. During the last three years, I have spent many hours, indeed days, [in] discussions with trade union leaders. I have got to know them well. I believe that most of them want this country to succeed . . .'

The great denunciation of the miners never came. Instead, Heath concluded like some dutiful, slightly reticent Victorian patriarch, with a passage of heavily veiled criticism and patriotic wishful thinking: 'I have spoken to you plainly tonight, and I will do so again when the time seems right . . . At times like these, there is deep in all of us an instinct which tells us that we must abandon disputes amongst ourselves. We must close our ranks, so that we can deal together with the difficulties which come to us, whether from within or from beyond our own shores. That has been our way in the past, and it is a good way . . . Our future and the character of our country depend on it.'

In practice, the three-day week's political effectiveness was dulled by the same lack of clarity that marred Heath's broadcast. For one thing, the drama of the measures' introduction on New Year's Eve was spoiled by the fact that more minor restrictions on energy use had been already been imposed, starting in the autumn. Some were voluntary, some compulsory, and they already covered everything from street lighting (dimmed to half its normal brightness on main roads) to television (evening closedown brought forward to 10.30 p.m.) to the appropriate temperature for offices (a slightly chilly 65 Fahrenheit). And then there was the sheer complexity of the three-day week itself: when its rules were published in late December, the government newspaper advertisements were almost indecipherable patchworks of small print, acronyms, legalese and statistical tables.

The prospect of living in a country with a speed limit of 50 miles per hour, with petrol rationing widely considered imminent, with no floodlighting for football matches or other outdoor events, with home heating and lighting kept to a minimum, and breaches of some of these and many other restrictions 'punishable', as a government ad in the London *Evening Standard* put it, 'by imprisonment or a fine or both', was not to everyone's taste. During the first two weeks of January, the New Zealand High Commission in London experienced three times its normal level of inquiries about emigration. On 4 January, the *Sun* reported that 'a blonde who drove a sleek blue Rolls-Royce' had been found guilty of 'keeping petrol without a licence'. Detectives, the paper went on, 'found a tank containing 540 gallons of petrol 30 yards from her luxury home at Holme Island Estate, Grange-Over-Sands, Lancashire . . . Police were told that the blue Rolls-Royce was making frequent calls at garages and drawing excessive amounts of petrol.'

The same month, a member of the Heath government was caught exhibiting a more embarrassing lack of patriotism. Patrick Jenkin, the confident young minister for energy, a new post created to deal with the oil crisis and the three-day week, suggested that people clean their teeth in the dark to save electricity. Even more injudiciously, he boasted to the *Evening Standard* that, 'Except for a glance at the papers, I can manage my whole morning routine without putting on a light.' The press needed no more encouragement to start spying on him. A photographer from the *Observer* found Jenkin's large house in north London with its porch light blazing and, it was widely reported, 'lights on in five windows'. Jenkin's wife told journalists that the pictures were deceptive, and he said that his toothbrushing advice had been a joke, but together they only dug a deeper hole. When I met him thirty-one years later, despite a subsequent ministerial career under both Heath and Thatcher, it was still capable of opening up under him.

As we got into the lift at the House of Lords – Jenkin was now a busy Tory peer – another peer squeezed in beside us. Jenkin, garrulous as ever, made introductions. 'We're going to talk about the three-day week,' he said cheerily.

'Oh, brushing your teeth in the dark,' said the other peer.

Jenkin gave a small cough of a laugh. 'Not too long on that, I hope.'

Up in his office, Jenkin avoided the issue for a while with a good anecdote about his department's struggles to enforce the three-day week. 'We got phone calls from members of the public,' he started. 'Plenty of people telling on somebody . . .' Amusement crinkled his full lips, and his rich voice turned mocking: 'There was a great deal of complaint that *saunas* were operating for a full five or six days, and of course they're quite heavy users of electricity . . . We asked [our civil servants] what we could do . . . and they said, "Well, there are really three categories of saunas. There are saunas which are part of hotels, and one can ask the hotels to observe the three-day week. Secondly, there are saunas attached to health clubs, and the clubs are all supposed to be on a three-day week. But there is a third category, dubious saunas . . . and they operate independently and are rather outside any of the normal rules and regulations, and people may not always know where they are . . ."'

Leaning back behind his desk, Jenkin laughed loudly and relished the phrase 'dubious saunas' for a few moments. 'Marvellous!' he said. 'Typical civil service!' Together we pictured nervous Whitehall functionaries peering through overlit doorways in the sex-trade citadel of seventies Soho. Then Jenkin lowered his voice to a near murmur and raised the subject of toothbrushing in the dark. 'What's never been reported', he said, 'is that I was cleaning my teeth by lamplight. The street lamp outside my house. It was a bright orange sodium lamp, on our side of the road. Street lamps were still on much of the time – well, urban street lamps. There were a lot of problems with dark rural roads . . .'

He began to explain why he felt the newspaper photographs of his house had been misleading. But then he stopped. 'The whole thing was very damaging,' he said. 'I have always described myself as the lightning conductor for the anger of the public. The anger turned from being anger against the miners . . . to being anger with the government in general. I have never had a correspondence anything like it. Five hundred letters a day. Particularly from small businessmen –

they were hit especially badly by the three-day week. And lots of them writing as loyal Conservatives: "What do you think you are doing? With your stupid remarks, you make it impossible for us to support the government."'

Less publicly, the strains of the three-day week were also felt deep in the machinery of the Heath government. One of the worst-affected ministries was the Department of the Environment. It had been a conspicuous symbol of the administration's early confidence, a new bureaucracy created by Heath overseeing a new area of state activity, with its headquarters in three clean-lined tower blocks that were completed in 1971 and rose among the dusty old spires and offices of Whitehall like great glass billboards advertising a more modern kind of government. But soon after the new ministry was occupied, the drawbacks of its design began to manifest themselves. The concrete corridors of the Marsham Street towers – or 'the three ugly sisters', as they became known – were windowless and dark. Meanwhile, the glassy offices were cold: in winter, the oil-fired boilers took forty-eight hours to warm up the complex. In an era of strikes and power cuts, these design flaws made some people in the ministry nervous. In May 1973, months before the onset of the oil crisis and the three-day week, an internal memo was circulated asking how many 'essential staff' would need emergency heating and lighting in the event of 'a severe electricity crisis'.

In November, with the oil crisis starting to bite, half the lifts in each tower were switched off to save power. The work of the ministry slowed accordingly. 'We now have to allow a full *10 minutes* to be sure of getting to a meeting on the top floors of the North Tower from here in the South,' wrote an irritated civil servant in early February. In December 1973, a few days before the announcement of the three-day week, personal kettles and electric heaters were banned from the premises. In the corridors, five out of every six lights were removed; civil servants spent the long midwinter evenings stumbling back and forth in near darkness. And from mid-January there were more of them: extra staff were moved into unused rooms to deal with the coupons that had been printed for petrol rationing.

Yet, in other ways, a strange entropy settled over the ministry. On 7 February, DOE representatives attended a general civil-service meeting about a government-wide shortage of paper. 'If the miners' strike continued for more than a month,' the meeting heard, according to the minutes, 'then paper mills might have to close. This would mean reliance on current stocks alone, which, at present, amounted to under one month's supply.' A vigorous discussion followed about the appropriateness or otherwise of civil servants using both sides of each piece of paper.

By mid-January, Marsham Street had reduced its electricity consumption by almost half. Candles and butane lamps had been distributed to staff, but the visibility of the towers with all their glass meant that, even when less than half-lit, they seemed to many outsiders to be setting a bad example. There were repeated complaints from members of the public and other ministries. The DOE had to enter into protracted correspondence about the lighting requirements for staircases and night-time cleaners. Yet the most persistent problem of all was the cold. The worst offices had no carpets or were in the towers' most exposed corners. Despite the extra jumpers, dressing gowns and bedroom slippers people were wearing at their desks – during the three-day week, the Whitehall dress code was relaxed, even at starchier ministries such as Defence – their feet were suffering. Then, on 1 February, a DOE civil servant announced that a suitably frugal solution had been found: 'The people in these rooms have now been given small pieces of carpeting for their feet, which have been of some help.'

In fact, the Heath government was lucky with the weather. After a typically cold December, temperatures in January and February were almost twice the average. On 17 January, the Cabinet was informed that fuel stocks at power stations were being used up at less than half the rate that had been anticipated. The trade and industry secretary Peter Walker, perhaps the sole remaining repository of the administration's early optimism, argued that there was 'room for cautious relaxation of the three-day week'. During the second half of January, there was talk in the Cabinet of a four-day week, even a five-day week for the most important industries. The more apocalyptic predictions about the oil crisis had proved unfounded: while the price remained damagingly high, the government refused to aid Israel militarily and saw Britain's Middle Eastern oil supply cut by a comparatively mild 15 per cent, before being fully restored in February. Petrol rationing did not have to be imposed. 'We are not in a state of continual crisis,' Heath defiantly told the *New York Times* on 6 January. He would not be the last British prime minister in the seventies to make that unavoidable but risky assertion. 'All they [American journalists] do is describe Britain as being in a state of decay . . . which does not bear any relationship to the facts. Most countries have their problems. We certainly have ours. But we have a good many blessings to count as well.'

Heath was at least partly right. Beyond the blighted towers of Marsham Street and the besieged home of the minister for energy, the impact of the three-day week on everyday life was destabilizing rather than disastrous.

In 1974, Colchester in Essex was representative of a lot of mid-seventies Britain and where it was going. A hilltop of old streets in faded orangey brick ringed by newer flat suburbs of neat lawns and passing cars, it had been a Roman town, a market town and an industrial town. Now it was turning into a town for office workers. Its population, like that of many places in southern England and close to London, had grown rapidly since the Second World War as the capital's had fallen. The University of Essex, with its tower blocks among trees like a Led Zeppelin album cover, had been built on the edge of town in the sixties. The railway line to London had been electrified. Commuting to work in the City was on its way to becoming the dominant local working pattern. The old docks and engineering works along the river had done well until the early seventies; now their fortunes were on the slide. But Colchester, unlike solely blue-collar places like Saltley, had prospects.

Politically, the town was calm on the surface. The council had been Conservative since 1950, while the parliamentary seat was comfortably Tory. Heath attended the Colchester Oyster Feast, the town's annual civic centrepiece, in October 1973, after the start of the oil crisis but before its implications had fully sunk in. Still looking tanned and quite slim, he performed one of his last smiling, vigorous walkabouts before the winter's emergencies confined him to London. He made a well-received speech about the value of Britain's armed forces, with reference to the long-established Colchester garrison and its soldiers' current service in Ulster. But away from such occasions other political currents were welling up in the town. Six weeks after Heath's speech, the local army recruitment centre was mobbed by demonstrators who plastered it in posters – 'Troops Out of Northern Ireland', 'Make Love Not War' – and forced it to lock its doors for the afternoon. At the university, which had been notoriously restive since the sixties, a substantial minority of students were seasoned practitioners of the rent strike and the sit-in, of the sudden barricade and picket, of the solidarity action. As a miners' strike loomed during the last weeks of 1973, the NUM was informed that, as in 1972, it would find eager allies on campus.

The build-up to the three-day week in Colchester was full of dark portents. Over the autumn, local shops had started buying in oil and gas lamps, both for their own use and for sale. The town's fire service issued a public warning that a cheap paraffin model from Hong Kong, which was selling for 50p, was leaky and too easy to knock over. By early November, the Colchester *Evening Gazette* reported, 'thousands' had been bought locally regardless. In mid-month came the first petrol panic. With petrol-rationing coupons printed and about to be distributed to post offices, drivers began to queue at garages, buying as little as half a gallon to keep their tanks full. Garages ran out of fuel and closed, or else imposed their own rules. On 5 December, the notice on one forecourt read, in twice-underlined capitals: 'Regular clients only served. No casuals served at all. Regular clients are those people who have drawn regular weekly or daily over the past 12 months.'

With hard times coming, people were circling their wagons. In mid-December, unscheduled power cuts – the miners' overtime ban was already hampering power stations – began to darken nearby parts of Essex. Industrial action by train drivers began to cut off the line to London. Colchester commuters got up hours earlier and queued on unlit platforms for trains that never came. In the town's shops, in the lamplight, with many locals too anxious to travel further afield for their Christmas shopping, there were intermittent shortages of everything from eggs – a hoarders' favourite – to toys (the oil crisis was reducing the production of many plastics). On 17 December, the vicar of a nearby village, a supporter of generally liberal causes called Andrew Hallidie-Smith, told the *Gazette* that thanks to Britain's political situation, the elderly and infirm 'could well be dying of starvation within the next year or two'. Union 'militants', he said, might have to be imprisoned or even shot if they 'persist in fomenting strikes'. He concluded: 'Sometimes there is a question of collective security and national survival.' His views secured him an interview on *The World at One*. A fortnight afterwards, with the three-day week finally beginning, an anonymous columnist in the Essex *County Standard* summed up the atmosphere in Colchester and its hinterland by quoting Shakespeare, and in particular part of a line from *Richard III* that would be much more widely cited later in the decade, during another national crisis and under another prime minister: 'This being the winter of our discontent . . .'

Yet in the event most people coped. Across Britain there was something of the besieged calm that Heath had commented on during his visit during the Spanish Civil War to a blacked-out Barcelona. In Colchester, some people even wrote to the *Standard* and the *Gazette* saying they preferred the darkness and the lack of traffic, the sense of life slowing down. On 18 January, the *Standard* talked to commuters at Colchester station. 'Everyone appeared resigned,' the paper found. 'One man even had a small Primus and heated up a tin of tomato soup on it.'

On 21 January, the *Gazette* published an article about the experiences of a typical Colchester family called 'Life on a Three-Day Week'. Graham and Gillian Bober owned a semi on a new private estate in the suburbs. They were in their mid-twenties and had a five-year-old and a baby. Gillian looked after the children, and Graham worked for a long-established local printers. They were both left-wing – she was the granddaughter of a miner, he was the chairman of the Colchester Labour Party – but they made Heath's three-day week sound quite harmless. 'It hasn't affected our budget that much,' Graham told the paper. Like many Britons during the three-day week, he was working three long days instead of five normal ones. 'All it means is that I don't smoke so much . . . [and] we haven't been able to put away the extra £5 each week.' On his extra days off he was doing 'some long-awaited decorating work' and helping Gillian. 'At least he can hoover,' she said. 'I don't mind him getting in the way . . . The nice part is that now we go shopping in town together on Thursdays and then the whole weekend is free for other things.'

In the Bober household and others like it during the three-day week, a temporary but suggestive shift in the gender balance was under way. Sometimes it simply involved men being at home more and finding it harder to avoid helping out; but sometimes it involved women's relative earning power. While businesses with predominantly male workforces – factories and other industrial concerns – were suffering selective shutdowns, the places where women tended to work – shops and offices – were less heavy users of energy and were therefore less affected by the power restrictions. 'Today it's no longer wrong for the wife to be a major contributor to household finance,' the *Daily Mail* acknowledged on 23 January, as the emergency entered its fourth week. In this respect, as in others, the three-day week was prophetic. Within a decade, many men's jobs in British factories would be gone altogether, and in parts of the country clerical and retail work for women would be all that remained.

The three-day week did not make instant feminists of the Bobers – Gillian was not working, after all. But their new life was intriguing. Through friends of friends, the Italian state television network RAI heard about the article on them in the *Gazette*, and Graham and Gillian were filmed with their boys for a programme on the three-day week. Graham wore a bold waistcoat and tie, Gillian wore a smart coat and scarf, and all of them sat for the cameras on their new cottage-style kitchen chairs with their new striped curtains in the background. Britain may have been in crisis, but it was not short of consumer durables.

When I met the Bobers three decades later, some of the confidence had gone from Graham's broad mouth. He was a taxi driver now.

'My printing company went bust five or six years ago,' he said. 'We were the last. There's not one manufacturing job in that part of Colchester now.' He slapped his knee and spilled some of his coffee on his armchair.

He and Gillian still talked about the three-day week with a degree of fondness. 'People took sides on it,' she said. 'We were living on a very right-wing estate. You'd go into a shop and people would say, "Bloody miners!" and you'd say . . .' Graham broke in: 'At the time I thought Ted Heath was very right-wing. We met him at the Oyster Feast. I spoke to him. We thought, "This bloke, he's dreadful."' He paused. 'I certainly never saw that they'd move as right as they did afterwards.'

During the three-day week, the Bobers and their neighbours looked after each other's children when there was no power at school. When there was no power at home, the Bobers would often go to Graham's parents, who were on the same part of the electricity grid as a local hospital and so almost never got cut off; or Graham, Gillian and their boys would sit together in their new kitchen-diner. 'Television wasn't so dominant then,' said Gillian. 'There was enough light for reading. We had gas lights from camping and a couple of antique oil lamps that had been my grandmother's.' There was a whiff of the Second World War about how they dealt with it all. Graham's employers did their best to keep him in work and earning. 'The company were good, they did a deal with the union,' he remembered. 'Our managers were local people. They weren't dictators.'

In the summer of 1974, after the three-day week was over, a firm of management consultants was commissioned by the Department of Industry to examine how British bosses and workers had responded to the crisis. 'A few companies consciously used the emergency as an opportunity to improve their industrial relations,' the survey discovered. Other employers found they were simply forced to 'set aside ongoing disputes' with unions and 'increase mutual cooperation'; in these cases the unions 'gained confidence, and benefits'. And this more collaborative economy was more productive: across all the companies surveyed, 'Output per direct labour hour did improve, generally by about 5%.' The report added, 'Thinking was stimulated

on the possibility of arranging a permanent four-day week . . .
Several companies began negotiations.'

The enhanced productivity of British business during the three-day
week is still an article of faith for many former members of the Heath
government. Peter Walker, Brendon Sewill and Heath himself all
cited it; Walker even told me, in his confident, broad-brush way, that
'Production in the three-day week went up to more than it had been
in the five-day week.' Looking down on London from his glass-
walled office, he accompanied his claim with a worldly chuckle: the
three-day week, he suggested, had confirmed what he and Heath had
been saying since the sixties about the slackness of the British economy. On their government's inability to alter this state of affairs,
except accidentally and during a national emergency, he had less to
say.

In fact, by most estimates, national output during the three-day
week fell by about a fifth. And the revolution in workplace practices
at the time was, at best, partial. The negotiations about a permanent
four-day week came to nothing. In other companies, the Department
of Industry report found, 'The duration of extra effort and cooperation was limited . . . by growing fatigue, the fading novelty element
. . . or the eventual intrusion of endemic problems.' Workers and
managers alike were resistant 'to Saturday working and also . . . [to]
starting work early or finishing late.' Among the men surveyed, 61
per cent said they disliked the three-day week's new working hours,
with only 10 per cent favourable. Women were only slightly more
flexible. People found the longer shifts tiring. They missed seeing
family and friends on those days. They were unsettled by the disruption of their domestic routines. Even Graham Bober found the
three-day week had its drawbacks. 'When I was doing my twelve-
hour shifts,' he said with distaste, 'I used to have a beard for three
days.'

All this contained hints of the more relentless British workplace
culture to come. But in Britain in 1974 that was still several governments away; commentators with an interest in the social implications
of the three-day week were quicker to identify its more bucolic
aspects. 'Now, at last, we've time to do all those lazy – and free –

things we always wanted,' wrote the columnist Jane Gaskell in the *Daily Mail* on 21 January. 'It already looks as if the 1974 crisis could, surprisingly, be good for us.' She cited a report from the Samaritans of a significant drop in the number of calls it was receiving from would-be suicides. Next she quoted Dr Antony Allbeury of Oxford University, an authority on 'leisure' – a growing preoccupation for social scientists, architects and planners in mid-seventies Britain – who spoke of the value of 're-reading an old book or digging a garden . . . not spending money . . . finding ourselves back in that almost peasant state'. Finally, Gaskell introduced Dr Richard Fox, a consultant psychiatrist from Colchester, to give a more modern hippy tinge to Allbeury's old-fashioned yearnings. Fox, she wrote, 'approves of the three-day week . . . as what he calls "a channel to husbands and wives" – to get together, be more spontaneous, to experiment more in their sex lives while the children are doing a five-day week at school'.

For all the period's problem-solving and difficulties, Britain did enjoy a sort of extended national holiday during the three-day week. Fishing-tackle shops reported big sales increases. Golf courses were busier; some driving ranges stayed open into the winter dusk and beyond, using car headlights for illumination. Audiences trebled for John Peel and Bob Harris's late-night BBC radio programmes of sprawling progressive rock because fewer people were having to get up for work in the morning. But like most holidays, the three-day week was not sustainable in the long run. 'Being political,' remembered Gillian Bober, 'I thought, "It's not going to go on."'

When the three-day week had been announced, public opinion had been evenly split as to whether it was needed. As the restrictions continued through January and into early February, support for them diminished. Labour claimed that the three-day week was politically motivated, unnecessary and economically crippling. At least parts of this critique were persuasive. With the oil crisis abating a little, petrol rationing not introduced in Britain after all and the country continuing to function despite the miners' overtime ban, the three-day week did increasingly seem like an overreaction – or, at best, a set of emergency measures so effective they had outlived their usefulness. At the same time, the economy was quietly suffocating. As early as the second week of the restrictions, the studiedly unsensational television current-affairs show *Weekend World* estimated that Britain's national income was down by between 10 and 15 per cent, a bigger fall, the programme pointed out, than during the General Strike of 1926 or during the worst year of the Depression in Britain, 1931. Almost a million people had lost their jobs – only temporarily, it was hoped – because their employers did not have enough electricity to use them. The earnings of everyone else were down, on average, by between a tenth and a sixth. And as the three-day week went on, many smaller businesses developed cashflow problems: they were still paying full-sized bills from before the emergency, but they were now only part-time enterprises. 'Many will not survive if the restrictions last for more than a very few weeks,' wrote the director of the Small Business Centre at Aston University in Birmingham in *New Society* magazine on 31 January.

Yet to the miners the economic news was not bad enough. During January, their pay talks with Heath and his ministers had continued, with a settlement, based on further concessions from the government, at times tantalizingly close at hand. But the NUM did not trust the government: in public, Heath's comments about the miners were still typically volatile. And just as importantly, the union was aware that its bargaining position was about to weaken. 'With fuel stocks holding out, and spring around the corner, our final card had to be played,' wrote Joe Gormley in his memoirs. On 5 February, 81 per cent of NUM members – a much higher proportion than in 1972 – voted in favour of a national strike. According to the Industrial Relations Act, a stoppage could not begin for at least thirty days after such a ballot, but the miners were in no mood to obey Heath's despised union legislation. They announced that the strike would start in four days. On 6 February, the energy secretary Lord Carrington briefed the Cabinet that

We shall enter on a coal strike . . . with a capacity to maintain electricity supplies until the end of March, provided that the power workers are not prevented [by pickets] from entering the power stations . . . Within 4–6 weeks, some coal-dependent industries will be in difficulties . . . The three-day week will also have increasingly severe effects on business confidence, liquidity and the balance of payments . . . As each month passes, the effect will deepen: lower stocks, more shortages of components, more danger of bankruptcies, unemployment . . .

The next day, Heath called a general election. He had been in power for not much more than three and a half years, and had enough of a Commons majority to have continued in office without an election, at least in theory, for another seventeen months. Instead, voting would take place, after an unusually brief campaign, on 28 February. Heath went on television to justify his decision and to appeal for support. 'The issue before you is a simple one,' he told viewers. 'Do you want a strong government which has clear authority? Do you want Parliament and the elected government to continue to fight strenuously against inflation? Or do you want them to abandon the struggle . . . under pressure from one particular group of workers?' He went on: 'This time the strife has got to stop. Only you can stop it . . . It's time for your voice to be heard – the voice of the moderate and reasonable people of Britain: the voice of the majority. It is time for you to say to the extremists, the militants, and to the plain and simply misguided: we've had enough.'

At first, the Tory papers were in no doubt that the election was about trade union power in general and about the miners in particular. This view of the contest was quickly distilled down to a single short question: 'Who governs Britain?' Since the previous November, when the NUM had started its overtime ban, a growing number of Conservative advisers and ministers had been urging Heath to respond to the coal dispute by abruptly calling an election and making the miners the central issue. These anti-NUM 'hawks' reflected the feelings of many Conservative MPs and party members, who wanted revenge for 1972, and also a belief that an election victory would enable the government to be much tougher with Gormley and the other union leaders.

However, the fact that Heath had resisted this pressure for over two months, and had kept on negotiating with the miners in the meantime, ought to have alerted the hawks and their allies in the right-wing press that the Conservative campaign in February 1974 was not going to be that satisfyingly tribal. Heath wanted to assert the government's authority over the miners, but he did not want to crush them utterly. He was exasperated by their stubbornness; he was alarmed by what he saw as their militant elements (in fact, according to Gormley, at least two of the communists on the NUM executive were opposed to a strike); and he sometimes talked publicly about the coal dispute in emotive, uncompromising language. But as had been demonstrated repeatedly since he had become Conservative leader, the confrontational right-wing side to his politics was essentially an illusion: Heath was a One-Nation Tory, much more interested in keeping the country together than dividing it. In December 1973, before the election was even announced, and with the Conservatives behind in the polls, Heath's speechwriter and confidant Michael Wolff told the *Sunday Times* journalists Stephen Fay and Hugo Young: 'Ted's real worry is about the consequences of a Tory landslide. It would sweep away the moderation which post-war Tories went into politics to defend.'

Creating exactly this scenario would be the central aim of the next Conservative leader. Yet over the three weeks of the February 1974 campaign, Heath attempted a more subtle, but no less ambitious political manoeuvre: winning a general election in the midst of a divisive national strike and a wider national emergency with the minimum of aggression and triumphalism. Thus, alongside the anti-union rhetoric in his election broadcast, he announced a major concession to the miners: while the campaign was going on, their pay claim would be examined by the Pay Board, a semi-independent body recently set up by his government to consider wage demands. The Pay Board would be permitted to offer the miners more money, and the government would accept its decision. On the first day of the election campaign, Heath also announced that the three-day week would be relaxed immediately in a small but highly visible way: the 10.30 p.m. television curfew would be lifted.

This nuanced approach was not pure high-mindedness; it also had a degree of electoral logic. British parties had a patchy record when they tried to win general elections by shaping their campaign around a single issue, as a small but telling *New Society* article had pointed out the previous month. Lloyd George and Ramsay MacDonald had won in 1918 and 1931, standing, respectively, as the leader of a victorious war effort and the head of an emergency cross-party coalition. But William Gladstone and Stanley Baldwin, equally formidable campaigners, had both lost, Baldwin in 1924 (campaigning for tariffs on imports to protect industry), and Gladstone in 1874 (advocating tax reform) and again in 1886 (advocating Irish Home Rule). Moreover, during the 1974 election, the NUM shrewdly took steps to minimize their strike's electoral impact. 'We were determined not to present the media with any free propaganda for the Tories,' Gormley wrote, 'and therefore put a strict limit of six men on any one picket line.' Jim Prior, one of Heath's closest Cabinet allies, recalls with frustration in his memoirs: 'Whether at the mines, power stations or docks, the miners were as quiet and well-behaved as mice.' There were no Saltley-style battles this time. During the election campaign, Gormley and his family received anonymous threats, and moved out of their London home as a precaution, but that was as far as the backlash went. Public support for the miners actually rose.

There were two other problems with Heath's strategy. The first was that it inevitably exasperated many Conservatives. 'I was furious,' remembered the usually loyal Brendon Sewill. 'Because I believed that if you were going to win the election, there had to be a [sense of] crisis . . . Instead of which . . . the crisis was cancelled for the period of the election. But if the crisis had gone away, why have an election?' He feared that the Tory campaign was too soft and subtle – or just incoherent – for many Conservative-inclined voters. In her memoirs, Margaret Thatcher recalls encountering some in late 1973:

Shortly before Christmas, Denis and I went to a party at a friend's house . . . There was a power cut and so night lights had been put in jam jars to guide people up the steps . . . The businessmen there were of one mind: 'Stand up to them [the miners]. Fight it out. See them off. We can't go on like this.'

But while the Conservative campaign disappointed such hopes, it still contained, from Heath's opening television broadcast onwards, enough abrasive moments to alienate more moderate Britons. This had always been one of the big flaws in Heath's public persona: he was a man of the centre, but with his impatience and air of certainty he often didn't seem like one. During February 1974, he copied Harold Wilson's successful tactic from the 1970 election of relentless public walkabouts. 'I enjoy meeting people,' Heath told a BBC news reporter with one of his enormous television smiles on 20 February. Yet on the same news item the cameras caught the irritation in his face whenever he was challenged by members of the public.

The shortcomings of his electioneering style and strategy were compounded by an unusually bad run of campaign setbacks. First, on the day Heath called the election, Enoch Powell resigned as a Conservative MP. Heath had sacked Powell from the shadow cabinet in 1968 for his racist 'rivers of blood' speech, but just as significant as their differences over immigration was their disagreement over economics. Since the fifties, Powell had been a pioneering supporter of the free-market counter-revolution that was brewing at the Institute of Economic Affairs. Now, in early February 1974, he accused the Heath government of initially pledging itself to this radical right-wing cause and then – via the 'U-turn' of 1971 onwards – feebly and dishonourably betraying it. In late February, Powell went further. This time the issue was Europe. Powell had long opposed British membership of the Common Market. Now he called publicly for people who shared his views to support the Labour Party, which wanted to renegotiate the terms of Britain's EEC membership and put them to a referendum. Two days before the election, he announced that he had already voted for a Wilson government by postal ballot.

In the final week of the campaign – a campaign in which a larger-than-usual number of voters changed their minds – there were further bombshells. A leak from the Pay Board appeared to show that the government had significantly overstated the level of miners' wages. The story that filled the newspapers turned out to be based on a statistical misunderstanding, but it was only belatedly and ineffectively rebutted by the Conservatives. Then, three days before polling

day, the British trade figures for January were published, their com-
pilation having been delayed by the three-day week. They were the
worst monthly ones ever recorded. The economic crisis, it appeared,
was even worse than the government had admitted. Finally, the following day, the head of the Confederation of British Industry, the
main lobby group for British business, offered what he thought was
an off-the-record opinion at a conference: that the Heath government's trade union laws were 'surrounded by hatred' and in need of
repeal. In fact, the speech was on the record. The BBC was taping it
for broadcast.

The Heath government had been unpopular almost from the start. Its
luck had been poor. Its response to the great economic and political
shocks it had suffered had often lacked conviction. It had failed to
achieve many of its ambitions. And it had an awkward leader. Yet
despite all this, from the beginning until the end of the campaign, it
recorded a narrow lead over Labour in almost every opinion poll. On
election day, the *Daily Mail* headline for a poll giving the Conservatives a lead of 4.5 per cent summed up the prevailing sense of how
the contest would conclude: 'A Handsome Win for Heath'.

Since the polls had underestimated Tory support in 1970, the
assumption was that they were doing so again. Such expectations
were reinforced by Wilson's performance for much of the campaign.
A lingering throat infection shrank his small voice. He did fewer
walkabouts. His wily bloodhound face had grown heavier and paler.
In public and in private, he seemed tired and withdrawn; over the
past four years he had not been energetic as leader of the Opposition.
Wilson was only fifty-seven, not old for a seventies politician, but
this was his fourth general election as Labour leader, and his
prospects looked bleak. Journalists covering his campaign events
commented on how stooped and elderly he seemed. There were
rumours about his health, that he did not want to win – or that, if he
did, he did not want to be prime minister for a full term. And if he
lost, as anticipated, he would almost certainly be quickly finished as
Labour leader. Six days before the vote, Tony Benn went with Wilson
to a campaign rally in London. 'I think he does realize that he is per-

haps within a week of the end of his political career,' Benn wrote in his diary. Bernard Donoughue, an academic from the London School of Economics whom Wilson had recently hired as an adviser, discovered that when he phoned 'leading party figures' to ask them to take part in campaign press conferences, 'Many of them saw little point in participating,' he wrote later, 'as they believed we were going to lose.'

The preoccupation with Wilson's political mortality meant that the strengths of Labour's campaign went almost unnoticed. Wilson retained his shrewdness. He had discreetly wooed Enoch Powell for months before the election, the two of them always meeting in the same men's toilets at the Commons. Once the campaign began, the precise timing and content of Powell's dramatic anti-Tory interventions was coordinated with Labour's plans. There was also an element of calculation to Wilson's subdued behaviour in public. With Heath making apocalyptic speeches, and the general sense of crisis that had been hovering since the autumn, there was advantage to be had from seeming unexcitable, familiar, even a bit boring. While the Labour manifesto reflected a leftward shift in the party since 1970 and sounded radical – it promised 'a fundamental and irreversible shift in the balance of power and wealth in favour of working people' – Wilson used the word 'socialism' only twice in his election speeches. Instead, the Labour campaign claimed he would be able to bring unions and management together. He would be able to calm everyone down. Perhaps the most important element of the manifesto was its anodyne title: 'Let Us Work Together'.

Wilson's enduring appeal was not the only key influence on the election to be underestimated: there was also the rise of the Liberals. During 1972 and 1973, under the sometimes flashy, often innovative leadership of Jeremy Thorpe – who on occasions travelled between campaign events by hovercraft – they had won a spectacular series of by-elections. Since the twenties, when the Liberals had last been in power, they had intermittently enjoyed such surges, usually when the government was in a mid-term trough, only to see this support largely evaporate at general elections. But during this campaign the opposite happened. In early February, the Liberals were at 12 per cent in the polls; by mid-month, they had climbed to near 20 per cent; by the end, they were scoring 25 per cent or even higher. In spite or perhaps because of a rickety electoral machine – whose overstretched components included campaign coordinators based in the cosy gloom of the National Liberal Club in London, and a party leader who looked like an angular Edwardian undertaker and was based many miles to the west in Atlantic-battered North Devon, where he had a tiny majority to defend and was only periodically contactable by telephone – the Liberals had considerable appeal in disillusioned times. 'Are you voting Liberal to get rid of Mr Heath or Mr Wilson?' one character asked another in 'The Stringalongs', the painfully accurate *Times* cartoon about trendy middle-class Londoners.

Thorpe's absence from the capital insulated him against hostile scrutiny, while the Liberals' long absence from government insulated them against blame for Britain's problems and meant that their more idealistic solutions – greater public 'participation' in government, 'partnership' between bosses and workers – were not mocked. Meanwhile, the drama and novelty of the third party's advance became a self-sustaining story. It was not until the last week of the campaign that the Conservatives saw the danger, and even then they attacked the Liberals only in the most general terms.

In the event, the Liberals did less well in the election than the polls suggested. They won 19 per cent of the vote and only fourteen seats – the British electoral system, with its crushing bias against smaller parties, making a mockery of Thorpe's climactic campaign rhetoric about forming a government. Nevertheless, 6 million Britons had voted Liberal, three times as many as in 1970. Exactly where those extra votes had come from was difficult to say, given the unusual volatility of the election, a substantial jump in turnout and the usual changes in the electoral register, but there were clues in the fates of the main parties. The Labour vote fell by half a million, yet the Conservative vote fell by over a million and a quarter. The Tory total was still narrowly ahead of Labour's, but translated into seats, with the electoral system interpreting the will of the people in its usual approximate fashion, the Conservatives now had 297 MPs to Labour's 301. Heath had lost his majority; the size of the vote for the

Liberals and other minor parties meant that Wilson had not acquired one.

There had not been a hung Parliament since 1929. For four days afterwards there was confusion. Heath did not resign. Instead, with some difficulty, he contacted Thorpe, who had been leading a victory procession around his constituency, and asked him to come to Downing Street. During two secret meetings and a series of telephone conversations, Heath suggested that the Liberals join the Conservatives in a coalition government or in a less formal 'understanding . . . on measures in a programme to be agreed'. In return, according to official minutes and transcripts of the exchanges, Heath offered Thorpe an official inquiry to consider the reform of the electoral system and two Cabinet posts for the Liberals. Thorpe was tempted: 'We may be moving in a somewhat helpful direction,' he told Heath after consulting with senior colleagues. 'I am sorry, this is obviously hell – a nightmare on stilts for you. Somehow I personally hope we can work something out.'

But there were two major obstacles. The Liberal Party as a whole wanted guaranteed electoral reform, not just the possibility of it, and Thorpe, for all his sympathetic words, thought that Heath, having called an early election and failed to win it, could not continue as prime minister. Heath was not prepared to meet either of these demands. Another sticking point was Thorpe's wish to be home secretary. 'I had been warned by the Secretary of the Cabinet', Heath writes in his autobiography, 'that there were matters in Thorpe's private life, as yet undisclosed to the public, which might make this a highly unsuitable position for him to hold.'

The secret talks continued. Wilson, knowing that the government's position was becoming less dignified and less tenable by the hour, simply waited and said little. As a last throw, Thorpe ambitiously suggested to Heath 'a conference of all the party leaders with a view to the formation of a national government'. The Cabinet decided that 'The time for it was not ripe.' Heath's options had run out. That evening, Wilson became prime minister.

It was not an outcome Heath had prepared for. 'I had been far too busy in the run-up to the election to make contingency plans for my own future,' he writes. 'So I was temporarily without a home. I tried to get the lease back on my Albany flat [which had expired in 1970], but a French couple had taken it up and were not enthusiastic about making way for me.'

Not all of right-wing Britain was cast into mourning by the election result. 'The squatter in No. 10 Downing Street has at last departed,' began an acidic editorial in the *Spectator* in March 1974. 'He clung with grubby fingers to the crumbling precipice of his power . . . Policy after policy was reversed, and disastrous alternatives were introduced . . . Mr Heath has spent nine years trying to ruin the Conservative Party, and three and a half trying to ruin the country.' Ralph Harris, the director of the Institute of Economic Affairs in the seventies, was still contemptuous about Heath's lack of right-wing backbone when I met him thirty-two years later. 'Heath deserved to lose,' he said. 'I voted Labour in '74. It was in the papers. We lost an IEA supporter, a sponsor, over it. It cost us the equivalent of £10,000 a year. But that's how angry I was. It was totally pathetic that Heath had given way to the miners.'

In Salisbury, I asked Heath why he thought he had lost. There was a monumental pause. Heath's big head was as still and expressionless as a sculpture on Easter Island. And then he spoke, more digressively than usual, as if he was still trying to work it all out. 'Well, the view is that if we had had the election a fortnight earlier, then we would have won. That's a very debatable point. But, from my point of view – you can say, there you are, I was always too considerate – we'd also got two leading figures [in the Cabinet] who were opposed to an early election. In fact, they wouldn't have had an election in 1974 at all. They'd have just faced the situation, and gone on for another year. But how one could have carried that off without . . . catastrophe, they've never really explained . . .' His voice trailed off.

The next time I was in Salisbury was for his funeral. It was another grey July day, almost exactly a year later. In London, 2005's second wave of terrorist bombings had just occurred and the most ominous preoccupations of the Heath era suddenly did not seem so distant. But in Salisbury the shopping streets were busy with schoolchildren and families, too young to make comparisons with, or probably to care about, the early seventies. Few people turned to look at the clusters of men of a certain age, all of them in dark suits, hurriedly making their way towards the cathedral. Until the cathedral green itself there was no one lining the pavements, and then only a thin curve of a crowd, perhaps 200-strong, politely waiting in anoraks behind the police barriers. On the other side of the green from the cathedral, behind its high gates, Heath's house was even more inscrutable than usual, all its window blinds right down.

Inside, the cathedral was a hushed museum of pinstripe and mid-twentieth-century haircuts. When the hymns started, they were sung with familiarity and gusto, a reminder of the old church-going Toryism and of the muted friendships and shared interests that sustained the private Heath. Seeing my notebook, the woman next to me whispered with a smile, 'My husband knew him from music groups in Broadstairs.'

The other whispers I heard between the hymns would have pleased Heath much less. Near the front of the cathedral, not far from where his large coffin rested under a mound of white lilies and a Union Jack, there was a row of politicians: a couple of Labour Cabinet ministers, the then Conservative leader Michael Howard, the last Conservative prime minister John Major – more recently beleaguered Tories whose struggles cast Heath's in a more favourable light – and then Margaret Thatcher. Beneath the dark overhang of her hat, her expression was a little fixed and uncomfortable. Her nose still jutted, proud as Arthur Scargill's, but some of the dominant gleam had gone from her eyes. Yet people's gazes were on her. They nudged neighbours in next-door pews to point her out. At the end of the service, when Thatcher was led from the cathedral, looking tiny and thin despite her high heels, there was a surge towards the police barriers: photographers, adult onlookers, even children all running across the green to get a glance. Afterwards, Douglas Hurd and the other loyal lieutenants of the Heath government emerged from the cathedral to what was left of the crowd.

A reception followed in Heath's house and garden. The rain had held off and the wind had dropped, so guests wandered out with their teacups and sandwiches onto the long, dipping lawn that ran down to the river. The party was for invited 'friends and colleagues', but many people looked around as if they were visiting for the first time. 'Is that his as well?' said one confident middle-aged man to another as they stared across the perfect glassy river to the meadows on the far bank. '. . . And Mrs Thatcher was here!' said someone else into their mobile. The mood was almost jolly: Heath might have been a rather original, intriguing, but ultimately embarrassing member of some great clannish family, who had, at long last, passed away. On the train back to London, I realized that during the funeral and the reception I had not seen a single damp eye.

7

Waiting for the Collapse

On the evening of 4 March 1974, Harold Wilson returned to Downing Street as prime minister. As he emerged from his official car, there were cheers and boos from the crowd waiting in the cold. The mild weather that had softened January and February had recently ended. Wilson walked slowly – almost trudged – the few yards to the front door of No. 10, with his shoulders slack and his back to the crowd. On the doorstep he turned and waved, a little woodenly, without any apparent joy. He gave the briefest flicker of a smile. He looked from side to side at the press of people and microphones; there was a wariness, and even a deadness, in his narrow eyes.

'Mr Wilson,' said a reporter, 'can we ask you, sir, what it feels like to be back here?' The prime minister began to open his mouth. Then he stopped and glanced twice at his wife Mary, pinned next to him by the flashbulbs and the television lights. There was a long pause. The crowd quietened. Wilson opened his mouth and shut it again. He swallowed twice. And then he finally spoke, flatly and with deliberation: 'We've got a job to do. We can only do that job as one people. And I'm going right in to do that job now.'

Taking Wilson at face value is a risky business. 'Harold Wilson always operated on several levels concurrently,' writes his former adviser Bernard Donoughue, who already had years of experience with tricky Labour politicians as an influential party member and politics lecturer. 'He was perhaps the most complex character I have met in my life.' On the last afternoon of the February 1974 campaign, with the polls seemingly predicting a Labour defeat, Wilson had 'astonished' Donoughue with a typically abrupt revelation:

He proposed . . . to switch secretly from the Adelphi to a smaller hotel . . . then to slip away unseen in our plane, indicating to the air traffic controllers that he was going to London, but during the flight to divert to a small airfield in Bedfordshire. Wilson would then race away by car to some secret hideaway in the country. He . . . was assuming that he would lose the election and was preparing his getaway . . .

The later years of Wilson's career are shadowed by many such conspiratorial, not fully corroborated stories. But as well as having their more solid elements – on election night that February, Donoughue records in his detailed diary of the period, Wilson and his entourage did leave the Adelphi for a smaller hotel without telling the press – these stories have a recurrent theme that fits with the broad, undeniable trajectory of Wilson's life. By the time he became prime minister in 1974, he and the political world he represented were winding down.

Like Ted Heath, he had been born in 1916 to striving, modestly-off parents in an unglamorous English town. Unlike Heath, Wilson came from an England that was northern and industrial: his father Herbert worked for a manufacturer of dyes and explosives just outside Huddersfield in Yorkshire. Herbert was a trained chemist with an interest in politics and ambitions for his son. When Harold was eight, they drove to London together in a motorbike and sidecar and took in the political sights of the capital. They parked in Downing Street, where Ramsay MacDonald was leading the first, short-lived Labour government, and Herbert took out his camera. Harold posed in front of the doorstep, slightly dwarfed by a large flat cap but with a beaky confidence. It was 1924, and his weary return to the same spot in 1974 was a long way off.

During the thirties, he received a less comfortable education in politics and economics. The Depression left his father without work for extended periods. In 1931, Harold closely followed the protracted, prophetic collapse of the second Labour government as it succumbed to a combination of recession, rows over public-spending cuts and terminal splits in the Cabinet. Yet his own course was briskly upward: grammar school, bookishness, Oxford. At university, he acquired a reputation for being self-contained and studious but also good company, a teller of tales, a show-off. His college, Jesus, was small and unselfconscious; Wilson had little to do with the grand-standing student politics that drew in contemporaries like Heath, Denis Healey and Roy Jenkins. He found the university Labour Club, he wrote to his parents, 'very petty: squabbling . . . with other sections of the labour party instead of getting down to something concrete'. He was asked to join the Communist October Club but refused. Instead, he took up with the Liberals. The party was in one of its frequent troughs, and he quickly became its Oxford university treasurer, known for his energy and efficiency rather than his politi-cal views. In his last year at Oxford, his involvement in the Liberal Club dwindled, but he did leave university with an aptitude for the more subtle political arts. In his finals, he scored a very good First in politics, philosophy and economics, the same degree as Heath. Wilson showed evidence, one of the examiners noted, of having researched the preferences of the dons who were going to do the marking and of tailoring his essays accordingly.

Wilson loved facts: collecting them, husbanding them, deploying them. After Oxford, his relish for data fitted in with an emerging official enthusiasm for social reform based on large-scale research. Between 1937 and 1941, he worked as an assistant to Sir William Beveridge, the revered social scientist and radical Liberal. Wilson found his boss prickly and exhausting, and turned down the chance to work on his famous 'Beveridge Report', which in 1942 set out the basic principles of the post-war welfare state. But working for Beveridge familiarized Wilson with the new British left-of-centre thinking, and gave him contacts and experience. His own interest in party politics was reawakened and he moved to the left. After Beveridge, he joined Whitehall's expanding bureaucracy and helped push the coal industry the first steps down the path to nationaliza-tion. In 1945, he became a Labour MP.

At first, Wilson rose in the party as an eager young technocrat. 'Socialism', he wrote in a book he published on coal, 'is the only means to full efficiency.' Within weeks of being elected, at the age of twenty-nine, he was appointed to his first government post, as parlia-mentary secretary to the minister of works. Within less than two years, he was in the Cabinet as President of the Board of Trade, over-seeing a huge, diffuse ministry with a staff of almost 13,000. Wilson quickly showed an adeptness at operating the state machinery – and a shrewd awareness of the good publicity to be had from sometimes switching it off. During 1948 and 1949, with the economy recovering from the war and opposition growing to the continuance of rationing, he presided over a high-profile 'bonfire' of government restrictions covering many consumer goods and foreign imports. Wilson retained an enduring belief in state planning to achieve the goals that the free market could not, yet he was also happy to be photographed ripping up a ration book.

In the fifties and early sixties, this ability to face both ways, to appear sometimes to be a politician of the Left and sometimes one of the more populist, pragmatic centre, acquired him enemies in the Labour Party but a growing following among voters. In public, he had his homely pipe and clever eyes, his charm on voters' doorsteps and his deadliness against debating opponents and hecklers. In private – where he smoked cigars – many Labour colleagues found him able, affable and increasingly plausible as a future prime minister, yet fundamentally untrustworthy. In 1963, after the premature death of the party leader Hugh Gaitskell and over a decade in opposition, Labour MPs chose Wilson as their next leader by a less than overwhelming margin. A year later, a stale, scandal-hit Conservative government narrowly lost the general election and Wilson was prime minister.

The party he had inherited from Gaitskell was alive with talent, rivalries and ideological divisions, with possible prime ministers and barons of Labour factions: James Callaghan and Tony Crosland, Barbara Castle and Roy Jenkins, Tony Benn and Denis Healey. Wilson's solution was to turn his leadership into an elaborate balancing act, playing off the different interests against each other, making temporary alliances, switching sides. It was a game he was very good at. From 1966, when it first became clear that his economic strategy was unravelling, there were almost perpetual plots to replace him as leader, most frequently with Jenkins or Callaghan. But he outwitted the plotters. Indeed, Wilson chose to make the game more elaborate still, by being the first prime minister to augment the conventional Cabinet with his own 'kitchen cabinet' of powerful and rivalrous advisers, such as Marcia Williams, his long-standing secretary, confidante and self-styled socialist conscience; his abrasive press secretary Joe Haines; and the sharp-elbowed Bernard Donoughue.

Yet however delicious the kitchen cabinet's manoeuvrings were for the political connoisseur – Donoughue and Haines could barely stand Williams, and vice versa, while she sought to bully Wilson – by the late sixties, and certainly by the seventies, all this jockeying was counterproductive when placed before a wider national audience, as it was frequently and in intricate detail by the national press. Increasingly, Labour under Wilson looked divided, introspective, even a little self-indulgent, at a time when more and more people considered the country in crisis. In the mid-seventies, moreover, unlike in the mid-sixties, Wilson offered no bold solutions to Britain's apparent decline; nor were his public persona or presentational tricks as fresh and energetic and appealing.

The consequences of all this were apparent at the February 1974 general election. Here the shock of the party's victory concealed the fact that the result was, in some significant senses, actually a defeat: for all the blunders of the unloved Heath government, the Conservatives had won almost a quarter of a million more votes than Labour. Wilson had been chosen as prime minister by barely 37 per cent of the participating electorate. Perhaps most alarmingly of all for Labour's future, the proportion of trade unionists voting for the party had plummeted from a steady three quarters in the sixties to little more than half. The defection of the skilled working class to other parties, which would be seen as fatal by politicians and commentators at future general elections, had already started.

However, Wilson in 1974 was no longer that concerned about the long term. 'For Harold it was about winning the election,' Donoughue told me when I met him. 'The defeat in '70 was such a personal humiliation, he only soldiered on to bury that.' Sitting on a sofa in the House of Lords, Donoughue suddenly fixed his fidgety blue eyes on mine and made his voice confiding: 'In 1974 I said to

Wilson' – the surname suggested a less loyal anecdote was coming – '"How much leave should I get from the LSE to work for you?" And he said, "Easter 1976."'

Denis Healey, who was Wilson's chancellor in the seventies, was even blunter about the returning prime minister's lack of ambition. 'In his second term he told many people that he planned only to stay for a few months. He told me in the lavatory at No. 10 just before a Cabinet meeting.' Healey giggled, characteristically delighting in the black comedy. Then, equally characteristically, he looked out of the window of his Sussex study and kicked Wilson's reputation in the shins. 'I thought, "About bloody time!" He was a terrible prime minister, actually.'

Wilson's memoir of running Britain in the seventies has a plain, perfunctory title: *Final Term*. It is a short book, given the period's importance and numerous dramas, and its tone alternates between a slightly lazy confidence – 'In 1974 the Cabinet was richer in previous experience than perhaps any incoming Government this century' – and a weary flatness – 'between 22 January and 11 February [1976] I had a number of speeches . . .' Quite often, Wilson's attention does not seem fully on the job of being prime minister. 'In the week after the 5 March [1976] sterling crisis,' he writes, 'I woke each day wondering whether something would occur to force me to postpone my resignation.'

'I think he was bored,' says Gavyn Davies, then a young Balliol economics graduate who had been hired by Donoughue to work in the Policy Unit, an influential body of Downing Street advisers. 'Wilson said a couple of times, "I've seen all this before." It was bloody odd – the prime minister was slightly an absentee prime minister.' In *Final Term*, Wilson justifies his reduced role with a metaphor that combines his usual wit and canny populism with an old man's digressiveness and nostalgia:

In the 1964 Government . . . I had to occupy almost every position on the field, goalkeeper, defence, attack – I had to take the corner-kicks and penalties, administer to the wounded and bring the lemons on at half-time . . . [In 1974] I explained to the Parliamentary Party soon after the Government was formed . . . [that] I would be no more than what used to be called a deep-lying centre-half – I instanced Roberts of the pre-war Arsenal team – concentrating on defence, initiating attacks, distributing the ball and moving up-field only for set-piece occasions (witness, as I had done, Roberts's famous winning goal in the sixth round of the FA Cup against Huddersfield in 1927) . . .

For a few former members of Wilson's seventies administration, all this was simply good delegation. 'In the Cabinet he was much more calm than in the sixties,' says Shirley Williams, who had been a fast-rising junior minister in his first government and from 1974 was secretary of state for prices and consumer protection. 'He left much more to Denis and Jim [Callaghan].' Both her position and the Policy Unit were innovations of Wilson's during the seventies – evidence that he had not lapsed into complete passivity – and, as in the sixties, he continued to pioneer the promotion of able women such as herself and Barbara Castle. 'Before Wilson the inner chambers of political decision-making were almost exclusively male,' Williams recalled. 'The seventies Cabinet was still very challenging for a woman, pretty sexist. There was a kind of premier club of moderates in the government, people like Crosland, that I was never invited to join. But Wilson was quite keen on me. He was quite exceptional regarding women.'

Yet most former colleagues are not complimentary. Donoughue told me: 'Harold was holding it together on the surface, but it was all cracking underneath. I sat in on Cabinet committees when inflation was approaching 20 per cent, but you didn't feel you could confront Harold with too much . . .' – he paused a little showily – '. . . as T. S. Eliot wrote in *Four Quartets*, "Man can't bear too much reality."' Joel Barnett, who was chief secretary to the Treasury, mentions in his memoirs 'a favourite phrase of Harold Wilson's: "A decision deferred is a decision made."' The journalist Peter Jay, a prominent newspaper and television commentator in the mid-seventies and a long-standing Wilson critic, suggests that the prime minister's working habits went beyond mere laziness. 'Ken Stowe, his private secretary, told me that during the last two years he wouldn't even receive three people in No. 10 without being given a full written text of what he was going to say.'

In *Final Term*, Wilson recalls that during his last months in office, 'Paper after paper was telephoning anxious inquiries about stories that I had this or that serious syndrome, most of them terminal . . . heart disease, one or more strokes, cancer in almost every part of the body, and leukaemia . . . every known affliction except housemaid's knee – the one thing I had. One Sunday popular paper had telephoned . . . about my "stroke", revealed by a slight limp for a day or two . . . I had twisted my knee playing golf.' Yet this account, at the very least, downplays the extent of concern about his health. There had been talk about it before he had even got back into Downing Street, and from the early months of Wilson's second government that talk became much louder. On 2 July 1974, the head of the National Economic Development Council, Ronald McIntosh

went to the House to see the PM . . . He was affable, relaxed and chatty and didn't seem to want to get to the point quickly – but though he may have slowed down I got the impression he was registering everything . . . There were no signs of the ill health that is talked of so much nowadays . . .

If, for now, Wilson seemed healthy, he was certainly not looking after himself perfectly. On 21 June, Donoughue records in his own diary: 'He is *drinking* more – brandy from midday till late evening, when he is very slow and slurred.' On 3 July: 'The PM . . . went out to lunch with the press and apparently was the worse for drink. This was embarrassingly obvious when the Cabinet committee on Energy met in the late afternoon. He rambled and ministers looked embarrassed.' There are many such subsequent entries.

Wilson's official doctor Joe Stone, who had been his GP since the forties, was also concerned. 'There were times when my father was a bit worried that Harold Wilson was not in control of himself,' recalled Stone's son Richard, also a doctor, who sometimes helped his father treat the Labour leader and took over as Wilson's GP in 1983. 'It might have been the alcohol. Harold didn't drink much when he was younger. But [in the seventies] Dad would come back from being with him, and he'd have had a couple of whiskies. That was not my dad at all – especially when he was driving.'

Lots of politicians drink. In the seventies, when booze pervaded

British life, from City of London lunchtimes to the onstage stumbles of bands like The Faces to the pissy terraces of football grounds, politicians almost certainly drank more than they do now. Yet Wilson's performance was deteriorating. 'Harold had been the master of the detail, and then he didn't have the detail,' Richard Stone told me. 'Heavy drinking cuts off one layer of your thinking. You lose sharpness, facts, precision. And it's the sign of someone who's burning out. In the seventies, Harold knew it was downhill from here.'

During 1975 and 1976, Wilson suffered a host of minor ailments. 'The toll was being taken,' writes Haines, a more sympathetic witness than Donoughue. 'Stomach disorders, returning colds and susceptibility to 'flu all testified to the cumulative effects of physical exhaustion.' In his diary, Donoughue records additional symptoms: a recurrent 'racing heart', problems with concentration, moments of unaccustomed bewilderment and forgetfulness. On 4 December 1975, Donoughue writes, 'Joe Stone has given him instructions to cut down his work . . . Joe Stone told Joe [Haines] and me that HW "is not the man he was a few years ago".'

'It might have been incipient Alzheimer's,' said Richard Stone. 'In the early stages you lose recent memories. You set out to do something and halfway through you think, "What am I here for?"' Within a few years of leaving Downing Street, Wilson would be diagnosed with both Alzheimer's and bowel cancer.

However, the precise state of his health in the mid-seventies will probably never be known for certain. When Stone inherited Wilson's medical records from his father, 'There was almost nothing there at all. Dad had tremendous loyalty to his patients. Harold's medical details were all kept in his head, apart from what dribbled out to me.' But, as prime minister in the seventies, it is widely agreed that Wilson did spend increasing amounts of time with Joe Stone. Stone accompanied him on foreign trips. He was a frequent visitor to Downing Street. 'My father had no ambition,' said Richard. 'Everyone else round Harold did. My father was a good socialist, and he was a listener.'

Often, the prime minister would simply arrive at the Stone family home in north London in an official car, accompanied only by his driver. The house was a very visible Edwardian semi on a busy corner of the Finchley Road, with six lanes of traffic going right past its front windows. But the house extended back a long way, and Wilson and Joe Stone would retreat to a sitting room at the rear that was shielded from prying eyes by a wall and a fenced garden. 'Harold would spend an hour, an hour and a half with my dad,' said Richard. 'Just go on talking and talking. Drink tea. I'd go upstairs, do my medical studies, come back down, and the prime minister's still there.' Part of an afternoon or an evening would slip by, the Finchley Road a distant, lulling drone. The prime minister's driver would wait outside in the car. Britain's many mid-seventies problems would await Wilson's attention. 'It was an escape', said Richard Stone, 'from being PM.'

There was a further reason for his diminishing effectiveness as prime minister. Wilson was convinced that he was being undermined by opponents from outside the familiar world of British politics. Shirley Williams told me:

I remember one day Harold took me into the Cabinet chamber. And he pointed to a beam that ran across the room. And he said, 'Look.' I looked up, and there was some sort of peculiar-looking bump. And I said, 'Yes?' And he said, 'That's a bug. They're bugging me.' So I said, 'Really, Harold?' And he said, 'Absolutely. They're listening to everything I say. And they're determined to get me out.'

Williams thought at the time that Wilson 'was off his trolley'. But afterwards she had changed her mind: 'There was a real attempt to try to undo him of a non-constitutional kind.' Since the mid-seventies, such allegations have generated a whole sub-genre of British political literature, running from credible investigations to lurid speculations. Wilson made possible its central text. In April 1976, he agreed to see two BBC reporters, Barrie Penrose and Roger Courtiour, who had been probing the alleged involvement of South African intelligence in the Jeremy Thorpe scandal, which was beginning to unravel publicly. Wilson had accused the South Africans of smearing Thorpe, a well-known opponent of apartheid. Yet what he told Penrose and

Courtiour was even more sensational. Wilson claimed that right-wing members of MI5, the British counter-espionage service, had been working with the South Africans and with American intelligence to smear him and his close allies as well as Soviet agents. Marcia Williams, whom Wilson had controversially made Lady Falkender in 1974, saw the reporters too and repeated the allegations. Penrose and Courtiour turned their material into a series of articles for the *Observer* in 1977 and then a book the following year, *The Pencourt File*. Such was its intention to cause a sensation, its title paid homage to 'Woodstein', the collective name for the American reporters Bob Woodward and Carl Bernstein, who had uncovered Watergate. Also in 1977, Wilson told a Royal Commission investigating illicit behaviour by the press (a commission he himself had set up as prime minister) that he and his family and close allies had suffered a series of unexplained burglaries in the weeks before his resignation and since. His enemies in the security services, he implied, were working in tandem with the right-wing press.

The impact of all this was less than Wilson and Penrose and Courtiour might have hoped. For one thing, Wilson served up his allegations in a dense, indigestible stew of self-justifications and strange riddles. 'I see myself as the big fat spider in the corner of the room,' he infamously told the reporters at one point in their taped conversations. 'Sometimes I speak when I'm asleep. You should both listen. Occasionally when we meet I might tell you to go to Charing Cross Road and kick a blind man standing on the corner. That blind man may tell you something, lead you somewhere.'

Wilson was widely considered to be in poor health. He was well known for his love of jokes, metaphors and concocted dramas, for his rhetorical halls of mirrors. He had also spent much of his time as Labour leader fending off plots against him by colleagues. He had an energetic sense of paranoia. As a young overseas trade negotiator for the Attlee government, he had even learned on trips to Moscow to search rooms for suspicious small objects. Three decades on, his claims about MI5 and the rest were not hard to dismiss as the embarrassing ramblings of a diminished old man. During 1977, Wilson made the task easier still by retracting his allegations – telling *The*

Times the statements attributed to him in *The Pencourt File* were 'cock and bull written by two journalists . . . with so little sense of humour that they cannot distinguish between disclosure and a joke' – and then making the allegations again. Finally, in 1978, Wilson stopped making the allegations altogether. Between then and his death seventeen years later, he never mentioned the topic in public again.

Yet since the seventies his claims have gained, not lost, credibility. For one thing, there is the long history in Britain of smear campaigns against left-wing politicians, involving members of the secret services, right-wing newspapers and allegations of Soviet connections, and sometimes a combination of all three: from the 'Zinoviev Letter' of 1924, the infamous forgery that helped drive the first Labour government from power, to 'Kinnock's Kremlin Connection', the 1992 *Sunday Times* story, later exposed as groundless, that sought to damage the Labour leader in the run-up to that year's general election. During the seventies, articles did appear in right-wing tabloids and *Private Eye* suggesting that Wilson had Soviet links. *Private Eye* in particular received packages of unsolicited documents from unknown sources that purported to show that the Labour leader was a traitor. In August 1975, Wilson held a meeting with the head of MI5, Sir Michael Hanley, to ask him about the rumour and its possible origin in the intelligence services. Wilson's biographer Ben Pimlott quotes 'a former adviser' of the prime minister 'who remembers speaking to Wilson immediately after the secret service chief had left'. The adviser says: 'Hanley admitted that there was a small group [in MI5] behaving oddly or out of turn . . . But [he] said they were getting back under control.'

Ten years later, a former assistant director of MI5, Peter Wright, alleged in his best-selling memoir *Spycatcher*, which came out in Britain after a protracted attempt by the then Conservative government to halt its publication, that he and some colleagues – and some officials in the CIA – believed during the seventies that Wilson was a Soviet agent. This school of thought found significance in Wilson's many visits to Russia as a trade minister in the forties and as a rising Labour politician in the fifties; in his numerous friendships with foreign businessmen who unusually retained interests in both the East and the West, including Joseph Kagan, the manufacturer of his trademark raincoats; and, most dramatically of all, in Gaitskell's early death, caused by the rare disease lupus, after which Wilson had succeeded to the Labour leadership.

According to the service's official historian Christopher Andrew, MI5 opened a file on Wilson when he became an MP in 1945 and maintained it in secret, referring to Wilson as Norman John Worthington, throughout both his premierships. And yet, the idea that Wilson was a Soviet agent was quite a mental leap. For one thing, the wildest version of this theory insisted that Gaitskell had been assassinated by the KGB so that Wilson could become prime minister, even though medical opinion considered such a killing impossible, a general election was some way off when Gaitskell died, and Wilson was not at the time the leading contender for the Labour leadership. The theory also depended heavily on the word of Russian defectors, who had a record of exposing Soviet agents but also an incentive to exaggerate and invent. Finally, there was the problem of Wilson's record in office, which, over issues from the state control of business to the war in Vietnam, was a perpetual disappointment to the Left. If Wilson was a Soviet agent, he was a very strange one.

Of course, the charge did not have to be true, or even very believable, to distract and damage Wilson and his administration, especially given the increasingly charged atmosphere of British politics in the mid-seventies. As his publisher Sir George Weidenfeld put it later, the Russian rumours 'came and went but they were . . . repeated in clubs, in drawing-rooms, in country houses, and retold, embroidered . . .' By Wilson's last weeks in office, even Donoughue, with his cockily untamed haircut and streetwise insider's air, was feeling slightly beleaguered. 'I believe that my room is bugged. Certainly my phone is tapped,' he wrote in his diary on 5 February. '[I] tried to resist the kind of paranoia which surrounds HW and Marcia. But the evidence is growing . . .'

With Wilson acting as an introverted, unusually passive prime minister, his talented lieutenants were left to deal with the many problems his government had inherited. And at this they proved less than expert.

The ejection of the Heath government had essentially solved 1974's most immediate crises. The miners quickly went back to work, and the three-day week was ended in March. But new crises swiftly took their place.

In Ulster, a 'power-sharing Executive' involving all the peaceful Catholic and Protestant parties had been coaxed into being by Willie Whitelaw during 1973, allowing the province to govern itself once more, but on a less sectarian basis than before. The new administration had been sworn in on New Year's Day 1974. It was a skilfully constructed, high-minded compromise – a last triumph of Heathite diplomacy, almost on the scale of the EEC entry negotiations. Yet the prospect of 'power sharing' in an Ulster which would have slightly closer ties to the Irish Republic but remain part of the United Kingdom did not appeal, at this stage in the province's history at least, to more radical republicans or loyalists. Their campaigns of violence continued, and in May the loyalists moved to overthrow the executive altogether. They formed a coalition, the Ulster Workers' Council (UWC), and called on all Protestant employees to oppose the executive by going on strike. Thousands complied; those who did not faced barricades manned by loyalist paramilitaries, and even death threats. Within a fortnight, much of the economy and daily life of the province had been brought to a halt. Wilson denounced the UWC as 'thugs and bullies' but was forced to dissolve the executive, and any chance of an end to the Northern Ireland crisis in the foreseeable future was gone.

The outlook for his government on the British mainland was almost as challenging. For one thing, Wilson did not have a parliamentary majority; he would have to call another general election to try to win one. And then there was Europe: in Opposition, as one of his opportunistic anti-Heath manoeuvres, Wilson had promised a referendum on Britain's Common Market membership when Labour got back into power. Now he would have to hold it, in a country that was not used to such votes and leading a party that was fiercely divided, as were the Conservatives, over the EEC issue. During 1974 and 1975, much of the government's attention was taken up by these ballots. Wilson, with the last glimmers of his electioneering brilliance, won both of them: the October 1974 election narrowly, leaving him with a disappointing and almost certainly temporary majority of three; the June 1975 referendum comfortably, with 67 per cent of Britons backing the European policy that he had finally settled on, that the country should stay in the EEC.

In the meantime, arguably the most fundamental domestic issue of all was left neglected: the economy. After returning to office in February 1974, Wilson had appointed Denis Healey as chancellor. 'I knew bugger all about economics,' Healey told me cheerfully when we met at his house in Sussex. 'I didn't understand it. It was very much secondary to me compared to foreign affairs – that was my passion. I had been defence secretary, but being chancellor is much harder. In defence, you control completely the million service people and the suppliers of arms and equipment, whereas in the Treasury you control nothing except your civil servants. Jim [Callaghan] said to me, "It's a bloody job, you know, Denis. You must leave it within two or three years."' In the event, Healey was chancellor for over five.

After political prominence as a student at Oxford, a sharp-elbowed rise through the Labour Party during the forties and fifties, and an unusually long and influential stint as defence secretary in the sixties, Healey did not lack confidence or ability. His politics had matured from a melodramatic left-wing socialism – 'the upper classes in every country are selfish, depraved, dissolute and decadent,' he had told the 1945 party conference, a handsome zealot still wearing his army uniform – to a much more pragmatic Labour tribalism. But he retained a bullying certainty and a relish for battle. He addressed opponents and other people he wished to dominate in his big, rich voice: slowly, unyieldingly, slightly mockingly, as if speaking to a small child. 'As chancellor I soon learned that economics is just a branch of social science,' he told me. 'The way people behave economically either as buyers or sellers or producers changes almost from year to year, from season to season. I was able to learn it all for myself.' How quickly had he got on top of his new role? 'Quite fast, really,' said Healey. 'Three months, I would say.'

In reality, the task proved less straightforward. The combination of his inexperience, the scale of the economic problems handed on by the Conservatives, the almost immediate need to win another general election, some hugely over-optimistic Treasury predictions about the economy and the government's finances, and the inability of most of the Labour Party, much of the Treasury and, to an extent, Healey himself to absorb the implications of the oil crisis and what it meant for a country with Britain's particular weaknesses – all this meant that 1974 and much of 1975 passed, very damagingly, without a major economic-policy rethink. 'For eighteen crucial months,' writes the historian Keith Middlemas in *Power, Competition and the State, Volume Three: The End of the Postwar Era*, 'the reserves of 1945–74 were dissipated.'

First-hand accounts of life at the Treasury in the mid-seventies contain, beneath their protective layers of mandarin understatement and irony, surprisingly bald confessions that disastrous things went on. 'We planned for too high a level of public expenditure,' writes Joel Barnett, then the department's chief secretary, 'in the expectation of levels of growth that, in the event, never materialized.' Sir Leo Pliatzky, a Treasury permanent secretary then and a civil-service veteran, writes that 'The first year or so of the new administration was . . . in some ways a period of collective madness. Public expenditure . . . rose by no less than 12.2 per cent . . . [in] a year in which GDP showed a small absolute decline.' In 1974, he notes, inflation reached a corrosive 16 per cent. In August 1975, it reached a peak of 26.9 per cent, approaching the sort of level for which struggling Third World economies were notorious. In the meantime, unemployment almost doubled. 'Stagflation' had arrived in Britain. 'The Treasury, as well as Wilson's ministerial team, seemed paralysed in the face of it,' records Peter Hennessy in his civil-service history, *Whitehall*. 'The lunch tables were very gloomy in 1974 with . . . talk about "the decline of the west" . . . [And] it was not just the Treasury that endured a crisis of confidence in the mid-1970s; it was the Civil Service as a whole.'

Healey himself was not given to crises of confidence. Yet even he was prepared to admit, albeit from the safety of his Sussex study three decades on, that his first two budgets as chancellor were flawed: 'They weren't deflationary enough.' Not, of course, that this was entirely his fault. 'I think it was partly that the figures were so unreliable,' he continued with barely a pause. 'I mean, *incredibly* so . . . If you look at the figures for the public sector borrowing requirement on which the whole of budgetary policy was based, they were *billions* out.' Nor had he been well served by Treasury civil servants in general: 'They tended to be anti-union, and they tended not to know much about the world. They didn't know about foreign affairs at all. And they didn't know much about the City . . .'

Many of Healey's Cabinet colleagues also seemed unwilling or unable to deal with the harsh new world. Barbara Castle and Tony Crosland, inspiring and original figures in Wilson's sixties governments, now seemed slightly world-weary, as if infected by the prime minister's mid-seventies lassitude. On 7 March 1974, less than a week into her new job as secretary of state for social services, Castle wrote in her diary of her 'own detached mood . . . [I] wonder all the time whether the game is worth that mass of paperwork'. Crosland's wife Susan wrote in her biography of him of the 'curious lack of exhilaration' that accompanied Wilson's re-election: 'We knew Labour couldn't achieve what the incoming 1964 Government had believed possible.'

In 1974, Crosland, now secretary of state for the environment, published 'Socialism Now', a long essay and sequel to his optimistic and influential 1956 book *The Future of Socialism*. The essay contained plenty of typically perceptive Crosland insights about how Britain had changed: the increasing importance of 'consumer choice' and of the service industries; the decreasing importance of social deference. But there were far fewer suggestions than in the *Future of Socialism* for how a Labour government might adapt itself. In places, the tone was close to defeatist. 'Developments in Britain during the last decade have been acutely disappointing to a democratic socialist,' Crosland wrote. 'British society . . . has proved much harder to change than was supposed . . . Britain in the 1970s is conspicuous for its persistent and glaring class inequalities, which an appallingly weak economy makes it hard to tackle.' The political journalist John Cole, who knew him well, sensed that between 1974 and 1976 Crosland was 'thinking a lot about his next holiday'.

One of the few ministers who seemed energized by the difficulties of the mid-seventies was the secretary of state for industry, Tony Benn, although his proposed economic remedies would quickly prove too radical to be politically practical. Benn's blueprint for industry was a more left-wing version of the state-led economic planning that had been tried and partly abandoned as ineffective by the Wilson government in the sixties. This time, the state would take 'direct control, through ownership, of a substantial and vital sector of the growth industries', in the words of a party-policy document with which Benn was closely associated, 'Labour's Programme 1973'. There would be a powerful National Enterprise Board, and planning agreements between the government and major companies. Business would be compelled to improve its performance; at the same time, Britain would take a significant step towards the long-standing left-wing goal of 'common ownership of the means of production' famously expressed in Clause IV of Labour's 1918 constitution.

Benn promoted his scheme by a combination of methods that would become his trademark: crusading public speeches, dogged advocacy in Cabinet, appeals to Labour Party members, provocative remarks to newspapers. But Wilson and most of his ministers considered the plan economically naive and politically counterproductive. During 1974 and 1975, it was steadily hollowed out by the Cabinet until it contained almost none of its original substance. Then Wilson demoted Benn to secretary of state for energy. Benn, loyal to the Labour Party and to the idea that he could best represent its left from inside the Cabinet, was humiliated but did not resign from the government. Westminster observers admired this demonstration of the old Wilson wiliness. 'All he [Benn] could do was visit oil rigs,' commented Neil Kinnock, then a left-wing MP and Benn ally. 'It was a walkover for the Prime Minister.'

Yet in many ways it was a pyrrhic victory, as Wilson's tended to be in those days. Benn was still in the Cabinet, in a job that would turn out to be rather more important than Kinnock imagined. As a senior minister he could continue to speak for a growing proportion of an increasingly left-wing and hard-to-control party membership. And, characteristically, Benn's demotion left him all the more certain that his sort of Labour politics would ultimately prevail. His public profile had been decisively raised, and so had that of his softly spoken but confrontational socialism. Both would terrify British businessmen, conservatives and floating voters for the rest of the decade and beyond, creating the impression that however compromising and unideological Labour might actually be in office, a very different party of class warfare and leftist dogma might seize power at any moment.

Finally, Wilson's defeat of Benn did not change the mood of the government. In the winter of 1974, the then foreign secretary Jim Callaghan attended an informal meeting of Cabinet ministers at Chequers. 'Everyone was free to express his views on the medium term outlook,' he records in his memoirs. 'I was feeling particularly gloomy: "Our place in the world is shrinking: our economic comparisons grow worse . . . The country expects both full employment and an end to inflation. We cannot have both unless people restrain their demands. If the [government-backed pay] guidelines are not observed, we shall end up with wage controls . . . even a breakdown of democracy."' Callaghan, like Healey one of the government's central figures, concluded his remarks with 'a joke' which had the air of a barely disguised truth. 'Sometimes when I go to bed at night,' said the foreign secretary, 'I think that if I were a young man I would emigrate.'

In 1974, the number of UK residents doing just that, which had been static or falling since the beginning of the decade, rose sharply. In each of the next three years, for the first time since annual statistics had been collected, the national population fell. The main cause was a decline in the birth rate. Other barometers of confidence in the country and its prospects also gave grim readings. The proportion of shares in British businesses owned by foreigners almost halved between 1969 and 1981. The main FTSE index plunged, from 544 in May 1972 to 146 in December 1974.

As the mid-seventies progressed, this pessimism about the economy spread far beyond the City of London. In 1977, *New Society* compared the results of two large-scale professional surveys of Britons' financial situations and expectations, one recent and one from four years earlier. The magazine found that the percentage of people expecting their standard of living to 'fall sharply' in the next ten years had more than doubled, overtaking the proportion of Britons expecting things to improve or stay the same. It also found that most people's sense of their current 'material position' had dramatically worsened. In 1973, 18 per cent of those surveyed had considered their position very strong. In 1977, the figure was 5 per cent. In 1973, only 13 per cent had regarded their position as very weak. In 1977, it was 26 per cent.

These perceptions were broadly accurate. During the mid-seventies, the median monthly disposable income of British households, allowing for inflation, which had been growing robustly in the early years of the decade, began to wilt: from £202 in 1974 to £198 in 1975, to £190 in 1976, to £187 in 1977. 'Living standards, for the first time in 40 years, are falling,' observed the *New Society* writer Tom Forester in a commentary on the 1973 and 1977 surveys. 'Age, class and party [allegiance] didn't seem to make much difference to how people rated Britain. They all tended to rate Britain . . . lower than their own position . . . [They] seemed to be saying that the country is going to the dogs . . .'

Yet in reality, and very significantly for the direction of British politics during the rest of the seventies and beyond, some Britons were affected by the bad times more quickly, and with more of a sense of shock, than others. Between 1974 and 1976, it was the comfortably-off who suffered. High inflation ate their savings. The low pound spoiled their holidays. A property crash – house prices fell 13 per cent in 1974, 16 per cent in 1975 and 8 per cent in 1976 – devalued their homes. The stock-market slump did the same for their shareholdings. Share dividends shrank or were not paid at all. During these years, disposable income fell considerably faster for the richest

tenth of British households than for everyone else, and by larger and
larger amounts the further you were up the financial scale. Even in a
severe recession, this was not a familiar situation. 'For the first time
since 1931,' writes Middlemas, 'London pawnbrokers . . . began to
receive assets of the former new rich.'

This sense of a world being turned upside down was sharpened by
the fact that other categories of Britons, traditionally not as well-off or
secure, were, at least at first, less affected by the crisis. Trade unionists'
wages were protected from inflation by their readiness to strike and by
the political leverage of their leaders. The jobs of public-sector workers
were protected by the continuing increases in government spending.
The political party that broadly represented these groups, Labour, had
won four of the last five general elections, while the party that broadly
represented the unsettled middle and upper classes, the Conservatives,
was still lumbered with the defeated Heath as leader for the whole of
1974 and into 1975. The following year, the City editor of the *Sunday
Telegraph*, Patrick Hutber, published a polemical paperback, the title
of which perfectly caught Tory Britain's air of beleaguerment: *The
Decline and Fall of the Middle Class – And How It Can Fight Back*.

Declinism was an established British state of mind, but during the
mid-seventies it truly began to pervade the national consciousness. It
filled doomy books aimed at the general reader. It became a melodramatic staple for newspapers, magazines and television programmes.
It darkened the work of artists, novelists, dramatists, film-makers
and pop musicians. It soured foreign commentary on Britain. It
spoke ominously to audiences beyond its traditional constituencies
of the elderly, the conservative and the instinctively pessimistic. And
it shifted in tone: from the anxious to the apocalyptic.

'The two main headlines in the *Times* this morning,' wrote Ronald
McIntosh in his diary on 15 March 1975, 'are, "Militant consultants
threaten to close NHS hospitals" and "Troops to move into Glasgow
tomorrow". This really does look like a collapsing society.' On 6
May, the American political sage Eric Savareid announced on CBS
television news, 'Britain is drifting slowly towards a condition of
ungovernability.' He went on to compare Wilson's government to

that of the Chilean socialist Salvador Allende in its final, chaotic days before its overthrow by General Pinochet. On 4 December, *The Times*' influential economics editor Peter Jay forecast that Britain would endure 'a remaining two or three years of phoney crisis, while our present Prime Minister continues to . . . paper over the cracks . . . before the breakdown of our present political economy'. In 1977, the respected political academic Tom Nairn wrote in his book *The Break-Up of Britain*, 'There is no doubt that the old British state is going down.' He went on to compare Britain to Prussia in its declining years, to the decaying Habsburg Empire, and to Tsarist Russia.

The credibility of the seventies declinists was enhanced by their political diversity: Nairn was an independent-minded Marxist, Jay was a well-connected social democrat, and Hutber was a tribal but forward-thinking conservative. They could not simply be dismissed as reactionary old nostalgics. Their analysis also fitted – and influenced, and was influenced by – an unmistakable cultural mood. 'The real keynotes of the seventies', wrote the astute social critic Peter York in *Harpers & Queen* magazine in January 1978, 'are fragmentation . . . and *paranoia* – impossible new situations like stagflation, the Arabs, [their] oil money and political power.'

In Britain, the most famous cultural consequence of this mid-seventies unease and volatility was punk. The Sex Pistols formed in 1975 in a rundown part of Chelsea, known appropriately as World's End, just as the Wilson government was drifting onto the rocks. But many British and British-consumed pop musicians who were not part of punk's roaring millenarian revolt also expressed a cosmic discontent: Pink Floyd, with their gloomy, plodding concept albums; and the keening prophets of mid-seventies Jamaican reggae. On 4 October 1975, David Bowie, another star whose albums during the decade were full of a half-fearful, half-delighted foreboding, infamously told the *New Musical Express*:

There will be a political figure in the not too distant future who'll sweep this part of the world . . . You've got to have an extreme right front come up and sweep everything off its feet and tidy everything up . . . It'll do something positive, at least, to cause a commotion in people and they'll either accept dictatorship or get rid of it.

Many novels published in Britain in the mid-seventies were also full of impatience with the present and with reckless political yearnings. 'There was a . . . reversion', wrote the literary critic Malcolm Bradbury in his editor's contribution to the 1977 volume *The Novel Today*, 'to a concern with the onerous pressure of history and the real.' In *The Family Arsenal*, published the previous year, Paul Theroux set amateur terrorists loose on a present-day London of 'ghostly rotting warehouses' and 'decay pushing towards ruin'. Theroux wrote of one of his protagonists:

The summer's disorder . . . made him wish for a cleansing holocaust . . . It was certainly coming . . . Hardship was a great sorter. He rather enjoyed the thought of deprivation, candlelight, shortages, paying with official vouchers and coupons.

The same year, in *The Takeover*, set in Italy but subtitled in some editions 'a parable of the pagan seventies', Muriel Spark imagined the panicking rich selling their paintings and letting their gardens go to ruin. '1973', she wrote, 'was in fact the beginning of something new . . . not merely to be defined as a collapse of the capitalist system . . . but such a sea-change in the nature of reality as could not have been envisaged by Karl Marx or Sigmund Freud.' In *The Summer Before the Dark*, published in 1973, Doris Lessing had her central character abandon a Britain plagued by strikes and power cuts and by a vigilante group called the British League of Action ('We need standards now . . . We will get things done.') Four years later, in *The Ice Age*, Margaret Drabble explicitly addressed 'the state of the nation' in the mid-seventies: 'Over the country depression lay like fog . . . [It was] a land passing through some strange metamorphosis . . . What next? The roping, the selling, the plundering?' A character comments: 'I think that the English are changing. I don't think they're going to go on finding life so funny. Because they've lost their superiority.'

Also in 1977, John Fowles published his own, more elliptical novelist's survey of contemporary Britain, *Daniel Martin*. His narrator, an English expatriate in California, says of his homeland, 'England is already a thing in a museum, a dying animal in a zoo.' Fowles prefaced the book with a celebrated quotation from the *Prison Notebooks* by Antonio Gramsci, the pre-war Italian Marxist thinker who was enjoying a sudden British vogue: 'The crisis consists precisely in the fact that the old is dying and the new cannot be born; in this interregnum a great variety of morbid symptoms appears.'

In the mid-seventies, there was a fashion, too, for the inventively dystopian but not always subtle novels of J. G. Ballard, such as *High-Rise* (1975), about a tower block collapsing into anarchy, and *Concrete Island* (1974), about a man marooned after a crash on an overgrown motorway roundabout. Both books were set in a recognizable contemporary London: in the unsettled Britain of the mid-seventies, Ballard's bleak science-fiction-tinged parables increasingly seemed more about the present than the future. The rising younger writers Martin Amis and Ian McEwan offered their own queasy novels, *Dead Babies* (1975) and *The Cement Garden* (1978), full of cruelty, *fin de siècle* decadence and social breakdown. Such themes always have an appeal, especially perhaps for young men like the seventies Amis and McEwan, with their desire to stir things up and make a name for themselves, but the sheer quantity and cross-generational quality of British 'crisis' fiction in the mid-seventies was striking. Novelists are not social scientists, or even necessarily good journalists – the long gestation periods of fiction and the need to consider character, place and plot, as well as topicality, see to that. But when so many novelists are saying the same thing they are usually on to something.

Dramatists were also preoccupied with Britain's decline and its consequences. Stephen Poliakoff's *Strawberry Fields* (1977) revolved around a road trip taken by two disillusioned political activists. With its scenes in abandoned buildings and its delphic, ominous dialogue, the play depicted the mid-seventies as 'a kind of turning point . . . the end of an era'. Like David Edgar in *Destiny* (1976), which dealt with the politics of race, and Howard Brenton in *The Churchill Play* (1974), set in the near future in an internment camp for political undesirables, Poliakoff saw right-wing authoritarianism as a likely response to the British crisis. Trevor Griffiths, another of the era's unusual number of high-profile, overtly political, usually left-inclined playwrights – itself a sign of the importance and compelling volatility of mid-seventies politics – focused instead on the internal tensions and philosophical dilemmas of a Labour Party very like Wilson's. The television series *Bill Brand* (1976) featured a Labour prime minister worn out by ill-health, and a Labour government with a tiny majority struggling to reconcile socialism with realism. Impossible to imagine now, its eleven episodes were broadcast by ITV in evening peak time.

Other cultural responses to the times were less earnest and party political. During the three-day week, the Scottish artist Jamie Reid made stickers to put in shops which read, 'Last Days . . . This store will be closing soon owing to the pending collapse of monopoly capitalism'. For their mid-seventies *Dead Boards* pictures, Gilbert and George took dusty black-and-white photographs of entropic, empty rooms: 'We were trying to do something that was absolutely hopeless, dead, grey, lost.' Meanwhile, films like Lindsay Anderson's *O Lucky Man!* (1973), Derek Jarman's *Jubilee* (1977) and Chris Petit's *Radio On* (1979) sent their protagonists on bleak, heavily symbolic tours of a poisoned Britain. There were lowering skies and boarded-up bomb sites; there was corruption and casual violence. And for viewers who liked their declinism with more laughs, there was always *Fawlty Towers* and *The Fall and Rise of Reginald Perrin*. Both hugely popular television series were first broadcast in the mid-seventies, and both featured middle-aged men trapped in a decrepit England and filled with rage or dreams of escape. Neither ought to have made comfortable viewing for Harold Wilson.

However, perhaps the most telling of all the dystopian Britains portrayed or predicted in the mid-seventies came from a less likely source. In July 1976, the sober, sometimes dry television current-affairs show *The Money Programme* devoted a special edition to exploring what sort of place Britain might be by the end of the decade.

The programme offered two scenarios. The first, relatively optimistic one was the 'do-it-yourself' society. 'Sooner or later, the spending had to stop,' the voice-over began. In an imagined 1980, one of the show's reporters drove an Austin Maxi, dumpy and dull-coloured like most British-made cars of the seventies, down a crumbling road past a long pile of rubbish. He stopped the car and started hauling bin bags out of the boot. Since the seventies, he explained, public spending had been radically cut: 'wealth creation' had become the government's main priority. There were no bin men any more, and little was spent on maintaining roads. He gestured towards the Maxi; it had been 'specially strengthened', he went on, so that like other Britons he could take his own rubbish to the dump over the pitted roads. 'Middle management now enjoys a more gracious lifestyle,' the voice-over interjected – there was a fleeting shot of white villas behind pampas grass and deep lawns – but for the less prosperous the times were more demanding. Modernization of the economy through automation and computers had left 2 million jobless for good. Overtime was close to compulsory for those in employment, and there had been 'a gradual erosion in the power of the trade union movement'. There were few strikes any more. In place of such communal struggles was the striving of the individual: little by little, the new Britain was 'making capitalists of us all'.

Especially for those on the left, this was an unsettling set of prophecies. But the programme's alternative forecast was much bleaker. This time, there was no reporter stoically unloading bin bags from his car; just footage of weeds and abandoned factories. In this 1980, the voice-over explained, Britain was enduring its 'worst ever economic crisis'. An incompetent left-wing government had nationalized the banks and allowed union pay demands to get out of control. Now there were 4 million unemployed and inflation was at 35 per cent. The pound was worth less than the dollar, and strikes had driven off foreign buyers of British goods. The stock market had almost ceased to exist: investors had taken their money abroad. Those people still in work owed their jobs to protective subsidies from the government. In much of the country, the voice-over continued, 'Capitalism is but a fond memory.' All that remained was a threadbare, isolated society: classes of sixty in schools, old city slums left half-demolished. 'We'll keep going, of course,' the voice-over concluded, a little unconvincingly, over a final shot of the shell of a factory, 'but the question is: "In what manner?"'

PART THREE
New Possibilities

8

The Great Black Hope

In the trough of the Wilson years, and during the rest of the British seventies, there remained one major source of optimism for anyone pondering the country's prospects. It was an economic opportunity, closely related to the economic calamity that had finally sunk Heath and which threatened to sink his successors. It involved oil. This time the fossil fuel was not buried under distant Middle Eastern deserts and available to Britain only on terms dictated by increasingly unfriendly Arab politicians; it was beneath a cold sea much closer to home, some of which was under Britain's direct control. Any government able to take full advantage of this great geological good fortune had a chance of surviving the seventies and, perhaps, even thriving in the decades beyond. But taking advantage of North Sea oil would not prove straightforward.

On the afternoon of 2 November 1975, a special train arranged by BP left King's Cross station in London for Aberdeen. On board were politicians, civil servants and industrialists invited by the company to the official opening of the first oil pipeline to Britain, from the Forties field in the North Sea. The journey did not go as planned. Before the train could reach Scotland, a crane collapsed across the East Coast main line. The train had to be diverted via Carlisle.

In Aberdeen, a Scottish nationalist group called the Tartan Army was threatening to disrupt the inauguration ceremony. Since 1973, there had been successful bomb attacks on overland sections of the Forties oil pipeline, for which the Tartan Army had claimed responsibility. With Harold Wilson, the Queen and Prince Philip due to take part in the official opening, the city was readied for one of the largest deployments in the history of Scottish policing.

But the day of the ceremony dawned blue and perfect. The royal family arrived at Aberdeen station at eleven and were driven west through the city towards Dyce, a booming suburb near the airport. There, on a large area of grass next to a new dual carriageway and BP's new Aberdeen headquarters, a dazzling white marquee had been erected. Its canopy, said to be the biggest ever made, was like some desert mirage in the flinty northern air, an infinity of Arabian swoops and diagonals. Inside the marquee there was a heating system, a lake of red carpet and, up on a pedestal, a towering, angular model of one of the Forties oil rigs. With the light coming through the canopy, and additional stage lights, everything and everyone in the tent, even the tired grey faces of Wilson and his ministers, was lent a clean, futuristic, vaguely uplifting glow. Outside, a crowd of oil workers waved Union Jacks, specially provided for the purpose, as the Queen and Prince Philip drove by. Then their Rolls-Royce came right into the marquee and braked smoothly to a halt, looking suddenly as old-fashioned as a horse-drawn carriage in its new white surroundings.

Wilson addressed the rows of dignitaries, his voice shrunken but faintly triumphant:

It is not often that one can point to a particular current event . . . and, without the benefit of hindsight, identify it as being of major long-term significance; 'the turning point' beloved of historians and journalists. Today's opening by the Queen of the Forties Field is one such occasion . . . It can truly be said to mark . . . the beginning of the end of our dependency on overseas supplies of energy.

Afterwards, in a spotless control room in the BP headquarters, with the Tartan Army nowhere in evidence, the Queen pushed a gold-plated button. A nearby screen began to flash. Along a transparent reconstruction of a section of the pipeline, a black mass began to move, inch by inch.

That evening, despite the chill which the heating had never quite banished, there was a party in the marquee to celebrate. 'It was one of the best parties I ever went to,' remembered a retired BP man I met in Dyce three decades later. 'There was a dance. They did it in style.' He nodded across his back garden towards the grass where the marquee had stood. He had helped put it up. 'Those were the days,' he said with a brightness in his narrow eyes, 'the early oil days, when everything was new.' Then he looked back at the window frame he had been carefully painting when I arrived, at his blocky but lovingly preserved mid-seventies house. He had lived in it ever since then, he said, ever since he had left farming as a young man and first come to Aberdeen to work in oil. Then he cut the reminiscence short and waved his paintbrush. 'Now be quick with your other questions,' he said, Aberdonian curtness returning. 'I've got to do this now because it's going to rain.'

Oil was first extracted on a small scale in Britain by the Romans. In Scotland, a slightly more substantial oil industry was created in the eighteen fifties around the laborious mining and processing of oil shale, or oil-bearing rock. This industry, which preceded by several years the better-known pioneering of the modern oil business in the US, survived until the nineteen sixties. In England, hundreds of oil wells were drilled between the First World War and the fifties, mostly in the Midlands and mostly with limited success. None of this land-based activity had a significant effect on the economy or on most Britons' perceptions of their country's important natural assets. As the post-war Labour politician Nye Bevan put it, Britain was 'a lump of coal, surrounded by fish'.

Then, in 1959, a huge underwater gas field was discovered off the Dutch coast. Since the geology beneath much of the North Sea was thought to be similar, a search for gas began in British waters. In 1965, it was found near the Humber Estuary. Further major British gas finds followed; geologists and oil companies, knowing that gas and oil deposits, formed in similar ways as ancient layers of rock trapped the decayed remains of prehistoric plants and animals, were often located close together, and knowing that oil was the more valuable of the two commodities, began to look for North Sea oil as well. In September 1969, a BP drilling rig chartered by the American Oil Company (Amoco) was prospecting 150 miles east of Aberdeen when it struck oil. 'None of us were prepared,' the on-board geologist Brendon MacKeown told the *Scotsman*.

We thought we might find some gas or at the most watery oil traces, so I didn't have any stainless-steel containers. I had to clean out an empty pickle jar from the mess hall to collect the sample. It was what we call sweet oil . . .

[A colleague] poured it into an ashtray on his desk and set it alight and it burned well. But unfortunately the heat caused the ashtray to crack and the bloody stuff spilled all over the floor.

Britain's rights over such underwater discoveries had only recently and belatedly been established. In 1964, after more than half a decade of Whitehall inertia, Britain had followed twenty-one other nations and ratified the United Nations Continental Shelf Convention, which permitted countries to explore and exploit natural resources found beyond their immediate coastal seabeds. Where two or more countries bordered the same continental shelf, as in the North Sea, the convention stated that the seabed should be divided by a boundary that followed the midway points between the national coastlines in question. Britain's long eastern seashore, running north to south down one entire side of the North Sea, with large eastward bulges in Norfolk and Scotland and the broad scatter of the Orkney and Shetland islands even further to the north and east, gave it a significant advantage, therefore, over the other nations hoping to secure windfalls from under the North Sea. When the sea was divided into national oil 'sectors', Britain's was by far the biggest in area, a great diamond of seabed and water, its grey surface glittering in good weather, stretching from Dover almost to the Arctic Circle.

For a country whose industrial revolution and long economic supremacy had been due, in large part, to the discovery and exploitation within its borders of another mineral – coal – North Sea oil seemed to offer another momentous opportunity. For a country whose economy, and whose heavy industries and northern territories in particular, had for decades been in seemingly terminal and accelerating decline, this opportunity seemed to have arrived in exactly the right place and at exactly the right time. Britain had long seafaring and engineering traditions; it had a national gift, at least according to its patriotic self-image, for mechanical improvisation and ingenuity; and it had many large ports and shipyards, which were increasingly available for work as much of their old custom disappeared to continental Europe and the Far East. Britain even had, at the start of the North Sea era, an existing industry making oil rigs and oil pipelines for use in other countries' offshore oilfields. Everything seemed in place for an oil boom.

In July 1973, the Labour MP and oil enthusiast Laurance Reed gave a lecture at Heriot-Watt University in Edinburgh, which was published as *The Political Consequences of North Sea Oil Discoveries*. Speaking before the oil crisis made the deposits vastly more valuable, he predicted: 'North Sea Oil arrives in time to save us from relegation to the third division . . . The 1980s will be Britain's decade. We shall become one of the most influential of nations.' The oil, he went on, would end Britain's dependence on the US and the Middle East, and it would provide Britain with a new empire, a chance for expansion comparable to the American 'opening of the West'. During the early and mid-seventies, forecasts like Reed's were common. A succession of huge oilfields were discovered in the British sector, estimates of the North Sea's total reserves surged accordingly, and all of this was reported by newspapers in the giddiest language. In the February 1974 election campaign, Wilson declared: 'By 1985 the Labour Secretary of State for Energy will be chairman of OPEC.'

Even Ted Heath in his final weeks in office, hemmed in by the miners, the three-day week and the economic crisis, was often preoccupied by the promise of North Sea oil. 'One thought, "There was a solution to our problems,"' he told me. Naturally, he and the other seventies prime ministers also thought about the windfall in party political terms. 'If we'd won the [February 1974] election,' he continued, his voice even lower and gloomier than usual, 'we'd have got it all.'

The discovery of the oil, and the dramatic economic benefits and rises in tax revenues it was expected to bring, had a profound influence on the British governments between 1970 and 1979: on their reluctance to abandon the old way of doing things; on their strong desire, even by the standard of governments in general, to cling to power. If you were in office when the oil came ashore in decisive quantities, the feeling persisted at Westminster, most of the difficulties and dilemmas of the British crisis might melt away. But when would that liberating moment be? Strikingly, even the boldest North

Sea oil advocates of the early seventies tended to talk about the eighties as Britain's promised land. They may have been trying to give their rhetoric a faintly science-fiction glossiness. Or they may have known that getting the oil was going to be a challenge.

The North Sea was, and is, one of the roughest and most unpredictable seas in the world. Weather systems approach it from several directions. Its waters are frigid, deep and murky compared to those in the places where offshore oil drilling was pioneered in the late nineteenth and early twentieth century, such as coastal California and the Gulf of Mexico. Its seabed is sandy and shifting. Its tides are large. It is prone to protracted storms, when 100-mile-an-hour winds are quite common and waves are regularly 70 feet tall. It is ringed but not sheltered by land masses, which can cause its currents and tides, as Bryan Cooper and T. F. Gaskell put it in *North Sea Oil: The Great Gamble*, to 'slop about like the liquid in a tea cup'. At other times, there is a dangerous calm: impenetrable mists descend in minutes and linger for days. In winter, which can last for more than half the year, there are often only a few hours of daylight anyway.

When I arrived at the heliport in Dyce in 2007 to take a flight to an oil rig, it was mid-September and a warm sun was shining, but the first storm of the winter was on its way. In the departure lounge, which was full of heavy-set men in their forties with glum expressions and restlessly bobbing feet, I picked up a discarded newspaper to look at the weather forecast; where the detail for north-east Scotland should have been, there was a carefully torn hole. Elsewhere in the paper there was a report that three men had been killed in uncertain circumstances the previous day, in an accident on a ship supplying North Sea oil rigs.

Before the flight, we put on rubber-sealed 'immersion suits' over our clothes in case the helicopter crashed into the sea. Officially, the suits would insulate you against the waves for a few, potentially crucial minutes; unofficially, one of the rig workers muttered to me as we pulled them on, they were known as 'body bags'. Out on the tarmac, our helicopter looked patched-up and old. After we had boarded, bulkily strapped and squeezed into our seats, earplugs in against the rotor din, it took the ground crew several tries to get the passenger door to close. Then the helicopter was quickly above Aberdeen, tidy and clean in the sunshine, and we headed out to sea.

For a few minutes the water was a benign Mediterranean blue. Then the first clouds came rushing in beneath us. The sea quickly turned steel grey, and the helicopter began to dip and lunge in the headwind. Rain crackled against the windows. The sea turned blue-black and disappeared. It was only mid-afternoon, but outside the helicopter the light was nearly gone. Inside the cold, draughty passenger cabin, no one spoke; most of the oilmen, veterans of hundreds of flights like this, sat with their heads in paperbacks or their eyes tight closed. After an hour and a half, the pilot spoke over the intercom: the weather at the rig was only 'fifty-fifty', he said; if he could not manage a landing, we would be flying straight back to Aberdeen. For another hour we battered through the clouds, then a ragged hole opened up in them below us, there was the tiny flame of a rig's gas flare in the murk, and the helicopter dropped erratically towards the waves.

Down on the rig's helipad, the wind was almost enough to flatten me. The air was wet and raw. Beyond the edge of the helipad, which had no parapet, heaving inky waves seemed to be advancing towards the rig from all directions. Otherwise, the horizons were empty, alien as a moonscape. Steep metal-mesh steps led down from the helipad to the main deck; through them I could see more waves, spitting and clawing at the legs of the rig a hundred feet below. I walked unsteadily down. When I finally stepped into the fuggy refuge of the rig's recreation room for the welcome briefing, I noticed there was only one tiny window with a sea view, and that all the chairs were turned away from it. 'The sea's up quite a bit tonight, then Tuesday through Thursday,' the man giving the briefing mentioned in passing. 'Waves of five to eight or nine metres.'

The North Sea has been familiar to trawlermen for centuries; but in the late sixties and early seventies little was known about how the far larger and less nimble vessels required for extracting oil, and the great numbers of non-seafarers involved, would cope with prolonged exposure to this unrelenting world. Oil rigs, unlike ships, could not head for the nearest port when the weather turned too perilous. The only fixed man-made structures already in the North Sea oilfields, underwater telegraph cables, had been known to shift half a mile in a storm. On 27 December 1965, there was a grim early example of the hazards Britain's new offshore industry was likely to encounter. Forty miles out to sea, the BP gas-drilling rig Sea Gem, a crudely converted barge, suddenly suffered the collapse of two of its supporting legs. The rig capsized and sank, throwing many of its crew into the water. Thirteen men died. Only the lucky presence of a cargo ship nearby ensured the toll was not greater.

To draw oil up through thousands of feet of rock and seawater; to pump it ashore via hundreds of miles of under-sea pipeline; and to do it in such a hostile environment, on a mass scale, for decades to come – all this required the invention and production of a whole new range of technologies, from giant semi-submersible rigs to tiny underwater cameras. During the early seventies, not enough British companies were able or willing to seize the opportunity, and much of this technology had to be imported. Professor Alex Kemp of Aberdeen University, a leading authority on North Sea oil since the beginning, told me: 'Bits of equipment were flown here straight from Texas to save time.'

Yet as the decade went on, British businesses started to catch up. Between 1976 and 1979, a quarter of all the country's manufacturing investment was North Sea-related. In effect, a new heavy industry was being created – after a long period when such enterprises had been increasingly thought of as doomed Victorian relics. Patriotic comparisons began to be made between the equipping of the oilfields and the American space programme. 'We flew over various pipe-laying barges etc,' recorded the usually downbeat Ronald McIntosh in his diary on 23 May 1975. 'The scale of the North Sea operations is very impressive and cheers me up every time I see it.'

One area of particular official pride, which was at least partly justified, was the design and assembly of the biggest, most expensive items of offshore equipment of all: the production platforms. These blunted Eiffel Towers of metal plate and mesh, as tall as skyscrapers and as heavy as Second World War battleships, were best suited to local fabrication, since they had to be towed into position in the oil-fields. But they were too bulky to be built in a conventional dockyard. Dockyards would have to be built for them, ideally as close to the North Sea as possible. The first to open was at Nigg, a waterfront hamlet just inside the mouth of the Cromarty Firth in the Scottish Highlands. In November 2004, I went to see it.

Driving north-east from Inverness, past white farmhouses, sloping cornfields and the glassy waters of the Firth, it was hard at first to imagine Nigg as an industrial centre of great significance. But as elsewhere in the Highlands, the silence and emptiness hid a lot of history. During both world wars, Nigg Bay had been an important Royal Navy anchorage. There were major military encampments in the area for decades before and afterwards. An aluminium smelter had been erected in 1970.

When the Nigg dry dock was completed in 1972, 1,000 feet long by 600 feet across – 'the biggest hole in Europe', according to *The Architectural Review* – another sudden local boom came with it. 'I used to travel this road to work at the yard at 3 a.m.,' my taxi driver told me. 'There were hundreds of other cars on it. Now you hardly see one.' He was in his late forties, with a moustache, long hair and slightly melancholy eyes. Seventies-style, he wore faded jeans that matched a short denim jacket. He was from Invergordon, an old navy town a few miles west of Nigg, he said. But in the seventies, 'There were a lot of Geordie boys up here. Even lads from the south of England. The wages in the yard were probably double the ones for other local jobs. It was good work. You wore earplugs and it was cold, especially when it was snowing. But you were kept so busy, you didn't feel it much.'

Across the Firth, a great windowless pale cube of a building – the old welding shed – drew nearer. But just before we reached it, we turned into a huge car park, empty except for a few cars in the corners. 'You used to be fighting for a space in this car park,' said the taxi driver. Now it was used by a couple of dozen workers making wind turbines in the welding shed; the rest of the dock complex was shut.

I got out and walked across the car park in the low sun. Moss was thickening against the kerbs of the parking spaces. At the far end, there was a pair of rusted gates and, past them, a stretch of waste ground scattered with rusted rig parts like the spines of dinosaurs. Beyond the waste ground stood the stump of a decapitated crane, the cube-shaped building and a distant rectangle of dark water flanked by long stiff fingers of concrete: the dock itself.

In the seventies, the dock was operated by Highland Fabricators, a subsidiary of the American conglomerate Halliburton. But in the Highlands and Whitehall it was regarded, nevertheless, as a kind of British miracle. Workers moved from the dying Glasgow shipyards to take jobs there, and Greek cruise ships had to be hired and moored in the Firth so that they had somewhere to live. The country roads around Nigg had to be regularly closed by police so that deliveries of rig components could be squeezed along them. The largest parts had to be floated in via the Firth. And all the while the yard built rigs: twenty-four hours a day, seven days a week. On 10 May 1974, Ronald McIntosh visited:

. . . [We] picked up a small helicopter for Nigg Bay . . . [The pilot] said that if you were prepared to work hard, the opportunities in north-east Scotland were unlimited now. I can quite believe this – you get a most exhilarating feeling of growth and expansion wherever you go here . . . At Nigg Bay . . . we were then shown the most impressive piece of ironmongery I have ever seen – the production platform they are building for BP for use in the Forties field. It is built on its side on the top of an enormous raft at the bottom of the biggest dry dock in the world. When it is finished they will fill the dock with water and float [the rig] out to the site, where they will fill one side with water until it is vertical. They will then fix it to the seabed . . . Special paints . . . are supposed to give it a life of twenty-five years.

When I got back into the taxi, the driver nodded at the remains of the dock in the distance. 'You can get two rigs in there, easy,' he said, slipping into the present tense. 'There were two rigs when I was there. Effortless.'

He offered to drive up the steep hill behind Nigg so that we could get a better look. Just below the crest, he switched off the engine. A cold wind rocked the gorse bushes outside and crept in through the car windows. We looked down at the dock in the sunshine. With its quaysides fully visible and its sheds as big as aircraft hangars, it seemed almost the size of a town. 'You can't really comprehend the size of that dock,' said the taxi driver. 'It was huge when you were in it.' But the dock was empty now except for water and rubble. The driver sighed, and rested his chin on a clenched fist. 'There's nothing here now. The yard closed two years ago. They tried for an aircraft-carrier contract last year, but they didn't get it. The smelter closed in '79. It's just call centres around here now. I know a lot of boys in the call centres who are trained welders. They need Nigg to reopen.'

The energies North Sea oil awakened in Scotland were not, however, simply economic. There were also political consequences. These would prove more problematic for the British government.

The Scottish National Party (SNP) was created in 1934. Its early membership was an uneasy coalition of left-wing and right-wing nationalists, of advocates of devolution for Scotland and advocates of full independence. The new party, moreover, had been founded at an unsuitable moment. With the Depression still lingering across northern Britain and authoritarian nationalism on the rise across Europe, to most voters the SNP seemed at best an irrelevance and at worst – the party had a fascist fringe – a politically toxic develop-ment. During the Second World War and the immediate post-war period, little changed. The SNP switched jumpily between tactics, endured splits, made sometimes crude attacks on the English, and won a single parliamentary seat at a by-election in 1945, which it lost again within months. At the 1959 general election, the party attract-ed 0.5 per cent of the Scottish vote.

Then it found momentum. During the sixties, the Scottish econ-omy showed signs of underlying decay – whole streets of factories shutting, industrial towns expiring – sooner than the English. The Conservative Party, which had seemed negligent about this issue when it was in government, began steadily to lose credibility and support in Scotland. Meanwhile, Labour turned against the idea of devolution. More political space had opened up for Scottish nation-alism. The SNP improved its fund-raising, broadened its party organization and curbed its wilder policies and members. At the

1964 general election it almost quintupled its vote, to 2.4 per cent. In 1966, it won 5 per cent. In 1970, 11.4 per cent. Labour and the Conservatives were alarmed by the trend and made concessions – in 1968, Heath announced his party supported Scottish devolution; in 1969, Wilson set up a Royal Commission to investigate the question – which further legitimized the idea of self-rule without actually satisfying the desire for it.

One major obstacle to independence, however, was the doubt surrounding Scotland's ability to sustain its own economy and its own acceptable level of government spending. The SNP had maintained for decades that both were quite possible, but during the late sixties the Wilson government and less biased British academics published evidence that Scotland was, in fact, heavily dependent on the rest of the UK. Then came North Sea oil. Its discovery gave the SNP a highly effective new argument. Most of the oilfields were off the coast of Scotland; if the country left the Union, the argument went, it alone would get most of the oil benefits. Scotland would no longer be one of the rustiest corners of a corroding UK; it would be a modern, rising nation, 'the most prosperous country in Europe', as the most ambitious SNP propaganda put it.

From 1971, the party put increasing emphasis on the oil issue at elections. From a memorable core slogan – 'It's Scotland's Oil' – populist promises poured out like so much North Sea crude: 'How would you like your granny's pension doubled? With £825 million every year from Scotland's Oil, self-government will pay.' The quadrupling of the world oil price during 1973 and 1974 massively amplified the appeal of the SNP's strong, graphic leaflets. In the February 1974 general election, the party's share of the vote in Scotland doubled again, to 21.9 per cent. In the October election, it reached 30.4 per cent, well ahead of the Conservatives and not far behind Labour.

The rise of the SNP, like the simultaneous revival of the Liberals, was both a cause and a symptom of the beginning of the end for the old post-war British politics, with its incrementally shifting ideas and predictable domination by two parties. More immediately, the SNP now had eleven parliamentary seats, at a time when the government had a majority of only three. Given the usual pattern of modern by-elections, this majority was unlikely to last long. Sooner or later, the Labour administration would be negotiating with the SNP for its survival.

'The Scots have really got us over a barrel here,' commented Peter Mountfield, a senior Treasury civil servant, in a confidential memo about North Sea oil in April 1974. There was a 'plausible case', a colleague wrote, 'for arguing that [the oil] is Scottish'. Mountfield concluded: 'An independent Scotland can go it alone.' During the mid-seventies, the SNP began to behave in some ways as if that situation had already come to pass. It established informal relations with OPEC and with Norway, the other main country with North Sea oil. It became friendly with the US consul in Edinburgh, a wily conservative called Richard Funkhouser, who saw Scottish nationalism as an understandable equivalent to the American 'states' rights' movement and wanted to reduce America's dependence on the Middle East by seeing North Sea oil extracted as fast as possible, whatever the means. The SNP also quietly secured allies and converts in the Aberdeen oil companies and in the Edinburgh banks that were thriving by financing them. In 1975, the party bought an expensive headquarters building in North Charlotte Street in Edinburgh's New Town, a quick walk from the traditional hub of Scottish banking in Charlotte Square.

A North Sea oil bonanza and Scottish self-rule, it seemed, were twin inevitabilities. In October 1973, a few weeks after the world crude price began to leap, the Royal Commission on Scottish devolution and other constitutional questions which Wilson had set up four years earlier finally reported. It supported the establishment of a Scottish parliament. In 1975, the proposed powers of the assembly were published in a White Paper, together with details of where it would be housed: in a handsome former school building with broad stone steps and neo-classical columns which stood, appropriately enough, on the same prominent Edinburgh hillside as the American consulate. The SNP continued to call for full independence but tacitly accepted the parliament as a stepping stone by arguing that the assembly should be granted more powers. In 1976, legislation for

Scottish and Welsh devolution was presented to the Commons with Labour and SNP support.

Yet, in the British seventies, little in politics or economics – perhaps even less than usual – was inevitable. As the rest of the decade would demonstrate, it was one thing to generate excitement and support for dramatic solutions to national decline such as devolution and North Sea oil; it was quite another to turn them into practical realities. For all the excitement about oil in North Charlotte Street, Downing Street and Fleet Street, for all the frenzied North Sea activity in Nigg and Aberdeen and elsewhere in the Scottish north-east, it was well into 1975, almost five years after the discovery of the first oilfield, that the crude actually started coming ashore. That year, British production was a tiny 34,000 barrels a day. In 1976, it was still insignificant – 253,000 barrels a day – compared to the major oil nations and to Britain's oil needs. It remained relatively small in 1977 – 792,000 barrels – and in 1978 – 1,119,000 barrels. It was not until 1979 that the output of the North Sea approached the level that it has maintained since, and it was not until 1985 that Britain's oilfields reached their first production peak.

By the oil-industry standards of the day, the whole process was impressively quick. Offshore drilling operations in difficult locations, when they were undertaken at all, often take decades to become properly productive. Yet for the often beleaguered and jittery governments of the seventies, the state of progress in the North Sea could be a torment. Even on the new frontier of the British economy, the country's old economic problems could not be easily escaped. Inflation in particular hugely swelled the cost of getting the oil. BP anticipated spending between £300 million and £350 million bringing the Forties field into full production, but spent £800 million. Meanwhile, the amount of foreign equipment imported for use in the North Sea meant that the offshore industry did not, as expected, reduce Britain's trade deficit – it increased it. Between 1974 and 1978, Healey writes in his memoirs, 'We were getting little benefit from North Sea oil. The capital investment required made it a net drain on our balance of payments . . . Even in 1978, North Sea oil was making good only half the impact of the [1973-4] OPEC price increase on our balance of payments, and was not yet producing any real revenue for the Government.'

During the sixties and early seventies, Conservative and Labour governments alike had rushed to parcel up the British sector of the North Sea into small rectangular 'blocks' attractive to oil companies. Licences to explore and extract oil from these subdivisions were – rather astonishingly, in retrospect – given away, except for a single auction under Heath which showed what a less panicky policy might have yielded: Shell and Esso were prepared to bid £21 million for a single block which turned out to contain no oil at all. The tax regime imposed on the North Sea oil companies by Whitehall was, at first, just as naive and generous: the conglomerates were allowed to reduce their British tax liabilities to almost nothing by combining their profits and losses in the North Sea with their profits and losses in the Middle East. 'Between 1965 and 1973,' the Public Accounts Committee of the House of Commons discovered to its horror in 1973, 'the oil majors' corporation tax liability in the UK was £500,000.'

Through the Scottish oil-shale industry, through BP and through the Anglo-Dutch conglomerate Shell, Britain had been heavily involved in the oil industry since the beginning. Yet by the early seventies, after decades of cheap Middle Eastern fuel and seemingly more pressing domestic issues, there were few British politicians who knew much about oil: the diminishing but politically charged business of coal mining was of much more interest. After the oil crisis, and as the scale of the North Sea's potential became obvious, this fog of ignorance started to lift. In 1974, Wilson appointed as a junior energy minister Thomas Balogh, a left-wing economist critical of the oil companies and of Whitehall's lenient treatment of them in the North Sea. In November, legislation was successfully introduced to tax their North Sea profits at 45 per cent. From a low base, the contribution of North Sea oil revenues to the government's income began to climb steeply: 0.3 per cent in 1976-7, 0.6 per cent in 1977-8, 1 per cent in 1978-9. By the North Sea's mid-eighties peak, a full tenth – and arguably a politically decisive tenth – of national tax receipts would be coming from its unlovely metal archipelago.

For a time in the second half of the seventies the Labour left's hopes for the oilfields moved beyond the purely fiscal: they also wanted to bring them under effective British government control. The chief architect of this ambitious strategy was a well-known Labour maverick who would quickly become even more unpopular than Balogh with the North Sea multinationals: Tony Benn. When Wilson made him energy secretary in 1975, the position may have been intended as a demotion – and may have been widely seen as a political dead end – but Benn, typically, acted as if it was the opposite. Still pursuing his enthusiasm for state intervention in the most important areas of British business, he proposed the partial nationalization of the North Sea. The oil companies, he envisaged, would work as contractors for the state-owned British National Oil Corporation (BNOC) in return for access to the North Sea's increasingly valuable deposits. Unfortunately for Benn, most of the Cabinet did not share his confidence that the particularly footloose and hard-nosed element of international capitalism that was the oil industry could be made the servant of British socialism. His colleagues' fears proved accurate. The multinationals responded to Benn's plan by threatening to hold back their North Sea operations, and his scheme was scaled down to a few measures – such as BNOC acquiring the right to buy and then sell on 51 per cent of the local crude – that established the impression of British government control of the oil territory but little more.

In 1978, another grand Benn scheme for the North Sea also sank with little trace. This time he proposed that the growing tax revenues from the oilfields should be put into a national Oil Fund and used to revive Britain's struggling onshore heavy industries. The Norwegian government was already pursuing a version of this strategy, husbanding its oil money in a kind of national deposit account for the decades to come. But Benn's idea was again rejected by the Cabinet. The state's immediate fiscal needs were too urgent, it was widely felt, for Britain to be able to afford such a policy. Instead, the great North Sea windfall would continue to be treated as an ordinary source of Whitehall revenue and be swallowed up by the day-to-day needs of hungry governments. Not for quite a time, until after the long British crisis of the seventies and afterwards was over, would it be obvious that this had not been a wise strategy. In 2008, the economist John Hawksworth of the accountants PriceWaterhouseCoopers calculated that, had Britain's tax revenues from North Sea gas and oil been invested rather than spent, they would now be worth £450 billion, and would give the British government control of one of the world's largest sovereign wealth funds.

There was one area of the country heavily involved with North Sea oil, however, that did take this path. The Shetland islands are a thin, shattered diamond of windy seashore and treeless grassland, 150 miles north-east of mainland Scotland and not that much further from Norway and the Arctic Circle. The islands are at the centre of ancient sea routes and fishing grounds, but they do not have a large, natural harbour and are too cold for most agriculture. Before the oil, Shetlanders lived by fishing, crofting, making knitwear and providing a strategic base for the British military in wartime. Prosperity arrived infrequently and did not linger; people often found adequate incomes only by joining the Royal Navy or by leaving Shetland altogether. Between 1901 and 1971, the population of the islands dwindled by almost half.

The discovery of oil nearby changed all this. First came the supply ships for the rigs, boxy and gleaming as tugboats on steroids, moored along new quays beyond the small grey harbour of the islands' small grey capital, Lerwick. Then came the oil industry's planes and helicopters, defying the fog and gales of Sumburgh, Shetland's tiny airport. By April 1979, there were more aircraft movements between Aberdeen and Sumburgh than between London and Paris. But the biggest transformation of the islands – and the one that was politically startling, even by the standards of the British seventies – involved a sea loch north of Lerwick called Sullom Voe.

During the early stages of the North Sea era, in 1971 and 1972, the islands' unusually powerful and far-sighted local authority, the Zetland County Council (soon to be renamed the Shetland Islands Council), worked out that the coming boom could be both a local economic opportunity and a social and environmental catastrophe. The council anticipated, correctly, that the oil companies would need a land mass as close as possible to the new oilfields to bring ashore their pipelines, refine their crude and load it into oil tankers. The council hired professional consultants to look at where the oil industry might best be accommodated. The consultants chose Sullom Voe, at the time little more than a disused base for Royal Navy flying boats. The council bought up land around the loch. Then its chief executive, Ian Clark, went to talk to the oil companies.

Clark was not a Shetlander. He was an unbending evangelical from 'the mainland', as the strongly independent islanders called Scotland. He was also a fearsome negotiator. Unlike Benn, he managed to persuade the oil industry that it needed his cooperation more than vice versa. Then Clark set his terms: only certain oil companies would be allowed to use the proposed oil terminal at Sullom Voe, and they would pay a fee to the council for every barrel that passed through, and another large sum to the council for the 'disturbance' which the construction and operation of the terminal would cause. The companies agreed.

For a local council to make such a deal, and to keep the proceeds, was probably unprecedented. In the House of Commons, where legislation had to be passed to allow the arrangement, the sharp-eyed Scottish Labour MP Tam Dalyell raised objections. 'It seemed to me far more than a fair deal,' he told me in 2002. 'I thought, "If Shetland can do this, then any part of the UK that finds itself suddenly favoured with natural resources can up and out."' But Dalyell was an isolated critic. The British government needed North Sea oil, and North Sea oil, inescapably, gave a new political leverage to the Shetland Islands Council, as it did to the SNP. In 1973, Jo Grimond, Shetland's shrewd MP and the former leader of the Liberal Party, introduced a private member's bill giving the council the powers it needed to make financial arrangements with the oil companies. The bill, despite being strikingly vague in its wording, became law with barely an alteration. In 1975, Richard Funkhouser summarized the saga for his State Department superiors in Washington, with a mixture of incomprehension, exasperation and admiration:

The irony of the North Sea . . . was that the tyrant which bestrode it was the Shetland County Council, a tiny group of home-spun farmers led by 'Fuehrer' Ian Clark who had reputedly hornswoggled some of the biggest multinationals and most sophisticated leaders in Britain out of terms which would make the Scottish Nationalists pale with envy.

Sullom Voe began receiving oil in 1978, after half a decade of construction work that outdid even the dockyard at Nigg in scale and extravagance. Over 7,000 people were employed on the building site at its busiest, sleeping in whole hillsides of mobile homes and, sometimes, inside sections of unused pipeline. When the terminal was completed, it is still said locally, scores of expensive imported diggers and dumper trucks were simply buried in the ground, because the local economy had no use for them and it was too complicated to ship them out. By the early eighties, the Shetland Islands Council was receiving enough income from Sullom Voe to fund over 80 per cent of its spending.

Two decades later, I visited the islands to see what use had been made of their North Sea millions. The road from Sumburgh airport to Lerwick was swerving and almost deserted, but as smooth and well-maintained as a road in a royal park. On the rocky windswept grass to either side were scattered bungalows. Many of them were large and looked recently built. In their driveways stood equally oversized and new-looking cars. In Lerwick, the buildings were prim Victorian stone, but along the main shopping street almost every second premises was a big branch of a bank.

At the council offices, the chief executive, a cheerful man without a tie called Morgan Goodlad, told me with characteristic Shetland directness that his was the wealthiest local authority in Britain after the City of London. When the oil money had started to come in during the seventies, he explained, the council had set up its own version of the Norwegian national deposit account and Benn's notional Oil Fund: the Shetland Islands Council Charitable Trust. The trust's aims – 'to improve the quality of life for Shetlanders, especially in the areas of social need, leisure, environment and education; to support traditional industries' – were so broadly drawn that they had implications for almost every aspect of the islands' existence. And so it had proved. Since the late seventies, the trust had paid for exemplary school buildings, generous subsidies to Shetland businesses, superbly equipped leisure centres and care centres for the elderly with five beds and six times as many staff – a whole self-contained world, barely known about in the rest of Britain, of lavish public provision and public expectation. 'The pressure comes up through our councillors for a new marina, a new village hall,' said Goodlad, trying to sound put-upon but not quite managing it. 'People think, "The council has so much money . . ."' Over the previous two years, a falling London stock market had devalued the trust's investments in shares by over a third, but it could still afford to give every Shetland pensioner a £262 Christmas bonus.

After the interview, I started off for Sullom Voe. On the outskirts of Lerwick, I spotted a modern-looking leisure centre. Inside, under the glass roof, the relentless Shetland wind was banished. The air was like a still, warm bath. A couple of people were bobbing in the pool; otherwise, on a weekday lunchtime, there was no one to enjoy the water slides and the well-fed palms and the expanses of spotless tiling. To my mainlander's eye, which had become accustomed to worn and crowded public amenities during the eighties and nineties, it all seemed disturbingly extravagant and deliciously utopian. I drove on. Again the road was immaculately surfaced and nearly empty. Every time I passed a cluster of bungalows big enough to be called a hamlet, there towered over them a school or a village hall or another leisure centre in a recent architectural style. Quite often builders were at work erecting more.

It was not until I reached Sullom Voe that there was any sign that all this might be vulnerable – that Shetland's alternative, more benign version of the British seventies might not continue for ever. On one of the terminal's endless quaysides, a line of council-owned tugboats stood idle. Offshore, the tankers were still queueing, but not as they used to: the annual number visiting Sullom Voe had halved since the peak years of North Sea oil production in the mid-eighties. In the terminal car park, letters were missing from the Sullom Voe sign and no one had bothered to replace them.

A few miles from the terminal, on the side of a steep headland overlooking where one of the North Sea pipelines came ashore, I found several neat rows of abandoned houses. They had been built by the council in the seventies, I learned later from the council's official history of the period, and were '100% oil-related'. The history went on: 'In view of the urgency with which these houses were required, lack of contractors on the islands, and difficult site and working conditions, the completed cost of the houses was . . . 50% over the cost limit of comparable housing types on the mainland.' Three decades on, their thick walls and chalet-style roofs and skylights with sea views had aged well. But their interiors had been stripped and their occupants were long gone.

I left their overgrown gardens waving in the wind and followed the road further uphill. After a few minutes, the road, which was no longer smooth but uneven and crumbling, veered sharply and ended in a bleak little plateau of tarmac. Facing the tarmac, flanked by nothing but miles of cold grass, was a great boarded-up hulk like a derelict supermarket. It was an old council leisure centre. In the seventies, Rod Stewart, that grainy-voiced cheerleader for boozy good times, had played a legendary concert in it for the Sullom Voe workers. Now, a local farmer used it to shelter his animals. I tried to find a way in, but all I found was boarded-up doorways and frightened sheep.

When I got back to Lerwick that evening, I thought about North Sea oil, about how its golden era was generally considered to be coming to an end, and about how Shetland might be affected. Then something Morgan Goodlad had said came back to me. I had asked him whether it had been wise for the council, given the volatility of its stock-exchange investments and the finiteness of the oil, to keep on spending quite so generously. 'The money', Goodlad had replied with a twinkle, nodding at the miniature Scandinavia outside his office windows, 'may have been well spent while it lasted.'

Elsewhere in Britain during the seventies, North Sea oil set in motion less gentle social and political experiments. Aberdeen, an old trading city of shipyards, paper mills and universities, famous for its plain granite streets and care with money, became a brash new oil town of overpriced taxis and binges by off-duty rig workers. Oil-company headquarters, like concrete and glass castles, occupied the hilltops in the richest suburbs. Those suburbs quickly got richer: in the seventies, house prices in Aberdeen rose by 50 per cent more than the national average, and the city created more jobs than any comparable place in Britain.

Oil fuelled a striking local appetite for electric gates and indoor shopping centres, for all-you-can-eat buffets and double garages, for a touch of Texas. Actual American oilmen – by 1976 there were 5,000 Americans in a city of 185,000 – bought or rented big Victorian villas in the villages along the River Dee west of Aberdeen. In 1973, they established the North Sea Petroleum Club in a white hillside lodge with a beech-lined drive. 'It was stetsons and cowboy boots at first,' the manager told me when I visited. The private dining club became a country club, with tennis courts and a car park full of Range Rovers and Porsches. The city became infamous for its traffic and impatient drivers.

This more jostling, more brazen Aberdeen gave a taste of how the more productive parts of Britain might turn out when, or if, the national economy turned around. But it was beyond the city's eastern horizon, far out to sea on the oil rigs themselves, that the starkest vision of a new competitive Britain was laid out.

Life on a rig is about work. Even when I visited one in 2007, thirty years after the North Sea's seventies gold rush, the routine was still all-encompassing and driven. Employees are aboard for between a week and a month at a time, and cannot leave, barring serious injury or illness, until their stint is done. They work twelve-hour shifts, starting at dawn or at dusk. There are no holidays on board, not even Christmas, and no days off. Between shifts, workers eat double portions of fat and starch in the mess hall. They try to sleep in tiny shared cabins. They watch television in the recreation room as the rig tannoys blast. But mostly they think about the job in hand. 'They finish their twelve hours,' a mess-hall steward on the rig told me, 'and all they do is talk about what they've done in their twelve hours.'

Drilling at sea is always expensive. People back onshore – politicians, consumers, oil company executives and shareholders – are always impatient for oil. And a rig is its own world. Even in 2007, the drilling platform I visited, a heaving, clanking maze of soaked decks and narrow corridors, had only one public telephone for a hundred crewmen and no reception for mobiles. Helicopters arrived at best once a day or, if the fog came down, not at all. When the weather lifted, another rig was just visible in the far distance. Otherwise, the outside world was nothing but the dark waves. 'People only really talk about the rig,' the steward told me. 'Not what's beyond.'

In the British sector of the North Sea during the seventies, a radically different balance of power between bosses and workers was established to what existed onshore. 'Industrial troubles have been rare,' wrote Leith McGrandle in his slightly rose-tinted 1975 book *The Story of North Sea Oil.* 'Casual signings-on [of workers] . . . have made union organization difficult . . . The Americans in the past have occasionally sacked a whole crew if they sniffed trouble ahead. This is one reason why there has only been one strike in the last four years.' A large proportion of oil-rig workers did relentlessly physical, relatively unskilled work for wages that were substantially better than on dry land. They were hired on short-term, insecure contracts. Often, they had been unemployed or in the armed services, or had left jobs as mechanics or farm labourers. They came from all over Britain, but particularly from depressed areas. Just as, in the following decade, Norman Tebbit would suggest the jobless should, they had 'got on their bikes' to find work.

Sometimes potential rig workers were scrutinized for their political views before being taken on. 'We are interested in identifying overt opponents of the system,' admitted Shell's personnel director Peter Linklater in 1978. 'The last thing we would want to do is to have political subversives on our payroll.' The screening was not always perfect. 'Before I went offshore I was on the executive committee of the Young Communist League,' remembered Chris Ramsey, a former oil man I met in 2004 who had first worked in the North Sea in 1977.

But on the rigs, where there were no daily newspapers and at first not even any television, he had had to accept he was in a different world: 'I used to keep my mouth shut. I covered stuff for the *Morning Star* using a false name. Everyone was working too hard, because of the American management. Safety was really bad – there was a diver killed every month then – but you wouldn't try a union offshore. Everyone was looking after themselves.'

In the Norwegian sector, the shop-floor culture was different. Oil platforms were unionized from the beginning. Some workers on British rigs have cast envious glances there ever since. 'The Norwegians have got it sussed,' said the engineer I shared a cabin with on my rig visit, as he sat hollow-eyed on his bunk after his night shift. 'Strong unions. Two weeks on, four weeks off, for everyone – not two weeks on, two weeks off, like us.' He shook his head and managed a weak, admiring smile: 'And now their unions are pushing for the next week off.'

But in the seventies, the British sector of the North Sea had no time for such old-fashioned industrial relations. The oil still did not flow quickly enough to save the decade's governments. Instead, the rigs acted as a kind of Trojan horse for a new, more right-wing version of workplace politics. Chris Ramsey, for one, detected an irony. 'It all happened when Tony Benn was energy minister!' he said with a bitter laugh. We were walking along the sand at Cruden Bay, north of Aberdeen, where the first oil pipeline of the seventies had reached land. A few hundred feet above our heads, helicopters still rushing to the rigs passed in a near-continuous, throbbing roar. When the next brief pause came, I asked Ramsey how long he had worked in the North Sea. Young Communist or not, he had stuck it out, he said, for thirteen years.

9

The Real Sixties

It is one of the conventional wisdoms about the seventies that the decade was a time when the rebellious energies of the sixties cooled and dissipated. In Britain and across the West, there is evidence for this view: in the shrinking, fragmenting underground press of the early seventies; in the frustration of the radical hopes expressed by the student uprisings of 1968; in the election victories of conservatives like Edward Heath and Richard Nixon; in the institutionalization of rock music and other sixties youth cultures; and in the retreat of many of those who would not be co-opted into introspection, or self-defeating factionalism, or the political and moral cul-de-sacs of terrorism. 'The time for play had passed,' writes Elizabeth Nelson about the early seventies in her book *The British Counter-Culture 1966–73*. Many other observers, both during the seventies and since, have competed to identify similar watersheds: phases or precise moments in the decade when, to take the most commonly used metaphor, the great party of the sixties ended and the hangover set in.

This liberal or left-wing melancholy about the seventies has, in many ways, been the mirror image of the doomy right-wing view of the same period. These different visions of national decline have complemented and given credibility to each other. They have helped ensure that the British seventies have not been widely mourned since their passing. And yet, both perspectives on the decade have always been dimmed by blind spots. The anti-seventies left, as you could call it, has a particularly large one. It fails to acknowledge that for many politicized Britons, the decade was *not* the hangover after the sixties; it was when the great sixties party actually got started.

Near the foot of Highbury Fields in north London, where the hand-some terraces facing trees and bushes begin to give way to office blocks and traffic, there is a small bronze commemorative plaque. Unlike those nearby for the eminent Victorians Joseph Chamberlain and Walter Sickert, it is not blue or green but matt black. It does not hang on a tall Georgian townhouse but on a low ungainly building, blank-looking and detached – a small set of offices, sometimes vacant with unopened post on the doormat – that was once a public toilet. And the plaque does not celebrate a long historical association but a single, relatively recent evening. In gold capital letters its inscription reads:

> The first gay rights demonstration
> in Britain took place here,
> in Highbury Fields, on
> 27th November 1970
> when 150 members of the
> Gay Liberation Front
> held a torchlight rally
> against police
> harassment

Above the inscription there is a political logo: a raised fist and, as if tattooed across it, the words 'Gay Liberation Front', a flower, and a pair of intertwined masculinity and femininity symbols. The plaque went up in 2000. Its manufacture and unveiling, funded by private donations, was recorded by the right-wing tabloids without complaint. Its significance is even explained in the house-buyer's guide to Highbury provided by the website findaproperty.co.uk. The buffed-up borough of Islington, of which Highbury is part, has for years been a popular area for prosperous gay men.

Yet there are things about the plaque – the actual phrase 'Gay Liberation Front', the logo's mixture of stridency and hippy dreaminess – that hint at a political world quite different from the present, and quite different from the seventies as experienced in Whitehall or Downing Street. For those active in this world, in its new politics of identity, individual experience and cultural allegiance rather than class, patriotism and economics, the decade was not a dead end but a maze of possibilities.

When the Highbury demo was suggested, the Gay Liberation

Front had been in existence for six weeks. It had been founded in a basement classroom at the LSE by a dozen students and academics. By late November 1970, its membership had mushroomed to over 200 'sisters and brothers', according to its campaigning newspaper *Come Together*, all of them impatient for a response to the 'hundreds of crimes committed against gay people by the police and the establishment every year'. On the 25th, the GLF held one of its regular and increasingly tumultuous meetings. Stuart Feather was one of those present. 'There was a discussion about having a demonstration,' he told me. 'But people said, "What are we going to have a demonstration about?" A guy suggested we went and demonstrated outside the American embassy against . . . [the] visa restrictions if you declared you were gay. I thought, "That's up to the American gays to get together." And the guy was, it turned out, very much of that old left, Vietnam, Grosvenor Square generation.' Feather paused. 'The other proposal – it was the only other real suggestion – was to go and protest the arrest of Louis Eakes.'

Sex between men had been decriminalized in England in 1967, in one of the path-breaking social – rather than economic – reforms for which the Wilson government of the sixties would be fondly remembered. But the liberalization of the law had only been partial: it remained illegal for men to have any sexual contact with each other in public. What constituted a public place was broadly defined, and prosecutions were pursued with vigour. Plainclothes policemen were sometimes assigned to favoured gay cruising spots such as Highbury Fields, which was dimly lit at night and had its bushes and public toilet. One autumn evening in 1970, Louis Eakes, who was a well-known Young Liberal, was seen by policemen approaching several men on the Fields and asking them for a light for his cigarette. Eakes denied that he had been looking for sex – he denied that he was even a homosexual – but he was arrested for 'gross indecency'.

Eakes was not a perfect martyr. When Feather heard about his arrest and his denials, 'I immediately thought, "This guy is gay, and he's just trying it on."' A few months later, Eakes would be arrested and convicted after a similar episode in another park. Yet for the Gay Liberation Front, Eakes's reliability and sexuality were beside the point. At 9 o'clock on a Friday evening, '150 beautiful gay people' (*Come Together*'s description) and reporters and photographers from several national newspapers met at Highbury and Islington station. Wearing multicoloured capes, flares and stage costumes, carrying torches, candles and balloons, smoking joints, shouting, chanting and playing musical instruments, the GLF protesters marched into Highbury Fields. At the far end of the park they halted and quietened. The group's demands were read out:

That all discrimination against gay people, male and female . . . should end . . . That sex education in schools stop being exclusively heterosexual. That psychiatrists stop treating homosexuality as though it were a problem or sickness . . . That gay people be legally free to contact other gay people, through newspaper ads, on the street and by any other means . . . as are heterosexuals . . . That employers should no longer be allowed to discriminate against anyone on account of their sexual preferences. That the age of consent for gay males be reduced to the same as for straights. That gay people be free to hold hands and kiss in public, as are heterosexuals . . .

After each demand, the GLF's newspaper recorded, 'We all responded with "Right on!", which echoed round the Fields.' The journalists, the protest's escort of standoffish policemen and a few perplexed passers-by – Highbury was still a traditional working-class area – looked on. Then, many of the marchers decided to make one of their demands into a reality on the spot, by kissing and holding hands. There were no arrests, but *Come Together* reported: 'A brother overheard a bunch of straight, grey reporters describe us as a bunch of "pooves". So we descended on this bunch and demanded a retraction.'

Next, Feather recalled, 'We marched around a bit, and then we all went off into the bushes and lit cigarettes.' Finally, most of the protesters headed to the nearest pub, the Cock – perhaps its proximity was not the only thing in its favour – for a few rushed euphoric drinks in the half hour before closing time. The whole protest had lasted ninety minutes. 'It didn't feel historic,' Feather told me. 'It was just exciting.'

I met him at his flat in Ladbroke Grove in the late summer of 2005. His pretty stucco corner of west London, associated for the last half century with social and political experiments, was steadily succumbing to pastel restaurants and upmarket bathroom shops. But on the fifth floor of Feather's slightly shabby white terrace, a whiff of sixties and seventies bohemianism lingered. Jimi Hendrix had lived in the flat below. Feather had been in his own housing association one-bedroom pad for twenty-six years. It had modular white sixties chairs, an easel in the living room and a mural on the bathroom walls and ceiling. Everything was a little faded, neatly arranged and preserved, museum-ish; not much in the flat seemed to have been bought after 1980.

Feather sat carefully in one of his vintage chairs, lean and crop-haired, wearing a paint-spattered T-shirt, smart shorts and sandals over tanned ankles. He was in his mid-sixties, but his eyes were still strong and blue, his recall of his radical life precise and unsentimental. He had grown up in Yorkshire: 'My dad was a lorry driver, and then he got a fish-and-chip shop.' As a teenager, he wanted to go to art school, but 'that was out of the question . . . I ended up as an apprentice engineer on a production line in a light engineering factory in York.' At this, Feather's confident, slightly mocking voice dropped and turned more halting: 'That job just got a bit too hairy because it was quite obvious I was gay, and I started getting a lot of, sort of, not aggro so much as . . . kind of being sent up and sort of pushed out of the way . . .' In the late sixties, he moved to London. 'I found myself a rather bourgeois life,' he continued, fluency returning. 'I wore Gucci shoes. I had a boyfriend and a job in an employment agency. And a cosy little flat down at World's End in Chelsea. Being gay to me was no longer a big issue. One of the demands of Gay Lib was the right to hold hands in public. Well, I'd been doing that with guys in Chelsea for a long time.'

Then, one day in the autumn of 1970, 'Two friends of mine went shopping down Oxford Street, and they were given a GLF leaflet. We all went along to a GLF meeting. They were the most extraordinary people. I'd never met people like them before. They were mainly young, beautiful and long-haired. I was sort of longhair-ish, but I had no political awareness at all. Here people were really talking about being gay, and how it affected their lives. They saw no point in any kind of parliamentary process for what they were trying to do. Their attitude was, "The government can change the law, they can give us rights – and then take them away. Our aim is to change public opinion, to change people's minds."'

Some of the style and confidence of the early GLF had, like other aspects of the British counter-culture, been imported from America. Gay-liberation groups had formed there first, in the aftermath of the Stonewall riots of 1969, when police raids on a gay bar in New York had for the first time provoked a militant response. In the summer of 1970, founding members of what would soon become the British GLF visited the US and were inspired by the new gay assertiveness they found. In America, they also sensed the potential for pioneering alliances between gay liberation and the era's other radical movements. In August, the Black Panther leader Huey Newton had emphatically included homosexuals in a rhetorical list of 'oppressed people' – and had then gone much further: 'Maybe a homosexual', he had written, 'could be the most revolutionary [of all].'

By 1971, the British GLF had too many members to hold its meetings in borrowed LSE classrooms. Its gatherings moved to Middle Earth, a huge labyrinthine basement in Covent Garden that had been a famous venue for counter-cultural events during the sixties. Up above, Covent Garden was still a fruit-and-vegetable market. When the GLF mounted one of its flamboyant demonstrations nearby, 'There were a few vegetables thrown,' Feather remembered dryly. Yet down in Middle Earth, with its endlessly receding rooms, its ceiling pillars and gloom, the meetings of GLF activists, usually seated in a circle and speaking in excited political slogans and insider-y gay slang, acquired a mystique, a certain fashionability even: celebrity bohemians such as David Hockney, John Lennon and even the Bloomsbury Group survivor Duncan Grant, then eighty-five years old, attended or lent support. 'There was an incredible warmth – you could really say love – between the early GLF people,' Feather recalled. 'Through the process of joining the GLF, by coming out, people were losing their places to live and losing their jobs. But we tried to live the GLF manifesto. And it seemed limitless.'

One aspect of the GLF creed, which was in keeping with the

broader mood of the counter-culture, was a slightly woolly but heart-felt anarchism. 'Oppression by the Big State Machine also affects gay people,' *Come Together* declared in early 1971, echoing Huey Newton, 'And they are as interested in fighting it as are all other groups that suffer from it.' In February, the GLF joined the great London march against Ted Heath's Industrial Relations Bill. Carrying placards that ranged from the sober – 'Homosexuals Oppose the Bill' – to the mildly cheeky – 'Poof to the Bill' – and hold-ing bunches of leaflets attacking homophobic discrimination in the workplace – 'nearly one million trade unionists are homosexual' – a hundred or so GLF activists presented themselves to the demonstra-tion's organizers. They were not made to feel entirely welcome. Since they were not a trade union, and since no one wanted to march with them, the GLF were informed, they would have to stay at the back of the demonstration.

The activists did as they were told, but the novelty of their pres-ence and the noise they made, chanting their way through Piccadilly with their Jesus beards and hippy centre partings, attracted media attention regardless. A cartoon in the London *Evening Standard* the next day sensed an unease in the trade union establishment about its new allies. A huddle of middle-aged men, heavy-set and with pipes and war medals, are in a union office wallpapered with press cuttings about the size of the demonstration. 'Well,' says one, 'I make it eighty to one hundred and fifty thousand, depending on whether you include the "Gay Liberation Front", or not!' *Come Together*, typical-ly, was more frank about the march: 'Many, in fact most, of the people on the demo were real male chauvinists . . . and therefore our enemy. We were there to CONFRONT the male chauvinism of working people.'

During 1971, the GLF's political exhibitionism acquired a bolder edge. 'I and a couple of others introduced the whole concept of drag,' said Feather. 'I saw it as much more direct than wearing a [GLF] badge, much more confrontational. With a badge, people would say, "What's the Gay Liberation Front?", and you would start talking about the concepts, rather than "Why are you wearing a woman's dress?", and then you saying, "Why are you wearing men's clothes?"' Yet with this new boldness – 'Among the drag queens we were really up for questioning . . . [even] what was gay and what was straight,' Feather remembered – came implications for the GLF membership. Not everyone wanted to wear drag or dismantle all the barriers between sexualities and genders; many of the activists just wanted to get a fair deal for gay men. From late 1971, the GLF's weekly London meetings turned into shouting matches between factions. 'There was a reaction against the drag queens,' Feather admitted. 'It came from the guys who just wanted' – a cutting note of mockery came into his voice – 'a male way of doing things, let us say.'

In 1972, the London meetings ceased. The GLF split into groups based in the north, south and west of the capital. Each group had distinctive characteristics: more working-class in the south, more middle-class and politically conciliatory in the north – where activists set up a late-night coffee stall for men cruising on Hampstead Heath – and most dogmatic and drag-orientated in the west. These groups quickly evolved into communes. The most experimental of these was in Ladbroke Grove.

7a Colville Houses was like thousands of other properties in the area and in neighbouring Notting Hill during the late sixties and early seventies: a big, balconied, once-grand Victorian house, vacant for years as this part of London had grown poorer and more transient, and now perfectly suited to serve the counter-culture's growing appetite for squatting and communal living. 'All that we did in the Colville commune was to take Gay Lib that one step further,' Feather told the oral historian Lisa Power two decades later, 'and say that all men should wear a frock. We thought that it was the answer. It almost was. It still is.' Andrew Lumsden, a sympathetic GLF activist but not a member of 'Colvillia', described visiting the commune to Power in less understated terms:

It was like stepping off the planet. You went into a no-daylight zone where there were places to sleep strewn all over the floor, posters to do with pop groups, endless sounds always on, you were always offered dope or acid. The welcome was lovely. It was unstructured to a degree that was terrifying if you had led any kind of structured life . . . None of the ordinary ways of coping seemed to be there. Somebody might be walking round without their clothes on, somebody else spending hours and hours making up. There was a wardrobe, a very large area for frocks and shoes and make-up and mirrors, people could spend hours in there . . . Somebody might be making love on one or another mattress, all in this twilight . . .

In Colvillia during 1972 and 1973, the transgressive games of the sixties, far from being played out, were energetically being taken further. 'The more we learn about each other in the commune, the higher we get: much higher than anything that came after flower power,' announced the Colvillia collective in a special issue of *Come Together* they produced. When the house was repossessed by the Notting Hill Housing Trust, the commune moved into a disused film studio down the road. The drag queens hung its interior so thickly with drapes that you could not hear the outside world. Money, sexism and maleness, privacy, ideology, personal identity and morality – all were scrutinized by the group and new approaches to them agreed. 'Sharing everything, our material possessions of course, our ideas, our energy, our minds and our bodies,' the collective wrote in *Come Together*, 'meant that we had to change ourselves . . . You never really know another person until you live with them. The question is, how much do you want to know? How much are you prepared to show? What are you afraid of hiding?' LSD consumption became close to compulsory. 'The police did come once,' Feather told me, 'but they were so shocked and embarrassed that they kind of retreated out of the door. Goodness knows what the neighbours thought. But we didn't have much contact with them.'

Yet as well as all this experimentation, there were less bohemian impulses in the commune. Many members were on the dole, putting their benefit money into the art deco teapot that served as Colvillia's bank account. But, Feather recalled, 'We [also] used to earn our money by going out on Fridays and Saturdays and buying and selling . . . a lot of women's clothes, lots of pottery, lots of art deco stuff . . . We'd doll up in the morning and load everything into prams, and parade down to Portobello market, and run the gauntlet of the stallholders.' Like the Middle Earth meetings, the drag queens' market stall attracted attention from beyond the usual gay circles. 'I remember selling brooches to Brian Eno,' said Feather, a very white, knowing smile edging across his tanned face. 'He was very nervous of us. He used to sort of eventually negotiate his way to the front of the stall.' The smile faded: 'We also had all these Italian tourists coming up and taking photographs of us. We got really stroppy with them. We chased them down the street, saying, "You fucking bourgeois Italians, what d'you think you're doing? You're taking our photograph, and you're not buying anything off our stall!"'

Colvillia did not last. 'There was one middle-class guy who decided that if he was free, as we all were, to do what he wanted, then he would refuse to sign on [for the dole] any more, or provide any more money . . . And he had a boyfriend as well who wasn't contributing anything. So the money was beginning to become abused . . . And then one of the younger ones and this woman started using the money to finance a drugs empire . . . There was a mad Afghan guy as well, who used to lope around, and he turned out to be a big drug dealer as well . . . And then we didn't know who was coming into the place and for what reason . . .' Sitting neatly in his immaculate flat, Feather paused. 'It just became very difficult indeed.'

By 1974, the commune was over, and so was *Come Together* and the GLF as a whole. Colvillia's two sites were redeveloped. The house was divided into flats by the Notting Hill Housing Trust. When I went to have a look at it after seeing Feather, I found five storeys of drawn net curtains instead of a drag queens' free-for-all. The film studio had also been replaced by social housing for families, for people who liked privacy. Tiny children's chairs warmed in the sunshine in heavily fenced-off back gardens. The tidying away of the old local bohemia had not been without social benefits, but that tidying away had also been very thorough and unsentimental: at neither site was there the slightest vestige of the commune.

Yet Gay Lib did leave traces in Britain. Some were small. 'There were one or two people one knew socially, who weren't involved in Gay Lib, who were suddenly appearing in magazines doing a bit of drag,' Feather recalled. 'And you thought, "That should've been me." I asked him if he still wore drag at all. There was an unusually long pause. 'The drag thing . . . One still dolls up in drag a bit and goes out, to a party or something.' But he didn't live in drag any more? 'That takes up too much time.'

Other legacies of the movement were more enduring. As well as its stunts and lifestyle experiments, the GLF had done less dramatic work: putting on dances for gay men and lesbians that were high-profile and no longer furtive events; publicizing these and other gay and lesbian happenings in *Come Together*; prompting the formation of GLF groups outside London, in Leeds, Manchester, Brighton and Birmingham. In July 1972, the feuding London GLF briefly put aside its differences to organize the first Gay Pride march, from Trafalgar Square to Hyde Park. In early 1974, an office the group had rented in the basement of Housmans, a well-known left-wing bookshop near King's Cross, was converted by former GLF activists into the London Gay Switchboard, a free information and legal advice service. By 1975, it had a staff of sixty volunteers and was receiving a thousand calls a week.

Other ex-GLF members stayed in politics. Peter Tatchell had joined within a week of arriving in London from Australia in 1971, after seeing a GLF sticker on a lamp post. During the eighties and nineties, he made himself into Britain's best-known gay activist, in part as a prominent member of OutRage!, which described itself as a 'queer rights direct action group' and retained the old GLF flair for confrontation and theatrical gestures. Angie Weir, an important GLF member later known as Angela Mason, became director of the lesbian and gay lobby group Stonewall and then, in 2002, director of the Labour government's Women and Equality Unit.

The GLF helped establish in modern Britain for the first time a visible, unapologetic and rapidly expanding gay culture. This had its commercial as well as its idealistic side. As even the Colvillia drag queens had discovered with their Portobello market stall, homosexuality could be a commodity as well as a crusade. In the seventies, the most obvious manifestation of this was the success of *Gay News*. It had been conceived as a 'national homosexual newspaper' in late 1971, at the height of the GLF's ideological civil war. Some of its staff were GLF members, and at first it operated as a collective, as *Come*

Together always did. But *Gay News* soon signalled its distinctive-
ness. 'News is not only the bad things that can happen to us,'
suggested the first issue's editorial, 'but knowing what others are
doing, sharing and achieving. Information . . .' The second issue
demonstrated this more upbeat, less politically radical sensibility by
giving over its front cover to contact ads. By Issue 40, *Gay News* was
calling itself 'Europe's Largest Circulation Fortnightly Newspaper
for Homosexuals', and carrying listings for gay pubs from Aberdeen
to York. By Issue 85, in 1975, the paper was featuring ads for gay
shops, gay pin-up calendars, mainstream Hollywood films with gay
characters and the 1976 Gay Spring Weekender in Torquay.

'I was against *Gay News*, the whole idea of it,' said Feather with
quiet force. He looked around his austere living room. 'We knew in
the GLF that capitalism had the ability to absorb dissidents.' In
Britain in the mid-seventies, true equality for gays – indeed, the satisfaction of even the more modest demands bellowed out by the GLF
in Highbury Fields – was decades off. But homosexuals, in part
thanks to the GLF, were now a recognized market – and a market
could be served. It was a sign of the Britain to come.

The other great seventies revolt over gender roles and sexuality
proved harder to commodify. Women's Liberation emerged as a
movement in Britain less suddenly than Gay Liberation. 'At regular
intervals throughout history, women rediscover themselves – their
strengths, their capabilities, their political will,' wrote Anna Coote
and Beatrix Campbell in their 1982 book *Sweet Freedom: The
Struggle for Women's Liberation*. They prefaced their assertion with
quotations from Mary Astell in 1700 – 'If all Men are born free, how
is it that all Women are born slaves?' – Mary Wollstonecraft in 1792
– 'Who made man the exclusive judge, if woman partake with him
the gift of reason?' – and Christabel Pankhurst in 1902 – 'The great
social injustices are the subjection of labour and the subjection of
women.'

The next wave of British feminism began to form during the sixties. By then, the fundamental grievances articulated by Astell,
Wollstonecraft and Pankhurst had been further sharpened by the

contradictions of life for women in post-war Britain. Families were getting smaller. Domestic chores, thanks to new home technologies, were becoming less all-consuming. More women were going to university. More women were working: in 1951, 36 per cent of those between twenty and sixty-four; in 1961, 42 per cent; in 1971, 52 per cent. More women were acquiring the sort of life expectations traditionally held by men. In many ways, these were not being met. Women's pay compared to men's fell between the early fifties and mid-sixties. The welfare state continued to assume that women were primarily carers rather than earners. Employers and trade unions did the same. The laws governing divorce and abortion were liberalized, cheap contraception became available and sexual freedom acceptable, but the greatest beneficiaries of this new permissiveness were men. About other, even more sensitive areas of gender relations, such as domestic violence against women, the reforming politicians of the sixties and counter-culture revolutionaries had little or nothing to say.

The injustice and frustration of the position of women in Britain and comparable countries was expressed, periodically, in brilliant books by foreigners. Simone de Beauvoir's *The Second Sex* (1949) was a monumental work of scholarship and polemic, written in an intoxicating grand style, about the domination of women through 'patriarchy', the fear and hatred of women that underlay it, and how only the 'liberation' of women could end it. Betty Friedan's *The Feminine Mystique* (1963) was more journalistic but equally potent. It was a vivid report, sometimes melancholy, sometimes furious, from 'the comfortable concentration camp' of female domesticity to which even the highly educated middle-class American women that Friedan interviewed had been confined soon after university, and where they acquired dishwashing sores and public personas that seemed 'listless and bored, or frantically "busy"'.

Then, in 1970, two more seminal feminist volumes appeared. Kate Millett's *Sexual Politics* took on Henry Miller, Norman Mailer and other revered male counter-culture figures and, with slashing literary criticism and bitter humour, showed their supposedly iconoclastic writing to be full of neuroses and bullies' assumptions about sex and women. Germaine Greer's *The Female Eunuch* was even more reve-latory. 'Women', she wrote, 'have very little idea of how much men hate them.' Greer's prose was as quick and concentrated as that of a good tabloid reporter, and effortlessly mixed the raw and demotic – 'tits' – with the analytical and academic. Her book, inspired in part by the rebellions of 1968, called for nothing less than a revolution in female consciousness. Woman must 'recapture her own will'. But Greer had no illusions that it would be easy: 'Take . . . joy in the struggle . . . For a long time there may be no perceptible reward . . . other than new purpose.'

The first British women's groups, in which women shared person-al experiences and 'raised' each other's consciousnesses, were established in 1968. As Gay Liberation would, the new political movement initially took its language, ideas and tactics from a precur-sor in America. And it quickly attained a momentum. The following January, the underground newspaper *Black Dwarf* declared 1969 the 'Year of the Militant Woman'.

A few weeks later, Marsha Rowe arrived in London from Aus-tralia. She was a young magazine journalist from Sydney with high hopes of the British counter-culture. She had grown up in a pretty harbourside suburb, 'not reading books' and with few intellectual or career expectations. 'I was brought up with the idea that it wasn't up to me to go to university.' But then one day, she told me, 'My life changed. I bought *Oz* magazine on a newsstand.' *Oz* was a kind of Australian *Private Eye* which had moved from straightforward ser-rated satire into the more freeform cultural and political iconoclasm practised by the underground press. Rowe paid for herself to go to university, did some work for *Oz* and more conventional magazines like *Vogue*, and joined Sydney's new sixties bohemia. It did not satis-fy her for long. By 1969, 'I had explored every bit. I was bored.' Other ambitious and rebellious Australians she knew had moved to London, so she followed them.

'I felt that I was arriving in a city . . . that was on the cusp of immi-nent changes, but I didn't know what. Everything did seem to be breaking up . . . The excitement and general hope of earlier in the six-ties had obviously gone . . . and it was like, "Where's it all going?"'

At first she hated the place: 'People were snooty about Australians.' After a brief stay, she fled to Greece for six months. There the military dictatorship – the reign of the 'Greek colonels' – and the brave opposition it provoked politicized her for the first time. 'When I came back to London, I thought, "OK, I've got to be engaged in some way."'

She began working for *Oz*, which had also moved to London. But it was not the radical experience she had hoped for. 'I did boring secretarial work. It was just assumed that women would. I typed bits of research, but I didn't think I could write at all.' A gust of remembered frustration lifted her soft voice. 'I *hated* having to be a secretary. But I really did have a sort of idea that maybe women were there to support men. In the counter-culture we still did all that stuff the men didn't. I ended up having all these crazy boyfriends, and I would be doing the boring job to pay for their creativity. You lived your creativity through the man.' And yet that inequality also felt increasingly intolerable. Rowe paused. 'I had very conflicted feelings that I couldn't articulate.'

She left *Oz* for another London-based radical newspaper, *Ink*, which had a slightly more considered and earthbound political agenda. Yet the gender imbalance seemed just the same. Despite her experience, she worked in production, not editorial; and when the paper acquired some new office technology, three women she had hired as typists were casually fired by the male editors. 'I could not believe it. I knew what some of these young women had given up. I didn't have any trade union background. So I resigned in protest.'

She had no idea what she would do next. For a few months she worked for a literary agent. Then, in December 1971, she and two other women who had had unhappy periods in the underground press, Louise Ferrier and Michelene Wandor, decided to call a meeting for women who had had similar experiences. It was held in Rowe and Ferrier's basement flat in Notting Hill and fifty people came.

'It was like the lid had been taken off,' Rowe remembered. 'We didn't really stay on the topic of work very long. Almost immediately, it was all about how you did all the shit stuff at home . . . about how we supported men . . . There were women who'd had to have children adopted, who'd had to have abortions . . . It was all about the sexual repression in the so-called liberated sixties. But none of us had ever said any of these things to each other . . . We didn't have any language to talk about what we wanted to talk about. The concepts weren't there. Sexism wasn't a concept. We just had to find a way by . . . mentioning experience. This was what consciousness-raising meant. You'd start describing your experience to each other. And then you'd come to an analysis.'

After the meeting, Rowe and Ferrier 'stayed up all night, thinking, "No one will ever speak to us again." That we'd crossed some terrible boundary. We were absolutely terrified, and ecstatic at the same time. It was very strange. And, of course, everybody did speak to us again, and there was another meeting, and another . . .' At the third gathering, Rowe recalled, 'I said, "I think we should start our own magazine."'

Spare Rib, the debut issue of which was published in July 1972, was not the first British feminist magazine of the era. A loose but rapidly expanding federation of women's groups called the London Women's Liberation Workshop had been producing *Shrew*, basic-looking and fierce in tone, and originally called *Bird* and then *Harpie's Bizarre*, since 1969. Nor was Rowe and Ferrier's meeting in Notting Hill the first significant gathering of the new British women's movement. In February 1970, the inaugural National Women's Liberation Conference had been held at Ruskin College, Oxford, with 400 women hungrily debating, discovering kindred spirits and daubing slogans – 'Sisterhood is powerful!' – across the university and the city beyond. The following November, a hundred feminists disrupted the Miss World contest at the Albert Hall by throwing flour bombs at the stage. The following March, the first demonstrations for women's rights took place in London and Liverpool, with men and children among the marchers and snow swirling around the banners calling for equal pay and free twenty-four-hour nurseries.

The early movement had elements in common with the Gay Liberation Front, with whom the feminists sometimes closely collaborated: it was theatrical, ambitious and sometimes utopian in its demands, effective in its guerrilla tactics, relatively small in scale. But even more than the GLF, the new British feminism was a profound challenge to the way that the British Left thought and behaved.

Some of this challenge lay in how the women's groups worked. 'We were very conscious of the fact that the [London Women's Liberation] Workshop's structure was completely different from the traditional Left from which many of us had come,' wrote the Belsize Lane women's group, looking back at their late sixties beginnings for *Spare Rib* in 1978. 'Our women's groups were deliberately small and federated to avoid the pitfalls of centralization and hierarchy.' Within the groups themselves, the emphasis on individual experience as the basis for forming political ideas was the exact reverse, in many ways, of how trade unions and other orthodox left-wing bodies functioned.

This was not the only point of difference with the unions. In October 1971, the second National Women's Liberation Conference took place in the less romantic surroundings of an out-of-season Skegness. By coincidence, the National Union of Mineworkers, which was gearing up for its strike that winter, was holding its annual conference next door. 'They had a striptease as part of their socializing,' Angie Weir, who was at the women's conference as part of a GLF delegation, recalled later. 'We zapped [disrupted] that and had discussions with the miners . . . I don't think they were very happy about it. I just remember getting onto the stage when they [the strippers] were on and then being hustled off.'

It was into this world of seemingly limitless political possibilities and difficulties for women that *Spare Rib* was born. Rowe was twenty-six. Her co-editor Rosie Boycott, another bruised veteran of the underground press, was twenty. 'Their temperaments, for the time being, meshed well,' wrote Boycott in her autobiography, characteristically writing about herself in the cool third person. While Rowe was self-deprecating but steely and principled, Boycott was pragmatic and mercurial, a rebel from an army family and Cheltenham Ladies' College who had already networked her way around the British counter-culture. When they were seeking funds and attention for the first issue of *Spare Rib*, wrote Boycott, 'Marsha

. . . joined a consciousness-raising group, attended the political meetings and versed herself in the law affecting the rights of women. Rosie went to a few meetings and a large number of parties and talked the whole idea up to anyone who would listen in the hope that they'd forget her age and inexperience and come over with the cash.'

Rowe got hold of desks and filing cabinets by visiting the offices of *Ink*, which had recently gone bankrupt, before the liquidators moved in. Partly by candlelight – the miners were now on strike – the two women drew up and distributed a questionnaire to find out what other women wanted from a feminist monthly, and from the responses and their own notions they distilled the magazine. 'We wanted to be accessible,' Rowe told me. 'We wanted to do a magazine that was largely professional, we wanted to be in WHSmith. We didn't want to bring it out . . . the way the underground press did, when they felt like it and when they'd got enough material together. We were going to produce it to a regular schedule, have things in it that were readable.' In her quiet, insistent voice, she went on: 'The whole idea was to do this bridging, this dialogue between what most women would accept in a magazine and what we were trying to explore.'

The first issue was dense and wordy, but unlike most underground publications it was clearly laid out on glossy paper. It had a cover photograph of two smiling, natural-looking women, and non-confrontational cover headlines – 'Growing up in the Bosom Boom', 'Georgie Best on Sex' – that could almost have come from a conventional women's magazine. Inside, the tone was sterner but eclectic. There was a feminist critique of romantic novels, a scattering of rude but pointed cartoons, a rather old-fashioned paean to Barbara Castle ('as slim as a girl . . . had a hair do before each battle with the toughies from the unions'), a lengthy article on the suffragettes, a recipe page ('banana and raw cabbage salad') and a supportive piece about a group of women in London 'fighting for a fair deal for women night cleaners'.

The first edition of 20,000 copies sold out. Two issues later, on the magazine's first full letters page, a reader wrote:

Dear Spare Rib,
After unsuccessful attempts to obtain your magazine in the early morning, I nipped out in my so-called 'lunch hour' (36 minutes!) and managed to buy a copy. Holding it proudly aloft I marched back into the office feeling liberated already, but, my boss was paying us a visit and had heard of you also, and the remainder of *my* lunchhour (his is later!) was lost while he was absorbed in *our* magazine. Very flattering . . . but not exactly 'Women's Lib!' . . . Carry on the good work and perhaps one day everyone will know we are equal, including ourselves!
Yours truly,
Elaine Rowland,
70a The Avenue,
Willesden, N.W.6

Not everyone was so positive. Other letter writers, and some prominent older feminists, found *Spare Rib* insufficiently bold. The magazine's launch party was disrupted by members of one of the GLF's more dogmatic factions, 'dressed', Boycott wrote, 'in clown outfits and smudgy make-up . . . "You're selling out," they said . . . "Your magazine is straight and bourgeois."'

There was some truth in this. *Spare Rib* was set up as a limited company with shareholders. Rowe and Boycott were both conventional figures by GLF standards: they both had boyfriends and plenty of contacts outside the counter-culture. For fund-raising purposes, Boycott wrote, 'Rosie had even dragged Marsha, protesting strongly, to see a rich Arab in Park Lane . . . Rosie thought it was fine to accept money from any source.'

Yet to focus on such compromises – or potential compromises: the Park Lane meeting came to nothing – was to miss the radicalism of *Spare Rib*. Article by article, and for the first time in a widely available publication, it laid bare the intricate workings of gender inequality in Britain: the discomfort of going to the pub as a woman alone (all the 'leeringly interested male faces'); the difficulty of being a sportswoman when sports insurers preferred men; the demeaning imagery of women's fashion magazines; the dismal working conditions in women's fashion boutiques; the drudgery of family weekends spent buried under washing and dishes. At the same time, *Spare Rib* suggested ways out: 'Do-It-Yourself Divorce', 'Working Without a

Boss', 'Seeing the Right Sort of Doctor', 'Discovering Women's History', 'Where Can You Turn When Criminal Assault Happens at Home?' And the magazine brought news from around Britain of a spreading wave of women's revolts. In June 1973, it reported,

Twenty mothers sat on playground swings and roundabouts stopping work from starting on the £6m Teeside Parkway road. They were protesting at a plan to turn the play area at Longbank estate, Ormesby into a compound for machinery. [In response] the council has suggested that the playground be resited in an area of the residents' own choice. They also pledged to rebuild the original play area when road works end . . .

This irreverent new politics was focused on the everyday and the local. 'I thought that people involved in big party politics were a bit irrelevant,' said Rowe. 'I thought, "What's happening that's real is what's on the ground."' And this new politics was as critical of the British state and its paternalistic assumptions as it was of male-dominated trade unions. After all, women had played little part so far in the post-war 'consensus'. Senior civil servants were almost always men. In the early seventies, there had never been a female party leader, let alone a female prime minister. *Spare Rib* may have praised Barbara Castle, but it also had to note that she 'lost the war' when she took on the unions. At the 1970 general election, only twenty-six women had made it into the Commons, less than a twentieth of the total number of MPs. At the February 1974 election, despite the prominence of the women's movement, the number dropped to twenty-three.

Yet while the new feminists felt justifiably alienated by the post-war consensus – and were one of the decade's first significant rebellions against it – they also shared some of its optimistic assumptions. Their movement had crystallized in Britain in the years before the oil crisis and the turmoil of the mid-seventies. 'Women's demands were formulated at a time when the economy was relatively healthy,' write Anna Coote and Beatrix Campbell. Arguments about equality in the workplace, for example, were made on the basis that women ought to share more fairly in this prosperity. How women might be better protected when and if this economic growth went into reverse was less discussed. When the unemployment rate surged in the mid-seventies, proportionally more women than men lost their jobs. Similarly, the feminist critique of the welfare state assumed that the government would continue to provide; it should simply do so with more sensitivity to women's needs. In practice, this was likely to mean more generously: the free twenty-four-hour nurseries demanded on the first march for women's rights would cost a lot of money. 'We tended to take the reforms of the 1945 government for granted,' wrote Sheila Rowbotham, the historian of British feminism and regular *Spare Rib* contributor, in her memoirs. 'It seemed to follow that only a fundamental transformation could alter social inequality. We never imagined that this was going to come from the right and actually make Britain *more* unequal.'

As *Spare Rib* became established, it started to take on more conventionally left-wing characteristics. In 1973, the magazine became a collective. 'I started going to political study groups and reading *Das Kapital*,' said Rowe. 'I did go to a few trade union conferences. The first one I ever went to, I just thought, "Oh, middle-aged men." [But] it seemed to be important what women could gain through the trade union movement.'

For all the unions' machismo, real and imagined, as early as 1961 a fifth of their members were women. By 1980, the proportion was approaching a third. Women disproportionately did the worst and lowest-paid jobs, so at least theoretically they had much to gain from joining. And unions were potentially powerful political vehicles, for Women's Lib as for other causes: during the seventies, 'Feminists [took] jobs in unions' expanding research departments,' record Coote and Campbell. '[There were] small but conspicuous incursions of women into manual trades, directly inspired by the women's movement . . . into such solidly male enclaves as the building workers' union.'

There was male resistance to this growing female interest in trade unionism. When Pat Sturdy, a shop steward from Burnley, set up the Women's Industrial Union in 1971, the first British union for female workers, 'The established union at the plant was even more hostile than management,' *Spare Rib* later reported. 'She was sent to Coventry by the shop stewards. Called everything from anarchist breakaway to reactionary.' After barely a year, Sturdy wound up her organization and reluctantly applied to rejoin her original, tradition-al union. The male orientation of such bodies can be gauged from the fact that it took until 1979 for the TUC to publish 'Equality for Women within Trade Unions', a charter calling for 'equality of job opportunity for women' and 'an end to all pay discrimination against women workers'.

But the charter *was* published. The increasing number of female trade unionists, and the notions about women's rights put into circu-lation by the new feminism, could not be ignored for ever. The changing nature of the economy also worked in their favour: with male-dominated heavy industry in decline and the more female-dependent service sector and government bureaucracy on the rise, the fastest-growing unions, such as APEX, the office workers' union, and NUPE, the National Union of Public Employees, had large pro-portions of women members and had to address their concerns. APEX campaigned successfully against discriminatory 'women's grades' of pay in several large companies, while NUPE negotiated better rates of maternity pay.

Even the maligned British government responded to the women's movement in its own halting way. Harold Wilson's relatively enlight-ened attitude to gender went beyond promoting charismatic figures such as Castle and Shirley Williams. In 1970, his first government passed the Equal Pay Act, which established that women should be paid the same as men if they were doing work that was 'the same or broadly similar'. The Heath administration that followed made a half-hearted attempt to introduce a law banning discrimination against women, but it was too full of exemptions, including clauses excluding education and training from its provisions which were introduced at the insistence of the education secretary – Margaret Thatcher – to have much credibility. The proposed act died with the Heath government.

With Wilson's return to office in 1974, the Westminster campaign for women's rights regained momentum. In 1975, the Equal Pay Act finally came into force. The same year, the government passed a much more comprehensive anti-discrimination law, the Sex Discrimination Act, which covered everything from housing to employment. That year also brought the Social Security Pensions Act, which preserved women's pension rights if they took time off work because of 'home responsibilities'; and the Employment Protection Act, which introduced paid maternity leave, outlawed dismissal on grounds of pregnancy and gave women the right to spend up to twenty-nine weeks off work after their baby's birth. Finally, the Wilson government set up an Equal Opportunities Commission to enforce the new gender laws.

Many of these initiatives proved flawed in practice. The Equal Pay Act was easily evaded by many employers, who divided their workers by gender and gave each group slightly different tasks and job titles, sometimes with union connivance. Between 1970 and 1977, women's wages as a proportion of men's did rise, from 65 to 76 per cent, but in 1978 the gap started to widen again. The Sex Discrimination Act, in turn, required individuals to prove that they had been unfairly treated in situations – a job interview, a loan application – where the decisive factors were often impossible to disentangle. Between 1976 and 1983, note Coote and Campbell, barely a tenth of the claims made about sex discrimination in the workplace were successful. Meanwhile, the Equal Opportunities Commission was overseen by a cumbersome and divided panel of grandees drawn from both the main parties, the unions, the business world and Whitehall. They were often cautious about women's rights and alienated their more committed young staff. During the commission's first eight years, it launched only nine anti-discrimination investigations.

Yet as in the unions, and as in society as a whole, the political weather in Westminster and Whitehall had unarguably changed for women. The change was often slow, and would remain so, but the world that existed before Women's Lib was not going to be restored.

One sign of this, in urban Britain at least, was the improvisation of a new physical and social infrastructure for bringing up children: community nurseries, one o'clock clubs, toy libraries, adventure playgrounds. Often these were created with limited official assistance and housed in temporary structures – self-built shelters of breeze blocks or rickety wood that stood on patches of waste ground, seemingly held together by little more than rainbow paint schemes and sunny murals. Yet these facilities were places where the grey-brown entropy of many British inner cities in the seventies was first challenged and reversed, and where new, more collaborative arrangements for parents were established. These community projects also proved surprisingly enduring. In Stoke Newington in north London, where Marsha Rowe was living when we met in 2005 and where I live now, most of the squats and shabby terraces that filled the area in the seventies are long gone: refreshed Victorian features and shiny Saabs are more the local rule. But there is still a community nursery and an adventure playground, both set up in the seventies, both a little saggy and peeling yet eagerly staffed and heavily used, within a minute's walk of my house.

'Feminism in the seventies was about all the things that now everyone takes for granted,' Rowe said. As in most revolutions, the gains came at a cost: 'I was exhausted at *Spare Rib*, absolutely on the edge the whole time.' In 1976, after four years on the magazine, she resigned. She carried on doing bits and pieces for *Spare Rib*, but her sense of political certainty, like that of the British women's movement in general, was ebbing.

Like Gay Lib, Women's Lib had split. On the one hand, there was radical feminism and its more dogmatic late-seventies variant, revolutionary feminism. They held that the oppression of women by men was so all-pervasive that only a fundamental change in how the genders related would end it. 'As long as women's sights are fixed on closeness to men,' warned the first high-profile British radical feminist manifesto, which was presented at the 1972 National Women's Liberation Conference, 'the ideology of male supremacy is safe.' Relationships with men, therefore, were at best potentially problematic and at worst impossible. Socialist feminism, meanwhile, saw such thinking as wrong and counterproductive: many men and women were inextricably linked through family or friendship or common class interest. The task of modern feminism, this second philosophy argued, was to build alliances with the mainstream left while challenging its male biases.

Rowe had more sympathy with the latter position. 'I was not a separatist. I was a coalitionist. I was in relationships with men. I found the radical feminists alienating.' In 1977, she left London for Bradford with her then boyfriend. After a year, she moved to Leeds. At the end of 1978, burnt out by a decade of activism, she got a serious kidney infection. 'I was ill for almost a year. I just disconnected completely.' When she resurfaced, feminism felt less central to her: she had also become interested in alternative medicine, in Jungian therapy, in French literary theory. She had embarked – she said this even more softly than usual – on 'a long inward journey. A lot of people went inward. It was very hard and painful. It took until about 2000 to look back at the seventies positively.'

She looked up from her living-room carpet. She was in her late fifties now, a freelance writer and 'life writing' teacher, slight and neat, in expensive black combat trousers and a dash of pale lipstick. She was sitting with her legs tucked up under her on the sofa, wild curly hair pulled back. Like Stuart Feather's, her small top-floor flat was immaculate: cream furniture, carefully preserved thirties windows, a view across a park. Perhaps there was something about people who had lived through revolutions that made them want orderly lives in the decades after. 'I've got a whole cupboard of the seventies,' she said. 'I'm writing a memoir of it all now.' And then, just as she had done in some of the photographs I had seen of the *Spare Rib* staff, she smiled an enormous, slightly intoxicating smile. 'We just thought', she said, 'that we were making our own world.'

10

Get Out of the City

Not all the new political movements of the British seventies were optimistic. Environmentalism was sustained instead by a sense of impending doom. This feeling began to gather the decade before, in books such as Rachel Carson's *Silent Spring* (1962) and Paul Ehrlich's *The Population Bomb* (1968), about the damaging effects of pesticides on wildlife and the dangers of global population growth. It gained political traction in Britain in 1967 with the wreck of the oil tanker *Torrey Canyon* near Harold Wilson's beloved Isles of Scilly, and his government's costly struggle to clear up the toxic tide that followed. And it became an international intellectual fashion by the early seventies, generating further polemics such as Gordon Rattray Taylor's *The Doomsday Book* (1970), which predicted both a new ice age and global warming; weighty reports such as The Club of Rome's *The Limits to Growth* (1972), which would go on to sell 4 million copies and be translated into thirty languages; and even its own popular BBC1 drama series, *Doomwatch* (1970–2), about a fictional government agency set up to deal with ecological disasters.

Some of this eco-pessimism was scientifically rigorous; some of it was scaremongering: 'The children of today's affluent Western societies', warned *The Population Bomb*, 'will inherit a totally different world in which the standards, politics and economics of their parents will be dead.' Often, the new thinking about the environment was a mixture of both. Either way, it found a receptive audience. After three decades of post-war growth, the cost to the planet – pollution, over-development, depleted natural resources – was increasingly hard to ignore. At the same time, the counter-culture and the rebellions of the sixties had accustomed many Westerners to questioning the values of industrial capitalism. Meanwhile, the disconcerting aspects of life in the late sixties and early seventies predisposed people to doomy thoughts: for America, where the new green politics, typically, crystallized first, there was the Vietnam War; for Britain, which soon sprouted an environmentalist movement of its own, there was the prospect of national decline.

As the brother of James, or 'Jimmy', Goldsmith, the restless, politically preoccupied British tycoon, Teddy Goldsmith grew up in the sort of circles where important men pondered the state of the world. The Goldsmiths were a cosmopolitan banking family who had diversified into public affairs and other businesses. Teddy and Jimmy's father had been a Conservative MP and friend of the young Winston Churchill. Jimmy, exploiting the complacency of the British corporate world in the fifties and sixties, aggressively bought and sold companies. Teddy followed a more circuitous route to prominence.

After leaving Oxford in 1950, he set up in business with his brother, but he lacked the focus for it. What excited him was science, specifically anthropology and ecology, not approached in the careful, empirical way he had been taught at university, but more expansively and intuitively. He read greedily. During the early fifties, he began taking notes for a book he titled *The Theory of Unified Science*, which would come to include over 200 words he had invented himself. He began travelling the world to see endangered species and what he reverently called 'tribal peoples'. Rich from investing in his brother's companies, he could afford to – and the obvious tension between where his money came from and his concern for the damage done by capitalism did not hold him back. Teddy, like Jimmy, had the ability of the very grand person to sustain a highly contradictory life.

However, his preoccupation with the disappearing natural world was a lonely one. In the West in the fifties and early sixties, economic growth was the orthodoxy, and his great book went unpublished. Then, during the late sixties, he became involved in a committee to 'save' the Brazilian Indians in the Amazon rainforest. Out of the committee came the idea of a magazine to popularize and develop his brand of environmentalism. Work on the publication started in 1969, and the first issue came out in July 1970. It was called *The Ecologist*.

Its story and significance would be almost as rich as *Spare Rib*'s, but in other respects the two monthlies were very different. While Marsha Rowe and Rosie Boycott's magazine was essentially a grass-roots operation, run by and for ordinary women, Goldsmith's was another important kind of seventies political initiative: a response to one of the era's perceived crises organized, away from Westminster, by members of the British elite. Teddy invested £20,000 of his own money in *The Ecologist*; his brother contributed £4,500. More funds came from Teddy's friend and companion on some of his environmental expeditions John Aspinall, the collector of endangered animal species, holder of extremely right-wing opinions and owner of the Clermont Club, the private gambling venue favoured by the more reckless alpha males of the London business world. 'A few thousand came from other people,' Goldsmith told me airily when we met. 'Some of it came from the son of a well-known tycoon who wanted to be anonymous. There was a fund-raising party at the Clermont. Laurens van der Post spoke . . .'

The Ecologist's early staff gave a seminar about the magazine at Eton. Nick Hildyard was in the audience. 'I was a rebel, taking lots of drugs, and I was looking for an intellectual package that made sense,' he remembers. He joined the magazine soon afterwards. Despite his schooling, he was a little astonished by some of the gentlemen's-club attitudes he encountered: 'The social milieu Teddy was involved with was Aspinall and all that. Teddy would relay to us what they were all saying at the Clermont. That Britain was on the verge of a revolution . . .'

The Ecologist initially defined its desired readership as 'the opinion makers'. Its offices were in Goldsmith's house on Kew Green, an idyll of plane trees and daffodils near the Thames in a prosperous part of west London. Hildyard recalls a sense of heavily subsidized radicalism in the early days: 'Teddy would be getting rid of a house somewhere to pay the next bill.' When I went to visit Goldsmith in 2005, he had moved downriver to Richmond, the next-door and even wealthier suburb. 'I'm at home this afternoon,' he told me on the phone one September lunchtime, after we had exchanged messages for several weeks. His voice was husky and commanding. 'Come and see me.'

*

It was a hot autumn day, of the kind that had become ominously common in the era of global warming. Hurricane Katrina had just swamped New Orleans. As I walked uphill from the station in the fierce sunshine, jets belching fumes passed overhead headed for Heathrow, and the houses got bigger. Goldsmith's was near the top of a slope of Victorian villas, two streets away from Mick Jagger's London residence. It looked no different from its broad, buffed-up neighbours: there were no eco-protest stickers in its sash windows. One ground-floor window, facing the pavement, was confidently wide open, giving onto a long shadowy living room.

Goldsmith came to the door in a tennis shirt. He was seventy-six now, very bony and with a white beard. One trouser leg was caught in his socks, but there was still a faintly messianic strength to his blue eyes. We sat down in the cool darkness of the living room, beneath heavy gold-framed paintings. I asked him about the house. He had had it for twenty years, he said. 'I thought there were going to be floods, so I didn't want a place in Chelsea,' he said with a twinkle. Then the twinkle was gone from his lean face. 'I don't see much of a future for the human race,' he seamlessly continued. 'I think we'll probably disappear in the next fifty years.'

From its first issue *The Ecologist* was tirelessly apocalyptic. The cover photograph was of a man drowning in quicksand, and the cover lines read: 'Population control for Britain?' and 'Can we avoid a world famine?'. Inside were pictures of poisoned industrial land-scapes, breathtakingly severe suggestions for ways out of the planetary crisis – 'why not offer [the public] . . . a bounty for submitting to sterilization?' – and a long editor's letter by Goldsmith that was monumental in its sweep, certainty and sense of doom:

. . . Human societies . . . like all other systems, have an optimum structure that cannot be maintained when growth is too rapid and when they are subjected to . . . the vast urban wastes that we refer to as our cities. When societies cease to display their correct structure they become disorderly . . . unhealthily preoccupied with the petty and the short-term . . . a situation which can only lead to further social disintegration . . .

Forty pages later, in the book-review section, the assistant editor Robert Allen voiced another of Goldsmith's preoccupations: the superiority of the hunter-gatherer phase of human history over what had followed. 'It is still an open question whether [modern] man will be able to survive the exceedingly complex and unstable ecological conditions he has created,' wrote Allen. 'If he fails . . . interplanetary archeologists of the future will classify our planet as one in which a very long and stable period of small-scale hunting and gathering was followed by an . . . efflorescence of technology and society leading to rapid extinction.'

In *The Ecologist*'s offices on peaceful Kew Green, such melodramatic thoughts were not uncommon. Hildyard remembers: 'My sense was, "There's this imminent crisis, unless we work together to change things." That's quite heady stuff.' But there was an awareness among the small staff – made up of long-standing Goldsmith acolytes like Allen and much younger volunteers like Hildyard – that their editor and their publication were also deliberately attention-seeking. 'The writing in the magazine was more aggressive than the feeling in the office,' recalls Hildyard. 'Teddy likes to shock.'

Here and there, *The Ecologist* also contained more measured and genuinely prescient environmental journalism. The first issue attacked nuclear power, citing its accident rate, the possible risk of cancer for those who lived near plants and the difficulty of storing radioactive waste. Detailed critiques followed of Alaskan oil drilling, industrial farming, supersonic air travel and the building of motorways to relieve congestion. By 1972, when the magazine's thinking was distilled into the best-selling paperback *A Blueprint for Survival*, *The Ecologist* was a potent mix of cosmic warnings and factual fuel for future green campaigns. And Goldsmith was in demand: 'I gave a talk to the Liberal Party, and to a mix of Labour and Conservative MPs on Commons committees. Eventually [the newly created environment secretary] Peter Walker asked to see me. I went with several academics. We talked to Walker . . .' Perched impatiently on the edge of one of the living-room sofas, Goldsmith gave a snort. '. . . He affected a certain interest in what we were doing. But the great problem was that our solution was just too difficult for him.' Goldsmith abruptly stood up, began pacing the room and switched to a campaigning present tense: 'For me economic development is a problem and not a solution. The only thing that can save us is the collapse of the economy.' He switched back to 1972: 'Our meeting with Walker – little came of it.'

One of the *Blueprint*'s recommendations was the establishment of a Movement for Survival, a coalition of green groups that would put pressure on the British government to take the measures – from imposing green taxes and increasing recycling to halving the country's population – that *The Ecologist* considered essential. 'If need be,' the *Blueprint* continued, this coalition should 'assume political status and contest the next general election'. The Movement failed to take off: the existing British conservation and organic-farming lobby groups found the *Blueprint* too alarmist and authoritarian, and decided against joining. Goldsmith was undeterred. When Walker and Heath's dream of a streamlined industrial Britain finally collapsed with the 1974 miners' strike, he ran for Parliament in the February general election.

'I had no idea where to stand, so I thought, "I might as well find my father's constituency." I only found out at the last minute that the seat [Stowmarket in Suffolk] didn't exist any more.' He contested a seat elsewhere in the county instead. 'We took hotels in Framlingham as our headquarters. Most of the people I found to help were hippies. Hair down to their knees, heads enveloped in a blue cloud of marijuana smoke. When I saw them my heart sank' – an unexpected note of self-deprecation had entered his voice – 'because these were the readers of *The Ecologist* at the time. I fought on the soil-erosion issue. The desertification of East Anglia. We needed a gimmick, as there were only a few weeks to the election, so I dressed all my hippies up as Arabs. The clothes came from theatrical costumiers in Jermyn Street. And my friend Aspinall found me two camels to ride on.' At this, without a flicker of embarrassment, Goldsmith took me upstairs to his bedroom, which was piled with papers and photo albums and books and files, even on the bed itself. He rummaged around for a minute, and then found an old picture of a cluster of long-haired men, wearing ankle-length Arab robes in low winter sunlight, lifting him onto a huge, hairy-faced camel. Goldsmith's one concession to the Westminster etiquette of February 1974 was that he was wearing a suit.

Back in the living room, gentlemen's-club charm in his blue eyes, he continued his account of the election. 'I used to harangue the local farmers: "Have a look at this camel. In twenty-five years' time, this will be the only mode of transport between Framlingham and Saxmundham." Aspinall sent me friends of his to help, sent me people from the Clermont Club. Didn't get on well with the hippies! Hordes of children followed us around. If children could've voted, we'd have won.' He paused for effect. 'I got 340 votes. I was somewhat dejected.'

But, by the mid-seventies, other people were also trying to establish a green presence in British mainstream politics. During 1972, shortly after the publication of *A Blueprint for Survival*, a small group of work colleagues and friends influenced by it began meeting in a pub in an industrial part of Warwickshire to discuss their fears for the environment. The Club of Thirteen, or the Thirteen Club, as they called themselves after the number of people present, soon produced an even smaller offshoot, made up of two solicitors, an estate agent and his assistant. After corresponding fruitlessly with the main political parties, they decided to set up a British green party. The PEOPLE Party announced its arrival with an advertisement in the Coventry *Evening Telegraph* on 31 January 1973. Candidates were asked to come forward to contest 600 seats at the next general election. In order to avoid an environmental catastrophe, the party's founders calculated, they would need to be in government by 1990.

The over-optimism and amateurishness of the project seemed to outdo even Goldsmith's political enterprises. The PEOPLE Party was predictably misspelled by the press as the 'People's Party' and assumed to be a new left-wing group. The party's chosen colour scheme of coral and turquoise confused things further by coming out as red and blue when reproduced, out of necessity, on cheap printing presses. Goldsmith himself, whom the PEOPLE founders had contacted, became an early member and gave the party his Movement for Survival mailing list. The party held a 'national conference' and adopted the *Blueprint* as its manifesto, with all its electorally indigestible demands and warnings.

At the February 1974 election, PEOPLE managed to put up five candidates, not 600. They did better than Goldsmith: one of the solicitors managed 3.9 per cent of the vote in Coventry North-West, which was respectable for a new minor party, and overall the five averaged 1.8 per cent. But at the October 1974 general election, the average shrank to 0.7 per cent. Goldsmith did not stand at all. In Britain that year, voters did not need environmentalists to tell them that the future was looking ominous.

Yet despite the Arab costumes, the foolish names for their political parties and the overblown campaign rhetoric, the new British greens were not just cranks – or some hippy version of the electioneering pranks of Screaming Lord Sutch. Their critique of the consumer-driven, chokingly industrialized post-war world was a profound and far-sighted one. At a time when the conventional political parties were primarily competing, as ever, over who could best deliver an economic boom rather than a recession, the environmentalists had spotted that man was, as the green thinker E. F. Schumacher put it in his 1973 best-seller *Small Is Beautiful*, 'living on the capital of living nature'. Even North Sea oil, the politicians' great black hope, was going to run out. And although *The Ecologist*'s circulation stayed in the low thousands, during the seventies its anti-urban, anti-industrial ideas reflected and influenced the broader culture.

Watership Down was published in 1972. Laura Ashley's peasant dresses sold in great quantities. Led Zeppelin and other hard-rock bands softened their albums with folky interludes. People watched *The Good Life* on television and spent their weekends visiting villages in the Cotswolds. They tried home brewing. They moved out of the tatty cities to East Anglia and the south-west, the only two English regions to show significant population growth. They talked about self-sufficiency and when the planet's resources might run out. Even at my old-fashioned boarding school in Berkshire, with its courtyard of parents' Bentleys and BMWs, we scratched out essays about the end of fossil fuels in double science.

In late 1972, Goldsmith and his magazine left Kew Green for Cornwall. 'We moved because we wanted to live the life we suggested,' he told me. 'We had a small farm, a hundred acres. Cows, an orchard with fifty-five varieties of apple trees. Few gadgets. No central heating. A composting lavatory. It never worked. It stunk to high heaven! Some guest we had poured a bottle of Chanel No. 5 down there. It smelled even worse!' Up in his bedroom, he showed me some photos of himself in Cornwall in the seventies. His beard was long and straggly, his eyes big and glittering under a dim Atlantic sky. There was a slight self-consciousness to his poses, a touch of the gentleman farmer, but also a pioneer's determination. Behind him stretched endless muddy fields.

During the mid-seventies, *The Ecologist* struggled to reconcile Goldsmith's patrician, sometimes very right-wing environmentalism with the more liberal, sometimes left-wing views of Hildyard and other young British greens, who increasingly saw capitalism rather than over-population or 'social disintegration' as the planet's main problem. In July 1975, Goldsmith's close ally Robert Allen wrote a notorious article for the magazine, 'The City Is Dead', which praised the Khmer Rouge for their recent forced evacuation of urban Cambodia. While acknowledging and regretting that this compulsory return to a rural way of life 'has probably killed thousands', and confessing a degree of unease and uncertainty about the Khmer Rouge's wider intentions, Allen's article was, in its title and some of its seemingly more heartfelt passages, recklessly and chillingly celebratory:

They [the Khmer Rouge] seem to be doing their best to ensure that urban parasitism cannot reoccur. They have closed the factories, destroyed the urban water supplies, and wrecked the banks, burning their records and all the paper money they can lay their hands on. They have returned to the barter system . . . If Cambodia succeeds in forging a decentralized rural economy, it will force us to reappraise the prison of industrialism . . . They deserve our best wishes, our sympathy, and our attention. We might learn something.

In his living room in Richmond, thirty years on, Goldsmith would talk about the politics behind his environmentalism only indirectly.

'There are a lot of taboo subjects that have to be dealt with,' he said, and then, a few minutes later: 'People who think population is the only issue tend to be right-wing. I've always considered myself a . . .' He paused. 'I don't see the Conservatives as true conservatives. I believe in family, locality, religion, in traditional societies very, very strongly indeed . . . I don't believe in nationalization, but privatization can make things very much worse. The problem is not who owns or runs the industries. It's the damage done.'

'I don't think Teddy's a fascist,' says Hildyard, who left *The Ecologist*, finally and acrimoniously, in 1997 after Goldsmith had given a speech to an audience including members of the French far right. 'I retain enormous affection for him. It's just that a lot of his model-based thinking lends itself to exploitation by very authoritarian groups.' Goldsmith was equally frank about his fall-out with his former protégé, now a director of the left-wing green campaigning group The Corner House. 'Nick Hildyard was a very capable young man, very bright,' he said, not acknowledging that Hildyard had since turned fifty. 'He was like a son to me. He lived with me for a long time.' Then came a flash of anger and defiance in Goldsmith's blue gaze. 'He belongs to a cult of fanatics of political correctness.'

From 1975, despite similar internal tensions, the PEOPLE Party made some progress towards political maturity. That year, it changed its name to the Ecology Party and abandoned its coral and turquoise colour scheme for a sensible, resonant green. The following year, it agreed a new manifesto. Out went the apocalyptic *Blueprint for Survival*; in came the milder, more positive *Manifesto for a Sustainable Society*. Rather than a Year Zero dismantling of modern industrial life, the latter argued for 'steady' rather than reckless expansion of the economy, and a green politics aligned with neither the Left nor the Right. The manifesto's unthreatening-sounding notion of sustainability remained the party's buzzword and guiding philosophy for the rest of the seventies and far beyond, eventually entering the language of Westminster politicians and corporations. Meanwhile, the more abrasive energies of British environmentalism were directed into specific campaigns: against nuclear power plants, against toxic waste dumps. 'I remember going on marches in the late seventies against [the nuclear fuel reprocessing plant at] Windscale, getting involved in direct action, sit-ins,' says Hildyard. 'It became more empirical.' At the 1979 general election, the Ecology Party fielded fifty-three candidates, ten times as many as it had ever put up before. Its vice-chairman and one of its main campaign coordinators was, like Hildyard, an Old Etonian, but of a smoother, less radical sort: Jonathon Porritt.

Yet while the British environmentalism of the seventies, even in its most unkempt phases, retained links with the Establishment and the professional classes, there was another potent new political movement, also anti-industrial and boldly utopian, which seemed to have no connection with mainstream British life at all. A fortnight before the October 1974 general election, newspapers and television stations received the following:

ALBION FREE STATE
(a kind of Alternative Society election manifesto)

. . .The dispossessed people of this country need *Land* – for diverse needs, permanent free festival sites, collectives, and cities of Life and Love, maybe one every fifty miles or so, manned and womaned by people freed from dead-end jobs and from slavery in factories mass-producing non-essential consumer items . . .

WE more or less ADVOCATE:

. . . [The] takeover of waste land, waste buildings . . . The 'true levellers' in 1649 grew corn by taking over common land . . . Regular weekly festivals . . . Festivals are for turning the world on its head . . . [for] a taste of music, dancing, love and anarchy . . . Community headquarters for conspiracies and radical activities and family festivities . . . Neighbourhood and workers' control of local factories, businesses, banks and supermarkets . . . The end result being a network (which already exists in embryo) of independent collectives and communities, federated together to form the Albion Free State . . .

There were pages more, of varying punctuation and coherence, concluding with the announcement that 'at the spring equinox, March 21st 1975, from rush hour (5pm) to sunset', the Albion Free State would orchestrate 'sheep grazing and people strolling naked down Piccadilly'.

It was not hard to dismiss the entire document as the wishful thinking of some hippy with a spare evening. Except that, by the mid-seventies, the Albion Free State was not just a phrase; it was one of several labels attached to a large and growing underground movement. And this movement was now coming into the open.

The British counter-culture, as was clear from the activities of the Gay Liberation Front, had not died with the sixties. Instead, it had spread and entrenched itself, often in the empty spaces that economic change or decline had opened up in the run-down inner cities. Ladbroke Grove, Notting Hill, Camden, Hackney, Islington: parts of London in particular in the mid-seventies contained whole dayglo streets of squats – obsolete industrial premises, houses unsold after the 1973–4 property crash – and it was from this milieu that the Albion Free State manifesto emerged. Yet, for some counter-culture activists and would-be visionaries, a city, with its hassle and many policemen, its claustrophobia and commercial pressures – as early as 1972, derelict buildings around Camden Lock, for example, were being converted into antique shops – was not the ideal place to build a new society. What was needed was more of a blank canvas. The revolution would be sown in the countryside.

There had been semi-autonomous, sometimes anarchic 'free festivals' of a sort in rural England – horse fairs, gypsy fairs – since the Middle Ages. From the late fifties, English crowds had assembled and camped in fields to hear trad jazz; from the early sixties, to hear the Rolling Stones and other rock bands. In 1970, these commercial but occasionally lawless events, with their press-baiting scuffles, drug-taking and particular dress codes, began to take on a more radical quality. At that year's Isle of Wight festival, the fences separating ticket-holders from non-payers camping nearby were torn down and the crowd became one. The same summer saw the first large, intentionally free festival, held outside the not very anarchic Sussex town of Worthing. As well as free music, there was free food and, in the festival's latter stages, free drugs. A whole rebellious subculture was forming which established its own temporary utopias – the Worthing festival was called Phun City – and rejected the norms of capitalism and the existing legal limits to pleasure.

In 1971, 10,000 people attended the first free festival at Glastonbury. In 1972, the free-festival movement selected a more politically charged site: Windsor Great Park, right below Windsor Castle, once common land but long since part of the Crown Estate. Led by William Ubique (or 'Ubi') Dwyer, a former civil servant who had become a formidable counter-culture activist and LSD enthusiast, a 'Rent Strike People's Festival' was planned for the August Bank Holiday weekend. No permission was sought from the Crown Estate commissioners, who promptly issued a banning order. Regardless, Dwyer had 100,000 promotional leaflets printed. 'The festival will finish,' the leaflets promised, or threatened, 'when those attending so decide.'

In the event, only 700 people turned up and were almost outnumbered by policemen. The festival ended quickly and without trouble. The following year, Dwyer tried again. Again the Crown Estate forbade a Windsor festival. Again Dwyer sought to provoke: 'The festival . . . is a revolution,' he told the Windsor *Express*. 'We want a new society . . . We want to replace the family with the commune. We want to stop all rent paying. It is a feudal relic from William the Conqueror . . .' This time, between 10,000 and 20,000 people came, and stayed for nine days. The policing was more aggressive, as was the response to it. Almost 300 people were arrested for drugs offences, officers were abused and threatened, and a police van was attacked. Only a shortage of policemen stopped the site being cleared by force.

In 1974, the apocalyptic year of the British seventies, the Windsor situation slipped from a tense stalemate into outright confrontation. That August, the police, the Crown Estate and the Director of Public Prosecutions responded to Dwyer's plan for a 'People's Free Festival' in the Great Park by considering closing off the site with barbed wire or flooding it with sewage. In the end, they erected a metal barrier to keep out vehicles. Dwyer, in turn, saw the festival as a vital opportunity to undermine the police and the drug laws. As one of his publicity leaflets put it, 'If two people, smoking dope, are approached by the police, they may well piss in their pants from fright . . . In a crowd of 1,000 all smoking dope together, you can tell the police to piss off.'

The August Bank Holiday arrived. A similar festival crowd to the previous year's gathered in the sunshine. There were Hell's Angels and ice-cream vans, bad trippers and children, free food stalls and no toilets. For five days the police kept their distance, maintaining a heavy-handed cordon around the Great Park and searching people as they came and went. A few officers disguised as hippies allegedly infiltrated the crowd to look for dealers. Newspapers and broadcasters, sniffing a story during a traditional lull for news, gave the festival, which like its Windsor predecessors was illegal, increasingly high-profile coverage. Then, the chief constable in charge of policing the event, David Holdsworth, decided he had had enough. 'The 1974 Windsor Free Festival was nothing more than a gigantic drug-inspired breach of the peace,' he told an official inquiry the following year, 'so I changed my mind about containing it and decided to bring it to an end.'

Blearily early on the sixth morning, his officers moved in. A representative of the welfare and civil-liberties group Release, who was on duty at the festival, gave an account in a Release newsletter of what followed:

At 7.30 [we] were rudely awakened by a hammering on and a rocking of our van. I leaned over to open the door, only to be greeted by about eight policemen who ordered me out of bed . . . Various reports were coming in concerning violence and arrests at the far end of the park, so [we] headed off to investigate . . . When we arrived at the middle-park stage, large quantities of policemen were accumulating . . . There were people on stage encouraging the crowd to enact a policy of non-provocation and non-violence . . . The police literally ploughed into the crowd . . . The front line of police had truncheons drawn and were swinging them viciously at anyone who got in their way . . . Bottles and cans were thrown [at them] . . . I immediately witnessed the police grab a man who climbed off the stage. He was carrying a guitar . . . As he was pulled round, his guitar brushed against a policeman who promptly wrenched it from him and hit it against the scaffolding . . .

[Later that morning] I could see that the cordon of police at the top of the hill had moved down slowly, making a clean sweep of the park . . . There were about 15 people on top of the scaffolding at the end, a token final protest . . . While these people were clinging on to the remnants of the stage . . . police encircled it and began to rock it. The structure was flimsy and I was surprised that it did not immediately collapse. I would not have rated the chances of the people on that scaffolding if they had fallen that forty odd feet. Eventually the people climbed down . . . The police succeeded in collapsing the stage by rocking it shortly after.

Some interpreters of the British seventies see the closing down of the 1974 Windsor festival as a turning point, the day when the 'permissive society' created in the sixties reached its limits and the coming moral counter-revolution first showed its teeth. In fact, there had been hostility in Westminster to disorderly pop festivals from the beginning. In 1970, the Conservative MP for the Isle of Wight, Mark Woodnutt, spent two days incognito at the island's festival, dressed, he later told the Commons, in a 'hippy outfit'. He was appalled at what he found. The following year, he secured legislation from the Heath government that required large-scale overnight festivals on the island to first obtain official licences. Other Tory MPs with robust views on law and order and pastoral constituencies that were vulnerable to hippy gatherings were impressed. Later that year, eight of them helped introduce a private member's bill to make the Isle of Wight restrictions apply nationally.

But then their Night Assemblies Bill ran into trouble. Its title, with its whiff of authoritarianism and moral panic, upset civil libertarians inside and outside the Commons, who considered the British right of assembly ancient and inviolable. *The Times* wondered out loud whether the bill might have made the Jarrow and Aldermaston marches illegal. The Heath government, which had initially been supportive of the bill, grew more ambivalent, designating the socially liberal Peter Walker as the minister considering the legislation. The TUC expressed its reservations and, in May 1972, Labour MPs blocked the bill's progress through the Commons for good. Three months later, Ubi Dwyer launched his first straggly-haired invasion of Windsor Great Park. Despite the escalating unruliness of the free festivals there, a significant residue of mainstream political sympathy for such events remained. 'Were the Police Too Tough?' asked the front page of the *Sun* after the crude clampdown of 1974. *The Times* also questioned the police tactics, and rosily summarized the business of the festival as 'the languid pursuit of music and sunshine'. The paper concluded: 'Festivals do tend to leave a mess . . . But they are basically amiable gatherings, which with a degree of tolerance it should be possible to accommodate.'

Starting in late 1974, a rather startling Whitehall experiment in liberal thinking and coalition-building took place. Faced with the prospect of another Windsor festival in 1975 – Dwyer was more determined than ever to stage one – the government slowly, haltingly, arrived at a bold conclusion: the state would have to join forces with the hippies and organize a rival free festival. One of the supporters of the plan was the home secretary, Roy Jenkins. By the mid-seventies, faced with IRA bombs and other worsening forms of public disorder, he was no longer as confidently libertarian as he had been in the sixties. But he remained a liberal where possible – and a political pragmatist. 'A mass pop festival', he wrote of Windsor in his memoirs, 'had been building up for a number of years into an annual semi-riot . . . and causing Prince Philip near-apoplexy.' To avoid a recurrence, the government would provide an alternative, less controversial site and whatever other assistance the free-festival movement might need. Over the winter of 1974–5 and the spring and early summer of 1975, this unlikely, unprecedented scheme gradually solidified. Its backers besides Jenkins included Release, the environment secretary and other notable Labour libertarian Anthony Crosland, and Stephen Verney, canon of the Royal Chapel at Windsor Castle, who combined Establishment contacts with a belief that young people could not and should not be prevented from going to free festivals.

However, for all this lobby group's liberalism and political leverage, it was not clear how it could do business with the slightly bug-eyed utopian visionaries calling for an Albion Free State. Dwyer utterly rejected the notion of a state-sponsored free festival: to him and many others in the counter-culture it was a contradiction in terms. In early 1975, he was jailed for promoting his next Windsor gathering in defiance of a legal injunction. But others in the free-festival movement were beginning to think more flexibly. Of these, the most prominent, and the most crucial to what would follow, was Sid Rawle.

Rawle was thirty, a big, bossy man from the West Country. He had already done a decade and a half in the counter-culture. He had been a Young Communist, an anarchist, a CND activist and a beatnik in Soho. He had been a founder of Tipi Valley in Wales, a famous settlement of hippies living in Native American tents. He had taken part in an even more famous commune on an Irish island owned by John Lennon. In 1974, 'The King of the Hippies', as Rawle liked to call himself, and as others sometimes called him, had helped Dwyer publicize that year's Windsor festival. In 1975, he had been jailed shortly after Dwyer for helping to advertise the next one.

But while in Pentonville prison, he had come to the conclusion that the free-festival movement might not survive further head-on confrontations with the government. He agreed to join a committee set up by Canon Verney to find an alternative to Windsor. He was released from Pentonville and went to see Dwyer in Oxford jail, but failed to persuade him of the radical value of a state-backed festival.

Rawle now found himself, only partly to his surprise, the most powerful hippy in the country, perhaps the most powerful there had ever been. 'At Windsor, Ubi Dwyer was the king of the hill,' he told me on the phone thirty years later, tiny prickles of competitiveness still detectable beneath his easy West Country burr. 'I didn't realize it at the time, but I ran a sort of coup.' A minute later, he added with more obvious relish: 'In 1975, we had the government by the balls.'

He was living in the Forest of Dean in Gloucestershire now, one of the few corners of southern England still remote and cheap enough for an uncompromised old hippy. One November morning, I drove there from London. After Cheltenham, the familiar Gloucestershire of sweet hills and prime properties receded. The road began to rise and twist back on itself and the forest closed in. There were huge, primeval beech trees and clearings full of rusted bracken; grey little ex-mining towns and dripping curtains of fir trees. There was a maze of brown lanes; at the top of one, guided by Rawle's precise instructions, I saw an old green hippy caravan, and then another, and then half a dozen other vehicles, some of them without wheels. Beyond them, half screened by trees, was a purple-painted bungalow with plants tangling on every windowsill.

Rawle came striding out of the doorway. He was tall and red-faced, with fierce eyes and an unkempt ginger beard. He wore wellington boots, blue mechanic's overalls from which a great prow of a stomach confidently protruded, and a small multicoloured ethnic cap of the kind favoured by very elderly British bohemians and jazz musicians. He spoke in a near-bellow, like a potentially belligerent hippy farmer. 'I tend to tell the story of the free festivals very self-centredly,' he began immediately. 'I tend to think I was in the middle of everything and leading it.' Then he ushered me off on a tour of his property. We squelched through his orchard with its medieval fruit varieties, paused at his standing stones and home-made pagan temple, and admired his three acres of winding paths and earthworks. Rawle told me he had once been 'the high priest of the hippies'. Then we went indoors to a long dim sitting room full of rugs and drapes and Celtic knick-knacks. He sat in a deep armchair at one end and pointed me to another.

'In 1975,' he said, 'I was trying to find an acceptable way to do the festival. Bill [Dwyer] wasn't into negotiating. But it's my gut feeling that the government cannot be seen to be beaten by us. Bill said, "You're a traitor, blah blah blah." But I thought, "If we lose this festival, we've lost the free-festival movement." I thought a festival was a way of getting the message over . . . a meeting place for a new culture. I thought it could propagate ideas.' He reached for a strikingly capitalist metaphor: 'I've always seen these things as trade fairs for alternative lifestyles.'

He found the Verney committee a welcoming environment. 'It wanted to find a solution. The civil servants on the committee became habituated to me. My drug-taking and drinking always was minute – I never was that interested. It gives me an advantage in the free-festival context. And I can sway a big crowd. One day, I'm sitting there on the committee, and someone said, "They want to offer you an old wartime airfield."'

Watchfield in Oxfordshire was a windy plateau near Swindon where RAF bomber pilots had learned bad-weather landing during the Second World War. It had been disused and left to vandals since 1946, but it still had a control tower and a huddle of other buildings, and tarmac strips that were suitable for vehicles. It was close to a village of the same name and was still owned by the Department of the Environment – and it was not in a Labour constituency. For Rawle and the large part of the free-festival movement who went along with the government plan, there was an additional draw: 'What we really liked was that [from there] we could see the white horse at Uffington. We said, "That's a sign."'

In late July, the government announced that a festival would be held at Watchfield. It would take place in less than four weeks – not long for any opposition to the event to organize itself – and would last from Saturday 23 to Sunday 31 August, three times as long as more conventional commercial rock festivals. The Albion Free State had been given a generous showcase for its wares. But getting the gathering organized was still a frantic, ideologically compromised undertaking. 'The government fought shy of giving us any money,' Rawle remembered. 'A big catering company got hold of us and said they were prepared to give us a few grand for the exclusive right to the commercial food stand.' Rawle agreed. 'Then we got turned down for the alcohol licence by Faringdon magistrates' court. We had sold the [alcohol] licence to another big catering firm for 2.5 or 5K. I said to my government minder, "If we don't get the licence, we ain't going to have a penny. I'm going to walk away." We got back in front of the same bench of magistrates within twenty-four hours and were given our licence.' In the meantime, the government arranged a temporary water supply and toilets for the festival. 'They provided huge amounts too much of everything,' said Rawle. 'When we got to the site, there were huge great water pipes all around.'

The approach of the festival was not greeted with universal delight locally. The nearby village was part of a safe Conservative seat. Watchfield had thatched houses, a stone church and 600 inhabitants, including a pub landlord who told the tabloids about his dislike of 'longhaired yobboes' and his plans to 'board up the windows and sit tight until they're gone'. A protest meeting against the festival attracted half the village, and a petition was delivered to the Home Office. The weekend before the event, the *News of the World* reported that Watchfield children were being 'evacuated' to stay with relations, and that pensioners in the village were 'leaving for reluctant holidays'. An Oxfordshire county councillor, Eric Bond, was also quoted: 'Lock up your daughters.'

The most high-profile opponent of the festival, though, was the local MP, Airey Neave. He was a war hero who had escaped from Colditz; a Machiavellian Tory close to the military and the intelligence services; and a member of many of the new right-wing groups and networks, some parliamentary and some not, beginning to form across Britain, from the Clermont Club in Mayfair to Norman Tebbit's Essex suburbs, which were fundamentally against Heath and Wilson and the whole liberal-leaning seventies consensus. In short, Neave was everything that the festival scheme – state-sponsored, almost Scandinavian in its symbolism and permissiveness: a Second World War airfield given over to pacifist hippies – was not. 'The conduct of the government in offering this site . . . is scandalous,' he told the *News of the World*. 'The taxpayer is going to pay and I am asking the [parliamentary] Ombudsman to investigate.'

But the time for Neave's sort of politics to shape British life had not yet come. The same edition of the paper noted that festival-goers had already started arriving in Watchfield, a week early. 'Two girls from Raynes Park, Surrey' had 'set up base in a derelict nissen hut' on the airstrip. Their manner and background suggested that the free-festival movement was both broader and less threatening than the likes of Neave imagined. 'Telephonist Vicki Scorpio, aged 20,' told the tabloid: 'I just hope there will be no trouble. I've come to listen to music.'

By 23 August, the dry grass and shadeless runway tarmac had been turned into a rudimentary town with room for 20,000 people. It had a nursery and an ecumenical chapel; its own radio station and newspaper, the *Watchfield Freek Press*; drinking water and on-site welfare services; camper van and car parks; a covered sleeping area in an old hangar; a giant sandpit, theatre and cinema; piles of firewood provided by the county council; and a 'Polytantric Stage', a 'Rent a Loony Stage' and a kids' play area. Around the perimeter and a short walk away in the village, 450 policemen and a droning police helicopter had been deployed. Seemingly almost as many bands were on the Watchfield bill: Hawkwind, Gong, Henry Cow, Human Abstract, Poltergeist, Wooden Lion, Solar Ben, Arthur Brown, Zorch, Tibet – the whole hairy spectrum of free-festival regulars, from the famous to the esoteric, from sixties-rooted psychedelic explorers to brow-furrowing left-wing improvisers. All these musicians would be providing their services to the Albion Free State for nothing.

At first, the utopian promise of it all proved less of a draw than expected. On the opening day, only 5,000 people turned up, to the derision of the many waiting journalists. The weather was unseasonably cold, with a frost forecast for the first night. The counter-culture grapevine was soon full of mutterings about the concessions that had made the festival possible. 'Almost a year of hassle, barter and disappointment', commented the underground paper the *International Times*, had produced 'a gloriously British compromise . . . A social democratic government has provided a site that can, in many ways, be regarded as liberated territory . . . within the terrain of dominant hostile culture. In some people's eyes, we have supped with the devil.' The *New Musical Express* was ruder and more concise: Rawle had been 'nobbled'.

But as the nine days of Watchfield passed, the unbuttoned norms of a long free festival gradually asserted themselves. The weather got much warmer. Men and women took their shirts off. The encampment thickened with vans and tepees, modern tents and caravans, shelters made out of corrugated iron or opened umbrellas or sheets of polythene. Zorch played a set that lasted from 11 p.m. to 5 a.m. Poltergeist played as a couple had sex under the stage to cheers from the audience. A dog fell into the toilets, and volunteers struggled to pull it out. Someone painted a huge smiley face on the control tower. The Bishop of Reading, Eric Wild, held a service of Holy Communion on the main stage and 'gained a generous round of applause', *The Times* reported, 'for his rendering of "The Lord Is My Shepherd"'. The commercial caterers were accused of overcharging. Chewy free bread was baked in an oil drum. Black-painted spaghetti was offered for sale as acid. Real LSD was in short supply, but a building was put aside for those having problems with it. 'In those days,' Rawle told me with an exasperated look, 'you put all the bad trippers together and created an even worse situation.' Every morning, there were public meetings for people to discuss the festival with him and the other organizers. A unanimous vote at one banned the *Daily Express* from the site for publishing a scare article headlined 'The Festival of Darkness'. There were a few muggings, tent robberies and drug busts. Hell's Angels, as they tended to at festivals, took over site 'security'. The police mostly kept their distance.

On the far side of the village from the airfield, there was a military training college which it was feared the hippies might invade. 'I was a squaddie there,' a man at the bar in the village pub told me thirty years later. He was still trim and correct, an ex-Ministry of Defence policeman, but he remembered the festival with an indulgent smile. 'The civilian police guarded the army houses,' he said. 'Everybody in the village was thinking there was going to be veg nicked out of their gardens. But it wasn't a rowdy pop festival. You could hear the music in the village. There was a bit of wacky baccy, but what's wacky baccy nowadays? We never heard of any hard-drug dealing. The police just slept in the army houses and drank in the mess.'

Meanwhile, he and some other soldiers went to have a look at the festival. 'We walked across the fields and walked in. I suppose we must have stood out. I'd never really been to a pop festival. We said hello to people and they spoke back. They were friendly people, a friendly crowd.' Did the villagers themselves go and have a look? His smile turned knowing: 'Oh yeah. Everybody went. They had to – they're nosy. One lad went to have a look, stayed over. And he ended up going off with the hippies for a few weeks.' He chuckled: 'Good old Arthur. He was a bit of a gullible sort of a bloke . . .'

During the second weekend of the festival, the *News of the World* ran a page of photos of women sunbathing topless on the airfield:

'Lanes near the site have been crowded with people in cars trying to see the bare girls.' Feminism or no feminism, in Britain in the seventies the sight of female flesh in public still turned a lot of people into Benny Hill. The *News of the World* interviewed 'four schoolgirls' from Swindon: '15 year-old Carol said, "We heard they were all taking their clothes off so we hitched a lift to have a look. Our parents don't know we're here. We've never seen anything like it."' The *International Times*' coverage also switched from grudging to excitable: 'Looking out on the swelling encampment . . . all seems worthwhile. Watchfield and its successors . . . will extend the psychological boundaries of our liberated territory as each day passes. One day the whole country will be a free festival, and a permanent one too!'

Even Neave's view of the event underwent an abrupt thaw. On 25 August, a stout fifty-nine-year-old man with a Brylcreemed gentlemen's-club haircut was improbably spotted among the festival crowd. The following day, *The Times* reported:

Mr Neave strolled round the site with his family, watching the bands and chatting to one or two rather bemused festival-goers. 'It is very orderly,' he commented . . . He [also] said . . . that he would like to see a permanent site [for free festivals] . . . so long as it was self-financing, and not an imposition on local villagers, ratepayers or taxpayers . . . His views echoed those of Mr Sidney Rawle as stated earlier in the day.

Civil servants also visited the site and held daily meetings there with Rawle. Lord Peter Melchett, a Labour junior minister who had helped conceive the Watchfield scheme and had now been commissioned to produce a government report on free festivals, camped on the airfield incognito. Eight months later, his working group, which included police and local-council representatives as well as more obviously pro-festival figures such as Melchett himself, published its conclusions. 'Pop festivals', the report began, 'are a reasonable and acceptable form of recreation.' Watchfield had 'passed off peacefully, with little trouble and relatively few arrests'. In fact, far from being a law-and-order problem, such events were of social benefit:

We think that festivals can offer useful experience to young people in living away, even if only for a short time, from the facilities of modern society . . .

People come together from different parts of the country and varied social backgrounds, and free festivals offer a valuable opportunity for broadening personal experience. In particular free festivals give people from inner city areas the incentive to get out into the countryside . . . It is [also] the experience of some members of the Working Group that some of the people who attend free festivals are disturbed or distressed – people who would not normally seek help from conventional sources but many find sympathetic help readily available at free festivals. We think that this ability to provide the right surroundings for such people is a useful function . . .

The report also saw free festivals as valuable cultural events, particularly for the poor: 'People who cannot afford to go to commercial festivals should have the opportunity of attending free festivals.' As for the allegation – for which there was considerable evidence – that much of the daily life of such gatherings was conducted outside the law, the working group shrugged its shoulders: 'Criminal offences, particularly drug offences, will inevitably be committed at free festivals . . . But we think that Government support for an event need not necessarily imply that the Government condones any crimes that individuals may commit while attending . . .' For those in any doubt by the end of the report about where the working group's thinking was leading, an appendix was included: 'What to take to a pop festival'. The advice included 'Wear a good pair of shoes' and 'If you intend to take a baby and/or young child make sure you have all the things that you will need. It may be difficult to buy them on, or near, the site.' The Albion Free State, it seemed, was virtually becoming an arm of the welfare state.

In fact, Melchett's May 1976 report and the idealism-tinged improvisation that was Watchfield marked the peak of Whitehall's enthusiasm for free festivals. 'At the end of Watchfield,' Rawle remembered, 'one of the government people there said to me, "This has been too embarrassing for the government. We are not going to be able to do this next year."' In his memoirs, Roy Jenkins portrays the 1975 gathering as no more than an awkward one-off: 'All passed off calmly. The disused airfield appeared to bore the pop fans and that festival was never heard of again.' In early 1976, before the Melchett report came out, the government announced that it would not provide funding or a site for a free festival that summer, in Watchfield or anywhere else. An uncharacteristically chilly sentence in the Melchett report acknowledged the government's rationale: 'Public expenditure on essential services is under severe restraint.'

In the more conventional Britain beyond the sun-struck hilltops the free-festival movement inhabited, the mid-seventies crisis was tightening. All the Melchett report could offer Rawle and his fellow hippy entrepreneurs was the vaguest prospect of official support: 'There is still scope for considering limited public assistance to free festivals . . . We propose to give further thought to how this might be done.' By the time the report came out, Melchett had been transferred from the Department of the Environment to the Department of Industry, which had no responsibility for festivals.

In August 1976, 1977 and 1978, a People's Free Festival was staged somewhere in southern England, but without government backing and with increasingly effective opposition from local councils, landowners and the police. Attendances dwindled: to 1,000, then 500, then 300 people. Rawle became less involved. 'The government missed a huge opportunity to use the energy of the hippies,' he said, getting up from his armchair and pacing his darkening living room. 'Why didn't bloody Roy Jenkins call me in and talk to me?'

In Watchfield a few weeks earlier, before I visited the pub, I walked out to the festival site. It was late August, thirty years exactly since the last day of the festival. But a business park had been built between the village and the airfield, full of high-tech companies unimaginable in the Britain of 1975. When I got to the festival site, there was nothing but ploughed-up stubble. The buildings had all gone. The closest I came to a relic of the festival was a bleached old wooden box with hippyish lettering that I found in a clump of weeds. The same corner of the site had been leased to a mobile-phone company for a fat humming aerial.

Yet the festival had left more than memories. 'There used to be a lot of hippy travellers on the airfield in the eighties,' said the first person I approached in the business park. He shrugged and pointed beyond the airfield: 'There's still a hippy festival at West Mill Farm.'

The farm was at the bottom of a lane of dusty nettles. The sign by the entrance was also in hippyish letters. Beside the farmyard two small wind turbines turned in the hot breeze. In one of the farm buildings I found a middle-aged man with a ponytail. 'We do horticultural therapy here for people who've had mental-health problems,' he said. I asked about the hippy festival I'd been told about. 'There's a gathering for Druids behind the farm every year,' he said matter-of-factly. 'It lasts for three or four days. It's been going on for years. They never cause any trouble.' I mentioned the 1975 festival and suggested it had established a local hippy tradition. 'That's right,' he said. ''75 was the first of the big green gatherings.'

He gave me a phone number for the owner of the farm, Adam Twine. Twine remembered only a little about the event – 'I was fourteen then' – but he explained that his family had leased the old airfield site for farming, on and off, for decades. His father had been running the farm at the time of the 1975 festival. 'I'm sure he was really fed up with it,' Twine said. 'Dad certainly wasn't sympathetic to those ideals.' Yet Twine himself had followed a different political path. He had become an anti-nuclear activist in the late seventies and early eighties. More recently, he had run for Parliament as a Green Party candidate. Now he was planning to turn the gusty old festival site into a wind farm. There had been opposition from some of the villagers, but he said he was undeterred. The local press had reported that he 'proposed painting the turbines in rainbow hues'. In a stony field in Oxfordshire some essence of the Albion Free State lived on.

11

Margaret and the Austrians

In 1975, Airey Neave had more success with another campaign he organized. This time, it was not against a hippy festival in his constituency; it was one that offered a bigger prize – the Conservative Party leadership.

Despite his general election defeat in October 1974, his second in a year and his third in four such contests, Ted Heath had not resigned. Labour's tiny majority, the ongoing economic crisis and the imminent referendum on EEC membership all helped convince him to continue as party leader, in the belief that the country would soon need him again as prime minister. His stubbornness and self-belief did the rest. But Neave and many other Conservatives were less persuaded. Four days after the election, the executive of the 1922 Committee, the party's most powerful internal body, voted unanimously that there should be a leadership contest.

Neave was a long-standing enemy of Heath: they had fallen out in the fifties, depending on which account you believe, either over Heath's lack of sympathy for Neave's sometimes delicate health or over Heath's poor estimation of Neave's political ethics and abilities. Neave was also a member of the 1922 executive. So was Edward du Cann, another Heath enemy and Neave's first choice as the next party leader, but he was a merchant banker with a problematic City reputation, and he eventually decided not to stand.

Neave's next preference for leader was Keith Joseph. Heath's former secretary of state for health and social security was now an increasingly outspoken critic of the economic policies of the Heath government and its post-war predecessors. Dark-eyed and nervily handsome, Joseph was an intense, brilliant speaker and thinker. He had taken over from Enoch Powell as the public face of the anti-Keynesian, pro-market movement that was building on the fringes of

British Conservative politics. But, like Powell, Joseph was an icono-
clast who did not know when to stop. Nine days after the October
1974 election, with his potential as a Tory leader beginning to be
seriously discussed in Westminster and the media, Joseph gave a
speech in Birmingham, where Powell had made his 'rivers of blood'
speech six years earlier. 'The balance of our population, our human
stock, is threatened,' Joseph warned with similar portentousness.
'Single parents from [the relatively poor] classes four and five are
now producing a third of all live births.' The pro-eugenics implications of the speech caused uproar in the press. Joseph was accused,
not entirely accurately, of advocating compulsory contraception,
even sterilization for the working class. For a month afterwards, he
alternated between trying to explain his position and trying to apol-
ogize. All the while, his reputation for poor political judgement and
intellectual contortions grew. On 21 November, he withdrew from
the leadership contest.

During October and November, other possible contenders were
talked up: confident liberal Tories like Jim Prior and Peter Walker;
the soft-spoken but ambitious Geoffrey Howe, a more diplomatic
spokesman than Joseph for the new right-wing economics; and the
revered negotiator and coalition-builder Willie Whitelaw. Neave, an
instinctive hedger of political bets, and increasingly desperate to get
rid of Heath, offered Whitelaw his services. But Whitelaw, like
Joseph and du Cann, decided not to run. Instead, in January 1975,
Neave ended up as campaign manager for the contender long considered the cleverest but also the most doomed: Margaret Thatcher.

The deputy to the shadow chancellor was forty-nine. She had been
an MP for sixteen years, a minister or shadow minister for fourteen,
and a major public figure since the early seventies. She was a fast
learner, a holder of fierce convictions and a highly distinctive speaker and political presence. She had made her way in a post-war
Conservative Party – and a post-war Britain – largely unsympathetic
to ambitious women and to politicians with her kind of right-wing
opinions. She understood much better than Joseph and Powell the
value of sometimes being patient or pragmatic. She had a growing

number of admirers in Westminster and the media, and was not closely associated with Heath.

Yet all these assets seemed to be far outweighed by her liabilities. To many, Margaret Thatcher was little more than a curiosity or an under-performing, ageing political prodigy. Her record as a minister was modest. She had held only one Cabinet position, education secretary between 1970 and 1974. During that time, she had disappointed her right-wing allies by failing to slow the expansion of comprehensive education and education spending. She had also failed to oppose the panicky lurch to the left of Heath's economic policy. An isolated and uninfluential figure in the Cabinet, her high profile outside it both at the time and since was in some ways closer to notoriety. In 1971, she had abolished free school milk for children aged seven to eleven and acquired an enduring nickname: 'Margaret Thatcher Milk Snatcher'. That year, the *Sun* called her 'The Most Unpopular Woman in Britain'.

There was often a crude misogyny behind how she was regarded, but in Britain in the seventies – and afterwards – for all the impetus of women's lib, misogyny remained a potent political and electoral force. And besides, when newspapers and the public did express enthusiasm for the prospect of a female prime minister, they often preferred Shirley Williams, with her easy warmth and unstyled air, her seemingly modern informality, to the colder, more old-fashioned-looking Conservative with her buttoned-up suits and big fixed smile. Margaret Thatcher was, essentially, not easy to be around: 'Thatcher was always tiresome,' remembers the political journalist Michael White, who spent a lot of time with her in the seventies. 'There was no romance, no self-analysis, no self-consciously epic quality like you would have got with Churchill.' In character, Thatcher the brilliant, chilly loner was like Heath in some ways, and by the autumn of 1974 many Tories thought they had had enough of that sort of leader. And even more than Heath, she lacked the class background and manner of a traditional Conservative grandee. In September, *The Times* published a quote from Powell that was close to the consensus view on her chances of leading the party: 'They would never put up with those hats or that accent.'

Contests for party leaderships, however, are rarely about ideal can-

didates. They are about who is bold enough to stand. On 21
November, Thatcher recalls in the first volume of her autobiography,
The Path to Power,

. . . I was working in my room in the House, briefing myself on the Finance
Bill, when the telephone rang. It was Keith [Joseph] . . . he had something he
wanted to come along and tell me. As soon as he entered, I could see it was
serious. He told me: 'I am sorry, I just can't run. Ever since I made that
[Birmingham] speech the press have been outside my house . . .' I was on the
edge of despair. We just could not abandon the Party and the country to Ted
[Heath]'s brand of politics. I heard myself saying: 'Look, Keith, if you're not
going to stand, I will . . .'

Her campaign began slowly. Until the end of the year, she insisted
that she would only formally stand against Heath – the vote was not
until February – if no one else did. It was widely assumed that this
seemingly tentative challenge would prompt a stronger candidate to
declare himself. And when no such figure did, it was widely assumed
that Heath, damaged as he was, would win by default. Polls showed
that Conservative voters preferred him; so did most of the shadow
cabinet; so did the Conservative Party in the Lords and in the constituencies.

Yet in reality these groups were either marginal or irrelevant to the
coming contest. Under the rules of Tory leadership races, which had
recently, with the party in a restive phase, been subtly but significantly tilted against incumbents, Conservative MPs alone decided the
fates of candidates. In February 1975, there were 277 Tory MPs.
Being chosen as leader required the support of a majority – a minimum of 139 votes – and also a victory margin over your nearest rival
of 15 per cent of the parliamentary party, or forty-two votes. If this
demanding electoral arithmetic produced no clear winner, further
rounds of voting would be held until one emerged. In effect, any significant degree of support for an alternative to Heath, plus a
reasonable number of abstentions, would prevent him winning a
clear victory and leave the wounded Tory leader at the mercy of a
second ballot.

Heath's position was further weakened by the ineptness of his
campaign. At times, it was gratingly overconfident, with his

lieutenants boasting publicly that he had the support of more than enough MPs to win comfortably on the first ballot; at others, it seemed clumsily, vulnerably eager to please, with the usually aloof Heath suddenly buying drinks in the Commons and holding awkward dinner parties for Tory MPs. By contrast, Thatcher's campaign quietly acquired momentum. Neave and Thatcher had known each other since the early fifties, when they had both been parliamentary candidates. Unlike her, he had spent the intervening decades carefully building Commons alliances and gathering information about fellow MPs. He knew who might be persuaded to support her, and who might be the best person to do the persuading. Sometimes it was himself; sometimes it was an MP already friendly with the intended convert; and sometimes it was Thatcher herself, low-voiced and ready to listen, more patient and less abrasive in private than she usually was in public.

While this discreet lobbying went on, Neave slyly played down her rising levels of support. He told potential backers that she was performing respectably but not strongly enough to defeat Heath. The implication was that MPs could use her candidacy either to teach Heath a lesson and make him behave better as leader in future, or simply to force a second ballot, at which point the rules still permitted other candidates to enter the race.

Thatcher also gathered votes by more straightforward means. In a Commons debate on inheritance tax in mid-January, she made a calculated and effective attack on one of Labour's most formidable public speakers, the chancellor Denis Healey: 'Some Chancellors are macro-economic. Other Chancellors are fiscal. This one is just plain cheap.' And she gave a glimpse of the new thinking she intended to bring to the Conservative Party. 'The future of freedom', she declared ambitiously, 'is inseparable from a wide distribution of private property among the people, not concentrating it in the hands of politicians.' In an article for the *Daily Telegraph* nine days later, she was more expansive:

I was attacked [as education secretary] for fighting a rear-guard action in defence of 'middle-class interests'. The same accusation is levelled at me now . . . Well, if 'middle-class values' include the encouragement of variety and individual choice, the provision of fair incentives and rewards for skill and hard work, the maintenance of effective barriers against the excessive power of the state . . . then they are certainly what I am trying to defend . . . If a Tory does not believe that private property is one of the main bulwarks of individual freedom, then he had better become a socialist and have done with it. Indeed one of the reasons for our electoral failure is that people believe too many Conservatives *have* become socialists already . . . Why should anyone support a party that seems to have the courage of no convictions?

This kind of confidence and aggression, of clarity and ideological frankness, had not been displayed in combination by a senior Tory for decades. Five days later, on 4 February, the first ballot for the party leadership took place. Heath got 119 votes and Thatcher 130. Heath resigned immediately, and it was announced that a second ballot would take place a week later, and that Willie Whitelaw, Geoffrey Howe, Jim Prior and Heath's former transport minister John Peyton would also be standing.

Thatcher and Neave's successful ambush of Heath sent a tremor across Westminster, but only a mild one. In Downing Street, Harold Wilson was with Ronald McIntosh, discussing how best to manage the investment programmes of the nationalized industries. 'While we were talking the news came in,' wrote McIntosh. 'Wilson said that like me he was surprised that Margaret Thatcher had got more votes than Ted. He said that the Conservative Party would not be willing to have her as leader and that Whitelaw would win in the second ballot.' The following day, McIntosh had lunch with the chancellor. 'Healey told me he had expected Heath to get more votes than Thatcher; and like the PM he expects Whitelaw to be the next leader.'

On 11 February, Thatcher beat Whitelaw, her nearest challenger in the second ballot by seventy-seven votes and became the first female leader of a major British political party. 'I rapidly scribbled some thoughts in the back of my diary,' she wrote later, 'because I knew I would now have to go and give my first press conference as Party Leader.' In the Grand Committee Room next to Westminster Hall, she faced a crush of slightly stunned male journalists. Her suit was severe and dark, her hair like a blonde battle helmet, and her answers were disconcertingly direct and short. She was asked, absurdly, if she had won because she was a woman. 'I like to think I won on merit,' she replied. Then she held poses for the photographers. 'I am now going to take a turn to the right,' she advised them half-jokingly, 'which is very appropriate.'

The next morning, the *Daily Telegraph* acknowledged that something momentous might have happened: 'Her accession to the leadership could mark a sea-change.' But as striking as the excitement of the most deeply Tory paper was its use of the word 'could'. For all her fame or notoriety, for all her campaign's public engagements, for all its statements about her personal beliefs, Thatcher was still a somewhat mysterious political figure. She had few well-known allies; she had a distinct tone but not many defined policies; and her suitability for the political environment of the British seventies, outside the peculiar hothouse of a Conservative leadership contest, was far from established. Another area of uncertainty concerned her social position and background. 'Since getting into Parliament in 1959 she had been happy to present herself as the archetypal Tory lady . . . quintessentially southern and suburban,' writes her biographer John Campbell. 'She had a rich businessman husband, sent her children to the most expensive public schools, lived in Chelsea and represented Finchley.' Yet this version of herself, while true up to a point, was far from the whole story. The real Margaret Thatcher was both much less polished and much more interesting.

She came from the East Midlands town of Grantham in Lincolnshire. It was a low-lying, ordinary place – part market town, part road and railway hub, part engineering works – and her father Alfred Roberts was a grocer. She was born in 1925 in a flat above his shop. Fifty years later, as the new Tory leader, she would begin emphasizing these biographical details for the first time: after Heath and Wilson, she realized a modest provincial upbringing was close to obligatory for a major British political figure.

Yet her childhood was more comfortable than theirs in small but significant ways. Her father had started out as a shop assistant, and her mother Beatrice as a dressmaker, but by the time Margaret was born – the younger of two daughters – her father had saved and worked his way to owning three shops, two of which had been knocked together, and he employed staff. 'My father was a specialist grocer,' she wrote later, '. . . the best-quality produce . . . three rows of splendid mahogany spice drawers with sparkling brass handles . . .' In the larger shop there was also a post-office franchise. Alfred Roberts was a contractor for the state as well as the dedicated small businessman his daughter would come to canonize.

He was also on the town council from 1927 to 1952, first as a councillor, then as an alderman, then as mayor. Officially, he was an Independent – there was a fading tradition in local government of not having party affiliations – but his politics were clear. 'The Independent group on the council was an anti-socialist coalition,' writes Campbell, and Roberts's 'overriding purpose in local politics was keeping the rates down. He very quickly became chairman of the Finance and Rating Committee, and retained that position for more than twenty years . . . He established a formidable reputation for guarding the ratepayers' pennies as carefully as his own.' After Labour took over the council for the first time, in 1950, as part of the post-war national surge of support for state spending and socialism, Roberts's political career was gradually terminated.

Margaret inherited his work ethic and much of his politics. She helped in the shop – 'there was, of course, no question of closing down for long family holidays', she wrote in her autobiography – and she helped the Conservative Party from the age of ten, delivering messages for them during the 1935 general election. The reined-in, conscientious quality of her childhood – 'nothing in our house was wasted, and we always lived within our means' – would furnish her with a whole political lifetime of morality tales. Yet she got out of Grantham as fast as she reasonably could. Quiet but self-assured, she studied hard at school, precociously read politics books and the *Daily Telegraph*, and won a place to study chemistry at Oxford. She arrived there in 1943, graduating in 1947. After several unsuccessful job interviews – in her autobiography Thatcher proudly quotes the notes from one: 'This woman has much too strong a personality to work here' – she obtained a job as a research chemist in one of the new British industries emerging away from the East Midlands. 'I was taken on by BX Plastics at Manningtree just outside Colchester.'

What was missing from this relatively smooth passage through the thirties and forties, compared to the experiences of Wilson, Heath and their generation of British politicians, was the decisive influence of the Depression and the Second World War. Bombs fell on Grantham, the unemployed queued outside the Labour Exchange – with Thatcher passing them on her way to school – but her life and outlook were not transformed. She was too young, her family slightly too comfortably-off, and she was the wrong gender to wear a combat uniform. She was not left with the same reverence as the likes of Heath for the state-led, essentially social-democratic way of doing things that had been the British response to the recession of the thirties and the threat of fascism, and which would be the basis for the post-war consensus.

Instead, from her time at Oxford onwards, she began to read and re-read a book that felt the opposite of reverence for the welfare state, Keynesian economics and other such left-of-centre notions: *The Road to Serfdom* by Friedrich A. von Hayek. Hayek's book was published in 1944, and Thatcher first encountered it soon afterwards. 'I cannot claim that I fully grasped the implications of Hayek's little masterpiece at this time,' she writes,

[but] at this stage it was the . . . unanswerable criticisms of socialism in *The Road to Serfdom* which had an impact. Hayek saw that Nazism – national socialism – had its roots in nineteenth-century German social planning. He showed that intervention by the state in one area of the economy or society gave rise to almost irresistible pressures to extend planning further . . . Nor did Hayek mince his words about the monopolistic tendencies of the planned society which professional groups and trade unions would inevitably seek to exploit. Each demand for security, whether of employment, income or social position, implied the exclusion . . . of those outside the particular privileged group – and would generate demands for countervailing privileges from the excluded groups. Eventually, in such a situation everyone will lose. Perhaps because he did not come from a British Conservative background . . . Hayek had none of the inhibitions which characterized the agonized social conscience of the English upper classes when it

came to speaking bluntly about such things.

The Road to Serfdom and its heretical notions caused a sensation. With wartime paper rationing, print runs were unable to keep up with demand. Hostile volumes were published in response. During the 1945 general-election campaign, Winston Churchill crudely distilled Hayek's already pungent thesis into his claim that the Labour Party, if elected, would require 'some form of Gestapo'. But what most of the book's early readers, including the chemistry student and president of the Oxford University Conservative Association Margaret Roberts, did not fully realize was that Hayek was much less of a voice in the wilderness than he liked to make out. He was part of an intellectual movement, radically right-wing in orientation and international in scope, that had been working towards a breakthrough for over half a century.

In politics, with all its competitiveness and restlessness, a set of ideas does not have to have reached its peak of influence for a counter-revolution to already be under way. Left-wing ideologies that threaten or seem to threaten powerful vested interests may be particularly prone to being usurped in this way. So it was in Britain in the late nineteenth century. Just as trade unions were beginning to become properly established, and just as government intervention to lessen the brutalities of the Victorian economy and society was beginning to be broadly accepted, so the first campaigns were launched for a return to a more robust national order. The Liberty and Property Defence League was typical. Founded by landowners and industrialists in 1882, its purpose, said one of its members, Lord Brabourne, was to oppose 'undue interference by the State, and to encourage self-help vs. State help'. As a brusque summary of what would become the modern right-wing mindset, it was almost worthy of Margaret Thatcher.

But the long rise of the British Left and British state had decades to run. Through the Edwardian era, the First World War and the inter-war period, both continued to expand. By the thirties, the Liberty and Property Defence League had disappeared, and the small scattering of writers, academics and pressure groups who continued to promote its free-market values were widely regarded as out-of-date cranks. Yet for these beleaguered right-wingers there was one remaining source of encouragement and intellectual nourishment. In Austria, an attachment to small government and unfettered capitalism endured in the universities. Economists such as Ludwig von Mises were fierce defenders of the principles of 'classical' free-market thought, as originally and famously set out by Adam Smith in *The Wealth of Nations* in 1776. Von Mises was also a penetrating critic of the growing vogue for state intervention in the economy, which had taken hold across Europe and the rich world, among political parties and governments of the Left and Right alike. State planning and capitalism, he argued, were fundamentally incompatible; combined, they would lead to inefficiency and, ultimately, an economic crisis.

This analysis was echoed and developed by Hayek, who was a colleague at the University of Vienna. 'The Austrian School', as the Viennese economists became known, began to attract international attention. In 1931, the LSE, the British university most receptive to free-market thinking, offered Hayek a professorship. For the next two decades, he and a few LSE allies mounted an often lonely campaign against the Keynesian orthodoxies that pervaded academia and government. There were occasional victories, such as the success of *The Road to Serfdom*, but most of the time it was the slow business of making converts and hoping they would achieve influence.

Margaret Thatcher may have been deeply affected by Hayek's book, but she spent the late forties and the fifties taken up with less philosophical matters. She married Denis, a divorced Tory businessman who ran a sometimes struggling paint and chemicals business. She gave birth to twins, the level-headed Carol and the more challenging Mark. She moved out of chemistry and into law, significantly specializing as a tax barrister. And she struggled on and off for almost a decade, until 1958, to secure a winnable parliamentary seat. Only in fleeting moments in her pithy, combative speeches – when she attacked excessive public spending, or portrayed socialism as a threat to freedom – did she reveal Hayek's influence.

A more charming young Conservative would act as the crucial go-between between the party and the Austrian economist through the post-war period and far into the seventies. Ralph Harris was a quick and irreverent working-class north Londoner who had been introduced to Hayek's work in the forties by one of the Austrian's few supporters at Cambridge University. In 1957, another Hayek disciple, a right-wing poultry magnate called Antony Fisher, made Harris director of the pioneering political think tank he had set up two years before, the Institute of Economic Affairs. Over the next quarter of a century, the IEA would act as the ideas factory and embassy of a new British conservatism. Harris would end up being nominated by Thatcher to go to the Lords as Lord Harris of High Cross. 'It was your foundation work which enabled us to rebuild,' she wrote to him and his IEA colleagues a few days after becoming prime minister. 'The debt we owe to you is immense.'

On a sparkling August morning in 2006, I went to see Harris at his home in the north London suburbs. He lived in High Barnet, at the end of the Northern line, among the big horse chestnut trees and detached houses that mark the outermost, most Tory-inclined parts of the capital. His flat was a few minutes' walk from the underground station, but he insisted on picking me up. As I waited outside the station in the sunshine, I thought uncharitable thoughts about the Thatcherites' famous love for the car. Then a brand-new hatchback drew up and an eighty-year-old man jumped out. Harris was wearing a yellow cravat, a pale, wide-brimmed hat, a tweed jacket in a dapper faint check, enormous black-framed glasses and a moustache straight from the forties. As we drove off, he immediately started talking about his new car and, more unexpectedly, about Nabokov. 'I've just read *Speak, Memory*,' he said in a high, quick, infectious voice. He smiled and shook his head in wonderment. A minute later, we pulled up outside a huge Georgian house on a hill. Harris ushered me into a long flat on the ground floor with a proudly suburban cream colour scheme and orchids in the rooms. 'We always have orchids,' said Harris with enthusiasm.

We sat down with biscuits and coffee, and he started by talking about his childhood in Labour Tottenham. 'My family were great Churchill fans, and I've always revelled in being part of the awkward squad. The Tottenham grammar school was right next to Tottenham Hotspur football ground. I affected to be a supporter of Arsenal.' He paused and gave a jolly smile. 'To stir up mischief and good argument.' After studying economics at Cambridge – 'I was already totally sure of the [pro-]market propositions' – he stood as a Conservative parliamentary candidate in Scotland at the 1951 and 1955 general elections. 'I was received as a bloody Tory,' he recalled. 'The atmosphere was wholly hostile to the right-wing position.'

In fact, the Conservatives, while in decline, were still the biggest party in Scotland in the early fifties. But a sense of embattlement, real or contrived, is often crucial to political crusades, and at least when it came to economics, the isolation of right-wingers like Harris was genuine: 'All the most publicized economists were on the left. The Keynesians claimed almighty power.' He leaned forward in his chair and a hint of contempt entered his voice: 'A lot of socialism is fine – well-expressed ambitions, lofty goals. But as for actual mechanisms for operating an economy, to get people working' – he threw up his hands – 'completely lacking. It was a kind of madness! You can't protect jobs that are going out of fashion. It was preposterous that intelligent people would defend this system. It couldn't last.'

By contrast, the insights of Adam Smith and the Austrian School seemed to him solid and rigorous. 'It was objective, the market view of the world. We had been getting wealthier right through the eighteenth and nineteenth centuries. At Cambridge, I had been influenced by the improvements in mortality that occurred during that period.' Harris leaned further forward, and his hand gestures grew bigger. 'The market is at once expansive and flexible . . . It's a marvellous mechanism. It's a cure-all. In the fifties and afterwards, I thought' – he slapped a fist into an open palm – '"Why won't they see it?"'

The idea of the IEA was threefold: first, to propagandize for market economics; second, to apply its insights to post-war Britain's problems; and, third, to make converts. The think tank was unglamourously funded by the large profits from Fisher's poultry business – he had been the first Briton to introduce American-style battery farming – and by donations from other right-wing businessmen, including James

Goldsmith. At the same time, the IEA insisted on keeping its distance from the Conservatives and partisan politics in general, hence the institute's bland, neutral-sounding name and its official status: 'The Institute is an educational charity,' pointed out Harris in a 1977 paperback summing up the IEA's work so far. 'In the early years . . . we reluctantly took and won four legal actions for libel against papers and politicians who mistook the findings of disinterested scholarship for the partisan promotion of interests.'

From the fifties until well into the eighties, Harris's most important collaborator in the production and dissemination of 'disinterested scholarship' – in the form of a near-constant flow of books and pamphlets – was the IEA's editorial director, Arthur Seldon. Seldon was another working-class Londoner and Hayek disciple, yet he was not a Tory; he had previously been a socialist and then a member of the small, frustrated wing of the Liberal Party that advocated free-market economics. He and Harris were different in other ways too. 'Arthur had a slight speech impediment,' Harris remembered, 'but he wrote marvellously clear, lucid, masculine prose. He loved correcting galleys, punctuation, grammar.' He paused. 'I am by nature very convivial. Like to get people cheerful. I work on my quips sometimes.' Residual political tensions also endured between them: 'Arthur believed in fixed exchange rates. I believed in floating ones. He believed in education vouchers. I believed in fees for education. We didn't ever argue against each other publicly. I was perfectly happy to argue for education vouchers in public. There had to be a collective view . . .' Because the IEA was trying to achieve influence? 'Yes. If you were forever bickering over nuances . . .' Harris made a sour face: 'The left wing were always bickering.'

The IEA's books and pamphlets covered subjects from shopping to trade unions to government control of the money supply, and were written by academics, politicians and journalists with left-wing as well as right-wing credentials. Yet there was a campaigning discipline about the publications. 'The titles were always two words, three words,' Harris remembered. And those words, and the words of the text that followed, were always attention-seeking, combative, direct, didactic. This is the opening of *All Capitalists Now*, written by 'an

independent economic consultant' and IEA trustee called Graham
Hutton in 1960:

> We all want to be better off. It is probably the first time in human history
> that everyone in the world wants to be better off at once. So there is a world-
> wide shortage of the things that make people better off: machines, vehicles,
> highways, human skills . . .

Free of the thickets of jargon and qualifiers that usually rendered
economic pamphlets impenetrable to all but the specialist, the IEA's
publications quickly laid out a seemingly open and fresh intellectual
landscape. 'The space devoted to [them] by newspapers, and particularly by the oft-despised popular press,' wrote Harris with
satisfaction in 1961, 'suggests that their subjects have been topical
and . . . attention-compelling.'

The IEA's output was not without its moments of poor judgement
and strained logic. The institute spent much of the early sixties arguing that, in Harris's words at the time, 'fears of unemployment and
widespread poverty' belonged to 'a vanished period', and that the
British economy was therefore healthy enough to be opened up to
more vigorous competition. By the seventies, the IEA was arguing
instead that the British economy was terminally weak – but still in
need of a dose of the same free-market medicine. Whatever the question the institute's pamphlets posed, their answer, it seemed, was
basically identical: less government, lower taxes, more freedom for
business and consumers. Harris did not think there was anything
wrong with such consistency. 'When you have a clear view of the
market,' he told me, sitting back in his chair now with his arms folded, 'you have answers to all occasions and situations.' Was the IEA's
degree of certainty akin to religious belief? 'Yes.'

Yet the convivial Harris recognized that, at least to begin with, the
institute's teachings would seem challenging and austere to non-
believers. 'The free market is rather a cold distillation,' he admitted
in a brief pause from singing its praises. 'Emotion is opposed to the
free market. It's rough and insensitive.' To win converts, the IEA
would need to seduce as well as lecture. It would need to invite people to lunch. 'I thought, "People are going to come to the IEA. They

ought to go away feeling they'd enjoyed themselves."'

Three times a week during the sixties and seventies, at 12.45 p.m. sharp, small groups of journalists, politicians and businessmen would arrive for drinks at the IEA offices. Since the fifties, the institute's premises had moved steadily upmarket, from a basement in Hobart Place in Victoria to Eaton Square in Belgravia to three knocked-together Georgian houses in Lord North Street – in all senses probably the best-connected street in Westminster, only a minute or two on foot from the Commons and both the Conservative and Labour Party headquarters. But the feel of the gatherings remained the same. 'We had a good table, as they say,' Harris recalled. 'A lovely family cooked the food downstairs, brought it to the table. They tended to give too large portions. I used to tell them, "Put less on their plates! We're paying for this!"'

There would be wine and coffee, and forthright discussion, either about the latest IEA publication or with a visiting free-market thinker. To keep things relatively amicable – and the identities of those attending private – politicians from opposing parties would never be invited to the same lunch. Conveniently for busy guests, the whole thing would be over by 2.30 p.m. Refusals were rare. 'The only person I ever remember saying "Do not ask me to your lunches" was a Labour MP.' Harris rolled his eyes. 'A totally uncivilized response. I thought, "Come, and argue it out!"' Occasionally, right-wing guests would be invited for a less free-ranging conversation: 'We had "punitive" lunches for people we thought had let the side down. I remember a chap from the Confederation of British Industry who had embraced [Wilson's] national plan . . .'

More often, Harris and Seldon would receive guests who were in varying states of readiness to become free-market converts. Brian Walden, in the mid-seventies still a Labour MP but moving rapidly rightwards, 'came on condition it would be private. He told us, "Wilson is a fraud and a cheat. I shall deny it completely if you go public. I'll pursue you and even sue you."' Harris stopped for a moment. 'Fascinating chap. Spoke with a strange accent. He became a scalp that we treasured. Later, he would often have our chaps on his television programmes.' There were other disillusioned left-wingers: 'A trade unionist came and talked of the madness of the government building unnecessary steel plants . . . An ex-Tribunite [socialist] MP gave us the phrase "the dignity of choice".' Harris beamed: 'Amazing turncoats! I would call them that privately,' he hastily added. 'They completely fulfilled our expectation that if people thought . . . they would come back to the market.'

However, even among the 'opinion makers' the IEA was focused on, assembling a critical mass of supporters was expected to be a protracted task. 'When we set up the institute, we thought this battle would occupy the rest of our lives,' Harris told me with slightly theatrical graveness. 'But twenty years later' – he suddenly beamed again – 'we had Thatcher. Far quicker than we imagined!'

Along with Geoffrey Howe, Keith Joseph and Enoch Powell, Thatcher began visiting the IEA and reading its publications during the early sixties. First as a junior pensions minister with an interest in trimming the welfare state, and then, later in the decade, as a shadow minister for power and then transport who made outspoken Commons speeches attacking the nationalized industries as oppressive and inefficient, she increasingly echoed the institute's thinking. Seldon wrote to Howe in late 1969: 'She said one day here [at the IEA] that she was one of a small group of Tory politicians like Enoch, Keith and you who saw the value of the market . . .'

A few months later, the Conservatives returned to power and Thatcher, Joseph and Howe were all given positions in Heath's Cabinet. Like the prime minister – 'I had hopes of him,' said Harris, 'but they dissipated quickly' – the three Tory right-wingers proved much less radical in office than the IEA had hoped, and their relationship with the institute loosened during the early seventies. 'I can remember Margaret Thatcher coming to an IEA lunch in the Heath [government] doldrums,' Harris recalled. 'She was wearing one of her spectacular hats. She made a very dogmatic statement about her reaction to people who supported socialism: where was the best place to do their shopping, the Co-op or Sainsbury's? she'd ask them. I thought it was pretty straightforward, direct stuff. I can't say I thought, "This is the woman."'

At times, communication between the IEA and the Tory right-wingers cooled to the point of frostiness. In February 1972, after reading an article Seldon had written about the excessive cost of the welfare state, Howe wrote to the IEA man: 'Opinion in favour of the [cost-cutting] policies you mentioned turns out to carry less weight than militant [public] response . . . to even quite modest applications of those policies e.g. on school milk . . .' In turn, Seldon wrote at the foot of Howe's letter: 'Not convinced by these public schoolboys!'

Thatcher was hardly that. But as education secretary, her first Cabinet position, she found herself in charge of a large and slow-to-change government department to which the insights of Hayek, Harris and Seldon could not be straightforwardly applied. Schools and universities did not (yet) constitute a market that could be liberalized. They consumed large and growing amounts of state spending, with the strong approval of the public, and they relied on members of the potent teaching unions to staff them. In her memoirs, Thatcher blames the alien political culture she found in education for 'my difficulties with the department': 'The ethos . . . was self-righteously socialist.' Her failure to make much impact could also be put down to inexperience and a political skin that had yet to achieve its later near-impregnable thickness: during the 'milk snatcher' row, she writes, 'I was hurt and upset.' Finally, there was Heath's lack of respect for her. When she talked too much in Cabinet meetings, as she often did, he would irritably drum his fingers on his blotter.

In her autobiography, Thatcher explains her broader failure to stand up for the free market during his government with some uncharacteristic self-criticism, and with some uncomfortable home truths for right-wingers about Heath's hold over British politics in the early seventies:

I was not a member of Ted's inner circle where most of the big decisions originated . . . Ted Heath [was] an honest man whose strength of character made him always formidable, whether right or wrong . . . [his policies] were urged on him by most influential commentators and for much of the time enjoyed a wide measure of public support . . . There were brave and far-sighted critics . . . But they were an embattled, isolated group. Although my reservations steadily grew, I was not at this stage among them.

Yet, in one sense, her readiness to ignore the IEA as a Cabinet minister was a sign not of weakness but of strength. By the early seventies, with her strong, unflappable voice and finishing-school posture, her immense private determination and ability to be disarmingly flirtatious, with what her speechwriter Ronald Millar called 'her senior girl-scout freshness' in a political world made up of increasingly tired, older men, Margaret Thatcher was already much more than a vehicle for the ideas of economists and think-tank geniuses. She was a political original, with her own ideas about when to listen to the theorists and when to follow her instincts. At one IEA lunch before she became Conservative leader, Harris told her grandly: 'Our aim is to create a new consensus about the market.' Thatcher shot back: 'Consensus? Don't use that word!'

With the collapse and humiliation of the Heath government in February 1974, the political climate was favourable again to less consensual forms of Toryism, and the ex-education secretary had time on her hands. 'I renewed my reading of the seminal works of liberal economics and conservative thought,' she writes. 'I also regularly attended lunches at the Institute of Economic Affairs where Ralph Harris, Arthur Seldon . . . [and] all those who had been right when we in Government had gone so badly wrong . . . were busy marking out a new path for Britain.'

Over the summer, she also became more formally involved with a new free-market think tank, as vice-chair of the Centre for Policy Studies (CPS). As with the IEA, there was a faintly cloak-and-dagger element to the CPS's activities, starting with its deliberately anodyne name. Founded by Keith Joseph with Heath's permission, its official purpose was to investigate how capitalism worked in continental Europe, and particularly in Germany, where more long-term business thinking and better cooperation between employers and trade unions than in Britain was producing enviable economic results.

In practice, the CPS did nothing of the sort. Instead, it became the base for the next stage of the British right-wing counter-revolution. While the IEA worked to change the intellectual status quo, the CPS took on a more practical role: to come up with radical policies that would get the Conservatives into government and enable them to change the country once they got there. In many ways, the task of the CPS was as forbidding as that of its predecessor. For the first year of the think tank's existence, Heath was still party leader. He and most Tories continued to dismiss the free marketeers as Victorian throwbacks and intellectual lightweights. 'When Keith [Joseph] made his first big free-market speech in 1974,' Peter Walker told me, 'I said to him, "What are you going to do about the velocity of money?", and there was a glazed look in Keith's face.'

Even after Thatcher became leader, moreover, it was by no means guaranteed that the Conservatives as a whole – let alone enough voters to elect a government – would learn to love the Austrian School. The CPS would need political operators with keen minds and sharp elbows. In the Tory politics of the mid-to-late seventies, there were few people, besides Thatcher herself, with a greater abundance of those qualities than Alfred Sherman.

A middle-aged woman with a stern expression answered the door at Sherman's Kensington apartment. 'You know that Sir Alfred is very unwell,' she said. It was a dim summer morning in 2006, and the hallway of his mansion-block flat was heavy with paintings. When the woman finished speaking, a deep silence came from the surrounding rooms. She showed me into the largest. It had leather sofas, a huge modernist glass table with a reading light in curved chrome, Japanese prints on the walls and a view of London rooftops. In a chair facing away from the bay window was an old man in boxer shorts and a half-buttoned shirt. His head was back and his eyes were closed, and his skin was like parchment wrapping bones. As I approached, the eyes opened to slits and, in a dry wheeze of a voice, hard to place except for a very faint East End rasp, Alfred Sherman told me to sit down.

There was no small talk. 'The Conservative Party in the seventies was unimpressive,' he said in answer to my first question, keeping his head tilted right back. 'The whole point about being a Conservative was that you didn't question. Margaret's shadow cabinet – the last thing they wanted was change.' What about Keith Joseph? 'Keith was all over the place. He wanted change, but he was frightened of change. And he didn't want to annoy his friends.' And Geoffrey Howe? 'Geoffrey swum with the tide.' Sherman took a long breath. Was there no one in the seventies that he considered an ally? 'No one. The IEA were in a narrow compass. And they were slightly jealous of me.' Surely he had intellectual allies? '[Milton] Friedman was a good economist. Hayek. That was all.' And Thatcher herself? Suddenly there was almost a smile on Sherman's thin lips. 'She came from Grantham with her mind made up. She brought Grantham with her. I doubt whether she ever read Hayek.' Could any conclusions be drawn from her rise? The smile turned to disdain: 'It was chance.'

Sherman's own rise to prominence as the effective head of the CPS and Thatcher's most important adviser in the mid- and late seventies was a political journey that made hers seem straightforward. He had been born in the East End in 1919. His parents were poor Russian Jewish immigrants, his father a Labour councillor. Alfred – precocious, always certain in his opinions – joined the Communist Party as a teenager. 'As a communist, I learned to think big,' he wrote in his memoirs, 'to believe that, aligned with the forces of history, a handful of people of sufficient faith could move mountains.' When the Spanish Civil War broke out, he went to fight for the Republicans and became a machine-gunner. His faith in communism survived the Republican defeat, the Second World War, and even a post-war period as an economics student at the LSE, yet it started to unravel when he visited Yugoslavia in the late forties. 'Communism as religion-substitute', he wrote later, with typically barbed terseness, 'has the disadvantage of susceptibility to judgement by results.'

The same could be said of free-market economics. Nevertheless, it became Sherman's new creed in the fifties. First in Israel and then back in Britain, he established a successful dual career as a freelance political adviser and polemical journalist, in particular for the Daily Telegraph. In the late sixties, he met Keith Joseph. Joseph was already becoming a free marketeer, but Sherman sharpened up his rhetoric and his thinking. 'I was able to "turn" him,' writes Sherman, revealingly slipping into the language of double agents and espionage. When Heath's government fell in February 1974, Sherman felt that Joseph's moment had come. For six months, the two intense men met and talked, conceived of the CPS and worked on Joseph's increasingly high-profile speeches. Also present and influential at some of the meetings was the iconoclastic right-wing British economist Alan Walters. He argued that one of the major causes of the country's rising inflation was the readiness of the Heath government and its post-war predecessors to simply print more money when in economic difficulties. Instead, he said, the money supply should be closely controlled, an economic philosophy that was beginning to become known as monetarism. Another intermittent guest at the gatherings was Margaret Thatcher. At this stage, she was publicly backing Joseph for the Tory leadership rather than standing herself. But, characteristically, she was eager to learn. And like any ambitious politician, she was keeping her options open.

During this period, Sherman hoped that a series of carefully staged attacks by Joseph on the post-war consensus, the first by such a senior Conservative, would transform the national economic debate and attract attention and funds to the CPS. Over the summer, Joseph's melodramatic rejection of Keynesianism – 'thirty years of good intentions; thirty years of disappointments' – and sudden announcement of his conversion to monetarism began to do just that. Then came his 'eugenics' speech. Sherman had helped draft it, but with reservations about the Pandora's box Joseph seemed intent on opening. Joseph's failure to cope with the speech's repercussions convinced Sherman he could not become Conservative leader, let alone prime minister. 'It was obvious he didn't have it,' Sherman told me, a sudden hiss of contempt in his voice, lolling back in his chair like some predator eyeing a weak and doomed animal. 'Not tough enough.'

In fact, the two of them remained close collaborators at the CPS, but Sherman transferred his primary loyalties to Thatcher. He did not know her well: they had not met until 1974. Yet even before then he had been impressed by 'the force of her beliefs', as he put it in his memoirs, and had been telling prominent Tories he knew that she had a chance of succeeding Heath as party leader. 'Margaret grasped opportunities when they arose,' Sherman said to me. 'She never worried and looked backward.' Thatcher identified in him a similar aggression and originality: 'Alfred had his own kind of brilliance,' she wrote. 'He brought his convert's zeal . . . his breadth of reading and his skills as a ruthless polemicist . . . The force and clarity of his mind, and his complete disregard for other people's feelings or opinion of him . . .' During her leadership campign, he informally advised her and lobbied for her behind the scenes at the *Daily Telegraph*. Afterwards, he assumed a larger role. 'I put the words into her mouth,' he told me. In his memoirs, Sherman offered a little more humility and detail: 'During her first two years as Leader . . . Mrs Thatcher made over a dozen speeches outlining her philosophy and policy prescriptions. We worked on these speeches day and night, particularly of an evening and weekend at her home in Flood Street, Chelsea . . .'

The Thatchers had bought their broad, almost gardenless terraced house just off the King's Road in west London in 1972. After her election as leader in 1975, it would prove increasingly useful to her as a private base and public symbol. Appropriately for a politician keen to associate herself with a particular version of 'middle-class values', the house looked prosperous but not grand or pretentious. Instead of the draughty sash windows and vulnerable Georgian stucco favoured by the capital's swelling left-inclined professional classes, Flood Street was solid to the point of blandness: a squat early-twentieth-century facade, almost characterless clean brickwork, roses in the small paved front yard. It could have been in a Surrey commuter town rather than still-gentrifying and bohemian Chelsea, with Malcolm McLaren and the Sex Pistols plotting a revolution of their own a little further along the King's Road. One evening in the late seventies, Kingsley Amis, then moving firmly and publicly rightwards in his politics, was invited to dinner, along with the right-wing historian Robert Conquest and a right-wing sociologist:

No. 19 Flood Street is one of those neat little joints between the King's Road and the Chelsea Embankment, comfortable . . . and decorated in a boldly unadventurous style . . . I was rather overcome with the occasion and the fairly close propinquity of Mrs T . . . very much a new face to me as to most people, too much so to take in a lot about the fare except that it was properly unimaginative, and, as regards drink, ample enough. The hostess wore one of those outfits that seem to have more detail in them than is common, with, I particularly remember, finely embroidered gold-and-scarlet collar and cuffs to her blouse . . . [She was] one of the best-looking women I had ever met and for her age . . . remarkable.

Sherman's encounters with the Tory leader at Flood Street were more focused but had the same backdrop of old-fashioned domesticity. 'Every phrase, every word', he wrote later, 'had to earn her approval (in contrast to Keith Joseph, who often accepted and delivered speeches after a cursory reading). In addition, she fed us, sometimes preparing the food in the kitchen while talking to us around the dining room table.' On these evenings and weekends, Sherman was often accompanied by Thatcher's parliamentary private secretaries John Stanley and Adam Butler. But he was the dominant influence on her: he gave her one-on-one lectures, he wrote her fierce memos, and he could type faster than anyone else when deadlines and late-night exhaustion beckoned.

However, like most rising opposition leaders, Thatcher had a huge and promiscuous hunger for advisers and lieutenants. Besides the Flood Street regulars, there was Joseph, still a mentor and the free marketeers' John the Baptist figure. There was Geoffrey Howe, whom she appointed shadow chancellor, and who had been a monetarist and a foe of over-mighty trade unions for at least as long as her. There was Norman Strauss, a marketing man from Unilever, who was almost as abrasive and clever as Sherman and advised Thatcher to be a confrontational 'conviction' politician. There was John Hoskyns, sometimes Strauss's collaborator, who had built up a pioneering computer business, developed an interest in cybernetics, the study of complex systems, and drawn up a giant diagram of the workings of the British economy, which concluded that the unions were the central problem. There were also Harris and Seldon, who had long been coming to similar conclusions at the IEA. There were all the less well-known pamphleteers and speechwriters at that think tank and the CPS. There were the growing number of noisy free-market converts working at British newspapers, such as Samuel Brittan, the senior *Financial Times* columnist, and William Rees-

Mogg, the editor of *The Times*. There was the continuing lineage of right-wing professors at the LSE. There was Milton Friedman, their more famous American counterpart and early monetarist, who won the Nobel Prize for Economics in 1976 and was part of the now-thriving international network of right-wing economists that had grown out of the Austrian School. And finally, there was Hayek himself, who had jointly won the same prize in 1974 and who, like Friedman, regularly came to London to visit the IEA and see Thatcher and her court.

Naturally, not all these people agreed with each other or uncritically supported the Tory leader. Some, such as Brittan, were libertarians and anxious about her apparent lack of interest in non-economic freedoms. Some, such as Strauss and Hoskyns, came from non-political backgrounds. Some, such as Howe, were privately appalled at the methods employed by the likes of Sherman: 'too zealous', wrote Howe in his autobiography. 'Good ideas all too often lost their charm.' And, of course, the natural competitiveness of politics and the sheer number of courtiers – by 1979, the Conservatives had ninety-six concurrent 'policy groups' – generated its own tensions and contradictions. Some of these would linger unresolved in Tory politics well after the seventies were over.

Yet, from the mid-seventies on, there was unmistakably a new mood in British right-wing politics: a new set of ideas and a new determination. 'Something had to be done,' said Sherman from his armchair, still wheezing but his diction, as always, clear, hard-edged. 'Britain had a ruling class that was no longer capable of ruling. The whole system, the trade unions, the civil service – third-raters.' For a few seconds, he lifted his head and leaned forward. 'You are put on this earth to do something, and you do it.' Then he picked up a dented old radio from a nearby table and switched on Radio 4 for the midday news. 'I think we've had enough,' he said. Four weeks later, he was dead.

Whether the abrasive new mood of the British Right matched the mood of the country was another question, and it was one to which the Flood Street and IEA radicals had so far devoted little attention.

'I didn't take much notice of opinion polls,' Ralph Harris told me. 'Didn't look at how the public were living.' He and his allies, like most revolutionaries, were in the business of leading, not following.

Yet there were some encouraging signs, if they cared to look. 'Liberal baiting by 1976 had become a major hobby,' wrote Peter York in *Style Wars*, his account of changing tastes and attitudes among fashionable Londoners during the seventies. 'You only had to talk about a social worker or an ethnic print dress . . . to get a laugh. Styles got really tight and aggressive, all the big floppy shambolic post-hippy styles started to disappear from 1975 on . . . [And] the Conservative radicals were sounding really sharp.' York expanded on these observations when I met him. 'People were fascinated by the Thatcher thing,' he said. 'She seemed to be confident, had shiny surfaces. People were very interested in the idea that Thatcher was a good business. She seemed to know about modern spin.' At the same time, Britain's sixties-derived hippy and liberal cultures were seen as both obsolete and suffocatingly ubiquitous: 'In Britain in the mid-seventies, mass hippiedom was all around. Yet the hippies and the liberals appeared to come from another age. A lot of people during the seventies absolutely lost sight of what the [sixties] struggle had originally been about.'

This impatience with the status quo and interest in the new Tory alternative to it was not confined to the cultural and nightclub elite York mixed with. At the February 1974 election, the *Sun*, until then a Labour paper, did not back a party: 'We're Sick of the Ted and Harold Show'. During the seventies, almost all the national newspapers were afflicted by bad industrial relations and the high rate of inflation – the price of newsprint, for example, doubled between 1970 and 1975. Consciously or unconsciously, these problems most likely contributed to the apocalyptic tone of much of their British news and comment. The *Sun* was a particularly troubled paper. Although its circulation and influence were growing rapidly, it had some of the worst facilities for staff and some of the most frequent union-orchestrated stoppages. Readers responded to incomplete or lost editions with letters to the paper full of fury towards unions in general. The editor Larry Lamb, once left-of-centre like his daily, became a committed anti-union campaigner. Margaret Thatcher, a few years earlier the *Sun*'s 'Most Unpopular Woman in Britain', would by the late seventies regularly come into the paper's offices to have a whisky with him after the first edition had been sent to the printers. The Tory leader would be at her most flirtatious and deferential. In return, Lamb provided her with advice about how to promote herself in the tabloids, and coverage so favourable that the *Sun*'s owner Rupert Murdoch, mindful of the paper's many remaining Labour readers, would phone Lamb and ask him: 'Are you still pushing that bloody woman?'

In some less direct, less tangible ways, too, British popular culture was becoming more hospitable again to right-wing conservatism. In 1971, Mary Whitehouse, the founder of the National Viewers' and Listeners' Association and campaigner since the sixties against 'moral collapse', revived her profile by helping to organize a large evangelical rally, the 'Festival of Light', at Westminster Central Hall in London. The illiberal nature of the event – homosexuality was among the 'sins' condemned from the stage – provoked a typically ingenious counter-demonstration by the GLF, including the infiltration of the hall by activists dressed as nuns, who kissed and released mice in the aisles. But Whitehouse was not deterred and, as the decade went on, and 'the permissive society' became a steadily more common term of abuse, it grew harder to say whether she represented the last of an old sensibility or the beginning of a new one. With her starchy appearance, Midlands origins and utter relentlessness, Whitehouse was even a little like an older, primmer Margaret Thatcher. In 1977, after *Gay News* published a poem about a Roman centurion's love for Jesus, Whitehouse became the first person for over fifty years to successfully sue for blasphemous libel. The jury split ten to two in her favour, and she won again in the House of Lords when *Gay News* appealed. The carefree iconoclasm of the early days of gay liberation suddenly seemed from another age.

There were other straws in the wind. In 1976, two non-traditional art exhibits at state-owned galleries attracted hostility on a scale that felt significant and political. At the Tate, a low, rectangular arrangement of 120 bricks by the American sculptor Carl Andre, ten years old and quietly titled *Equivalent VIII*, was vandalized and condemned by the tabloids as a decadent waste of taxpayers' money. At the Institute of Contemporary Arts, the more obviously provocative *Prostitution* by the artists' collective COUM Transmissions, which included used sanitary towels and pictures of a member of COUM in porn magazines, became an overheated metaphor in newspaper editorials about Britain's economic and spiritual decline. The Conservative MP Nicholas Fairbairn denounced COUM as 'Wreckers of Civilization'. And, as with 'the Tate bricks', the fact that a challenging artwork had obtained government assistance received particular condemnation. Since the early sixties, the British state had steadily become more liberal in many ways. Now, limits to that permissiveness seemed to be being set by the media and the broader culture.

A disenchantment with liberalism and a fascination with something fiercer began to show up everywhere, from comics – *2000AD*'s strip about a lantern-jawed, semi-fascist lawman of the future, Judge Dredd, which started in 1977 – to prime-time television dramas. In the hugely popular cop series *The Sweeney*, first broadcast between 1975 and 1978, the central theme, always there amid the screech of brakes and beery backchat, was the need for the police to get round the rules imposed on them by decades of soft-hearted bureaucrats: to put the fear of God into criminals again, take part in gun battles, behave like a gang themselves. And there was often time as well for a little bleak comment on other issues. As one of the detectives put it in the third series, like Hayek in a laddish brown leather jacket, 'What's inflation going to do to your cut by 2001?'

But the most promising evidence of all for a political sea change was the number of prominent converts to the Tory cause. By 1978, there were enough defectors from the Left for their stories to fill a book, *Right Turn*, edited by the Conservative MP Patrick Cormack. They included Reg Prentice, a Labour Cabinet minister only two years earlier; Lord Chalfont, a Labour minister in the sixties and, until 1974, a Labour peer; the ubiquitous journalist Paul Johnson, who had been editor of the *New Statesman* from 1965 to 1970; Kingsley Amis; and the historian Hugh Thomas, a famous authority on the Spanish Civil War and a former Labour Party member and prospective parliamentary candidate.

They gave diverse reasons for moving rightwards. Prentice cited Margaret Thatcher's 'courage and integrity': 'She is making no attempt to offer false comfort and easy options . . . She is challenging the British people to choose the bumpy ride to a free society.' More often, he and the others emphasized their dissatisfactions: at the trade union 'mob' they saw at work in recent industrial disputes; at the whiff of class warfare in Labour's recent general-election manifestos; at the rise of Tony Benn; at the whole recent expansion of the British state – in Johnson's words, '. . . The burgeoning bureaucrats of local and central government; the new breed of "administrators" who control schools, hospitals and even the arts; sociology lecturers . . . so-called social workers with their glib pseudo-solutions to non-problems . . .' Unifying all these arguments, which were not always individually convincing, was the allegation that the British post-war consensus was evolving into a kind of socialist one-party state, the sort of monolith Hayek had warned about in *The Road to Serfdom*. 'The authors of these essays have turned right,' Cormack wrote in his introduction, 'because they believe there is a *real risk* that our society will be replaced by the sort of . . . tyranny that so many millions suffer under, and seek to escape from, in Eastern Europe.'

Johnson, characteristically, went further. One element of this 'tyranny', he wrote, had already arrived: 'the manifest preference' of the Labour government for 'determining policy not in the arena of Parliament . . . but in secret and unrecorded talks with union leaders'. Johnson was correct that such meetings took place, and that they were central to the workings of the Labour government in the mid- and late seventies. This arrangement between Labour and the unions even had an official name: the social contract. But it was not the impregnable alliance he imagined.

12

A Relationship of Forces

In the south-east corner of Smith Square in Westminster stand a pair of ponderous twenties buildings. Seven storeys of dull brick, rows of narrow windows, fussy little columns at the entrances: the offices of the Local Government Association are uninspiring even by the standards of the area's bureaucratic anthills. On a wet February lunchtime, a determinedly enthusiastic press officer gave me a tour. There was not much to detain us. We passed glass partitions, new pale wood, aubergine walls – the bland esperanto of modern office decor. 'This place was in a really, really poor state when we took it over in '98,' the press officer said briskly. 'Derelict. Lots of tiny offices. No furniture. Mess on the floor. We went round with torches.' She raised her eyebrows. 'It used to be a real warren when the T&G and Labour had it.'

Between 1928 and 1981, Transport House, as the interlinked complex was then known, was the headquarters of both the Transport and General Workers' Union and the Labour Party. The TGWU acquired the land for the offices and had them built. It then invited the party to be its tenant. Over the decades the arrangement grew so familiar that 'Transport House' became political correspondents' shorthand for the Labour movement in the same way that Downing Street was shorthand for the government. And for anyone who wondered about the balance of power between the unions and the party, the landlord–tenant relationship in Smith Square gave pause for thought.

During the Labour administrations of the seventies, however, the political interconnections within Transport House became more significant still. At 10.30 a.m. on the third Monday of every month, the top-floor Board Room hosted the meetings of the TUC–Labour Party Liaison Committee. It was a new body, and it oversaw a new and unprecedented collaboration between the unions and government. The arrangement covered everything from workers' pay to state pensions, from food prices to rent. It was known as the social contract.

I asked the press officer if I could see the room, but she said it was in use. Instead, she gave me a photograph. It showed a long, slightly claustrophobic penthouse with panelled walls, high windows and a vast C-shaped conference table. What went on in this space between the Liaison Committee's half-dozen union leaders and half-dozen Labour ministers has not had a good press. This entry for 22 April 1974 from the diary of Barbara Castle, then the social services secretary, is typical:

Up to London early for a meeting of the Liaison Committee . . . The two sides faced each other across that rather bleak boardroom at Transport House which makes it so difficult to engender enthusiastic intimacy. The TUC anyway are hardly noted for forthcoming enthusiasm at the best of times . . .

Shirley Williams, another member of Harold Wilson's seventies Cabinet with reservations about the unions, was also on the committee. 'I thought the whole idea of the Liaison Committee was a big mistake,' she told me. 'On constitutional grounds – that union leaders, people with outside interests, should be able to veto things that the government wanted. The meetings were very dull most of the time. I found the TUC conservative, self-interested, fairly sexist, not all that interested in poverty or those not in full-time work. I came away with a slightly stale feeling in my mouth. This was not what I thought democratic socialism was going to be.' Denis Healey just made a face when I asked him about his time on the committee. 'The meetings were a chore,' he said. 'They were often quite difficult.' How did he get on with the union leaders generally at the time? Healey gave a world-weary laugh. 'When I had them to No. 11 Downing Street we used to have beer and sandwiches. But Hugh Scanlon [the engineering workers' leader] asked for *goujons de sole*.'

The idea of a 'social contract' between a Labour administration and the unions was first raised by Tony Benn in a pamphlet he published shortly after the party's defeat in the 1970 general election. Relations between the 1964–70 Wilson government and the unions had gone from cool to near-catastrophic, culminating in the public battle over 'In Place of Strife' and the unions' successful rejection of the government's proposals for calming Britain's increasingly volatile industrial relations. 'What is required', concluded Benn in response in 1970, 'is a much closer link . . . so that there is a two-way flow of information about policy all the time. This information flow is an essential ingredient of all systems . . . and it has the merit of avoiding the much-publicised eyeball-to-eyeball crunches and confrontations.'

Benn's vision of a smoothly efficient collaborative socialism – he had been minister for technology before the election – was highly optimistic, and his influence on Labour Party policy was limited. But Wilson's union difficulties in the sixties and Ted Heath's even greater ones in the early seventies persuaded Labour that a new approach was needed. At the same time, the fact that the Conservatives were in office and passing anti-union legislation such as the Industrial Relations Act concentrated minds at the TUC. In 1972, the TUC–Labour Party Liaison Committee was set up and the social contract began to solidify. Its precise terms were vague at first. Up to and during the 1974 general elections, the social contract's main purpose was to suggest to voters that Wilson, unlike Heath, could get on with the unions. Yet once Labour were back in office the nature of the party's deal with the TUC became much clearer. In essence, the social contract committed the government to policies the unions wanted – the repeal of the Industrial Relations Act, increased spending on welfare benefits, state-imposed restrictions on the prices of essentials – in return for an undertaking from the unions to accept modest pay rises, agreed with the government, which would not worsen the inflation rate and the already perilous economic situation.

There was from the start an element of wishful thinking about the social contract. Wilson was weakening as a political figure and had a tiny majority, and many union leaders were hard-nosed and pragmatic. Those same trade unionists were having increasing difficulties with militant shop stewards, and with the pay demands of their members in general. Finally, employers and other business interests were excluded from the whole balancing act. 'The social contract was a godsend device at the '74 elections for beating the Tories,' Bernard Donoughue told me. 'But deep down I didn't believe in it.' Yet in the Britain of the mid-seventies, with a government recently deposed by the miners, with the oil-price rise biting, with near-panic infecting parts of Whitehall and the City of London, the social contract seemed to offer a way out of the crisis. Besides, similar alliances between groups of unions and left-wing governments had existed for years and had worked effectively elsewhere in northern Europe. 'The Social Contract', wrote the trade union historian Robert Taylor in 2004, 'looked [at first] to many observers like a far-sighted and practical arrangement.'

That it did owed much to a dry little man from Liverpool with an unyielding murmur of a voice and an instinctive dislike of disorder. Jack Jones had been elected General Secretary of the TGWU in 1968. By the mid-seventies, his union's growing membership, Britain's largest, was approaching 2 million. One trade unionist in six was a member. The TGWU had long been known for its assertive recruiting – it was, after all, a union for 'General Workers' – and its particularly close connections to the Labour Party, but under Jones these characteristics grew much stronger. As Britain's rising unemployment and inflation made life harder for small unions, which lacked the political and shop-floor clout reliably to protect their members, so the TGWU attracted defectors. At the same time, the TGWU's internal political culture – increasingly left-wing, with a strong leader but few other checks on the activities of its shop stewards – was in tune with the mood of British trade unionism from the late sixties to the late seventies.

In February 1973, the Strawbs, a so far modestly successful folk-turned-rock band who had been around in Britain since the early sixties, released a single called 'Part of the Union'. A raucous, ambiguous singalong that was either a satire or a celebration or a condemnation of union power – and quite possibly all of these – it spent three weeks at Number 2 in the charts. Its chorus and best verses went:

Oh you don't get me I'm part of the union
You don't get me I'm part of the union
You don't get me I'm part of the union
till the day I die, till the day I die.

. . . And I always get my way
If I strike for higher pay
When I show my card
To the Scotland Yard
This is what I say:

Oh you don't get me I'm part of the union
You don't get me I'm part of the union
You don't get me I'm part of the union
till the day I die, till the day I die.

. . . So though I'm a working man
I can ruin the government's plan
Though I'm not too hard
The sight of my card
Makes me some kind of superman.

Oh you don't get me I'm part of the union
You don't get me I'm part of the union
You don't get me I'm part of the union
till the day I die, till the day I die.

When I met Jones in 2004, he was ninety-one, but as he talked about the status of unions in the mid-seventies he raised and clenched both fists. 'The unions were growing stronger and stronger,' he said in his soft insistent voice. 'They thought they could grasp the world.' A few minutes later, he described the British work-force at the time as a 'huge solid phalanx of industrial workers'. And his hands swept the air as if he was a general gesturing towards his troops from a hilltop.

Jones's authority was personal and moral as well as crudely political. He had grown up in a slum next to the Mersey, in a house that was condemned as unfit for habitation the year he was born. His mother took in lodgers: one ended up as a dead gangster in Chicago.

His father drank, worked in the docks and was a low-ranking but committed TGWU activist. Jones himself had 'no more than average educational ability', as he put it in his autobiography *Union Man*, and followed his father into trade unionism and heavy industry. He spent the Depression years of the twenties and thirties finding and losing jobs, drawing the dole and leading unofficial strikes in the Mersey docks. As a shop steward, he quickly developed a contempt for what he saw as the excessive deference shown to employers by many of the TGWU's more senior officials. But the General Secretary Ernest Bevin earned his approval: 'He did not take a narrow view of trade unionism or his duties as General Secretary . . . [During] the abdication crisis Bevin considered that Edward VIII was letting down the country . . . He suggested that Edward was profligate and implied that he was an alcoholic.'

A similar combination of puritanism, patriotism and political expansionism would mark Jones's time as General Secretary. But that was decades away. In 1936, still in his early twenties, he became a Labour city councillor in Liverpool. Then he went to fight in Spain, where he met Ted Heath. He was wounded in his right arm and shoulder, and had to crawl to safety after waiting for nightfall on the battlefield among the dead and dying. Back in England, he resumed his career as a councillor and TGWU official, first in the Mersey docks and then in the Midlands. In Coventry, he found thriving car and aircraft factories and weak union branches, and steadily transformed the TGWU's position: between 1939 and 1955, its membership in the city rose more than tenfold. During the Second World War, with Bevin now minister of labour, Jones also had his first experience of cooperating with the government to further his left-wing goals, winning better wages for local toolmakers in return for recruiting skilled workers for the war effort.

Occasionally, he returned to the rabble-rousing methods of his youth. During one dispute at a car factory in the fifties, he 'lay down in the road and encouraged others to do the same' to stop delivery trucks from entering. But mostly he advanced by conscientiousness and a keen appreciation of the geometries of power. He worked eighteen hours a day. He spoke in an unhurried, level voice as if he expected people to pay attention. He listened carefully, blinking slowly and with his thin lips set in a straight line. There was nothing obviously macho about him: his face was round and owlish, and he dressed reassuringly like a trade unionist from the forties, the labour movement's heroic era. 'Mr Jones must be the last major trade union leader to wear a cloth cap regularly,' noted the *Guardian* in a 1968 profile. By then, already well into his fifties, he was like a very composed elderly uncle. As an unnamed union leader told Stephen Milligan for his 1976 book *The New Barons*, 'Jones has a smile like the sunlight glinting on the brass plate of a coffin.'

At ninety-one, his persona was little changed. The TGWU headquarters had moved from Smith Square to Holborn, further from the centre of power, and was housed in an anonymous modern office block with corporations as neighbours. But Jones sat behind a desk, arms folded and watchful, in the corner office he still used several days a week as chairman of the National Pensioners Convention, an organization he had set up for retired trade unionists. He wore a blue suit and waistcoat, and looked about seventy. His cloth cap hung from the coat stand. A plaque commemorating the service of Liverpudlians in the Spanish Civil War hung from the wall. A sense that his life was part of an ongoing, age-old struggle lingered strongly in the room.

I started by asking him about his first years as TGWU General Secretary in the late sixties and early seventies. 'We had our difficulties,' he began, deadpan. 'With Barbara Castle particularly . . . If it had been left to Barbara, the unions would have been tied up in all sorts of legislation' – he meant the 'In Place of Strife' proposals – 'and the trade union movement could've been considerably curtailed.' In 1969, Jones and his union were crucial to the sinking of 'In Place of Strife' and, with it, Castle's prospects, previously good, of becoming a truly front-rank Labour politician. But behind his desk Jones simply shook his head at her folly and said no more. We moved onto his relationship with Harold Wilson. 'He was a peculiar fellow,' said Jones after a long sigh. 'I never got much out of him. I mean, he wasn't unsympathetic. If I went to see him in Downing Street, he had a little barrel of beer, and we'd have a couple of half pints, as it were. For him, I suppose, that felt friendly enough . . . But he was a cold, cold man, very cold. You couldn't make the measure of him. Wilson showed no enthusiasm about anything. It was like dealing with a rather cold civil servant all the time, which he was to some extent. There was no passion there. Never was.'

In the early seventies, Jones got on better with Ted Heath. Their Spanish link had a little to do with it, but more significant was Heath's unvarnished manner and his desire, intermittently expressed, for the unions and the government to cooperate in the face of the growing economic crisis. The latter appealed to Jones's patriotism and to his openness to political arrangements that would cement the unions' position. During 1972, Jones was a guest at Chequers, discussed 'wages restraint' with Heath, and helped the Conservative government end a highly damaging national dock strike. 'Heath was not unsympathetic to labour,' Jones wrote with typical calculation in his autobiography, before adding with a dash of equally typical tribal sentimentality: 'He genuinely wanted to get on with working people.'

But their efforts to establish some sort of social contract came to nothing. Heath fell, Thatcher replaced him, and Jones, for all his doubts about Wilson, did the deal with the new Labour government instead. In part, he saw the social contract as an economic and electoral shield against the free-market ideas that were now taking hold of the Conservative Party. 'Once you took Heath out of the Tory crowd, they were very antagonistic towards the labour movement,' he told me. As the mid-seventies turned into the late seventies, and the political appeal and right-wing themes of Thatcher's policies became clearer, this defensive aspect of the social contract became increasingly important to the TGWU leader.

Yet the arrangement also had a more confident, expansive side. One of Jones's political heroes was Clement Attlee, whose government he revered for its radical and long-lasting redistribution of income and social opportunity. Since Attlee's defeat in the 1951 general election, Jones, like many in the unions and on the Labour left, had frustratedly endured almost a quarter of a century of less egalitarian administrations. 'We wanted a Labour government that would act for labour, for working people,' he told me; now, with the social contract, he saw an instrument to make such a Labour government a reality. The vulnerable state of the Wilson administration and of the British economy, Jones calculated, only enhanced his political leverage. 'We have a right to expect action,' he told the 1975 Labour Party conference, in a speech that ranged far beyond the usual concerns of unions by calling for more government action on unemployment and restrictions on imports, 'because we are playing our part in solving the nation's economic problems as never before.'

Between 1974 and 1978, Labour adopted a series of Jones's favoured policies. Despite the government's already overstretched finances, there were increases in the state pension and freezes on rents for council tenants. There were state subsidies to keep down food prices. There was the Health and Safety at Work Act, which Jones proudly describes in *Union Man* as 'the most comprehensive legislation ever drafted covering people at work'. There was the establishment of the Advisory, Conciliation and Arbitration Service (ACAS), a body of which he had conceived, as an independent mediator for industrial disputes. More than any of these gains, there was a sense that Jack Jones was making much of the political weather, both in the government and in the labour movement. On 19 June 1974, the *Guardian* diary recorded:

At the Department of Employment yesterday, arriving five minutes early for a noon meeting with Michael Foot, a CBI [Confederation of British Industry] delegation . . . noticed a shiny TGWU limousine parked outside, being given a good polish by the chauffeur. Inside, with the Minister, was Jack Jones, whose important official deliberations kept the representatives of the tycoons cooling their heels for a good 20 minutes.

A fortnight earlier, Hugh Scanlon, who as head of the Amalgamated Union of Engineering Workers (AUEW), was probably the second most influential union leader and usually a Jones ally, complained to Tony Benn that Jones had the ear of the prime minister. 'I think Harold Wilson, Michael Foot and Jack Jones run the country,' Benn replied. Frequently there were rumours that Jones was about to be asked to join the Cabinet. In *Union Man* he confirms one of them, with his usual blunt and impregnable self-assurance. At the 1974 TUC conference, he writes,

Sitting beside me on the platform Jim [Callaghan] whispered: 'You've performed miracles. You should be with us in the Government. You could go into the Lords and be with us in no time.' I whispered back: 'I don't want to go to the Lords and I don't want to be in the Government, but I'll help it all I can.'

Jones's idea of helping out was not always what the government had in mind. In the autumn of 1977, he hinted heavily in the press that ministers and trade union leaders should set a 'personal example' as socialists in a time of economic stress by not living in 'big houses'. The papers immediately printed pictures of the substantial country residences of Denis Healey, Wilson and Callaghan. In January 1975, Jones suggested that ministers should consult the unions in advance before making speeches addressed to their members. 'Far better that they [ministers] should talk to us', Jones said, an air of superiority unmistakable in his tone, 'before they make speeches which are often a little bit away from reality.' He used the same television interview to chastise Healey for calling on trade unionists to restrain their wage demands. 'We worked out a TUC policy [on pay],' Jones began. 'We are trying to apply it . . . I think that's the priority and not some Minister attempting to re-write something that is a matter for the trade union movement.' The fact that in this case 'some Minister' was the chancellor of the exchequer, the second most senior member of the Cabinet and the traditional steward of the economy, did not seem to trouble the TGWU leader in the slightest.

'A lot of Labour ministers were either afraid of the unions or felt respectful of them,' remembered Bill Rodgers, who was transport minister in the late seventies. 'They were older than us. Jack Jones – he fought in Spain. I was a young schoolboy then. They had little education, often. They had climbed up the ladder. Our ministers . . . were often apprehensive. Callaghan came in to see me once and said, "You're seeing Jack Jones this morning. You won't forget about the [Labour] conference, which is in ten days' time?" What Callaghan meant was: "Don't upset him unnecessarily. Because we need him onside."'

Three decades later, Jones leaned right forward across his desk, round face immobile and long fingers intertwined, and characterized his dealings with the governments of the seventies. 'It was a relationship of forces,' he said in his precise voice. 'If government wanted to talk to unions, it was a recognition that the unions must have been fairly strong. They wanted something from the unions . . . And one's conscious of that all the time.' He flapped a hand dismissively: 'I always suspect politicians. You don't become drunk because the prime minister sends for you.'

Did this relationship between the unions and the government feel sustainable at the time? Jones maintained his poker face. 'It was always going to be a bit abrasive, you understand that. It was never a question of, because I was a Labour Party member and a Labour Party supporter, conceding to Labour things I wouldn't concede to the Tories.' His first duty, after all, was to the swelling and restless TGWU: 'If the union membership was strong, you obviously had to get some results from that.' Jones sat back and out came his coffin-lid smile. 'That's what a union's about, isn't it?' he said with a knowing laugh. 'We want more.'

In the seventies, the nakedness with which Jones exercised his power was compensated for, at least to a degree, by the modesty of his manner and by his widely perceived personal integrity. Jones was not an upstart with a loudhailer like Arthur Scargill. Nor was he, unlike some union leaders, and despite his public appetite for TGWU limousines and *goujons de sole*, even faintly baronial in his private life. Although he led the biggest union, he did not draw the biggest union leader's salary. He and his wife Evelyn, a Labour activist who like him had risked her life fighting fascism in the thirties, took most of their holidays in a caravan in Devon. When they went to the Algarve in 1976, on a six-day package in the cheap period before Christmas, the *Daily Mail* considered the trip newsworthy enough for a two-column story with three photographs.

Back in England, the couple lived in a 'one and a half bedroom' flat on an estate in Denmark Hill in south London. He had bought the flat from the Greater London Council in the early seventies – the then Conservative-controlled GLC was a pioneer of council-house sell-offs – but otherwise his home life was plain and old-fashioned. He often walked into work at Transport House. While he was out, Evelyn, who was the local Labour ward secretary, would sometimes arrange for party events to take place in the flat. In the evenings, Jones recalled, 'I'd come home from a bloody meeting with a minister, and the living room would be full of people. It wasn't a big flat, so I'd have to sneak to bed.'

He was still living in the flat when I met him and, a few months later, I paid his estate a visit. I found a hillside of unusually handsome old blocks, with brass fittings on their doors and views of central London framed by rose bushes. There was almost no graffiti or litter; instead, there was a sense that some core of mid-twentieth-century municipal idealism had been preserved. I asked one of the estate's gardeners if he had heard of Jack Jones. 'Oh yes,' he said, carefully putting down his wheelbarrow. 'The union man.' The gardener pointed out a flat with net curtains, a neat row of mugs along one windowsill and a folded-up chair on its balcony.

'I believe trade union leaders should identify with the workers you represent,' Jones told me. 'You're much the same. You're part of them . . . I never moved out of a working-class background.' For almost the only time, his voice took on a slight hesitancy: 'I tried not to, anyway. I had the flat, and I had a council house in the Midlands . . . Other union leaders, they move away from working people – even Joe Gormley had a big house – so their outlook becomes quite different. They begin to have *friends* amongst the middle class. I think you should continue to be . . . with your own class.'

During the seventies, Jones's power and dedicated proletarianism discomfited some. He campaigned for the abolition of the House of Lords. He advocated higher taxes for 'the landed gentry, who don't contribute anything to society'. Some of his opponents in the press took to calling him the Emperor Jones, after the doomed self-made autocrat in the play of the same name by Eugene O'Neill. Other critics found him bafflingly colourless: in 1976, the *Spectator* described him as 'that earnest, bespectacled figure with the curious speech impediment'. In 1977, the Social Democratic Alliance, a new pressure group on the right of the Labour Party – which would ultimately play a part in the forming of the SDP – produced a dossier alleging that Jones was 'a dedicated opponent of Western Parliamentary Democracy'. Between 1966 and 1977, MI5 compiled forty volumes of material on Jones and the AUEW leader Hugh Scanlon, and repeatedly sought to block their appointment to positions on government bodies.

Yet, just as often, Jones received extraordinary praise from parts of the press and political establishment usually critical of trade unions. 'Jones . . . with the social contract, has emerged as a national statesman,' declared the *Financial Times* in 1975, 'devoted to doing what he believes to be best for Britain's workers and their families . . . confounding his critics who had dismissed him as a negative man of the Left.' In 1974, the head of industrial relations at the textiles conglomerate Courtaulds wrote to the *Guardian*: 'Everyone with first-hand experience of industrial relations will agree with much that Mr Jack Jones says . . .' That March, Paul Dacre, the future editor of the *Daily Mail* and scourge of the British Left, interviewed the TGWU man for the *Daily Express*: 'James Larkin Jones . . . probably the last of the cloth-cap union leaders, possessor of a blunt, rough-edged Scouse charisma, is very far from being a monster.' In December 1977, a *Sun* editorial described Jones as 'one of the nicest men anyone could hope to meet'.

In 1975, and again in 1977, Gallup polls found that a comfortable majority of the public considered him more powerful than the prime minister. During the 1974 general elections, graffiti appeared: 'Vote Jack Jones, cut out the middle man.' In 2004, I asked him how he had felt during the seventies about the idea that he was running the country. He looked at me unblinkingly. 'It was utter nonsense, of course. The press are always inclined to simplify. I was reflecting the point of view of the members . . .'

Jones was due to retire in March 1978. During his final months as TGWU leader, his public statements grew increasingly philosophical.

In December 1977, he gave the Richard Dimbleby lecture on BBC1, a rare honour for a trade unionist, and proposed a new model of British industrial relations centred on the election of 'ordinary shopfloor and office workers' to company boards. 'We must develop the idea of the Talk-In rather than the Walk-Out,' Jones concluded, as if a scaled-down version of the social contract could be introduced in every business in the land. In February 1978, he talked more ambitiously still to the *New York Times*. 'There's no use', he told America's establishment paper, in unions 'going after the wage full stop'; the work of such bodies for their members 'doesn't end at the plant gates'. Instead, unions should continue to press as well for a shorter working week, for longer holidays, for 'a civilized life' for 'the working man . . . with a home, time for the wife and kids, leisure, fun'.

Jones did not mention it, but there was a place in Britain where this enlightened vision of working-class ease and fulfilment was already a reality. When Bevin had been head of the TGWU, he had conceived of setting up a holiday centre for his members somewhere on the south coast of England. The scheme was not pursued: the Depression and the Second World War meant the union had other priorities. Yet the idea endured. When Jones became General Secretary, he broadened the project to encompass 'a combined centre for convalescence, holidays, and union education' and began looking for a location. 'Almost by accident, I came across a vacant site on the seafront at Eastbourne,' he writes in *Union Man*. 'A group of speculators had "caught a cold" over their plans for a new hotel . . . The land was to be sold. A "For Sale" sign caught my eye and we were able to buy the site at a reasonable price.' In 1974, he laid the foundation stone, and in 1976 the TGWU Centre opened, a miniature workers' utopia built on the site of a capitalist failure in a traditionally Tory resort town, in the middle of the traditionally Tory-dominated south of England. As a symbol, and as evidence of the unions' advance in the seventies, it was hard to better.

In February 2005, the centre was still open. I arrived in Eastbourne on the coldest morning of the winter, with pensioners hurrying between shops and snow in the forecast. The seafront was deserted:

palms absurd in the stinging wind, grey waves humping shingle onto the beach, an endless succession of white stucco hotels. Gradually as I walked, a taller, more modern, more angular structure revealed itself in the distance, a great dark honeycomb of smoked glass. When I reached its main entrance, there was a salt-stained sign: 'T&G Centre'. Above the sign rose ten storeys of balconied rooms, piled up in the heavy, hard-edged architectural style I had seen in seventies oil-company headquarters in Aberdeen, as if the decade called for fortresses after the breezy glass boxes of the fifties and sixties. Below the sign, at doormat level, was the foundation stone Jones had laid, still crisp, dedicating the complex 'to the working people of all lands'. Up on a third-floor balcony a lone guest, white hair thrashing in the wind, was taking a picture of the sea. Otherwise, the building's brown glass skin hid its inner life almost completely. The first snowflakes began to fall, and I stepped inside.

The lobby was warm and dim. There were TGWU pens and polo shirts for sale. A muzak version of 'Yesterday' was playing, and there was the faint chink of coffee cups. A few men with lived-in faces sat contentedly in deep armchairs. Everything looked faintly institutional but spotless. Then the manager appeared, grey-suited, young-looking but twenty-two years in the job, and showed me into his office.

'This was Jack Jones's brainchild,' he began, sitting down at a pristine modular seventies table and offering me tea or coffee, his manner somewhere between a vicar and an estate agent. 'It was his baby . . . One hundred and thirty bedrooms. Designed by the union's architects. No outside paintwork for ease of maintenance. Built by British workers with British materials. The slates are Welsh, the tiles are from Stoke-on-Trent. It was built to a very high standard for the time. The carpets lasted for twenty-five years. Every room was en suite – in the seventies, it was unheard of. Fitted radios in the headboards. We had a projector in our conference room . . .' He beamed. 'Unheard of!'

Room rates were low – between £6 and £6.50 a night for full board in the beginning, depending on the season – and subsidized by the union. Many guests did not have to pay at all. Some were convalescing: any TGWU member off sick from work for more than two weeks was entitled to a free fortnight at Eastbourne for them and a partner, with food and travel also paid by the union. Other guests came to the centre for TGWU conferences and seminars. 'Shop stewards will be able to benefit from educational services,' as Jones put it in a speech at the opening ceremony in September 1976 which cleverly blurred the political, the personal and the pleasurable, 'while their families benefit from a holiday.' Showing his unusually clear-sighted understanding, for a union leader, of the relationship between unions and everyday life in the seventies, he went on: 'Many wives who have criticized their husbands for spending too much time in trade union activity will see the Union in a new light when they enjoy a holiday here – and vice versa . . . because these days it is often the women who are the strongest advocates of trade union rights. The shop steward wife will be able to explain "all about it" to her husband and children very convincingly in these surroundings.'

Jones envisaged TGWU activists being schooled at Eastbourne in negotiating techniques, in how companies worked, and in the whole widening social, economic and political role he envisaged for unions. He envisaged foreign trade unionists coming to stay to 'exchange ideas' and aid 'international understanding'. At times, as the noon sun shone on the crowd of middle-aged TGWU officials gathered for the opening ceremony, his rhetoric turned panoramic and idealistic. 'This building', he said, 'epitomises our hopes and our dreams . . . the forward march of the people towards a richer and fuller life . . . the increasing demands for shorter working hours and earlier retirement . . . the maximum participation of all our members not only in union policy . . . but also in decisions which determine their standard of living and conditions of employment.' He concluded: 'This centre charts a new path for trade unionism. It is an encouragement to abandon pessimism and gloom.'

The actual life of the complex in the seventies was sometimes more prosaic. 'Eastbourne is a very Conservative town, a very Conservative town,' the manager told me in his office. 'The building was nicknamed the Kremlin. It was very much, "The Reds are here on the seafront." You'd just gone through the early seventies . . .' – he scratched his knee – 'all the disruption from the unions. I don't think we were that welcome. We used to have hordes of people trying to look in through the glass. We had one local sea captain – sadly passed on – who liked to drink and see how far he could get into the building without being caught.' Regardless, the guests played snooker and sat on the sun roof. They took notes in seminars and drank in the bars. They ran into old colleagues. They spotted visiting dignitaries: often Jones, sometimes Scargill. They relished the colour TV in their rooms and the one-to-four ratio of staff to guests. 'The restaurant was designed as self-service, but that arrangement only lasted a matter of weeks,' the manager said. 'People in the seventies didn't want to stand up and queue.'

He took me on a tour. We walked up staircases with rich wooden bannisters and through mahogany doors. We looked at en suites still with their original raspberry and avocado decor. We saw the kitchens – 'built above ground, to be better for the staff' – with their cauldrons of cabbage and chips. We talked about the in-house carpenters, engineers and cleaners, and the centre's model workforce: still unionized, largely self-sufficient, loyal. We passed delegates attending a TGWU conference – 'Winning in the Global Workplace' – with their coats thrown over the chairs in one of the bars and the union religion still in their eyes. We saw a man peering in from the street through the smoked glass. Then we stopped for a few minutes in a huge corner bedroom. 'Two walls of glass!' said the manager. Below us, a white sun caught the pier and the curve of the beach, but a cold draught crept across the carpet. 'We lose a lot of heat in winter,' he conceded, 'but the complaint we have about these rooms is that people can't see the TV from the bed. It's too far.'

The room was unoccupied. It was February, but filling the centre was getting harder all year round. 'When I started there were 2,500,000 members in the T&G,' the manager said. How many did the union have now? He dropped his voice: 'About 800,000. Last week, I was given the go-ahead to look further afield for guests – people from other unions, possibly non-union members . . . Since the mid-nineties we have looked at our staffing levels.' He sighed. 'Like every industry. We have looked at it quite radically. We now have thirty-two full-time members of staff.' At the busiest times in the seventies there were sixty.

He left me in the restaurant. Lunch was over and the room was empty; the muzak had switched to 'Bridge Over Troubled Water'. Yet the room still had a certain grandeur. Great bulb-lit glass globes hung in clusters from the high ceiling on black cords, as if in some modernist concert hall. A long mezzanine level faced out to sea. Along its curving parapet there was a mural from the seventies, all bold reds and blues and greens, and a plaque ascribing it to something called the Art Workers Cooperative. Three artists' names were listed – Simon Barber, Christopher Robinson and Michael Jones, one of Jack Jones's sons. Then the plaque explained that the mural told the story of trade unionism in Britain.

It started with men ploughing fields. Then the fields became a gloomy forest of mill chimneys, and the men became bent-backed factory workers and miners. A cartoon capitalist in a top hat squatted on a Monopoly board. Then there were policemen in early-twentieth-century uniforms beating union demonstrators with truncheons; thunderous scenes from the Spanish Civil War and the Second World War; and then a new sunlit post-war landscape, with jets streaking overhead and smokeless modern factories. On an idealized production line a clear-eyed worker looked at his watch, as if timing some high-tech process or thinking of his next tea break. Then there was the silhouette of the TGWU Centre in Eastbourne, with a saxophonist playing to guests and the English Channel glittering. Finally, there was a man in a flat cap with his shirt off, lying against a tree, eyes half-closed. Another man ran across a nearby beach with two women in bikinis. More off-duty trade unionists lounged on a yacht in the blue distance.

The whole painting was slightly absurd. Its lack of subtlety, its crude historical transitions, its mixture of travel-brochure and socialist-realist imagery – it verged on the kitsch. Yet there was something moving about its idealism and mistaken confidence. In September 1976, as Jack Jones was opening the TGWU Centre in the sunshine, hopes for the advance of the unionized working class in Britain were still very much alive.

13

Marxism at Lunchtime

Bolder left-wing visions also survived deep into the British seventies. In the autumn of 2008, as I was making some of the last alterations to this book, a slim envelope arrived in the post from my cousin Simon. I vaguely knew he had been politically active in the seventies, but somehow I had always been too busy to talk to him. Inside the envelope was a tiny yellowed, creased booklet. 'A bit late but might be interesting!' said a Post-it note attached to the cover. I carefully peeled off the note, and on the front of the booklet were four words in heavy black and red capitals: 'The Little Red Struggler'. And then, in smaller type: 'A handbook for student militants 30p'.

The handbook did not have a publication date, but inside it no years were cited after 1975. There was also an inky photo of some protesters with beards and thick sideburns in the style of serious young men in the mid-seventies, and a caricature of Richard Nixon turning into Gerald Ford. The handbook had been printed in Manchester, at somewhere called the Progress Bookshop, and its publisher was listed as the National Student Committee of the Communist Party.

For sixty busy pages a whole dead political world sprang to life. There were London contact details for Marxists in Medicine, the Women's Liberation Workshop, the Angola Solidarity Committee and the British Campaign for Peace in Vietnam. There was a surprisingly objective guide to 'political groupings in the student movement', from the Workers Revolutionary Party to the International Marxist Group to the Communist Party itself. There was a sober and detailed guide to campus occupations:

DO . . .
Decide whether the action is to be *demonstrative* or disruptive . . .
Have specific demands which are negotiable, as well as raising issues which question the role of education in society . . .

Look forward to the initial organisation inside [the occupation], eg food, entertainments, sleeping arrangements, study facilities . . .

DON'T . . .
Rely on a small elitist/vanguard invasion . . .
Allow [campus] staff, particularly security staff, inside the occupation . . .
Smoke dope; get drunk; damage the place; leave a mess when it's all over.

Most strikingly of all, the booklet gave a chronology of notable political interventions by British students since the mid-sixties:

1968: Feb. Leicester. 200 students in sit-in . . . 1970: May. Keele. Situationists, helped by Edgar Broughton Band and spraycans 'liberate' Keele . . . 1972: Oct. Queen visits Stirling . . . Students union concerned over cost of visit . . . less than sober demonstration takes place. Press uproar . . . 1974: Mar. Essex. Police break student picket . . . 1975: Mar. Lancaster . . . students occupy administration block . . . May. Warwick students sit-in over rents issue . . .

*

By the mid-seventies, in Britain, as in many other countries, campus radicalism of a loosely Marxist nature was no longer the shock to the system it had been in the sixties. It was becoming something equally interesting: a new political orthodoxy, with its own confident patterns of thought and public rituals. Some of this confidence came from the apparent advance of the Left and retreat of the Right in the wider world. In 1974, fascist dictatorships in Greece and Portugal had been overthrown by left-inclined rebels. In 1975, the Americans had withdrawn, humiliated, from Vietnam. Africa was full of left-wing liberation movements. The Soviet bloc and China, whether you approved of their version of communism or not, seemed increasingly strong as Western capitalism struggled with the oil crisis and economic downturns. In Britain, the media, more interested in foreign affairs then than it is now, conscientiously brought news of it all.

Intellectually, too, the British campus left had a momentum in the mid-seventies. The Tory right and the free-market think tanks may have been plotting their counter-revolution, but their publications were still far less prominent on university bookshelves than those of their ideological opponents. Since its establishment in London in

1970, New Left Books (now Verso) had been successfully importing the ideas of left-wing thinkers from continental Europe, such as Walter Benjamin and Louis Althusser. More mainstream British publishers moved into the same market. In 1975, Jonathan Cape issued *Leninism Under Lenin*, a long didactic book by a Belgian Marxist historian, Marcel Liebman, which described the leader of the Russian Revolution over half a century earlier as 'one of the men who did the most to shape the world of today'. In 1977, Penguin included in its Modern Masters series, alongside studies of Einstein and Gandhi, a stylishly designed layman's guide to the thoughts of Antonio Gramsci, the Italian Marxist of the twenties and thirties.

The increasing 'hegemony', to use Gramsci's then fashionable term for cultural dominance, of left-wing notions at British universities in the seventies was famously satirized by the liberal academic and novelist Malcolm Bradbury in *The History Man*, the exquisitely black campus comedy he published in 1975. Bradbury's villain and main protagonist was Howard Kirk, a bullying, philandering Marxist sociology lecturer. Kirk taught at a fictional college which closely resembled the most politically combustible British campus during the seventies, the concrete-and-grass crucible of the University of Essex. In an interview decades later, Bradbury said he had always thought of Kirk as the kind of Marxist who was more 'opportunist' than ideological: 'He reads political trends, perceives the political flow and goes with it.' Kirk was the 'history man' of the book's title – academic shorthand for a believer in inevitability. The novel was set in 1972, but it did not date quickly. For the rest of the decade, for more British students and academics, almost certainly, than at any time before or since, the one inevitability in political life was the victory of world socialism.

My cousin Simon arrived at Middlesex Polytechnic in 1974. He was nineteen and already had a head full of politics. His parents were both mildly left-wing and had sent him to a private but radical Quaker school, where underground papers like *Oz* had been passed around. He studied politics for A-level and cut out general-election results from the *Guardian*. He sent off for all the parties' literature, and chose Labour.

But at Middlesex he found politics being conducted on a different level. The polytechnic was only a year old, and had been formed out of a scattering of facilities across north London, including Hornsey College of Art, which in 1968 had been the site of the biggest British student rebellion of that revolutionary year. An occupation of the college had lasted two months, and the students had temporarily set up their own university there with the aid of a few sympathetic staff. At Middlesex in the seventies, the Hornsey sit-in lived on as a memory and a mythologized happening, and as a model for further actions.

'The campus I was taught at was a pretty tatty old technical college with a few Portakabins stuck on the back,' Simon, in his early fifties now but still skinny like a student, told me as he cooked me supper at his semi-detached house outside Watford. 'The whole diaspora of left-wing groups there was a bit mind-boggling to me compared to where I'd come from. There was the International Marxist Group, the International Socialists, Militant. The Communist Party were always regarded as fairly mainstream. I aligned myself' – he was still fluent in the jargon – 'with a group called the Broad Left, which dominated the National Union of Students.' The Broad Left was an alliance of communists, left-wing Labour supporters and more free-floating socialists which had been established in 1973. Like the other radical student groups, its policies ranged from the relatively parochial – a big increase in the student grant – to the revolutionary and universal – the 'nationalisation of all building land'. 'I wouldn't have called myself a Marxist when I arrived at the poly,' said Simon, 'but, theoretically, I got very Marxist.'

At Middlesex he grew his hair halfway to his waist, had a beard 'on and off', and cultivated a Che Guevara moustache. Officially he studied 'humanities', an adventurous new type of degree which let students do modules in different subjects. He chose history, law and English literature. Yet really he studied Marxism. 'The teaching staff all called themselves Marxists. They were young academics, probably radicalized in '68. In history, we learned to point at the majority

1 Edward Heath celebrates winning the June 1970 general election. 'We were returned to office to change the course of history of this nation,' he told the Conservative Party conference that autumn. (David Cairns/Hulton Archive)

2 Heath's dream of the future: an early model of Maplin airport, planned by his government to be built on an artificial island off Southend-on-Sea. (Peter Johns/*Guardian*)

3 'They just overwhelmed us': striking miners swamp the police cordon and close the Saltley coke depot in Birmingham in February 1972. (copyright unknown)

4 'This isn't Aden, or Cyprus. It is . . . Britain's own backyard': a Belfast street on a bad day in the seventies. The war in Northern Ireland was the most severe test imaginable for natural compromisers like Heath and Wilson and Callaghan. (Don McPhee/*Guardian*)

5 When the lights went out: Piccadilly Circus partly blacked-out during the three-day week, 1 February 1974. For two mid-winter months the Heath government drastically restricted the supply of electricity to all 'non-essential' shops and other businesses. (PA/PA Archive)

6 'A relationship of forces': Harold Wilson (centre), a fading prime minister by 1975, in the custody of (left) Jack Jones, General Secretary of the Transport and General Workers' Union, and (right) Vic Feather, Secretary of the Trades Union Congress. Jones was widely considered so powerful that during the 1974 general elections graffiti appeared: 'Vote Jack Jones, cut out the middle man.' (PA/PA Archive)

7 Salvation from a cold grey sea: North Sea oil rigs under construction at Nigg in the Scottish Highlands, mid-seventies. The Nigg dry dock was 'the biggest hole in Europe' according to *The Architectural Review*. (Don McPhee/*Guardian*)

8 Members of the Gay Liberation Front protest on behalf of arrested members of the Women's Liberation Front outside Bow Street Magistrates Court, 4 February 1971. (Central Press/Getty Images)

9 Sid Rawle, hippy anarchist and organiser of the 1975 Watchfield free festival, arrives for a meeting at the Department of the Environment, 20 August 1975. (PA/PA Archive)

10 Waiting for the next Britain: the newly-built Civic Centre in Milton Keynes, May 1977. Conceived by idealistic socialists, the brand-new city voted Conservative as soon as it became a parliamentary constituency. (Edward Hamilton West/*Guardian*)

11 Police shove back pickets so that a bus carrying Grunwick employees who are still working can get through, 11 July 1977. Like the miners at Saltley in 1972, the Grunwick strikers were joined on their picket line by thousands of other trade unionists and assorted left-wingers. Unlike at Saltley, the police won. (Peter Johns/*Guardian*)

12 Jayaben Desai, one of the leaders of the strike at the Grunwick plants between 1976 and 1978. The mainly Asian and female strikers wanted a union to represent the workforce. Their employer George Ward emphatically did not. (Homer Sykes/Network)

13 The limits of seventies union power: pickets stuck outside 'Fort Grunwick', as George Ward called his premises, summer 1977. Rupert Murdoch and other employers would follow Ward's example. (Kenneth Saunders/*Guardian*)

16 The shape of things to come: Margaret Thatcher speaking two months before becoming prime minister. Saatchi & Saatchi's famous posters attacking the Callaghan government's poor record on unemployment back her up. But under Thatcher the jobless figures would get far worse. (PA/PA Archive)

14 Prime Minister Jim Callaghan speaking in Tamworth during the 1979 general election. During the campaign his personal lead over Margaret Thatcher in the opinion polls, already substantial, more than trebled. Enthusiasm for his party was less infectious. (Rolls Press/Popperfoto/Getty Images)

15 Public Enemy Number One: Jamie Morris, ex-Tory, militant shop steward, and leader of the infamous strike at Westminster Hospital during the Winter of Discontent. After his period of national notoriety between January and March 1979, Morris soon left politics for property renovation and running an off-licence. (PA/PA Archive)

of historians as apologists for capitalism. Most of the books on our reading list were written by Marxists.' He read *Das Kapital*. He read *Parliamentary Socialism* by Ralph Miliband, father of David and Ed Miliband, yet a ferocious critic of Labour's compromises with capitalism when in office. He read *The World Turned Upside Down* by Christopher Hill, an influential Marxist reinterpretation of the seventeenth-century English revolution which saw immense potential in its small radical sects, such as the Levellers and the Diggers. He read books about the Spanish Civil War; about 'colonialism and imperialism'. And he saw what happened to students at Middlesex who questioned such categories: 'You could be howled down for disagreeing with Marxism in a seminar. Even in law. That was funny: students doing law modules from these quite staid backgrounds, coming up against these Marxist law lecturers who were trying to explain that the law was a blunt instrument of capitalism.' Simon smiled to himself, and it was hard to tell whether the memory left him delighted or appalled, or both. I mentioned Malcolm Bradbury's book, and he nodded. 'There were lots of "history men" lecturers at Middlesex.'

Away from seminars and lectures, the political education continued. 'You couldn't get away from it. There would be political speeches being made in the refectory as you were having your lunch. Someone would get up. There would be a crude PA. People would listen. People would get up and argue. I don't ever remember a Conservative student making a speech.' Did the dominance of the Left at Middlesex feel at all unusual? 'I assumed that was just the way it was at colleges everywhere.'

Frequently, the political satisfactions of public rhetoric and student elections would not be enough and the undergraduates would go on strike. The spark was usually fees for foreign students: with the government's finances under pressure, these were increasing rapidly, and Middlesex had a lot of overseas pupils. But the strikes quickly took on a more all-encompassing quality. Pickets would be established simultaneously at the gates of all the Middlesex campuses. 'I wasn't the most confident or outgoing of people, but I went on the picket lines,' Simon remembered, 'and they were 100 per cent effective.

Most students didn't even try to cross.' College buildings would regularly be occupied for days at a time. 'We had a whole alternative counter-curriculum during the occupations. Some lecturers joined in with us and gave lectures they said they weren't usually allowed to give: about the role of art in the revolution, about the last stages of capitalist decline.' During one sit-in, Simon and the other students watched *Winstanley*, a 1975 British film about the leader of the Diggers, Gerrard Winstanley, who had briefly put into practice an early version of communism by leading land occupations and setting up communes in England during the 1650s. Sid Rawle, of the free-festival movement, the Diggers' closest seventies equivalents, had a substantial part in the film. All the strands of British left-wing utopianism seemed to be coming together.

'I don't think I ever slept overnight in the college buildings,' said Simon, 'yet I remember occupying the college offices during the day. It was exciting . . . There were often police at the college, at the entrances . . .' He stopped. 'It would sometimes get boring after a while. There were no pitched battles.'

But in some ways the very normality of the strikes and occupations and their left-wing participants seemed the most significant thing about them – the sign, it seemed, that a new political world was coming into being. Simon was even able to keep up with his studies. The flexibility of the modular degrees at Middlesex, with their emphasis on coursework and with few compulsory events to attend, meant they could tolerate a great deal of campus disruption. In 1977, he took and passed his finals: exams were never boycotted. Yet before he left the poly there was time for one more radical gesture. 'I never collected my degree,' he remembered. 'There was no ceremony because the students were threatening to disrupt it. The year after, the poly invited me back again to collect my degree. But I boycotted the ceremony.'

By then, the summer of 1978, he had moved seamlessly into another part of the counter-culture: a condemned flat in Notting Hill. It was in Colville Houses, the street where the Gay Liberation Front had had their commune in the early seventies, and the area seemed little changed, still full of squats, swirly-painted vehicles and hippy food stores. Simon's flatmate was involved in the Chile Committee for Human Rights, and touring anti-Pinochet musicians from Chile slept on their floor. Simon was working as a community volunteer in nearby Kensal, 'championing the rights of the oppressed people of west London', he recalled with a self-mocking smile.

How did his revolutionary certainty in the seventies look to him now? There was a long pause. We both looked at our empty plates. Finally, he blew out his cheeks. 'It looks ludicrous.' Simon was a senior social worker now. He had a daughter of his own at university, and she wasn't taking part in any sit-ins. He still had his moustache, but it was trimmed and neat, and his beard and straggly hair were long gone. He was still politically active, but for a more modest goal: arranging practical aid for the Palestinians.

Yet then Simon went on: 'I was thirteen in '68. I remember thinking, "There is an irreversible momentum to this." The revolution was around the corner. It was only a matter of time. That feeling was still around in the mid-seventies. The feeling was that things had quietened down a bit, but the general trend was still towards the overthrow of global capitalism. The feeling was, "We're still going to win." At Middlesex, I used to think about my course, "If this is what's being taught, there's no way back. These Marxist lecturers are the opinion-formers." Even the existence of publications like *The Little Red Struggler*, which I read avidly, created the impression that the movement was building, that it's not going to go away. It just didn't make sense that you could go back to' – and he said the next words with a hint of the old campus venom – 'a militarist and capitalist system. It didn't seem to have anything in its favour, morally, and I didn't understand anything about economics. I thought that '68 had blown the lid off a Pandora's box for equality and liberty and human potential . . .' He cut short his speech. 'What I didn't know in the seventies was that there were plenty of people who were keen to get the lid back down again.'

PART FOUR

The Reckoning

14

William the Terrible

In the summer of 1944, as the Second World War was entering its final phase, the economist and British Treasury adviser and envoy John Maynard Keynes, his health failing, made one of his last and most important visits to the US. At Keynes's request, the conference he was due to chair was not held in airless, sticky Washington but far to the north-east, in the more bracing summer resort of Bretton Woods in New Hampshire. In late June, he and over 700 other delegates and office staff from forty-four countries travelled there in official trains and were put up at the grand and slightly chaotic Mount Washington Hotel. Over the next three weeks, despite malfunctioning microphones, countless cocktail parties, and committee sessions that did not end until 3.30 a.m. and then resumed at 9.30 the same morning, the delegates negotiated a new set of arrangements for regulating the international economy, intended to rescue it from a decade and a half of deep recession and world war and to minimize the chances of such traumas recurring. They agreed that exchange rates between currencies should be fixed, and they created the International Bank for Reconstruction and Development, or the World Bank for short. They also created the International Monetary Fund, or IMF, to promote global economic growth, prevent global economic crises and lend money to countries on a temporary basis if they encountered serious economic difficulties.

In some ways, the Bretton Woods Agreement was a triumph for Keynes. For years he had been promoting schemes for disciplining capitalism through new international institutions; even the term 'International Monetary Fund' was his. Now, such a machinery had been assembled, and the other delegates treated him as a visionary. At the concluding Bretton Woods banquet, the *Listener* recorded, as the sixty-one-year-old Keynes 'moved slowly towards the high table, stooping a little more than usual, white with tiredness, but not unpleased at what had been done, the whole meeting spontaneously stood up and waited, silent, until he had taken his place'.

Yet in other ways Bretton Woods marked his and Britain's defeat. Keynes had long been aware that the burden of the Second World War, the relative decline of the British economy and the cost of the post-war welfare state envisaged by the Labour Party – and a decisive proportion of British voters – made it likely that the country would have to borrow heavily in future decades. He wanted the IMF, therefore, effectively to provide overdraft facilities for Britain and other creaking, left-leaning nations, with the minimum of strings attached. He wanted it to have a small, independent staff and to be based in London. But the Americans had a different vision. They wanted the IMF to be large, based in Washington, close to the US government and tough with the countries to which it lent money. This partly reflected the more free-market mindset of the American government, and partly the changing balance of world power. 'We are putting in twice as much money [to the IMF] as anybody else, three times as much,' commented America's chief negotiator Harry White to one of his colleagues at Bretton Woods. 'It is preposterous that the head office should be any place else [than America]. We can vote it any place we want . . . New York has become the financial center of the world. These British are just fighting uphill.'

Over the IMF and much else at Bretton Woods, the Americans got their way. The text of the Agreement hid this to a degree through ambiguous language and sheer length: Keynes did not have time to read all ninety-six pages before he and the other delegates were unceremoniously asked to vacate the hotel within hours of the end of the conference. Back in London, some Bank of England officials, some members of the Cabinet and some Conservative MPs with a particular sensitivity to threats to Britain's superpower status spotted the implications of what had been agreed. But Keynes and the government, optimistic about Britain's relationship with the US and watching Britain's economic position deteriorate almost daily, argued for the Bretton Woods Agreement with conviction. In December 1945, together with a proposed emergency loan from the

American government, it was presented to Parliament. The whole package, Keynes told the House of Lords in a string of elegant euphemisms, was 'a workable compromise between the certainty they [the Americans] wanted and the measure of elasticity we wanted'. The Bretton Woods Agreement was approved by the Lords without a vote, and passed by the Commons with a majority of 243.

Four months later, Keynes died. But the intimate, always potentially problematic, triangular financial relationship between British governments, the IMF and the US endured. As Keynes had anticipated, Britain was a frequent supplicant to the Fund in the post-war decades. Loans were obtained under Labour in 1947, 1948, 1965, 1967 and 1969; and under the Conservatives in 1956, 1957, 1958, 1961, 1962, 1963 and 1964. Between 1947 and 1971, Britain borrowed more from the IMF, in fact, than any other country.

Much of this took place without great controversy in Britain, one indignity among many in the country's general economic slide. Chancellors became accustomed to the transatlantic, highly technical rituals of IMF negotiations, with loans divided into 'tranches' and provided on terms set by the Fund ('conditionality'), and 'letters of intent' written by grateful British governments promising to manage the economy better in future. So regular and intricate were these dealings that some of the British Treasury and Bank of England officials involved went on to work for the IMF. In the mid-sixties, the chancellor Jim Callaghan even helped oversee the creation of a new currency for the Fund to use in its lending operations called the Special Drawing Right, or SDR. In 1973, out of government and, temporarily, tired of British politics, the canny, avuncular Callaghan was a serious candidate to become the IMF's managing director until he was vetoed by the French. The Fund then approached Callaghan's successor as chancellor Roy Jenkins to see if he was interested in the position. Jenkins decided not to put his name forward. The job was taken instead by a more austere figure, a former Dutch finance minister and professor of economics, Johannes Witteveen.

Yet by the mid-seventies, the many links between Britain and the IMF could no longer conceal a growing tension in the relationship. In the harsher international climate created by the oil crisis and the financial cost to America of the Vietnam War, the Fund was becoming sterner in its thinking. One aspect of the new economic situation was affecting the IMF directly: the system of fixed currency-exchange rates which had been established at Bretton Woods, and which the Fund had overseen, was now disintegrating. But there was much else worrying the bankers in their white ziggurat of a headquarters in Washington. There was the worldwide surge in inflation; the recessions under way in many wealthy countries; the apparently unstoppable rise of trade unions and public spending in such societies; and, finally, the state of the IMF's relations with the US itself. Free marketeers in the American government such as the Treasury secretary William Simon and the chairman of the Federal Reserve Arthur Burns were putting strong pressure on the Fund to impose right-wing economic policies on the countries receiving its loans. By the mid-seventies, this pressure had been effective. The IMF had never been exactly sympathetic to socialism, yet now its view of the world economy – pessimistic, verging on the apocalyptic – and what should be done to revive it – crudely, conquering inflation by cutting public spending – had much in common with monetarists such as Milton Friedman and the capitalist counter-revolutionaries of the IEA.

In this context, Britain, with its long-standing dependence on IMF loans and its especially troubled economy, became the object of particular concern and even derision in Washington. 'Even before the oil price rise . . . the Fund staff considered the problems of the UK economy basic and in need of resolution over the long term,' writes the IMF's official historian Margaret Garritsen de Vries. 'The United Kingdom highlighted some . . . increasingly debated questions about the economies of industrial countries. Could governments continue to support the wide range of social welfare programs that had come into being since World War II? Were large government claims on the economy [such as taxes] retarding private investment? . . . Could government-owned industries be run in the same efficient and profitable way as private industry?'

William Ryrie, an IMF director in the mid-seventies who had previously been a senior official in the British Treasury, put it more bluntly to me: 'The Fund were pretty appalled, really, by the management of the economy. I was ashamed, really. There was a deep-rooted belief in the Treasury and elsewhere in Whitehall that the IMF was there for us to use, as well as poor countries.' Indeed, in right-wing American circles, Britain was increasingly talked about as if it *was* a struggling Third World country. On 29 April 1975, the *Wall Street Journal* carried an influential editorial:

The British economy . . . is sinking . . . Britain's current contribution to the world is to reveal the ultimate result of economic and social policies . . . [which insist that] the state must fulfill all needs . . . [and all] income must be redistributed . . . We learn that *The Economist* does not think it fair of Margaret Thatcher . . . to describe the budget as 'typically socialist'. After all, Mr. Healey did not increase the 52% corporate tax rate. Nor did he increase the 83% marginal tax rate on earned income above $48,000 [then £24,000] or the 98% marginal tax rate on 'unearned income' – interest and dividends, for example – above $48,000 . . . The British government is now so clearly headed toward a policy of total confiscation that anyone who has any wealth left is [taking] any chance to get it out of the country . . . The price can only be still slower economic growth and still lower living standards for all the British, rich and poor. Goodbye, Great Britain, it was nice knowing you.

Less than a year later, on 16 March 1976, with the pound in midplunge on the currency markets and the government beginning to face no-confidence motions in the Commons, Harold Wilson abruptly resigned as prime minister. He had been back in office barely two years. He told the Cabinet, most of whose members had had no hint of his intentions, that he wanted to avoid getting stale in the job and to make way for one of his talented colleagues. He also insisted that the worst of Britain's mid-seventies economic crisis was over, and therefore it was safe for him to go. On television afterwards he looked pale, his eyes even more furtive and half-closed than usual. His voice was flat and perfunctory.

And yet, despite the gloomy consensus about Britain in America, among the currency traders and at the IMF, Wilson's economic optimism was partly justified. Inflation was falling. The social contract was holding. Share prices were recovering as the City's worst fears failed to materialize and pension funds, flush with cash thanks to trade unionists' previous big wage increases, invested in the stock market. 'The bottomless slump', writes the historian Keith Middlemas in *The End of the Postwar Era: Britain since 1974*, 'had been something of an illusion.'

Some of this recovery was also down to Denis Healey. By 1975, his initial ignorance about economics as chancellor was giving way to a characteristic intellectual efficiency and curiosity. His previous Cabinet position as defence secretary had been dominated by tricky issues connected to Britain's decline, such as how to end the country's colonial deployments 'east of Suez' in an orderly fashion, and Healey, clever, sure of himself and not personally very constricted by ideology, had approached these dilemmas with something close to relish. 'I've always been a loner,' he told me in his Sussex study. 'I saw so much damage done to the party by infighting when I was an official of the party after the war. I was never a member of the Gaitskell group or any other.' Instead, he valued improvisation and flexibility: 'One of the things you learned from [serving in] the war was the importance of planning, and of knowing that planning will go wrong, so then you have to be very quick on your feet.' Above all, he sought to avoid being incompetent. Repeatedly in our interview he used a phrase for this which had the trademark Healey combination of white-collar machismo, calculated vulgarity and suppressed insecurity: 'making a balls'.

As chancellor, Healey showed diminishing loyalty to the economic creed that had dominated British government thinking since the forties. 'I'd been very pro-Keynesian before I knew anything about economics,' he said. He looked from his desk towards one of his many bookcases. 'I've got the first edition of *The Economic Consequences of the Peace*. Keynes lived at Tilton Manor, five minutes from here . . .' Healey quickly turned back to me. 'But the world changes, dear boy. Keynesianism had really had its day by the seventies.' Heretically, the chancellor paid attention instead to the rising right-wing economists. 'I was very hostile to the monetarists at first.

But . . . I believed that keeping control of the money supply was very important. And I believed that the market had a major role to play.' He arched his caterpillar eyebrows: 'Milton Friedman said that I was a monetarist without knowing it.'

In April 1975, just as the *Wall Street Journal* was despairing of Britain's ever-expanding state, Healey cut public spending. Later that year, he effectively cut it again by imposing 'cash limits' on his fellow ministers: unlike previously, government departments would now receive an annual sum to spend from the Treasury and, regardless of what happened to the inflation rate that year, no more. In January 1976, Healey reduced public spending again. In July, he repeated the exercise on the largest scale so far. There was substantial opposition in Cabinet, notably from Tony Benn and Tony Crosland, but the chancellor prevailed. That he did so was due not only to his powers of persuasion, but also to a new mood in the less left-wing and more pragmatic parts of the Labour Party. 'We realized that we couldn't go on as in 1974,' remembered one of the most influential pragmatists, Tom McNally. 'There were going to have to be new things tried.'

Healey aside, the Labour figure most central to this fundamental change in economic policy was the man McNally advised, the new prime minister, Jim Callaghan.

Callaghan was four years older than the fading Wilson, and thirteen years older than Margaret Thatcher. He was chosen as Labour leader only after three rounds of voting by Labour MPs. In the first ballot, which showed how divided the party had become, with Healey and Jenkins standing from the Labour right, Crosland and Callaghan from the centre of the party, and Benn and Michael Foot from the left, Callaghan attracted less than a third of the votes and came second. Foot won. In the next round, Callaghan beat Foot by only eight. In the final round, Callaghan won by a less than overwhelming thirty-nine. In his autobiography *Time and Chance* he describes his state of mind in the period leading up to the leadership contest:

Ten years earlier I would have been avid for the Party leadership, and the prospect of leading the nation, but now I was almost 64 years of age. For nearly 30 years I had served continuously either in Government or in the

Shadow Cabinet, and for 20 years on the Party's Executive or as its Treasurer. I had been at the centre of all the controversies, but since becoming Foreign Secretary . . . I had begun to feel a little detached, especially as my visits abroad prevented me from attending Cabinet and Party meetings as frequently as before. I had assumed . . . that the time would come before long when the Prime Minister would tell me in a kindly way that he would like me to make way for a younger man.

In contrast with the other candidates – and with Thatcher the year before – Callaghan gave no interviews during the leadership election and offered no clear personal manifesto. Instead, he simply continued with his duties as foreign secretary. And yet his apparent diffidence was as deceptive as his Billy Bunter cheeks and kindly old man's smile. Callaghan, in a less overt way than Wilson, was a man of great ambition, an operator, a delicate weigher of situations, a relisher of political manoeuvres. In the leadership contest, he had correctly calculated that his high profile and extensive connections made traditional campaigning unnecessary. Instead, his parliamentary private secretary Jack Cunningham, with a sleight of hand worthy of Airey Neave, set up two parallel teams of MPs to promote Callaghan, one openly and one behind the scenes. Together they created a sense of inevitability around Callaghan's candidacy, suggesting that he was the man who could unite the party and keep the unions happy. Then, when it came to the actual voting, Callaghan and his backers played the long game. They realized he did not have to win in the first round; a strong second place would be enough, provided he then attracted the supporters of the other, less successful candidates of the right and centre, who would be alarmed at the prospect of Foot as the Labour leader.

By 5 April, all this had come to pass and Callaghan was prime minister, having won the support of parts of the left and many of the unions, as well as more predictable supporters. 'I must tell you, there is no other feeling like it in the world, to be sitting in the seat of the prime minister of the United Kingdom,' he told the television journalist Michael Cockerell a decade and a half later. 'I had no doubts at all about my capacity. I had watched so many others. It's not altogether a very difficult job to do if you use elementary common sense, if you have a knowledge of how your fellow human beings think and feel.'

In 1976, Callaghan already felt that his life and career had given him such knowledge. He had been born in 1912, with British power only just beginning to dip from its late Victorian peak. He grew up in Portsmouth, the pride of the Royal Navy moored just beyond the close-packed streets. His father, one of ten children in a family that was half Jewish English and half Catholic Irish, had run away from home to join the navy and risen to chief petty officer. During the future prime minister's early childhood, Callaghan senior served on the royal yacht *Victoria and Albert*, the predecessor to *Britannia*.

But there were other lasting influences on the younger Callaghan besides his father's patriotism. His mother was a Baptist, properly puritan in outlook, and when his father died suddenly of a heart attack in 1921, she, Callaghan and his older sister Dorothy struggled along together in rented rooms. Like Jack Jones, and unlike Ted Heath, Wilson and Thatcher, Callaghan did not easily escape the privations of his upbringing. He was a solid rather than outstanding school pupil, and anyway his mother was far too poor to send him to university – an opportunity denied that would linger in him, especially when he entered the well-educated world of British politicians and Westminster reporters. Instead, in 1929, with the Depression filling the streets of Portsmouth with the unemployed, he left and became an employee of the state, working as a clerk for the Inland Revenue in Maidstone in Kent, on the opposite side of the tax game from the future tax barrister and Tory leader Margaret Thatcher. He was already a socialist – for one thing, his mother had received a widow's pension for the first time thanks to the first Labour government – and he quickly joined a civil-service union. During the thirties, he became an activist of repute and assistant secretary of his small union by 1936, at the age of twenty-four. While in the position, he recalled later, he learned a lasting political lesson:

On one occasion I led a small team to conduct negotiations with the Board of Inland Revenue . . . We had a good case and . . . [I] pressed it to the extreme . . . altogether gave what I thought was a brilliant display of fireworks . . . . At the end of the afternoon . . . our team came away without having gained a single halfpenny. I was furious and could not understand what had gone wrong. But D. N. Kneath, one of the older and more silent members of the negotiating team from south Wales, knew. And the next day he told me, 'Remember, my boy, more flies are caught with honey than with vinegar.'

Callaghan became an unlikely admirer of Stanley Baldwin, the Conservative who was prime minister twice in the twenties and again in the thirties, and whose moderation and apparent blandness concealed a great ability to defuse crises and appeal across classes. In 1945, after a quiet war service, Callaghan got his chance to start following in Baldwin's footsteps, winning the marginal Tory seat of Cardiff South – part working-class, part middle-class, part retired – by a comfortable margin. Within a year and a half, he was already being seen in the Commons as a young man with prospects. Tall, with a confident jutting nose and a quick smile that could become a smirk in repose, he was a junior transport minister by 1947. While generally loyal to the frugal left-wing policies of the Attlee government, he sometimes struck a more populist note, writing in 1948, for example, that one of the functions of the tax system should be 'encouraging the maximum production of wealth'. As a transport minister, he oversaw the introduction of cats' eyes and zebra crossings, and posed with an actress in Parliament Square for a road-safety campaign without looking the slightest bit embarrassed.

When the Attlee administration began to disintegrate, Callaghan made vain efforts to help hold it together, and emerged with a keen understanding of how embattled governments live and die. 'The whole of politics is about taking decisions that are either bad or worse,' he told Cockerell later. 'You rarely take good ones.' After Labour's defeat at the 1951 general election, he spent thirteen years in opposition. He was effective on television, popular with female voters, and forward-thinking: 'The accent for socialists must be on the consumer,' he said in a speech criticizing the unresponsiveness of the nationalized industries as early as 1950. He was also known for his robustness on law and order, always useful for an ambitious British politician, and worked for the Police Federation for almost a decade as a consultant. And usefully, too, he had unusually reliable health for a mid-twentieth-century Labour figure, preserving his rosy, unlined features with catnaps, hiking holidays and a famously contented marriage. In 1964, Callaghan returned to office as chancellor; like Wilson's new government as a whole, he seemed a formidable political mixture of the modern and image-conscious and the shrewd and old-fashioned.

Yet his time as chancellor proved close to traumatic. 'We had been in office for only three weeks,' he records in his autobiography, 'when the first large attack against sterling was launched from the Continent . . . an attack by speculators which I had been half expecting and had believed I was mentally braced to overcome. But in all the offices I have held I have never experienced anything more frustrating than sitting at the Chancellor's desk watching our currency reserves gurgle down the plughole day by day and knowing that the drain could not be stopped.' For the next three years, he was dogged by economic problems inherited from the Conservatives, by Wilson's impractical schemes for solving them and by recurrent panics over the pound. 'I was always aware of the weakness of sterling,' he told Cockerell. 'It was something that lived with you the whole time.' In *Time and Chance*, Callaghan describes his experience of one sterling crisis as a kind of political drowning: 'It was like swimming in a heavy sea. As soon as we emerged from the buffeting of one wave, another would hit us before we could catch our breath.' In 1967, he finally went under, devaluing the pound, being booed by an outraged crowd in Downing Street and giving gulping, tetchy interviews in support of the policy on television. Left with profound 'feelings of failure', he resigned as chancellor soon afterwards.

Between 1967 and 1976, Callaghan rebuilt his career. As home secretary in the late sixties, he reversed the liberalizing drift of government policy on law and order and public morality. In 1968, he supported the fierce policing of the Grosvenor Square riots. In 1969, he opposed the legalization of cannabis, telling the Commons he wanted to 'call a halt to the rising tide of permissiveness'. The same year, he stood up for a different, more left-wing traditionalism by helping sink Barbara Castle's proposal for taming the unions, 'In Place of Strife'. Unlike many Labour politicians, Callaghan had a

genuine union background, and his attitudes and closeness to Jack
Jones and other union leaders reflected that. He also enjoyed exercis-
ing his political muscle and making a successful political kill. 'I
wasn't stabbing them in the back,' he told Cockerell of his behaviour
towards Castle and her allies over 'In Place of Strife'. 'I was stabbing
them in the front.'

As foreign secretary during Wilson's listless seventies government,
Callaghan was able to maintain a useful distance from the troubles at
home. He made himself into an international statesman, and was on
particularly good terms with the Americans: with Gerald Ford, who
took over as president from Richard Nixon in 1974; and with Ford's
slippery Secretary of State Henry Kissinger, whom Callaghan
admired, as he put it in *Time and Chance*, for his 'negotiating skill
and persuasive powers' and his 'flexibility'. The admiration was
mutual: in 1975, Kissinger flew specially to Cardiff to see Callaghan
given the freedom of the city.

By the mid-seventies, Callaghan's smooth eagerness as a young politician had given way to a more cunning, more homespun charm. He
had developed an unhurried, almost cosy public speaking style, full
of plain sentences and wise, grandfatherly vowels. It could sound
patronizing, but to many it sounded reassuring. He had lost his smirk
and taken to wearing elderly, thick-rimmed glasses. He had been
married for almost forty years and was known for his devotion to his
children and grandchildren. Since 1967 his main British home had
been a small Sussex farm, only an hour from London and just a few
miles from Healey's house but usefully unworldly, for personal and
political purposes, in its domestic routine and outward detail.
Sometimes in front of photographers and sometimes not, Callaghan
would put on a tweed hat and, heavy shoulders stooping slightly,
walk the 140 acres checking on his barley and cattle and keeping a
daily account of the rainfall. Close colleagues regularly speculated
that he might give up politics and become a farmer.

He did not, of course, but in one important area of his political
thinking Callaghan became increasingly receptive to ideas emphasizing good husbandry. Like Healey, he was not dogmatic about

economics: 'I am no theologian in monetary doctrines,' he wrote in his autobiography. But his puritan streak inclined him in a certain direction: 'I was always prudent in economic affairs, and agreed with a view expressed by Bernard Donoughue [whom he had kept on as head of the Downing Street Policy Unit] that ". . . monetary disciplines were essential to good economic management, and conversely that monetary laxity would undermine the foundations of sustained economic growth".' As early as 1970, Callaghan attended an IEA lecture – one of the first senior Labour politicians to do so – by Milton Friedman on the benefits of monetarism and the bankruptcy of Keynesianism. Callaghan was not instantly or completely converted; instead, he later told his biographer Kenneth O. Morgan, as the seventies went on he came to believe, like Healey, that some of Keynes's ideas were beginning to show their age. And during that decade Callaghan did find himself increasingly in agreement with the monetarists on the identity of the main threat facing the British economy: 'He thought that eventually inflation undermined the whole fabric of society,' his adviser Tom McNally told me.

Callaghan and Healey's new thinking about the economy was supported by a growing body of opinion in the Treasury. Some civil servants there were sceptical, almost by definition, about the ability of other government departments sensibly to consume the revenues the Treasury helped gather. Others were intrigued or persuaded by the new right-wing economics. Still others had found the barely controlled surge in public spending during the first half of the seventies simply too alarming.

Yet, abroad, many observers of British economic policy continued to believe throughout the mid-seventies, and often long after that, that nothing had really changed. Strong impressions of foreign countries, once formed, can linger, often in defiance of shifting realities. This was perhaps especially true of how the Americans, with their relatively insular media, saw Britain then, with its socialist government, which was so alien to the American political tradition.

In 1975, Margaret Thatcher confirmed the views of Labour's foreign critics on her first visit to the US as Conservative leader by breaking with the Commons tradition that opposition leaders do not attack Britain when abroad. The country, she said, was being stifled by socialism, and might even fall apart: 'If Britain were to break, a well-nigh mortal blow would be struck against the whole Western world.' Callaghan chastised her for a lack of patriotism, but in America Thatcher's self-possession and dramatic turn of phrase was, for the first time in the US, widely noted and her message widely heard.

On the increasingly important international currency markets, meanwhile, confidence in Britain had already drained away. 'The dealers thought the state of the economy in the UK was weak,' recalled Dennis Weatherstone, then head of the foreign-exchange operation at the influential American bank JPMorgan. 'The markets are pretty smart. They're not full of economists, but they talk to economists. And they smelled that something wasn't quite right in Britain. The country was declining – I hate to say that. I had come to the States from England in 1971. I found that in the bank in New York we had lots of young people being promoted. In London we had had none of that.' More specifically, 'There was a recognition that sterling was less and less the world's reserve currency, that it shouldn't be as strong [in value] against the dollar.' He paused. 'I didn't think the pound would go into free fall. But one thing you know about markets is they always overreact.'

In 1972, before the start of Britain's mid-seventies crisis, a pound was typically worth $2.60. By January 1976, the exchange rate had eroded to just above $2. Until early March, the rate held. Then, in the fortnight before Wilson's resignation, it began to lurch downwards. By mid-month the rate was $1.90 – the first time it had ever fallen below $2; by mid-May, it was $1.80; by early June, not much more than $1.70. Often, a fall of several cents occurred in a single day. On 8 March, a fall of over five cents occurred in a single hour.

Besides the general disenchantment with the British economy, there was a specific explanation for all this. In March, the Bank of England and the Treasury, believing that Britain's inflated wages were making its exports too expensive, had decided that a modest further drop in the value of the pound could ease the situation. On the 4th, the Bank cut interest rates, which was a traditional prompt to the currency markets to lower the price of sterling, and began selling pounds, which was another. Exactly who in the Bank and the Treasury favoured this course of action, and the precise detail of what was done, has been a matter of protracted and intricate dispute, but the effect on sterling was unambiguous: other major holders of the currency, in particular the newly rich oil-producing countries, suddenly took fright at what they saw as the fragility of sterling and the British economy in general. They sold their pounds. As the currency slid further on the foreign exchanges in consequence, the Bank of England abruptly changed course and began using its reserves, often in vain, to buy pounds and prop up the value of sterling. Between February and April alone, the Bank's reserves shrank by a third.

It took until mid-June, over three months in total, for the Callaghan government and the Bank of England to halt the pound's fall. They did so by borrowing money, not from the IMF – Britain had just done that the previous December – but from the central banks of other rich countries, notably America, Germany, France, Switzerland, Canada and Japan. On 7 June, Healey announced to the Commons that a loan had been secured from these countries with a combined value of $5.3 billion, or approximately £3 billion. The money, it was intended, would buy the government breathing space. It would replenish the Bank of England's depleted reserves; restore the markets' confidence in sterling – a country with a truly weak currency and economy, the thinking went, would not be offered such credit; and it would also give the government's new economic policies time properly to take effect and demonstrate their worth to the outside world. Considering the potentially shaming symbolism of the deal, it was done with relatively little public comment. But there was a catch: the loan would have to be repaid, in full, within six months.

Over the summer, the soon-to-be-famous hot summer of 1976, with its parched parks and standpipes, its freakish ladybird swarms and languid Alabama skies, the crisis seemed to recede. The pound rose back to $1.80 in late June, and stayed near that level into September.

In July, Healey forced his latest cuts in public spending through the Cabinet. The same month, with a typical mixture of bluff and confidence, he told the current-affairs TV programme *Panorama*: 'We're now in a better position to achieve our economic miracle than any time since the war.' Did the chancellor, the presenter asked, think the pound was now basically out of trouble? 'My own view is it will settle at a rate which will hold for quite a long time.'

In August, Healey went on holiday, staying in Britain so that, should the state of sterling require it, he could easily be contacted or even return quickly and discreetly to Whitehall. In his autobiography, he recalls,

. . . not a drop of rain even in the Highlands until the very end of our tour. We drove through Wales and the Lake District . . . then on to Skye, and up the west coast to Ullapool, where we stopped at a little hotel on the quay . . . After a pleasant supper of Loch Broom smokies, we went to bed, to be woken by a series of telephone calls. Each time I had to plod downstairs with my pyjamas covered by a raincoat, since the only telephone was in the hall, where the front door was wide open. First, a call from the police to say that there had been a bomb threat against me . . . Then a series of calls which I had to take more seriously . . . Sterling was under pressure; I agreed [the Bank of England] should spend up to $150 million on intervention, but then let the pound fall. Finally I got back to bed for a few hours' sleep. Next day the flurry was over . . . I spent a couple of days at the Edinburgh Festival meeting actors and singers, including Teresa Berganza, who had been an impeccable Cherubino in *Figaro* . . .

By late August, the currency traders were having doubts about sterling again. There were fears on the markets that the drought would threaten water supplies and force a return to the three-day week. The sopping autumn that suddenly set in at the end of the month put an end to that, but traders remained spooked about impending strikes by the National Union of Seamen and at British Leyland; by the announcement in September of poor trade figures; and by the adoption of a policy by the National Executive Committee of the Labour Party, against Callaghan and Healey's wishes, that called for the nationalization of the insurance companies and leading banks. To make matters worse, on 9 September the Bank of England stopped supporting the pound on the foreign exchanges, on the basis that it had spent over £200 million doing so in the last week alone, and that such an effort was unsustainable in the long term. 'We had discussions: "What did national bankruptcy mean?"' Gavyn Davies, then a young but influential member of the Policy Unit, told me. 'We were on the verge of it. We used to do analyses on the rate at which our reserves would be used up. The answer was ... basically in no time.' Unprotected by the Bank, the pound fell almost immediately from $1.77 to $1.73. By the last Monday of the month, 27 September, the pound was at $1.68, a record low.

It was the first day of the Labour Party conference. In the echoing, restless hall in Blackpool, with cigarette smoke drifting in the television lights, Callaghan survived hostile motions on his policies from the left and the right of the party, thanks to union support. But the pound kept falling.

The following morning, Healey was due to fly to Hong Kong for a conference of Commonwealth finance ministers, and then on to Manila for the IMF's annual meeting, which finance ministers and the Fund's senior management traditionally attended. As he left the Treasury in front of the cameras, Healey tried to look relaxed, even jaunty. He wore a casual jacket and summer trousers, not a suit, and kept a hand in his trouser pocket. In the other hand he swung a briefcase. He stood and smiled. His official car waited, black, tank-like, authoritative.

Yet over the currency markets that morning Healey had no authority at all. As he was driven to Heathrow, he heard on the car radio and in updates by car telephone from the Treasury that the pound had gone, as he put it later, 'into a free-fall ... About every quarter of an hour, the pound dropped another cent ... It seemed like the end of the world.' He was exaggerating the extent of the falls, but not that much: in the time it took him to get to the airport, a journey of not more than three quarters of an hour, sterling fell two cents. During 28 September as a whole, it fell by four and a half. On the foreign exchanges that day, *The Times* noted 'the absence of almost anybody wanting to buy pounds'.

At Heathrow Healey got out of the car and walked quickly, still smiling, straight past the waiting journalists and into the terminal. But – a rarity in his political life – he was no longer sure what to do. 'If I took the plane,' he wrote in his memoirs, 'I would be cut off from all contact with London for seventeen hours.' If he did not leave for Hong Kong, he might seem to be panicking and the pound might sink further. For twenty-five minutes he conferred with his aides and the governor of the Bank of England in the VIP lounge. He also phoned Callaghan in Blackpool. Callaghan later recalled:

I was about to leave the hotel to deliver my speech to the Conference . . . Denis told me that Bank of England experts were forecasting gloomily that sterling would continue to fall . . . as low as $1.50 and no one could tell whether it would then stop. He said . . . he was uncertain whether he . . . should leave for the Far East at such a moment. My view was that if staying in London would make the situation easier, he should do so . . .

A quarter of an hour before take-off, Healey decided that getting on the plane was too risky. Outside the terminal, one of his subordinates, stooping awkwardly in his suit, with one foot on the pavement and one foot in the gutter, slowly lifted a series of black suitcases back into the boot of the official car. A policeman watched impassively with his hands behind his back. Then Healey emerged, walking much less briskly than before, smile intact but distinctly fixed. He stopped briefly to speak to the reporters. He told them he had not ruled out flying to Hong Kong the following day, or to Manila later – the IMF meeting did not start for another six days. But when his smile slipped a few times, his broad, strong face looked numb.

He went back to London. That evening, he held an emergency meeting with his Treasury advisers. 'It took us three hours to agree that our best course was to announce that we were applying to the IMF for a conditional loan.' Callaghan agreed, but the announcement of the decision was held back until the next day, in order not to upstage the Commonwealth conference. In the meantime, the markets reacted to Healey's retreat from Heathrow with – Callaghan's phrase – 'hysterical panic'. Even Healey was badly shaken: 'It was the lowest point of my period at the Treasury,' he wrote later. 'For the first and last time in my life, for about twelve hours I was close to demoralisation.'

In Manila, with Healey absent, the IMF gathering was addressed instead by Sir Douglas Wass, a senior Treasury civil servant who looked down at his notes and spoke to the huge, half-empty hall in a precise accountant's tone, with none of the chancellor's boisterous charisma. 'The lack of frank, face-to-face talks at this stage', suggests the Fund's official historian with some understatement, 'may have added to the difficulty of later negotiations.'

Yet in the other conference hall of the moment, in Blackpool, the first signs had already come of an effective response to the crisis from the Callaghan government. Shortly after taking Healey's phone call from Heathrow, Callaghan had given his maiden speech to the Labour conference as party leader and prime minister. Aware that it might also be his last, he decided to be frank.

For too long, perhaps ever since the war, we [have] postponed facing up to fundamental choices and fundamental changes in our society and in our economy . . . We have been living on borrowed time . . . Governments of both parties have failed to ignite the fires of industrial growth in the ways that [other] countries . . . have done. Take Germany, France, Japan . . .

The cosy world we were told would go on for ever, where full employment would be guaranteed by a stroke of the chancellor's pen – that cosy world is gone . . . We used to think that you could spend your way out of a recession . . . by cutting taxes and boosting government spending. I tell you in all candour that that option no longer exists, and that insofar as it ever did exist, it only worked on each occasion . . . by injecting a bigger dose of inflation into the economy, followed by a higher unemployment . . .

Now we must get back to fundamentals. First . . . our labour costs being at least comparable with those of our major competitors. Second . . . significantly improving the productivity of both labour and capital. Third . . . [by not] printing what Denis Healey calls 'confetti money' to pay ourselves more than we produce.

The delegates listened to his words in near silence. When Callaghan finished, he did not receive the leader's usual standing ovation. Some members of Labour's National Executive Committee and some ministers sitting with him on the stage – the conference slogans behind them read, 'With Your Help Labour Will Go from Strength to Strength' and 'Labour Gets to the Heart of Matters that Matter' – did not clap at all. On the currency markets, to which the speech was transparently also addressed, the response was contradictory. 'Dealers said, everyone was "waiting for a sign",' *The Times*' economics editor Peter Jay reported. 'The PM's speech at Blackpool was not construed as such a sign . . . in part because those who were engaged in hectic dealings had very little idea of what he had said. When questioned about it . . . they tended to "assume" that Callaghan had said "the same old things". When asked what he should have said, they gave a fair summary of what he had said. When told that he said it, they expressed surprise.'

Then again, the very confusion of these responses confirmed Callaghan had said something unexpected. In his slightly fussy, schoolmasterish way, and with stiff, sometimes awkward turns of phrase – 'in all candour', 'insofar as' – that gave away all the redrafting and intellectual gear shifts that lay behind the final text, the Labour leader had made an attack on the post-war consensus at least as coherent and bold as anything by Margaret Thatcher. The ability of a struggling Labour prime minister to toughen up the whole British attitude to the economy could be questioned; so could the extent of Callaghan's conversion to or understanding of the new right-wing economics; and so could the wisdom of that thinking in the first place, as the less economically successful Britons of the next decade and a half would find out. But after Blackpool nothing would be quite the same again in British politics. On 10 December, the new right's economic guru Milton Friedman acknowledged as much, telling *The Money Programme*: 'The most hopeful sign I have seen in Britain was the talk which your Labour prime minister gave to the Labour conference at the end of September. That was, I think, one of the most remarkable talks – speeches – which any government leader has ever given.'

Callaghan's Blackpool address, like any leader's party-conference speech, was the work of many hands. Bernard Donoughue and Gavyn Davies of the Policy Unit had influenced its contents, as had Tom McNally; and so had the prime minister himself, with his growing alarm about sterling and the state of the economy. Yet the author of the speech's most iconoclastic passages was not officially a member of the government but rather a less formal, more intimate ally of the Labour leader and a man of many usefully overlapping political and media guises: Peter Jay.

The Jays were about as close as Labour came to royalty. Peter's mother Peggy had long been one of the most powerful women in the party in London, as a councillor, Hampstead activist and the confidante of Labour grandees. His father Douglas, meanwhile, had been a prominent left-wing journalist in the thirties, a Labour economics minister in the forties, fifties and sixties, and remained a Labour MP. Douglas was known for his quick and certain mind, for his pioneering ideas about modernizing the party – in the early sixties, he argued it should abandon nationalization and its 'working-class image' – and for his icy relations with Harold Wilson, who terminated Jay's career as a minister in 1967 with a meeting at a railway station in the south-west of England. Jay, halfway through a Cornish holiday, had refused to come back to London to be fired.

Peter Jay had inherited many of his parents' attitudes and connections, and had updated them. In 1961, at the age of twenty-four, he married Callaghan's daughter Margaret. From 1961 to 1966, he worked as a senior civil servant at the Treasury. In 1967, still only thirty, he became economics editor of *The Times*, a position he held until 1977. In 1972, he also began presenting *Weekend World*, the most rigorous and respected – if not the most watched – current-affairs programme on British television. Throughout, Jay behaved as if born to such roles. Lanky and drawling, with a faintly spoilt, handsome face and a big, confident mouth, he was articulate, inquisitive and increasingly pessimistic about Britain. He was fundamentally loyal to the Labour Party but capable of being stingingly critical. Callaghan considered his son-in-law 'brilliant' and, from the early sixties, intermittently sought his advice.

When I met Jay in 2006, he seemed little changed. He collected me from a station outside Oxford in an unkempt Mercedes. As we surged out of the car park he immediately began explaining that

1976 was the true turning point in modern British politics. 'At the time I called the change of attitude the New Realism,' he said. Beneath his craggy, tanned forehead his eyebrows went up. 'Later, Thatcher used that phrase quite a lot.' He paused briefly. 'I call the twenty years beforehand, 1956–76, the years of the two Harolds [Wilson and Macmillan]. Disgusting, horrible, contemptible people. They alienated a whole generation of people like myself who might otherwise have gone into politics.'

We pulled up outside a large stone house with several cars in the driveway. Next to it was a converted barn full of books on politics and economics and framed caricatures of Jay, who since the seventies has had a high-profile media career without quite recapturing his Callaghan-era influence. He sat down at a long messy desk, folded his tanned arms and continued. 'At Oxford and the Treasury I was a twenty-four-carat Keynesian. My father was a great influence in that. Then, during the late sixties, I noticed that the trade-off between inflation and unemployment was worsening in the UK. I went to the States for *The Times* and became interested in monetarism. I visited the University of Chicago, the Hoover Institution in Stanford, the Federal Reserve in St Louis, the great centres of monetarism. I liked their flow of statistics – very useful for a journalist, well-presented. I met Friedman. He's a very attractive character. He has that wonderful Jewish humour and intellectuality. He became a good friend. He signed my application for a green card . . .'

Jay stopped. Then his deep, smooth broadcaster's voice rose a little: 'I was absolutely conscious that on a number of issues . . . the monetarists were on the political right. I entirely disagreed with them on those issues – as I did with the lot on Lord North Street, the IEA. But the macroeconomic question was a factual question. Ideology can't be against the facts.'

From the late sixties on, Jay became increasingly convinced that British economic policy required a complete overhaul. 'You needed a healthy economy for there to be redistribution of wealth. So you had to stop the crisis.' He began advocating monetarism in *The Times*, with dire warnings about what would happen to the economy, and to British democracy itself, if there was no change of course. He said the same things to his father-in-law and to Healey in private. When Callaghan replaced Wilson as prime minister, Jay became a direct influence on both No. 10 and No. 11 Downing Street. Callaghan's Blackpool speech was merely the most famous instance.

'He rang me up,' Jay said, leaning back in his chair, legs stretched right out. 'I recall it being the day before the speech. He said he'd got a rubbishy draft. Would I send him something? I sat down and wrote a whole speech. The first part said, "Keynesianism has no future," and all that. The second half said, "So the way forward for socialists is . . . to change the role of labour so it becomes entrepreneurial." I called this market socialism.' Jay's big mouth bent into an unexpected self-mocking grin. 'Callaghan, wisely, did not use that part of the speech.'

Even the part of the speech Callaghan did use was a little too radical for Healey. In his memoirs, he calls Jay's contribution 'a notorious passage . . . [which] appeared to reject the very concept of Keynesian[ism] . . . in principle and at all times'. The chancellor did not want to go that far. For one thing, he did not wholly trust Callaghan's judgement on economic matters. 'The thing about Jim was,' Healey told me with one of his knife-plunging smiles, 'he wasn't a great success in his earlier jobs before he became prime minister. In fact, he was a disaster at the Treasury and had to resign . . .'

For his part, Callaghan had misgivings about Healey's retreat from Heathrow. He had hesitated before agreeing that the chancellor should miss his flight, and the negative reaction of the currency markets and the media to the decision confirmed these doubts. Callaghan wrote later in his memoirs: 'I should have encouraged the Chancellor to go.'

Instead, for the whole of 29 September and the morning of the 30th, Healey stayed in London. 'Jim doesn't want me in Blackpool,' Healey wrote in his diary. '[Would] weaken repair of calm.' The 29th had brought the official announcement that Britain was applying for an IMF loan of $3.9 billion (£2.3 billion), the biggest sum the Fund had ever been asked for. On the foreign exchanges that day and the day after, with Callaghan's speech still being digested and the Labour conference still restive, the pound was wildly up and down but no longer in free fall. At breakfast time on the 30th, with a debate on the economy due that day in Blackpool, Healey phoned Callaghan to ask if he could come to the conference and make the case for the IMF loan and the government's changing economic strategy, but Callaghan said no. To take his mind off things, Healey went to the National Gallery for the morning. He had a meeting with the curator, he wrote later, 'to choose an Ostade and a Wouwerman for my office at the Treasury, and a Van den Neer for No. 11'. Then suddenly, at 11.30 a.m., he told me, 'Somebody came in from my office – rushed in – and said, "The PM wants you up right away. There's a plane waiting for you at Northolt."'

When Healey got to the RAF base in west London, he found the runway flooded and unusable after a downpour. His plane was grounded for over an hour, and he did not make it into the Blackpool conference hall until 3 p.m. 'When I came in, they started booing,' he remembered. For another hour and a half he was not permitted to give his speech. At the previous year's conference, delegates angry at his cuts in public spending had voted him off the party's National Executive Committee, so he no longer had the right to jump the queue of speakers at party conferences. Instead, he had to wait, his suit crumpled and his great bullish cheeks red, while the delegates debated the NEC's call from earlier in the autumn to nationalize the banks. As a succession of speakers condemned the whole structure of modern banking and demanded its replacement with 'a state monopoly of finance', the British chancellor and supplicant to the bankers of the IMF took notes and, a little theatrically, put his head in his hands. When his turn came, he had to speak from the floor, not the stage, like an ordinary delegate. And, like an ordinary delegate, he was given five minutes. He rose from his seat with his tie loose and walked to a microphone.

'I do not come with a Treasury view,' he began, almost shouting, his voice echoing. There were boos and cheers, then silence. He looked from side to side. 'I come from the battlefront . . . The government have decided to go to the IMF . . . to give us time for our strategy to work. To get Britain to stand on her own feet for good and all . . . There are some people who would like to stop the world and get off . . .' – there were isolated shouts from the hall – '. . . I do not blame them. It has not been an easy world in the last few months . . . [But] we have got to stick to the policy we have got . . .' – there were shouts of 'a Tory policy!' – '. . . I am going to negotiate with the IMF on the basis of our existing policies, not changes in policy . . .' – now there was applause – '. . . But when I say "existing policies" I mean things we do not like as well as things we do like.' Healey began to nod his big head rhythmically. 'It means sticking to the very painful cuts in public expenditure . . .' – shouts of 'No!' – '. . . It means sticking to a pay policy . . .' – shouts of 'Resign!' – '. . . And I ask conference to support me.'

There were cheers, boos, hisses and an abortive attempt at a standing ovation. The chancellor walked slowly back to his seat and sat down heavily. Then, adrenalin still surging, he quickly stood up again and threw his arms aloft, waving his notes and spectacles in the air. For several seconds he held the pose like a victorious boxer: both hands waving, shirt cuffs slipping down, shirtfront coming untucked and stomach showing, sweat all over his face, triumph and amazement in his eyes.

That evening, Callaghan went on television and struck a different note about the coming negotiations with the IMF. 'If we were to fail, I do not think any government could succeed,' he said, sober as an undertaker. 'I feel it would lead to a totalitarian government of the Left or the Right.'

A jittery October followed. With the IMF negotiators not due to arrive in London until November, there was plenty of time for press speculation and political tension to build up in Britain. On the 6th, Healey's still-uneasy relations with Callaghan abruptly worsened, when the prime minister refused to let him raise interest rates to protect the pound. For several hours Healey considered resigning – a potentially fatal blow to such a beleaguered government. But before he could, Callaghan relented. His private secretary informed Healey, coolly, that the prime minister had been 'testing the strength of your conviction'.

Independently of Healey, Callaghan also tried to find an alternative to an IMF loan and the politically perilous conditions which were certain to come with it. He was on good terms with the German chancellor Helmut Schmidt, and he retained the goodwill of Kissinger and Ford. During October, Callaghan deployed all his careful diplomatic skills, and these three foreign allies offered hints that financial assistance might be forthcoming. But Schmidt was unable to persuade his government, and Ford was unable to persuade the right-wingers in his administration who wanted Britain to change its ways. On 25 October, Callaghan switched to his other negotiating mode – overt menace – and suggested in an interview that Britain might not be able to afford its NATO commitments, such as stationing soldiers in Germany, if a German or American loan was not provided. The threat, however, had little effect other than to irritate the Americans. A week later, on 2 November, any remaining chance of an easy deal with them disappeared when Ford was defeated in the presidential election by Jimmy Carter.

In the meantime, the Conservatives and the British right-wing press were doing their best to make the impending talks with the IMF seem even more ominous. Margaret Thatcher suggested that the Fund could reasonably seek public spending cuts of between £5.5 and £6 billion, or over a tenth of state spending. The *Sunday Times* reported that the IMF wanted to see the pound devalued to $1.50 before granting a loan. The next day, sterling plunged by seven cents and, despite a denial from the IMF, kept on falling. On 28 October, a Thursday, the exchange rate hit a new low: $1.535. The following Monday, the IMF negotiators arrived in London.

There were six of them. They rejected a suggestion from the Treasury that they hold a press conference, and checked into Brown's hotel in Piccadilly under assumed names. Brown's seemed a shrewd choice: it was prestigious but discreet, several Georgian townhouses knocked together in a dark side street. It had been a choice of visiting American presidents in the past, and was not far from the American embassy. It had an interior of rich panels and shadows and, if the press found out who was staying there, multiple exits for guests. Standing among streets full of art dealers and jewellers and dapper gentlemen in taxis, streets that had been rich and seemingly unchanged for centuries, the hotel was also usefully distant – for IMF negotiators who wanted to remain firm during the talks to come – from Britain's current economic turbulence, and from the Britons who would be hurt by the tough loan conditions the Fund was likely to demand.

And yet in the dour grey autumn of 1976 the negotiators stayed rather longer at Brown's than they would have wished. Traditionally, a visit from the Fund to arrange a loan lasted about a fortnight. The IMF team would examine a country's economic data, diagnose the underlying problems, ask the government in question to suggest solutions, and offer a loan when a solution to the Fund's liking was found. But this time the IMF negotiators spent virtually a fortnight doing very little. On their fourth day in London, Healey met the head of the team, Alan Whittome, and told him that some of the crucial economic figures were not ready yet. Otherwise, for the first week and a half, there was no meaningful contact. The IMF people hung around in their rooms, gave empty updates to their superiors in Washington and worried about whether their telephones were being bugged. Meanwhile, Callaghan and Healey let the Cabinet and Labour MPs know that the Fund was being kept waiting, in order to dignify a little what would follow. 'The atmosphere in London was tense,' writes the IMF's usually deadpan official historian. 'Negotiations . . . were protracted.'

Whittome was a bony, upright man of fifty who had been with the Fund since the early sixties. Appropriately, given the intertwined relationship between Britain and the IMF, he was an Englishman. He had a diplomat's manner, a dry sense of humour and, at least until he joined the Fund, an old-fashioned Establishment background: head boy at Marlborough, war service in the Royal Armoured Corps, degree at Cambridge, and then a successful first career at the Bank of England, where he had risen to deputy chief cashier by his late thirties. It was as if a representative of an earlier, more dynamic Britain had returned to pass judgement on what his country had become. 'Last night a relative warned: "He is a very tough man who will be very blunt,"' the *Daily Mail* reported on 1 November. Whittome had wide experience of arranging loans for European countries, including France in the economic turmoil following the revolutionary events of May 1968. During 1976, he was also involved in loan negotiations with Italy. He did not seem likely to be too intimidated that autumn, therefore, by Britain's needs and difficulties. His second-in-command in London was a frank Australian, David Finch. Other members of the team came from New Zealand, America and Germany – former British colonies, former British enemies. If nothing else, the IMF was a superb arranger of national rematches.

When the Fund and the British government started meeting in earnest, on 10 November, Healey quickly recognized in Whittome another keen mind and untangler of problems. 'I liked him,' Healey told me. 'He was direct and courteous.' But did he expect Whittome to be tough? Healey let out his snorting, man-of-the-world laugh. 'Oh yes.'

The IMF had been informed by the Treasury that the official forecasts for the public-sector borrowing requirement for the next two financial years were a huge £10.5 billion and £11.5 billion respectively. The Fund responded by proposing that British state spending be cut by £3 billion in 1977–8 and by £4 billion in 1978–9, drastic reductions of 6 per cent and 8 per cent. Callaghan and Healey responded that annual cuts of £2 billion represented the absolute maximum that they could force the Cabinet, the unions and Labour voters to accept. The Callaghan administration was already effectively a minority government: Labour's tiny majority at the last general election had been steadily eroded by defeats in by-elections, and in early November the government lost two more. However forcefully the IMF, Margaret Thatcher and the right-wing press on both sides of the Atlantic argued for the salutary effect on Britain of a reduction in public spending, the economic crisis of the mid-seventies was only just beginning to pass, and many of the Britons who relied on state services were not feeling prosperous enough to tolerate cutbacks.

Between 10 and 25 November, the IMF team repeatedly met senior Treasury civil servants. Whittome drank a great deal of whisky with Healey. Callaghan invited Whittome to Downing Street for midnight chats, and tried to coax him towards a more understanding position. Whittome even met trade union leaders. But the basic disagreement between the Fund and the government remained. Discouraging hints appeared in the press: on 22 November, *The Times* reported that the talks 'have not gone as smoothly as had been expected'. Leo Pliatzky, one of the civil servants involved, found Whittome, for all his urbanity and experience, 'increasingly weary and frustrated'. Late in the month, four of the IMF team went back to Washington temporarily, so poor was the progress in London. Yet the Fund, like Healey and Callaghan, felt that it could not afford politically to shift its position. 'It was extremely important that the Fund officials not weaken the policies expected of the United Kingdom,' writes the IMF's historian. 'Otherwise the policies expected of Italy might also have to be weakened.'

The British negotiations seemed stuck, gummed up by the range of competing groups they needed to satisfy. And all the while a non-negotiable deadline loomed nearer. Britain needed the IMF's money by the end of December, in order to repay the massive loan from the central banks of America, Germany and other rich countries which it had secured over the summer. By late November, even some of the American right-wingers who had previously relished the Callaghan government's struggles were getting anxious. During the autumn, the chairman of the Federal Reserve Arthur Burns had warned Ford that 'from an international point of view, it would be catastrophic for Great Britain to go down the drain financially'. The world economy was still delicate after the oil crisis, and Britain was still one of America's key European allies. On 26 November, another powerful American free marketeer, the Treasury secretary William Simon, went a step further than Burns. He flew to London to rescue the IMF talks.

If Whittome seemed 'tough' even to the *Daily Mail*, Simon was something else altogether. 'William the Terrible', as he was known in America, was the son of a rich heir and industrialist who had dissipated his fortune. Simon was left with a stringent work ethic and built a famous career as a bond trader on Wall Street during the fifties and sixties. He came to regard markets in general with reverence, and the seemingly less competitive areas of modern professional life, in particular the 'cocoon of bureaucratic life in government', as he called it in his autobiography, with such contempt that in 1978 a polemical book of his about all this had a preface by Milton Friedman *and* a foreword by Friedrich von Hayek.

Nevertheless, Simon left Wall Street in 1972 to serve in the Nixon and Ford administrations. He made himself the ultra-capitalist conscience of both governments, arguing for cuts in public spending even in the depths of America's mid-seventies economic crisis. In 1975, most notoriously, he responded to the catastrophic debt problems of the New York municipal government by suggesting that the federal government should exact the highest possible political and financial price for bailing New York out. 'The city had lived beyond its means for years,' he wrote afterwards. He told a Senate hearing during the crisis, 'I would urge . . . that the financial terms of assistance be made so punitive, the overall experience be made so painful, that no city, no political subdivision would ever be tempted to go down the same road.'

A year later, Simon arrived in London. After New York, Britain had become his favourite example of the damage caused by profligate left-leaning politicians. He was familiar with the work on the subject done by Ralph Harris and the IEA. And he was not feeling merciful. 'Callaghan came to us pleading for an IMF loan,' he wrote in his autobiography. 'Historically, the United States has always been there to assist its (often ungrateful) friends . . . But there is a difference being a charitable benefactor and host to a parasite.'

Simon's British visit was only a weekend stopover on his way to an official engagement in Moscow, but at Heathrow that Friday he cut a swaggering figure, especially when compared to the retreating Healey of a few weeks earlier. Officially, Simon's was a relaxed 'private visit': the *Sun* noted that he arrived wearing red tartan trousers. But he also came with an 'entourage of 43 people', the paper reported, including his wife and sons, three secretaries and at least fourteen Secret Servicemen. The following day, he posed for a photo for the *Sunday Times* in the driveway of the American ambassador's palatial residence in Regent's Park. Simon leant on the bonnet of an enormous, shark-like Ford, smiling hugely, hair perfectly parted, pipe in hand, like some Wall Street superman about to go for a weekend drive.

'It was kind of funny,' he confessed to the paper two years later, 'because I dressed in a pair of golf pants. The Press were all over the place and I told them: "I'm just here to see the sights . . . I thought I might go to the Tower and even do some shopping."' The British government also did its bit to maintain the fiction of a recreational trip: 'Whitehall officials stressed that there was no direct connection between Mr Simon's visit and . . . any fundamental disagreement between the IMF experts and the British government,' *The Times* reported that Saturday. 'Mr Simon's visit is not seen, therefore . . . as intended to rejuvenate discussions . . . in spite of [its] timing.'

That afternoon, Simon did go shopping, but that was not his main purpose. Like an increasing number of wealthy Americans in the post-war years, he had a London tailor, Wells of Mayfair. For almost 150 years, Wells had been in the same premises, a deep set of tiled and panelled rooms in a twisting street close to Savile Row. Since the sixties, Simon's cutter at Wells – the man who shaped his suits – had been a tall, correct man called Richard McSweeney. 'Bill liked a fairly quiet suit,' McSweeney told me when I met him, retired and a little husky now, in his small, neat house in the outer London suburbs. 'Charcoal greys. We used to call it the mid-Atlantic suit. Not quite as fitted as an English suit, not as baggy as an American suit.' On Saturday afternoons, when McSweeney would lock the door at Wells and work on, alone, Simon was one of the few customers allowed to disturb his seclusion. And so it was on the afternoon of 27 November 1976.

A few days earlier, McSweeney remembered, Simon had phoned him unexpectedly at work: 'That you, Mac? Bill Simon here. Are you still doing your Lone Ranger act on Saturday afternoons? Can I come next Saturday?' McSweeney had said it would be a pleasure. 'I'll have two or three other guys with me,' Simon went on. 'Is that OK?'

At 3 o'clock that Saturday, the doorbell at Wells rang. When McSweeney opened it, 'The road was full of black limousines. A great big athletic guy got out and said to me, "I'm accompanying Mr Simon." Then Bill appeared, shepherding a little group of elderly, heavy and dark-suited men with briefcases.' McSweeney smiled knowingly at me in his armchair and quoted Harold Wilson's famous old phrase for foreign bankers: 'I took them to be the gnomes of Zürich.'

McSweeney went on, 'Bill said, "I've got a bit of business to do with these guys. Can you give us half an hour?" I didn't know what the meeting was going to be about exactly, but I knew that there was this iffy business [with the pound] – every time we sent a suit to America the price was going up for us – and that Bill was going to be involved in negotiations. Great Britain was nearly broke, and Bill was one of the white knights.' McSweeney showed Simon and his dark-suited companions to the back of the shop and into a fitting room. The size of a small bedroom, it had a window onto a light well and a heavy door, but no lock. McSweeney squeezed in as many chairs as he could around the fitting room's table. Then a Secret Serviceman shut the door on Simon and his companions and stood outside, while other American agents took up positions elsewhere in the shop and in the street.

'I carried on working,' McSweeney recalled. 'I was thinking, "Clever old Bill."' Less than half an hour later, after more comings and goings involving the fitting room and more men in dark suits, the fitting-room door opened for good and Simon came out. 'Bill was all smiles.' McSweeney paused. 'The men in suits were poker-faced.' Simon shook his hand and gave him 'a huge wink'. Then he ordered two suits, he and the others got into the limousines, and they were gone.

When I visited Wells's old premises in 2005, they had been turned into a restaurant. It was part of the Brown's chain – appropriately, given the building's part in the IMF saga – but the connection with the hotel was in name only. The fitting room which Simon and the men with briefcases had borrowed was now a staff rest area, full of empty yoghurt pots and half-eaten apples.

Exactly who was present and precisely what was agreed in there in

1976 remains a little uncertain, but some things can be deduced. Simon's tailor was a few hundred yards from Brown's hotel and from the American embassy. It was also less than a mile from the Treasury. Simon himself told the *Sunday Times* in 1978 that he and his Treasury under-secretary Edwin Yeo 'met the [British] Treasury people' at Wells. 'Then we went off and talked to Whittome for a few hours and I met all the senior [British] government officials.' Simon summed up his day's work: 'We pretty well set the parameters.'

By 'the parameters', the *Sunday Times* inferred, Simon meant the principle that the IMF should not soften its position too much. Yet the American government remained anxious about what might happen if the IMF negotiators in London failed to reach a deal with the British. Back in Washington, the Fund's historian records, 'US Treasury authorities' – Simon or his subordinates – 'transmitted to Mr Witteveen President Ford's belief that it would be desirable for Mr Witteveen, in the interest of the international community, to go to London.' Although Ford had lost the November presidential election, he was not due to leave office until January, as is the custom in America, and he was still preoccupied by the London talks. On 1 December, Witteveen flew to Britain and met Callaghan.

To enable both men to speak as freely as possible, neither the British Cabinet nor the executive board of the IMF were told about the encounter. As it turned out, the discussions between Witteveen and Callaghan verged on the acrimonious. The many different versions of what happened variously have Callaghan losing his temper, threatening to put restrictions on imports to Britain if a loan was not provided, and even calling the director of the IMF 'boy'. But by the meeting's conclusion both sides had made potentially decisive concessions. Witteveen now wanted cuts in British state spending of around £2.5 billion over the next two financial years, less than half what the Fund had originally asked for. Meanwhile, Callaghan, according to the IMF's historian, had 'finally agreed to support a reduction' in public spending which, while 'not as large as that proposed by the [Fund] staff . . . was, nonetheless, substantial'.

Now all he had to do was convince the Cabinet.

*

Since the IMF's arrival in London, Callaghan's roomful of able, quarrelsome ministers had not simply been sitting quietly. Divisions and positions on public spending can be dry to the layman but, particularly in hard times and especially for left-wingers, they are the essence of politics. Over the last year and a half, as Healey had repeatedly forced through his cuts, ministers' stances had hardened. During November 1976, the Cabinet polarized further.

On the left, and utterly opposed to the Fund's demands, were Tony Benn and his half-dozen allies. In the centre, but also against the IMF cuts, were Tony Crosland and another faction of half a dozen ministers. On the right, and prepared to do some of what the Fund wanted, were Healey and three relatively junior colleagues. And then there was Callaghan: coming round to Healey's position in private, but in public keeping his cards close to his chest. 'It would have been best if we [the Cabinet] could have reached a quick decision,' he writes in his memoirs, 'but I knew this would not be possible if we were to remain together.' He also knew that any senior ministerial resignations over the issue would be the end of his fragile government. 'So . . . I decided not to bring matters to a head but to allow time to work and Ministers to become familiar with the problems, with the arguments and with the possible solutions . . . And so although I knew how far I was ready to go to secure agreement with the IMF, I saw no advantage in making my position clear at an early stage.'

Instead, between 23 November and 14 December Callaghan held a succession of carefully orchestrated Cabinet meetings. Simultaneously, negotiations continued between the government and the IMF: the pivotal Cabinet meeting of 1 December started half an hour late because, unknown to ministers, Callaghan was in his meeting with Witteveen. But even Benn was impressed by the thoroughness of the Cabinet debates. 'Callaghan was very fair,' he told me. 'He said, "This is a very important thing." He put me on to speak first. I put up my alternative to the IMF cuts, then the others put theirs.' He paused. 'They were the most interesting discussions I ever attended in my life.'

Benn's case against the cuts was simple and dramatic. 'This is a political decision as grave as any in our history,' he began at the meeting of 1 December. 'We are in the middle of a slump . . . We've got to reduce unemployment . . . We've got to expand our manufacturing base. We've got to safeguard the benefits of the welfare state . . . We cannot fudge the issue . . . Cuts and deflation will not be acceptable.' As a cautionary tale, he cited the 1929 to 1931 Labour government, still remembered with a shiver in the party, which had split and then been crushed in a general election after succumbing to pressure for cuts in public spending in the midst of a sterling crisis and a recession. This time, Benn went on, Labour should be more streetwise and resilient: rather than accept the IMF's demands, the government should shield sterling and the economy by putting limits on currency trading and foreign imports until the economic pressures eased.

Benn was fiercely cross-examined by Callaghan and other less left-wing members of the Cabinet. He defended his arguments determinedly, and made some telling points against those who would do a deal with the IMF. 'They said, "Your proposal is a siege economy,"' he told me. 'I said, "Yours is a siege economy too, except the bankers will be inside the castle, and your supporters will be outside, besieging."' Yet ultimately his plan was too similar to other schemes for Britain's economic salvation that he had unsuccessfully proposed earlier in the seventies. Moreover, behind his clear, defiant rhetoric there appeared to lurk an uncertainty about whether or not to ignore the IMF altogether. According to Benn's diary, at the 1 December meeting, 'Jim [Callaghan] asked [me], "Do you think we need the loan?" I said I would prefer to have the loan rather than not.' But in the very next sentence Benn seems to adopt a different position: 'I reminded the Cabinet of the famous cartoon in 1940 of a soldier after Dunkirk waving his fists and saying, "Very well, alone."' And in the next sentence he seems to adopt another position still: 'I said that I thought the IMF would help us because it would be in their interests to do so.'

Benn did not win over enough of the Cabinet. Next to argue against the IMF cuts was a less charismatic, more pragmatic left-winger, the environment secretary Peter Shore. He proposed two years of restrictions on imports to protect the British economy, until, he anticipated, significant North Sea oil revenues started to flow and removed the need for such emergency measures. Shore's plan, being less ambitious and ideological than Benn's – and not being proposed by Benn – fared slightly better under cross-examination, but other ministers still worried it might provoke a trade war with Britain's allies or bankrupt the country before its measures could take effect by endangering the loan from the IMF. Shore, too, failed to convince a Cabinet majority.

With the momentum of the meeting established, Callaghan called on the final and potentially most formidable opponent of the IMF to speak. Tony Crosland, unlike Benn and Shore, was ideologically close to a large proportion of the Cabinet. He had an enduring reputation – probably still the pre-eminent one in the party – for panoramic but nuanced political thinking. And he could not be typecast as a financially unrealistic socialist. The previous May, he had been one of the first major Labour figures to call for belt-tightening, telling a local government conference in Manchester that councils should curb their spending: 'We have to come to terms with the harsh reality of the situation which we [the Labour government] inherited. The party's over.'

Yet by the late autumn of 1976, after a year and a half of much more penny-pinching Labour government, Crosland felt that the cuts proposed by the IMF were unnecessary and would be counterproductive. 'I want us to stick to our existing strategy,' he told the Cabinet on 1 December. 'We have . . . deflation . . . We've got a wages policy, and it will work. There is no case for a change.' Far from reviving the apparently all-important currency markets' faith in the government, 'New cuts would have a disastrous effect . . . because they'd damage wages policy and destroy confidence.' If the IMF absolutely insisted on the cuts as a condition of the loan, he went on, Britain should 'threaten a siege economy, or talk about . . . our troops in Germany . . . membership of the EEC, etc. Schmidt and Ford would soon give way.' Or, alternatively, the government should 'do a presentational job to the IMF by announcing now the cuts we had decided on in July but which have not yet become known, and possibly some extra cuts . . .'

Crosland was a confident man, and often signalled the fact. He smoked cigars, wore loud shirts and used irreverent words. Callaghan had made him foreign secretary, but he had long-standing ambitions to be chancellor. Yet at the Cabinet meeting of 1 December the casualness of Crosland's language and the unevenness of his arguments – some of them penetratingly logical, some of them barely sketched out – suggested a talent on the wane. In the Labour leadership contest the year before, he had come last and been eliminated after the first round. As foreign secretary he was often abroad, even during the IMF crisis, and his political, as opposed to intellectual, influence had not recovered. He was only fifty-eight in 1976, not old for a senior politician then, but there was a weariness and passivity in his handsome face. The year before, Barbara Castle had caught his mid-seventies mode in her diary: 'a mixture of brilliant analysis and suspended action'.

By the climax of the IMF crisis, Crosland was not the only Cabinet member who was worn out. 'The IMF negotiations were the most tiring part of my life,' Healey told me. 'I would often work sixteen hours a day or even longer. Get up at six in the morning, and go to bed maybe about two or three in the morning.' He lowered his voice. 'I got shingles, which is a famous nervous disease . . . Unpleasant, but you use an ointment.'

Yet the chancellor proved tougher than his Cabinet opponents in the end. The day after Benn, Shore and Crosland had presented their arguments, the Cabinet met again. Healey told them that the government would have to start repaying its non-IMF loan from the summer in exactly a week. If it did so without borrowing more money from the IMF, he continued, the Bank of England would be left with less than £2 billion in reserves. Earlier in the autumn, the Bank had sometimes spent over a tenth of that sum in a single week, defending sterling on the foreign exchanges.

Healey next urged the Cabinet to accept the £2.5-billion reduction in state spending that Callaghan had secretly agreed with Witteveen on 1 December. The cuts would be scheduled to delay the pain as much as possible: £1 billion in the financial year 1977–8 and £1.5 billion in 1978–9. The prime minister then confirmed to the Cabinet for the first time that he supported his chancellor. In another astute piece of stage management by Callaghan, Michael Foot, the Cabinet's most popular left-winger and closest link to the unions, then announced that he too agreed with Healey. Finally, Callaghan records that he 'went round the table one by one, inviting the opinion of every member of the Cabinet'. The IMF cuts were accepted by eighteen out of twenty-three ministers.

It took another fortnight for the detail of the deal to be agreed by the Cabinet and the IMF, and for it to be accepted by Parliament and the unions. There were still delicate moments. On 3 December, in a meeting with Healey, Whittome appeared to increase the IMF's demand for cuts again, to almost double what the Cabinet had just reluctantly conceded. 'I told Whittome he should tell the Managing Director [Witteveen] to "take a running jump",' Healey wrote afterwards. 'He smiled and said, "We seem to have reached an impasse."' Healey warned that if the Fund did not back down, the government would 'call a general election on the issue of the IMF versus the people', not a prospect the officially apolitical IMF would welcome, and an unconscious echo of Heath's challenge to the miners two years earlier. As chancellor, Healey had no authority to threaten elections, Callaghan noted later,

But I was quite happy that he should have done so. He and I sat for some time in my bedroom talking over the various drastic policy changes that would be needed if a loan was not forthcoming . . . On that night anything seemed possible . . . The next morning we parted and I travelled to Chequers for the weekend, and on arrival was handed a message . . . The IMF negotiators had reported back [to] Washington and had shortly afterwards telephoned London, suggesting a renewal of contacts . . .

When the Commons debated the final terms of the loan on 21 December, twenty-seven Labour MPs voted against the government, despite a three-line whip, and thirty abstained. But the Conservatives, caught between wanting to paint Healey as a pawn of the IMF and their own basic agreement with much of what the Fund was demanding, abstained rather than opposed, and the loan terms were passed comfortably.

The biggest cut, £320 million, would come in spending to stimulate employment; then defence, £300 million, with the chancellor showing his lack of political sentimentality by squeezing his old department; then housing, £280 million; nationalized industries, £240 million; food subsidies, £217 million; and road building, £125 million. Reductions in the budgets for education, the NHS, and welfare benefits and services were relatively small or non-existent. The IMF may have questioned Britain's 'wide range of social welfare programs', but the Callaghan government was not going to dismantle them.

In Washington, William Simon declared the planned cuts 'excellent' regardless. At Transport House in London, Jack Jones was more guarded: 'The unity of the Labour party and the trade unions, despite our concern about a lot of these measures, will be maintained.' It was left to a less senior but rising union leader, Alan Fisher, of the rapidly expanding National Union of Public Employees, to strike a more ominous – and prescient – note. 'In meeting the conditions made by the IMF', he said, 'the Government have accepted a cheque that may bounce at the next general election.'

During the IMF crisis, the government had broadly accepted the Treasury's forecasts about the economy, in particular concerning the public-sector borrowing requirement (PSBR). When the PSBR for the financial year 1977–8, which had been pivotal in the IMF negotiations, turned out to be £5.6 billion rather than the £10.5 billion the Treasury had predicted, suspicions were sown in the Labour Party that have flourished since: that the Callaghan government had been the victim of a subtle campaign in 1976 by right-wing Treasury officials to make it accept cuts in public spending. When I asked Bernard Donoughue about this theory in 2005, he dropped his customary insouciance for a moment and looked at me fiercely. 'The Treasury and the Bank of England wanted cuts,' he said. 'They were exaggerating everything. In 1976, I remember a Treasury friend said to me, "Look, you can't manage the economy tightly over a long period. You only get a chance once every decade to get the economy under control. What you need is a crisis that frightens ministers into accepting [your ideas]. The bigger the crisis, the more you can frighten ministers. [It's] what we call the Treasury bounce.'"

A few weeks later, I asked William Ryrie, who had been in the Treasury from 1963 until 1975 before joining the IMF, whether he thought there had been a 'Treasury bounce' in 1976. 'History isn't made that way,' he said. 'It's always cock-up more than conspiracy.' But a few minutes later, when I asked less directly about how the Treasury had seen the IMF crisis, he said cryptically: 'The window had opened.' What did he mean exactly? Ryrie, now Sir William and retired to an idyllic private estate in south London, sat very upright in a pink shirt and cream trousers in his vast living room. A distant clock ticked. 'An opportunity to pursue better policies,' he said.

Finally, I asked Healey about the Treasury figures. 'The figures were unreliable,' he said. 'I mean, *incredibly* so. If you look at the PSBR . . . billions out.' He looked at the ceiling of his study in mock outrage. Then he told me a story about his war service. 'When I was in the army, I ruptured myself. [To convalesce] I was sent to replace a drunken bombardier as a railway checker on Swindon station. And on six platforms in the blackout, it was very difficult to count the number of soldiers getting on and off . . . So I made up the number who were getting on, and I went to the ticket collector [on the trains] to get the number getting off. But I found he made up his too.' Healey chuckled. 'So I always had a distrust of statistics.' Did he think the Treasury had duped him in 1976? 'The big problem they always have in the Treasury is getting governments to control spending,' he said calmly. 'So any excuse they can find for getting spending cut they will take. It wasn't so much a conspiracy against the government so much as an attempt to get the policies they believed in.'

It seemed rather a fine distinction. Perhaps sensing this, Healey immediately changed the subject. When the IMF crisis was over, he continued, he soon discovered that 'We didn't really need the money at all.' How soon did he come to that conclusion? 'About six months afterwards.' In the end, the Callaghan government used less than half the IMF loan, and paid it back well ahead of schedule. 'The whole thing was unnecessary,' said Healey. 'If I'd had the right figures, I needn't have gone to the IMF. Very irritating, but there you are . . .'

His voice trailed off. Then, after a second or two, his usual domineering cheeriness returned. 'But of course, once we got through it all, people outside Britain thought I could walk on water . . .' Healey warmed himself with a proud smile. Then he got up from his desk, fetched some glasses and poured me a huge late-morning whisky to drink before my train back to London.

By the end of 1976, sterling was back above $1.70. During 1977, it reached $1.80, then $1.90. There was a slight worry that its value was now too high, and that the exchange rate was making British exports more expensive, but the anxiety passed. In September 1977, Healey was chosen to head an important IMF committee. The following year, he writes in his memoirs, 'I was approached several times to see if I would be prepared to take Witteveen's place as Managing Director of the IMF when he retired [in 1979].' Perhaps unwisely, Callaghan's chancellor declined the offer.

15

Brent vs the Cotswolds

With the IMF's bailiffs back in Washington, less exotic but equally formidable opponents lay in wait for the British Left. One was a moon-faced London businessman called George Ward. Short and slightly plump, with big glasses, tight clothes and a voice like a slow, buzzing wasp, Ward was a factory owner in his early forties. He came from a middle-class Anglo-Indian family who had hit hard times. His father had been a prosperous New Delhi accountant who died young with unexpected debts, and Ward had grown up shuttling uneasily between India and England, between boarding schools and bedsits. He studied economics at a polytechnic, considered academia, and settled for accountancy. For a time in the late fifties, he had emigrated to Brazil to escape London's racism. He came back to England for good in 1963: he had liked the entrepreneurialism of Brazil but not its coups and inflation. Finally, he set up a company with two men he met at a Catholic Mass in London, John Hickey and Tony Grundy. From parts of their three surnames they contrived an inelegant but moderately memorable company name: Grunwick.

Grunwick developed photographs. They opened for business in a garage in St John's Wood in north-west London in 1965. 'At the outset,' Ward wrote later,

we had to do everything by hand, and dipping the strips of photographic prints into one trough after another made me feel that I was working in a Chinese laundry . . . But little by little, by offering better terms and quicker delivery times than our competitors, we managed to get ahead . . . We moved up and down the mews as other tenants moved out . . . The properties in the street were owned by the Council, which proved to be a tolerant landlord. We would knock down the walls of adjacent houses to give ourselves bigger rooms to work in. Our only real problem was the neighbours, some of whom would complain when the machines were whirring away in the dead of night, especially since we could not afford air conditioning and would keep the doors open in summer . . .

By the early seventies, with cheap cameras, family snaps and foreign holidays part of everyday British life, Grunwick was one of the biggest independent photo-processing firms in the country. Its mail-order services, which had snappier, Americanized names like Bonuspool and Trucolor, were speedy, good quality and cheap. Ward was managing director, and he and his relations were the biggest shareholders. Between 1972 and 1976, the company moved from St John's Wood into two factories a few streets apart, further west in Willesden.

Willesden, like its borough, Brent, was one of the last heavily industrialized corners of the capital. It was in gradual decline: in its threadbare red-brick streets businesses were closing and unemployment was rising. Yet for Grunwick it seemed a shrewd choice. The expanding firm needed more staff, especially in the summer, when a single hot weekend could threaten to swamp it with films to develop, and it needed those staff to be unusually hard-working and flexible. One group its recruitment concentrated on was Brent's large Asian population, which had grown especially fast in the late sixties and early seventies with the expulsion of the Indian communities from Uganda and other former British East African colonies. 'Grunwick advertised door-to-door in Brent,' Jayaben Desai, who joined the company in 1974, told me. 'They said, "Any education, any caste, any experience." I was working at home, sewing and dress-making, and I was depressed. I was afraid to go out. My big son said to me, "Mum, you need to go out."'

Desai, who was tiny and slight, and in the mid-seventies still spoke erratic English, had come to Britain half a dozen years earlier. Like Ward, she did not find immigrant life in London easy at first. Her husband, who had previously been a manager in a tyre company when they lived in Tanzania, had to settle for work as an unskilled labourer. His reduced wages and the boredom of sewing at home drew her to Grunwick, first in the evenings and then full-time. As she stuffed films into envelopes and processed cheques, complaints and invoices, she watched the workforce alter. 'Gradually the white girls left and were replaced with Indian people. The white girls would not do overtime.'

Life for the few hundred employees at Grunwick was less dirty and physical than in Willesden's heavy industries. The mostly female staff, joined by students during the university holidays, sat at rows of desks piled with envelopes and boxes, under bright lights, like a cross between workers in a postal sorting office and a typists' pool. The company's two premises, in Cobbold Road and Chapter Road, were better equipped and less bodged-together than the St John's Wood garages where it had started out. In April 1976, Grunwick moved many of its staff, including Desai, into Chapter Road after a refurbishment costing £70,000. At both plants, 'Physical working conditions were reasonably good,' concluded a government report the following year. But then the report continued: 'Compulsory overtime was at times a burden . . . The management was strict in its insistence upon overtime during the summer season. Although it was clear that some applications for relaxations on overtime . . . had on occasions been granted, there was on other occasions a lack of human understanding in dealing with such requests.' The report also found fault with the pay rates at Grunwick ('low'); with the turnover of staff ('high' and 'disquieting'); with 'petty restrictions' on workers, such as '"no talking" in the mail order department'. Above all, the report found a 'lack of effective machinery for handling grievances'.

The company did not recognize the right of unions to represent its employees. Even in the seventies, this was quite common in small firms, especially those with fluid workforces like Grunwick's. Yet by 1973, the year before Desai joined the company, enough tension had already built up around the issue, both inside and outside the firm, for there to be a public battle. The spark was the sacking of a handful of staff. Ward said the redundancies were because 'work was short'. The unions said the workers had been fired for trying to organize a TGWU branch at Grunwick. Either way, between fifteen and twenty other employees went on strike. The dispute lasted seven weeks and drew in workers from other Willesden factories as pickets.

It became a struggle, even Ward was forced to concede, about whether there should be a union in his factories.

But he prevailed. It was winter, the company's slackest season and the worst time to picket, and an inconclusive industrial tribunal failed to interpret the original sackings as his opponents wished. Attitudes on both sides were left to harden. Ward was marked down as a dangerous reactionary by the unions; meanwhile, he was left convinced that the union movement was, as he put it later, 'an arrogant establishment . . . claiming that it stands for workers' solidarity and the "sacred right" of collective bargaining when what it wants is more power'.

In 1975, Grunwick set up its own, highly watered-down version of a union: a works committee, to which each department in the company could elect representatives. 'This committee was not encouraged as a forum for the handling of individual grievances,' the 1977 government report found. 'The minutes . . . do not create the impression that it was a very effective body for dealing expeditiously with collective issues.' The report concluded that some staff did not even know the works committee existed, and that other employees had no faith in its power to challenge the management. The mail-order department where Desai worked and whose staff 'consist[ed] largely of Asian ladies . . . never did elect a representative', the report discovered. Instead, the department was spoken for by its manager, Malcolm Alden. He was close to Ward, young and abrasive, and 'the source of many of their grievances' in the first place.

On Friday 20 August 1976, the latest in a long succession of sweaty days that heatwave summer, with the recently installed air conditioning at Chapter Road not yet functioning and the films to be processed piling up as they always did at that time of year, Alden had a confrontation with an employee called Devshi Bhudia. Bhudia was nineteen, a 'boy' in Ward's later description, who had been with Grunwick for almost a year. He had become so dissatisfied with the pay and conditions that he had lined up a job elsewhere, but he had yet to hand in his notice. Instead, earlier in August, he had agreed with three students who worked in his department and shared his resentments that they should mount a protest of some sort, which would provoke the management into sacking one of them; then the rest of them would publicly walk out.

At 1 o'clock on the 20th, the opportunity presented itself. Ward had left that day for a fortnight's holiday in cooler, greener Ireland, but in his absence a certain high-handedness towards the shop floor remained. As Bhudia was about to go out for lunch, Chapter Road having no canteen, he was suddenly instructed by Alden to sort an additional thirteen crates of mail for posting by 2 o'clock. Bhudia had the students to help him, and the difficulty of the task would later be disputed, but his response was unambiguous: he and the students began a go-slow. At 3.30 p.m., Alden noticed that the crates had not been dealt with and called Bhudia into his office. 'There was a scene,' as the 1977 government report put it, and Bhudia was fired on the spot. As he was leaving the premises, on his own, the students told Alden they were resigning in protest at Bhudia's treatment. They followed Bhudia out of the factory.

They went through the main gates and found him standing just outside in the hot afternoon. Like him they were angry and excited, and they discussed letting down the tyres of Alden's Jaguar. But as their adrenalin began to subside, it dawned on all of them that they had lost their jobs without having any clear idea about how to take their campaign for a fairer Grunwick any further. So they just stayed where they were. In front of them, down the long straight expanse of Chapter Road, the shadows of the street's trees and terraced houses slowly lengthened. Afternoon became evening.

At 6 o'clock, with Bhudia and the students still at the gates, Desai started packing up to go. She knew nothing about the earlier incident, but she wanted to get home. She lived two bus rides away in more respectable, more suburban Wembley. 'My husband objected to me doing overtime in Willesden,' she told me, 'because the area is not good.' Yet that evening, unusually, one of Alden's junior managers told her she could not leave until she had done at least another half an hour's work. Desai, whose dislike of Alden and Grunwick's style of management had been steadily building, objected and lost her temper. Alden appeared and took her aside. There was an argument, and Desai announced she was resigning. It was a spur-of-the-moment decision, but before she exited the building she was joined by her son Sunil, who had a temporary job in the same department as a student. 'The two of them stood in the middle of the floor like soap box orators,' Ward wrote. '"Can't you understand what these managers are doing to us?", Mrs Desai demanded. Malcolm [Alden] requested them to leave the premises, and eventually he and Peter [another manager] escorted them to the main gates.'

The Desais found the original four Grunwick dissidents talking to the company's personnel manager. He was making conciliatory noises about speaking to Alden on their behalf, but Jayaben Desai dismissed his chances and his likely motives. Then, she told me, she dissuaded Bhudia and the students from having a go at Alden's car. 'I said, "Don't do that. It will involve the police." They said, "What should we do then?" I said, "We don't know anything about involving a union, but let's find out."'

Over the weekend, Desai spoke to her husband. He had a new job with the unionized film company the Rank Organisation, and was confident that a union could civilize Grunwick. Sunil had vaguely discussed the same idea with some of his co-workers there a few weeks before. So the Desais and the other dissidents resolved that they would find and join an appropriate union the following Monday, 23 August. They also decided to draw up a petition in favour of a union representing the Grunwick workforce, and to invite the staff at Chapter Road to sign it as they arrived for work.

When Monday morning came, Desai and her five allies mounted a rudimentary picket outside the gates and collected signatures. Even Ward later conceded that 'many' of his employees agreed to sign, although he insisted that the petition was deliberately blank where the detail of its demands should have been. During the rest of the morning and the early afternoon, the Desais made plans with sympathizers inside the plant for a mass walkout of Chapter Road staff. At 3 o'clock, over fifty people, just over a tenth of the Grunwick workforce, got up from their desks and joined the picket. Press photographers were also present outside the gates. 'There was shouting and excitement,' records the 1977 government report. In small, unselfconscious, only vaguely political stages, a famous strike was crystallizing. Next, the participants decided to take it further. They were going to march on the other plant at Cobbold Road.

The second Grunwick premises, which contained the company's colour-processing and transport departments, was ten minutes' walk away across several busy roads. The Chapter Road rebels had supporters there, but so far work had continued at the Cobbold Road premises uninterrupted. Before the marchers could reach Cobbold Road, one of Ward's allies raced over by car from Chapter Road and warned the management what was coming. According to Ward, the arriving 'crowd' of strikers then proceeded to 'shout, scream, swear and spit' at one of the Cobbold Road managers. 'One woman [striker] tried to climb through a window into one of the offices,' he continued, 'and had to be shoved back. People ran back and forth along the side of the building, smashing reinforced windows and hacking at doors with sticks, iron bars and heavy plastic tubing . . .' The account in the 1977 government report on Grunwick is less graphic but probably more accurate: 'Although there was some violence, it was short-lived – no more than an explosion of excitement following upon the Chapter Road walk-out . . . The strikers were calling upon those who were inside [Cobbold Road] to come out and join them. Some fiery spirits tried to force an entry . . . The management resisted and it is possible, though by no means certain, that . . . a girl striker was hit. The police were called and the strikers went away. Only a few from Cobbold Road joined the strikers that afternoon.'

Nevertheless, for the rest of the week the dispute gained momentum. By Friday 27 August, 137 Grunwick staff, approaching a third of the total, had stopped work. Ward was still on holiday with his family in Ireland. It had taken him four days even to hear about the initial Chapter Road walkout, and he would remain away on holiday until 6 September. 'No one could have foretold', he wrote afterwards, 'that [the strike] was to grow to the proportions it later assumed.' Yet, by the end of August, talks between his managers and the strikers about a return to work, something both sides in theory still desired, had in effect already reached a dead end. The strikers

wanted a union established at Grunwick to deal with their grievances, and the management did not. On 2 September, the company
sent a formal letter to all the strikers: 'Your participation in strike
action has brought [your] contract to an end, and accordingly your
employment with this company has ceased.'

The Grunwick walkout had provoked the response of tough employers down the ages to industrial action: a lock-out. Meanwhile, inside
the gates of the Grunwick plants, between two thirds and three quarters of the staff were still working. Given the nature of the company's
workforce, and the local unemployment rate, it was not hard to
envisage Desai and the other dissidents being quickly replaced, and
their campaign fading away.

Yet the world outside the gates would prove much more hospitable
to their cause than they or Ward initially imagined. The first sign of
this came when the strikers inquired about joining union. On 23
August, Sunil Desai had cycled to the Wembley branch of the
Citizens' Advice Bureau and had been given three phone numbers:
for the TUC, for the Brent trades council, and for the Association for
Professional, Executive, Clerical and Computer Staffs, or APEX, the
union that seemed most suitable. Sunil called the TUC first; a few
hours later, a TUC staffer rang back and confirmed that APEX was
the best union to try. The following day, a Tuesday, over sixty of the
strikers held a meeting, elected a delegation to talk to the union's
London organizer and filled in APEX application forms. By Friday,
every single striker who had been on Grunwick's permanent staff was
an APEX member.

The person who more than any other made this swift coming
together of forces possible, and who would lead the resulting coalition against the company management, was an ambitious young
Brent activist called Jack Dromey. Like Ward, Dromey was a fleshy
man with a flat voice and a liking for open-necked shirts, coupled
with a defiant, relentless manner that won him both enemies and
admirers. And like Ward, he was a mixture, politically speaking, of
the past and the future: someone who would continue the eternal
power struggle between employee and employer by new means. Yet

unlike Ward, Dromey regarded Brent as home territory. He had been born and brought up there in a family of poor Irish immigrants. After university, and a noted career in student politics, he had returned to the borough as secretary of the trades council. The position sounded workaday but in fact the trades council was radical, run by a combination of communists and Labour left-wingers like Dromey, and it was energetic and innovative in its alliances and activities. When it first became involved in the Grunwick dispute, Dromey wrote in his 1978 book *Grunwick: The Workers' Story*, the trades council 'was simultaneously fighting hard against cuts in the National Health Service in Brent, and cuts in education, and . . . in support of the long-running strike for equal pay [for women] at the TRICO-Folberth factory in Brentford, an effort which involved 24-hour picketing . . .'

As trades council secretary and often the fulcrum of these efforts, the bearded Dromey, sometimes photographed on picket lines with a loudhailer and a leather jacket like a militant polytechnic lecturer or a younger, more fashionable Arthur Scargill, had an intimate knowledge of the borough's industrial estates and how their employees could be mobilized. 'There was Rolls-Royce next door to Cobbold Road, *fiercely organized* by the T&G,' he remembered when we met in 2006. 'They were *passionate* in support of Grunwick. White men, quite chunky, well paid' – he smiled – 'supporting these diminutive Asian women. You had that very powerful combination. We arranged for the strikers to visit other workplaces. Women in saris meeting workers who'd never met women in saris before. They would go in and simply tell the Grunwick story. They were without any kind of guile or jargon. They were brilliant. There had not been that sort of mobilization before for a local dispute.'

In 2006, Dromey was slimmer and much less hairy. He wore a suit. He was treasurer of the Labour Party and deputy general secretary of the TGWU, and was married to the equally prominent Labour politician Harriet Harman. He had acquired a national reputation, perhaps the best of any senior trade unionist, for mounting successful campaigns for low-paid immigrant workers. But, in 1976, such campaigns by unions were virtually unknown. 'In the five years before Grunwick,' said Dromey, as we had coffee in an anodyne meeting room at the TGWU's London headquarters, 'there had been a succession of disasters where unions had let down black and Asian workers. The big battalions were oblivious to the fact that there was a world of super-exploitation in 1970s Britain – exploited migrant labour.'

Officially, British unions had been sympathetic to immigrants and opposed to racism for decades. In 1955, the TUC condemned 'all manifestations of racial discrimination or colour prejudice whether by governments, employers or workers'. But until Grunwick such laudable declarations had very limited effect in practice. At best, the unions took the same sort of guarded interest in the politics of race as they did in feminism and gay liberation. At worst, racism lingered in unions as it did in other parts of British society.

The post-war labour shortage, which had prompted the British government to encourage mass immigration in the first place, had ended in the sixties. In the seventies, with unemployment rising instead, competition for jobs between the white and non-white working class became more intense. Between the early sixties and the mid-seventies, the Labour Party to which the unions were tied gradually abandoned its earlier liberal stance on immigration and, in opposition and in government, engaged in a competition with the Conservatives to bring in the toughest, or at least the toughest-sounding, restrictions. At the same time, for many white trade unionists, class politics and the interests of existing union members took precedence over supporting immigrants or recruiting them into unions – particularly as the places where immigrants often worked were, like Grunwick, frequently a difficult environment for union activism. When Enoch Powell made his 'rivers of blood' speech in 1968, he was condemned by some union leaders, but many union members, notoriously, took the opposite view. An official of the Association of Scientific, Technical and Managerial Staff in Birmingham who had attacked Powell was quickly telephoned by members of his union telling him to 'mind the union business instead of looking after those nig-nogs'.

Less crudely but just as insidiously, records the historian Dilip Hiro in his 1971 account of race relations *Black British, White British*, right through the sixties 'Trade unions at the factory level worked in league with management to restrict equal opportunity for black and Asian settlers – in recruitment, types of job available, promotion and redundancy.' This collusion diminished but did not disappear during the seventies. In 1974, the radical race-relations periodical *Race Today* commented: 'The section to benefit most from the trade unions are white men over the age of thirty-five. Nowhere is this as clearly illustrated as in the struggles of black workers.' When the economy weakened in the mid-seventies, non-white workers suffered disproportionately: between 1974 and 1980, Hiro notes, the number of unemployed Asian and Afro-Caribbean Britons rose by 290 per cent, over twice as fast as the jobless total as a whole. The mid- and late seventies also saw the National Front marching through London and other British cities. The party enjoyed sudden surges of support at local and national elections, and infiltrated union branches. Between 1975 and 1977, the number of assaults, robberies and violent thefts suffered by Asian and Afro-Caribbean Britons increased by almost a third. Not all these developments were directly related – the National Front, for example, took most of its support not from trade unionists but from disgruntled right-wing Tories – but they formed a political climate which, until Grunwick, seemed much less than multicultural.

Dromey, who sometimes calls himself 'a Brent nationalist', was quick to tell me that, in the seventies, his borough's unions were more enlightened than most when it came to race. 'From the sixties, there was a union-backed, inter-race group in Brent, the Willesden Friendship League,' he said with a proud bob of his head. 'Grunwick was a dispute that might've struggled to get off the ground in most parts of Britain, but Brent was the borough to have it in.' Yet even he admitted there were some awkward moments between the strikers and their allies. 'I remember a meeting in week 12 of the strike when Len Gristey [an APEX official] said to some strikers who were Muslims, "No power in Christendom will defeat you." I slid under the table.'

Yet at Grunwick, and for decades before, British Asians were not simply the passive recipients of political assistance. The first Indian Workers' Association in Britain was set up in Coventry in 1938. One of its founders, Udham Singh, was already a member of a union and the local trades council. He was also concerned with larger political issues. In London two years later, he assassinated Sir Michael O'Dwyer, who as governor of the Punjab in 1919 had supported the Amritsar massacre of Indian nationalist demonstrators. Singh was hanged, but other Indian Workers' Associations were formed in Britain; by the late fifties, there were so many of them that they received official advice from the Indian prime minister, Jawaharlal Nehru, and held a national conference, in 1958, which pledged them to campaign for better working and living conditions, oppose racism and form alliances with the Labour Party and trade unions.

By the early seventies, British Asians were going on strike to secure their equal treatment in the workplace, whether the unions supported them or not. In 1972, the semi-skilled staff of Mansfield Hosiery Mills in Loughborough, many of them, as at Grunwick, recently arrived East African Asians, downed tools to protest against their exclusion from the better-paid, more comfortable jobs done in the same premises by white workers. Local union officials opposed the strike, but an industrial tribunal found both the union and the mill's owners guilty of unlawful discrimination. Two years later, at Imperial Typewriters in Leicester, another group of mainly East African Asian workers, faced with unfair treatment compared to their white colleagues over everything from production targets to tea breaks, mounted round-the-clock pickets, organized strike rallies and won national attention. Again, local union officials opposed their action. After a three-month struggle, the strikers returned to work having won only relatively minor concessions.

Both disputes, however, seemed to mark the arrival in Britain of a new and potent workplace militancy. They showed that East African Asians, often employers or relations of employers before they became immigrants, could, with their understanding of the managerial mentality and their resistance to being intimidated by it, turn themselves into stubborn and inventive shop-floor rebels. And the disputes showed that the East African Asians' extended family and friendship networks, which had appealed to British employers seeking a quick and reliable supply of recruits, could also be used to sustain strikes. An atmosphere of solidarity and cooperation did not have to be created between the strikers; it already existed. Finally, the disputes stood out for the part played in them by women. Of the first thirty-nine workers to walk out at Imperial Typewriters, twenty-seven were female. Often doubly discriminated against, used to balancing domestic and workplace burdens, and more awkward to confront aggressively than their male counterparts, Asian women could seem infuriatingly dogged, disconcerting strikers to unthinking British employers.

In 2006, Jayaben Desai was still living in the same semi in Wembley as in the Grunwick days. On the way there, walking through the area's neat, quiet streets, with the North Circular moaning in the distance and the sky turning from white to grey, the other pedestrians were mostly Asian women in Asian dress. Soon after Desai answered the door her phone rang and she began a long, unhurried conversation in Gujarati. Her living room was plain: no political posters or memorabilia, not much furniture, a faded colour scheme of seventies brown, a single electrically heated cushion on a hard sofa. Desai's bird-like frame was swaddled in an oatmeal cardigan despite the mildness of the day, and she wore glasses attached to a neck-cord. She was seventy-three and her health had not been good recently; a few months earlier, when I first wanted to contact her, I had found a speech on the internet, recently given by a well-known trade unionist, which paid tribute to her Grunwick heroics in the obituarist's past tense.

Now, however, her voice was loud and clear as she spoke on the phone, and when she finally looked around from her conversation, her huge eyes and strong nose were the same as in the Grunwick photographs. She came over and sat down right next to me on the sofa. I asked if what she had done in the seventies had changed her. 'No. Not much,' she said, curling her legs up under her. 'I am the same person. I am a capable person. I can handle home, I can handle work. I can explain things – always the words come to my mouth. I always put my foot first on the threshold. I was born like that.' She flapped a hand and laughed: 'Determination is always there.'

She was born in Gujarat in India. 'My father was a landowner. He was involved with Gandhi before I was born. I was involved in the independence movement when I was ten years old. A flag was always in my hand. In the seventies, a BBC journalist said to me, "Aren't you oppressed by men?" I said, "I don't think that way. We have a woman prime minister in India. We have had women warriors in India who fight with children on their backs."' She suddenly poked me in the ribs to underline the point. 'I didn't know anything about strikes to begin with, but the fighting power was there.'

In her late thirties, she was forced to leave Tanzania with her family. 'My father said, "Do not go to England. It is not a good country, because the people there are very racist."' When she became one of the leaders of the strike at Grunwick, 'My husband said, "Do you know what you've done? They'll kidnap our children." I said, "God will help me. And I haven't had any telephone calls abusing me."'

From the first weeks of the dispute, the strikers and their allies in the unions dug in for a struggle. APEX was a cautious, politically moderate body – 'right-wing' by Dromey's left-wing standards – but it had been recruiting rapidly in recent years, especially among women, as the white-collar and light-industrial sectors of the British economy were becoming a greater proportion of the whole. In mid-September 1976, less than three weeks after the Grunwick rebels had submitted their union-membership applications, APEX began giving them strike pay: only £8 a week at first, about a quarter of the typical basic wage at Grunwick, but backdated and soon increased to £12, supplemented by another £2.50–6 a week depending on each striker's needs.

Desai remembered, 'We made a rota for the picket: nobody stands on the picket line for more than two hours, then they can go home. Two hours meant women could do housework, people could do other jobs. I was doing the cooking at home, everything. My husband didn't do anything. He was working night shift, so he was getting very good wages, but he was asleep during the day. He would leave for his shift at seven. Sometimes I didn't get home for good until nine, ten o'clock in the evening. He and my sons had to heat the food up.' To sustain this dual life as mother and activist – as the strike went on *Spare Rib* and other British feminists began to show an interest in what the magazine called the 'Grunwick women' – Desai rushed back and forth between Wembley and Willesden. 'I used to go to the picket and back twice a day. I couldn't drive then. It was a twenty-minute journey, if I was lucky with the buses. But the buses were unreliable then, and there was a fifteen-minute walk to and from the bus stop . . .'

Her husband and sons quickly accepted her new life as a strike leader – 'I have a very good family' – but the families of some of the other strikers were less supportive. 'A number of the women said to Jayaben that they were having trouble going away from home to [picket] the factories,' Dromey told me. Despite the growing involvement of Asian women in British industrial disputes, Desai told the Asian feminist writer Amrit Wilson in 1978, 'Our Gujarati women are often weak. Their husbands don't want them to do anything which is not passive, and in the end women end up believing . . . that their life must revolve around dressing up, housework, wearing jewellery and other things like that.' The fathers and fathers-in-law, too, of some of the Asian women who had walked out at Grunwick pressed them not to continue the strike. Besides the 'traditional attitudes' to gender that Wilson found among British Asians – and which, for all the advances of feminism, persisted among many other Britons – there were good economic reasons not to take part in a protracted industrial dispute. Poor immigrant families like those of many of the Grunwick women usually needed two incomes.

So Desai and a core of equally committed strikers visited the waverers and their families at home. Dromey, who from early in the dispute began attending the strike leaders' daily meetings, helped set up larger gatherings where doubters could be won over. For him, the gender and ethnicity of the Grunwick workforce were not obstacles but opportunities: 'I wanted a clear statement that there were going to be no no-go areas for unions.' Yet for all his leather-jacketed bravado in public, in private he was less confident about the strike's prospects. 'I knew that we were in for a tough fight from the start:

the fact that less than half the workforce had walked out; the fact that we started with no organization at Grunwick. We didn't know about the early seventies walkout at Grunwick, but we quickly found out. When we did, we were, "Hmmm . . ." One of our union conveners said to me, "This is going to be a difficult one, Jack."'

Ward had not seen the dispute coming, but after he returned from his holiday in Ireland, halfway through the strike's second week, he proved a formidably stubborn opponent. He gave slow but unyielding television interviews in front of his factories, belly out and tie unfussily askew. In 1977, while the strike was still going on, he published a book about himself and the strike called *Fort Grunwick*, which, as the dispute continued, was what the Chapter Road plant in particular came to resemble. Its tight little compound – a concrete courtyard and a few almost windowless buildings hemmed in by high walls and the backs of houses – had never looked that welcoming; now, with extra wooden panels fitted to the metal mesh of its gates, with razor wire strung around its brick perimeter, with security spotlights and essential supplies stockpiled, the factory began to suggest a new architecture for strike-defying businesses, ugly and crude but functional, that would become familiar in British industrial disputes in the decade to come.

Ward was every bit as ingenious as Desai and Dromey. When the strikers persuaded the main suppliers of Grunwick's photographic chemicals and paper to boycott the company, Ward sent out his managers to buy small quantities from other sources and drive them back to his plants in the boots of their cars. When trade unionists at British ports and airports, and at the equivalent facilities in Belgium, the Netherlands and Germany, refused to handle Grunwick's mail-order business with continental Europe – in the seventies, such were the levers some well-organized strikers in Willesden could pull – Ward bought a six-seater aircraft, took out the back four seats and hired a pilot to fly deliveries back and forth to Rotterdam from a shifting selection of small British airfields.

He also fought a shrewd propaganda war. During 1977, the Queen's Silver Jubilee year, he hung Union Jack bunting above the

Chapter Road razor wire. He presented himself to the media as a typical British underdog. In February, shortly after announcing a 15 per cent pay increase for the Grunwick staff who were still working, he commissioned the respected polling firm MORI to survey them about being represented by a trade union. Two hundred and sixteen employees said they were against a union, and only twenty-one were in favour. Given the pay increase and the skewed nature of the sample – by definition it excluded the employees who were most in favour of having a union, as they were on strike for that very reason – the poll result was not that surprising. The strikers and their sympathizers inside the plants also alleged to the press that the survey had been conducted in less than neutral conditions. On 18 March, the *Kingsbury News*, a local Brent paper, reported that the poll had been 'taken department by department . . . People [who took part] felt they could easily be identified. They said Mr Ward told the staff that all in one particular department had voted against [having a union] except for one person. They were disturbed that he knew the results so precisely. They also said managers had . . . shown the voters specimen ballot slips.'

However, for the national media and the public the result of the survey was easier to absorb and remember than its questionable context. For the rest of the dispute, Ward's anti-union stance had at least the appearance of democratic legitimacy; the Grunwick workforce was assumed to be utterly divided; and Ward was able solemnly and repeatedly to invoke as an argument 'a worker's right . . . *not* to join' a union, as he put it in his autobiography – despite the fact that compulsory union membership at his factories was not a goal of the Grunwick strikers and, he had to admit in his book, only a distant and possible consequence if they won. 'Granting an official status to the union by "recognition"', he wrote, 'in practice . . . means the union is likely to seek to negotiate not just for its own members but for the whole workforce, and eventually it may try to impose a closed shop, excluding from employment all those who refuse to join.'

In these slightly stiff, paranoid sentences, as in the fortifications at Chapter Road, was embedded a whole new right-wing approach to strikes and unions. In time, it would come to dominate Conservative

Party thinking. But in 1976 and 1977, with Margaret Thatcher and her free-market allies not yet in full command of the Tories, let alone in government, it was left to Ward and, most dramatically, an unexpected group of Ward backers to put the new approach into practice.

In September 1976, the APEX general secretary Roy Grantham made a speech at the TUC conference alerting other unions to what was happening in Willesden and urging that they make a contribution. The delegates from one other union in particular paid Grantham's speech close attention. Grunwick, as a company with a thriving mail-order business, was highly vulnerable to any action taken against it by the Union of Post Office Workers (UPW), the main postal union and, at local level at least, a more radical organization than APEX. By September, members of the UPW branch that dealt with Grunwick were already refusing to cross the picket line to deliver the company's mail. On 1 November, UPW members at the sorting office in nearby Cricklewood began refusing to receive the Grunwick mail as well, or to let the company come and collect mail that had already arrived at the sorting office.

'This was a threat to our jugular,' Ward wrote later. 'Eighty-four per cent of our trade depended on mail order.' But help was at hand. On the evening before the postal boycott of Grunwick began,

I . . . heard a programme on BBC [radio] 4 about the closed shop. The man who was leading the debate against compulsory unionisation was a Roger Webster, who had been sacked some time before by British Rail for refusing to join a union . . . He argued with spirit, but also with a dry humour . . . I found myself in total agreement . . . He was described on the radio as the National Branch Organiser for the National Association for Freedom . . . After hearing Roger Webster talk I decide to get in touch with NAFF.

While Ward was trying to find a phone number or an address, NAFF's director, John Gouriet, had by coincidence just found out about the threatened postal blacking at Grunwick. 'I had read a tiny little style column item, hardly an inch, on the back of the [London] *Evening Standard*,' he told me in 2006. 'It was one little company that was being bullied. I rang up George Ward and said, "Can we help?"' Roger Webster completes the anecdote in his memoirs: '"Answer to prayer!" was George's reply. "I've been trying to get hold of you since I heard your man on the radio. How soon can we meet?"

'"I'll be with you in an hour," replied Gouriet.'

During the late sixties and early to mid-seventies, a certain feverishness seized some of those involved in British right-wing politics. The fever, which intermittently infected the Conservative Party itself, started during Harold Wilson's sixties government, hit a peak with the defeat of Ted Heath by the unions, continued at a high level throughout Wilson's second, crisis-hit administration, and only slowly abated as Callaghan began to run the country with relative competence and moderation – and, more importantly from an anxious right-wing point of view, Thatcher began to look like a radical and electable alternative. Some of the preoccupations of this feverish right-wing politics were relatively short-lived: whether Prime Minister Wilson was a Russian spy; the threat to true Conservatism represented by Prime Minister Heath. But others were enduring: the belief that British decline had worsened into national crisis; the need for a strong, quite possibly authoritarian right-wing government to stop the slide; and, above all, the need to take on the trade unions, which were at best, the argument went, a working-class interest group that had grown too powerful or, at worst, part of a global left-wing conspiracy that led all the way back to Moscow.

The holders of this world view were a mixed bunch. There were City grandees, and restless Tory MPs such as Nicholas Ridley and Airey Neave; new bourgeois pressure groups such as the Middle Class Association, and members of MI5; and distinguished former soldiers, such as the founder of the SAS Colonel David Stirling and General Sir Walter Walker, until 1972 head of NATO's northern command. There were also the less distinguished tycoons and landowners who gambled and plotted at the Clermont Club; and even survivors from previous busy periods on the far-right fringe of British politics, such as the veteran anti-Semite and anti-immigration campaigner Lady Jane Birdwood. The organizations these people formed came and went. The Middle Class Association had 5,000 members at its peak and existed from 1974 to 1976. Stirling's GB75 and Walker's Civil Assistance were both intended to be larger, country-wide networks of volunteers, ready to 'act', in Walker's usually undefined terms – interpretations of his intentions varied from helping the government maintain essential services to mounting a military coup – 'in the event of a breakdown of law and order'. These organizations attracted national attention: Labour politicians warned about 'private armies', and letter-writers to right-wing newspapers expressed rare excitement.

But such publicity always seemed to lure the likes of Walker into overconfidence and the other vices of hastily assembled political crusades: claiming vast but unconvincing memberships, splitting and merging, impatiently adjusting their names and aims. It was one thing to airily plan the counter-revolution in a gentlemen's club, it seemed; quite another actually to do something concrete in the Britain of the late sixties and the seventies, which was preoccupied by the state of its economy and still had a strong Left.

The National Association for Freedom was the one right-wing fringe group with a practical mindset and genuinely potent political connections. It had been officially launched in December 1975, and Margaret Thatcher attended its first subscription dinner in January 1977. But NAFF's roots ran much deeper, back to the forties, when Norris McWhirter, one of the identical twin sons of a right-wing Fleet Street editor, had campaigned against Clement Attlee as a teenager. At Oxford, Norris was taught by Tony Crosland and found the future Labour philosopher 'able' but 'quite unconvincing', he wrote later; after university, Norris and his brother Ross established a precocious, abrasive double act as entrepreneurs, journalists and political and legal campaigners, specializing in dogged court actions against unions and the state which made successful use of obscure parts of the law and were accompanied by a fierce rhetoric about defending the individual against the collective. In the late sixties, the brothers fought against the introduction of comprehensive education to the prosperous north London suburb of Enfield and formed a lasting alliance with one notable local right-winger, Ralph Harris of the

Institute of Economic Affairs. By the mid-seventies, the McWhirters' less overtly political activities, as the co-editors of *The Guinness Book of Records* and the cold but compelling stars of its television spin-off *Record Breakers* – both of which put an anti-egalitarian emphasis on ranking individual achievement – had made them rich enough to set up their own right-wing organization.

It started in 1975 with a publishing company for anti-union tracts, the Current Affairs Press, and a news-sheet, *Majority*, which stood up for the 'free' capitalist economy and suggested that private citizens should husband food and set up 'self-help' groups to counter strikes. In October, Ross McWhirter successfully intervened against members of the National Union of Seamen when they refused to let passengers' cars off a strike-bound ferry in Southampton, by using legal writs and despatching Gouriet to the port as his envoy. In November, the Current Affairs Press was renamed Self-Help. The same month, plans were drawn up to turn Self-Help into NAFF, and Ross McWhirter, a vocal opponent of the IRA, broadened his organization's remit further by offering a £50,000 reward for information leading to the arrest of the notorious Republican cell, later known as the Balcombe Street Gang, then at work in the capital. The IRA gang travelled to McWhirter's house in Enfield, waited for darkness, and shot and killed him beside his doorstep. In the Commons the next morning, Margaret Thatcher said, 'We on this side of the House . . . knew Ross McWhirter well and admired him a great deal. He was one of the finest people of his generation . . . He was active each and every day in protecting and preserving individual liberty.' A week later, still in the glare of publicity sparked by McWhirter's murder, NAFF was launched by his brother.

From the start, the Association had close links with the Conservatives, from Thatcher right down to the party membership, which was NAFF's main recruiting ground. It had money: membership was £5 a year, high for a political organization in the seventies, and wealthy supporters were prepared to donate much larger sums – a 1978 appeal for £90,000 to pay for some of NAFF's activities at Grunwick raised the cash in three weeks. It had a vigorous newspaper, *The Free Nation*, with articles about the Tory leader ('Mrs

Thatcher, Please Don't Sell Out to the Union Left') and the policies she should adopt ('Council Houses: Give 'Em Away!'), and others by some of her more radical advisers (Ralph Harris and Alfred Sherman). It had articles about the socialist threat abroad as well as at home ('Why the Zambezi Is OUR Front Line'). It featured appeals from NAFF for information about bullying by unions ('Are you fed up with blackmail and intimidation from militant minority groups in your place of work? . . . Do you want to take action but don't know how? WHY NOT GET IN TOUCH WITH US FAST? 01-836-8553 Ansaphone in operation. WE WILL HELP IF WE CAN'). For light relief, and perhaps revealing of its readers' income and location, *The Free Nation* also had 'Stable Talk', a column about racehorses.

NAFF's other high-profile publication was a Charter of Rights and Liberties. Reflecting the mixture of libertarian thinking and traditional right-wing fixations found in *The Free Nation*, these included:

The Right to be defended against the country's enemies.
Freedom of speech and publication.
Freedom to withdraw one's labour, other than contrary to public safety.
Freedom to belong or not to belong to a trade union . . .
The Right to private ownership.
Freedom to exercise personal choice . . . in spending, and from oppressive, unnecessary or confiscatory taxation.
Freedom from all coercive monopolies.
Freedom to engage in private enterprise . . .

In the spring of 1976, Graham Smith had just finished a law degree when he came across the first issue of *The Free Nation* in WHSmith in Leicester. He had not been involved in student politics but was considering joining the Conservatives and, he told me, 'I'd always been interested in libertarianism. I was intrigued by *Free Nation*. I wrote off to them: "I've got six months free. Would you be interested in me doing a summer job?"' He started as 'a gofer' for NAFF, before becoming its first research officer. 'The offices were in Upper Berkeley Street [in Marble Arch]. Couple of smallish rooms. There was a mixture of young people like me and older figures like Norris McWhirter – a delightful character, quietly spoken, great integrity. It had a sense of something completely different. We felt like radicals.'

At first, much of this radicalism boiled down to selling papers in shopping streets in other parts of London. It was something left-wing sects like the Socialist Workers Party did all the time, but a brave initiative for a right-wing organization – an indication of where Britain's political centre of gravity still lay. Unlike their left-wing counterparts, the NAFF paper-sellers worked in groups. 'We went to Brixton once,' Smith remembered. 'The local SWP got unhappy. We beat a retreat . . . We even went up to one TUC conference. Sold the papers outside the front door. Dromey was there, over on the other side of the road, with a bunch of his Grunwick pickets. He started shouting with his loudhailer, and a great bunch of people started coming over, and the police suggested we beat a retreat . . .'

The junior NAFF activists tended to be middle-class and clean-cut but less conventional than the typical young Conservative. Instead, they looked like hippy-ish young Christians. Smith had a Jesus beard and wore tight T-shirts over his lanky frame. Thirty years on, he had naturally broadened a little. Like Dromey, he was clean-shaven and wearing a suit when I interviewed him, in another corporate-style meeting room, and like Dromey he had done well since Grunwick: he was a partner in the international law firm Bird & Bird. It was an uncomfortably close London summer evening but that did not completely account for his initial jumpiness. 'I haven't been active in any of this stuff for years, really,' he told me, looking at the table. Getting him to agree to meet had taken months.

John Gouriet was a different matter entirely. Since his time as NAFF director in the seventies, without ever entering conventional politics, he had never stopped fighting for right-wing causes. He was much older than Smith, ex-army, and he lived in rural Somerset. When I rang him in 2006, he invited me down for lunch without hesitation.

In a winding valley north of Taunton, the slow bus from the station got stuck in a traffic jam. When I called Gouriet to say I would try to carry on by foot, he immediately offered to drive and intercept me. 'Red Peugeot 406,' he added crisply, as if we were embarking on a minor military operation. 'Number plate ending in FYB.'

Gouriet was wearing an old-fashioned check farmer's shirt when he picked me up. He had side-parted hair like Prince Charles, a proud nose like Edward Heath and an intermittent excitement in his eyes. In the car, he talked about where he went shooting, about the pointlessness of speed limits – 'people, if left to their own devices, will do the right thing' – and about 'the hoi polloi in Minehead' on the nearby coast. Then we turned off into a sweet village, where a white house stood, looking out over the valley, full of dogs, antiques and prints with imperial themes, and with its front door wide open in March. 'We're having pheasant,' Gouriet announced.

'I came out of the army in January '73,' he began as we sat in his bracing kitchen. 'Armoured-car regiment. Converted to tanks. Started in Malaya, active service '56–'57. It didn't interfere with our polo and racing, but I'd never seen a dead body until I'd seen one strung up on a tree, looking like a sieve. A Chinese informer.' Gouriet paused over his cream sauce. 'I was in Aden. Borneo in '65, one of two intelligence officers. One was looking at the enemy, listening to the enemy. I put it to good use at Grunwick. I was in Northern Ireland for a year. I went briefly to Saigon – I was cadging a lift to Hong Kong with the RAF. It was the most extraordinary scene, several huge runways, aircraft landing, taking off, at the same time as mortar attacks . . .'

Like a significant number of British army officers who had witnessed the advance of communism and Irish republicanism at first hand, Major Gouriet entered civilian life in Britain in the mid-seventies with a sense that the world was tilting dangerously towards leftism and anarchy. 'I went into the City. I was there watching the FTSE fall to that ghastly figure of 146 [in 1974]. Too many people were wringing their hands. I joined the [Conservatives' hard right] Monday Club. I became chair of its economic committee. I was by then a good friend of Ralph Harris [of the IEA] . . .' Gouriet smiled. 'It's not what you know but who you know . . . And I joined what would become NAFF – I discussed it all with him. I originally called it Link. I wanted to link everything up, to pull the right-wing fringe groups together, build up substantial pressure points to persuade the government of the day . . .'

There was a division in the NAFF hierarchy between the young libertarians like Smith, who were opposed to authoritarianism of all kinds, and some older members like Gouriet, who had army backgrounds or right-wing intelligence connections and did sometimes think of British politics in military terms. 'There's a clip of Dromey addressing his troops at Grunwick,' Gouriet volunteered as we finished the pheasant, 'and he says, "Gouriet may look like Colonel Blimp but he's a General Pinochet."' Gouriet laughed: 'High praise indeed!' After we had finished pudding and covered numerous other subjects, he volunteered again: 'Going back to that comment about me and Pinochet' – he smiled almost wistfully – 'perhaps Dromey had a point.'

At Grunwick, the assistance NAFF gave George Ward was at first behind the scenes and narrowly legal. In response to the November 1976 postal boycott, or 'blacking' as such union actions were often called, 'They recommended solicitors,' Ward wrote. 'After consulting Counsel [the solicitors] advised me that legal action [against the Union of Post Office Workers] would prove effective.' Following the usual McWhirter method of using forgotten parts of the law as political levers, NAFF and the solicitors drew Ward's attention to the 1953 Post Office Act, which made it a criminal offence for 'any officer of the Post Office' to 'wilfully detain or delay' the mail. 'They suggested that we should apply at once for an injunction to stop the blacking,' Ward wrote. An injunction was obtained and served, and the UPW called off their boycott. It had lasted for only four days.

But NAFF did not depart from Willesden in search of a fresh cause. Instead, Gouriet became a regular presence at Fort Grunwick. 'I spent three days a week in the factory,' he told me, 'and I was in touch with Ward by phone every day.' The press and pickets soon came to recognize him. He walked as if still on a parade ground and wore a tie and pocket handkerchief. In front of the cameras, he smiled confidently and talked to those still working – even to the pickets – a little like a royal visitor. Even thirty years later, Dromey could not conceal his irritation: 'They parachuted from nowhere, NAFF, with their cut-glass decanter accents. No one knew to start with that they were part of a wider Conservative network. I thought they were cranky at first, but NAFF were very astute tactically.' In a passage about NAFF in Dromey's 1978 account of the strike, there is a sudden sense of an era of union supremacy ending:

Every time the union applied the ordinary trade union pressures of blacking and picketing some upper-class twit appeared on the television screen with a court writ in his hand. The NAFF was breaking the ground rules of industrial relations, not 'playing cricket.'

Winter started, Grunwick's slow season, and the strikers were still outside the gates of the two Willesden plants. They stood in thin lines, rarely more than a dozen people at each entrance, the Asian women with coats over their saris and small home-made placards, with small numbers of other Grunwick strikers and supporters from other unions reinforcing them. The doggedness of the strike, the growing sense in Willesden and beyond that a pivotal confrontation between the British Left and Right was building up at Grunwick, the relatively novel identity of the strikers – all this continued to attract media attention. 'I was going on TV, on the radio, to meetings,' Desai recalled. 'Grunwick was a test case for everyone. I and my husband were already Labour supporters, but I learned a lot about politics. I thought we could win.' How did she feel about becoming a public figure? 'There was no feeling in my mind, "I have to go on television." In my mind it was all about the struggle – that's it.' But a few minutes later, she volunteered, 'In India – oh my god – a daughter of a friend said, "I saw your picture on a big poster in the station." She sent me a big cutting from the Indian *Times*.'

In early 1977, the strikers tried another tactic. Over the autumn, they had written repeatedly to chemists across London, asking them to stop collecting and sending films to Grunwick. Some chemists agreed; from February 1977 those that did not were picketed. 'In Brent this picketing was very effective,' wrote Dromey. 'Of sixteen shops discovered still to be using Grunwick, ten agreed to stop . . . With the help of trade unionists all over London, coordinated through the Greater London Association of Trades Councils, most of Grunwick's four hundred outlets . . . received a visit. The biggest store in Oxford Street, Selfridges, chose to ponder [its attitude to the strike] at first but quickly abandoned Grunwick when Jack Dromey rang up to say that thirty pickets would be arriving the following Saturday.'

Yet the rest of Grunwick's activities continued virtually uninterrupted. The fact that the company had separate premises several streets apart – the Chapter Road factory even had entrances opening onto two different streets – made it hard to picket. Grunwick's delivery vans and managers' cars drove past the strikers, sometimes not bothering to slow down. As the dispute dragged on, the police on duty at the picket appeared to grow impatient with the strikers: in October 1976, they had abruptly announced restrictions on the number of protesters they would allow at the gates. A few days later, nine pickets were arrested and charged with obstructing a public highway. By March 1977, despite the picketing rota and Desai's rushing back and forth and stirring pep talks from Dromey, the number of strikers was dwindling: 'Students had left the strike, others had found new jobs,' he wrote. 'The strike lost all momentum . . . The picket lines . . . on occasion, were non-existent.'

But if the strike was fading in Willesden, its reputation in the labour movement was still growing. The support that resulted revived Desai and her comrades. In April, 1,000 trade unionists from as far away as Wales and Liverpool came to Willesden for the day to march on behalf of the strikers. In May, Shirley Williams and two other government ministers, all three of them APEX members, stood for a symbolic hour on the picket. Desai smiled at the memory. 'A government minister who was on the picket line that day said to me, "You haven't eaten, drunk all day. How do you do it?" I said, "I've got energy. It comes from flesh and bone, not food." The minister said, "My wife told me that precious things come in small packets. Now I believe her!"' And at that Desai's smile split into a great laugh.

In June, APEX decided to mobilize the whole pro-strike coalition on the streets of Willesden by calling a mass picket. 'Apart from Russian tanks and sex education there was nothing in the 1970s which frightened the right more,' wrote Dromey with nice wit later, 'than the dreaded "mass picket".' One precedent from earlier in the decade would soon be in the minds of the Right and Left alike at Grunwick. Dromey spelled it out: 'the "Battle of Saltley Gates".'

At 6 a.m. on 13 June, two hours before the remaining Grunwick staff were expected to start arriving for work, the first members of the first mass picket emerged from Dollis Hill station and lined up in front of the Chapter Road gates. Many of the pickets were women: the Communist Party Women's Group had suggested at a recent meeting of British feminist organizations that women should show their support for the strikers on 13 June, and the strike committee had agreed. 'Its members considered that the presence of a large number of women would emphasize the peaceful intention of the picket,' wrote Dromey, 'and have a restraining influence on the police.' By breakfast time, there were about 700 pickets, spread between the two entrances to the Chapter Road plant and the two entrances to the Cobbold Road plant, and about 300 policemen, many of them sitting in police buses parked along the main road that separated the factories. Ward watched through the net curtains of his first-floor office, which faced down Chapter Road and was right next to the most heavily picketed gates.

It was there that trouble started. According to Dromey, 'The "loyal" workers . . . passing [on foot] through the gates were shouted at and called "scabs" but got into work with relative ease.' Ward's account differs: 'Every time one of our employees got near the gates, moving through the gap in the picket lines that the police were struggling to keep open, toughs would surge forward in an effort to get to him; there would be three or four arrests required in order to get a single worker through to the plant.' Both accounts agree, however, that relations between the police and some of the pickets quickly degenerated into shoving and grappling. By the end of the morning, eighty-four pickets, many of them women, had been arrested, most of them for obstruction. Plenty of the television and newspaper reporters present were taken aback by the aggression of the police. The London *Evening Standard*, usually no friend of left-wing protesters, recorded: 'One demonstrator was dragged to a police van by his hair and several others were clearly punched during the arrests.'

The next morning, faced with another mass picket, Ward's workers unexpectedly arrived by bus. Malcolm Alden, the fierce young Grunwick manager who had helped provoke the strike in the first place, had discovered, in a moment of ingenuity worthy of Ward or Gouriet, that you could drive a bus with an ordinary car licence as long as you owned it and did not collect fares. Alden's son had recently been driven to a school camp in an old red single-decker; the school, Ward wrote, 'let us borrow it for a while'. When the loan expired, the company bought several double-deckers – despite the strike Grunwick still had the spare funds – to create a strike-breaking fleet that would allow for maintenance and breakdowns. On a double-decker, its staff would also be a safer distance from the boiling crowd.

That morning, and each weekday during the rest of June, the Grunwick ritual was played out. Shortly after dawn, the pickets would come: the ease of the journey from other parts of London and the brevity of the confrontation with that day's bus meant that the protest could be fitted into busy diaries. 'I used to take the kids to school, then go to the picket,' a mild, middle-aged woman who had been in the International Socialists told me at a celebration of the strike's thirtieth anniversary. Left-wing barristers came on their way to court: John Platts Mills QC, president of the Socialist Lawyers' Society, dressed in a bowler hat and suit, hectored the police through a megaphone for their alleged pro-Ward bias. Radical actors came on their way to rehearsals – and were too tired out by the early rise and the picketing to rehearse properly afterwards. Trade unionists from across the capital came before going to work.

While the pickets were massing, chatting and standing around, the bus would be kept carefully out of sight. 'My husband found it in a side street once,' the woman at the anniversary remembered with a smile. 'He put sugar in the petrol tank.' Then, often driven by Alden, and with Gouriet on board to gee up the strike-breakers, it would zig-zag a dozen miles across north London, picking up workers at pre-arranged points. At the last rendezvous, a journalist from *The Times* travelling on the bus reported on 24 June, 'Two or three special patrol group [SPG] police vans start following close behind. The driver confers with the police, who are in radio contact with the commander at the scene [outside the Chapter Road factory]. It is then decided which is the best route and whether to use the back or front gates.'

Finally, the bus would make its approach. Often this was down the straight stretch of Chapter Road. The tight tree-lined pavements would be crammed with pickets and banners. The road itself would be screened off by policemen. The police would lock arms, and the more aggressive pickets at the front of the crowd, always a minority, would stop chatting and push inwards, onto the roadway, into the path of the bus. The bus, if it could, drove fast, and the pickets had to get out of the way; if it could not, it had to inch through the crowd. 'Scabs! Scabs! Scabs!' went the chant. There was banging on the windows, furious faces up against the glass. But the bus usually got through. It would stop as close to the gates as it could, and the workers would hurry out. The gates would be quickly opened to let them in, and then shut. Alden would dismount from the cab and have a fag.

In many ways, the whole televised routine was indeed reminiscent of the confrontation between trucks and pickets at Saltley five years earlier. But two things had changed. After Saltley, where the police had been outmanoeuvred and outnumbered, and so publicly humiliated, there had been a rethink of their approach to mass pickets. Police commanders in such situations were now encouraged to use cat-and-mouse tactics – suddenly closing off roads, switching the entrances used by picketed factories – to throw the blockading crowds off balance. And the police began to use a degree of intimidation.

During the dock strike of the summer of 1972, a river wharf in the Midlands had been besieged by pickets. 'Our lot were really struggling,' an anonymous chief inspector told the police sociologist Roger Geary. Then, the chief inspector continued, 'More officers drove [onto the wharf] in a bus and got out . . . They were all six foot men and they marched up and they changed the whole complexion of the situation.' Here, as at Saltley and Grunwick, the police did not use truncheons or riot shields, but they were much more ready to make arrests. In *New Society* on 30 June 1977, the left-wing writer and activist Stuart Weir produced a convincing eyewitness account of a day at Grunwick, during which 'two phalanxes of police' made 'a series of charges' against the crowd and 'dragged pickets out one by one'. Most of the part-time pickets in Willesden were keen to avoid physical confrontations, but more arrests were made on the first day of the Grunwick mass picket than in the whole week-long 'battle' at Saltley.

On occasions at Grunwick, the police were pelted with flour and eggs, cans and paper cups. Dromey and most of the pickets disapproved of such behaviour, but they did regard the police as a less than neutral presence. 'George Ward's rent-a-mob' went one of the picket-line chants, and Dromey alleged in his book that there was a 'special relationship' between the company and the police. Grunwick's personnel manager in the summer of 1977 had previously been a Brent policeman, and Scotland Yard used the company to process crime-scene photographs. No collusion was ever proved, but Ward was certainly happy with what he called 'the courage and efficiency of the police' during the mass pickets. Gouriet felt the same: 'The policing was terrific, absolutely terrific,' he told me. 'Beyond the call of duty.'

On 23 June, the police made an arrest at Grunwick to gladden any British right-winger's heart. Earlier that month, Jayaben Desai had decided to recruit further supporters. 'I went to Yorkshire without telling my husband,' she recalled with one of her big white smiles. 'To see Arthur Scargill.'

Scargill was now president of Yorkshire NUM. 'Mrs Desai and members of the strike committee accompanied by Jack Dromey came to my house unexpectedly on a Sunday afternoon,' he told a BBC documentary in 2002. 'Mrs Desai said, "We've had all the messages of support that you can think of. The problem is that no one's coming to really help us." I said that we would.' During the 1972 and 1974 miners' strikes, for the first time, the overwhelmingly white NUM had received generous donations and support from black and Asian trade unionists and members of the public. Scargill had woken up to the political potential of ethnic-minority Britons – and to the potential for alliances with them in the future. Now, in late June 1977, Desai's request and the possibility that Grunwick might be another Saltley was too good to resist. On the evening of the 22nd, Scargill and two coaches of miners set off from Barnsley and drove through the night to Willesden.

'Almost from the first day, we had been waiting for the miners,' wrote Stuart Weir in his account of his time with the mass picket. On the morning of the 23rd, they appeared: 'Eight abreast, below broad scarlet and red banners, [they] seemed to fill the road.' Dromey described the arrival of a bigger contingent of miners three weeks later in even more heroic terms:

Women with shopping baskets and local workers out for a lunch-time stroll stared in silence as the miners' delegation approached. They marched in grey and brown working clothes . . . not in groups, but in a solid line of power-ful arms that stretched from pavement to pavement without a break. There were no placards . . . no hurry . . . They made no noise and sang no songs but just occasionally as they rounded a bend permitted themselves a deep growling chant in thick Yorkshire: 'Easy! Easy!' and 'We'll be back! We'll be back!'

The police were less awestruck. After the miners' march-past on the 23rd, Scargill joined a knot of pickets in Cooper Road, outside the back entrance to the Chapter Road plant. The strike-breakers' bus approached, and the police began to shove the pickets back. Scargill, wearing a tie under his donkey jacket and his usual shiny black shoes, was first caught in the middle of the crush of pickets, and then thrown forward, open-mouthed. He gulped, stumbled, looked round to see who had pushed him, and then braced himself with a slightly tentative hand against the back of a policeman. A second or two passed. Then another officer, helmetless and much taller than Scargill, came lunging in at him from the side and seized his arm. In one well-honed move-ment, this policeman, an SPG man, pinned Scargill's arm behind his back, yanked him round, and with two other officers pushed him towards a police bus and bundled him in. BBC television news filmed it all; and then they filmed the feared union militant sitting behind a barred window on the police bus, looking pale. Scargill gave a pained wink to the cameras. Then he looked straight ahead.

The fact that this new picket-challenging policing could occur under a Labour government was a source of frustration and disbelief to the Grunwick strikers and their allies. Since the party had returned to power in 1974, the unions had gained a great deal: the repeal of Heath's Industrial Relations Act, the establishment of ACAS, the almost daily influence over government policy provided by the social contract. And yet, as Grunwick would vividly demonstrate, union strikers and pickets had done less well out of the government. They were still required to act 'peacefully' – an adverb which gave a great deal of leeway to watching policemen. And when the unions lobbied hard during 1974 and 1975 for pickets to be given the right to detain vehicles, a power which could have proved decisive at Grunwick, the police and the home secretary Roy Jenkins, the latter concerned about the implications for the liberty of individuals, successfully blocked the proposal. In the second half of the seventies, the trade union dictatorship envisaged by some on the British right and left was not quite at hand.

Nonetheless, for the residents of Willesden during the Grunwick mass pickets it sometimes felt like that. In 2006, I followed the route that many of the pickets took to get there. The tube journey from central London was barely a quarter of an hour. At Dollis Hill station, the nearest to the site of the Chapter Road plant, I got off the train and walked up a short exit tunnel. The gates of the old Chapter Road plant were right in front of me.

They were padlocked and rusted in places, and beyond them were weeds and an abandoned fridge in the factory courtyard. But the street outside the gates seemed much as it had been in the seventies: narrow and residential, with small terraced houses behind tiny front gardens. There was little through traffic, a newsagent, a slight air of transience and tattiness – here and there a dumped sofa beside a doorstep. I asked the newsagent, a middle-aged Asian man, if he remembered the strike. He shook his head. He'd never even heard of Ward's company. He nodded across the road at the Chapter Road site. 'It used to be an Indian catering firm a few years ago,' he said. 'And then it was an old people's day centre.'

I began knocking on the doors of the houses. At the seventh one I tried, about fifty yards from the derelict plant, a slightly older Irish woman answered. She certainly remembered the pickets. 'There were too many of them,' she said. 'They'd be standing on your window ledges.' Was it frightening? 'Actually, it was. There'd be people fighting. When you got up [in the morning], the pickets would be here. You'd open the curtains, you'd see them here. My husband – he was in a union – he agreed with the strike. I didn't.' She looked at me firmly in her turquoise cardigan. 'I didn't know what they were fighting for. I remember the police having to take us through the station when we wanted to use it. Otherwise we stayed indoors.'

In fact, Dromey and others in the strike coalition had had anxieties about mounting a mass picket on Willesden's narrow residential pavements. For one thing, what exactly was the aim of it? Should the mass picket be to stop the remaining Grunwick staff going into work? Or to stop the company obtaining supplies? Or simply to draw attention to the strike and attract more support for it? Or a combination of all three? During the summer and autumn of 1977, as mass pickets were repeatedly mounted at Grunwick, the strike committee – let alone the thousands of supporters who converged on Willesden – never quite decided. Instead, Dromey wrote, the committee 'varied its [strategic] emphasis from week to week'.

And there was another worry about the tactic. 'It could easily lead to confrontation with the police,' Dromey wrote, 'and to the involvement of elements who were not as interested in democratic rights as they were in punch-ups. The mass picket was therefore a risky weapon unless good discipline was maintained.'

On 23 June, a police constable called Trevor Wilson, a member of the special patrol group, was hit on the head by a bottle during a fight with some pickets. For several minutes afterwards – 'some say a quarter of an hour', wrote Dromey – he lay limp and unattended on the ground, in his crisp dark uniform, as a great crescent of blood spread out across the pavement and the pickets, in their flapping jeans, walked past or stood watching him from a distance. The cameras framed the scene like a religious painting. Wilson was hospitalized and given ten stitches. Pickets had received comparable injuries at Grunwick, but it was the policeman who made the front pages. Wilson's wife was pregnant, even the relatively unsensational *Times* reported the next day, and the recovering constable would 'miss a charity sporting event which he had helped to organize . . . for an electro-cardiogram machine for a hospital in Northampton'.

The violence at Grunwick had a lasting impact far beyond Willesden. In March 1997, as Labour nervously prepared to return to office for the first time since the seventies, Tony Blair wrote an opinion piece about industrial relations for *The Times*. It was headlined 'We Won't Look Back to the 1970s' and included this characteristic passage:

Let me state the position clearly, so that no one is in any doubt. The essential elements of the trade union legislation of the 1980s will remain. There will be no return to secondary action, flying pickets . . . The scenes from Grunwick . . . could no more happen under our proposals than under the existing laws.

In 1977, as Blair almost certainly knew, the confrontations outside Ward's factories were a gift to the Conservatives. After ignoring the strike during its early stages, the House of Commons had been discussing the dispute with increasing intensity since November 1976. The afternoon after the assault on Trevor Wilson, there happened to be a session of Prime Minister's Questions. During it Callaghan, usually unruffled in the Commons, was caught between condemning the pickets' violence – 'does he think I want to stand here and defend policemen being hit over the head with bottles?' – and condemning Ward for his Victorian approach to industrial relations – 'it seems to me deplorable [that] . . . people have been dismissed for joining a union'. Callaghan concluded unconvincingly by demanding that 'Those who latch on to this industrial dispute to turn it into a political battle . . . should keep clear . . . This situation is getting extremely serious.' That month a special Cabinet committee was created to monitor events at Grunwick, meeting daily and sometimes twice daily. Ten Downing Street also began to receive daily reports.

Margaret Thatcher, for her part, was quick to grasp the significance of the Grunwick battle. In *The Path to Power*, she devotes almost six pages to it:

> What came to be known as the 'Grunwick affair' . . . was a clear case of the outrageous abuse of trade union power . . . Grunwick was a medium-sized business run by a dynamic Anglo-Indian entrepreneur . . . A left-wing coalition emerged to . . . punish Grunwick. Every part of the socialist world was represented . . . The National Association for Freedom took up the case . . . I gave NAFF as much support as I could, though a number of my colleagues regarded it with deep distaste and made public criticisms of its activities. Without NAFF, Grunwick would almost certainly have gone under.

Her Finchley constituency was not far from Willesden. 'I would ring her up from time to time and brief her [about Grunwick],' Gouriet told me. 'And she had me in to brief the shadow cabinet.' The Conservative shadow education secretary Rhodes Boyson was the MP for Brent North, a NAFF member, and a strong Ward supporter. Keith Joseph, too, was sympathetic to NAFF, and made speeches defending Ward in the Commons.

Yet, as Thatcher acknowledged in her memoirs, not all Tories were comfortable with NAFF's militant anti-trade-unionism. The shadow employment secretary Jim Prior, one of the many shadow ministers she had retained from the Heath era – such, for now, was her incomplete authority over the Conservatives and her caution about appearing too radical to voters – favoured a less confrontational approach to the unions and, like Dromey at first, regarded NAFF as 'cranks'. Moreover, much of the public and the media retained the traditional British aversion to political organizations that looked even a little like 'private armies'. It was an aversion that the mid-seventies antics of General Sir Walter Walker and the other paramilitary right-wingers had only strengthened, so, during 1976 and 1977, Thatcher's support for NAFF and what it was doing at Grunwick remained largely tacit. Messages were quietly passed on praising NAFF's efforts, while in public the Conservative leader and her lieutenants concentrated on the issue of the Grunwick violence. Her memoirs record that during the mass pickets, 'I wrote to John Gouriet . . . "We feel that the scenes of wild violence portrayed on television . . . are enough in themselves to put most of the public on the side of right and are doing more than hours of argument.'''

On 11 July 1977, she appeared on an edition of *Panorama* entitled 'The Alternative Prime Minister'. Questions about Grunwick dominated the programme. 'Mass picketing cannot be peaceful picketing,' she began, boldly. Did she think, the interviewer probed, that the laws on picketing needed changing? Thatcher paused. 'I do think some of the laws of picketing . . . need . . . if I say changing . . .' She drew back: 'I think we need a voluntary code of practice.' Yet later, when the interviewer asked her whether she sympathized at all with Jayaben Desai and the rebellion she had led against Grunwick's working culture, Thatcher's eyes suddenly blazed, her big forehead creased with irritation and her voice deepened:

I must say that I have had the greatest admiration for those people who in the bus have gone through the picket lines *day after day*. Their courage and the courage of the bus driver . . . is very great indeed . . . A few days ago . . . I wanted to know what it felt like as a person to have to run the gauntlet of that sort of behaviour, and so I did ask my PPS to go in on the bus through the picket lines.

Adam Butler, then a young Conservative MP, was the PPS in question. 'I went in on the bus with Jim Prior's deputy,' he remembered. 'The workers were nervous. Everyone was nervous. But it was over very quickly. The bus was not stopped. There were a lot of angry faces. The bus shook. There were no bricks thrown or anything like that.'

By the high summer of 1977, Grunwick was an international as well as a national story. The strikers were receiving letters of support from China and America. Yet Ward showed no sign of backing down. The government and the TUC began to adjust their priorities: restoring order to the streets of Willesden began to take precedence over securing all the strikers' wishes. On 30 June, Lord Scarman was appointed to lead an official Court of Inquiry into the origins of the dispute and the issues between Grunwick and APEX. Public hearings would be held throughout July, and Scarman would publish his conclusions in late August. In the interim, it was hoped, the situation would calm down.

However, the sheer number of interest groups on both sides made a complete ceasefire unlikely. And so it proved. In mid-June, with much of the media's attention on the mass pickets, the postal workers at the Cricklewood sorting office had again begun blacking Grunwick's mail. For the next three weeks, their illegal action was ineffectually challenged by the Post Office and the national leadership of their union. On 5 July, the Post Office began to suspend the Cricklewood workers without pay, but, since they had not been sacked and could not instantly be replaced, locking them out of the sorting office had the effect of stopping the movement of post throughout Cricklewood and Willesden.

By 8 July, Ward wrote, 'There were nearly a thousand mail bags containing about a hundred thousand packets of processed [films] piled up in every available corner in the Chapter Road works. There were also some bags at Cricklewood that we had been unable to retrieve.' It was a Friday, and there was no immediate prospect of shifting the backlog. With a neatness that any defender of workplace rights could appreciate, a company which had provoked a strike by demanding that an employee delay his lunch hour to ready some parcels for posting was now choking, steadily, on a build-up of unposted mailbags.

Except that Gouriet had had an idea. It had long been the view of NAFF and *The Free Nation* and other libertarians in Britain and America that a single, state-run postal service was an oppressive and inefficient monopoly. The blacking of Grunwick's mail, in addition, had helped NAFF realize that an unchallenged Post Office also gave great power to the postal unions. The previous winter, shortly after the first Grunwick blacking, *The Free Nation* had launched a campaign 'to allow voluntary groups like the church and the scouts to take around people's Christmas mail without breaking the law'. The campaign came to nothing but, eight months later, the notion occurred to Gouriet again. 'George was running out of money. I'm a soldier. If you're faced with a problem, you solve it. I'd hunted with over forty packs of hounds. Once you get networking through the hunts' – Gouriet grinned at his Somerset dining table – 'they're game for anything, those sort of people. And it was a very simple concept, the sort of thing that we were taught to do in the army . . .'

He called it Operation Pony Express, after the mythologized nineteenth-century mail business that overcame the human and natural perils of the Wild West. 'I planned it all in the Waldorf Hotel [in London]. I took a room there, for three or four days, made lots of phone calls. I didn't want to do it from my own office [at NAFF]. There were no written instructions, just verbal ones.' At first, he continued, 'Ward wasn't keen. He thought Pony Express might exacerbate things, end in disaster.' But Gouriet persuaded him.

On Thursday 7 July and Friday the 8th, Ward sent out 'a team of girls' from Grunwick to buy £12,000-worth of stamps. 'A girl would breeze into a London post office,' he wrote, 'ask the clerk if they had "plenty of stamps" and then slap in an order for £600 or £700 worth.' No suspicions were aroused. In the meantime, Gouriet hired two large trucks and a minibus from a haulier in Andover, far enough from the capital for discretion. He also asked two dozen NAFF members – 'sixteen people from the City, one or two from the office', and the Conservative MP and Ward advocate John Gorst and his wife – to meet him in north London. 'They didn't know what they were in for,' Gouriet recalled with a pleased look. 'I told them we were having a party.' Instead, on the Friday evening, he briefed them and told them to get into the minibus and the trucks. After midnight, with Gouriet leading in a car like the cavalry officer he was, they drove in a convoy through Willesden. At 1 a.m., they arrived outside the Chapter Road plant.

Graham Smith was in the minibus. 'I'm not sure we gave any thought to it turning nasty,' he told me. But the road was empty. The Court of Inquiry had just begun its public hearings, and there had been no mass pickets that week; and since Grunwick was closed at night and at the weekend, smaller-scale picketing was patchy at these times anyway. The only people waiting for the convoy were Ward, a couple of his managers and a few policemen outside the plant. For the next hour and a quarter, with the lights of the factory fully on, the Grunwick men and NAFF volunteers heaved the mailbags into the trucks. Then Gouriet, Ward, Gorst and his wife posed for a hurried photo – Gouriet in shirtsleeves, beaming, he and Gorst doing victory signs, all of them crowding the frame with excitement. Finally, at 2.20 a.m., the convoy drove off into the thin summer darkness.

They left London and headed into the countryside. Smith fell asleep. When he woke, the convoy had pulled up in front of a large new corrugated iron barn. Outside were dozens more NAFF volunteers and a farmyard full of newly parked estate cars, Land Rovers and horseboxes. When I asked Gouriet where the barn was, his lunchtime jolliness disappeared for a moment. 'You don't need to know,' he said. 'The farm owner was very worried he'd be duffed up. He died eighteen months ago.'

The location of the hub of the Grunwick strike-breaking scheme has been kept quiet since 1977. 'A secret depot sixty miles from London' – Ward's description – is as concrete as the participants have been prepared to be, at least in public. However, it has been possible to make a rough guess. In the right-wing milieu inhabited by Gouriet in the seventies, the West Country is a recurring motif: General Sir Walter Walker lived and schemed in Somerset; Airey Neave did the same from his home near Swindon; the even more hardline Conservative MP Nicholas Ridley – 'a good friend of mine', said Gouriet – made hints about coups to army acquaintances in his constituency in Gloucestershire. The rural West Country was politically conservative, full of military bases and retired officers, and easy to reach from the smart parts of London where the capital's rich right-wing doom-mongers tended to live.

A few weeks after seeing Gouriet, I found out from someone else the full truth about Pony Express. When Gouriet had been planning the operation, he had contacted another 'good friend' in Gloucestershire, and asked if he could borrow a barn for a night and a day. The Honourable Robert Wills had said yes. The Wills family had barns to spare. They had made their money in tobacco in the eighteenth and nineteenth centuries, first in Bristol and then across Britain: Woodbine and Embassy were Wills Tobacco brands. By the seventies, their tobacco business was in decline, but the family still owned thousands of acres of Gloucestershire, and their political allegiances had shifted from the Liberals to the Conservatives. Robert Wills was a 'traditional squire', in the words of his *Daily Telegraph* obituary; 'bluff, slightly eccentric', he ran 'one of the best shoots in the country' on his estate.

I drove there from London on a cold sunny April day in 2006, following the same route as the Pony Express convoy. After an hour and a half, I knew I was approaching Gloucestershire when the road rose with the Cotswolds and I saw the first pro-hunting poster – 'Liberty & Livelihood', it read with a NAFF-style libertarian flourish – on the windy grass verge. Just past Burford, I turned off into a valley of hidden dips and branching country roads. Then, next to an empty stone bus shelter, came the beginning of a grand tree-lined drive and a weatherbeaten sign: Broadfield Farm. At the end of the drive was a big honey-coloured farmhouse, almost a manor house. Behind it was a thick screen of conifers and a crescent of barns around a large rutted yard.

I parked in the yard, got out of the car, and a burglar alarm started. After a few minutes, a rather correct woman appeared. 'Can I help you?' she said, and I explained that I had come to see the farm manager. She told me to wait. For a quarter of an hour I stood and watched the cold wind make dust devils in the yard, and thought about the old class loyalties that British right-wingers in a crisis could call upon. Then the farm manager appeared, friendly and barely old enough to have been alive for Grunwick. But he knew what had happened at the barn. First, he took me to his office and showed me a photo of Robert Wills in the seventies, a hawkish middle-aged man with command in his eyes. 'Mr Bob was very much in the Conservative mindset,' said the farm manager. 'Tony and Blair were swear words.' Next he offered to show me the barn.

It was at the back of the yard, windowless and partly dug into the hillside. He hauled the doors open. The barn was feet-deep in dusty brown animal feed. Its high walls and ceiling were a dull grey and quite blank. It was hard to envisage the installation of a commemorative plaque. But then the farm manager gave me a phone number for a retired Broadfield foreman who had got the barn ready for the strike-breakers. I called him straightaway from the yard, and he was happy to talk.

'On the Friday evening, the boss [Wills] wanted the barn unlocked,' he remembered. 'He didn't say why, and I didn't ask, but when I came to take the padlock off, the key was lost. The boss had to come with the cutters. When he had cut through the lock, he picked it up and gave it to me and said, "One day that may be a piece of history."' Then, the foreman remembered, Wills gave all his farm-workers the weekend off.

But one of them, a shepherd, had ignored the order. The foreman gave me his number, and the shepherd, too, agreed to talk – as long as he could remain anonymous: 'I'm still renting from them.' Then he told his story. 'My dad went up to the farm on the Friday night,' he began, 'and a security man stopped him, told him to keep away. But I had to drive through the farm to get to the fields at eight o'clock on the Saturday morning. There was a lorry there, and all these different vehicles, and loads of people about. And those bits you get down the edges of sheets of stamps – there were dustbins full of those. I couldn't believe it. I was just ignored as I drove through. Later, I was told it was none of my business what had been going on. But we knew the postal strike was on [in Cricklewood]. We saw the [Grunwick] pickets on TV. We weren't that thick. We guessed.' Was it a shock? 'It made us all realize at the time that when the working man was striking, how much was engineered against him. My cousin was a miner, and it didn't surprise me that Mr Bob was involved. He was very Tory and against the unions.' Another former Broadfield Farm employee told me: 'Mr Bob used to say to us, "If I knew any of you voted Labour, I'd sack you."'

To the NAFF activists who had converged on the farm on that warm July night, however, a more daring, idealistic conservatism was in the air. Half a century earlier, during the 1926 General Strike, large numbers of anti-union students had come forward as strike-breakers. They had been organized with some fanfare by retired military officers, and had used hired trucks and private cars to distribute food and other essential supplies. Now, after years of the Left making the running in British street politics, a radical right-wing volunteer network had finally been activated again. 'It was revolution,' remembered Graham Smith, suddenly reverent, looking up from the table in his law firm's conference room. 'There was a lot of shared excitement. People were very talkative.'

The trucks were driven into the barn. Long tables and chairs were set up. Other volunteers sat in groups on the floor. 'It started off a bit chaotic,' said Smith, 'but then we divided up tasks.' The hundred thousand parcels had to be unloaded, individually weighed and stamped, then sorted by address and put back into mailbags for posting. There were 250 volunteers altogether: Smith, with his Jesus beard and a sweatshirt; a young woman with an Alice band and a tank top, heaving mailsacks, almost like a Second World War Land Girl; and lots of older men in shirtsleeves like Gouriet. It was hot in the barn, even with the door open. There was the odd Thermos of soup, tea or coffee, and an atmosphere like a particularly eager election count. 'It was revolting licking thousands of stamps,' Smith remembered, 'but there was a very strong sense that we had to get it all done. The mail had to be out in the postboxes the next morning.'

During the early hours of Saturday, the finished sacks were loaded into the smaller vehicles in the farmyard. 'Then the horseboxes and shooting brakes were despatched,' recalled Gouriet. They went down the long drive of Broadfield Farm, with instructions to deposit Grunwick's mail in modest, hopefully not-too-noticeable quantities at postboxes from Manchester to Truro. 'We were euphoric,' he said. 'It was the same spirit as in the war. I drove a load myself before heading home. I remember stopping in Burbage to post the last bundle. Then I had a very large whisky.' He looked wistful: 'They didn't have as many breathalyzers in those days.'

For the rest of the weekend he and the other NAFF volunteers kept quiet about what they had done. The Grunwick mail, now sitting in thousands of postboxes a safe distance from London, still needed to be collected, sorted and delivered by postal workers who were in the same union, the UPW, as the Cricklewood militants. And the mail was all in branded Grunwick envelopes; it was still possible that a national blacking of it could be organized if the existence of Pony Express got out too soon. On Sunday, a BBC film crew visited the Chapter Road plant and were puzzled and suspicious to find the factory no longer piled with mailbags, but they did not work out what had happened. It was not until the Monday, when postmen began to find postboxes jammed with Grunwick mail, and sorting-office workers began receiving it in vast, unusual quantities, often incorrectly stamped, that the penny began to drop. Dozens of UPW branches outside London now refused to touch the Grunwick envelopes, but the union's national executive, more politically cautious than many of its members, narrowly voted against supporting the blacking or extending it to every sorting office. In the Commons, Gorst made a gloating announcement: 'Is the Secretary of State [for Industry] aware that over 1,000 bags of backlog mail . . . were posted last weekend? Will he agree that the action of the Post Office workers at Cricklewood is [now] completely irrelevant?'

'To be frank, we were stunned,' Dromey recalled. 'We thought there was no way out for George Ward, and then suddenly . . . we were in serious difficulties. We hoped Operation Pony Express would be a one-off. But it was a huge morale boost for the forces of reaction in Britain.' In his living room in Somerset, over coffee and chocolates, Gouriet savoured the memory. 'We outwitted them. We outfoxed them. We ran rings around them.' In 1977, his favourite British politician, described with a wink as 'one NAFF enthusiast', even gave an anonymous quote to *The Free Nation*, comparing Pony Express to a famous recent hostage rescue by Israeli commandos. 'Margaret,' remembered Gouriet, 'said it was "the best thing since Entebbe".'

The Grunwick strike was not over. On the same day as Gorst's announcement, the company endured the biggest mass picket so far. Around 20,000 strike supporters, unaware of Pony Express, swamped Willesden and succeeded, for once, in preventing the Grunwick bus from reaching the factories for several hours. 'We stopped the bloody plant,' Scargill told me. Mass pickets continued into the autumn. In August, the Court of Inquiry published its report and recommended the reinstatement of all the strikers who had held full-time jobs at the plants. The report also recommended that the company should let APEX represent its workers. In addition, during the autumn, 'There was still a hope that we could somehow resuscitate the postal blacking,' said Dromey. 'And a simple defiance, a determination to carry on.' Through the winter and the following spring, and into the summer of 1978, Desai and the hardcore of strikers maintained their picket. 'I lost my health. I had a gallstone operation after the strike,' she told me. 'But during the mass pickets – oh my god – the spirit was very high.'

After Operation Pony Express, the momentum of the dispute had altered, however. 'We were never able to regain the initiative,' Dromey admitted. Grunwick's mail was not blacked again. Ward, confidence restored, simply rejected Scarman's recommendations; he had already rejected a similar conclusion from the government conciliation service ACAS. Such consensus-seeking bodies, with their carefully balanced panels of trade unionists, business leaders and thoughtful liberal lawyers like Scarman, had no place in his concept of industrial relations. He did not reinstate the strikers or recognize a union. Grunwick survived and grew, and established new brands such as Bonusprint and other London premises. It survives to this day. Ward is still in charge but no longer grants interviews.

'Ward was the vanguard,' said Dromey. 'Others followed: Murdoch, Eddy Shah, Thatcher herself during the [1984–5] miners' strike.' Dromey made a final attempt in the autumn of 1977 to orchestrate the cutting off of Grunwick's essential services – not just its post but also its water, telephones and electricity – but failed. By early 1978, he wrote, 'The "loyal" workers were no longer being bussed in . . . They walked through the picket lines and many talked to the strikers as if nothing had ever happened.' After 'some really difficult discussions' with the strike committee, Dromey decided that ending the action would be 'the dignified thing to do'. Desai and a handful of others disagreed. They went on hunger strike, were suspended by APEX for refusing to wind up their campaign, and ended up demonstrating outside the TUC headquarters against what they saw as their abandonment by the unions. A visiting Jack Jones shook hands respectfully with Desai and her comrades. The TUC general secretary went a step further: '[Len] Murray called us inside,' she told me. 'He said, "Who is asking you to do this?" I said, "It is my tradition. And now you hang us on the wire."' By 14 July 1978, her defiance and her memorable plain-speaking were no longer enough. After almost two years, the strike committee declared that its action was at an end.

In the TGWU meeting room twenty-eight years later, Dromey looked for a silver lining. 'You never really lost a dispute like Grunwick,' he said in his flat Brent tone. 'Did we achieve our objectives? No. Was it a landmark event? Yes. There's not been a month since when I haven't met Asian workers who mention 1976–1978.' The argument seemed a bit rehearsed.

When I heard him speak at the Grunwick thirtieth anniversary celebration a few months later, however, he was more convincing. He was not wearing a suit, and there was a touch of the old leather-jacketed Dromey in his stage manner. With a lift in his voice, he pointed out that in 1977 London dockers had joined the mass pickets in support of Desai and the others. 'Nine years earlier,' he added, after a pause for the audience make the connection themselves, 'dockers had marched in support of Enoch Powell.'

After I interviewed Dromey, I put an advertisement in *The Miner*, the journal of the NUM, or what was left of it, asking to talk to miners about their experiences at Grunwick. A few weeks later, an ex-miner called Glyn phoned.

'I was seventeen then,' he began. 'Born and bred in a mining village. I was at a union meeting when they asked for volunteers to go down. We met up in Rotherham. It was a jolly. I think that were my first time in London.' He spent a day on a mass picket. 'I'd never seen anything like it. There were students, women demonstrators shouting . . . an actual gay group, who we got talking to. A group of guys standing there who were obviously gay. Standing there in unity with the sacked workers. I'd never met people like that. There were good feelings there. There were working-class people regardless of race, age, colour . . .'

For the British Left, such coalitions would become commonplace in the decade to come. And so would charging policemen.

16

Getting Away with It?

In some ways Grunwick was a deceptive political event. Away from Willesden and its acrid controversies, 1977 and 1978 proved to be a surprisingly good time for the British Left, or at least the milder parts of it. The Labour government suddenly found itself in a more benign economic and political climate than had been the case for years. 'The stock markets came roaring back,' remembered Gavyn Davies of the Downing Street Policy Unit. 'North Sea oil was about to arrive. The social contract seemed to be working well. We had got rid of the IMF. We were optimistic that we had turned a very big corner.' This optimism was not just private. 'The pendulum has swung our way,' Jim Callaghan told a BBC interviewer on *The World This Weekend* in late 1977. And it even affected the government's more downbeat members, such as Bernard Donoughue. 'In the summer of 1978, there was quite a good atmosphere,' he told me. 'I thought it was just possible that . . . we'd got away with it.'

There were a surprising number of reasons to come to this conclusion. Some of them, as Davies suggested, were economic. Most obviously, inflation finally seemed to be coming under control: in January 1978, it dropped below 10 per cent for the first time since October 1973, when the oil crisis and the whole mid-seventies economic meltdown had begun. In early 1978, too, unemployment began to fall, after rising continuously over the previous four years. Working days lost to industrial action – almost 6.5 million in the most turbulent quarter of 1974 – were down to barely 1.5 million, despite Grunwick, by the second quarter of 1978. And the average Briton's real disposable income, often an equally potent political influence, having shrunk during 1975 and 1976, started to grow again in late 1977. By the following year, it was expanding once more at the comfortable rate to which Britons had been accustomed in calmer post-war decades.

The opinion polls registered this sense of a storm passing. During the IMF crisis, the Conservative lead over Labour recorded by Gallup had surged to 20 per cent. But then it steadily receded: to 10 per cent in mid-1977, 5 per cent in early 1978, 1 per cent that spring. By the autumn, with possibly as much as a year of the government left to run – a phase of the electoral cycle in which governments usually gained in popularity – Labour were narrowly ahead. This trend was confirmed by actual elections. In 1976 and 1977, the party had lost by-elections in seats it had held since the Second World War. In 1978, in more vulnerable constituencies, it won. In October, in Berwick and East Lothian, it even increased its support, the first time a government had managed this in a by-election for a dozen years. In her memoirs, Margaret Thatcher summed up her feelings about the state of British politics in late 1978:

So a difficult year approached its end. We were behind in the polls and seemed all too willing to behave like a permanent Opposition rather than a potential Government, a failing on which the actual Government readily capitalized . . . We had made some progress towards converting the Party and public opinion in the direction I knew was required. Events too had contributed – the scenes at Grunwick . . . What mattered far more was that our programme lacked the clear commitment to changes, particularly in trade union law, which I believed were necessary . . . We still had a long way to go.

Another major obstacle was Callaghan. 'Jim Callaghan had been dealt a bad hand by history and Harold Wilson in 1976,' Thatcher wrote. Despite this, 'He was a formidable opponent . . . He adopted in the House [of Commons] a manner that appeared avuncular, was in fact patronizing and made it hard for me to advance serious criticism of Government policy without appearing to nag . . . He proved extremely talented as a party manager; he had a real feel for public opinion.' She also considered the prime minister 'brave' for supporting a new, post-Keynesian economic policy; and 'tactically brilliant' – a 'poker player' who 'employed skill, gamesmanship and simple bluff'. Her shadow chancellor and close ally Geoffrey Howe was even more admiring. 'Callaghan was a much more confident creature than Wilson had become,' he told me. 'He did begin addressing the real problems of the country.'

During 1977 and 1978, 'Sunny Jim', or 'Steady Jim', or 'Uncle Jim', or 'Farmer Jim' – the public nicknames all suggesting the valuable political qualities of likeability or shrewdness – oversaw a skilful balancing act. His government continued the curbing of state spending which had begun in the final, more sober phase of the Wilson administration. Callaghan justified the policy with a cunning mixture of priggishness and party point-scoring: contrasting his government's financial prudence not with the profligacy of the Wilson Cabinet – in which he and his chancellor Denis Healey had, after all, both served – but with the almost equally free-spending administration of Edward Heath, one of whose most extravagant ministers had been its education secretary, Thatcher herself.

In the late seventies, Callaghan and Healey also both sensed that voters were turning against state spending. Voters in Healey's Leeds constituency complained to him in blunt West Yorkshire terms about what they saw as the overgenerosity of welfare benefits. In the country as a whole, the proportion of people who took this view increased from 34 per cent in 1974 to 50 per cent in 1979. Meanwhile, the balance of public opinion between those who preferred cuts in spending and taxation as the broad aim of government and those who preferred increases was also shifting rightwards: from a 16 per cent margin in favour of the spenders in 1978 to parity in 1979.

For this reason, and to stimulate the economy, the Callaghan government reduced taxes from the notorious peaks they had reached under Wilson. For those on ten times average earnings – the rich – the proportion paid in income tax and national insurance fell from 70 per cent to 65 per cent; for those on one and a half times average earnings – the middle class – it fell from 35 per cent to 32 per cent; for those on half average earnings – the poor – from 22 per cent to 18 per cent, proportionally the biggest drop. In 1978, the government further asserted its distance from socialist orthodoxy by selling some of its shares in BP, a partial privatization which the Conservatives favoured but had been too cautious to argue for in public.

On other issues, Callaghan challenged current liberal thinking. In October 1976, in a famous speech at Ruskin College in Oxford – six years earlier the venue for the first National Women's Liberation

Conference – he questioned the value of the 'new informal methods of teaching' and argued for 'a basic curriculum with universal standards' of numeracy and literacy. When it came to personal morality, he was even more traditional. 'In the [Policy] Unit we produced a paper for his first Easter holiday reading about the restoration of responsible values in our society,' wrote Donoughue later. 'He telephoned me from his farm to say how much he liked it and asked me to join in the writing of his future speeches to incorporate this dimension. Sometimes these "values" emerged as a touchingly old-fashioned prudery. He once cautioned Tom McNally and me not to tell bawdy stories in front of [his wife] Audrey . . . and he told me that he had been totally unaware of homosexuality until well into adult life . . .' The prime minister, Donoughue recorded, hummed hymns to himself as he walked stooping down the corridors to crucial meetings.

Callaghan, as much the son of a naval officer as of a Baptist mother, also increased the share of state spending that went on defence. Unlike his successor as prime minister, and despite opposition from the Ministry of Defence, he insisted on maintaining a permanent naval presence in the South Atlantic: a small, soon-to-be-infamous vessel armed with missiles and helicopters called HMS *Endurance*. The Argentinian government had repeatedly suggested it might invade the Falkland Islands during the mid- to late seventies, and Callaghan wanted to deter them. In December 1977, during a period of particular tension between Buenos Aires and London, 'A force was despatched' to support *Endurance*, Callaghan recalls in his memoirs, including frigates and 'a nuclear-powered submarine'. The British government made sure that Argentina learned of its deployments, and sought legal advice about establishing an exclusion zone around the islands. The Argentinian government backed down, and the episode was quickly forgotten. 'The force was able to return, the only misfortune being that the ships' companies missed Christmas with their families,' writes Callaghan with some restraint, given the consequences for British politics the next time a London government sent a task force to the Falklands.

In 1977, Callaghan also enthusiastically took part in the celebration of the Queen's Silver Jubilee:

The Queen kindly invited Audrey and me to join [the royal yacht] *Britannia* when she reached my home city of Portsmouth on 27 June for the Naval Review at Spithead. I was determined not to miss this . . . The Queen held an evening reception aboard *Britannia* and the Royal Marines beat the Retreat, marching and playing as only they can . . . I felt my spine tingle as dusk fell and the ceremony drew to an end with the tune 'Sunset' blowing softly on the bugles . . . On the next morning *Britannia* threaded her way through the long lines of ships drawn up for review . . .

At the end of the year, Tony Benn wrote in his diary: 'Callaghan is riding high. The press loves him because he's openly right-wing.'

In March 1977, Callaghan increased his independence from the Labour left by forming an alliance with the Liberals. The Lib–Lab pact, like many of his manoeuvres as prime minister, deftly turned a position of weakness into one of at least temporary strength. From the start, Callaghan's government had been hampered by its lack of a Commons majority. By early 1977, he had accepted that getting legislation through the Commons, let alone staying in office until the economy and Labour's poll ratings properly healed, would require a deal with one of the minor parties. The Liberals proved amenable. Since the onset of the mid-seventies crisis, there had been persistent talk among some centre-right and centre-left politicians of the need for a 'national government' – a cross-party governing coalition as there had been in the thirties – to cope with the recession and the threat to British democracy from the extreme left and right. A decade earlier, prominent Liberals had considered such an alliance with Wilson's first, relatively fragile sixties government. But the Liberal Party as a whole had not backed the proposal and, wrote David Steel, then a rising young Liberal MP and a supporter of the deal, had then seen 'influence slip from our grasp' as Wilson increased his majority at the next general election. Yet now, in 1977, the time was riper still: Labour needed a Commons ally, and Steel was party leader, his predecessor Jeremy Thorpe having resigned amid allegations about his sexuality, his involvement in financial irregularities, and his part in a plot to have his lover Norman Scott murdered.

On 23 March, Callaghan and Steel ambushed the Conservatives by announcing the Lib–Lab pact, immediately after Margaret

Thatcher had put to the Commons what she hoped might be a dead-
ly motion of no confidence in the government. All thirteen Liberal
MPs voted against the motion, and the government survived comfortably. For the next year and a quarter, until the Liberals
terminated the alliance in July 1978, Labour were protected by their
new parliamentary allies, without conceding much to them beyond
the establishment of 'a joint consultative committee' involving the
two parties to 'examine Government policy'. A frustrated and irritated Thatcher was 'astonished', she wrote, that the Liberals 'had
signed up to such a bad deal'. Benn was enraged by the pact for the
opposite reason, feeling that Labour had conceded too much, but
when he threatened to denounce the alliance publicly, Callaghan
threatened in turn to sack him from the Cabinet, and Benn was
silenced. For now, 'Uncle Jim' had outfoxed all of them.

Moreover, for all his right-wing gestures, he could not simply be
dismissed as a sort of counterfeit Tory. The Lib–Lab pact suggested a
way forward for centre-left politics that would directly and indirectly lead, for good or ill, to the creation of the SDP in the next decade
and of New Labour the decade after that. Callaghan also continued
to give the unions unprecedented influence over government policy.
After all, in his mixture of social conservatism, patriotism and reverence for trade unionism he shared the world view of many of their
members. With his heavy head and thick-rimmed glasses, his careful
manner of speech, his affability in public and occasional menace in
private, he could easily have been mistaken for a senior union official.

Finally, and most significantly, he presided over a Britain that was
probably more equal than it had ever been before – and certainly
more equal than it has ever been since. Authorities on poverty rates
and income distributions differ as to precisely when the optimum
moment came, but some of their statistics for the period leap out.
The Gini coefficient, a common measure of income inequality,
reached its lowest level for British households in 1977. The proportion of individual Britons below the poverty line did the same in
1978. Social mobility, measured as the likelihood of someone becoming part of a different class from their parents, also peaked in the

Callaghan era. The causes were various and hard to disentangle: the social contract, the tax system, the post-war expansion of higher education and white-collar employment, even the seventies economic crisis, which had depressed the incomes of many of the wealthy for an extended period. But the egalitarian Britain of the Callaghan years was an achievement, not much trumpeted at the time, which would seem larger and larger after he left office, as its social trends were relentlessly reversed.

In 1978, that did not seem imminent. In July, the TUC–Labour Party Liaison Committee published 'Into the Eighties', a pamphlet confidently laying out a path for continued Labour government. The pamphlet envisaged a 'high productivity, high investment, high wage economy' with good industrial relations, progressive tax rates and, repeated in almost every rose-tinted paragraph, growing prosperity from North Sea oil. In a lull over the summer, the prime minister went for a walk along the South Downs near his farm with his son-in-law and confidant Peter Jay, whom he had recently approved, with a hint of nepotism and hubris, as Britain's new ambassador to Washington. Callaghan told Jay that he sometimes thought of himself as a Moses figure: a leader who set vital changes in motion and hoped to guide his followers to the promised land.

In the summer of 1978, his chances of doing so certainly seemed better than Margaret Thatcher's. By then, she had been leader of the Opposition for three and a half years, a long time in the accelerated politics of the seventies. And her years in charge had not been easy. In her memoirs, the chapter covering 1975 to 1977 is titled 'A Bumpy Ride'.

Some of her difficulties derived from how she had been elected: surprisingly, less than overwhelmingly and, for some Tory MPs, accidentally, as their intended protest against Heath misfired. '"My God! The bitch has won!" exclaimed a Vice Chairman of the Party when the news came through,' recorded the Tory historian John Ranelagh, then a member of the Conservative Research Department, which remained doggedly Heathite for the rest of the seventies regardless. Once Thatcher's victory had sunk in, he continues, 'There was a

great shrugging of shoulders and an assumption that Thatcher would
lose the next election because her policies were "silly" and out of
tune with political realities, notably that getting along with the trade
unions was a *sine qua non* of political life. Within the Party bureaucracy it was felt essential to . . . indicate privately to journalists that
the new leader was an aberration . . . that she would soon be out and
Willie Whitelaw would replace her.'

Thatcher, it was often said within the party during 1975, would be
'gone by Christmas'. The Conservatives had been quick to change
failing leaders in the past. Some senior Conservatives, including
members of her shadow cabinet, doubted whether a woman had the
mental and physical stamina to lead the party. Others felt that, like
Heath, she would eventually be forced into policy U-turns. Still others simply thought her policies were crude and appalling. Former
party leader Harold Macmillan was one of them. In the autumn of
1975, Peter Walker, undeterred by Heath's fall, was at work on an
update of Macmillan's thirties argument for liberal Toryism, *The
Middle Way*. 'I used to go down to Harold's house in Sussex with the
latest chapter,' Walker told me.

One day after Margaret's first party conference I was down there, and he
said, 'Peter, were you at the party conference?' I said, 'Yes I was.' And he
said, 'I watched on television. An *extraordinary* affair. I've always been to
these conferences. You sat on the platform, and you would listen to incredible remarks being made from the floor. You know, they wanted to birch
them before hanging them, things like that. Then you'd get up and make
your speech. You wouldn't mention anything that had been said from the
floor. And they were terribly nice, they'd give you wild applause . . .
Watching her last week, I think she actually agrees with them.'

Yet while Thatcher's robustness on law and order and rhetoric
about 'middle-class values' delighted many party members, that did
not necessarily mean they preferred her to Heath. At the same party
conference, Ranelagh notes, 'Heath was given a rapturous reception
. . . and was widely reported, both in private and in the press, to have
described Thatcher and Joseph as traitors and as crazy, with right-
wing views that would, if implemented, destroy the Party and the
country . . . Pointedly, Heath left the Conference before she gave her

speech.' Heath's distaste for Thatcher and her type of Toryism, often openly expressed, would hang over her leadership like a dark plume of pollution from some obsolete but stubbornly surviving old factory, never quite dispersing even on the brightest days. His hold over the party membership and bureaucracy, over Tory MPs and the shadow cabinet, over Conservative and Conservative-leaning voters would not prove quite as enduring, but it remained strong right through the seventies. In late 1978, almost four years after he had been deposed, a Gallup poll gave the Conservatives a narrow 3 per cent advantage over Labour. But the lead grew to 14 per cent if Heath replaced Thatcher.

For her, iconoclastic advisers like Alfred Sherman and upstart think tanks like the Centre for Policy Studies were an alternative to the traditional Tory power centres and networks, at least until she could gain control of them, as well as sources of ideas. Another favoured method of outflanking the Heathites was the direct, sometimes emotional appeal to the public on issues such as the mass picketing at Grunwick, which could be used to suggest changes in Conservative policy which had not been cleared with colleagues. She was not a natural on television; she was working too much to watch it very often. There remained a stiffness in her posture and a monotony in her voice. But she worked hard on her screen presence during her first years as leader. She hired Gordon Reece, a former television producer, and followed his advice to slow down and deepen her voice, to shed what she had learned from a set of elocution lessons in her youth, which had left her sounding like a Tory lady from the shires. With Reece's coaching, she now sounded more like a kind of supremely authoritative suburban housewife. She even learned to show glimpses of a rather dominating humour. On the Yorkshire Television programme *Calendar* in February 1978, an interviewer asked her a question that ended with the words 'if you get to Downing Street'. Thatcher snapped back: 'What do you mean, "if"?' There was a pause. The leader of the Opposition looked at the camera, her hair enormous and sculpted, her expression utterly deadpan. Then she broke into a huge sharkish smile. A few moments later, the interviewer asked her: 'Are you difficult to work with?' Out came the shark smile once more: 'Are you having difficulty with this interview?'

The Conservative leader was now compelling television. The problem was, as the seventies crisis eased during 1977 and 1978, a compelling leader was not necessarily what voters wanted. Thatcher's personal ratings were consistently much lower than Callaghan's. On ominous foreign-policy issues, such as how to deal with the Russians, her certainty and fierceness sometimes went down well with the public. In early 1976, in a speech written for her by Robert Moss, a leading member of NAFF, she accused the Soviet Union of being 'bent on world dominance' – virtually a heresy for a senior Western politician in the era of detente. The Russian army newspaper *Red Star* condemned her as 'the Iron Lady'. The following month, her approval rating jumped seven points. Yet this kind of bluntness and fresh thinking seemed less well suited to British issues. On key questions such as what to do about the unions, the Conservatives were divided. 'I often felt that the shadow cabinet and Conservative Central Office were like the Tower of Babel,' wrote Sherman. 'We spoke different and mutually incomprehensible languages. Leading members of the shadow cabinet were . . . less concerned with opposing the Labour government than in internal manoeuvres, and clipping Mrs Thatcher's wings.' Meanwhile, in other important policy areas, such as the economy, the Callaghan government and the IMF already seemed to have set the country on a new course.

Unlike Sherman or Keith Joseph, Thatcher was a sensitive enough political operator to realize that there was a limited public appetite in the Britain of 1977 and 1978 for further transformation of the post-war order. During this period – indeed during the whole period between her election as leader and her first general-election campaign – she permitted the publication of only a single guide to her party's policies, 'The Right Approach', a 1976 document so carefully designed to strike a balance between Thatcherite and Heathite Toryism that it was actually written by her enemies in the Conservative Research Department. 'It was a fudge,' wrote Thatcher later of the document's ambiguous, detail-free proposals for controlling wages and prices, 'but temporarily palatable.'

Between 1975 and 1978, her own speeches, while full of bold generalizations about the failings of the Left and the virtues of the free market, were quite often vague – if not downright misleading – about what a Thatcher government would actually do. 'Let me make it absolutely clear that the next Conservative government will look forward to discussion and consultation with the trade union movement about the policies that are needed to save our country,' she told the Conservative Party conference in 1976. Such are the necessary evasions of most governments-in-waiting with big ambitions; her biographer John Campbell calls this period 'Thatcherism under Wraps'. During these years, her appetite for radical right-wing ideas and advisers never really diminished, but some of the free marketeers did begin to worry about her: 'Cautious Margaret' was the phrase they used. Previous Tory politicians with an interest in the new right's ideas, such as Joseph, and Heath in the sixties, had let the movement down once they took office.

And when would Thatcher take office? Since 1974, Labour had survived despite the economic crisis, despite Wilson's resignation, despite the IMF crisis, despite deep troughs of unpopularity, defeats in by-elections and local elections, the loss of its Commons majority, profound Cabinet splits, and despite an almost constant feeling that the government could fall at any moment. 'Margaret's stint as Opposition Leader, the hardest job in British politics, was to last longer than any of us had expected,' Geoffrey Howe confessed in his memoirs. 'We were obliged to maintain the weary routines of opposition well into a fifth year.' And by that fifth year, with many things going better for the government and North Sea oil finally about to start delivering its benefits, the mood among many Conservatives was shifting from frustration and anxiety to something worse. 'There was certainly an air of defeatism,' wrote Norman Tebbit of the feeling among his fellow Tory MPs in June 1978. Even Thatcher herself was prone to occasional dark thoughts. After Kingsley Amis had dinner with her at Flood Street, he wrote,

The bit [she said] that stayed with me most ran roughly, 'People have always said that the next election is going to be crucial. But this one really will be, and if it doesn't go the way Denis and I want then we'll stay [in Britain], because we'll always stay, but we'll work very hard with the children to set them up with careers in Canada.'

Yet, outside the Thatcher family, leaving the country was slipping out of fashion by the late seventies. Between 1974, a peak year for emigration as for other bleak socio-economic indices, and 1978, Britain's annual population loss slowed by almost a third, according to the Office for National Statistics. 'The future looked tastier,' wrote Peter York in December 1977, summing up the national mood at the end of the year for *Harpers & Queen*. 'There was a feeling that things were starting to go up again, and indeed the indicators suggested at the very least a consumer boomlet for 1978.' The Conservative Research Department agreed with him. In a confidential advisory note on the party's strategy for that year, written in February and marked 'MT to see ASAP', the department conceded that in early 1978, 'There was a surprising amount of euphoria about the country's economic prospects and Labour and Mr Callaghan seemed in calm control of events.'

Perhaps the most complete expression of this renewed optimism about Britain was a book published that year by the *Washington Post*'s London correspondent, Bernard D. Nossiter. Nossiter was an experienced reporter, suspicious of orthodoxies, and the author of two previous books: one on the subservience of President Kennedy and American unions to corporations, and one on the inadequacies of India under the often admired rule of Mrs Gandhi.

Britain: A Future that Works began with refreshing irreverence, by mocking all 'the scribes and prophets of disaster' who had predicted a British collapse over the previous half-dozen years. Nossiter made some persuasive, or almost persuasive, points: that all wealthy countries had found the seventies hard going; that the declinists tended to omit the decade's better years from their plunging graphs about Britain; that the country's levels of state spending and taxation were average rather than crushing by European standards; and that the

British economy had grown faster between 1945 and 1975, despite its much-trumpeted post-war troubles, than it had between 1855 and 1945. 'Is it possible', asked Nossiter of Britain's seventies crisis, 'that the whole episode is a case of hypochondria?'

He listed signs of national well-being: increasing life expectancy, growing meat consumption, more universities, shrinking poverty, cleaner air, the return of fish to the Thames, the oil riches in the North Sea. But then his argument took a less predictable turn. Looking at London, he saw 'the last inhabitable great city. Productivity is higher in New York, Düsseldorf, Paris and Stockholm. There is a nervous intensity in these towns; crowds hustle along . . . heads down . . . People in London streets tend to amble, look around . . . This hurts the growth rate but it may ease the psyche.' Critics of Britain's economic performance were right when it came to some of the raw statistics, Nossiter conceded, but they were missing the bigger picture: 'Britons . . . appear to be the first citizens of the post-industrial age . . . [They] are choosing leisure over goods.'

Some of A Future that Works felt too Anglophile to be rigorous, and some of its observations – that there was a unique sense of 'kinship' and 'decency' among Britons; that 'union members see their well-being now requires a measure of restraint' – would look rather misjudged in a few years. Yet Nossiter's 'leisure over goods' thesis did pick up something about Britain and its surprising level of contentment in the late seventies. In 1977, an international survey by Gallup showed that Britons considered themselves among the happiest people in the world. The same year, New Society published a more scientific assessment of British attitudes to material goods and other forms of fulfilment.

'Do the British Sincerely Want to Be Rich?' drew its conclusions from two comprehensive surveys conducted in 1973 and 1977. 'The British seem to have lowered their sights since 1973,' the magazine found. 'The British are remarkably unambitious in a material sense. Very few sincerely want to be rich . . . Even if they could . . . the vast majority do not seem prepared to work harder for it . . . Most people in Britain neither want nor expect a great deal more money.' The 1977 survey asked its subjects a long-winded but interesting question: 'Do you think that it is best for people to work as hard as they can for as much money as they can get, or for people to work only as much as they need in order to live a pleasant life?' By a consistent two to one margin, across all social classes, genders and party political groupings, people considered 'a pleasant life' the better option. The fact that citizens of comparable countries appeared to be doing better materially – nine tenths of those surveyed felt that West Germany had a superior standard of living to Britain – did not seem to bother many of the respondents. Less than a sixth of those surveyed said they were 'very worried' about falling behind other nations, and approaching half said they were 'not worried' at all. Britons, *New Society* concluded, 'seemed to be saying that the country is going to the dogs, but they themselves aren't doing too badly'.

In Britain in 1960, almost all full-time manual workers got two weeks paid holiday. By 1970, between two and three weeks was the norm. By 1975, it was three to four. By 1980, four to five. The length of the British working day underwent a similar change: in 1961, a man in full-time employment spent an average of 460 minutes a day at work, and a woman 420 minutes; in 1975, the respective figures were 420 and 380 minutes. A steady shortening of the working week had been under way in Britain since Victorian times, and during the sixties and seventies a growing literature announced the imminent arrival of a 'leisure society'. Diverse causes were identified: labour-saving technology, higher unemployment, the diffusion of hippy anti-work ideas and the dominance of union power – after all, what was the TGWU Centre in Eastbourne, with all its sea views and sun terraces, if not a monument to the unions' ability to win an easier life for the working man?

In the seventies, less overtly political leisure facilities became a normal state-run amenity for the first time. In 1970, there were twenty-seven sports centres in England. In 1974, there were 167, with plans for another 612 by 1981. At a 1975 conference for architects and construction companies called 'Building for Leisure', one participant suggested that sports centres were the 'fourth wave' in the modern development of Britain after industrial towns, railways and suburbs. In a 1976 book called *The Sociology of Leisure*, Stanley

Parker, a British academic specializing in 'leisure studies', predicted that 'the long weekend will probably grow in popularity' and treated 'the 30-hour week' as an inevitability. Even the senior British politicians of the seventies, despite all the emergencies they faced, seemed in tune with what Parker speculated might become 'a golden age of leisure': Heath with his sailing, Callaghan with his farm, Healey with his famed 'hinterland' of opera and poetry. The workaholic Margaret Thatcher, with no appealing leisure habits to publicize, seemed at a disadvantage.

Yet there were other aspects of life in late-seventies Britain that better fitted Thatcher's politics. Not all observers agreed with Nossiter and *New Society* that Britons were becoming more contented and less materialistic. In 1978, the year that Nossiter's book came out, the British left-wing journalist and social explorer Jeremy Seabrook published an account of a journey he had recently undertaken through working-class parts of Britain.

What Went Wrong? Working People and the Ideals of the Labour Movement was a disillusioned book. In Wigan, following in George Orwell's footsteps, he found 'a place of ruined Victorian splendour'. It had 'a new denim bazaar and delicatessen', and 'shopping arcades full of consolations for the convulsive changes that [had] occurred' in the local economy. Over the last few decades, he wrote, a whole side of Wigan based on coal mining and textile manufacturing had simply 'vanished'. There had been all-pervasive political consequences:

Few young people visit the Labour clubs. There has been a dramatic break in the transmission of the working-class tradition . . . The young are products of a given world, just as their parents were, when mine, mill and neighbourhood determined their lives; only now it is image and fashion, the endless spool of excitement and novelty that has been unwound before their eyes since they were born . . . The young feel passive and purposeless . . . They are anchored in a culture of commodities.

Seabrook described an atomized, depoliticized Britain, where close-knit working-class streets had been demolished in the name of slum clearance, where glassy new shopping centres towered over disused mine workings, where elderly Labour activists despaired about the party's compromises with capitalism under Healey and Callaghan, and where 'the stridency of the market-place is the most significant influence' on working-class attitudes. Seabrook even questioned whether the unions wanted a less materialistic Britain: 'The growth of the trades unions, the anger and militancy of recent years, are not necessarily the radical phenomenon which the Left makes them out to be.' He quoted an unnamed union leader: 'The most beautiful four letter word in the English language is MORE.'

What Went Wrong? was a brave and prophetic book. It began to suggest a truth about modern Britain that many people on the left and the right are uncomfortable with to this day: that much of the social, economic and political landscape which would come to be associated with 'the eighties' – either perjoratively or triumphantly – was already visible in the second half of the seventies, if you cared to look. 'It was all there, waiting,' Peter York, a less disapproving authority on the two decades than Seabrook, told me. 'There was less wealth. Less upper-middle-class wealth. The whole of London wasn't done up or for sale. But all of those things were there in embryo. All of those [eighties] people were there, waiting – for the economy to change, for taxes to change.'

In his ostentatious memoir *The Way We Wore*, the writer, broadcaster, intimate of eighties pop stars and ubiquitous eighties man-about-town Robert Elms describes walking through Soho, the streets piled with uncollected rubbish, to a nightclub with a new gang of friends in early 1979:

You'd see us, if you knew where and when to look . . . Tuxedos and wing collars, padded shoulders and cummerbunds . . . silk scarves . . . diamante brooches, taffeta gowns . . . There were maybe only thirty or forty elaborate souls at most, gathered up by the bush telegraph . . . The nucleus of what would become known as new romantic, which would go on to define the 1980s stylistically . . . was weaving its way through the wreckage of the winter of discontent to get to Billy's on Tuesday nights . . .

The consumerism of the late seventies was not just for trendies. The recovery in average disposable income from 1977 onwards released new appetites. That year, Freddie Laker began his Skytrain service to the US, offering flights at a third of the price of his rivals. Demand for tickets so outstripped supply that an encampment of youthful would-be customers, complete with sleeping bags and 'We Love You Freddie' placards, built up on the pavements outside the Skytrain offices in London. It was almost as if the free-festival movement had finally come to the capital, but this was a festival offering transcendence of the everyday wholly through consumption. In 1978, Callaghan gave Laker a knighthood. The same year, a new record was set for the total number of foreign holidays taken by Britons.

In 1976, the unprecedentedly vast Brent Cross shopping centre opened in north London, with a cathedral-shaped floor plan, commentators noted, and innovative evening opening hours so people could come after work. In 1979, the final phase of the equally large Arndale centre opened in Manchester, giving the city two dozen acres of shops, flats and offices combined in a single structure. Across the country in these years, the big retailers rolled out their chain stores.

In east London, a decade before the regeneration of the rest of the capital's docklands, the developer Peter Drew turned St Katharine's dock next to Tower Bridge, defunct and sparsely inhabited by artists, into a proto-yuppie paradise of expensive warehouse flats, hotel bars and moorings for yachts. Between 1975 and 1980, the average British house price increased by more than half.

Some Labour figures felt the party should do more to adjust to this new world. In 'a comprehensive school in a northern city', Seabrook memorably encountered Dave Ransome, a young teacher and would-be councillor from an active Labour family. Ransome told Seabrook that his middle-aged parents – a weaver and an engineer – were 'rather defeated and apathetic' now, but he wanted to carry on their crusade by new means, means that sound eerily Blairite to twenty-first-century ears:

We've got to change the image of the Labour Party. It's too much identified with the cloth cap, the industrial worker. We've got to get out and reach people in some of the up-market posher areas, or we shall just become a party of the ghetto, the enclaves of poverty. A lot of things we worked for have been achieved. We've got to show we can cope with the problems of the end of the twentieth century. Otherwise, there is a danger people will think we're irrelevant.

In the Downing Street Policy Unit, Bernard Donoughue and Gavyn Davies were having similar thoughts. 'I went to the right-wing think tanks,' Donoughue remembered. 'They treated me very well. I went to the opening of the Centre for Policy Studies. I was interested in the monetarists. I wouldn't call myself' – he gave a characteristically sly look – 'a convert. I'd call myself intrigued. I felt that what Thatcher was saying about needing to give people more incentives, liberalize the economy, control the public bureaucracy, was correct. What the Callaghan government offered tided Britain over difficult times. But we didn't have the answer to Britain's long-term decline.'

Davies was more optimistic about Labour's ability to reinvent itself in office. He was younger and slightly newer to government than Donoughue, a Welshman with a soft manner that disguised a political durability and a love of hard numbers. When he finished working for Callaghan in 1979, he took his feel for economics into the City and made vastly more money than any other former member of the seventies Labour governments. Since the seventies, he has stayed loyal to the party, becoming a living embodiment of the adaptability to capitalism of a certain kind of worldly left-of-centre figure, more common in continental Europe than Britain, and of the talent and potential sometimes hidden from view in the Callaghan government.

We met in Mayfair in 2006. Davies had an office on the top floor of a huge, gutted terrace in which unspecified but highly successful financial operations were performed. It was a weekday morning, but he was in chinos and a check shirt, his body language floppy and unmacho, his voice unshowy and flat. Sitting slouched across an armchair, he described how he came to work for Harold Wilson and Jim Callaghan. 'Bernard phoned me at Balliol and said, "Come and join." I thought, "One year at Downing Street, then come back and be an academic. No one's going to offer a twenty-three-year-old the chance to see this again."' In both governments Davies was an influential economic adviser – 'a bit like Ed Balls' under Gordon Brown in the nineties – and like Donoughue and Peter Jay, Davies was at least a partial convert to the economic ideas of Milton Friedman.

He also sensed that the new free-market thinking had implications for how the Labour government should behave in other areas. An unexpected hint of emotion entered his voice: 'I spent a humungous amount of time – 50 per cent of my time, even during the 1974 crisis – working out what would happen if we sold off council houses. The public-accounts advantages of selling council houses. The political liberation for urban working people – our people. We had schemes absolutely fully developed, ready to launch. The schemes helped the buyers with their mortgages, through subsidies. The schemes put the proceeds back into [council] house-building.' The rationale was still socialist, he felt: 'In housing, state provision was going wrong. Bernard and I thought council housing didn't bring equality between people in public housing and people in private housing.'

Joe Haines, Wilson's powerful press secretary, was another advocate of widening property ownership in this way. But his argument for the policy shift was more obviously party political. Since the fifties, both local and national Conservative politicians had intermittently supported selling off council houses, and, where the policy had been implemented – notably in London, where properties had been sold to their tenants at a small discount in the late sixties and early seventies – it had proved quite popular. In 1972, under the Heath government, 60,000 council homes had been effectively privatized across Britain, a forgotten but suggestive piece of Heathite radicalism. In 1975, Haines warned Wilson that if Labour did not match the Conservatives in responding to the growing working-class desire for property, 'Our very substantial block vote' – a revealing choice of words – 'among council tenants might be significantly eaten into.' In 1978, Margaret Thatcher was photographed having tea in a sunlit front garden with the 2,000th person to buy their home from the Conservative-controlled Greater London Council.

Yet selling off municipal housing had its critics. Whatever the discounts and mortgage subsidies offered to buyers, the fact remained that many council tenants – generally the poorer ones – would be unable or unwilling to take advantage of them. And the bigger the discounts and subsidies, the less worthwhile the exercise would be, at least financially, for local authorities and the government. 'Labour local authorities thought the idea was inegalitarian,' said Davies, irritation suddenly creasing his mild face. 'A lot of their arguments were self-serving. Crosland supported the local Labour authorities. He didn't want the row. Bernard got Wilson to almost launch the policy. But from the moment Jim [Callaghan] came in, council-house sales just didn't happen.'

Behind Davies, through the glass wall of his office, colleagues at immaculate desks grappled with the abstractions of early-twenty-first-century financial capitalism. But his mind was still in the seventies. Between 1974 and 1979, he went on, council-house sales were discouraged by the government; while not completely forbidden, they were allowed to dwindle. 'It was an own goal. A monumental own goal. Bernard and I are still somewhat obsessed by it. There is still bitterness over it, on both sides. Sure as hell, it was frustrating when we saw the Tories do council-house sales [in the early eighties]. It gave me a sinking feeling.' He paused, and then gave a look halfway between disbelief and admiration. 'Thatcher priced the council houses', he said, 'in a way that meant you were insane if you didn't buy.'

There was one place in Britain where the great subterranean seventies shift from public to private, and the struggles and determination of forward-thinking left-wingers to adapt to it, was demonstrated to perfection. It happened in the damp low hills of north Buckinghamshire, in an invented city with a mouthful of a name that seemed, entirely appropriately, to suggest both the old economic order and the new.

In fact, the name Milton Keynes had nothing to do with Milton Friedman or Maynard Keynes. It came from a small village that was effectively abolished in the mid-sixties, when the Wilson government announced the development of the surrounding thirty-four square miles for a new settlement. Yet from the start this second Milton Keynes involved two competing visions of Britain. On the one hand, it was a New Town, the latest in a series established from East Kilbride to Basildon for redistributing the population and improving the social and economic life of Britain. The New Town programme had been set in motion by the Attlee administration. It involved state planning and funding, and the construction of a great deal of state-owned housing, and was regarded with scepticism by many British right-wingers, Alfred Sherman prominent among them.

At first, Milton Keynes seemed set to follow the same template. The settlement was envisaged as a long rectangle of public housing and industrial and retail developments, 'a linear city' held together by a loop of public-transport routes. This being the sixties, the public-transport system selected was a futuristic monorail, which would glide between the tower blocks and the north Buckinghamshire treetops and would be free to use, with funding coming from local ratepayers. The 250,000 residents envisaged for this new 'monorail city', as it quickly became known, would all live within five minutes' walk of a monorail stop, and the longest journey from there to the city centre would take fifteen minutes. People would rent flats, or houses built close together with small walled gardens. Private space would be limited; public amenities would come first.

But the monorail Milton Keynes did not take account of how Britons were increasingly living, and of one development in particular. During the sixties, car ownership doubled. 'There's no way in life you're going to get rid of the car,' Derek Walker, who became chief architect of Milton Keynes in 1970, told me. 'I thought the monorail city was terribly flawed. Linear cities become a kind of corridor, and I was never sold on high blocks.' So, instead of this vision of Milton Keynes, Walker and a decisive number of the new city's planners argued for another, partly based on what they saw as the key social trends in Britain, and partly on how things were done in a distant but charismatic foreign city that many British architects, journalists and consumers in the sixties and seventies saw as the society of the future: Los Angeles.

'I doubt whether any part of the world . . . has ever packed such an extraordinary emotional punch, a feeling of a place that was leading the world in technology, in economic achievement, in the forging of a new and different lifestyle,' wrote the influential British city planner Peter Hall about sixties and seventies California a quarter of a century later. 'The Los Angeles experience had profound effects . . . on an entire generation of us.' Derek Walker was one of a stream of young British architects and city theorists who visited southern California in the sixties and fell in love with the freeways and the spaciousness and the uninhibited buildings, with the apparent ease of movement and the consumer riches. Walker had grown up in a Yorkshire village in the forties and fifties. 'This is a tight-arsed country,' he said with typical directness. 'I saw the sixties as a time of aspiration, dissolving class structures. People were getting wealthier. They'd started seeing American kitchens. The whole system of consumerism was being born, big time . . . In Milton Keynes, we did a continuous household survey, asking people what they wanted, and their horizons were rising, rising, rising.'

By 1971, the new city's first few hundred homes were finally being built and the concept of Milton Keynes had been transformed. It was now to be a great, spread-out, American-style grid of streets, with each 'grid square' containing a residential, recreational or business district, screened off from the traffic and from neighbouring districts by landscaping and thick belts of trees. Within this dispersed, suburban, consumer-driven city – a shopping centre was scheduled for completion before a hospital or a railway station – it was hoped, nevertheless, that the left-leaning ideals of the post-war New Town programme would be maintained. Jock Campbell, the first chairman of the Milton Keynes Development Corporation, was a Labour lord and 'a real socialist', Walker told me. Walker himself was a *Guardian* reader who saw no contradiction between consumerism and egalitarianism. 'I was about thirty-five in 1971,' he said with a knowing laugh. 'You bloody well think you can do anything.'

In 2006, he was still living in Milton Keynes, as he had done throughout the seventies. But, like many modernist architects, his faith in the new had its limits. His house was a medieval rectory in Great Linford, one of several villages which had been absorbed into Milton Keynes. Great Linford remained a mixture of old Buckinghamshire dwellings and large seventies houses, and was one of the city's most sought-after districts.

We sat at a table surrounded by delicate, slightly faded architectural illustrations and models. 'Linear Parks, Milton Keynes 1970' was the label on one dusty, utopian assemblage of cardboard and green netting propped against a wall. Walker leaned back in his purple shirt and swirly tie and told the story of Milton Keynes in the seventies with infectious enthusiasm and amused eyes.

'As a north countryman, I always thought it was a bloody dull area, flat as a bathboard,' he began. 'Never built on because of flooding. Poor farming land.' In addition, in its first years, the construction was hampered by a local labour shortage: 'You needed something like 30,000 building operatives to build 3,000 houses a year. We had 600 building operatives in this area.' During the early seventies, the property bubble inflated by the Heath government made this labour shortage worse. In 1972, there was a national builders' strike. Meanwhile, inflation was high and rising and building materials were scarce: 'There was a period when we couldn't get bricks.' Then the mid-seventies brought the three-day week and deteriorating government finances, which reduced the money available for Milton Keynes. Walker and his colleagues learned to be frugal. 'You get more for your money out of landscaping than anything else, hence the emphasis on that.' Then came the drought of 1976 and Dutch elm disease. Milton Keynes's newly planted shrubs and trees died in their tens of thousands.

In July 1974, the conservative journalist Christopher Booker joined the multitude of British and foreign reporters, architects, planners, social scientists and curiosity-seekers visiting the partly built city. 'These are bleak days for the . . . "prestige projects" which were such a disastrous legacy of the overblown fantasies of the sixties,' he wrote. 'The dinosaurs of Maplin and the Channel Tunnel seem on the edge of extinction.' At Milton Keynes, he found

. . . rolling farmland criss-crossed with mile upon mile of half-finished roads, labelled V8 or H7 . . . On nearby hilltops stand the first housing estates . . . Not the sprawling, leafy, affluent suburbia of a Los Angeles, but hundreds of grim little misshapen boxes, in brick or corrugated metal . . . In the present economic climate . . . the chances must be that over the next decade Milton Keynes will simply become a pathetic national joke, falling ever further behind its ambitious schedule, and finally grinding to a stop in a sea of mud

and rusting contractors' equipment, unsold houses and half-finished factories . . . Such a horrible mistake must never be made again.

Building sites can be lowering places for life's pessimists – or for
those who have to live on them. Histories of Milton Keynes call the
city's seventies inhabitants 'pioneers'. Their 'reservations' about the
housing they moved into 'appear to have surfaced quite quickly',
writes Mark Clapson in *A Social History of Milton Keynes*:

The absence of windows in bathrooms was disliked . . . Many dwellings
[were] not found to be well designed for warmth . . . Another common complaint was that noise insulation . . . was often poor . . . External features of
housing produced some strong reactions. People were generally conservative
in their tastes, expressing . . . a marked dislike of such materials as cedar
boarding or aluminium.

Milton Keynes was muddy in the winter and dusty in the summer.
Unlike previous New Towns, anyone could go and live there – it was
not being built as an overspill settlement for a specific city or town –
but in the early years almost half the pioneers came from London.
They came to find work. Milton Keynes's good road connections and
position near to both the capital and Birmingham made it appealing
for offices and light industry. It also attracted the headquarters of the
Open University – 'a nest of Marxists', as Margaret Thatcher
described it, half-jokingly, to the development corporation chairman
Jock Campbell. Between 1971 and 1981, more jobs were created in
Milton Keynes than in any British city apart from the oil-boom town
of Aberdeen. Yet other pioneers came for bleaker reasons: hoping 'to
solve family problems by a change of residence', as the development
corporation's annual report put it in 1975, or to get away from overcrowded, apparently deteriorating parts of inner London, with their
tight grey-brown streets and clogged council-housing waiting lists.
Many incomers were 'disadvantaged', said the 1977 annual report.
Incomes in Milton Keynes were lower than in the capital and other
parts of the south-east. 'Too many new residents', thought the
corporation, 'have difficulty making ends meet.'

Milton Keynes promoted itself vividly and innovatively. An exhibition in London used Astroturf and architectural models to suggest

both an energetic new city and a bucolic retreat. There were beckoning ad man's slogans – 'Come to Milton Keynes' – seductively designed brochures and a magazine, *New City*, which showed a world of clean-lined houses and greenery, of 'integral carports' and 'safety for children'. But some incomers arrived with no furniture and no friends to find a largely unfinished city with few amenities – the shopping centre did not open until 1979 – and, where the work was done, a completely new kind of urban landscape for Britain. Disorientation, loneliness and the break-up of marriages are frequent features in the accounts of the pioneers. 'People travelling through the city complain that it seems to be deserted,' recorded the development corporation's annual report in 1978. 'The citizens, when driving about, lose their sense of place.'

Netherfield, half a dozen miles south of Derek Walker's rectory in Great Linford, was one of the first and least popular grid squares of housing. I went there the week before I met him. In the taxi I asked the driver, who had been taking fares in Milton Keynes since 1971 and knew his local history, what he thought of the estate. 'It was built with alternative materials because of the builders' strike and the brick shortage,' he said. 'It was built as a slum.' And what was its reputation now? 'Sink,' he said.

For several more minutes we continued along the dual carriageway with only the odd roof visible above the high grass verges and tree-tops – the usual backdrop to journeys between different parts of Milton Keynes. Then we turned off, passed through the curtain of trees and drew up next to a set of buildings that looked like a cross between a moon colony and an army encampment. In long, absolutely parallel lines, terraced houses with identical flat fronts and flat roofs, side-by-side grey shoeboxes of wood and corrugated aluminium, marched into the near distance. The land they stood on rose and fell quite sharply – Milton Keynes was not as flat as Derek Walker said it was – but the continuous roof line of each row of terraces remained exactly horizontal, so that, seemingly at random, some houses were one storey, some two and some three. The rows of terraces were quite far apart, further apart than in a London street, with strips of green in between and lots of sky to see; and the endlessly repeating facades, catching the March sunshine, had a certain geometric beauty. But a more unyielding piece of city planning was hard to imagine. And it had not aged well. There was rubbish in many of the front gardens, some of the garages under the houses were disintegrating, and on one house the aluminium panels were coming away, showing nothing but wood and nails beneath. In the middle of the estate was the 'local centre', to use the jargon of the Milton Keynes planners: some dispiriting shops, a few pedestrians and a pub with a warning on its blackboard: 'No Travellers'.

Walker confessed he was disappointed with Netherfield. 'It really was a lovely plan and should have worked,' he said. 'But it hasn't. It had the poorest builders who worked in the city. It had problems – the local housing officers, if they didn't like somewhere in the city, they would put all the trouble there.' It did not exactly add up to an admission of responsibility, yet he and the other architects of Milton Keynes learned from Netherfield and the other barrack-like estates they built in the city in the early seventies. The obligation to consult and respond to residents was, unusually for a large public-housing development in post-war Britain, a central element of the Milton Keynes project, and the city's household survey found that people wanted privacy and individuality in their houses, and a villagey, 'traditional' feel to their streets – not a place in some monumental modernist scheme. Walker and his colleagues listened, and Milton Keynes began to change again.

After we had talked about Netherfield, Walker suggested I visit Heelands, another local council estate which had been built later in the seventies. It was close to his house, and Milton Keynes is full of footpaths – in the seventies, Walker knew about environmentalism as well as consumerism, and made provision for walkers and cyclists as well as drivers – so after the interview I set off on foot. It was a sleety afternoon with a bitter headwind, but within a few minutes I had almost forgotten about the cold. First, on all sides, there were small white houses, arranged in squares among the trees. Each house had a built-in garden shed, a terracotta roof and a faintly Mediterranean air. Then there were more English streets of updated half-timbered houses, each with a slightly different front and a different steeply pitched roof. There were areas of benches and landscaping, like the houses carefully placed and well-preserved. Everything was on an intimate scale; there was almost no graffiti and no vandalism. Heelands was not southern California – assuming LA was a city model still worth following – but unlike a lot of public- and private-housing developments from late-twentieth-century and early-twenty-first-century Britain it felt solid and cared for and unshowily modern.

On a similar estate nearby I talked to an elderly woman who was approaching her front gate with a bag of shopping. 'I moved here from Wimbledon in 1980,' she told me. 'For more space, for my kids – I had four of them. I started in a council property. It was beautiful. Fields all around. No road signs. Everybody took pride. The original ones of us still do.'

Despite the unfamiliarity and unfinished quality of the city in the seventies, and the scorn of commentators like Christopher Booker, most incomers came to like the early Milton Keynes. In 1975, a development-corporation survey of five estates found that 'between 83 and 95 per cent of residents were pleased with life in Milton Keynes, and only four families out of the 290 covered wanted to return to wherever they had come from'. In some ways the blank-slate feel of Milton Keynes, which the likes of Booker found so alienating, was actually a strength: in Britain in the seventies, traditional cities, despite the beginnings of gentrification in parts of inner London, were losing popularity and population. 'The public', said Walker, 'voted with their feet.'

And then there was Milton Keynes's improving housing. 'By the mid-seventies, the quality of the public housing was very good,' Walker continued. 'Good spaces. Extremely good landscaping.' His busy eyes became still and sober for a moment. 'All your socialist principles tell you that public housing is very important.' The Milton Keynes architects and planners also learned how to squeeze the maximum funding out of the period's cash-strapped governments. 'We used to take the big schemes to central government on Christmas Eve,' Walker recalled, his cheeky glint returning. 'The civil servants were so anxious to get off to their kids, their mulled wine, we got the schemes through with a minimum of fuss.'

However, the 'socialist principles' which underlay Milton Keynes were increasingly of the Gavyn Davies rather than the Arthur Scargill variety. 'We were trying to build the public housing as being available for purchase,' Walker told me. This was a major change of philosophy. In the late sixties, there had been tensions between the development corporation and the Wilson government over the ratio of public to private housing in Milton Keynes: the government wanted a 50:50 split, to save money and promote property ownership; the left-wing development corporation wanted more council dwellings. But, as the seventies went on, Jock Campbell and Derek Walker steadily adjusted their ideas about what socialism meant, and the distinction between public and private housing in Milton Keynes became increasingly blurred. The city 'must become more responsive to home ownership', Campbell said in 1977.

Yet, at the same time, he and Walker wanted to avoid the 'total commercialism', in Walker's words, that they saw filling other British cities up with shoddy, overpriced properties. Walker tried to insist on high standards of construction and design, and the development corporation sought to make the house prices fit the city's demographics. 'Ways of providing low cost housing for sale to people in the lower income groups are being explored,' recorded the corporation's annual report as early as 1972. Like the more modern-minded members of the Wilson and Callaghan governments, such as Davies, Donoughue and Tony Crosland, the planners of Milton Keynes were searching for a political holy grail: a way of combining freedom of choice and consumer satisfaction with social justice. In 1975, the development corporation declared that it wanted the city to have more property owners *and* to accommodate more of Britain's poor.

This vision of property-owning socialism was only partly realized. The decade's frequent recessions, high interest rates and government restrictions on council-house sales held it back. In 1972, there were 8,000 owner-occupied homes in Milton Keynes; by 1979, the total had grown only modestly to 13,000.

The real take-off in local home ownership would have to wait for a new political era. 'In our housing surveys in the eighties, we would ask, "Why did you buy your council house?"' Walker remembered. 'And people would say, "Because everything in the house has been done for me. It's got a nice garden. It's safe."' He gave a world-weary chuckle. 'When Margaret Thatcher sold off council estates, our houses went like bloody hot cakes!'

In late 1978, despite Callaghan's recovery in the polls, the development corporation began reluctantly to acknowledge that it might soon be dealing with a Conservative government. A weekend brainstorming session produced a paper on the corporation's future strategy. It was called 'Here comes Maggie!'. During the last months of the Callaghan administration, the corporation started to put more emphasis on the building of private homes in Milton Keynes and less on the building of council ones, whether they were going to be sold off ultimately or not.

But there was a clearer sign of the more money-orientated Milton Keynes and Britain to come: the opening of the shopping centre in 1979. Walker was heavily involved in the design. It was more elegant and more careful with public space – more high-minded, you could say – than other shopping centres. The 'shopping building', as he and the other architects called it instead, rose from the still half-empty centre of Milton Keynes as a series of airy glass boxes. They were only a few storeys high and undecorated on the outside except for their slim cream frames: no logos, no gimmicks, nothing but a near-infinity of glass and, reflected in it, passing cars and the shifting north Buckinghamshire sky. On the inside, even in 2006, after three decades of consumerism in Milton Keynes beyond the city planners' wildest seventies imaginings, the shopping building still seemed comparatively civilized and calm. The halls linking the shops were very broad and smooth, with views of the outside world. There were benches and flower beds in frequent clusters, less token and pathetic-looking than usual. People sat talking on the benches, holding proper conversations, not just pausing for breath. Birds even sang in the palms. Other people strolled past, sometimes with no shopping bags at all. The building felt as much civic as commercial; like the Heelands estate, still faintly utopian.

On 25 September 1979, four months after taking office as prime minister, and five years after its construction had begun, Margaret Thatcher formally opened the shopping building. 'Lunch was arranged in marquees for a thousand people while the building itself was packed,' record Terence Bendixson and John Platt in their history of the city. 'Light poured through the glass walls and bounced off the honey-coloured travertine floor as Mrs Thatcher toured the shops and bought some oranges.' Walker met her. 'She was very kind about the building,' he said. How did he feel about meeting her? 'I was . . .' His voice trailed away to nothing.

Thatcher told the crowd, 'Building a city for nearly 100,000 people is an immense and complex undertaking . . . Here in Milton Keynes we can see success.' Then she quickly moved on to more political themes. 'This morning, at Willey Court in the Galley Hill Estate, I visited Mr and Mrs King, who are buying their house from the [development] corporation. Encouraging people to own their homes . . . is something to which this government attaches great importance. We shall be making the necessary changes in the law . . .' That morning she had also visited a local centre for small businesses. 'This government,' she said, 'aims to create the conditions in which . . . free enterprise generally can flourish.' But first, she went on, 'More people' needed to 'accept some simple economic truths'. As she was listing them, the Milton Keynes *Standard* reported, 'Several hundred trade union members barracked Mrs Thatcher . . . forcing her to shout. After declaring the centre open she commented: "I think we won". She received an ovation from the crowd.'

At the next general election, in 1983, the first in which Milton Keynes had its own constituency, the Conservative candidate won with a majority of 11,522.

17

Pressures Building

A new Britain was emerging in the late seventies. Yet its hopes and fears, as the unresolved political mood of 1977 and 1978 showed, did not necessarily imply a change in Downing Street. There were two things that gave Margaret Thatcher rather than Jim Callaghan the chance to mould this new Britain for the long term. One was an unease about the direction of the country, encompassing everything from the unemployment rate to the unwinnable war in Ulster to the state of race relations, an unease which persisted in the late seventies despite the economic recovery and the growing confidence of the government. The other, more decisive factor in Callaghan's downfall was a sudden nationwide revolt against the social contract.

It was made possible, in part, by Jack Jones's retirement. In March 1978, at the age of sixty-five, he stepped down as general secretary of the TGWU. The occasion was marked the month before by a ceremony at the Royal Festival Hall in London attended by Callaghan, Michael Foot and 2,700 other Labour and union dignitaries. Important government business, including a meeting of the TUC–Labour Party Liaison Committee, was suspended to make room for the day-long tribute to the Emperor Jones. The left-wing actress Prunella Scales read out messages of appreciation from trade unionists around the world. Entertainment was provided by a Chilean dance troupe – opposing Pinochet was a favourite Jones cause – the Nolan Sisters and the impressionist Mike Yarwood, who put on a cloth cap and told a joke to happy applause about Callaghan needing permission from Jones to form a government.

The prime minister himself sat next to Jones, both of them beaming like amused old patriarchs in the front row of the stately Attlee-era auditorium. The rest of the audience, reported the *Daily Mail*, was 'friendly-looking, respectably dressed . . . mostly middle-

aged . . . very like an oversize diocesan meeting'. Jones was presented with a cheque for £10,000 donated by TGWU members. He
immediately handed it back, to be spent on a campaign for pensioners and on the union's convalescent homes.

Yet the standing ovation Jones received for his altruism was deceptive. In the TGWU and other unions such an approach to money
matters was already falling out of fashion. At the Festival Hall,
Jones's successor as general secretary, Moss Evans, a less shrewd and
flinty left-winger and a self-proclaimed 'man of the shop floor', told
the audience: 'We must hold fast to free collective bargaining to get
the best obtainable return for our members.' Stripped of the traditional pipe-smoking, passive-aggressive jargon of union wage
negotiators, this meant: I want to get the largest possible annual pay
increase for the 2 million people in the TGWU, regardless of the
effect on inflation, on the economic and political situation in general, and on the government's finances; and I want to negotiate that
increase directly with my members' employers, unhindered by any
government limits on wage settlements, of the sort in place until now
under the social contract.

There was a celebratory, nostalgic atmosphere that day in the
Festival Hall. Even the *Sun* had qualified praise for 'Emperor Jack':
'He is straight. He is always frank.' His successor's ominous words
about the future of British industrial relations went largely unre-
marked upon. In fact, abandoning the social contract was already
TGWU policy. Eight months earlier, in a less famous hall on the Isle
of Man, and while Jones was still general secretary, a TGWU conference had voted to go back to the pay 'free-for-all', in Jones's
disapproving phrase, that had existed before the Wilson and
Callaghan governments began making their annual deals with the
unions. In his memoirs, Jones presents the vote as a watershed:

The alternative composite motion called for 'a return to unfettered collective
bargaining' . . . An avalanche of delegates spoke out for [it] . . . Towards the
end of the debate I was asked to speak. I realized that whatever I said would
not change the minds of the majority in the hall, and yet I felt that when they
returned to their homes many would reflect on my words . . . I warned that
a mad scramble for larger wage increases would only make our troubles ten

times worse in the years to come. 'The benefits of North Sea oil . . . are on the horizon. If this Government fails you will hand these to the party of privilege. You will put back the mighty in their seats and kick the people of low degree in the teeth.'

In 2004, I asked Jones how he felt about the vote now. 'I understand why I was defeated,' he said calmly. 'As it happens, you know,' he continued less evenly, 'I could say, "Well, I was right after all, because the Tories got in, and the unions"' – he let out a sudden stuttery laugh – '"lost."' After a short pause his calm returned. 'But I think I'd have probably been against [continuing with pay restraint] if I'd been on the shop floor. I would've identified with those who thought they could get better.'

Under the social contract, wage increases for union members had been consistently at or below the rate of inflation – controlling inflation being, in large part, the contract's *raison d'être*. Between July 1975 and July 1976, the first year of pay restraint, or 'phase one' as it was officially known, average earnings rose 13 per cent and so did inflation. Between July 1976 and July 1977, 'phase two', earnings rose 9 per cent while inflation rose by twice that. The result was a brutal cut in the standard of living of some of the Labour Party's most natural and loyal supporters, and, sometimes, anger towards those considered responsible – regardless of their political status. During 1977, the political journalist John Cole wrote afterwards, 'when [Jones] went round factories workers knew what was happening to prices . . . and they simply shouted at him'.

The better-paid, better-skilled members who had always been influential in British unions had an additional grievance about the social contract and its pay agreements. Although the latter were voluntary, administered by the TUC rather than the government, and vulnerable to a degree of rule-bending by unions, with the effect that wage settlements usually ended up higher than the officially acceptable percentage – which was 12 per cent in 1975–6 and 5 per cent in 1976–7 – limits were also set on pay increases in cash terms: £6 a week in 1975–6; £4 a week in 1976–7. One consequence of these cash limits was to erode the skilled workers' precious 'differentials', the gap between their wages and those of less valued colleagues. For the low-paid, and egalitarians like Jack Jones, this levelling was a good thing. Shirley Williams told me that in the late seventies her ministerial postbag was full of letters from badly paid women urging her to fight to keep the social contract. But egalitarianism was not and never had been the main business of British trade unionism.

Nor, for that matter, was helping struggling Labour governments to stay afloat. As the miners' leader Joe Gormley put it bluntly in his autobiography, the social contract 'put us [the unions] in a false position . . . Our role in society is to look after our members, not run the country.' In the second half of the seventies, British trade union membership was higher than ever before, and still rising: exceeding 50 per cent of the national workforce in 1975, and reaching 55 per cent in 1979. (Despite the result of the next general election, membership would not actually peak, according to an authoritative official survey, until the middle of 1980.) Yet, if the TUC and the government were going to set wages, what was the point, you could ask, of having individual unions? And if the TUC and the government were going to run the country jointly, what was the point, you could just as well ask, of having independent political parties? Or of normal democratic government? During 1977 and 1978, these questions began to trouble people beyond those who were always crying wolf about the state of British democracy. 'I thought the social contract was extremely dangerous,' Bill Rodgers, Callaghan's transport secretary, told me. Was there something humiliating for a Cabinet minister about the social contract? 'Good word,' said Rodgers quietly. 'Good word. It *was* humiliating.'

Jones and other supporters of the alliance disagreed. They argued with some force that the economic crisis Britain and many other countries faced in the mid-seventies justified the suspension of normal politics. In a way, the social contract was the temporary 'national government' called for by commentators and politicians of many persuasions, just as the Lib–Lab pact was. However, this argument became harder to make during 1977 and 1978 as the crisis began to pass and the social contract lingered on. In August 1977, a third year of pay restraint began. It was less rigorous than before: the TUC was no longer prepared to tell its member unions to hold back their wage demands to the government's chosen figure, this time 10 per cent, except in the most general terms. But the arrangement just about worked. Between August 1977 and August 1978, average earnings rose by 14 per cent, while inflation rose by 8 per cent. In the gap between these two numbers much of the period's sudden surge in goodwill towards the Callaghan government was generated. Perhaps the social contract, or some improved version of it, would endure after all.

But then 'Sunny Jim', his personal popularity soaring, his confidence as prime minister strengthening, had a moment of boldness. 'Shortly before Christmas' in 1977, he writes in his memoirs,

At the Cabinet Meeting on 22 December, I threw out the idea that from August 1978, we should aim to get pay settlements down to 5 per cent . . . As far as I can recall, because no formal proposal was before the Cabinet, there was no discussion . . . Ministers probably assumed that I was thinking aloud – as indeed I was. However, when I made my New Year Broadcast . . . the 5 per cent idea hardened and popped out when the interviewer tempted me . . .

Several explanations have been given as to why Callaghan insisted on this soon-to-be-notorious figure. In his memoirs, he cites the inflation rate: though much lower than it had been earlier in the seventies, it was still 'too high when compared with . . . other major industrial countries', and tighter restrictions on wage increases would be needed to get it down to a more competitive level. Denis Healey, sometimes as barbed about his allies as about his enemies, told me that the 5 per cent was a symptom of Callaghan's general overconfidence: 'Jim wanted 3 per cent originally.' Peter Jay told me that Callaghan, an old union man himself but also a moralist, had simply had enough of the unions' recurring tunnel vision about pay: 'He said to me, "They don't deserve 1 per cent. They deserve zero per cent."'

There was also a machismo about Callaghan as a politician – you could see it in his later remarks to Michael Cockerell about 'stabbing' his Labour opponents in the sixties 'in the front' – which his gentle, lulling voice and considerable patience and cunning could not always disguise. In early 1978, when he decided for good on the 5 per cent figure, there were still over six months to go until a new pay target was actually required. Callaghan had not consulted the TUC or individual unions. But, by early 1978, in less than two years as prime minister, he had already gone against Labour and union orthodoxy twice on fundamental issues: over the IMF cuts and over Keynesian economics. Both times he had got his way and, it seemed, been proven right. Why not a third time?

As well as a political ego, there was some original thinking behind the 5 per cent limit. In 1978, Callaghan and the Downing Street Policy Unit had hopes that Britain could learn from abroad, not from America as it usually tried to, but from a more comparable country. 'We looked to Germany a lot,' Gavyn Davies recalled. 'The Social Democrats were in power. Germany was doing well surviving the oil shock. It had high productivity, low inflation; consensus between trade unions, management and government.' Influenced by this much-publicised West German 'miracle', Callaghan envisaged a Britain where, rather than the bumpy back-and-forth of the social contract, smooth annual pay discussions took place between these three interest groups.

Coming from a leader so familiar with the combative industrial relations of post-war Britain, there was an air of unreality about this vision. And so there was about the 5 per cent figure. In July 1978, the Cabinet agreed to it, such was Callaghan's authority and the absence of other ideas, but without much enthusiasm. However, the TUC and the unions refused to support it or even treat it seriously. Most trade union leaders, like most ministers, political journalists and politically interested Britons, expected there to be a general election in the next few months. The economy was relatively healthy, and so were the government's poll ratings. The termination of the Lib–Lab pact over the summer had removed Labour's Commons majority. The real argument about pay, it was widely assumed, would take place after the election. At the TUC conference in September, a resolution was put forward calling for Britain to adopt the German approach to industrial relations, but it was easily defeated. The margin was so large it was not felt necessary to count the exact number of votes. By now, writes trade union historian Robert Taylor, 'There was little support among the unions for any form of wage understanding with the government.' The social contract was effectively over, at least for the foreseeable future. Callaghan's stated desire for a 5 per cent pay limit remained, but in reality only as a provocation to the unions. It would prove hugely effective.

Yet, until the winter of 1978–9, the Conservatives could not quite see how to turn the end of the social contract to their advantage. For all Margaret Thatcher's periodic, blazing-eyed condemnations of the power and supposed excesses of the unions, the fact that she kept the much more pro-union Jim Prior as her shadow employment secretary and chief spokesman on union matters revealed her party's hesitancy and divisions over Labour's pay policy, over what should replace it, and over government relations with the unions in general. 'The unions do pose a real dilemma,' admitted an internal Conservative briefing on election strategy in 1978. 'It seems to most observers . . . that the Tories can either challenge the trades union status quo – and risk losing the election in the subsequent rumpus; or they can promise to govern on the unions' terms, and probably win the election on safer issues, knowing that they are then almost certain to fail the country in office.' At a meeting of the Leader's Steering Committee in late January, the minutes record that when a colleague 'argued that if we told the truth about the unions we should certainly lose the election, Mrs Thatcher acknowledged that this could not be the centre-piece of our election strategy'.

This Tory nervousness about taking on the unions persisted at least until the end of 1978, and in some instances – well-publicized at the time but forgotten now – into the early eighties. It can seem puzzling to the modern political mind, filled with tales of the mid- and late-eighties confrontations of 'the Iron Lady', rather than the earlier compromises of 'Cautious Margaret'. For even in the seventies there was already a potent union-bashing impulse in British popular culture and the British media. In fact, there had probably been such an impulse for as long as potent unions had existed. *I'm All Right, Jack*, the famed, extremely funny British film about a factory strike, featuring feeble ministers, bullying pickets, grasping pay negotiators, lazy workers, unjustified sympathy walkouts, and Peter Sellers as a pompous shop steward with a love for the Soviet Union and a Hitler moustache – in short, almost all the favoured motifs of the anti-union argument – was released in 1959. Even then, when Jack Dromey was still in short trousers, the casual intricacy of the satire and the success of its title catchphrase suggested that a large audience knew exactly what the film was talking about.

By the late seventies, the attitudes of many Britons to unions had hardened further. The difference between the relatively reverent treatment of the massed Saltley pickets by the press, public and police and how their counterparts at Grunwick were generally received only five years later demonstrated the shift. And yet, as the Conservatives recognized, it was one thing to think the unions were too powerful, another to know what to do about it. Margaret Thatcher's shadow cabinet was full of politicians, herself included, who had seen at first hand what happened to Heath, and since the miners' strikes of 1972 and 1974, even more Britons had joined unions. 'Trade unionists' were not, yet, political bogeymen who could be invoked with little risk; they were a majority of the workforce and a large minority of the Conservatives' own voters.

In 1978, moreover, with the number of British working days lost to strikes down by three quarters from its early-seventies peak, public interest in industrial relations had faded somewhat. In January, in a Gallup poll cited by Conservative strategists, the issue was ranked fifth in importance, well behind law and order, inflation, unemployment and taxation. Despite the fraying of the social contract, the survey gave Labour a 9 per cent lead over the Conservatives on the union issue, its largest advantage in any policy area. By the following month, John Hoskyns, the Thatcher adviser keenest to confront the unions and the co-author of 'Stepping Stones' – a radical, intoxicatingly confident blueprint for achieving 'a Tory landslide' and then 'national recovery', with the political neutering of the unions the precondition to both – was despairing about the shadow cabinet's resistance to his strategy. 'In my heart I know the country's finished and the Tories aren't going to save it,' he wrote in his diary. In

March, Sir Ian Gilmour, the most outspoken and influential of the many union-friendly Conservatives still in the shadow cabinet, felt able to dismiss Hosykns' scheme by asking: 'Do we even agree that there is a need to change union behaviour at all?'

There was at least agreement in the party about the importance of the coming general election. The Conservatives had lost four of the last five. 'Our last chance is nearly here,' 'Stepping Stones' warned in one of its many melodramatic passages. 'If we speak with an uncertain voice, the collectivists will . . . continue to impose their minority solutions on a majority tranquilised with the North Sea bonus.'

In the absence of a Tory consensus about the unions, or of an economic crisis to sink the government, the Conservatives turned in 1978 to an even more fraught political theme. 'We must not shirk the immigration issue,' wrote the promising young Tory MP and leader's adviser Nigel Lawson to Thatcher on 15 January, underlining the entire sentence. '[It] is almost the acid test of whether a political party is in tune with the ordinary people.' Twelve days later, on the high-profile television current-affairs programme *World in Action*, the Conservative leader answered a question about immigration with the following:

People are really rather afraid that this country might be swamped by people with a different culture . . . We do have to hold out the prospect of an end to immigration, except, of course, for compassionate cases . . . Everyone who is here must be treated equally under the law . . . [But] quite a lot of them [immigrants] are fearful that their position might be put in jeopardy, or people might be hostile to them, unless we cut down the incoming numbers.

It was ten years since Enoch Powell's 'rivers of blood' speech, and ten years since a mainstream British politician had said anything as racially provocative. Thatcher was condemned for the language and content of her remarks by Callaghan and Healey, by bishops, by the Liberal leader David Steel and even, in private, by some shadow cabinet colleagues. Powell expressed his 'hope and relief' at her words. As he had in 1968, Thatcher received thousands of letters, most of them supportive. 'I was taken aback by the reaction to these extremely mild remarks,' she writes in *The Path to Power*, but she also admits that before the interview she had been giving immigration 'a good deal of thought'.

By the late seventies, she had come to feel that the mass immigration to Britain since the Second World War was causing 'real problems', principally among 'Poorer people . . . [who] watch their neighbourhoods changing and the value of their house falling.' Politicians who 'dismissed the anxieties of those who were directly affected as "racist"' were 'dishonest and snobbish'. She also considered her comments on *World in Action* justified on broader political grounds. 'Before my interview, the opinion polls showed us level-pegging with Labour. Afterwards, they showed the Conservatives with an eleven-point lead . . . It provided a large and welcome boost at an extremely difficult time.'

When the Tory leader made her 'swamping' intervention, the total number of immigrants settling in Britain was not rising, in fact, but falling quite sharply. In 1977, 44,000 had entered the country, compared to 55,000 the previous year, most of them the dependants of existing British citizens, and this downward trend continued during 1978 and 1979. Post-war immigration had been in large part a consequence of Britain's economic good times and of the sharp rises in state spending during the late forties, the fifties and the early sixties. The mills of Bradford needed nightworkers; the new National Health Service needed nurses. Now, in the late seventies, with the economy and the state in a less expansive phase, immigration was easier to criticize.

Prejudice and tensions about race had long been present in Britain: the first British race riot took place in Liverpool in 1919, three decades before the start of mass immigration. The fact that many of the post-war immigrants came from Britain's colonies and former colonies had initially eased the process. But by the sixties and seventies, with British imperial pride receding fast and a debate about national decline established in its place, Commonwealth immigration could look, to a certain kind of British patriot, less like a healthy post-imperial exchange and more like a national defeat: an invasion of territory of the kind previously mounted by Britain against other states. To sharpen the immigration issue further, the overcrowded and worn inner-city areas and industrial centres where immigrants tended to live and work, together with many white working-class Britons – the places where the opportunities for immigrants, such as they were, had originally been – were precisely the places which the recessions and economic changes of the seventies damaged most. It was not the best setting for racial harmony.

The Conservatives had imposed the first restrictions on immigration as early as 1961, beginning two decades of competition between the two main parties, in opposition and in government, to devise politically advantageous clampdowns. Periodically, both parties drew back from this form of politics: the Conservatives when they allowed the East African Asians into Britain in the early seventies; Labour when they introduced the Race Relations Acts of 1965, 1968 and 1976, which cumulatively outlawed discrimination in employment, education and the provision of goods and services, and established the Commission for Racial Equality (CRE). Powell apart, until Thatcher's *World in Action* interview senior politicians did not condemn immigration. Yet their basic attitude to it and to the race-related questions with which immigration was inextricably linked – the immigrants on whom debate focused were never the many white Europeans, Americans and Australians settling in Britain – was not fundamentally liberal. 'Callaghan', writes his biographer Kenneth O. Morgan, 'felt that immigration was an issue to be handled in a way attuned to public opinion rather than on the basis of abstract liberal political theory.' And that public opinion Callaghan took to be broadly hostile: 'He was unsentimental on the principle of restricting immigration into Britain.' Ambalavaner Sivanandan, the director of the Institute of Race Relations then and since, and a harsh but perceptive critic of many British governments, was dismissive even of Labour's best work for racial equality. 'The 1976 Race Relations Act had no teeth,' he told me. 'Never mind no teeth, it had no gums.'

The 1976 Act, conceived by the Wilson government and made a reality by Callaghan's, outlawed not only racial discrimination but racial segregation. It required local councils actively to promote equal opportunities, and it made the publication, distribution or public use of language 'likely to encourage' hatred against any 'racial group' a criminal offence. On paper, the Act seemed in tune with the new, racially progressive left-wing politics coming into being at Grunwick. Yet, by the end of 1978, the CRE, one of the main tools for enforcing the Act, had launched only twenty-nine investigations into racial discrimination and concluded one, against a restaurant. More damaging still to the Act's credibility, for all its potent-sounding provisions regarding incitement to racial hatred, the legislation was having little effect on the activities of a recently established, increasingly influential British political party whose central function, as demonstrated almost daily on the pavements from Leeds to London, appeared to be racial incitement at its rawest.

The National Front had been founded in 1966. Its first leader, A. K. Chesterton, was a former editor of *Blackshirt*, the journal of Oswald Mosley's British Union of Fascists, in the thirties, and the National Front also brought together members of other far-right groups which had been struggling for political impact since Mosley's heyday: the Racial Preservation Society, the British National Party, the League of Empire Loyalists. Initially, the National Front struggled, too. It was full of quarrelling, conspiracy-minded factions, ranging from English nationalists to Nazi sympathizers to anti-Semites, but, by the late sixties, they had rallied around the idea of opposition to immigration. The recent success of the Campaign for Nuclear Disarmament as a single-issue pressure group was their unlikely but well-chosen model. Powell's spectacular 1968 attack on immigration, and his advocacy of repatriation for those already living in the country, gave the National Front, whose policies were often hard to tell apart from Powell's, momentum and the beginnings of a mass membership. With Powell effectively disowned by the Conservative leadership, Tory voters and activists who strongly agreed with him found in the National Front a new political home. The Heath government's acceptance of the East African Asians, and its growing tendency to alienate right-wing Conservatives, pushed the process further.

Between 1968 and 1972, the National Front's membership swelled from 4,000 to 17,500. It started to do strikingly well in elections for a so-called minor party. In the West Bromwich by-election of 1973, a constituency with a history of hostility to immigrants and support for Powell, it won a sixth of the vote. In local elections the following month, in wards from Staines to Blackburn, it won as much as a quarter. At the 1974 general elections, the National Front contested enough constituencies – ninety in the October contest – to be permitted a party political broadcast. In 1977, the then *Guardian* journalist Martin Walker published a breathless but well-researched paperback which described the National Front as 'the country's fourth largest political party'.

In reality, the NF was too unstable a coalition, always splitting and arguing with itself even in this period of electoral promise, to be a successful party in the conventional sense. 'The membership', Walker admitted, 'is rather like a bath with both taps running and the plughole empty. Members pour in and pour out.' The same went for NF voters: apart from a hardcore of committed racists and extreme right-wingers, at best a few hundred people in a parliamentary constituency, the majority could always potentially be drawn away by less erratic, more mainstream parties. Usually – and this was what Margaret Thatcher's 'swamping' comments tacitly acknowledged – that party was the Conservatives.

In *The Path to Power*, she writes of the immigration issue in the seventies: 'I felt no sympathy for rabble rousers, like the National Front, who sought to exploit race.' But what was her *World in Action* interview, with its disapproving reference to 'people with a different culture' if not a politician doing something at least very close to that? Yet in her book, after this brief reference to the NF's racism, she immediately moves on, focusing instead on one of the party's much less significant characteristics: its occasional tendency in the seventies to advocate vaguely left-wing policies such as the nationalization of North Sea oil. 'I found it deeply significant that such groups [as the NF] . . . were just as much socialist as they were nationalist. All collectivism is always conducive to oppression . . .'

After the 'swamping' interview, the Conservatives did not start advocating repatriation for immigrants or an end to Britain accepting any new ones. Thatcher did not speak so negatively about immigration again. But a signal had been sent. Four weeks after the interview, a by-election was due to take place in Ilford North, a Labour seat in one of the NF's strongest areas, the Essex–east London borders, and a seat where the NF had been doing well in the early campaigning. In the event, the Conservatives won; a rare and welcome election success for them in 1978. Enoch Powell, reflecting later on Thatcher's *World in Action* comments, told an interviewer: 'If you're trying to convey what you feel to the electorate, perhaps you only have to do it once.' At the 1979 general election, the NF vote fell by more than half from what it had been at the 1974 general elections.

Almost as harmful to Labour as Thatcher's reaching out to the most race-conscious segment of the electorate was what the NF did away from the ballot box. There had always been a street-corner machismo to the NF – not least from its links back to Mosley's Blackshirts – but from 1974 onwards deliberately provocative marches through immigrant neighbourhoods, intimidating pavement meetings and other aggressive occupations of public spaces became key NF tactics. Brick Lane in east London, a narrow, busy, mainly Bangladeshi street close to several areas known for decades as centres of racist politics, was a frequent target. During June 1978, a report by the local trades council recorded, 'There were more and more racists selling *National Front News* and *Spearhead* each week on the corner.' On 11 June,

Skinhead youngsters, many wearing badges saying 'NF rules OK', NF T-shirts, or with copies of *NF News* in their pockets, had been gathering at the top of Brick Lane since about 11am . . . Some had come from Peckham, Ealing, Putney. Some came in minibuses . . . At about 12 noon . . . after an NF meeting . . . a group of white youths marched down the Lane . . . clapping and shouting 'the National Front is a White Man's front' . . . The police had all suddenly disappeared . . . [Then] 150 white youths ran down Brick Lane shouting 'Kill the Black Bastards' and smashing the windows of a dozen shops and the car windscreens of Bengali shop keepers. 55 year-old Abdul Monan was knocked unconscious by a hail of rocks and stones hurled through his shop window. He ended up in hospital and needed five stitches . . . Some Asians and anti-racists fought off the attackers. It was perhaps ten minutes before the police arrived. They held 20 of the white youths,

447

but released all except three whom they eventually charged only with the minor charge of threatening behaviour . . . The police said the 'spontaneous outbreak' happened just at the time they were changing shift and they were totally unprepared . . .

The trades council report, which was titled 'Blood on the Streets: Racial Attacks in East London', gave the details of over a hundred such incidents, including two murders, between January 1976 and August 1978.

A number were directly attributable to members of racist groups like . . . the National Front. However, the great majority of the attackers . . . are largely 'apolitical' youths, usually white. They have no direct involvement with racist politics except in their almost unconscious absorption of the relentless propaganda . . .

Whether those involved were 'apolitical' or not, such scenes had consequences for British politics. Regardless of the improving economy by the late seventies, and of Callaghan's reassuring qualities, regardless of the promise of North Sea oil and the bright new vistas seemingly opening up for consumerism and leisure, it was hard to feel that Britain was entirely on the right track with the NF on the streets, immigrants being assaulted and the police apparently able – or willing – to do little about it. Did these things happen in healthy, contented countries? In Europe in the early twenty-first century, anti-immigrant violence, both physical and rhetorical, is depressingly close to being an accepted fact of political life. But in Britain in the late seventies, which was only partially emerging from its mid-decade panic about mass pickets, 'private armies' and the possible collapse of the whole comfortable post-war order, what was occurring in Brick Lane and elsewhere was taken more seriously. It was seen as the kind of thing that happened in Germany – not in the broadly peaceful and prosperous Germany of the mid-seventies, which Callaghan and Gavyn Davies hoped might be a model for Britain, but in the Germany of the thirties.

'It was a real chance in the seventies for the Nazis,' Roger Huddle, one of the founders of Rock Against Racism, told me. 'When the Nazis came out in Britain, it was necessary to move very, very quickly.' Rock Against Racism began as a letter to the *NME*. During the mid-seventies, Huddle and a friend of his called Red Saunders, both of them restless veterans of the sixties Vietnam protests and British left-wing activism, and both with an interest in the political possibilities of popular culture, began worrying about the apparent surge of the far right in Britain. 'We talked about the rise of the Nazis, [David] Bowie's flirtation with fascism,' Huddle remembered. 'We came up with the name Rock Against Racism. We talked about doing a one-off gig.' Then, in August 1976, they read about a recent Eric Clapton concert in Birmingham where the guitarist had made an impromptu speech in support of Powell's immigration stance. Saunders decided to write to the *NME*. 'Red read the letter out to me over the phone', said Huddle, 'and asked me to sign it.' Half a dozen friends of theirs agreed to sign too. The letter was published on 11 September. It began,

When we read about Eric Clapton's Birmingham concert . . . we nearly puked . . . Come on Eric . . . you've been taking too much of that *Daily Express* stuff . . . You're a good musician but where would you be without the blues and R & B? . . . Rock was and still can be a real progressive culture . . . not a nightmare of mediocre garbage . . . We want to organise a rank and file movement against the racist poison in music. We urge support for Rock against Racism.

At the end of the letter was an east London PO box number. 'We got so many letters, 200 or 300 in the first week, mainly from soul fans and mixed-race couples, that we felt confident,' Huddle remembered. Rock Against Racism quickly turned into a real campaign. Huddle was working as a graphic designer for the Socialist Workers Party (SWP), as the International Socialists now called themselves. By the late seventies, the SWP was the radical left-wing group with the largest membership and the most energy. Along with supporting strikes and opposing the social contract, anti-racism had long been a favoured SWP cause. The party also saw Rock Against Racism as an opportunity to widen its influence and form coalitions, both of which were perennial SWP ambitions. 'The SWP let us use their PO box,' said Huddle. 'They gave us their whole infrastructure, their ability to book coaches for demonstrations. The SWP print shop became the powerhouse for RAR propaganda.'

Huddle is a short man with cropped grey hair and an appealing energy about him. In 2006, he was working for a trade union and doing an art MA, and was still ready to cite Marx and Lenin and use the phrase 'dialectical relationship' in his quick sentences without a hint of embarrassment. But he was keen to emphasize, setting out the intricate political geometry of Rock Against Racism with neat choppy hand gestures over our cheap restaurant table in King's Cross, that the campaign was much more than an SWP front: 'RAR was very independent. Red was a fellow traveller, not an SWP member.' Such distinctions were important to Rock Against Racism's chances of success because the SWP was a controversial body in the seventies, not just for its empire-building, but for its confrontational approach to the National Front. In his history of the street politics of the period, the SWP activist and author David Widgery describes a typical stand-off:

The NF's first big demonstration of 1977 was planned for April, through a multi-cultured inner city suburb . . . Wood Green [in north London] . . . The SWP led the argument for direct confrontation . . . While the worthies . . . of the Labour Party and the Communist Party and the official ethnic bodies . . . addressed a rather small audience in a local park, the Front and their police protectors were faced with much more numerous, better organised and determined opposition armed with smoke bombs, flares, bricks, bottles and planned ambushes. At Ducketts Corner . . . there was a spontaneous move to block the road and physically attack the Front . . . Conventional anti-fascist politicos had been augmented by North London tribal gangs, rockabillies, soul girls and tracksuited Rastas . . . [and] a squad of black kids accurately hurling training shoes borrowed from Freeman, Hardy and Willis . . .

The concerts by reggae and punk bands which Rock Against Racism put on across Britain from late 1976 onwards still had some of this confrontational quality. National Front supporters would turn up – the activities of the SWP and the NF often seemed symbiotic – as well as anti-racists and politically uncommitted music fans. Sometimes even the bands themselves became contested ground. 'The battle for Jimmy Pursey became crucial,' said Huddle, quite deadpan, about the singer of punk group Sham 69, whose mixture of mouthy working-class pride and a raucous football-terrace sound had attracted a large NF fanbase which Pursey seemed unsure whether to welcome or disown. 'He was a weird lad. I think he was a good lad,' said Huddle. 'But at one show' – his voice lifted at the memory – 'we had to hold the [anti-racist] dockers back from attacking the skinhead Sham fans with pickaxes.'

Other members of the Rock Against Racism coalition were milder. The singer Tom Robinson, who wrote Top 10 hits with socially conscious lyrics and clever choruses, joined the campaign after being involved, years before, in the more herbivorous activities of the Gay Liberation Front. 'I saw the RAR letter. I wrote to the address: "What is this Rock Against Racism? Where do I join?" I had seen skinheads around. I'd read up my history about the rise of Hitler. The SWP were the only band of people prepared to roll up their sleeves. If it had been the Young Conservatives, I'd have gone along as well.'

Like many of those involved in Rock Against Racism, Robinson was contemptuous of Labour's caution, or worse, on race and other social issues. 'The Callaghan government was a wretched fucking government,' he told me as we had lunch in a rather grander London restaurant than the one where I met Huddle. Robinson sat back in his jeans and leather jacket – he was by now a well-known radio DJ and presenter – and continued with slightly studied candour: 'In RAR we thought, "The government are the enemy as well as the NF. This reactionary Labour home secretary [Merlyn Rees, the less liberal successor to Roy Jenkins] is as bad as it gets. How could the government get any worse?"'

The climax of Rock Against Racism was a demonstration in Trafalgar Square in April 1978. It was followed by a march to Victoria Park in east London and a free open-air concert. By midday in Trafalgar Square, wrote Widgery, 'The sun was out and the whole lot were there . . . punks and hippies and skins, vicars and trade unionists, blacks, browns and pinks. It was certainly the biggest anti-fascist rally since the thirties.' Along the six-mile route to Victoria Park, a flat windswept space fringed with tower blocks which was the only park the organizers could get permission to use – and was where the Chartists had rallied in 1848, and the GLF had held 'Gay Days' of picnicking and public kissing in the early seventies – the march fattened and the crowd listened to bands playing from the backs of trucks. It was almost as if the demonstrators were at a left-ist rally in the pre-Pinochet Chile of the radical socialist Salvador Allende, and not in London under careful old Callaghan. Giant pa-pier mâché heads of Hitler and the NF's leaders, made by Roger Law, who would give Margaret Thatcher the same treatment on *Spitting Image* a few years later, were rolled along the tarmac. The organizers claimed an attendance of 80,000, even 100,000. 'We expected 20,000,' said Robinson, whose band played in the park, 'so the PA system was for 20,000. When 80,000 came, they couldn't hear.'

There were backstage arguments about the running order for the bands, and the stage had to be guarded in case of National Front attack. But none of this mattered much. Billy Bragg was in the audi-ence as a nineteen-year-old Clash fan. 'Almost everyone I know who went, went to see the Clash,' he told me. 'It was a style trip . . . [But] Rock Against Racism did engage me. Through RAR I engaged with race, with gay rights, women's rights.' Widgery writes a little mock-ingly but also excitedly:

As the park slowly filled up one could float through three generations of the Left. At the outskirts there were couples who might have . . . been in Trafalgar Square when Bevan spoke against the Suez invasion . . . Their sen-sible footwear had been learnt on the Aldermaston march but the thermos flask and binoculars came from bird-watching outings . . . The middle [group] was the generation of 1968 . . . They had henna on for the occasion even if it did remind them of a commune they'd rather forget and they were slightly worried about the whereabouts of their eight-year-old whom they had arranged to hand over to its other single parent by the inflatables . . . They had quite liked Tony Benn's speech . . . [And finally there were] the front-line punks [who] had been on amphetamine for days and were living for this moment. This was their Woodstock and their Grosvenor Square. The punks didn't like any of the speakers but knew exactly what the music was saying.

Victoria Park, part hippy-tinged free festival, part sequel to the multiracial pickets at Grunwick, part precursor to the fusions of pop music and celebrity with good causes achieved at Live Aid and Live 8, was a culmination of sorts for the new left-leaning political movements of the British seventies. It was a sign that their ideas and tactical innovations would, regardless of who won the forthcoming general election, remain influential for years to come.

In the long term, Rock Against Racism succeeded in a broad sense. In its racial attitudes and level of integration, 'London now is *unbelievable* compared to thirty years ago,' said Huddle. Yet the creativity of Rock Against Racism – from its sharply designed campaign newspaper, a little like an eighties style magazine before its time, to its clean-edged modern logo – did not mean that racism had ceased to be a force in Britain by the end of the seventies. In 1982, a credible survey by the Policy Studies Institute found that since 1974, 'The British job market has changed little in its hostility to black workers, except that it now excludes more of them from work altogether.' When the survey asked its respondents whether life in Britain had improved for their ethnic group over the last five years, only 20 per cent of West Indians and 15 per cent of Asians said it had. Three times as many people in both groups said things had got worse.

In local politics during the seventies, especially in London, there was the beginning of a reaction against these inequalities. At the 1974 borough elections, the number of non-white councillors in the capital rose from none to ten; at the next such contests in 1978, to thirty-five. But even the latter figure was nothing like a reflection of the city's ethnic make-up. Despite these small election successes, despite Rock Against Racism, despite Grunwick, the seventies did not fundamentally change the political position of non-white Britons. It would take an expression of their discontent on British city streets in 1981 that was much fiercer, and on a much greater scale, than 'black kids hurling training shoes' at the NF to get that process started.

In Northern Ireland, too, the late seventies brought not resolution but a sense of pressures building. In July 1979, the *New Statesman* published an article by the respected investigative journalist Duncan

Campbell based on a leaked British army document written in November 1978. 'Northern Ireland, Future Terrorist Trends' predicted that for the foreseeable future, 'Any peace [in Ulster] will be superficial and brittle.' Instead, the briefing paper continued, 'We can expect to see increasing [IRA] professionalism and the greater exploitation of modern technology for terrorist purposes.' During the 1979 general election campaign, the *Guardian*'s political reporter Michael White told me, 'There was a rumour the IRA had a Sam-7 [anti-aircraft missile]. The press flew in a separate plane from the party leaders. We all joked that it was the decoy. But we were quite relieved to land after the last flight of the campaign.'

Across the Irish Sea, an 'acceptable level of violence' continued in Ulster through the late seventies, in all its unacceptable forms. The number of soldiers killed in 1978 was the same as it had been in 1975; in 1979, it was much higher. In March 1979, the Bennett Report, an official inquiry into the interrogation techniques used by the Royal Ulster Constabulary, had 'no doubt' that many injuries recently sustained by Republican prisoners 'were not self-inflicted and were sustained during a period of detention at a police office'. The report recommended that prisoners detained for terrorism-related questioning should be seen by a doctor every twenty-four hours, and that CCTV should be installed in the RUC's interview rooms. The Callaghan government agreed, but its Northern Ireland secretary Roy Mason, the most pro-military and least conciliatory holder of the position in the seventies, nevertheless insisted: 'The Bennett Report has not said that ill-treatment has taken place.'

It was in South Armagh, the southernmost part of Ulster, a mazy borderland of hills and high blackthorn hedges, where unmarked roads led to the Irish Republic and watchful IRA supporters had farms on the vantage points, that the near-stalemate in which the British government and army found themselves by the late seventies was most obvious. 'The law', wrote A. F. N. Clarke, a captain in the Parachute Regiment, in a memoir of serving in the area during 1976, 'does not apply here . . . We are right in the heart of their country.'

In 2005, South Armagh still felt a little like that. From the railway station at Newry, which was still a damp temporary box of plasterboard and wire mesh – 'It kept being blown up,' said my driver – I took a taxi to Bessbrook Mill, in the seventies the largest British base in South Armagh, and now one of the few left. For a few minutes we drove past off-white housing estates and small wet fields. Then, in the middle of a village, at the top of a short steep lane, the taxi stopped. At the bottom of the lane, blocking the road, was a wall of green corrugated metal as high as a bus. There was a gap in the wall, a narrow, twisting chicane of an entrance, with floodlights and cameras covering it. The fortifications were still a slight shock to come across, for a first-time visitor to Ulster, as if the army occupation of the British Isles that people were always worrying about in the seventies had actually happened. Beyond them was a long grey Victorian building with blocked-up windows and a roof covered in radio aerials. A bright orange wind sock flapped in the grey wind. From behind the wall came the rising sound of a helicopter.

Bessbrook Mill was built by Quakers in the nineteenth century as part of a model community for linen manufacturing. In the mid-seventies, a less pacifist body, the SAS, started using it. Bessbrook quickly became a centre for regular British army operations as well. On this dark December lunchtime in 2005, its main gate was being guarded by a private with a Liverpool accent, pink cheeks and not even his first hint of stubble. He treated my request to visit (I had phoned ahead) with mild puzzlement, but he let me in. Inside the gate were half-empty helipads. In the seventies, they were said to be the busiest in Europe – in South Armagh then, as in Vietnam, it was not safe for soldiers to travel on the ground. Between the buildings were signs of a long and settled military presence: a trimmed lawn, some topiary, three gravestones. In the guard room a tanned army press officer 'just back from Iraq' looked at my notes and answered my questions politely but not very concretely. When I asked if there were any army border watchtowers nearby that I could easily go and look at that afternoon, before they were dismantled, he shrugged. 'You know what the weather's like in Northern Ireland,' he said, as if Bessbrook was still a kind of cursed imperial posting. 'Probably not.'

He offered to phone me a taxi. While I waited for it by the main gate, I chatted through the slit window of the sentry post to the private I had met earlier, and to another soldier who had joined him. They talked about army chocolate bars, stolen cars and bored local teenagers. Occasionally they checked a car as it drove into the base. After three quarters of an hour, the taxi had not come. One of the soldiers made an anti-Irish joke about it. Realizing belatedly that South Armagh taxis were still perhaps not that keen on collecting passengers from British army bases, I walked uphill into the village. Almost immediately I saw a taxi passing and hailed it.

The driver was a freckled talkative man of about thirty. 'I had a cousin who married a soldier twenty years ago,' he said when I mentioned where I had just been. 'She had to leave the country. You don't want to be out here if you're not staunch Republican.' I asked if he would show me some army watchtowers, and he agreed. As we drove off in the failing light towards the border, he told me about South Armagh in the seventies.

'I grew up in Newry,' he began. 'On any given night you'd hear gunfire. I remember the soldiers shitting themselves. I saw one guy start to cry. Another one drop his gun. I felt sorry for a lot of the soldiers – only normal kids . . .' He gestured at the farms dotting the green slopes and ridgelines. 'Every single house would have someone who would see the soldiers coming, tell the IRA. There were always twenty other roads to use to avoid the army checkpoints. Roads you paid people to use, smuggling roads. South Armagh had some fucking super-terrorists. Fucking bad men.'

We drove fast through a puddle. 'My dad and uncle were both in the H-blocks,' the taxi driver continued matter-of-factly. 'My dad moved here from Belfast in the late sixties. Burned out by Protestants. In the late seventies, he went to Donegal [in the Irish Republic] for a week of basic weapons training. He was arrested in 1979. Convicted on the evidence of one tout. My dad did eleven years. My uncle a bit longer.' What was it like having his dad in prison? 'It was shit. It was shit. But I wasn't the only one. One day a week at my school, half the kids wouldn't be there. They would be going to see their daddies.' What did he think about his dad being in the IRA? 'He was a brave man,' the taxi driver answered without a pause. 'Big balls. Fought for what he believed in. Proud of him. Absolutely.' Then, much more softly: 'Absolutely.'

The light was too bad to do more than glimpse the tall spidery outlines of British surveillance posts on distant hilltops. In one pretty, blustery village we passed a great angular bunker like the hull of a battleship. Northern Ireland in the seventies, like North Sea oil, had required the British government to improvise a new architecture with an ugly but lasting charisma. But the soldiers were already gone from most of the villages we drove through. On one hill which the army had abandoned there was a Republican flag on an enormous flagpole. 'They took the towers down by helicopter,' said the taxi driver with satisfaction, 'just like they built them.'

In the late seventies, another unhealed sore for the Callaghan government was unemployment. Although the total had started to fall, the fall was slow. The number of jobless remained much higher than Britons had been used to in the years before the oil crisis. And it could not be attributed solely to that event: there were also unforgiving long-term forces at work in the British labour market, such as mechanization and increased competition from abroad. 'I had a strong sense that the traditional industries were all contracting simultaneously in the seventies,' recalled Callaghan's adviser Tom McNally. 'The mills in my constituency in Stockport were just melting away.'

In 1977, a promising young Liverpool playwright started work on a series of black, bitterly funny television plays about a gang of unemployed tarmac-layers in his home city and their battles with the dole office and their own demons. Alan Bleasdale's *Boys from the Blackstuff* was not completed and broadcast until 1982, when it was taken to be a commentary on a different political world altogether, but the origins of the series showed, to the contrary, that there were grim continuities between the Callaghan era and what came afterwards.

Another powerful condemnation of unemployment in the late seventies did make it into public view while Labour was still in government. In March 1978, while the Conservatives were in one of their low periods for morale, popularity and energy – and Callaghan, partly for this reason, was widely thought to be planning to call a general election in the near future – Margaret Thatcher's presentation expert Gordon Reece hired the advertising agency Saatchi and Saatchi to refresh the Tories' image. Saatchi's was a cocky, ingenious, relatively new agency, set up in London in 1970. It was one of several in the city which had established Britain during the decade as the world centre for clever ad men and talked-about campaigns – another sign of the gaudy rise of British consumerism beneath the bleak headlines. Saatchi's specialized in stark, memorable images: for example, a rueful pregnant man for a famous 1970 ad suggesting men should think more about contraception. Labour were quickly warned about the agency's political potential by Edward Booth-Clibborn, an authority on British advertising whom the party had recruited in 1977, along with a few other ad men, to do publicity work on a more ad hoc basis. But the poster campaign Saatchi's mounted for the Tories in August 1978 was still a shock.

'Labour Isn't Working' was one of a dozen ideas developed for the Conservatives by the agency that summer. Maurice Saatchi and the agency's then managing director Tim Bell considered it merely a 'possible', and it only became part of their presentation to Margaret Thatcher because the copywriter who had come up with the theme, Andrew Rutherford, found out that it had been downgraded in importance and covertly slipped a summary of his concept back in among Saatchi and Bell's presentation notes. Bell's biographer Mark Hollingsworth records that when the rough poster was shown to Thatcher,

She stared at it for a long time; the convention in party propaganda was not to mention the opponent directly. 'Why is the biggest thing on the poster the name of the opposition? We're advertising Labour,' she said. Bell and Maurice replied, almost in unison, 'No, we're demolishing Labour.'

Thatcher agreed to the poster. Then Saatchi's hired a large group of Young Conservatives from South Hendon and photographed them standing in a snaking, despondent, seemingly endless line, the dole queue of every insecure worker's worst imaginings. With 'Labour

Isn't Working' printed in huge, heavy capitals hanging over the queue, and 'Britain's Better Off with the Conservatives' in smaller, lighter letters underneath, the poster was ready. Senior Tories apart from Thatcher still had misgivings, and the party had not budgeted for an advertising blitz before the actual election campaign, so Saatchi's had to be persuaded to accept delayed payment, and only twenty posters were put up across the entire country. But the tone and timing were perfect. Denis Healey – possibly stung by the attack on one of the weaker points of his record as chancellor – called the posters a 'fraud' because they did not show a real dole queue, and claimed that the line was made up of Saatchi employees. The agency, which had indeed filmed some of its workers for another Conservative ad, gleefully entered a war of words with the chancellor. Since it was August, the silly season, the media covered the row, and the political effect of the posters was magnified far beyond even the best hopes of Saatchi's and the Tories.

Unemployment, like Britain's racial tensions, like Northern Ireland, was damaging to the Callaghan administration but unlikely to be fatal. All three problems would be as bad, and often much worse, in the next decade without bringing down the government. But the Saatchi campaign unsettled Labour at a crucial moment.

For most of August, Callaghan was at his farm in Sussex, going for walks, looking after his animals and weighing up whether to call a general election in the autumn. There were strong arguments in favour: the difficulty of carrying on as a minority government; the divisions among the Conservatives; the dramatic improvement in the economy, which might not last into 1979; the absence for once of any big ongoing political crises; and, above all perhaps, the fact that the unions' annual pay negotiations started in November, and were unlikely to be comfortable. During the spring and summer of 1978, McNally remembered, 'Jim let me start putting preparations in place. Recruiting people. There was an advisory group that met. October 5th was the popular choice for the election. We had a poster ready. It was just a picture of a candle, with words saying, "Remember the last time the Tories said they could work with the unions."'

But there were arguments, too, against a quick autumn poll. Firstly, an election did not have to be called until October 1979. Why risk a contest a year earlier? In 1978, Callaghan had been in office barely two years, and was enjoying the job more than most incumbents. 'Jim liked being PM,' Gavyn Davies recalled. More tangibly, if the government waited until 1979, it might benefit from the tax cuts it had made, which would take effect in late 1978, and from the introduction of a new electoral register, which tended significantly to favour Labour, in early 1979. Waiting could also demonstrate confidence: that the economic recovery was going to continue, that the government could keep the unions reasonable. 'Jim said to me,' McNally remembered, '"It'll be easier to get another round [of pay restraint] from them with an election looming than with an election settled."'

Finally, there was the evidence of the opinion polls. Callaghan spent much of his time in Sussex that August reading microscopically detailed surveys and analyses of British voting intentions, with a particular emphasis on marginal constituencies, provided by Robert Worcester of MORI, Labour's favourite pollster. This material revealed that the government's recovery in the polls since 1976 was not as impressive as it looked, thanks in part to the Saatchi poster campaign. Labour was at best level with the Tories, at worst still slightly behind. 'I did my own amateur calculations [for an October 1978 election] and came up with 303 Labour seats and 304 Conservatives,' Callaghan wrote afterwards.

The most probable result would be another 'hung' Parliament, a prospect I did not relish . . . I had no wish to undergo once again the frustration and uncertainty of having no Parliamentary majority . . . I made up my mind. The Government should aim to consolidate the progress we had made and then ask the country to confirm us in office . . . in the spring. I looked at the 1979 calendar . . . British Summer Time would begin on 18 March; Good Friday was on 13 April. I drew a ring around Thursday 5 April 1979, the last day of the income tax year. This seemed as auspicious as any other day. Having decided, I telephoned the Chancellor who was my near neighbour in Sussex and invited myself to tea . . . It was a lovely summer's afternoon, and we sat in the garden while I told him what I had decided. We then reviewed the winter's prospects.

Callaghan's biographer Kenneth O. Morgan says that the chancellor responded evenly to the news from Callaghan: 'Healey gave the opinion that the . . . economic argument was neutral . . . between having the election in the autumn and in the spring.' But Healey told me, 'I was worried, because I knew we were liable to have trouble with the unions again [over the winter].' Either way, between this teatime meeting on 18 August and the first week of September, Callaghan said nothing definite about his decision to any of his other colleagues. Instead, he dropped hints. On 1 September, he held a dinner for union leaders in Sussex, and put the case against an October election to them – but not strongly enough for them to believe he meant it. For in the unions and the Cabinet, in the Labour Party and the other parties, in the media and among the public, there was a conviction that an election was coming.

It had been building for months. In July, before the start of the parliamentary summer recess, the transport secretary Bill Rodgers 'gave what was understood to be a farewell party for my own departmental staff', he wrote later. Like many politicians and commentators, of all denominations, Rodgers assumed that the election would be soon after Parliament returned, and that Labour would win narrowly: '[I] discussed idly with my permanent secretary which office of state I might next occupy.'

On 5 September, a tanned and confident Callaghan spoke to the TUC conference in Brighton. After carefully summarizing the state of the economy and the arguments for keeping the pay rises of trade unionists to 5 per cent, arguments which were received without much excitement and a little heckling, he slowed his voice to a teasing half-murmur. 'I understand', he said, 'the reasons for the present spec-u-lation about the prospect of a general election.' In response to this speculation, he went on, he was going to sing a verse from an old music-hall song by Marie Lloyd. 'As far as I remember, it went like this: "There. Was. I. Wait-ing at the church . . ."' – the prime minister played the rhythm with an upturned finger – '"Wait-ing at the church, wait-ing at the church."' In the hall there was laughter and applause, then puzzled silence. Callaghan, poker-faced as the driest comedian, sang on: '"When I found he'd left me in the lurch, Lor' how it did upset me."' Callaghan paused. 'Perhaps you recall how it went on: "All at once he sent me round a note. Here's the very note. This is what he wrote"' – the Labour leader savoured the mockingly simple rhyme – '"Can't get away to marry you today. My wife won't let me!"' As his words died away, there was a final bout of clapping and laughter, and Callaghan looked down. The television cameras just caught a smile.

'Uncle Jim' loved old songs, and so did the middle-aged delegates at the TUC conference. Yet his speech baffled many of them. Callaghan had meant to imply that Margaret Thatcher was going to be left 'waiting at the church' for an autumn election that would never come. But this message, conveyed so eccentrically and unexpectedly, was lost on most of the delegates – and on most of the journalists present. Their heads were already full of noise about an October election, so they did not hear him. The following day, 6 September, the conference voted to set up an election fund, and *The Times* reported that the Cabinet meeting on 7 September would see the announcement of an October election, on the 5th.

In his memoirs, Callaghan mentions the 1978 TUC conference only fleetingly, and his singing to it not at all. On the subject of the autumn election, he admits: 'I made a mistake in allowing the speculation to build up . . . without uttering a word to cool it.' Soon after the conference, the comedian Roy Hudd wrote to him pointing out that the song to the TUC was not by Marie Lloyd at all but by Vesta Victoria, another music-hall legend. Callaghan wrote back, telling Hudd that he had deliberately misattributed the song to Lloyd because she was better known. Through overconfidence or tiredness, or both, the great fox of sixties and seventies Labour politics had begun chasing his own tail.

On 7 September, the Cabinet met as scheduled. 'After the holidays . . . Ministers were in a mood of good-humoured tension,' wrote Rodgers. 'The Secretary of the Cabinet . . . was teased about the further vacation he would shortly enjoy.' When Callaghan briskly asserted that there was not going to be an autumn election, 'We almost rose from our chairs in astonishment.' There was disbelieving laughter. Later that day, a slightly fidgety Callaghan, in a dark suit and dark tie, broadcast to the nation. 'Now I'd like to tell you, personally, how I see it,' he began, trying for his best bedside manner.

'Things have been going much better . . . These can be lasting, not temporary, improvements if we follow through . . . Would a general election now solve inflation? . . . No.' Authoritatively, a little patron-izingly, he sketched out the reasons for his decision. Then he quickly moved on. 'We can see the way ahead. We will face our difficulties as we come to them. I can already see some looming on the horizon.' A final resolute look came over his face, which had lost some its full-ness over the last two years. 'Let's see it through together.'

Callaghan's advisers immediately sensed the risk. 'I said to him, "You'll either be remembered now as a political genius,"' McNally recalled later, '"or as the man who missed the boat."' The unions' feelings were more clear-cut. David Basnett, head of the General and Municipal Workers and of the loyal union group Trade Unionists for a Labour Victory, had already given a press conference endorsing Callaghan's 'decision' to hold an autumn election. He and other union leaders now felt humiliated. Callaghan's song to the TUC now seemed like mockery – the unions, it was clear, had also been kept 'wait-ing at the church' – and the postponement of the election seemed like the prime minister's secretiveness, political game-playing and disregard for the unions at its worst. Many trade unionists also thought Callaghan had made a catastrophic electoral misjudgement. Many of his Labour allies felt, or have come to feel, the same way. 'To my dying day I believe we could have won an election on 5 October,' McNally told me. Gavyn Davies and Bill Rodgers said much the same.

In her memoirs, Margaret Thatcher comes close to supporting their analysis. 'I shared the general sense of anti-climax which the Prime Minister's [election] announcement caused . . . [Yet] would we have won a general election in the autumn of 1978? I believe that we might have scraped in . . . But it would only have needed one or two mistakes in our campaign to have lost.' More interestingly still, she goes on: 'Even if we had won, what would have happened next? . . . The TUC had voted against a renewal of the Social Contract – and the following month's Labour Party Conference would vote to reject all pay restraint . . . If we had been faced with that [pay revolt] over the winter of 1978/79 it might have broken us, as it finally broke the Labour Government . . .'

18

The Peasants' Revolt

On 21 September, exactly a fortnight after Jim Callaghan's election announcement, workers at Ford rejected a 5 per cent pay offer, roughly half the rate of inflation, and went on unofficial strike. By 25 September, 57,000 of them were out, from Dagenham to Bridgend. 'Stuff the 5%', said their placards. In early October, their union, the TGWU, once so loyal to the government, declared the strike official. In mid-November, Ford, until now so close to Callaghan that they employed his son Michael as an executive and had recently opened a car plant next to his constituency, agreed to give the strikers 17 per cent to get them back to work. The strikers accepted. The government responded to Ford's flouting of its 5 per cent pay guideline by withdrawing the subsidies it paid the company. On 13 December, the Commons voted on whether the government could impose penalties on employers in such situations. With the Conservatives, the Liberals, the Scottish Nationalists, the Ulster Unionists and Labour left-wingers all either voting against the government or abstaining, the government lost by six votes. The sanctions against Ford were withdrawn, and the government was left close to defenceless against any workers who followed the Ford strikers' example. 'We've acted as a spearhead,' a triumphant TGWU official at Ford told the Communist Party journal *Marxism Today*. The Winter of Discontent was under way.

This simplification of Shakespeare's phrase, which had been fleetingly used during the three-day week, first resurfaced in September 1978 in a series of speeches by trade union leaders warning about the consequences of any government attempt to restrain pay. 'The unions' scriptwriters are reduced to dusting off old clichés for the coming pay battle,' sneered the *Sun*'s industrial correspondent Peter McHugh. But from the Ford strike onwards, the phrase rapidly became less of a joke. 'In no time at all in November 1978, Jim's pay target fell apart,' Bernard Donoughue remembered. 'In four or five weeks it just went.'

The Winter of Discontent lasted from November 1978 to March 1979. It was the biggest British labour stoppage since the General Strike of 1926, and in Britain there has not been a remotely comparable strike wave since. In 1979, which included the Winter of Discontent's two most militant months, January and February, almost 30 million working days were lost, more than three times as many as the previous year and the equivalent of every employee in the country taking a day's strike action. On 22 January 1979, the Winter of Discontent's single most militant day, 1.5 million public-sector staff refused to work.

But the Winter of Discontent was not really about such carefully choreographed, centrally directed 'days of action'. It was more shapeless and anarchic. Many of its strikes were unofficial, undertaken without the approval of the union hierarchies. The Winter of Discontent fed off its own energies, spreading suddenly and unpredictably. There were strikes by truckers and traffic wardens. There were strikes by ambulancemen and dinner ladies. There were strikes by binmen and local newspaper reporters. There were strikes by hospital cleaners and people who operated rubbish incinerators. There were strikes by nurses and Fleet Street printers. There were strikes by Heathrow pilots and civil servants. There were strikes by school caretakers, train drivers and gravediggers. There was an overtime ban by oil-tanker drivers. There were even strikes far out at sea, among the usually cowed workers on oil rigs.

Many of these industries had rarely experienced such stoppages, even in the seventies, while many of those who went on strike had never done so before. Some of the strikes were national and attritional, lasting several weeks or months. Some of them were local and short, almost comic in their contagiousness, their paper-thin rationales, their air of feverishness. 'London's traffic wardens disappeared from the streets this afternoon,' the London *Evening Standard* reported on 15 January 1979, 'because of a lightning strike . . . so that [they] can attend a mass meeting . . . to negotiate a pay deal.'

The government wanted wage settlements of 5 per cent, and inflation was just under 10 per cent, but the strikers paid little or no attention to these figures. The truckers demanded more than 20 per cent; the nurses 25 per cent; the tanker drivers 40 per cent. Such demands were, depending on your political perspective or your position in the labour force, either the result of pent-up and justified pay grievances, or a Darwinian workers' free-for-all.

The winter weather added to the sense of panic. Heath had been gifted a mild January and February during the three-day week, but Callaghan was much less lucky. November 1978 was warm, while December was a little colder than average. But January and February were Arctic by British standards: barely above freezing, even during the day. In central London, for the first time in years, roads were blocked by snow. Airports, motorways and trains were slowed or brought to a halt; whole towns were isolated; food prices went up. And the weather stayed raw into the spring and beyond. In May, when the day of the general election finally came, Tony Benn reported 'hail and snow' in his constituency in normally temperate Bristol.

In Britain in the seventies, strikes in winter were hardly new. The dark season, every streetwise striker and strike victim knew, was when strikes had teeth. The disruption of everyday life by industrial disputes was also a familiar ritual. But this time the effect of the strikes was more universal and dramatic than before, and all the more so for being presented by a press with anti-union biases and industrial disputes of its own – and which was inclined to be harsh on the Callaghan government after the anticlimax of the autumn. Journalists, like politicians, had cleared their diaries for the election that never was.

From November to March, the papers, when they came out at all, were full of sudden school closures and struggling hospitals; of queues at petrol stations and panic buying in supermarkets; goods stuck in docks from Hull to Southampton; commuters unable to get to work; south London council tenants without heating or hot water; drivers on the M4 having to cope without de-icing trucks; parks and shopfronts sinking, infamously, beneath accumulations of uncollected rubbish; and, even more infamously, happy rats feeding on it. The right-wing tabloids, in particular, went to great lengths to make all of this look as nightmarish as possible – the rats, near Leicester Square in central London, were only caught by a photographer after hours of waiting – but the consequences of the strikes were painfully real. Over a million people temporarily lost their jobs as a result of the stoppages. And the effects of the strikes even touched the inner sanctums of government and union power. 'At the TGWU headquarters in Smith Square,' the *Evening Standard* reported on 1 February, 'the side entrance had almost completely disappeared behind a wall of rubbish sacks.' On the 23rd, Tony Benn wrote in his diary,

Pickets were standing at the end of Downing Street. One picket looked through my car window and asked if he could speak to me. The driver went on but I stopped him and got out. I assured [the picket] I was not going in [to 10 Downing Street] to do their job or replace their work, and I went in. I sat down at the table outside the Cabinet Room and worked on my papers . . .

Despite the months, even years, of warning signals, the strike wave had taken the government largely unawares. The successes of 1977 and 1978, the distracting obsession with an autumn election, the fact that the government had already improvised its way through so many crises, the fact that the unions had grudgingly stayed in line since 1974 – and the belief that with an election unavoidable in the next year they surely would continue to do so now – all of these contributed to the government's unpreparedness. 'I don't think we had really planned for the winter of '78–'79,' Gavyn Davies told me. 'We had no plan for the strikes, no PR approach.' Donoughue wrote later that the postponed election had left the government 'flat'. Afterwards, Callaghan had not reshuffled his Cabinet. The Policy Unit, which had been expecting an autumn contest, had few policy ideas left. The hope was to muddle along until a spring election, win it, and then start afresh. There was even press speculation in early 1979 that Denis Healey would replace Callaghan as prime minister soon after Labour won another term. That, it was said, was why the chancellor had recently turned down the job of managing director of the IMF.

The strike wave put a torch to such hopes. Yet the government's standing, contrary to the conventional wisdom since – and there is more conventional wisdom about the Winter of Discontent than about any other episode in the British seventies – did not go up in flames immediately. Through November and December, and into the first week of January, some opinion polls continued to show small Labour leads, as they had done since mid-1978.

'The Conservatives don't seem to be doing all that well,' said Brian Walden, the ex-Labour MP turned free marketeer who had become a forensic interviewer of British politicians, as he introduced *Weekend World* on 7 January 1979. 'This isn't a happy situation for Mrs Thatcher,' he went on, over footage of empty supermarket shelves and closed petrol-station forecourts. 'The public fear the power of the unions,' but the Conservatives, he reminded viewers, did not have a good record when it came to taming them: Heath had been 'smashed'. Would Margaret Thatcher, if she ever became prime minister, do any better?

He turned to his guest. The Conservative leader smiled her calmest, most ready-to-pounce smile. Recently, she said softly, she had been looking at British trade union law, all the way back to the Trade Disputes Act of 1906. Ever since that date, she had concluded, unions had been 'above the law'. They had had 'licence to inflict harm, damage, and injury on others'. She paused. 'This is a problem. We've got to meet it . . . Someone's got to grasp this nettle.' Then she made a series of nearly jaw-dropping suggestions: that strikes in 'essential services' could be outlawed; that social security benefits paid to strikers could be sharply reduced by making them subject to taxation; that strikers could have their benefits taken away altogether if they acted without a secret ballot in favour of industrial action. None of these radical ideas were Conservative policy yet, but by floating them so publicly and suddenly she knew, as she put it in her memoirs, that anti-union legislation would be instantly 'higher on the agenda than some of my colleagues really wanted . . . I had broken ranks. People could see that I was going to fight.'

The interview continued. Walden, well-briefed and provocative, belittled her proposed reforms as 'peripheral' to the union problem. Thatcher became visibly angry – as usual, it was in her eyes – but lost none of her crispness. Unions, she said, should go back to their original ideals of simply looking after their members, not 'strike against the weakest members of society'. The fact that the former sometimes meant exactly the latter did not detain her. Since the early seventies, when it came to unions, 'Public opinion has changed tremendously,' she concluded. 'It is ready for things which it was not ready for.'

From this point on, as much as these things can be fixed precisely, the Winter of Discontent and union power in general began to stop being a dilemma for the Tories and started to become their key to office. After years of expressing a vivid but rather impotent outrage at union behaviour – over the mass picket at Grunwick, for example – Thatcher had finally demonstrated that she had the will and the ideas to do something about it. Meanwhile, the unions, too, at last appeared to be behaving with the political self-destructiveness that 'Stepping Stones' and countless other union-curbing blueprints produced by the British Right since the fifties had always predicted, and perhaps secretly hoped, they would. 'Party in grip of mild euphoria,' wrote Thatcher's adviser John Hoskyns in his diary on 18 January, 'because country beset by strikes . . . Idea of special relationship between Labour and unions a joke.' The chapter in his memoirs about the Winter of Discontent and the 1979 general election has a frank title: 'Saved by the Unions'.

Jamie Morris arrived in London from Fife in Scotland in 1970. He was seventeen, five foot three, and had 'little formal education', as the London *Evening Standard* would later put it. He liked horses, the Conservative Party and the countryside, but in the capital he had to settle for a flat with his dad in a council tower block. For four years Morris did menial jobs in department stores. He renounced Conservatism for socialism. Then, in 1974, he started working for the state, as a telephonist at Westminster Hospital.

Five minutes' walk from the Houses of Parliament, and a street from the Labour and Conservative Party headquarters, Westminster Hospital was a looming thirties fortress, the latest site of a famous institution that had been in the area since the 1700s. It was where MPs were taken if they fell ill in the Commons; and where

Westminster journalists, if a politician's plight was sufficiently compelling, could easily keep an eye on them. A week after starting at the
hospital, Morris joined the Labour Party and the National Union of
Public Employees, or NUPE. Like the other unions which represented people in state-funded or white-collar jobs, NUPE was expanding
and open to new talent in the seventies. Within three weeks, Morris,
who was a conscientious organizer and a good talker, had become a
shop steward. 'There were problems to sort out,' he explained terse-
ly to the *Evening Standard* later. 'I was around . . . People seemed to
like my ideas. It was as simple as that. I didn't want to become a full-
time union official.'

Instead, by the winter of 1978–9, Morris had been promoted by
the hospital to domestic supervisor, with responsibility for the cleaners and non-medical care staff. Besides his union duties – he was now
branch secretary at the Westminster and looked after NUPE matters
at two other nearby hospitals – he was a Labour borough councillor,
council-committee member and school governor. He had also spent a
year at the LSE studying industrial relations. He sometimes worked
seventy or eighty hours a week, but he seemed to have the energy for
it: he was still only twenty-six, with puppy fat in his face, flicked and
styled longish hair and a handsome young man's beard. In his little
time off, he went back to his council tower block, listened to Bob
Dylan and Woody Guthrie, and read horror novels.

He sometimes talked about becoming a Labour MP. He had a touch
of Callaghan's moralism: speaking about teenage vandals to the East
London *Advertiser* in early 1979, he said, 'I'd fine the parents and give
the kids a bucket of water to clean off the graffiti.' But in other areas
his political stances were less helpful to the government. In 1975, in a
dispute over the use of his hospital by private patients, he led a campaign of industrial action so high-profile and provocative that he
received a letter bomb. Four years later, he told the *Advertiser* that the
Labour social services secretary '[David] Ennals and his minister
Roland Moyle . . . should be on the *Muppet Show* – they've no idea
what's going on in the health service.' The very picture of a cocky
young shop steward, he concluded with a flourish: 'I'm a rebel and I'll
only shut my mouth when they put the lid on my box.'

Morris sat out the first few weeks of the Winter of Discontent. Then, in mid-January, his moment came. In 1979, the British welfare state and political status quo contained an often-forgotten weakness and injustice. Despite decades of relatively generous state spending, manual workers in the public sector such as the cleaners and carers Morris supervised were not well paid. A typical weekly wage was between £49 and £54, at a time when the average manual worker in industry earned £90. In 1978, his union, NUPE, decided it wanted a weekly minimum of £60 for its members, an increase, depending on their starting wage, of between 10 per cent and over 20 per cent – smaller than many other pay claims during the Winter of Discontent, but still far in excess of the government's 5 per cent guideline. The government resisted. From mid-January, NUPE responded with an unpredictable national campaign of overtime bans, strikes and work-to-rules, the severity of the action in each workplace dependent on the attitude of the union's local officials.

Hospitals were among the places worst affected. Almost half were suffering disruption by the end of January, the *Daily Mail* reported. The great brick citadel of the Westminster was one of them: 'Dirty linen stood in piles around the corridors. Patients ate meals off paper plates.' On 30 January, the hospital announced that it could not admit any new patients, including emergency cases. Even the patients already in its wards might have to be moved if the dispute went on. Then the hospital would be shut down completely until the pay claim was resolved.

The next day the *Evening Standard* identified Morris as the union official leading the industrial action. It was a public role he seemed happy to fulfil. 'I think the management will find it hard to carry on,' he told the paper, beside a photo of him coming out of a NUPE meeting at the hospital, wearing an open-necked shirt and dark glasses and with a small crowd of more conventional-looking union members standing behind him, like followers. As well as refusing to do their usual duties, NUPE members at the Westminster were also refusing to allow deliveries of heating oil. 'I feel sorry for the patients of course,' Morris went on. 'It is not that long since I was a patient at the Westminster Hospital myself, suffering from a broken ankle.' But until his union's grievances were addressed, nothing could be done for them. 'The feeling at the [union] meeting', he summarized melodramatically, 'was one of anger.'

The following day, the *Standard* reported that two hospital delivery vans with their tyres slashed had been found blocking the service entrance to the hospital. NUPE members had refused to unload them: they were now blacking deliveries of sterile medical supplies and fruit and vegetables, as well as oil. The Westminster's managers had tried and failed to persuade ambulancemen, the police and the Automobile Association to help, and had finally resorted to calling a local army barracks. Soldiers in berets had unloaded the vans. 'Sabotage Hospital Calls Army', said the *Standard*'s front-page headline with equal measures of distaste and excitement. Those responsible for the tyre-slashing were not named by the paper, but a picture of Jamie Morris with the caption 'He ordered the total walkout' directly above a photo of the vans unsubtly implied a connection.

The paper also reported Morris's reaction to a concession from Alan Fisher, the slightly ineffectual general secretary of NUPE, that his members could, after all, assist hospitals in medical emergencies. 'Mr Morris said he had been told by NUPE officials that [this concession] did not apply to Westminster Hospital.' Morris was then asked about a code of conduct for strikers recently issued by NUPE headquarters. 'I hope it's been sent in the post to my home address,' he said with taunting sarcasm, 'because it won't get to me here. Our pickets are stopping the mail.'

Since the early stages of the Winter of Discontent, the right-wing papers had been looking for union ogres, and now the *Standard* had found one. 'What is left of the moral capital the miners drew on in 1972 and 1974 has been squandered by the likes of Mr Jamie Morris,' declared a *Standard* editorial. Even the *Guardian* condemned Morris by name, out of the many millions of trade unionists on strike, for his 'boasting' and 'willingness to put patients at risk'. On 31 January, the day that what was happening at the Westminster was first widely reported, Margaret Thatcher appeared on the *Jimmy Young Programme* on Radio 2, one of her favourite soapboxes.

'Some of the unions', she told the show's large and electorally significant audience, 'are confronting the sick . . . If someone is inflicting
injury, harm and damage on the sick, my God, I will confront them.'

But Jamie Morris's notoriety had not yet peaked. On 6 March,
with timing worthy of the blackest satirical novel, as the industrial
action Morris was orchestrating at the Westminster continued, the
social services secretary David Ennals, who was responsible for the
NHS, including its pay disputes, was admitted to the hospital. Ennals
was a protégé of Callaghan's, a slightly soft-hearted, not especially
competent minister with vulnerable health who had been shot in the
Second World War and left with a crooked right arm and circulatory
problems. He had spent a month in hospital in 1978 for a thrombo-
sis in his leg, from which bone had been taken thirty years earlier to
rebuild his arm, and in early 1979 the condition painfully recurred.
He was advised to go to the Westminster for two days of tests.
Despite the situation at the hospital, he felt he had no choice, and
despite the restrictions there on receiving patients, which alternately
tightened and loosened in the general disorder, he managed to get
himself admitted, discreetly, via a back entrance. Then his troubles
started.

Morris declared the fifty-six-year-old Ennals 'a legitimate target
for industrial action'. As the minister sat stranded in bed in a public
ward, propped up with pillows and wearing green pyjamas, unable
to walk without a stick or a wheelchair and with official papers still
arriving for him in red boxes, Morris roamed the corridors of the
Westminster, young and trim and relishing his power, promising
reporters that Ennals' stay 'would be made as uncomfortable as possible'. NUPE's hospital porters, Morris told the *Guardian*, would not
help the minister to the X-ray department. He would not have newspapers or mail brought to him. 'He won't get the little extras our
members provide patients. He won't get his locker cleaned or the
area around his bed tidied up. He won't get tea or soup.' Morris told
the *Daily Mail*: 'He won't see a single smile.'

Morris said he blamed Ennals personally for the pay dispute.
'Don't you think he has been mean-minded?' he asked the *Guardian*.
'People who work in hospitals . . . have to fight for a decent living

wage, but the miners can walk into an office and be given 15% just like that.'

For all Morris's gloating, his arguments had some force – and some unexpected supporters. The *Daily Telegraph* agreed that Ennals, as the minister in charge of NHS pay, made a 'legitimate target' for aggrieved NUPE members. Peter Jay was away in Washington as British ambassador but was still closely following events at home. He told me, 'The Winter of Discontent came from [the desires of] very low-level people. Individuals governed the Winter of Discontent. They were thinking, "Why be restrained in our pay demands? I want to be re-elected as branch secretary." When I was at *The Times*, I would often spend the morning with the National Union of Journalists, fighting for a higher pay increase, trying to negotiate the best result we could, and the afternoon writing a leader calling for pay restraint and a national incomes policy.'

Even Margaret Thatcher, faced with the volatile politics of the winter and conscious of the need not just to attack trade unionists but also to win some of their votes at the coming election, and the need to discredit Callaghan, found herself occupying an unexpected position on pay restraint. She opposed the 5 per cent guideline and refused to condemn 'free collective bargaining'. 'Although opposition to centrally imposed pay policies meant that we would find ourselves with strange bedfellows, including the more extreme trade union militants,' she wrote later, 'the revolt [by unions during the Winter of Discontent] against centralization and egalitarianism was basically healthy. As Conservatives, we should not frown on people being well rewarded for using sharp wits or strong arms . . . Of course, such an approach was described . . . as being opportunist . . . But in fact it was an essential part of my political strategy to appeal directly to those who had not traditionally voted Conservative.'

Over pay, it seemed, she and Jamie Morris were temporarily on the same side. As Ted Heath, Jim Prior and other more cautious Tories pointed out in public and in private over the winter, this was a risky and contradictory stance. Thatcher was loudly chastising unions for their excesses, except when those excesses happened to hurt the Labour government. At the 1978 Conservative conference, the shadow chancellor Geoffrey Howe came up with a cumbersome form of words to summarize the Tory pay policy. In government, he said, the Conservatives would permit not 'free collective bargaining' but 'realistic, responsible collective bargaining, free from government interference'. Yet in fact there was a shrewdness to the piled-up euphemisms: they sounded bland and uncontentious, but gave a future Tory administration plenty of room for manoeuvre against the unions. 'Free from government interference' would not be how most would describe British industrial relations in the coming decade.

But in the Westminster, from the 6th to the 8th of March 1979, Ennals remained stuck in bed in his green pyjamas. He read his official papers through thick-rimmed glasses. He looked a little flushed, but he kept his hair neatly parted and managed to smile for the cameras. Nurses who were not NUPE members brought him tea and tidied his locker. Members of the public who had been volunteering in the hospital since the start of the dispute did the same. His tests were carried out. 'I am being treated magnificently,' he told the *Daily Telegraph*, 'and that includes doctors, nurses, administrators, porters, domestics, volunteers . . . I have seen no sign of discrimination [against me]. I have seen nothing but professional skill and human kindness.' In this interview and the dozen others he gave while in hospital, he did not criticize or mention Jamie Morris.

After two days, Ennals left the Westminster in a wheelchair, getting into his ministerial Rover to be driven straight to an official engagement. As a parting gift, the *Telegraph* reported, he had 'received a red carnation and a note from Jamie Morris [which] referred to him as Comrade Ennals and asked him to attend, if possible, one of the union's future branch meetings'. Ennals' response was not recorded.

Yet soon afterwards a reconciliation of sorts between the minister and the militant was achieved, as it turned out. NUPE's national negotiator Bob Jones helped effect it. 'Jamie came to see me,' he recalled when I met him, retired now, at his house in a quiet south London suburb. 'Strange fellow. Very young. Wild . . . but quite serious.' In early March 1979, Jones already knew all about the situation at the Westminster. 'There wasn't another hospital that produced a dispute in quite the same way,' he said in his soft but exact Scouse voice. 'The governors of the hospital were inflexible. They didn't want to let Jamie into the negotiations.' But the governors were eventually persuaded.

The climactic meeting took place in the boardroom of some borrowed government offices in Paddington, not far from the Westminster. It was a Sunday teatime and the heating was off. 'It was freezing,' Jones recalled. 'We blew all the fuses trying to plug in electric fires. People were huddled in coats.' Besides Jones and Morris, there was Alan Fisher, the head of the TUC Len Murray, the Westminster's managers, and a man from the conciliation service ACAS, who was dressed for a dinner that evening. He never got to it; instead, deep into the night, the negotiations spluttered and stalled. At 11 p.m., the TUC gave everyone fish and chips – 'good piece of organization, that', said Jones in his armchair, hands across his stomach – but still NUPE and the Westminster's management were at odds. In the small hours, as a last resort, Ennals was summoned. 'We got him out of bed,' recalled Jones with a slow smile. 'He was properly dressed but he had his pyjamas on underneath. They were poking out. I remember Jamie said, "Look, he's got his pyjamas on."' Did they find it funny? 'Yes, Jamie did.' But the minister's arrival ended the stalemate. 'Ennals turned up at four. The thing was over by five.'

In the second week of March, NUPE staff at the hospital began working normally again. The government had agreed to give all NUPE members a 9 per cent pay rise, plus an official review of the differing levels of public- and private-sector pay which would publish its findings in August and was likely to award NUPE members between 5 and 10 per cent more. Morris had accepted the deal and convinced his colleagues to do likewise. 'I have done an about-turn', he explained to the *Sun*, 'simply because I am a realist.' He told the *Daily Mail*: 'Okay, so I have been accused of betrayal but I can take it. Just as I've had to take death threats and obscene letters in recent weeks.' Shortly after the Westminster returned to normal, a motion of no-confidence in Morris as NUPE branch secretary was proposed by some of the hospital's other shop stewards. Morris survived it by thirteen votes to four. 'Mr Morris', the *Standard* reported, 'said that his role as NUPE leader at the hospital was coming under fire from militants . . .'

Soon afterwards, Morris disappeared from the national press. But the revolt he had led enjoyed quite an afterlife. In 1981, the television satire *Yes, Minister*, a beautifully sustained attack on seventies and early-eighties Whitehall which was Friedrich von Hayek's favourite programme and was co-written by Anthony Jay, a close associate of the British free-market think tanks, included an episode called 'The Compassionate Society'. Its plot revolved around an implacable young Scottish hospital shop steward called Billy Fraser, 'an odious man' to civil servants, who had shaggy hair and shop-floor clout and kept his hands in his pockets in the presence of ministers. 'We can bring London's hospitals to a complete standstill,' this Morris looka-like warned in his key scene. 'There will be no cancer treatment, nothing . . . Until we have brought back the compassionate society.'

The following year, Lindsay Anderson's even more caustic film *Britannia Hospital*, a state-of-the-nation piece set in a nightmarishly troubled hospital, featured another shaggy-haired young union offi-cial, this time called Ben Keating, with complete power over the ancillary staff and a large appetite for industrial blackmail. Like Morris, Keating wore an open-necked shirt, was fixated on the use of his hospital by private patients, and had a half-hidden traditional streak. At the end of the film he is bought off with an invitation to a royal luncheon. According to the film writer Gavin Lambert's mem-oir about Anderson, 'The idea for *Memorial Hospital* [*Britannia Hospital*'s original title] . . . had occurred after he read a news story about a labour union official who organized a strike . . . at a nation-alized London hospital. Pickets actually refused to admit ambulances . . . or delivery vans with medications . . .' The trade union scenes in the film were based on events in several late-seventies hospital dis-putes, but Lambert recalls that Anderson specifically researched the Westminster battle.

Anderson was an anarchist, albeit of the rather gilded sort: he dis-approvingly watched what he called the 'increasingly sectarian, increasingly materialist' behaviour of the unions during the Winter of

Discontent from various sunny locations in Australia, India and California. Anthony Jay, meanwhile, was an urbane early Thatcherite. But Jamie Morris seems to have got to both of them.

After the Westminster dispute, Morris followed a more complicated political and personal path than his public image suggested. A few months after the 1979 general election, he got married. In 1980, he bought a wreck of a three-storey Georgian house in Bow in east London and began doing it up. In 1982, he became a father. For a time he stayed at the Westminster, continued as NUPE branch secretary and remained a Labour councillor in the East End. He had a left-wing reputation on the council and, in 1981, with the Labour left at its peak, he was selected for the party's panel of potential parliamentary candidates. But his political and NHS careers went no further. Labour began to move rightwards. In 1983, he left the health service and the council, citing low pay and bad health. A public row over his property ownership – he was still living in his council flat – may also have contributed to his retreat from politics.

Later that year, he began running an off-licence in Bethnal Green. The East London *Advertiser* carried a photograph of him behind the counter, still a local celebrity, holding a bottle of champagne, clean-shaven and wearing a jumper with reindeer dancing across it. In 1989, the *Sunday Times* interviewed him for a tenth-anniversary piece about the Winter of Discontent. Morris was still running his off-licence. 'I suppose I enjoyed the Winter of Discontent,' he said. 'I certainly don't regret it.' But the Thatcherite paper happily noted that the scourge of the Westminster now had a Filofax and a house worth £250,000.

Morris did not appear in the press again. In 2006, I tried for several weeks to find him. A television producer who had spoken to him for a documentary a decade earlier told me Morris had been 'in Liverpool' in the late nineties. He said Morris was unemployed at the time and living on a council estate, 'involved with unions still . . . doing not a lot . . . lazy but intelligent'. I called some union officials, past and present. 'Ahhh . . . Jamie,' said one former union leader with feeling. But he had no information, and nor did the other union men. The LSE, where Morris had studied, had an old address, and agreed to write to it for me, but nothing came back. I tried hospitals in central London, but nobody remembered him. I went to the Westminster, but it had become a block of flats. 'Businessmen and a few students with rich parents,' said the security man. I went to the East End and looked up at Morris's old tower-block flat. Pebble-dashed and raw, looking out across miles of London's poor, it was not hard to see how it had turned him from a Scottish Tory into a radical young man.

Finally, I went to his old off-licence. It stood at the foot of another council block: Morris had ended up providing the workers with booze rather than better wages. It was a hot, sapping late-summer afternoon, but eventually I found an Asian couple who ran another off-licence nearby and remembered him. 'Nice fellow,' they said with knowing smiles. 'He was a talker. Very good at talking.' A slight roll of the eyes: 'Always talking politics.'

It was not a complete surprise that the accident-prone Ennals should end up helpless before the likes of Morris. It came as more of a shock when Callaghan's response to the strike wave showed a similar com-bination of timidity and fixed-smile denial. The denial came first. On 4 January, with the Winter of Discontent still in its relatively early stages and the government's poll lead still holding, but the overall sit-uation visibly worsening – a road hauliers' strike was spreading across Britain – the prime minister left the country to attend a sum-mit in the Caribbean.

The gathering was held on the palmy French territory of Guadeloupe and was attended by Chancellor Helmut Schmidt of West Germany, President Giscard d'Estaing of France and the American President Jimmy Carter. There was plenty for them and Callaghan to talk about. In his memoirs, with the gusto of a former foreign secretary, he devotes almost twenty pages to the issues: Britain's need for American permission to replace its 'independent' Polaris nuclear weapons with Trident; America's need for Britain and West Germany to approve its possible deployment of cruise missiles in Europe; and the desirability or otherwise of imposing sanctions against apartheid South Africa, another brewing issue. Most urgent of all, there was the situation in Iran, where the Shah's regime was collapsing, an Islamic revolution was building, and the second oil crisis of the seventies was already starting. Some of these matters would be prominent in global politics through the eighties and, in the case of Iran, far beyond.

'Guadeloupe was a big, international, slightly glamorous, certainly high-octane summit,' remembered Tom McNally, who went there with Callaghan. 'Does the PM go? If he doesn't, what does that say about the state of Britain?' The summit had been months in the arranging. Callaghan relished such meetings and usually performed well at them. 'It seemed OK to go,' said McNally. 'We wanted to say it was business as usual. The government must govern.'

So, on 4 January, the prime minister and a small entourage went to Heathrow, the slightly shabby backdrop, in the absence of Maplin, for so many pivotal moments in his premiership. There he found his official jet deep in snow. 'British Airport Authority men armed with shovels and brooms dug it out,' the *Standard* reported. 'Mr Callaghan himself ventured outside at one point to lend a hand.' Then he flew off to 'the sunshine summit . . . according to the official patter, to achieve closer cooperation in tackling the problems of mankind. Mr Callaghan's friends [also] saw the excursion hopefully as a good lift for election year.'

From a conventional British foreign-policy perspective, the summit was fruitful. Callaghan talked one-on-one to Carter about replacing Polaris with Trident: '[The] cost . . . I remarked . . . would be beyond our means. The President responded that he thought it should be possible to work out satisfactory terms . . .' In return, Callaghan, in the usual manner of post-war British prime ministers, helped smooth the frictions at the meeting between Carter and the continental European leaders. The sessions lasted two days and took place in a large thatched hut circled by palms, with, Callaghan wrote, 'staffs kept carefully out of earshot and only the sound of the sea to distract us'. There was a minimum of the paperwork that normally choreographed summit discussions, only one official reception, and no issuing of a communiqué afterwards. The hut was in a commandeered holiday camp, and journalists were kept at a distance.

Between sessions the four leaders 'gossiped on the grass outside our huts, ate together informally . . . Carter jogged, Giscard played tennis, and I sailed a small dinghy'. Like the other leaders, Callaghan had had a hard seventies and his batteries needed a little recharging.

But his relaxation was only ever partial. Each day after lunch a slight, precise Englishman would come and see him. Sir Clive Rose was a senior civil servant who had recently been a British negotiator in arms talks with the Russians. He was now chairman of the Civil Contingencies Unit (CCU), a drily-named but rather ominous official body set up secretly by Heath in 1972, after Whitehall had been unable to cope with the miners' strike and Scargill's victory at Saltley. In fact, the British government had had a machinery for keeping the country functioning during major strikes for over half a century, ever since trade union militancy and the official fear of it had hit one of its periodic peaks in 1919. But the CCU, or the 'Winter Emergencies Committee' as Heath revealingly preferred to call it, was a more sophisticated entity, designed to maintain essential supplies and amenities if they were seriously threatened by industrial action, natural disasters or nuclear war. It was run by ministers, civil servants and a former brigadier, and met in the Cabinet Office Briefing Room A, or COBRA, an underground communications centre which, like the CCU, still exists, is periodically used and tends to leave journalists who write about it slightly awestruck. Heath's CCU divided the country into regions, each overseen by a committee drawn from local councils, the civil service, the military and the police. The CCU's existence was not officially admitted until four years after its foundation. In many ways the whole set-up was a more concrete, more professional, less publicized version of the volunteer networks for saving the country from the unions that some British right-wingers spent the seventies trying to assemble unofficially.

The CCU had found the Winter of Discontent less of a surprise than other parts of the Callaghan government. 'It was obvious we were going to have a difficult winter,' Rose told me. 'We had had a difficult winter the winter before. Twenty thousand troops had been used in the firemen's strike.' By the Guadeloupe summit, the CCU had been fully activated, and Rose was in the Caribbean to keep the prime minister informed. 'I got a cable from Britain every day,' Rose remembered. 'Callaghan would be relaxing after his long mornings at the summit, and I had to turn up with ill news from the home front. Callaghan used to feign anger: "Go away." But he listened. He took seriously what was happening.'

Unfortunately, back in Britain this conscientiousness did not show in the pictures from the Caribbean. Instead, the photographs showed Callaghan sitting in the sun. The lack of a communiqué to set out the summit's achievements added to the impression that the gathering had been something of a political luxury. Yet it only lasted two days; greater damage was done by Callaghan's decision to stay on in the tropics for a further three, for an official visit to Barbados. The island was a former British colony, Callaghan knew the prime minister Tom Adams, Adams had invited him, and there were matters for the two men to discuss. But the leisure element of the stay was more pronounced than in Guadeloupe. Callaghan and his party, including his wife Audrey, stayed at the famous and famously expensive Sandy Lane resort. With even the *Financial Times* taking an interest in Audrey's choice of sun hat, the Callaghans' short holiday felt like a potential disaster from the start. 'The beach next to the hotel', McNally remembered, 'was a kind of rest and recreation place for Belgian hookers. Some of the best-looking girls you've ever seen, sunbathing topless.' Callaghan tried to avoid being photographed beside them, but a tabloid caught him and McNally emerging bulkily from the waves after a swim. When the pictures appeared, 'I remember him saying, "How on earth have they got this photograph?"' McNally recalled. 'I said, "I believe it's with a camera with a range of 400 metres, Prime Minister."'

Callaghan slept on the flight back to Heathrow on 10 January. He woke up, feeling purposeful, with some hours still to go before landing. He held an impromptu meeting with McNally and his own long-standing personal press officer, the low-key but sure-footed Tom McCaffrey. Callaghan asked them whether he should hold a press conference at Heathrow about the situation back in Britain, where the road hauliers' strike was prompting panic buying and walkouts were now threatened by public-sector workers. 'I was in favour,' said McNally. 'I thought he was going to say, "Jim's back. I'm in control." And not get into the details.' McCaffrey was against: he wanted the prime minister to get back to Downing Street first, be thoroughly briefed, and then assert himself. Callaghan, for once, ignored McCaffrey's advice. He would speak to the press at the airport.

It happened not in a prepared room, with the reporters seated and kept at a distance, and the prime minister at a table, calm, behind microphones and with a glass of water, but in one of Heathrow's charmless corridors. Callaghan, looking tanned but tired – it had been a night flight and he had only had a catnap – was pressed against a wall by the journalists and the flashbulbs. McNally stood to his left, watching. Almost immediately, he looked aghast.

Callaghan was asked about the pictures of him in the sea in Barbados. He tried to brush off the implication of the question, first with light sarcasm – '. . . and d'you know, I actually swam . . . I know that's the most exciting thing of the visit . . .' – and then with slightly pompous irritation – 'I think you should put all that kind of criticism in perspective. One mustn't allow jealousy to dissuade you from doing what you know is the best thing.' Then he tried to sound fatherly and reassuring, the way he usually did when addressing the media and the public, but succeeded only in sounding patronizing: '[In the Caribbean] I kept very closely in touch with domestic affairs. Indeed, thanks to the miracle of modern communications, I was able to lift a telephone and press a button and I was through to Number 10 before you could say "Jack Robinson", and talk to ministers and others . . .'

As his fifteen-minute interrogation went on, Callaghan seemed increasingly uncomfortable. He blinked in the flashbulbs; between questions, he looked impatiently at the ceiling, or from side to side, as if he wanted to walk away. His head movements were slightly unsteady and slow. He rambled. Finally, a junior reporter from the *Evening Standard* interrupted: 'But what is your general approach in view of the mounting chaos in the country at the moment?' The prime minister replied as if addressing a schoolboy. 'Well, that's a judgement that you are making. I promise you that if you look at it from outside' – Callaghan was not even bothering to meet the gaze of the cameras – 'perhaps you're taking a rather parochial view. At the moment, I don't think that other people in the world would share the view that there is mounting chaos.'

It had not been an easy question: almost any answer was a potential liability. Yet Callaghan's words – prickly, a touch complacent, too long-winded for the papers to properly quote his actual argument – were about the most politically vulnerable ones imaginable. The next morning, the front page of the *Sun* had the snap of a good line from *Fawlty Towers*: 'Crisis? What Crisis?' Thirty years on, the phrase is still regularly used to accuse British politicians of complacency.

While Callaghan was in the Caribbean, there was one place in Britain where the stresses of the Winter of Discontent seemed at their clearest. Hull, even now, is a slightly emaciated, isolated city, out beyond the East Yorkshire flatlands on a narrowing neck of land between the vast, muddy Humber and the cold North Sea. The railway station is the end of the line, a great arched roof with too few trains beneath. The wide streets, especially at night, can be spookily empty. Hull's population has been falling for decades. The revival of England's northern cities has not changed it like Manchester or Newcastle or Leeds.

But, in the seventies, Hull was even more of an island. Its old port and old fishing fleet were shrinking. The Humber Bridge was not yet finished (there had been delays with the construction). By road, remembered Fred Beach, then a local truck driver and TGWU shop steward, 'There were only two primary routes in: the A64 for traffic from the south and the Midlands; and the A1059 for traffic from Scotland and the north. The B-roads were slow . . .' They were especially slow during the Winter of Discontent, when snow fell heavily and regularly in the north-east. That winter, Beach continued, with unionized hauliers like him on strike, 'You had [non-union] trucks sneaking into Hull from all over the place. But eventually they had to come onto the main road.' He grinned. 'And that's when we collared them.'

During January 1979, as part of the road hauliers' strike, Beach and a handful of other Hull T&G officials organized a blockade of the city so complete and unyielding that Hull became known as 'Stalingrad' and 'siege city' in the press. Salt, sugar and dairy products had to be rationed in shops. Animals starved on nearby farms. Cargoes froze in the docks. All the while, the strikers ignored instructions, from government and T&G leadership alike, to loosen their grip. Instead, for five weeks the economy of Hull was effectively run by a 'dispensation committee' of shop stewards, Beach among them, that commentators on the left and the right compared to the revolutionary Soviets of Russia in 1917. The feelings of some of those affected by the blockade lingered for years afterwards. Hull, in short, was the Winter of Discontent at its most all-encompassing and alarming; and also, perhaps, at its most exhilarating. If I couldn't find Jamie Morris, then perhaps Beach and his colleagues could explain why they did for Callaghan and gave the country Margaret Thatcher.

Beach met me at the station wearing a blue suit and a blue tie. He had a pocket watch on a chain and a T&G badge on his lapel. It was August 2006, and he was seventy-nine. He had recently retired after a quarter of a century as the local branch secretary, but that was only officially, and he had never had that much time for the official way of doing things. He was still wiry and upright, with a penetrating voice that expected to be heard, and he drove me straight to the new TGWU headquarters in the city centre. Once inside, he checked on the progress of someone who was fixing the lights, and then sat me down in a small kitchen with a humming fridge. He made mugs of tea and tilted his glasses forward.

Normally in the seventies, he said, 'You couldn't get lorry drivers to go on strike. You couldn't get lorry drivers angry. To lorry drivers, low pay and long hours was just a way of life. Drivers were ten-a-penny. Ex-army men with heavy-goods licences. Easy sacking, easy hiring. Weak regulatory authorities. Sixty, seventy, eighty hours a week was normal. The lorry driver was a mobile tramp, a nonentity. The lorry driver didn't have any respect; their employers didn't have respect for them. If you don't like it, lump it. A heater in your cab?

Never heard of it.' He paused over his tea. 'Good training for a cold picket line.'

Hull, he went on, had been a low-pay economy 'for centuries'. But, in the winter of 1967–8, there had been a rebellion against it: an unofficial strike by TGWU members that started in Scotland and spread southwards. He and the Hull T&G had been involved, and had gained useful experience. By the winter of 1978–9, another decade of resentments had accumulated in the port city's greasy world of haulage firms and freelance truck drivers. 'If you went into a cafe, everyone was saying, "This effing job." We'd had three years of pay restraint, and people had got fed up of it. You'd get back after going down to London and back again in one day, and see the gaffer go off home in his nice car, to his detached house in the country, and his daughter getting her pony out. And you said: "We want a bit of that."' Britain might have been at its most egalitarian in the late seventies, but for the discontented truck drivers, like the low-paid public-sector workers, it was not nearly egalitarian enough.

During 1978, lorry drivers around the country began talking about a national strike. 'Low-level officials in the T&G were sympathetic. At first, T&G headquarters were not keen. We thought, "We'll go without them." There's a big gap between us and them in London. They get down south and – it must be the air or something – they change their principles. The leadership were in that golden room down there in Smith Square. They only knew what was under their noses. Moss Evans was too nice a man to be leader of the T&G. Headquarters were frightened to death of a strike. They and the TUC were virtually part of the government. There was an election due . . .' And that hadn't worried him? 'Oh no,' said Beach emphatically. Immediately he slightly changed the subject. 'The political nuance of the average lorry driver is zero. They were working too hard. Too tired. You'd go to meetings and mention something political, and nobody would know what you were talking about.' Beach was no radical in the seventies; he was, he said, a 'broad left' man. But he became part of something that would have large political consequences. 'By the end of 1978, there was a vast and efficient communication between shop stewards.' A kind of union within a union? 'Yes. Of shop stewards. We were disciplined. We knew people everywhere. Lorry drivers do. The mood was very, very strong, and it was universal. I think it was unstoppable.'

In November 1978, the Road Haulage Association, which represented lorry drivers' employers, told the transport secretary Bill Rodgers that they were aiming to keep the annual pay rise for British truckers within the government's 5 per cent guideline. Rodgers told Callaghan the good news, but the transport secretary thought it might be too good to be true. The Association, he knew, was not a tough or united body but a loose alliance of small firms without a strong leader or much in the way of negotiating skills. At the start of January 1979, alarmed by the lorry drivers' anger and their plan to go on strike, it suddenly offered them a 13 per cent pay rise. It was not enough. The strike went ahead.

In Hull, it had a particular fierceness. 'We didn't just want to hurt the haulage companies,' said Beach calmly, sitting with his mug of tea. 'We wanted to hurt everybody. To describe our actions as vicious sometimes would not be an exaggeration.'

The Hull strike committee put pickets on the docks and on the main roads in and out of the city. They put pickets on the oil-storage depots at Salt End at the eastern end of the waterfront. They put pickets everywhere a lorry might pass and where its driver might need persuading not to make his delivery. The pickets were there every day, all day and all night, in all weathers, with braziers and Primus stoves and flasks of Heinz soup that 'fell off the back of a truck', Beach remembered. He and the other members of the strike committee drove round checking on the pickets, right up until midnight. 'The gaffers were getting up to all kinds of naughties,' recalled Barry Andrews, another truck driver who was on the committee. 'Their trucks would come after midnight. But the lads were there waiting for them. The longer it went on, the worse the lads got. They almost pulled off a door off a [lorry] cab. They knocked fish off the back of fish trucks when drivers refused to cooperate. All over the road. Useless.' Beach broke in: 'There was one particularly nasty incident . . . when the lad put the concrete thing over the flyover into the windscreen.' He continued more softly: 'That could have been a death job.'

Beach had driven me from the TGWU building to Andrews' house near the centre of Hull. It was a small red-brick terrace with a minibus parked outside. Andrews was much younger than Beach and looked more like a trucker – tattooed, thickset, with a check shirt, sweatpants and a big stud earring – but nowadays he did something gentler for a living: he used the minibus to take people to hospital for dialysis treatment. He had an air of weary contentment about him. As we sat in his front room, with the August evening sun coming in, a clock ticked; his wife sat there too, with her feet up, knitting. Occasionally she got up to feed a parrot in a cage by the back window. After an hour or so she brought out plates of pastries, sandwiches and chicken drumsticks.

Yet the Winter of Discontent was still raw in the room. 'We told the pickets, "Violence is out,"' Beach went on. 'But if a factory had to close because they weren't getting supplies in, I don't think there was any sympathy from our lads.' Andrews cut him off: 'They never worried about us!' Hull in the seventies was a Labour city, with a Labour council and Labour MPs. There was a struggling Labour government, and Beach, like a lot of the strike committee, was a Labour supporter. Yet the truckers' strike in Hull, like many of the other strikes that winter, had an almost millenarian quality that went beyond politics – or at least beyond electoral and party politics. It was a kind of peasants' revolt, inward-looking and based on ancient grievances. 'I wasn't interested in what the rest of the country was doing,' said Beach. Did he worry that the government would bring in the army to drive their trucks? 'We weren't worried. We thought, "If the army comes in, well, they come in. But the threat of them won't stop us."' Despite months of rumours and Cabinet discussions during the Winter of Discontent about the deployment of soldiers, the army never came.

Beach drove me to where the picket had been at Salt End. Under an endless North Sea sky, we passed miles of docks, still operating but fringed with sunken businesses. Then, in a lay-by at the top of a long straight road that led down to the Humber, we stopped. Beach turned off the engine. In the distance, on the waterfront, were the fat grey cylinders of the oil depots. 'The tankers would come out in sixes or sevens, up this road from the depot,' Beach said. 'We would have six or seven cars in the lay-by here, with drivers, fuelled up, waiting to go. Working in shifts, twenty-four hours a day. When the trucks eased down for the traffic island' – he nodded at a small nearby roundabout where the depot road met the road into Hull – 'their drivers would wind down a window, give a flash of their lights, and throw out a piece of paper.' The tanker drivers were union men themselves who had recently returned to work after their own pay dispute. 'They would leave gaps between the tankers,' Beach continued, 'so the paper could be picked up. The paper would have the address of their destination. It could be a petrol station fifteen miles away. One of our cars would beat the tanker to the garage. We'd set up a picket there. And the tanker driver would say, "I won't cross a picket line."' Beach smiled. 'Every tanker driver, virtually . . . The depot managers were furious – the tankers would come back full. On their way back the drivers would wave to our pickets, sometimes give a thumbs-up . . .'

He fell silent. Then he turned his lean, proud face away from me and looked out through the windscreen at the horizon. 'What we did,' he said in a new, grave voice, 'in many ways and on many occasions, I've regretted it. But it was so effective. We stopped everything. The employers, they were so humiliated. Humiliated! Some of them were country people, so of course rank Tories . . . I wasn't feeling sorry for 'em. Later on in life came more realization about what we'd done.' He waited while a few clouds passed. 'It was the world turned inside out.'

During the Winter of Discontent, the dispensation committee of the Hull TGWU sat from 8 a.m. until 4.30 p.m. at Bevin House, then the union's local headquarters. It was a heavy, slightly charmless two-storey building with a big car park just outside the city centre. Beach was the committee's chairman. Early each morning, in the grudging winter dawn, the car park would fill up with cars, trucks and farm vehicles, and then a queue of local employers would form across the tarmac, into the TGWU building, along its dark central corridor, and into a chilly, strip-lit room that was normally the canteen. 'The corridor was 145 yards long,' Beach said with characteristic precision, 'and they were often stood two and three deep.' It was not unusual for people to stand in line all day. 'When the dispensation committee closed at 4.30, we told the people still in the queue, "Come back tomorrow."'

Those that reached the front found themselves facing a long white table with three shop stewards sitting behind it, drinking mugs of tea and rolling cigarettes. Beach was usually in the middle. The three of them would be wearing smart jackets rather than their usual driving clothes. Elsewhere in the room, Beach remembered, 'We had a couple of handy lads. One of them was the doorman. Behind him was another, not showing his knuckledusters. Once or twice they had to take a couple of paces forward. But there was never any violence.' Instead, as the *Sunday Telegraph* reporter Nicholas Roe memorably described it in a front-page piece about the committee on 21 January, 'Business was conducted with a taut formality.' Beach recalled: 'We would say, "Take a seat, sir," to the employers. Everything was done right. They had to prove that the destination of the load was OK. Deliveries to nursing homes and pensioners were OK. Hospitals were OK. Perishables were OK – but not much was perishing: it was very cold. But the employers had to have the paperwork to prove it.' Lists would be consulted, pens pointed at the supplicants. Roe depicted a typical negotiation, between the committee and a man wanting to move a truckload of wood for coffins:

. . . There were smiles at the request and someone murmured that they were not going to stop coffins. So the company representative, who had been waiting outside in the corridor, was brought in . . . He was very polite, as were the committee, and he appeared nervous and watchful. He sat before the table as before a tribunal and answered questions . . . It was suggested that some of the load of boards might in fact be a little short for coffins . . . But no, coffins came in all sizes. Smiles. The request was granted in principle, but the man was told to return later to finalize details . . .

. . . Back came the coffin man. He was told: 'We would like you to make arrangements to move the load, and we would like . . . you to ask [your driver] if he would be prepared to donate money to the widow of the picket who died in Aberdeen [when a strike-breaker ran him over].' The arrangement was agreed, the dispensations signed and stamped.

The committee kept a record of their decisions and the names and vehicle number plates of those concerned. They also kept a log of any TGWU lorry drivers who broke the strike, so that action could be taken against them when the dispute was over. The bureaucratic fussiness of it all, the determined good manners, the mugs of tea – there was an old-fashioned quality and an Englishness to the workings of the committee that defused its tensions. But only partly. 'Some of the gaffers took it personal,' Beach said. 'The effing! The "what they were going to do to us". Twenty years later, I was in a drivers' room, and there was a lad in the doorway with a camel coat on. Filled the doorway. He gave me a threatening nod. I said, "Yeah?" And he said, "You are the person that humiliated my father."'

As in any revolution, scores were settled and a rough class justice imposed. 'A lot of these gaffers were out and out bandits,' said Beach. 'They'd tell you black was white. This fellow, we'd stopped his transport for some reason. His transport manager was making a fuss, telling us his boss was hard up. Afterwards, we were having a meeting. Tap on the door. It's the boss, with a suntan. He had been on holiday in Barbados. But he can't give his drivers a rise!'

In Whitehall, there was horror at what the lorry drivers were doing across Britain. 'Pickets were blocking materials for the manufacture of penicillin; preventing the collection of propane gas required to de-freeze railway points; and refusing to allow the movement of chlorine for water purification,' recalled the transport secretary Bill Rodgers in his memoirs. No government or modern society could let the movement by road of such essential supplies be interrupted for long. Rodgers, moreover, was not the sort of Labour politician to be even secretly excited by the class warfare being waged by Fred Beach and his comrades. He was a donnish, slightly pained figure on the right of the party who was already sceptical about unions and would soon leave Labour to help found the SDP. He particularly distrusted the TGWU. 'Moss Evans was a slippery character,' Rodgers told me. 'He wasn't in control of his own union.'

But as long as the Road Haulage Association was unable to put together a pay deal that would satisfy the lorry drivers, the TGWU leadership offered Rodgers and the government their only chance of at least keeping the strike within certain bounds. So pressure was applied to the union. On 12 January, Alex Kitson, the TGWU official coordinating the strike, sent a telex to the union's regional offices advising them that in order 'to prevent intervention of emergency powers and calling in of troops', a list of 'priority' items drawn up by the government should be allowed free passage through picket lines. A week later – the delay showed the weakness of the government's leverage – the TGWU issued a 'Charter for Pickets':

1. Pickets should not try to prevent, hinder or delay vehicles carrying the following priority goods:
2. Supplies . . . for the production etc of food and animal feeding stuffs.
3. Supplies for medical and pharmaceutical products . . .
4. Fuel . . . for the heating of schools.
5. Materials essential for gritting or snow clearing.

'Union officials', the document went on, 'will decide where pickets should operate. They will also fix the number for each picket. Pickets will be told to wear identifiable armbands and have a responsible leader . . .' To make sure that these rather optimistic instructions were being followed, Kitson and Eric Hammond, another national TGWU official, were to hold daily meetings with senior members of the Civil Contingencies Unit, including Clive Rose, who had come back from the Caribbean with Callaghan. Such close cooperation between a striking union and the British government was unprecedented – it was like a last-ditch version of the social contract – but in practice, predictably, the alliance was a flaky one. 'We would meet early every morning', Rose remembered, 'and pick up the places where the rules were not being observed. Then I would say to the union, "Call off your dogs." I found Hammond reliable, a first-class chap. I was never sure with Kitson how effective he would be – or try to be.'

Rose and Rodgers were stuck in London for most of the Winter of Discontent, partly because of the pressure of work and partly through political caution. 'I don't think I went outside London,' Rodgers recalled, as we talked in his drawing room in Highgate, with its art books and busts. 'It would've been provocative. What you saw of the pickets was on television, of course . . .' In Hull, I asked Fred Beach what he had thought of the 'Charter for Pickets'. He looked at me blankly. 'If headquarters did send one to us,' he said, 'nobody took any notice.'

Instead, the strike committee was lost in the struggle. They worked eighteen-hour days: eight and a half hours at the dispensation committee, and hours more spent planning, talking to the press and checking on the pickets. 'Sometimes . . . men came in from the cold', wrote Nicholas Roe in the *Sunday Telegraph* after watching the pickets come and go from Bevin House, 'like troopers from the Eastern Front with real snow on their boots, to say hello, warm up, or seek advice . . .' Some Hull residents had less empathy with the strikers. A local farmer dumped the carcasses of animals, which he said had starved to death because the lorry drivers were stopping his supply of feed, on the pavement in front of Bevin House. On 10 February, a more famous Hull citizen, Philip Larkin, wrote about the Winter of Discontent to his friend Kingsley Amis:

Yes, it's all very interesting, isn't it. Up to a century ago, if you wanted more money you just worked harder or longer or more cleverly; now you *stop work altogether*. This is much nicer, and anyone can do it. In fact, the lower-class bastards can no more stop going on strike now than a laboratory rat . . . can stop jumping on a switch to give itself an orgasm . . . It's a funny old world for an old man . . . 'I want to see them starving, the so-called working class, Their wages yearly halving, Their women stewing grass . . .' I sing my dreary little hymn quite a lot these days . . .

By then, the lorry drivers' dispute was finally over. From late January, one by one, the haulage firms agreed to give the truckers a pay rise of 22 per cent. The government reluctantly accepted the surrender. 'When cabinet was over,' wrote Rodgers afterwards, 'I sent my official car away and walked back from Number 10 . . . through St James's Park. I summoned my Private Secretary . . . and telephoned [my wife] Silvia. "I'm about to resign," I announced.'

But he didn't. 'The practical problems of dealing with [the aftermath of] the strike were too absorbing . . . It was very exciting . . . In the cabinet we got past the time where you had to be friendly. Once I threw some papers across the cabinet table to Callaghan and said, "That's what has to be done."'

In the second half of February, the strike wave began to subside. On Valentine's Day, a loosely worded 'concordat' on pay was announced between the TUC and the government. The gravediggers went back to work in mid-month, after a fortnight on strike, with a 14 per cent pay rise. The binmen went back later in February with 11 per cent. Ministers, worn down and thinking increasingly about ending the strikes relevant to their departments rather than about the government's position as a whole, let employers hand out whatever pay rises were necessary to end strikes; or, in the case of public-sector workers, acted as beaten employers themselves. Even so, other stoppages flared up or continued until the middle of March.

And all the while the prime minister seemed becalmed. 'In February, Bernard [Donoughue] and I went to Jim', said Tom McNally, 'with about eight initiatives . . . and he said, "No, we'll just go on." A bit of the fight had gone.' At Downing Street, Callaghan spent increasing amounts of time alone in his study. There he read official papers and, he told his close colleagues, 'fiddled around with this and that'. Speeches for him to make criticizing the unions' behaviour were written, but not given. He did not go on television to make great appeals to the nation. When he did appear, even after the Winter of Discontent was finally over, he seemed alternately exasperated and distracted. Asked about the recent strikes on the BBC's current-affairs programme *Nationwide* on 27 April, his answer wandered from a nostalgic digression about 'the old Department of Labour *Gazette*' and the supposedly benign unions of his youth, to a finger-pointing denunciation of the modern union attitude to pay – 'There's so much sloppy thinking about in this country!' – that was too fleeting to have much force.

The overconfident Callaghan of the Caribbean trip, of the postponed general election, of the 5 per cent pay guideline; the bold and competent Callaghan of the IMF crisis, of the break with Keynesianism, of the seemingly effortless Commons victories over

Margaret Thatcher – these versions of the prime minister had been replaced by a new one: the worn-out and disillusioned veteran. There was even a touch of the seventies Wilson about him. He was almost sixty-seven. It was half a century since he had first joined a trade union, and now the unions had probably destroyed his premiership. In his autobiography, with its fatalistic title *Time and Chance*, the section on the Winter of Discontent is strikingly brief and flat:

The only redeeming features that I could discern throughout the whole affair were the remarkable ingenuity with which those affected set about improvising arrangements to beat its adverse effects, and the stoicism with which the general public met the hardship . . . Ministers considered whether we should declare a state of emergency. My instinct was in favour . . . but it was argued that it was very uncertain whether a declaration would do much practical good. The Conservative Government of 1970–74 had declared five such states of emergency, and it was pointed out that none of them had made any significant difference. After a time signs began to appear that the fever was running its course . . .

Of the mood in the government in March 1979, he writes:

For three years we had believed in ourselves and in our capacity to govern and to win, despite all the odds against us. Now I sensed this was no longer true. Nearly thirty years earlier, as a Junior Minister in the Attlee Government, I had watched demoralisation set in and a thick pall of self-doubt begin to envelop Ministers as they and the increasingly paralysed Government Departments and Civil Service waited for the inevitable election . . .

Apart from Rodgers and a few other ministers who relished taking on the unions – and who were effectively thinking their way out of the Labour Party – the Winter of Discontent was as miserable an experience for the Cabinet as it was for Callaghan. In late January, Donoughue writes,

There was a deathly calm in No. 10, a sort of quiet despair. No papers were being circulated through Whitehall apart from the depressing minutes of . . . an ever longer list of pay negotiations . . . Moving among [ministers] as they gathered for Cabinet in the hallway . . . their sense of collective and individual depression was overwhelming. There was none of the usual buzz and banter . . . Many of them, especially Michael Foot, appeared genuinely puzzled. Denis Healey was very tired . . . puffy and florid . . . David Ennals was at times slightly emotional. It was felt that one or two Ministers, particularly Tony Benn . . . were playing at politics in advance of a future party leadership contest. Others were clearly inhibited by their membership of . . . the unions most damagingly involved in the current strikes.

The Winter of Discontent did not quite lead to national catastrophe. The food shortages caused by the lorry drivers' dispute remained local and brief. Other feared walkouts never happened. Clive Rose remembered: 'The two strikes that never materialized, that we were terrified of, that could have brought the country really to a halt, were the electrical power workers and the water workers. We had contingency plans but we knew they'd be fairly ineffective. Only palliatives.' Power stations and sewage plants were too complicated for soldiers to operate, and much of the British army was stationed in Germany and would take weeks to redeploy in a civilian role in Britain. Or at least this was what its high command told ministers. For all the talk of the army 'taking over' in Britain in the seventies, with all the shades of meaning that implied, when it came to the decade's climactic crisis, the army, already stretched by the Cold War and Ulster, was keen to stay in its barracks. Rose recalled: 'I was terrified of the PM saying, "I want the army to take over gravedigging." I called the chief of general staff early one morning to test the waters. His reaction was an expletive. I said, "Thank you. You've given me my brief."'

Some senior Labour figures felt that when the Winter of Discontent was at its iciest, the civil service, too, was not as cooperative as it might have been. On 18 January, Donoughue wrote in his diary, 'Whitehall has come to a total halt while they wait to see which way the cat will jump politically.' In 2008, when I interviewed him again, with another Labour government apparently entering its terminal phase, he recalled of the Callaghan administration's worst days: 'It was like being on a liner in mid-ocean when all the engines have stopped. Just drifting silently. The civil service just backs off. If they thought Gordon Brown was going to lose power imminently, that would happen again.'

Rose denied that the civil service's motives in early 1979 were so political and self-preserving. At the time, he remembered, 'Rodgers said to me, "Your job is to make sure the government's policies are carried out, to keep the government in office." I felt my role in these circumstances was slightly wider. I said, "My job is to save the country's bacon, to see the country isn't destabilized."' Rose also had a testy late-night meeting at the House of Commons with the home secretary Merlyn Rees and the abrasive junior minister Gerald Kaufman. 'At the end, Rees said to me, "Clive, we found your advice helpful, as usual. The usual soft-soaping stuff. Now what advice would you have given if I'd been a Conservative minister?" I said, "Exactly the same." It wasn't the answer he expected.'

Rose gave a small satisfied smile. He was long retired from Whitehall now, to a peach-coloured house in a Suffolk tourist town, but his desire to seem even-handed politically had not left him. 'I had great respect for Callaghan,' he assured me early on, as we talked in his spotless drawing room. 'There was relief in the civil service when Callaghan replaced Wilson.' But British prime ministers aged fast in the seventies. At the end of the interview, Rose delicately suggested that by 1979 it was perhaps time for the Callaghan administration to make way for something different. 'Callaghan wasn't exactly the best dresser,' Rose volunteered, immaculate on a scorching day in pressed caramel trousers, red socks and a pink shirt in a tiny check. 'His suit was usually a bit crumpled. He used to slump a bit in his chair.' Rose said he also remembered watching Shirley Williams arrive for Cabinet, usually out of breath, with things spilling out of her handbag. Then the faint look of contempt in his cool eyes turned to one of admiration. 'Margaret Thatcher,' he said, 'at her first Cabinet meeting, was wearing what looked like a brand-new Chanel suit. Amazing hairdo. It felt like a change.'

19

Last-ditch Days

In March 1979, Margaret Thatcher's adviser John Hosykns noticed that senior Conservatives were finally assuming they would win the general election. They were worrying instead about how they would govern. But when would the election actually happen? Before the Winter of Discontent, Callaghan's preference had been for April, and what he had been through over the winter had not increased his appetite for hanging on much longer, let alone until the last possible election date in November. 'I did not wish', he wrote later, 'to drag out the next few months, surviving only by wheeling and dealing.'

Yet to other members of his administration 'surviving by wheeling and dealing' was what the Callaghan government had always been about; in fact, it was the central task of politics – especially in difficult times. As long as there was a chance that the Conservatives, so divided and unpopular only months before, would self-destruct – and even if there was none – this Labour rearguard wanted to hold on to power for as long as it could, because that was what democratically elected governments did until the voters told them otherwise.

Walter Harrison was one of the diehards. The Labour deputy chief whip had been in the party since 1936. He was a terse Yorkshireman who had been coaxing and frightening MPs into line since the midsixties. By 1979, with the Lib–Lab pact over and Labour's Commons majority long gone, he was known as a worker of parliamentary miracles, 'a genius', in Callaghan's estimation, 'at conjuring majorities out of thin air'. By 2006, he was eighty-five, and sounded frail on the phone. But he gave me directions to his house outside Wakefield. 'I like to navigate by pubs,' he said, momentarily brightening. Then his voice hardened: 'What books have you read? Who have you seen?'

I went to meet him a week before I met Sir Clive Rose, on a day forecast to be the hottest ever in England. South of Wakefield the train stopped for a long time without explanation. Outside the windows the former Yorkshire coalfield was hummocky, yellow-green in the heat. 'KILL THATCHER' said some ghostly old graffiti on a bridge. Harrison's house was in the last street of a country suburb, with a corn field at the end of the garden and, beyond that, a ruined castle. When I knocked on his door, it was early afternoon but all the curtains were drawn. For a few minutes no one came. In the porch I could see two new-looking Labour placards propped against a wall. The sun hammered down. Then Harrison appeared and led me bonily to a dark sitting room, where trade union journals and House of Commons magazines were piled and a creaking fan turned slowly, back and forth.

We sat down and he leaned in very close. 'Are you ready with your pen?' he said. 'In 1974,' he began, 'I was offered [ministerial jobs in] employment, trade and industry, and local government, and I refused them all. Then I accepted the job of deputy chief whip. I knew with the majority we'd got that I would be required. There had been a fragmentation in the Labour Party . . . a deterioration . . . We had people in high positions who thought they were exempt from strong discipline . . . I had the attitude that irrespective of how high up the ladder MPs were, they were all equal in keeping the Labour government in power.'

Harrison came from a family of ten. His father died when he was young, and one of his brothers died of malnutrition in the thirties. 'The atrocities that were done in those days,' he said with a sudden intensity, 'they were everlasting memories. I considered it my duty to sustain a Labour government that I knew to be better for the people of this country.' His thin face relaxed a little. 'As deputy chief whip,' he said, 'I worked seven days a week. I rang MPs at home. I got to know their mothers, their sisters. I had contacts all over. The Welsh Nationalists – I was talking to them. I had a good relationship with the Scottish Nationalists. I had a dossier on every Tory MP. What their hobbies and interests were. I persuaded one Tory MP with an interest in the navy to witness a naval exercise off Norway when there was a crucial vote. And I tried to help people with their problems. If anybody was in domestic trouble, I became a welfare officer

. . . I knew the Commons staff, the Commons police. I knew all the cafes. I knew all the restaurants, the bars. I got round everywhere.' He gave a sly smile. 'It once came to me that two civil servants were talking, and one said to the other, "I saw Walter in the upstairs committee room." "Oh, that's funny," said the other, "I saw him on the library corridor at the same time. D'you think he's got one of those cardboard cut-outs?"'

Harrison helped allocate offices for Labour MPs, a potent form of patronage. He noted which ones liked freebies: flights on Concorde were a favourite, usually secured by claiming an 'interest in aerospace'. He insisted that he and his fellow whips maximize their Commons authority by refusing any freebies themselves. He divided Labour MPs into interest groups and sought to keep them separate and satisfied. 'I knew all the personalities,' he said, 'I knew all my men that I could rely on and trust.' And when there were crucial parliamentary votes, he kept them hidden in rooms around the Commons until the last possible moment, so that the Conservatives would underestimate the likely Labour attendance. 'I had old men staying in the House all night,' Harrison said. 'Sir Alfred Broughton, even though he was ill, he used to come down.' Broughton was a dying Yorkshire Labour MP with a constituency close to Harrison's. 'I had to turf a minister out of his office so Sir Alfred could stay there and Lady Broughton could look after him,' Harrison continued. 'I remember the night when we brought five sick men in.' He held up five skeletal fingers. 'Five! Three of them from hospital! I have records of a dying man and a fit man who had an equal Commons attendance record. A fit minister!' Harrison's chin was wet with spit. 'That's what grips me,' he said. 'That's what grips me.'

But, by the late seventies, he knew that one day all his fierceness and diplomacy would not be enough. A no-confidence motion would be put, and the Callaghan government would lose it. That moment came on 28 March 1979.

The government lost for many reasons. One was Broughton. 'I spoke to him at 1.20 p.m. on the day of the vote,' Harrison recalled. The vote was that evening. 'He said he was too unwell to travel from Yorkshire. I said, "OK." My father had emphysema. I could read what the problem was.' It was a Commons convention that when an MP was too ill to vote, an MP on the opposite side abstained. But when Harrison approached his Conservative counterpart Bernard Weatherill – 'a very good friend of mine' – the Tory deputy chief whip told him that the informal rule could not possibly apply in such a pivotal vote and that, besides, it would be impossible to find a Conservative MP prepared to abstain. Then Weatherill changed his mind. 'He offered not to vote,' said Harrison. 'But I didn't want him put on the rack.' A pause. The fan creaked. 'So I said no.'

Four days later, Broughton died. Yet a bigger part in the no-confidence defeat was played by other MPs from northern Britain: the Scottish Nationalists. Since their surge at the 1974 general elections, life had become more complicated for the SNP. The party now had eleven MPs, but they were inexperienced. And, as often with electoral breakthroughs by minor parties, a distracting number of possible paths had opened up for them. Should the SNP, as its leadership wished, remain a broadly left-wing party, partly out of conviction, but also to attract some of Labour's huge Scottish vote? Or should the SNP acknowledge the fact that most of its MPs represented former Tory seats, and move to the right? Between 1974 and 1979, the SNP tried to do both in the Commons, siding sometimes with the Conservatives and sometimes with the government. Attacked by Labour as 'Tartan Tories' and by the Conservatives as old-fashioned left-wingers, the SNP lost support. Meanwhile, the inflated expectations and more complex party organization generated by the successes of 1974 also pressed on the Nationalists. Should they back the Scottish parliament which their election victories had made a possibility, or should they still work for full independence?

During the Callaghan government, the idea of Scottish devolution, which both Labour and the Conservatives had flirted with since the late sixties, slowly acquired legislative flesh and bones. It was not a straightforward process. The Liberals were initially opposed. The Conservatives, swiftly reversing their position under Ted Heath, were hostile. The Labour Party was divided. The Commons contained plenty of determined supporters of the Anglo-Scottish union as it stood; plenty of left-wing MPs who saw devolution as a distraction from the class struggle; plenty of northern English MPs with industrial seats who feared a Scottish parliament would secure preferential treatment for its declining heavy industries; and plenty of Tories who simply wanted to trouble a vulnerable Labour government. The SNP, after an agonized internal debate – exacerbated by the fact that the party often rose in the polls when progress towards devolution seemed to have stalled – decided to back Labour's proposals for a Scottish parliament with modest powers, as a 'stepping stone' towards independence. Despite this temporary alliance, in 1977 the first devolution bill was defeated in the Commons. A second bill was passed the following year, but only after Labour rebels had amended it, so that the establishment of a Scottish parliament would require the support of 40 per cent of the total Scottish electorate at a referendum. Any abstentions, intentional or otherwise, would effectively count as votes against.

The referendum was set for 1 March 1979. In the weeks beforehand, campaigning took place in virtually the worst circumstances imaginable for securing a 'yes' vote. The Winter of Discontent and disillusionment with the Callaghan government had soured the Scottish electorate. The weather was atrocious, with snow on polling day. Senior Labour figures, taken up with the aftermath of the strikes and with ensuring the government's survival in the Commons, contributed little to the 'yes' campaign: Callaghan made a single brief visit to Glasgow. The sagging popularity of the SNP weakened the 'yes' campaign's impact further. The much-hyped Scottish football team had recently been humiliated in the World Cup, which had stirred up feelings of national inadequacy and self-loathing, which in Scotland were never that far below the surface. And all the while, the opponents of devolution campaigned with great intensity and stubbornness. Their cause was personified by Tam Dalyell, the Labour MP for West Lothian, Commons personality and professional contrarian, who relentlessly posed what had become known as the 'West Lothian Question': how could devolution be just if it left English and Scottish MPs with unequal Commons voting rights?

Given all this, the result on 1 March was respectable for support-ers of devolution – a 64 per cent turnout, of whom 52 per cent voted 'yes' to a Scottish parliament – but not nearly good enough: this added up to less than 33 per cent of the electorate, well short of the 40 per cent required. The elegant old Edinburgh school that had been earmarked for the parliament was left empty on its hillside, its closed-up facade in plain sight.

The SNP blamed the government's distracted contribution to the 'yes' campaign for the outcome of the referendum. The fact that a simultaneous vote on a parliament for Wales, conducted against a similar political backdrop, had produced a far worse result for devo-lution supporters there – less than 12 per cent of the Welsh electorate had voted 'yes' – cut no ice with the Scottish Nationalists. Nor did the fact that their Welsh counterparts Plaid Cymru, who had three MPs and had undergone their own pro-independence surge during the sixties and seventies, continued to support the Callaghan admin-istration. The SNP demanded that the government ignore the referendum's 40 per cent rule and establish a Scottish parliament, otherwise the party would put down a motion of no confidence in the government.

In the days immediately after the referendum, both sides made an effort to avoid this outcome. The SNP met with Michael Foot, now Callaghan's Commons fixer and a stronger advocate of devolution than the prime minister. After the meeting, Foot proposed an intri-cate parliamentary manoeuvre whereby the government would encourage the Commons to reject the Scottish referendum result and then delay the official abandonment of the devolution project until after an autumn general election, thus luring the SNP into supporting the government in the interim. But Callaghan rejected Foot's plan as too complicated and constitutionally questionable. Instead, the gov-ernment proposed that there should be 'a short interval for reflection', in Callaghan's words, 'for talks between the parties . . . to see if any accommodation could be reached on how to carry Devolution forward'.

Unsurprisingly, the SNP found this proposal far too airy. As threat-ened, they put down a motion of no confidence in the government, to be debated in late March. The Conservatives, seeing an opportunity, then let it be known that they were planning to put down their own no-confidence motion. As the main opposition party, theirs would be debated first. 'When assurances of SNP support . . . seemed to be forthcoming,' wrote Margaret Thatcher later, 'I agreed that it [our motion] should be tabled.' The SNP had joined forces with the one British party that was opposed to devolution altogether, 'the first time in recorded history', as Callaghan witheringly put it in the no-confidence debate that followed, 'that turkeys have been known to vote for an early Christmas'. Scotland, even more than the rest of Britain, would feel the consequences of the SNP's decision.

In his hot living room Walter Harrison got up and retrieved an old cassette player from where it had been resting on top of a coal scuttle next to Callaghan's autobiography. 'I'm going to put something on for you,' he said. The recording of the no-confidence debate of 28 March 1979 was crackly and raw, the cassette player, turned up full, distorted it even more, and the fan in the living room creaked distractingly back and forth. But the moods and rhythms of the six-and-a-half-hour debate were still easily decipherable. We sat in our sticky armchairs and listened to the main passages, as the drawn curtains kept out the sun and the rest of the world. Harrison was quite still, his hollow chin resting on a single fingertip, looking into the fireplace.

Margaret Thatcher opened the debate with a mediocre speech. Her sentences, usually biting and direct on less formal occasions, were stiff and long-winded, full of unnecessary historical digressions and economic jargon. She sounded as if she had been waiting too long for this moment: simultaneously stale and nervous. She was heard in near silence. Callaghan, responding, was much better: loud, alternately jokey and contemptuous, seemingly uninhibited. He mocked his would-be executioners: 'So, tonight, the Conservative Party which wants the [Scotland] Act repealed and opposes devolution, will march through the lobby with the SNP, which wants independence . . . and the Liberals, who want to keep the Act. What a massive display of unsullied principle!'

On the tape Labour MPs cheered frequently and strenuously. In his armchair Harrison smiled. But the bounce in Callaghan's rhetoric – he sounded relieved that the day of judgement had finally arrived for his government – could not completely disguise the weakness of his position. The SNP and the Liberals, he was being forced to acknowledge, were about to vote to bring down his administration. Meanwhile, the unions remained at least partly outside Labour's control: 'The government have reached a new agreement with the TUC [the recent and vague Valentine's Day concordat]. It is not perfect, and it may be breached on occasion . . .' In other areas, too, the government had little new to offer: 'We shall make most progress by adapting and broadening the policies that have served so far . . . and not by sudden switches or reversals . . .'

Yet it was partly the government's existing policies which had left it so vulnerable. Deep into the debate, long after Callaghan had finished speaking, one of his Commons allies stood up and announced that he had become utterly alienated by what Labour had done in office. Gerry Fitt was a Catholic MP from Belfast, a left-winger and moderate Irish nationalist who usually voted with the Labour government. He had even escorted Callaghan when, as home secretary ten years earlier, Callaghan had gone on a risky walkabout in the Bogside in Derry. But now Fitt had had enough. 'I believe', he said, 'that the policy on Northern Ireland adopted by the Labour government since 1974 has been disastrous . . . I made up my mind the Friday before last when I read the Bennett report on police brutality in Northern Ireland . . . I have a loyalty to this government . . . But . . . I cannot go into the lobby with them tonight.'

The disorder and fragmentation of British politics in the seventies, which had left so many governments with tiny or non-existent majorities, also meant that by 1979 Callaghan had to deal with forty-three MPs from small parties, an unprecedented number by post-war standards. In the days leading up to the no-confidence debate, and even during it, frantic, close to farcical negotiations went on between the government and the minor parties. The Ulster Unionists, who had ten Commons MPs and a sharp appreciation of how best to exploit their parliamentary leverage, had already won from the Callaghan administration an increase in the province's representation at Westminster, from twelve to seventeen. Now, in March 1979, they requested that, in return for their support in the no-confidence vote, the government agree to lay a gas pipeline between Northern Ireland and the British mainland. The pipeline was not an outlandish idea. The government had already independently thought of building one, and the plan was acted on a few years later. But Callaghan, perhaps now with an eye on his reputation after he left Downing Street, felt that agreeing to a pipeline at such a climactic Commons moment would seem too transparent a political bribe, and said no to the Unionists' suggestion. Two of their MPs, Harold McCusker and John Carson, indicated that they might still back the government anyway. Roy Hattersley, the prices and consumer-protection minister, was given the task of securing their votes. On the morning before the no-confidence debate, which was due to start at 3.30 p.m., he had a meeting with the two Unionists.

They wanted a special Retail Price Index which monitored the higher cost of living in Northern Ireland . . . They asked for Price Commission enquiries into the cost of those commodities which made life particularly expensive in the six counties . . . We agreed the policy in about ten minutes. Working out the joint communiqué was far more difficult. By lunch I had begun to suspect that they wanted the negotiations to drag on into the afternoon. The Chief Whip was sure they were looking for an excuse to renege. He told me not to let them out of my sight. Mercifully they wanted to lunch alone. The two men presented themselves in my House of Commons room at just after three . . . and asked for a drink. They drank whisky all afternoon as they stared at, argued with and changed the draft text. At six we ran out. [The Labour whip] Anne Taylor went across the corridor to obtain fresh supplies from [the trade secretary] John Smith – who always had plentiful stocks . . . At eight they agreed to sign . . . McCusker wrote his Christian name and then, discovering he was using green biro, tore up the entire document. We stuck it together with sellotape . . .

At 10 p.m., the Commons voted on the confidence motion. Gerry Fitt abstained, but McCusker and Carson supported the government. So did the three Plaid Cymru MPs and the two MPs of the breakaway Scottish Labour Party, who had left Labour in 1976 over its slowness to introduce devolution. Added to the 303 MPs Labour could muster, in Sir Alfred Broughton's absence, this made a total of 310. In the crush of the Commons that evening – Callaghan 'had never seen the Chamber as crowded', and the ailing Broughton would have struggled – many Labour and Conservative MPs thought that the pro-government vote would be just enough. A strike by Commons catering staff had led some Tory MPs to go off to their gentlemen's clubs for dinner and, deliciously for supporters of militant trade unionism, a few had not got back in time for the vote. Those who did 'returned to the Chamber looking rather crestfallen', remembered the Tory MP Kenneth Baker in his memoirs, 'while the Labour benches looked very cheerful'. No British government had lost a vote of confidence since the first, flimsy Labour administration in 1924. As the votes were counted, Callaghan recalled,

The wait seemed never-ending. At last one of the Government Whips, Jimmy Hamilton, a Scot from Bothwell, emerged from the Lobby which had counted the Members who had voted for the Government. He struggled through the almost impassable crowd . . . and as he went to the clerk's table he gave me an almost imperceptible thumbs-up. For one moment I wondered whether, as in *The Perils of Pauline*, we had escaped once more, a prospect I would have greeted with mixed feelings . . .

But Hamilton and many of the other Labour and Conservative MPs who had been doing the parliamentary arithmetic in their heads had not included in their counts the two Tories who had been acting as tellers for Margaret Thatcher. The number of MPs in favour of the no-confidence motion – 279 Conservatives, thirteen Liberals, eleven Scottish Nationalists and eight Ulster Unionists – was actually 311. The government had been defeated by one.

'The terrible anticlimax when we realized,' said Harrison quietly, still looking into the fireplace. On the tape, immediately after the result was announced, there was a brief chasm of silence, followed by a landslide of shouts and cheers from the Conservatives. Then, half-lost in the noise, the slightly dirge-like sound of 'The Red Flag' being sung spontaneously by Labour MPs, led by a promising young left-winger, Neil Kinnock. That night, Harrison recalled, Michael Foot, another of Callaghan's doomed successors as party leader, held a wake to mark the defeat. 'Very good party,' Harrison said with feeling.

'I slept well that night,' wrote Callaghan, who did not go to the wake, 'for the uncertainty was over.' The next day, 29 March, he announced that the general election which the government's no-confidence defeat necessitated would be on 3 May. This meant an unusually long campaign. Over its five weeks, the government hoped, the Winter of Discontent would recede day by day. Already the opinion polls were showing the Tory lead over Labour shrinking, from around 20 per cent during the winter's most chaotic phase to around 10 per cent in late March. It was also hoped that the extended campaign would expose the Conservatives' weaknesses, and those of Margaret Thatcher in particular. 'We thought Thatcher was the weak link,' Gavyn Davies told me. 'Shrill, totally out of touch with mainstream thinking. In a presidential contest, people would've voted for Jim.'

The election was not a presidential contest, but Labour tried to make it one. Like Wilson in 1970, Callaghan was the smiling, strolling centre of their campaign, dropping in on shopping centres and housing estates, clasping hands and holding casual conversations, his gaze friendly but knowing, and making low-key speeches about the perils of change. He wore sharper-than-usual dark suits and took care with his haircuts. He made no gaffes. After the gloom and paralysis of the winter, he had recovered his poise. On 12 April, the polling firm Gallup published its answer to the question, 'Who would make the better Prime Minister?' Callaghan led Thatcher by 39 per cent to 33 per cent. By the end of the campaign, his lead on this question had more than trebled: 44 per cent to 25 per cent.

Apart from persistent hecklers who wanted the British troops out of Northern Ireland, Callaghan was treated respectfully by the public. No trade unionists with placards pursued him. Nobody threw ink or stubbed out a cigarette on him, as had happened to Heath in the early seventies. The 1979 campaign, wrote the veteran general-election observers David Butler and Dennis Kavanagh, was 'exceptionally orderly'. Part of this was due to increased levels of security. Two days after the no-confidence vote, Thatcher's mentor Airey Neave had been blown up by a car bomb as he drove up the ramp from the House of Commons car park, with the Irish National Liberation Army, an IRA splinter group, thought to be responsible. But the Labour campaign also had a deliberately sedative quality. The manifesto, cosily titled 'The Labour Way Is the Better Way', was Callaghan's last triumph over the left of his party. It ignored policy proposals from Tony Benn and other senior Labour figures for getting rid of Britain's nuclear weapons, for more state intervention in the economy and for the abolition of the House of Lords, all of which were receiving growing support in the party as a whole. The word 'socialist' barely featured. Instead, the document offered a mild, modernized, rather optimistic version of social democracy:

We will take great care to protect working people from the hardships of change . . . We must keep a curb on inflation . . . [We] will continue to reduce the burden of income tax, and raise the tax threshold below which people pay no income tax . . . We shall continue to help those who wish to buy their own homes . . . We will seek to implement the UN target of 0.7% of the Gross National Product for official [overseas] aid as soon as economic circumstances permit . . .

The manifesto concluded: 'We reject the concept that there is a choice to be made between a prosperous and efficient Britain and a caring and compassionate society.' With this argument, and in its bright, almost apolitical underlying tone, the manifesto prefigured what would be offered a decade and a half later, to a more receptive country, by New Labour.

Callaghan's manifesto also prophesied with some accuracy what would happen to Britain if he was defeated: 'A Tory government . . . would mean soaring prices and growing unemployment . . . At work . . . confrontation . . . free market forces . . . misery for millions of the most vulnerable . . . a drastic reduction in all our social services.' During the campaign, the prime minister carefully avoided making personal attacks on Margaret Thatcher, but his whole demeanour and almost all of what he said was intended to contrast Labour's inclusiveness with her divisiveness, Labour's caution with her recklessness, Labour's pragmatism with her dogma. This approach could be questioned. Labour, in truth, contained plenty of divisive, reckless and dogmatic figures. One of them, Tony Benn, argued during the campaign that, in the polarized Britain of the late seventies, Labour should match the Conservatives' new abrasiveness under Thatcher with their own.

Yet as April went by, Callaghan's strategy seemed to be at least partly working. The Tory poll lead eroded: in the first week of the month, one survey had the Tory lead down to single figures; in the second week, two did; in the third week, three. In the fourth week, a MORI poll put the Conservatives only 3 per cent ahead. NOP actually gave Labour a 0.7 per cent lead. 'During the campaign, I felt, "It's going well,"' Tom McNally told me. On 29 April, Bernard Donoughue sent Callaghan a memo titled 'Strategy: Last Three Days'. 'The genuineness of Labour's appeal was getting through,' he wrote. 'But we must not let up. Harold made that mistake in 1970 . . . We need one last big heave to get home.' In the *Guardian* on 2 May, the respected political commentator Peter Jenkins wrote, 'It would no longer be amazing to see Mr Callaghan win by a whisker.'

In the Conservative Party during these weeks there was an intermittent but widely felt anxiety: that the politics of 1977 and 1978 – of the Tories still seeming a little green and divided, of Callaghan catching enough of the national mood and mounting an unlikely political escape – might be returning despite all the recent Labour calamities. In part this nervousness was an occupational hazard for opposition parties entering elections with opinion-poll leads after a long period out of office. In part it was the unreliability of British opinion polls in the seventies. Yet even Margaret Thatcher found the 1979 campaign at times worrying and frustrating:

I . . . believed that we should be bold in explaining precisely what had gone wrong [in Britain] and why radical action was required to put it right. I was soon to be aware, however, that this was not how [the Conservative Party chairman] Peter Thorneycroft and Central Office in general saw things.

Their belief was that we should at all costs avoid 'gaffes', which meant in practice almost anything controversial – in particular, attacks on trade union power . . .

In fact, Thatcher was partly complicit in her own muzzling. Unlike Callaghan, she only addressed public meetings to which friendly audiences, usually Conservative Party members, had been given tickets. She declined to take part in a televised debate with him and the Liberal leader David Steel, worrying that 'I might make a mistake.' Since the early sixties, it had been the norm in Britain that opposition leaders actively sought such confrontations. Instead, she presented herself to the cameras in more controlled circumstances. On a farm in Norfolk, she held a newborn calf in the air for thirteen minutes, smiling determinedly and keeping its dangling legs away from her suit. In Milton Keynes, which she and Callaghan both visited, she had her heartbeat and blood pressure tested for the photographers. 'They can't find anything wrong with me,' she said as the reading came up, adopting a public style – a little self-mocking but, more importantly, domineering and utterly confident – that would become crushingly familiar to Britons over the next dozen years. 'They never can.'

She did as few serious interviews as she could get away with. The one proper television interrogation she agreed to, for Thames Television's *TV Eye* on 24 April, was not an overwhelming success. The show's regular interviewer Llew Gardner had questioned her roughly three years earlier, and she only agreed to appear this time on the condition that he was not used. But his replacement, Denis Tuohy, felt obliged to stand up to her and probed her hard about taxes and trade unions. 'This was the most hostile interview of the campaign,' she wrote afterwards, 'but it allowed me to give a vigorous defence of our proposals.' Her biographer John Campbell's evaluation of the encounter is less positive: the would-be prime minister, he writes, came across as 'angry' and 'evasive'. Margaret Thatcher, like her brand of Conservatism, with its contradictory mixture of free-market radicalism and market-town moralism, was not impregnable when properly challenged. But, from 1979, increasingly few British journalists and politicians would manage to do so.

The Tuohy interview, nonetheless, was not quite a gaffe, and after-wards she reverted calmly to her usual electioneering style: energetic, slightly shameless, a production line for easily digested political sym-bols. In Halifax, she held up two mesh bags of groceries for the cameras, one with a piece of paper tied to it reading 'February 1974' – the date Labour had come to power – and one reading 'Today'. The 1974 bag was twice as full as the 1979 one. The message was as unsubtle and potent as a graphic in a tabloid: under Labour, inflation had stripped voters' kitchen cupboards. Callaghan was scornful of such photo opportunities. 'It's not my style,' he said. 'If I do [it], I'll sound as phoney as she does.' Given the way his personal advantage over her in the polls grew during the campaign, a lot of voters evi-dently preferred his more muted, less cartoonish public manner. However, just because people did not particularly warm to Margaret Thatcher did not mean that they ignored her arguments about what was wrong with the country. Over the campaign, MORI found that the Conservative poll leads over Labour on inflation, taxation and law and order all widened.

Moreover, Thatcher could not really be dismissed as 'phoney'. In 1979, as throughout her career, she was minutely styled, either by herself or by others, and eerily photogenic. In public, she was always in character. But then that *was* her actual character – minus her occa-sional moments of self-doubt and her famously sparse outside interests. The would-be prime minister was conscientious, abrasive, sure of herself, slightly priggish, controlling, occasionally flirtatious, a break with the past, a woman – all this was there in plain sight. And Thatcher was happy to draw attention to how different she was from most other seventies politicians. When journalists and voters, as they often did, asked her whether a woman could cope with being prime minister, she compared herself to Elizabeth I, or said that only a woman could balance Britain's books, or give the country a good spring-cleaning. It was not exactly a feminist answer. In the May 1979 edition of *Spare Rib*, published before the election, an editorial headlined 'Is Margaret Thatcher for Women?' pointed out that the Conservative leader had a poor Commons record when it came to voting for bills that benefited women; that the union she had been most critical of during the Winter of Discontent, NUPE, had a 65 per cent female membership; and that if she was elected she was likely to cut the welfare state on which women especially depended. 'We at *Spare Rib* have no illusions about Labour,' the magazine concluded. '[But] we want to keep the Tories out.' And yet, in its next issue, published in June, *Spare Rib* had to concede that during the election the Conservative leader had skilfully used feminist themes in her rhetoric. Beside her Callaghan had looked 'paternalistic'.

Set against her challenging political persona the Conservative manifesto also seemed less than radical. Short, untitled and published almost a week after Labour's, it seemed, like the other policy documents the Conservatives had put out since she became leader, more an exercise in smoothing over the party's splits and not alarming the voters than in providing a fresh right-wing formula for government. The Conservatives promised to cut taxes, public spending and inflation, but the lack of precise figures and policies in the manifesto – Denis Healey said with some justification that finding the latter was 'like looking for a black cat in a dark coal cellar' – made the leaner, more responsible government the Tories envisaged quite hard to differentiate from the one Callaghan was already leading, and which he had been leading ever since the IMF called time on Labour's mid-seventies extravagances in 1976.

There were only glimmers of the new political thinking that would dominate the eighties: a promise to sell off shares in the nationalized shipyards; to increase police pay sharply; to encourage private transport companies; and to help council tenants to buy their homes. There were a few ominous words for strikers and trade unionists: 'We shall . . . make any . . . changes that are necessary so that a citizen's right to work and to go about his or her lawful business free from intimidation or obstruction is guaranteed.' And, almost buried among all the generalities, there was this brief sentence: 'We may be able to do more in the next five years than we indicate here.'

Would hints about change and Margaret Thatcher's singular political qualities be enough? There were doubts among senior Conservatives. On 25 April, barely a week before polling day, these doubts reached a peak. That night, after an arduous day's campaigning, Thatcher had a late dinner in her hotel at Glasgow airport with her husband Denis, daughter Carol and the party's deputy chairwoman Janet Young. Thatcher was tired but reasonably content: 'Although the opinion polls suggested that Labour might be closing on us, the gap was still a healthy one and my instincts were that we were winning the argument.' There were jokes and gossip around the table. Then Young got up to take a phone call. She 'returned with a serious expression', Thatcher wrote,

to tell me that Peter Thorneycroft . . . felt that things were not too good politically and that Ted Heath would appear on the next Party Election Broadcast. I exploded. It was as about as clear a demonstration of lack of confidence in me as could be imagined. If Peter Thorneycroft and Central Office had not yet understood that what we were fighting for was a reversal not just of the Wilson–Callaghan approach but of the Heath Government's approach then they had understood nothing. I told Janet Young that if she and Peter thought that then I might as well pack up . . .

Thatcher got her way – although the Heathites and their descendants would get her in the end. Heath did not appear in the broadcast. The politics of the British seventies did not come full circle. Instead, in the last week of the campaign, the opinion polls turned back in favour of the Conservatives. There were no more surveys forecasting a Labour victory. The final predictions were that the Tory vote would exceed Labour's by between 5 and 8 per cent, enough, even given the unpredictable British electoral system, for a proper majority. The British, it appeared, still liked Callaghan; but they did not like him enough to remain loyal to the politics he represented.

On the evening of 1 May, Thatcher spoke at her final campaign rally, in Bolton, which had two especially marginal seats, last won by the Conservatives when they last won a general election, in 1970. Her speech concluded:

There's a world-wide revolt against big government, excessive taxation . . . An era is drawing to a close . . . At first . . . people said, 'Oh, you've moved away from the centre.' But then opinion began to move too, as the heresies of one period became, as they always do, the orthodoxies of the next . . . It's said that there is one thing stronger than armies, and that is an idea whose time has come . . .

The next day, Bernard Donoughue waited for the end in 10 Downing Street:

On the eve of the poll the weather was as awful as it had been for most of our final four months . . . with widespread snow, hail and rain to remind the electorate of the horrors of the Winter of Discontent. I concluded that God was, if only for the time being, a Tory. With the Prime Minister in Cardiff [his constituency], Number 10 was totally quiet. Private Office had already prepared the thick briefing files for the incoming Tory Government. I felt completely drained as I overheard [the principal private secretary] Ken Stowe discussing with . . . Caroline Stevens, Mrs Thatcher's Diary Secretary, how to arrange her positive vetting to get security clearance to work in Number 10.

Conclusion: The Long Seventies

Shortly before midnight on 3 May, the BBC's election-night pro-gramme *Decision '79* announced the result of an exit poll in one of its 'barometer seats', Derby North. There had been a swing of 0.7 per cent from the Conservatives to Labour. 'If this is right,' said one of the presenters, with only a little drama in his voice, 'Callaghan is back. With a tiny majority.' But, a few minutes afterwards, another presen-ter broke in with more news on the Derby North poll. 'It's been adjusted,' he said calmly. 'It's a 2 per cent swing to the Conservatives.'

Moments later, Margaret Thatcher came gliding out of the front gar-den at Flood Street wearing an ocean-blue suit and a great predatory grin. 'Do you know, Mrs Thatcher, that the polls are in your favour?' a reporter asked from somewhere in the pavement crush and the dark-ness, as loud cheers and boos jostled for prominence. The Conservative leader, conscious that no actual results were in yet, said that she was 'cautiously optimistic'. But her face said otherwise. By the following afternoon, her party had 339 seats and a majority of forty-three.

In some ways it was a tremendous victory. Margaret Thatcher was the first woman to be elected the leader of a Western democracy. The national swing from Labour to the Tories was the largest between the major British parties since Clement Attlee's watershed victory in 1945. In seats won, it was the best Conservative performance in a general election for twenty years. The party had done particularly well with women voters – a 12 per cent lead over Labour compared to 1 per cent at the last election; with young voters – a 1 per cent lead among eight-een- to twenty-four-year-olds compared to an 18 per cent deficit in October 1974; and, above all, with skilled workers or C2s, whose votes were divided equally in 1979, eradicating Labour's 1974 advan-tage of 23 per cent in this crucial electoral category. Geographically, the Tories did best in the south of England and the Midlands, in new towns and, wrote Butler and Kavanagh, in 'East London and its sur-rounding areas, particularly previously strong National Front areas'. Racists, feminists, teenagers, trade unionists, Milton Keynes residents – all had voted in large numbers for the fierce woman from Grantham.

And yet an emphatic majority of Britons had not. The Conservative share of the vote was only 43.9 per cent, the lowest to elect a British prime minister since the war, apart from Wilson's two paper-thin man-dates in 1974 – hardly the most encouraging of precedents. Nor did the turnout suggest a country that suddenly felt a change of government would solve its problems: at 76 per cent it was below average for a post-war general election. And, most awkwardly of all for those who argued in 1979, and have argued ever since, that Thatcher's arrival in Downing Street marked a moment of profound disillusionment with what had gone before, the number of Labour voters did not collapse on 3 May. It increased, going up by 75,000 compared to October 1974.

As much as movements of votes can ever be conclusively traced, the Conservatives had won instead by taking support from the Liberals (down over 2 million), the Scottish and Welsh Nationalists (down 370,000), and the National Front (down by more than half in the seats they fought). In fact, among the segment of the population you might expect to have become most alienated by Labour in the seventies, the middle class and the rich, support for Labour at the 1979 general election was up by more than a quarter. Not until Tony Blair's election in 1997 would the party appeal as successfully again to Britain's ABC1s. The tax cuts, social conservatism and growing interest in consumerism of the Callaghan government marked the beginning of something in British left-of-centre politics, however long it would take the defeated Labour Party to recognize it.

In other ways, too, May 1979 was less of a boundary between two political worlds than is commonly accepted. General elections, like the beginnings and ends of decades, are rarely as decisive as they seem.

Like almost all post-war British prime ministers, Margaret Thatcher entered Downing Street with a bold vision for national revival. She gave her co-visionaries central roles in it: Geoffrey Howe as chancellor, Keith Joseph as industry secretary, John Hoskyns as head of the Downing Street Policy Unit. Early on in her government, she found the time to contact and thank even the wilder figures who had helped her to power. In late May, John Gouriet, the architect of Operation Pony Express at Grunwick, received this letter:

Dear John,
Thank you very much for your kind letter. I am grateful to you . . . for being such a great help during our years in Opposition. I very much hope that you will be able to give your support to our cause over the next few years. It would be greatly appreciated if you would.
Every good wish,
Margaret

Quickly, too, she sought to signal to the unions that times had changed. Bob Jones, NUPE's national negotiator in the seventies, had dealt with Heath – 'He was all right,' he told me – and Callaghan – 'He said to us, "Help me."' Now he encountered the new prime minister. 'I met Thatcher five times, and we were never offered tea.' There was still indignation in his usually level voice. 'Once I complained,' he continued, the indignation turning to disbelief, 'and she just turned her head away.'

But this sense in 1979 of an omnipotent new government lasted no longer than it had for previous post-war administrations. Instead, between the autumn of that year and the spring of 1982, and arguably well into the mid-eighties, Britain endured a period of economic, social and political crisis that matched, and often eclipsed, anything in the seventies – indeed, anything in peacetime in the modern era. This crisis included a recession deeper and longer than Britain had known since the thirties; a rise in unemployment that reached a peak three times higher than any under Callaghan, Wilson or Heath; another surge in inflation and another oil crisis; another surge in IRA violence; another sterling crisis; race-related riots in thirty British towns and cities; a collapse in the average Briton's disposable income so prolonged that by 1983 it still had not recovered to its level when Labour left office; an open rebellion against Margaret Thatcher's policies involving almost half her Cabinet; repeated threats of resignation by Thatcher; and a collapse in her government's popularity so steep that, in a Gallup poll in October 1981, she received the lowest support ever recorded for a British prime minister.

That January there was an episode, forgotten now, which seemed to epitomize the young Thatcher administration's haplessness. The National Coal Board, with the government's approval, announced plans to shut down an unspecified number of mines which it considered uneconomic. The NUM, under its president Joe Gormley and its president-to-be, Arthur Scargill, responded menacingly. 'I was appalled to find that we had inadvertently entered into a battle which we could not win,' wrote Thatcher in her memoirs. 'There had been no forward thinking in the Department of Energy about what would happen in the case of a strike . . . The objective had now become to avoid an all-out national strike at the minimum cost in concessions.' The Coal Board withdrew its closure programme, and the government, in Thatcher's words, 'undertook to reduce imports of coal . . . improve the redundancy terms for coal miners . . . agree to an [increased annual industry subsidy] of well over £1 billion . . . and draw a ring fence around the coal industry by arguing that coal was a special case'.

The 1981 miners' dispute, with its sense of official panic and unpreparedness, with its policy U-turn by the government, with its apparent demonstration that decisive political power in Britain still lay with the unions, and with its vain efforts by leading Conservatives to dignify defeat, made the Thatcher administration look uncannily like that of Edward Heath. On 22 February, a whole edition of Weekend World was devoted to the NUM's third victory in a row over a Tory prime minister. With the unconcealed excitement of a political journalist who had recently seen a lot of short-lived governments, the programme's usually shrewd host Brian Walden, eyes glittering, asked the question on many commentators' lips: 'Is this the beginning of the end of the Thatcher experiment?'

In the early eighties, Thatcher tried to dismiss her difficulties with defiant speeches. 'You turn if you want to,' she famously told the Conservative conference in 1980, 'the lady's not for turning.' But it was hard to argue with great confidence that the British seventies, in a political or economic sense, were over. As late as June 1985, a Punch cover cartoon could feature two pinstriped businessmen looking out of the window of a City of London skyscraper at a formation of flying pigs. 'It's the economic recovery!' one businessman was saying to the other. 'It's the economic recovery!'

Of course, we all know better now than to write off Margaret Thatcher's first years in government. We know that by 1985 she was already well into the run of luck and ruthless decision-making which would carry her through the Falklands War, through Michael Foot's frail Labour leadership, through Scargill's ill-timed summer strike and through the craze for the SDP, and which would change Britain during the eighties, year by year, law by law, Tory election victory by Tory election victory. By the end of this ascendancy the country would seem to have less in common with its seventies self, in its political assumptions, in its social structure, in its economic life, in its industrial relations, in its financial and physical landscape, in its sense of a national trajectory – who in 1989 still talked about British decline in the same way that they had in 1979? – than any comparable nation.

This erasure of the seventies continued after Thatcher's fall in 1990. By the late nineties, let alone by the first years of the twenty-first century, after eighteen years of Conservative government, after the creation of New Labour, after the endless tranquilizing boom of the Blair era, the British seventies were a foreign country. They fascinated us, they contained lessons for us, they influenced us. But we didn't live there.

When I started researching this book in 2003, the seventies often felt much more than three decades away. Trade unions had been wound up or amalgamated. Whole industries had been restructured or no longer existed. Leading figures kept turning up in the obituaries. Drawing parallels between the British present and the British seventies seemed a slightly esoteric interest, a game mainly for historians, like making comparisons between the present day and the fifties, say, or the twenties.

Yet between 2005 and 2008 this began to change. Largely unnoticed at first, another oil crisis began to develop. Inflation and unemployment began to rise. The Labour government began to struggle. The Conservatives began to revive. A recession began to bite. Sterling and the FTSE index began to slide. Trade unionists concerned about their living standards began, regardless of the government's difficulties, to go on strike. Certain forgotten seventies phrases – 'stagflation', 'oil shock', 'government pay policy', 'government bail-out' – began to be taken out of their display cases. Collapsing banks were even nationalized. The will of the 1976 Labour conference, as an old left-wing delegate might have put it, had finally been recognized.

Other seventies notions made unexpected returns. In March 2008, the *Sunday Times* gave over two pages to explaining why the solution to the problems at Heathrow was an airport on an artificial island in the Thames Estuary. On *Newsnight* ten days later, Irwin Stelzer, Rupert Murdoch's chief political adviser, previously known for his profound faith in free markets and his fierce dislike of state meddling in them, suddenly announced that the answer to the international economic downturn was 'fiscal stimulus' – a right-winger's euphemism for governments coming to the rescue of capitalism. He almost sounded like a member of one of Ted Heath's or Harold Wilson's economic committees. Stelzer ended his contribution by quoting Richard Nixon, in his phase as a sceptic about the free market while US president in the early seventies: 'We are all Keynesians now.'

During 2009 western rulers of all ideological stripes, from the liberal Barack Obama in America to the conservative Nicholas Sarkozy in France, faced with an economic crisis threatening to dwarf anything in the seventies, responded with stimulus packages and other state interventions of a distinctly pre-Thatcherite type. In Britain, for a time, even the rightwing and financial press were startlingly ready to condemn the excesses of unshackled capitalism – the economic orthodoxy in the West, and far beyond, since Thatcher's election in 1979. It seemed possible that the era of Margaret and the Austrians was finally coming to an end. By the autumn, with a recovering City of London promising vast bankers' bonuses again, and all the British political parties seemingly unable or unwilling to curtail them, and focused instead on emergency cuts in public spending, this great swing back to the left seemed less inevitable. But either way, a very seventies unease has seeped back into how we see the world.

Economic crises, floods, food shortages, terrorism, the destruction of the environment: these spectres, so looming in the seventies, did not go away during the eighties and nineties; yet they faded – they were quite easy to forget about. Now they have returned - there is even newspaper talk of another visit from the IMF - it is possible to wonder how many of Britain's seventies problems were ever really solved.

These days Britons no longer mourn their empire. They are more comfortably European. They are more relaxed about race, sexuality and gender. Their government is no longer fighting a war in Ulster. The British population is rising rather than falling. The feel of national life is more feverish than entropic. The look of things is gaudy and skin-deep, rather than heavy, worn-out and grey.

And yet Britain is still a polluted, often tatty country with a dependence on Middle Eastern oil. It still veers between boom and recession. It still has an unstable currency. It still has an economy with relatively low productivity. It still has a comparatively class-bound society. Its south is still richer than its north. It still invests for the long term only reluctantly. It still lacks modern infrastructure. It still panics about national security when a bomb goes off. It still harbours the National Front's successor, the British National Party. It is still arguing about Scottish devolution. It is still arguing about the European Union. It is still not quite sure of its place in the world.

But if these remain Britain's underlying problems, some of the solutions the seventies offered are gone. David Cameron, Old Etonian, calm rather than confrontational in his manner and not a politician, you suspect, for argumentative lunches at right-wing think tanks, is not a new Margaret Thatcher – however often he echoes her simplistic but potent seventies arguments about the need for good economic housekeeping. There is little sign, so far, of an intellectual revolution behind his rise. There seems little of her intensity or singularity behind his charm and poise.

The modern Labour Party, meanwhile, despite its return under Gordon Brown to a politics which is recognisably left-of-centre, does not contain a messianic dissident like Tony Benn, or even a mouthy pragmatist like Denis Healey. The Liberal Democrats, their shadow chancellor Vince Cable apart, are rather timid, over-disciplined, and close to the Tories in many of their ideas. Nowadays, if you talk to promising new MPs, it can sometimes be quite hard to tell which party is which.

And outside Parliament, for now at least, British politics is a shrunken thing compared to the seventies. In Hull in 2006, after I had finished talking to Fred Beach about the Winter of Discontent, I walked into the city centre to get some dinner. It was a mild dry summer evening but the streets were almost empty. The city centre was nothing but lads outside bars. Beyond it, by the new marina, I found a promising-looking restaurant, but it was shut. Instead, I watched the sky dim over the Humber for a few minutes. The lights of the North Sea oil facilities that Beach had helped blockade in 1979 quivered faintly in the distance.

I walked back towards my hotel. Halfway there, I found a Chinese restaurant with a buffet, but it was all too congealed. Instead, I followed an unlit road that passed along the oldest part of the waterfront. There were derelict Georgian facades, and I could hear the slap of water out in the shadows. Then I turned a corner and saw a huge floodlit sign: 'Napoleon's Customer Car Park'. For a moment, I thought it meant somewhere I might want to eat, but then I saw the premises Napoleon's occupied. 'Casino & Restaurant' it said above the door, beside a stretch of mirrored glass and flashing red and white lights. And framing the doorway in the darkness there was an ungainly two-storey building which I had only seen in photographs. It was Bevin House, the old TGWU headquarters. Here Beach and his comrades had run their strike. Here the T&G dispensation committee had mounted a kind of revolution. Here the power of the British Left had reached a kind of peak.

But that was over a quarter of a century ago. In 2006, the TGWU's existence as an independent organization was drawing to a close. It would soon merge with another shrinking union and take on a new, anodyne, unthreatening-sounding name: Unite. And Bevin House had already been renamed, I noticed. In keeping with the casino's Napoleonic theme, it was called Elba House. It was a name that conjured up exile, powerlessness, and eventual defeat.

*

A few weeks earlier that summer, I had seen Callaghan's former intimate and son-in-law Peter Jay at his house outside Oxford. After the interview, he offered to drive me to the station. At the last minute, as we were sitting in the car in the driveway and Jay was starting the engine, another passenger got in. He was in his gangly late teens, had short spiky hair like the bass player of the Clash in the late seventies, and, like quite a lot of teenagers in 2006, was carrying a guitar case with his bags. Jay introduced us: the teenager was Tommy, one of his children from his second marriage (he and Callaghan's daughter Margaret had divorced in the eighties). Tommy was getting the train to London, too, so that he could catch a flight to Ibiza. As Jay drove, he explained that he and I had been doing an interview about the seventies, 'when politics was interesting'. We all laughed knowingly.

Jay dropped us at the station and drove off. The station was small and deserted, and the train was late. As we stood on the platform, it seemed crass to probe Tommy about his father's famous connections with Callaghan, so I asked him instead about his plans for the summer. He said he wanted to go travelling before he started studying architecture. The sun went in and out. Then he asked me what I thought about David Cameron. I said I thought that Cameron was getting quite an easy ride from the press.

'He's good news for the Right,' Jay's son broke in. 'I'm on the left,' he went on. 'But my girlfriend is from the other end of the political spectrum. Her father says Thatcher did lots of good things for this country. I'd never heard that before. In my family there was never a good word about her.' He looked at me intently. 'If someone said, "Thatcher saved Britain," what would you say to them?'

I started talking about unemployment in the eighties, about the economy's erratic growth under her administration, about how lucky she had been with the Falklands War, with Labour's split and the formation of the SDP. 'She had a lot more political luck than your dad's first father-in-law,' I said. The train came before I could say any more.

After we got on, Jay's son went and sat on his own with his guitar case. He seemed quite content to end the history lesson.

Acknowledgements

First, I would like to thank everyone who agreed to be interviewed. I hope I have represented each of their versions of the seventies fairly. I would like to thank the people who helped make three of the most important interviews possible: Peter Walker, Dan Hillman and Rebecca Stone. I would like to thank the staff of the Science 2 reading room at the British Library, and Kathleen Dixon at the British Film Institute. I would like to thank the friends who listened to me going on about the seventies and gave me ideas: Adam Curtis, Andrew Bagley, Stuart Kerr, Conrad Leach, Charlotte Higgins, Alex Butterworth, Paul Laity, James Meek, Sarah Walsh and John Dugdale. For specific pieces of assistance, I would like to thank Larry Elliott, John Blundell, Jonathan Glancey, William Keegan, Michael White, Rebecca Carter, Mariam Yamin, Robin Christian and Mark Bygraves; and for tolerating my absences from the *Guardian* and giving me seventies-related commissions, Ian Katz, Katharine Viner, Charlie English, Claire Armitstead and Merope Mills. At Faber, I am grateful to Walter Donohue, Neil Belton, Anna Pallai, Stephen Page, Hannah Griffiths, Sarah Savitt and Rachel Alexander for their constant enthusiasm and occasional reality checks. I am grateful to my agent David Godwin for his calm and expert support. Jon Riley helped the book into being when it was only a vague idea; Ian Bahrami expertly improved the manuscript. I would also like to thank Sinead and Tim Marsh and Tina Muller for enabling me to write on Thursday afternoons, and Jean and Richard Holloway and Elizabeth Beckett and Robert Milnes for helping so much at other times. And, most importantly, I would like to thank Sara for being this book's ideal reader, reviewer and editor; and Lorna and Gillen for distracting me so deliciously during the half-decade it has taken me to understand a whole one.

Chronology

1970
February: First National Women's Liberation Conference held in Oxford
June: Edward Heath wins general election with majority of thirty
July: First issue of *The Ecologist* published in London
October: Gay Liberation Front founded in London

1971
January: First British soldier killed in Ulster for half a century
November: National Union of Mineworkers begins overtime ban

1972
January: Miners begin national strike. British soldiers kill fourteen
   unarmed people during Bloody Sunday in Derry
February: Thousands of miners and other pickets, led by Arthur Scargill,
   force closure of Saltley coke depot in Birmingham, despite the efforts of
   hundreds of police. Miners' strike ends in total union victory
March: British government takes direct political control of Ulster
July: Abortive secret talks between British government and IRA leadership.
   First issue of *Spare Rib* published in London

1973
January: Britain admitted to EEC. Foundation of the PEOPLE Party, later
   the Green Party
October: Egypt invades Israeli-occupied Sinai Peninsula, sparking the oil
   crisis
November: Miners begin another overtime ban

1974
January: Three-day week to ration electricity consumption imposed by
   Heath government
February: Miners begin national strike. Heath calls early general election.
   Loses
March: Harold Wilson becomes prime minister without a majority. Ends
   three-day week

October: Wilson calls general election to win a majority. Wins majority of three. Scottish National Party (SNP) wins 30 per cent of Scottish vote
November: IRA kills twenty-one civilians in Birmingham pub bombings

1975

February: Margaret Thatcher defeats Heath in Conservative Party leadership contest
June: Referendum on whether Britain should remain in EEC. Pro-Europeans win by 67 per cent to 33 per cent
August: Watchfield free festival jointly staged by hippy anarchists and Wilson government. British inflation rate peaks at 26.9 per cent
November: Wilson and the Queen attend official opening of first British North Sea oil pipeline

1976

March: Wilson resigns as prime minister
April: Jim Callaghan wins Labour leadership contest and replaces Wilson as prime minister
August: Strike begins at Grunwick photo processing plant in London over employees' wish to be represented by a union
September: Sterling plunges against the dollar on the currency markets. Chancellor Denis Healey, on his way to a meeting of the International Monetary Fund (IMF), turns back from Heathrow. Callaghan tells Labour Party conference: 'The cosy world is gone.' Healey tells Labour conference Britain will ask the IMF for the biggest loan it has ever granted
November: IMF negotiators arrive in London demanding huge cuts in public spending in return for loan. Callaghan and Healey argue for smaller cuts. Majority of Callaghan's Cabinet want no cuts at all
November–December: Callaghan and Healey persuade Cabinet and IMF to accept more moderate cuts in public spending. Britain obtains IMF loan

1977

March: Callaghan negotiates Lib–Lab pact to shore up government's position in the Commons
June: First mass picket at Grunwick. Battles between pickets and police
June–July: Boycott of Grunwick mail by postal workers brings strikers to verge of victory
July: The National Association for Freedom, a radical right-wing group close to Thatcher, secretly collects and distributes the Grunwick mail. Possibility of strike victory recedes

1978

January: Inflation drops below 10 per cent for the first time since the oil crisis

March: Jack Jones, Callaghan's most powerful union ally, retires

April: Rock Against Racism campaign holds mass rally and festival in London

July: Lib–Lab pact ends. Grunwick strikers concede defeat

August: Conservatives and Saatchi and Saatchi launch 'Labour Isn't Working' poster campaign

Autumn: Labour overtakes Conservatives in opinion polls

September: Callaghan decides against calling widely expected autumn general election

November: Jack Jones's union goes on strike for higher pay. Other unions do the same. The Winter of Discontent begins

1979

January: Callaghan travels to the Caribbean for international summit and holiday. Probed by reporters on his return. The *Sun* summarizes his response: 'Crisis? What Crisis?'

January–February: Peak of the country-wide strike wave. Exceptionally cold weather

March: Winter of Discontent ends. Government's devolution proposals for Scotland and Wales rejected in referendums. SNP stops supporting Labour in the Commons. Government loses vote of confidence in the Commons. Callaghan calls May general election

April: General-election campaign. Large Conservative opinion-poll lead steadily narrows

May: Thatcher wins general election with majority of forty-three. Liberal vote collapses. Labour vote increases slightly

Sources

This is a selection of the sources I have found most useful. Those with a broad relevance to my book I have listed beside the first chapter to which they contribute. The abbreviation PRO is for the Public Record Office; HMSO for Her Majesty's Stationery Office.

INTRODUCTION: OUR WEIMAR?
Blair, Tony, Labour Party Conference speech, 27 September 2005
Cameron, David, 'Modern Conservatism', Demos, 30 January 2006
McIntosh, Ronald, *Challenge to Democracy: Politics, Trade Union Power and Economic Failure in the 1970s*, Politico's, 2006
New Economics Foundation, *Chasing Progress Beyond Measuring Economic Growth*, 2004
New Musical Express, 23 December 1978
Time Out, 24 January 1970

1 CHAMPAGNE AND RUST
Benn, Tony, *Office Without Power: Diaries 1968–72*, Arrow, 1989
Brittan, Samuel, *Steering the Economy: The Role of the Treasury*, Secker & Warburg, 1969
Butler, David, *The British General Election of 1970*, Macmillan, 1971
Campbell, John, *Edward Heath: A Biography*, Cape, 1993
Cobden, R., *England, Ireland, and America by a Manchester Manufacturer*, Ridgway & Sons, 1835
Coleman, Terry, *Movers & Shakers: Conversations with Uncommon Men*, Deutsch, 1987
Critchley, R. A., *The British Household in the Seventies*, International Publishing Corporation, 1975
Economist, The, 13 June 1970
Heath, Edward, *The Course of My Life: My Autobiography*, Hodder & Stoughton, 1998
Hurd, Douglas, *An End to Promises: Sketch of a Government, 1970–1974*, Collins, 1979
Koestler, Arthur, *Suicide of a Nation?*, Hutchinson, 1963

Middlemas, Keith, *Politics in Industrial Society: The Experience of the British System since 1911*, Deutsch, 1979

Middlemas, Keith, *Power, Competition, and the State, Vol. 1, Britain in Search of Balance 1940–61*, Hoover Press, 1986

Pimlott, Ben, *Harold Wilson*, HarperCollins, 1992

Prior, James, *A Balance of Power*, Hamilton, 1986

Shanks, Michael, *The Stagnant Society: A Warning*, Penguin, 1961

Stewart, Michael, *The Jekyll and Hyde Years: Politics and Economic Policy since 1964*, Dent, 1977

Thatcher, Margaret, *The Path to Power*, HarperCollins, 1995

2 THE GREAT WHITE GHOST

Alan Clark's History of the Tory Party, 'From Estate Owners to Estate Agents' (Part 3), BBC2, 28 September 1997

Heath, Edward, author interview, 27 July 2004

Heath, Edward, *Travels: People and Places in My Life*, Sidgwick & Jackson, 1977

Macmillan, Harold, *The Middle Way: A Study of the Problem of Economic and Social Progress in a Free and Democratic Society*, Macmillan, 1938

Sampson, Anthony, *The New Anatomy of Britain*, Hodder & Stoughton, 1971

Sewill, Brendon, author interview, 8 December 2004

Walker, Peter, author interview, 1 June 2004

Walker, Peter, *Staying Power: An Autobiography*, Bloomsbury, 1991

York, Peter, author interview, 7 February 2006

3 HEATHOGRAD

Arnold, P., 'The Maplin Sands', Essex County Archive (Southend), February 1970

Ball, Stuart, and Anthony Seldon (eds), *The Heath Government 1970–1974: A Reappraisal*, Longman, 1996

BBC News, BBC1, 13 November 1969

Bromhead, Peter, *The Great White Elephant of Maplin Sands: The Neglect of Comprehensive Transport Planning in Government Decision-Making*, Elek, 1973

Buchanan, Colin, 'Note of Dissent by Colin Buchanan in the Report of the Commission on the Third London Airport', HMSO, 1971

Cashinella, Brian, and Keith Thompson, *Permission to Land: The Battle for London's Third Airport and How the Whitehall Planners were Beaten to their Stripe-Trousered Knees*, Arlington Books, 1971

Crick, Michael, *Michael Heseltine: A Biography*, Penguin, 1997

Defenders of Essex Association, Accounts and Newsletters, Essex County Archive (Southend), 1969–1990

Department of the Environment, 'Maplin Population Projections', PRO CM 33/14, 1973

Department of the Environment, 'Maplin: Preliminary Design of Sea Wall', PRO CM 33/13, 1973

Department of the Environment, 'The Maplin Project: Designation Area for the New Town', PRO AT 25/175 1973

Department of the Environment, 'Public Consultation on Motorway and High Speed Rail Link Routes', HMSO, 1973

Department of Trade, 'Maplin: Review of Airport Project', HMSO, 1974

Dobson, John S., *'Fowlness': The Mystery Isle, 1914–1939*, Baron, 1996

Fenton, James, 'The Last Chance for Foulness', *New Statesman*, 2 February 1973

Hansard (Commons), 4 March 1971, 9 August 1972, 8 February 1973, 13 June 1973, 23 October 1973, 16 January 1974; (Lords) 22 February 1971

Heseltine, Michael, *Life in the Jungle: My Autobiography*, Hodder & Stoughton, 2000

Hunt, Donald, *The Tunnel: The Story of the Channel Tunnel 1802–1994*, Images, 1994

'Maplin Development Act', HMSO, 1973

'Maplin Development Authority (Dissolution) Act', HMSO, 1976

Maplin Development Authority, 'Maplin Trial Bank Report', PRO CM 33/40, 1974

'Maplin Development: Plan and Section and Plan of Location of Runways', HMSO, 1972

Maplin Movement, Accounts, Essex County Archive (Southend), 1973

McKie, David, *A Sadly Mismanaged Affair: A Political History of the Third London Airport*, Croom Helm, 1973

Roskill, Eustace Wentworth, 'Report of the Commission on the Third London Airport', HMSO, 1971

Tebbit, Norman, *Upwardly Mobile*, Weidenfeld & Nicolson, 1988

Thames Estuary Development Corporation, 'Maplin (Foulness): The British Air Gateway of the Future for Western Europe, with Deep-Water Docks, Oil and Industrial Facilities', Essex County Archive (Southend), 1971

Town Committee on Maplin, Minutes of Meeting of 27 March 1973, Essex County Archive (Southend)

Walker, Peter, *The Ascent of Britain*, Sidgwick & Jackson, 1977

Walters, Alan, *Maplin: The End?*, Bow Publications, 1974

Wentworth-Day, James, 'The Headland of Birds', *Sunday Times* magazine, 17 December 1972

4 CLOSE THE GATES!

A Force to Reckon With, Yorkshire Television, February 1983

Allen, V. L., *The Militancy of British Miners*, Moor, 1981

Ashworth, William, *The History of the British Coal Industry. Vol. 5, 1946–1982: The Nationalized Industry*, Clarendon, 1986

Barratt, J., 'Coal Stocks Memorandum', PRO, 7 January 1972

Barratt, J., 'Situation Report at the End of Week Five', PRO, 11 February 1972

BBC News, BBC1, 8 February 1972, 10 February 1972

Beckett, Francis, *Enemy Within: The Rise and Fall of the British Communist Party*, John Murray, 1995

Bellingham, Richard, author interview, 24 August 2004

Birmingham *Evening Mail*, 10 January 1972–11 February 1972

Birmingham *Post*, 8–11 February 1972

Birmingham *Sunday Mercury*, 9 January–13 February 1972

Blue Peter, BBC1, 21 February 1972

Cabinet Minutes, 6 January 1972, PRO CAB 130/533

Cabinet Minutes, 10 February 1972, PRO CAB 128/50/7

Carrington, Peter, *Reflect on Things Past: The Memoirs of Lord Carrington*, Collins, 1988

Clutterbuck, Richard, *Britain in Agony: The Growth of Political Violence*, Faber, 1978

Crick, Michael, *Scargill and the Miners*, Penguin, 1985

Department of Employment and Productivity, 'In Place of Strife: A Policy for Industrial Relations', HMSO, 1969

Ffoulkes, F. L., 'The "Saltley" Incident: A Report', British Gas, 1985

Geary, Roger, *Policing Industrial Disputes: 1893 to 1985*, Cambridge University Press, 1985

Gormley, Joe, *Battered Cherub: The Autobiography of Joe Gormley*, Hamilton, 1982

Hansard (Commons), 18 January 1972, 3 February 1972, 11 February 1972, 14 February 1972

Harper, Roger, author interview, 27 September 2004

Howe, Geoffrey, *A Giant's Strength*, Inns of Court Society, 1958

Industrial Relations Act, HMSO, 1971

Jeffery, Keith, and Peter Hennessy, *States of Emergency: British Governments and Strikebreaking since 1919*, Routledge, 1983

Ledger, Frank, and Howard Sallis, *Crisis Management in the Power Industry*, Routledge, 1995

Maudling, Reginald, *Memoirs*, Sidgwick & Jackson, 1978

McLaren, Charlie, author interview, 1 September 2005

Memorandum on 'Police Views', PRO FV 38/119, 16 February 1972

Milligan, Stephen, *The New Barons: Union Power in the 1970s*, Temple Smith, 1976

Miner, The, October/November 1971, December 1971/January 1972

Miners' Last Stand, The, Thames Television, 20 January 1972

Morning Star, 10 February 1982

Robens, Alfred, *Ten Year Stint*, Cassell, 1972

Routledge, Paul, *Scargill: The Unauthorized Biography*, HarperCollins, 1993

Samuel, Raphael, 'The Lost World of British Communism', *New Left Review*, September/October 1987

Scargill, Arthur, author interview, 17 September 2006

Scargill, Arthur, and Robin Blackburn, 'The New Unionism', *New Left Review*, August 1975

Taylor, Robert, *The Fifth Estate: Britain's Unions in the Seventies*, Routledge, 1978

Times, The, 10–21 February 1972

True Spies: Subversive My Arse, BBC1, 27 October 2002

Watters, Frank, *Being Frank: The Memoirs of Frank Watters*, Monkspring, 1992

Webb, Richard, author interview, 27 September 2004

Who Likes Arthur Scargill?, Yorkshire Television, 21 November 1974

Wilberforce, Richard, 'Report on the Miners' Wage Claim', PRO COAL 26/1110, 18 February 1972

Yorkshire Matters, Yorkshire Television, 10 June 1970

5 QUESTIONS OF SOVEREIGNTY

Adams, Gerry, *Before the Dawn: An Autobiography*, Heinemann, 1996

Army in Ulster – Men in the Middle, The, Thames Television, 18 September 1969

Asher, Michael, *Shoot to Kill: A Soldier's Journey through Violence*, Viking, 1990

Bardon, Jonathan, *A History of Ulster*, Blackstaff Press, 2001

Bardon, Jonathan, *A Shorter Illustrated History of Ulster*, Blackstaff Press,

1996

Barzilay, David, *The British Army in Ulster Vol. 1*, Century, 1973

Bew, Paul, and Henry Patterson, *The British State and the Ulster Crisis: From Wilson to Thatcher*, Verso, 1985

Brenton, Howard, *The Paradise Run*, Thames Television, 6 April 1976

Callaghan, James, *A House Divided: The Dilemma of Northern Ireland*, Collins, CRE, 1973

Catterall, Peter, and Sean McDougall (eds), *The Northern Ireland Question in British Politics*, Macmillan, 1996

Commission for Racial Equality, 'Discrimination and the Irish Community in Britain', 1997

Coogan, Tim Pat, *The IRA*, HarperCollins, 2000

Curtis, Liz, *Ireland: The Propaganda War: The British Media and the 'Battle for Hearts and Minds'*, Sasta, 1998

Curtis, Liz, *Nothing but the Same Old Story: The Roots of Anti-Irish Racism*, Information on Ireland, 1984

Daily Mirror, 1 January 1973

Dewar, Michael, *Brush Fire Wars: Minor Campaigns of the British Army since 1945*, Hale, 1984

Eighteen Months to Balcombe Street, LWT, 19 February 1977

Dillon, Martin, *The Enemy Within*, Doubleday, 1994

Dudley-Edwards, Ruth, *The Faithful Tribe: An Intimate Portrait of the Loyal Institutions*, HarperCollins, 1999

Elliott, Phillip, 'Misreporting Ulster: News as a Field Dressing', *New Society*, 25 November 1976

Evelegh, Robin, *Peacekeeping in a Democratic Society: The Lessons of Northern Ireland*, C. Hurst, 1978

Fisk, Robert, *The Point of No Return: The Strike which Broke the British in Ulster*, Deutsch, 1975

Forging the Union, BBC Radio 4, 7 August 2006

Gallagher, Tom, *Glasgow: The Uneasy Peace: Religious Tension in Modern Scotland*, Manchester University Press, 1987

Garnett, Mark, and Ian Aitken, *Splendid! Splendid! The Authorized Biography of Willie Whitelaw*, Jonathan Cape, 2002

Guardian, 4 January 1973

Hoggart, Simon, 'The Army PR Men of Northern Ireland', *New Society*, 11 October 1973

Holland, Jack, *Hope Against History: The Course of Conflict on Northern Ireland*, Coronet, 1999

Kitson, Frank, *Low Intensity Operations: Subversion, Insurgency, Peace-*

keeping, Faber, 1971

Labour Party, 'Now Britain's Strong, Let's Make It Great to Live in: The Labour Party's Manifesto for the 1970 General Election', Labour Party, 1970

Mac Stíofáin, Seán, *Memoirs of a Revolutionary*, Gordon Cremonesi, 1975

McGarry, John, and Brendan O'Leary, *Explaining Northern Ireland: Broken Images*, Blackwell, 1995

Mason, Roy, *Paying the Price*, Robert Hale, 1999

Money Programme, BBC2, 11 February 1977

Neuman, Peter R., *Britain's Long War: British Strategy in the Northern Ireland Conflict 1969–98*, Palgrave, 2003

Newsinger, John, *British Counterinsurgency: From Palestine to Northern Ireland*, Palgrave, 2002

O'Neill, Terence, *The Autobiography of Terence O'Neill*, Hart-Davis, 1972

Panorama, BBC1, 8 November 1971

Parker, Tony, *May the Lord in His Mercy Be Kind to Belfast*, Jonathan Cape, 1993

Pettitt, Lance, *Screening Ireland: Film and Television Representation*, Manchester University Press, 2000

Phillips, Paul T., *The Sectarian Spirit: Sectarianism, Society and Politics in Victorian Cotton Towns*, University of Toronto Press, 1982

Rees, Merlyn, *Northern Ireland: A Personal Perspective*, Methuen, 1985

Renwick, Alistair (ed.), *British Soldiers Speak Out on Ireland*, Information on Ireland, 1978

Rich, Paul B., and Richard Stubbs, *The Counter-Insurgent State: Guerilla Warfare and State Building in the Twentieth Century*, Macmillan, 1997

Rose, Richard, Ian McAllister and Peter Mair, *Is There a Concurring Majority about Northern Ireland?*, University of Strathclyde, 1978

Seymour, Gerald, *Harry's Game*, Collins, 1975

Short, K. R. M., *The Dynamite War: Irish-American Bombers in Victorian Britain*, Gill and Macmillan, 1979

Taylor, Peter, *Beating the Terrorists? Interrogation in Omagh, Gough and Castlereagh*, Penguin, 1980

Taylor, Peter, *Brits: The War against the IRA*, Bloomsbury, 2001

Times, The, 1 January 1973, 3 January 1973

Troops Out Movement, 'Alternative White Paper on Ireland', Literature Committee of the Movement, 1974

Troops Out Movement, 'Tom-Tom', Bulletin of the Troops Out Movement, 1975

Troops Out Movement, 'Troops Out', Paper of the United Troops Out Movement, October 1977, November 1977, December/January 1978

Waller, P. J., *Democracy and Sectarianism: A Political and Social History of Liverpool 1868–1939*, Liverpool University Press, 1981

Weekend World, LWT, 17 November 1974

Whitelaw, William, *The Whitelaw Memoirs*, Aurum, 1989

Wilson, Harold, *The Labour Government 1964–1970: A Personal Record*, Weidenfeld & Nicolson, 1971

Winchester, Simon, *In Holy Terror: Reporting the Ulster Troubles*, Faber, 1974

Young, Hugo, *This Blessed Plot: Britain and Europe from Churchill to Blair*, Macmillan, 1998

6 LIGHTS OUT

Atkinson, Kate, *Emotionally Weird*, Doubleday, 2000

BBC News, BBC1, 13 December 1973, 14 December 1973, 11 January 1974, 12 January 1974, 15 January 1974, 14 February 1974, 20 February 1974

Beloff, Michael, *The Plateglass Universities*, Farleigh Dickinson, 1970

Bober, Gillian, author interview, 10 January 2005

Bober, Graham, author interview, 10 January 2005

Burton, Graham, 'Red Essex', *Park Life*, 13 February 2001

Cabinet Minutes, 16 October 1973, 1 November 1973, 13 November 1973, 22 November 1973, 29 November 1973, 4 December 1973, 12 December 1973, 13 December 1973, 20 December 1973, 3 January 1974, 17 January 1974, 24 January 1974, 31 January 1974, 7 February 1974, 1 March 1974, PRO CAB 128/53

Colchester *Evening Gazette*, 3 October 1973–8 March 1974

Constable, David, author interview, 10 December 2004

Daily Express, 3–5 January 1974

Daily Mail, 5–28 January 1974

Daily Mirror, 8–21 January 1974

Department of Energy, 'Memorandum from Secretary of State', PRO CAB 129/174, 6 February 1974

Department of the Environment, 'Effect of Power Restrictions on Marsham Street', PRO AT 55/57, 10 December 1973–28 February 1974

Department of the Environment, 'The Electricity (Advertising, Display, etc.) (Restriction) Order 1973', PRO AT 55/57, 14 November 1973

Department of the Environment, 'The Electricity (Industrial and Commercial Use) (Control) Order 1973', PRO AT 55/57, 13 December

1973

Department of the Environment, 'The Electricity (Lighting) (Control) Order 1973', PRO AT 55/57, 10 December 1973

Department of the Environment, 'The Fuel and Electricity (Heating) (Control) Order 1973', PRO AT 55/57, 8 December 1973

Department of the Environment, 'Licence for Avoiding Three Day Restrictions', PRO AT 55/57, 13 December 1973

Department of Trade and Industry, 'Companies in Financial Difficulties & Contingency Planning', PRO FV 79/135, 31 December 1973–1 March 1974

Department of Trade and Industry, 'Effects of Three Day Working', PRO FV 86/02, 8 March 1974

Department of Trade and Industry, 'Policy on Selective Financial Assistance in Relation to the Three Day Week', PRO FV 79/134, 5 February 1974

Dow, Christopher, *Major Recessions: Britain and the World 1920–1995*, Oxford University Press, 1998

Drabble, Margaret, *The Ice Age*, Knopf, 1977

Durgan, Shirley, *Colchester 1835–1992*, Ian Henry, 1994

Essex *County Standard*, 1 October 1973–8 March 1974

Fay, Stephen, and Hugo Young, *The Fall of Heath*, Sunday Times Books, 1976

Fifty Years of BBC TV News, BBC2, 6 July 2004

Frayn, Michael, *A Landing on the Sun*, Viking, 1991

Guardian, 14 December 1973, 1 January 2005

Hansard (Commons), 9 January 1974, 10 January 1974, 25 March 1974

Harris, Ralph, author interview, 9 August 2006

Heath, Edward, Prime Ministerial Broadcast, 13 December 1973

Inbucon-AIC Management Consultants, *The Three-Day Week*, HMSO, 1976

Ingham, Bernard, *Kill the Messenger*, HarperCollins, 1991

Jenkin, Patrick, author interview, 12 January 2005

Kynaston, David, *The City of London Vol. 4: A Club No More 1945–2000*, Chatto & Windus, 2000

London *Evening Standard*, 2–16 January 1974

Middlemas, Keith, *Power, Competition, and the State, Vol. 2: Threats to the Postwar Settlement, Britain 1961–74*, Macmillan, 1990

Midweek, BBC1, 6 February 1974

Neale, Kenneth (ed.), *Essex: 'Full of Profitable Thinges'*, Leopard's Head Press, 1996

New Society, 3 January–28 February 1974, 18 July 1974

Odell, Peter R., *Oil and World Power: Background to the Oil Crisis*, Penguin, 1974

Panorama, BBC1, 8 October 1973, 28 January 1974, 4 March 1974

Potter, Dennis, TV Column, *New Statesman*, 18 January 1974

Rothschild, Victor, *Meditations of a Broomstick*, Collins, 1977

Rothschild, Victor, *Random Variables*, Collins, 1984

Sloman, Albert, *A University in the Making*, BBC Books, 1964

Sun, 3–31 January 1974

Thorpe, Jeremy, *In My Own Time: Reminiscences of a Liberal Leader*, Politico's, 1999

Venn, Fiona, *The Oil Crisis*, Longman, 2002

Weekend World, LWT, 2 December 1973, 6 January 1974, 13 January 1974

Wilson, Harold, Shadow Ministerial Broadcast – Power Crisis, 14 December 1973

7 WAITING FOR THE COLLAPSE

Amis, Kingsley (ed.), *Harold's Years: Impressions from the New Statesman and the Spectator*, Quartet, 1977

Amis, Martin, *Dead Babies*, Jonathan Cape, 1975

Andrew, Christopher, *The Defence of the Realm: The Authorised History of MI5*, Allen Lane 2009

Ballard, J. G., *Concrete Island*, Jonathan Cape, 1974

Ballard, J. G, *High-Rise*, Jonathan Cape, 1975

Benn, Tony, *Against the Tide: Diaries 1973–1976*, Hutchinson, 1989

Bradbury, Malcolm (ed.), *The Novel Today*, Fontana, 1977

Brenton, Howard, *The Churchill Play: As It Will Be Performed in the Winter of 1984 by the Internees of Churchill Camp Somewhere in England*, Eyre Methuen, 1974

Brittan, Samuel, *The Economic Consequences of Democracy*, Temple Smith, 1977

Brittan, Samuel, *Is There an Economic Consensus? An Attitude Survey*, Macmillan, 1973

Castle, Barbara, *The Castle Diaries 1974–1976*, Weidenfeld & Nicolson, 1980

Cole, John, *As It Seemed to Me: Political Memoirs*, Weidenfeld & Nicolson, 1995

Crosland, Anthony, *Socialism Now, and Other Essays*, Jonathan Cape, 1974

Crosland, Susan, *Tony Crosland*, Jonathan Cape, 1982

Dell, Edmund, *A Hard Pounding: Politics and Economic Crisis*

1974–1976, Oxford University Press, 1991

Donoughue, Bernard, author interview, 2 March 2005

Donoughue, Bernard, *Downing Street Diary: With Harold Wilson in No. 10*, Jonathan Cape, 2005

Donoughue, Bernard, *The Heat of the Kitchen: An Autobiography*, Politico's, 2003

Donoughue, Bernard, *Prime Minister: The Conduct of Policy Under Harold Wilson and James Callaghan*, Jonathan Cape, 1987

Edgar, David, *Destiny*, Eyre Methuen, 1976

Fall and Rise of Reginald Perrin, The (Series 1), BBC1, 1976

Fawlty Towers, BBC2, 1975

Forester, Tom, 'Do the British Sincerely Want to Be Rich?', *New Society*, 28 April 1977

Fowles, John, *Daniel Martin*, Jonathan Cape, 1977

Gilbert & George, Gilbert & George Major Exhibition, Tate Modern, 2007

Griffiths, Trevor, *Bill Brand*, Thames Television, 1976

Haines, Joe, *The Politics of Power*, Jonathan Cape, 1977

Harpers & Queen, January 1978

Healey, Denis, author interview, 29 March 2005

Hennessy, Peter, *Whitehall*, Secker & Warburg, 1989

Hutber, Patrick, *The Decline and Fall of the Middle Class – And How It Can Fight Back*, Associated Business Programmes, 1976

Jubilee, Megalovision, 1977

Lessing, Doris, *The Summer Before the Dark*, Jonathan Cape, 1973

McEwan, Ian, *The Cement Garden*, Jonathan Cape, 1978

Middlemas, Keith, *Power, Competition, and the State, Vol. 3, The End of the Postwar Era: Britain since 1974*, Macmillan, 1991

Money Programme, 16 July 1976

Nairn, Tom, *The Break-Up of Britain: Crisis and Neo-Nationalism*, New Left Books, 1977

New Musical Express, 4 October 1975

O Lucky Man!, Memorial Enterprises, 1973

Office for National Statistics, 'Distribution of Real Household Disposable Income 1971–2001', ONS, 2002

Panorama, BBC1, 4 March 1974

Pearce, Edward, *Denis Healey: A Life in our Times*, Little, Brown, 2002

Penrose, Barrie, and Roger Courtiour, *The Pencourt File*, Secker & Warburg, 1978

Pliatzky, Leo, *Getting and Spending: Public Expenditure, Employment and*

Inflation, Blackwell, 1982

Poliakoff, Stephen, *Strawberry Fields*, Eyre Methuen, 1977

Radice, Giles, *Friends and Rivals*, Little, Brown, 2002

Radio On, Plexifilm, 1979

Savage, Jon, *England's Dreaming: Anarchy, Sex Pistols, Punk Rock, and Beyond*, Faber, 1992

Seldon, Anthony, and Kevin Hickson (eds), *New Labour, Old Labour: The Wilson and Callaghan Governments, 1974–79*, Routledge, 2004

Spark, Muriel, *The Takeover*, Macmillan, 1976

Stone, Richard, author interview, 27 October 2008

Theroux, Paul, *The Family Arsenal*, Hamilton, 1976

Walker, John A., *Left Shift: Radical Art in 1970s Britain*, I. B. Tauris, 2002

Williams, Shirley, author interview, 15 March 2005

Wilson, Harold, *Final Term: The Labour Government 1974–1976*, Weidenfeld & Nicolson, 1979

Wright, Peter, *Spycatcher*, Viking, 1987

8 THE GREAT BLACK HOPE

Aberdeen Press and Journal, 3 November 1975, 4 November 1975

Alvarez, A., *Offshore: A North Sea Journey*, Hodder & Stoughton, 1986

Architectural Review, August 1974

BBC website, On This Day: 3 November 1975, news.bbc.co.uk/onthisday/hi/dates/stories/november/3/newsid

Cooper, Bryan, and T. F. Gaskell, *North Sea Oil: The Great Gamble*, Heinemann, 1966

Corti, Gerry, and Frank Frazer, *The Nation's Oil: A Story of Control*, Graham & Trotman, 1983

Daily Mail, 4 November 1975

Dalyell, Tam, author interview, 5 July 2002

Document, BBC Radio 4, 30 January 2006

Goodlad, Morgan, author interview, 10 July 2002

Harvie, Christopher, *Fool's Gold: The Story of North Sea Oil*, Hamilton, 1994

Harvie, Christopher, *The Road to Home Rule: Images of Scotland's Cause*, Polygon, 2000

Harvie, Christopher, *Scotland and Nationalism: Scottish Society and Politics from 1707 to the Present*, Routledge, 2004

Hawksworth, John, *Dude, Where's My Oil Money?*, PriceWaterhouse-Coopers, 2008

Kemp, Alex, author interview, 5 November 2004

Lynch, Peter, *SNP: The History of the Scottish National Party*, Welsh Academic Press, 2002

McGrandle, Leith, *The Story of North Sea Oil*, Wayland, 1975

Marshall, Elizabeth, *Shetland's Oil Era*, Shetland Islands Council, 1977

Marshall, Elizabeth, *Shetland's Oil Era: Phase Two*, Shetland Islands Council, 1978

Ramsey, Chris, author interview, 4 November 2004

Reed, Laurance, *The Political Consequences of North Sea Oil Discoveries*, Heriot-Watt University, 1973

Shetland Islands Council, *Shetland in Statistics*, Shetland Islands Council, 2001

Tartan Army, The, www.electricscotland.com/history/tartan_army12.htm

Theroux, Paul, *The Kingdom by the Sea: A Journey Around Great Britain*, Hamish Hamilton, 1983

Times, The, 4 November 1975

Wasted Windfall, A, Fine Art Productions, 1994

9 THE REAL SIXTIES

Blasius, Mark, and Shane Phelan, *We Are Everywhere: A Historical Sourcebook of Gay and Lesbian Politics*, Routledge, 1997

Boycott, Rosie, *A Nice Girl Like Me: A Story of the Seventies*, Chatto & Windus, 1984

Come Together, issues 5, 7–10, 12–13, 15–16, 1971–3

Coote, Anna, and Beatrix Campbell, *Sweet Freedom: The Struggle for Women's Liberation*, Blackwell, 1982

De Beauvoir, Simone, *The Second Sex*, Jonathan Cape, 1953

Engel, Stephen M., *The Unfinished Revolution: Social Movement Theory and the Gay and Lesbian Movement*, Cambridge University Press, 2001

Feather, Stuart, author interview, 23 August 2005

Fountain, Nigel, *Underground: The London Alternative Press 1966–74*, Routledge, 1988

Friedan, Betty, *The Feminine Mystique*, Gollancz, 1963

Gay Left, issue 1, Autumn 1975

Gay Liberation Front Manifesto, Gay Liberation Front, 1971

Gay News, issues 1–4, 24, 40, 43, 75, 85, 1971–6

Greer, Germaine, *The Female Eunuch*, MacGibbon & Kee, 1970

Jeffery-Poulter, Stephen, *Peers, Queers & Commons: The Struggle for Gay Law Reform from 1950 to the Present*, Routledge, 1991

Jivani, Alkarim, *It's Not Unusual: A History of Lesbian and Gay Britain in the Twentieth Century*, Michael O'Mara 1997

Lewis, Jane, *Women in Britain since 1945: Women, Family, Work and the State in the Postwar Years*, Blackwell, 1992

Millett, Kate, *Sexual Politics*, Doubleday, 1970

Nelson, Elizabeth, *The British Counter-Culture 1966–73: A Study of the Underground Press*, Macmillan, 1989

Power, Lisa, *No Bath but Plenty of Bubbles: An Oral History of the Gay Liberation Front 1970–1973*, Cassell, 1995

Rowbotham, Sheila, *A Century of Women: The History of Women in Britain and the United States*, Viking, 1997

Rowe, Marsha, author interview, 14 September 2005

Rowe, Marsha, *Spare Rib Reader*, Penguin, 1982

Shrew, April 1970–Autumn 1976

Spare Rib, July 1972–July 1979

Walter, Aubrey (ed.), *Come Together: The Years of Gay Liberation 1970–73*, Gay Men's Press, 1980

Weeks, Jeffrey, *Coming Out: Homosexual Politics in Britain from the Nineteenth Century to the Present*, Quartet, 1977 and 1990 editions

10 GET OUT OF THE CITY

Beam, Alan, *Rehearsal for the Year 2000 (Drugs, Religions, Madness, Crime, Communes, Love, Visions, Festivals and Lunar Energy); The Rebirth of Albion Free State (Known in the Dark Ages as England); Memoirs of a Male Midwife (1966–1976)*, Revelaction Press, 1976

Carson, Rachel, *Silent Spring*, Houghton Mifflin, 1962

Clarke, Michael, *The Politics of Pop Festivals*, Junction, 1982

Collin, Matthew, *Altered State: The Story of Ecstasy Culture and Acid House*, Serpent's Tail, 1997

Daily Mail, 18–25 August 1975

Department of the Environment, 'Free Festivals: First Report of the Working Group on Pop Festivals', HMSO, 1976

Doomwatch, BBC1, 1970–2

Ecologist, issues 1–6, 8, July 1975

Ehrlich, Paul, *The Population Bomb*, Ballantine Books, 1968

Fallon, Ivan, *Billionaire: The Life and Times of Sir James Goldsmith*, Hutchinson, 1991

Goldsmith, Edward, author interview, 1 September 2005

Goldsmith, Edward (ed.), *A Blueprint for Survival*, Penguin, 1972

Goldsmith, Edward (ed.), *The Doomsday Fun Book: Seven Years of Satirical Comments from the Ecologist*, Wadebridge Press, 1977

Guardian, 19–25 August 1975

Hildyard, Nick, author interview, 8 September 2005

International Times, August 1975

Jenkins, Roy, *A Life at the Centre*, Macmillan, 1991

Macnaghten, Phil, and John Urry, *Contested Natures*, SAGE, 1998

McCormick, John, *British Politics and the Environment*, Earthscan, 1991

McCormick, John, *The Global Environmental Movement*, Belhaven, 1989

McKay, George, *Senseless Acts of Beauty: Cultures of Resistance since the Sixties*, Verso, 1996

Maddox, John, *The Doomsday Syndrome*, Macmillan, 1972

Meadows, Donella H., *The Limits to Growth: A Report for the Club of Rome's Project on the Predicament of Mankind*, Universe Books, 1972

New Musical Express, 26 July–13 September 1975

News of the World, 17–31 August 1975

Parkin, Sara, *Green Parties: An International Guide*, Heretic, 1989

Rawle, Sid, author interview, 8 November 2005

Release, Monthly Newsletter, September 1974

Routledge, Paul, *Public Servant, Secret Agent: The Elusive Life and Violent Death of Airey Neave*, Fourth Estate, 2002

Schumacher, E. F., *Small Is Beautiful: A Study of Economics as if People Mattered*, Blond and Briggs, 1973

Swindon *Evening Advertiser*, 13 March 2002

Talshir, Gayil, *The Political Ideology of Green Parties: from the Politics of Nature to Redefining the Nature of Politics*, Palgrave Macmillan, 2002

Taylor, Gordon Rattray, *The Doomsday Book*, Thames & Hudson, 1970

Times, The, 20–30 August 1975

Twine, Adam, author interview, 13 September 2005

Wansell, Geoffrey, *Tycoon: The Life of James Goldsmith*, Grafton, 1987

Watchfield Festival photographs, www.butterworth01.f2s.com/watchfield.html, tinpan.fortunecity.com/ebony/546/jan-2002-updates.html

Watchfield Freek Press, Special Bank Holiday Edition, 25 August 1975

11 MARGARET AND THE AUSTRIANS

Amis, Kingsley, *Memoirs*, Hutchinson, 1991

Calendar, 'Profile: Margaret Thatcher', Yorkshire Television, 23 February 1978

Campbell, John, *Margaret Thatcher, Vol. 1: The Grocer's Daughter*, Jonathan Cape, 2000

Chippindale, Peter, and Chris Horrie, *Stick It up Your Punter! The Rise and Fall of the Sun*, Heinemann, 1990

Cockett, Richard, *Thinking the Unthinkable: Think-tanks and the Economic Counter-revolution 1931–1983*, HarperCollins, 1994

Cormack, Patrick (ed.), *Right Turn: Eight Men who Changed their Minds*, Pen & Sword Books, 1978

Daily Telegraph, 31 January, 12 February 1975

Denham, Andrew, and Mark Garnett, *Keith Joseph*, Acumen, 2001

Harris, Ralph (ed.), *Ancient or Modern: Essays in Economic Efficiency and Growth*, Institute of Economic Affairs, 1964

Harris, Ralph (ed.), *Radical Reaction: Essays in Competition and Affluence*, Hutchinson, 1960

Harris, Ralph, and Arthur Seldon, *Not from Benevolence: 20 Years of Economic Dissent*, Institute of Economic Affairs, 1977

Harris, Ralph, Arthur Seldon and Stephen Erickson, *A Conversation with Harris and Seldon*, Institute of Economic Affairs, 2001

Hayek, Friedrich A., *The Road to Serfdom*, Routledge, 1944

Hoskyns, John, *Just in Time: Inside the Thatcher Revolution*, Aurum, 2000

Howe, Geoffrey, author interview, 4 July 2006

Howe, Geoffrey, *Conflict of Loyalty*, Macmillan, 1994

Judge Dredd, *2000AD*, 1977

Krugman, Paul, 'Who Was Milton Friedman?', *New York Review of Books*, 15 February 2007

Millar, Ronald, *A View from the Wings: West End, West Coast, Westminster*, Weidenfeld & Nicolson, 1993

Moore-Gilbert, Bart (ed.), *The Arts in the 1970s: Cultural Closure?*, Routledge, 1994

Ranelagh, John, *Thatcher's People: An Insider's Account of the Politics, the Power and the Personalities*, HarperCollins, 1991

Sherman, Alfred, author interview, 1 August 2006

Sherman, Alfred, *Paradoxes of Power: Reflections on the Thatcher Interlude*, Imprint Academic, 2005

Sweeney, The, Thames Television, 1975–8

White, Michael, author interview, 1 March 2007

York, Peter, *Style Wars*, Sidgwick & Jackson, 1980

12 A RELATIONSHIP OF FORCES

Benn, Tony, *The New Politics: A Socialist Reconnaissance*, Fabian Society, 1970

Guardian, 19 June 1974

Jones, Jack, author interview, 10 January 2004

Jones, Jack, *A World to Win*, Birkbeck College, 1975

Jones, Jack, 'The Human Face of Labour', The Richard Dimbleby Lecture 1977, BBC, 1977

Jones, Jack, *Union Man*, Collins, 1986

New York Times, 27 February 1978

O'Neill, Eugene, *The Emperor Jones*, Cincinnati, 1921

Pittaway, J. G., *The Story of Transport House*, TGWU, 1978

Rodgers, Bill, author interview, 23 June 2006

Spectator, 31 January 1976

Taylor, Robert, *The Trade Union Question in British Politics: Government and Unions since 1945*, Blackwell, 1993

TGWU Record, October 1976

13 MARXISM AT LUNCHTIME

Bradbury, Malcolm, *The History Man*, Secker & Warburg, 1975

Hill, Christopher, *The World Turned Upside Down: Radical Ideas during the English Revolution*, Maurice Temple Smith, 1972

Joll, James, *Antonio Gramsci*, Penguin, 1977

Liebman, Marcel, *Leninism Under Lenin*, Jonathan Cape, 1975

Miliband, Ralph, *Parliamentary Socialism: A Study in the Politics of Labour*, Merlin Press, 1964

Richards, Huw, 'Malcolm Bradbury Interview', Economic and Social Research Council, www.esrcsocietytoday.ac.uk

Walshe, Denis (ed.), *The Little Red Struggler: A Handbook for Student Militants*, Communist Party of Great Britain, National Student Committee, 1976

Winstanley, British Film Institute Production Board, 1975

14 WILLIAM THE TERRIBLE

Benn, Tony, author interview, 20 March 2005

Browning, Peter, *The Treasury and Economic Policy 1964–1985*, Longman, 1986

Burk, Kathleen, and Alec Cairncross, *'Goodbye, Great Britain': The 1976 IMF Crisis*, Yale University Press, 1992

Callaghan, James, *Time and Chance*, Collins, 1987

Cockerell, Michael, *Callaghan: A Film Portrait*, BBC2, 1992

Cockerell, Michael, *Denis Healey: The Man Who Did the Dirty Work*, BBC2, 12 October 1989

Daily Mail, 1–27 November 1976

De Vries, Margaret Garritsen, *The International Monetary Fund*

1972–1978: Cooperation on Trial: Narrative and Analysis, Vol. 1 and Vol. 2, International Monetary Fund, 1985

De Vries, Margaret Garritsen, *The IMF in a Changing World: 1945–85*, International Monetary Fund, 1986

Financial Times, 18–26 November 1976

Guardian, 15–29 November 1976

Harmon, Mark D., *The British Labour Government and the 1976 IMF Crisis*, Macmillan, 1997

Healey, Denis, *The Time of My Life*, Michael Joseph, 1989

Hickson, Kevin, *The IMF Crisis of 1976 and British Politics*, University of Southampton, 2002

Jay, Peter, author interview, 7 July 2006

Jefferys, Kevin, *Anthony Crosland: A New Biography*, Richard Cohen, 1999

Keegan, William, and Rupert Pennant-Rea, *Who Runs the Economy? Control and Influence in British Economic Policy*, Temple Smith, 1979

Ludlam, Steve, 'The Gnomes of Washington: Four Myths of the 1976 IMF Crisis', *Political Studies*, December 1992

McNally, Tom, author interview, 13 October 2006

McSweeney, Richard, author interview, 30 May 2005

Moffitt, Michael, *The World's Money: International Banking from Bretton Woods to the Brink of Insolvency*, Joseph, 1984

Money Programme, BBC2, 21 May 1976, 1 October 1976, 29 October 1976, 12 November 1976, 10 December 1976

Morgan, Kenneth O., *Callaghan: A Life*, Oxford University Press, 1997

Pardee, Scott, author interview, 14 July 2005

Pimlott, Ben, *Labour and the Left in the 1930s*, Cambridge University Press, 1977

Ryrie, William, author interview, 25 July 2005

Sampson, Anthony, *The Money Lenders: Bankers in a Dangerous World*, Coronet, 1981

Simon, William E., *A Time for Action*, McGraw Hill, 1980

Simon, William E., *A Time for Reflection: An Autobiography*, Regnery Publishing, 2004

Simon, William E., *A Time for Truth: A Distinguished Conservative Dissects the Economic and Political Policies that Threaten Our Liberty – And Points the Way to an American Renaissance*, Reader's Digest Press, 1978

Skidelsky, Robert, *John Maynard Keynes, Vol. 3: Fighting for Britain 1937–1946*, Macmillan, 2000

State of the Nation: The Cabinet in Conflict, Granada Television, 15
    February 1977
Sun, 1–27 November 1976
Sunday Times, 28 November 1976, 14–28 May 1978
Times, The, 25 September–29 November 1976
Van Dormael, Armand, *Bretton Woods: Birth of a Monetary System*,
    Macmillan, 1978
Walker, Richard, *The Savile Row Story: An Illustrated History*, Prion,
    1988
Wall Street Journal, 29 April 1975
Weatherstone, Dennis, author interview, 30 July 2005
Whitehead, Phillip, *The Writing on the Wall: Britain in the Seventies*,
    Joseph, 1985

15 BRENT VS THE COTSWOLDS
BBC News, BBC1, 16 June 1977, 17 June 1977, 23 June 1977, 27 June
    1977, 11 July 1977
Beckett, Andy, *Pinochet in Piccadilly: Britain and Chile's Hidden History*,
    Faber, 2002
Butler, Adam, author interview, 30 March 2006
Daily Mail, 24 June 1977
Daily Telegraph, 2 May 2005
Desai, Jayaben, author interview, 17 May 2006
Dromey, Jack, author interview, 12 May 2006
Dromey, Jack, and Graham Taylor, *Grunwick: The Workers' Story*,
    Lawrence and Wishart, 1978
Durkin, Tom, *Grunwick: Bravery and Betrayal*, Brent Trades Council,
    1978
Free Nation, The, March 1976–August 1977
Gouriet, John, author interview, 29 March 2006
Gouriet, John, *Checkmate Mr President!*, Maclellan, 1981
Grunwick 30th Anniversary Celebration, Tricycle Theatre, London, 17
    September 2006
Guardian, 20–22 December 1976, 17–18 June 1977, 11 July 1977, 13 July
    1977
Hansard (Commons), 27 November 1975, 4 November 1976, 20 June
    1977, 23 June 1977, 24 June 1977, 30 June 1977, 12 July 1977
Hiro, Dilip, *Black British, White British: A History of Race Relations in
    Britain* (updated edn), Grafton, 1991
King, Roger, and Neill Nugent (eds), *Respectable Rebels: Middle Class*

Campaigns in Britain in the 1970's, Hodder & Stoughton, 1979

Kingsbury News, 21 January–11 November 1977

Layton-Henry, Zig, *The Politics of Race in Britain*, Allen & Unwin, 1984

McWhirter, Norris, *Ross: The Story of a Shared Life*, Churchill Press, 1976

Money Programme, 24 June 1977

Morris, Margaret, *The General Strike*, Penguin, 1976

Moss, Robert, *The Collapse of Democracy*, Temple Smith, 1975

National Association for Freedom, *The National Association for Freedom*, NAFF, 1977

Panorama, 11 July 1977

Pychon, Thomas, *The Crying of Lot 49*, Jonathan Cape, 1967

Rogaly, Joe, *Grunwick*, Penguin, 1977

Scarman, Leslie, 'Report of a Court of Inquiry under the Rt Hon. Lord Justice Scarman, OBE into a Dispute Between Grunwick Processing Laboratories Limited and Members of the Association of Professional, Executive, Clerical and Computer Staff', HMSO, 1977

Sivanandan, A., *From Resistance to Rebellion: Asian and Afro-Caribbean Struggles in Britain*, Institute of Race Relations, 1986

Smith, Graham, author interview, 6 September 2006

Time Out, 12–18 August 1977

Times, The, 21–24 June 1977

Timeshift: The Grunwick Strike, BBC4, 28 December 2002

Tory! Tory! Tory!, BBC4, 8–22 March 2006

Walker, General Sir Walter, *Fighting On*, New Millennium, 1997

Ward, George, *Fort Grunwick*, Temple Smith, 1977

Webster, Roger, *When Britain Waived the Rules and Sampled Anarchy: A Battle Won for Freedom-loving Britons*, R. Webster, 2000

Weekend World, LWT, 16 October 1977

Weir, Stuart, 'A Picket's Eye View', *New Society*, 30 June 1977

Willesden & Brent Chronicle, 13 August 1976–8 November 1977

Wilson, Amrit, *Finding a Voice: Asian Women in Britain*, Virago, 1978

16 GETTING AWAY WITH IT?

Architectural Design, 'Los Angeles: Architecture and Culture', Autumn 1982

Banham, Reyner, *Los Angeles: The Architecture of Four Ecologies*, Allen Lane, 1971

Barker, Paul, Peter Hall, Cedric Price and Rayner Banham, 'Non-Plan: An Experiment in Freedom', *New Society*, 20 March 1969

Bendixson, Terence, and John Platt, *Milton Keynes: Image and Reality*,

Granta, 1992

Bishop, Jeff, *Milton Keynes: The Best of Both Worlds? Public and Professional Views of a New City*, University of Bristol, 1986

Booker, Christopher, *The Seventies: Portrait of a Decade*, Penguin, 1980

Boyne, George, 'The Privatisation of Council Housing', *Political Quarterly*, April–June 1984

Brent Cross history, www.brentcross-london.com

Chester, Lewis, Magnus Linklater and David May, *Jeremy Thorpe: A Secret Life*, Fontana, 1979

Clapson, Mark, *A Social History of Milton Keynes: Middle England/Edge City*, Frank Cass, 2004

Clapson, Mark, Mervyn Dobbins and Peter Waterman (eds), *The Best Laid Plans: Milton Keynes since 1967*, University of Luton Press, 1998

Clark, Tom, *The Limits of Social Democracy? Tax and Spend Under Labour, 1974–79*, Institute for Fiscal Studies, 2001–4

Conservative Research Department, Leader's Steering Committee: Minutes of 51st meeting, 30 January 1978; of 54th Meeting, 27 February 1978

Conservative Research Department, 'The Right Approach: A Statement of Conservative Aims', Conservative Central Office, 1976

Construction Industry Conference Centre, Building for Leisure: A Major Conference on the Design and Construction of Indoor Recreation, Sports and Leisure Centres, University of Nottingham, 1975

Davies, Gavyn, author interview, 8 March 2006

Elms, Robert, *The Way We Wore*, Picador, 2005

Forester, Tom, 'Do the British Sincerely Want to Be Rich?', *New Society*, 28 April 1977

Galbraith, J. K., *The Affluent Society*, Deutsch, 1977 edition

Gershuny, Jonathan, *After Industrial Society? The Emerging Self-service Economy*, Macmillan, 1978

Gershuny, Jonathan, and Kimberly Fisher, 'Leisure', in Halsey, A. H. and Josephine Webb, *Twentieth Century British Social Trends*, Macmillan, 1999

Hall, Peter, 'It All Came Together in California: Values and Role Models in the Making of a Planner', *City*, 1996

Halsey, A. H. (ed.), *British Social Trends since 1900: A Guide to the Changing Social Structure of Britain*, Macmillan, 1988

Marwick, Arthur, *British Society since 1945*, Allen Lane, 1982

Milton Keynes Development Corporation, Annual Reports, 1972–8

Morgan, Kenneth O., *Britain since 1945: The People's Peace*, Oxford

University Press, 1990

Mynard, Dennis C., and Julian Hunt, *Milton Keynes: A Pictorial History*, Phillimore, 1994

Nossiter, Bernard D., *Britain: A Future that Works*, Deutsch, 1978

Parker, Stanley (ed.), *The Sociology of Leisure*, Allen & Unwin, 1976

Patten, Chris, 'Further Thoughts on Strategy', Conservative Research Department, 23 February 1978

Philo, Chris (ed.), *Off the Map: The Social Geography of Poverty in the UK*, Cultural Geography Study Group, 1995

Rapoport, Rhona, and Margaret Sierakowski, 'Recent Trends in Family and Work in Britain', Policy Studies Institute, 1982

Seabrook, Jeremy, *What Went Wrong? Working People and the Ideals of the Labour Movement*, Gollancz, 1978

Smith, Michael A., Stanley Parker and Cyril S. Smith (eds), *Leisure and Society in Britain*, Allen Lane, 1973

Steel, David, *Against Goliath: David Steel's Story*, Weidenfeld & Nicolson, 1989

TUC–Labour Party Liaison Committee, 'Into the Eighties: An Agreement', Labour Party, 1978

Turner, Jane, and Bob Jardine (eds), *Pioneer Tales: A New Life in Milton Keynes*, People's Press, 1985

Walker, Derek, author interview, 16 March 2006

Walker, Derek, *The Architecture and Planning of Milton Keynes*, Architectural Press, 1981

17 PRESSURES BUILDING

Bethnal Green and Stepney Trades Council, 'Blood on the Streets: A Report on Racial Attacks in East London', Bethnal Green and Stepney Trades Council, 1978

Bleasdale, Alan, *Boys from the Blackstuff*, BBC2, 1982

Bragg, Billy, author interview, 10 January 2006

Brown, Colin, *Black and White Britain: The Third PSI Survey*, Heinemann, 1984

Brown, Colin, and Pat Gay, *Racial Discrimination: 17 Years after the Act*, Policy Studies Institute, 1985

Callaghan, James, Prime Ministerial Broadcast, BBC1, 7 September 1978

Campbell, Duncan, 'The British Army's Secret Opinion', *New Statesman*, July 1979

Clarke, A. F. N., *Contact*, Secker & Warburg, 1983

Clarke, Alan, *Contact*, BBC2, 6 January 1985

Daily Mail, 21 February 1978

Daily Mirror, 21 February 1978

Denselow, Robin, *When the Music's Over: The Story of Political Pop*, Faber, 1989

Fallon, Ivan, *The Brothers: The Rise and Rise of Saatchi & Saatchi*, Hutchinson, 1988

Hollingsworth, Mark, *Tim Bell: The Ultimate Spin Doctor*, Hodder & Stoughton, 1997

Huddle, Roger, author interview, 1 March 2006

I'm All Right Jack, 1959

Kettle, Martin, and Lucy Hodges, *Uprising! The Police, the People and the Riots in Britain's Cities*, Pan, 1982

Lawson, Nigel, 'Thoughts on "Implementing our Strategy"', internal Conservative Party memo, 15 January 1978

New Musical Express, 11 September 1976, 6 May 1978

Robinson, Tom, author interview, 12 September 2005

Rodgers, Bill, *Fourth Among Equals*, Politico's, 2000

Sivanandan, Ambalavaner, author interview, 5 September 2006

Sun, 21 February 1978

Temporary Hoarding, spring 1978, summer 1978, March/April 1979

Thurlow, Richard C., *Fascism in Britain: From Oswald Mosley's Blackshirts to the National Front*, Tauris, 1998

Walker, Martin, *The National Front*, Fontana, 1977

Widgery, David, *Beating Time*, Chatto & Windus, 1986

World in Action, Granada Television, 27 January 1978

18 THE PEASANTS' REVOLT

Anderson, Lindsay, *The Diaries*, Methuen, 2004

Anderson, Lindsay, *Never Apologise: The Collected Writings*, Plexus, 2004

Andrews, Barry, author interview, 3 August 2006

Battle of the Giants, Yorkshire Television, 1 May 1979

Beach, Fred, author interview, 3 August 2006

Benn, Tony, *Conflicts of Interest: Diaries 1977–1980*, Hutchinson, 1990

Britannia Hospital, EMI Films, 1982

'Callaghan "On the Spot"', *Nationwide*, BBC1, 27 April 1979

Calvert, Hugh, *A History of Kingston upon Hull*, Phillimore, 1978

Can the Government Survive?, Thames Television, 20 November 1978

Daily Mail, 31 January–9 March 1979

Daily Telegraph, 2–9 March 1979

Donoughue, Bernard, author interview, 30 August 2008
Donoughue, Bernard, *Downing Street Diary: With James Callaghan in No. 10*, Jonathan Cape, 2008
East London *Advertiser*, 2 February 1979–4 February 1983
Gillett, Edward, and Kenneth A. MacMahon, *A History of Hull*, Hull University Press, 1989
Guardian, 7–10 March 1979
Hansard (Commons), 16 January 1979
Hobsbawm, Eric, *The Forward March of Labour Halted?*, New Left Books, 1981
Hull *Daily Mail*, 3 January 1979–5 February 1979
Humble, J. G., and Peter Hansell, *Westminster Hospital 1716–1974*, Pitman Medical, 1974
Jimmy Young Programme, BBC Radio 2, 31 January 1979
Jones, Bob, author interview, 2 August 2006
Lambert, Gavin, *Mainly about Lindsay Anderson: A Memoir*, Faber, 2000
Larkin, Philip, *Selected Letters of Philip Larkin 1940–1985*, Faber, 1992
London *Evening Standard*, 2 January–8 March 1979
Marxism Today, February 1979
Money Programme, BBC2, 17 January 1979
Rodgers, Bill, 'A Winter's Tale of Discontent', *Guardian*, 7 January 1984
Rose, Clive, author interview 25 July 2006
Secret History: Winter of Discontent, Mentorn Productions, 1998
Suddaby, John, 'The Winter '79 Strikes in Camden', *New Left Review*, July–August 1979
Sun, 7–9 March 1979
Sunday Telegraph, 21 January 1979
Sunday Times, 20 January 1989
Weekend World, LWT, 7 January 1979, 14 January 1979
Yes, Minister, 'The Compassionate Society', BBC1, 23 February 1981

19 LAST-DITCH DAYS

Baker, Kenneth, *The Turbulent Years: My Life in Politics*, Faber, 1993
Butler, David, and Dennis Kavanagh, *The British General Election of 1979*, Macmillan, 1999 edition
Conservative Party, 'Conservative Manifesto 1979', Conservative Central Office, 1979
Evans, Gwynfor, *The Fight for Welsh Freedom*, Y Lolfa, 2000
Hansard (Commons), 28 March 1979

Harrison, Walter, author interview, 19 July 2006

Hattersley, Roy, *Who Goes Home? Scenes from a Political Life*, Little, Brown, 1995

Jones, Mervyn, *Michael Foot*, Gollancz, 1994

Labour Party, 'The Labour Way Is the Better Way: The Labour Party Manifesto 1979', Labour Party, 1979

McAllister, Laura, *Plaid Cymru: The Emergence of a Political Party*, Seren, 2001

Morgan, Kenneth O., *Michael Foot: A Life*, HarperPress, 2007

Party Election Broadcast, the Labour Party, 20 April 1979

Spare Rib, May 1979, June 1979

CONCLUSION: THE LONG SEVENTIES

Butler, David, and Dennis Kavanagh, *The British General Election of 1983*, Macmillan, 1984

Decision '79, BBC1, 3–4 May 1979

Downing Street Years, The, Fine Art Productions, 1994

MORI, *How Britain Voted since Labour Last Won*, MORI, 2005

Punch, 12 June 1985

Weekend World, LWT, 22 February 1981

Index

Aberdeen, 185–7, 205–6
ACAS *see* Advisory, Conciliation and Arbitration Service
Adams, Gerry, 105, 115
Adams, Richard, 241
Adams, Tom, 482
Adley, Robert, 45
Advisory, Conciliation and Arbitration Service (ACAS), 297, 402, 476
air travel, cheap, 420
airports, 35–46, 521
Aitken, Ian, 109
Albion Free State, 244–59
Alden, Malcolm, 361–3, 386
Allbeury, Dr Anthony, 144
Allen, Robert, 238, 242
Allen, V. L., 64
Althusser, Louis, 309
Amalgamated Union of Engineering Workers (AUEW), 80–1; *see also* Scanlon, Hugh
Amis, Kingsley, 282–3, 287, 414–15, 493
Amis, Martin, 180
Anderson, Lindsay, 181, 477–8
Andre, Carl, 286
Andrews, Barry, 487–8
APEX *see* Association for Professional, Executive, Clerical and Computer Staffs
Argentina, 407
Armstrong, Sir William, 48–9, 131
Arnold, P., 36
art, 181, 286–7
Art Workers Cooperative, 306

Article 5 (play), 122
Ashworth, William, 60
Aspinall, John, 236, 239, 240
Association for Professional, Executive, Clerical and Computer Staffs (APEX): description and growth, 371; and Grunwick, 365, 371, 375, 384, 401, 402; women members, 230
Association of Scientific, Technical and Managerial Staff (ASTMS), 367
Astell, Mary, 220
Atlee, Clement: death, 355; government of, 44, 326, 424; Jones on, 296
AUEW *see* Amalgamated Union of Engineering Workers
Austrian School, 268–72, 284

Baker, Kenneth, 507
Balcombe Street Gang, 119, 378
Baldwin, Stanley, 148, 326
Ballard, J. G., 180
Balliol College, Oxford, 20–1
Balogh, Thomas, 199
Banner Theatre company, 85–6
Barbados, 482, 483
Barber, Anthony, 47, 127, 128
Barber, Simon, 306
Barcelona, 24
Barnett, Joel, 163, 172
Barnsley Miners' Forum, 70
Basnett, David, 463
BBC: Northern Ireland coverage, 122

Beach, Fred, 484–91, 493

Beatles, 16, 120–1; *see also* Lennon, John

Beauvoir, Simone de, 221

Beckett, Andy: childhood in army family, 96–8; education, 241

Belfast, 99, 100, 105; Falls Road, 101–2, 103; Maze Prison (Long Kesh), 110; Stormont, 108–9

Bell, Tim, 458

Bellingham, Philip, 78, 85

Bendixson, Terence, 433

Benjamin, Walter, 309

Benn, Tony: and 1970 election, 12, 13; and 1974 (Feb) election, 150–1; and 1979 election, 509, 510; Blair on, 1; on Callaghan's popularity, 408; economic ideas watered down by Wilson, 174–5; and the EEC, 92; and Healey's public expenditure cuts, 323; and IMF cuts, 350–1; on Jones's influence, 297; and Labour Party 1976 leadership contest, 323; and Lib–Lab pact, 409; and North Sea oil, 200; and RAR, 452; and rise of right-wing conservatism, 288; and the social contract, 290–1; on weather in 1979, 466; in Wilson's sixties governments, 18; and Winter of Discontent, 467, 496

Bennett Report, 454

Berganza, Teresa, 332

Bessbrook Mill, 455–6

Bevan, Nye, 187

Beveridge, Sir William, 157

Bevin, Ernest, 294, 302

Bhudia, Devshi, 361–2, 363

Bill Brand (TV series), 181

Birdwood, Lady Jane, 376

Birmingham: CP in, 72; IRA pub bombs, 118, 120, 124; Saltley coke depot, 66–9, 71–86

Blair, Tony, 1, 392

Bleasdale, Alan, 457

Bloody Sunday, 111–13

Blue Peter (TV programme), 65–6

Blueprint for Survival, A, 38, 238, 239

BNOC *see* British National Oil Corporation

BNP *see* British National Party

Boardman, Tom, 126

Bober, Graham and Gillian, 140–2, 143, 144

Bond, Eric, 253

Booker, Christopher, 426–7

Booth-Clibborn, Edward, 458

Bowie, David, 178, 449

Boycott, Rosie, 225–7

Boys from the Blackstuff (TV series), 457

Boyson, Rhodes, 393

BP *see* British Petroleum

Brabourne, Lord, 269

Bradbury, Malcolm, 179, 309

Bragg, Billy, 452

'brain drain', 15

Brenton, Howard, 180

Bretton Woods Agreement, 317–19

Britannia Hospital (film), 477

British Army: and Northern Ireland, 95–7, 100, 102–7, 109–14, 120–3; and Winter of Discontent, 496

British National Oil Corporation (BNOC), 200

British National Party (BNP), 46

British Petroleum (BP), 128, 185–6, 187, 192, 194, 198, 406

Brittan, Samuel, 283, 284

Broad Left, 310

Broadstairs, 19

Broughton, Sir Alfred, 500–1

Brown, Gordon, 496

Buchanan, Colin, 38

building schemes, 35

Burns, Arthur, 320, 345

Bush, George W., 521

Butler, Adam, 283, 394
Butler, David, 509, 517

Cabinet Office Briefing Room
    (COBRA), 481
Callaghan, Audrey, 407, 482
Callaghan, Jim: and 1979 election,
    508–10, 512, 514; appearance
    and dress, 328, 497; background,
    323, 325–8; on being chancellor,
    171; Blair on, 1; character, 324,
    326–7, 407, 438–9; civil-service
    attitude to, 497; and council-
    house sales, 423; economic
    measures, 323, 328–57, 404,
    406–7; equality under, 409–10;
    fall of government, 498–508; and
    Grunwick, 392; at Guadeloupe
    summit, 479–82; homes, 298,
    328; and IMF, 319, 339–57; and
    immigration, 442, 444, 451; and
    industrial relations, 56; and Jay
    (Peter), 337, 339; and Labour
    Party 1976 leadership contest,
    323; Labour plots to replace
    Wilson with, 160–1; and Lib–Lab
    pact, 408–9; nicknames, 406; no-
    confidence vote, 504–8; and
    Northern Ireland, 98, 100; post-
    pones election from 1978 to
    1979, 459–63; public-speaking
    style, 328; Ruskin College
    speech, 406–7; and Scottish devo-
    lution, 502, 503; speech at 1976
    Labour Party conference, 335–7,
    339; Thatcher on, 405; and trade
    unions, 298–9, 327–8, 434,
    438–40, 461, 463; in Wilson's
    sixties governments, 98, 100; in
    Wilson's 1974 government, 163,
    175; as Wilson's chancellor, 18,
    327, 339; and Winter of
    Discontent, 464–5, 479–84,
    494–5
Callaghan, Michael, 464

Cambodia, 242
Cameron, David, 1, 522, 524
Campbell, Beatrix, 220, 228, 229,
    231
Campbell, Duncan, 453–4
Campbell, Jock, 425, 427, 431–2
Campbell, John, 266, 267, 414,
    511
Canada, 112
Cann, Edward du, 260
CAP see Common Agricultural
    Policy
Capper, Sir Derrick, 81, 82, 83, 84
car industry, 464
car ownership, 424
Carlisle, 48
Carr, Robert, 58
Carrington, Peter, 12, 145–6
Carson, Edward, 108
Carson, John, 506
Carson, Rachel, 234
Carter, Jimmy, 342, 479, 480, 481
Castle, Barbara: on Crosland, 353;
    reasons for career stall, 295;
    Spare Rib on, 226; and trade
    unions, 56, 290, 295; in Wilson's
    sixties governments, 18, 56, 295;
    in Wilson's 1974 government,
    173
CCU see Civil Contingencies Unit
Cement Garden, The (McEwan),
    180
Centre for Policy Studies (CPS),
    278–83
Chalfont, Lord, 287
Channel Tunnel, 35
Charter of Rights and Liberties,
    379
Chesterton, A. K., 445
chief whip: role, 498–501
child care, 231–2
Chile, 178, 313
China, 308
Churchill, Winston, 89, 97, 235,
    269

Churchill Play, The (Brenton), 180
cinema, 181
cities: inner-city decay, 15
'City Is Dead, The' (Allen), 242
Civil Assistance, 377
Civil Contingencies Unit (CCU),
    481–2, 492
civil service: and Winter of
    Discontent, 496–7
Clapson, Mark, 427
Clapton, Eric, 449
Clark, Ian, 202–3
Clarke, A. F. N., 454
Clash, The, 452
Clermont Club, 236, 376
Clutterbuck, Richard, 77
coal *see* mining and miners;
    National Union of Mineworkers
Cobden, Richard, 14–15
COBRA *see* Cabinet Office Briefing
    Room
Cockerell, Michael, 324, 326, 328
coke, 66
Colchester, 138–42
Cole, John, 436
Coleman, Terry, 13
Collins, Michael, 114
Colvillia Commune, 216–18
Commission for Racial Equality
    (CRE), 444–5
commodification: homosexuality,
    219–20
Common Agricultural Policy
    (CAP), 91
Common Fisheries Policy, 91
communism *see* Marxism
Communist Party of Great Britain
    (CP): and 1972 miners' strike,
    72, 75; in Birmingham, 72; and
    NUM, 62–3; and Scargill, 69; *see
    also* McGahey, Mick
Communist Party Women's Group,
    385
Concrete Island (Ballard), 180
confrontation: reasons for in sev-

enties, 55
Conquest, Robert, 282
Conran, Sir Terence, 46
Conservative Party: 1975 confer-
    ence, 411–12; 1975 leadership
    contest, 260–6, 410–11; 1979
    manifesto, 513; analysis of 1979
    success, 516–17; 'Labour Isn't
    Working' campaign, 458–9;
    mood in 1978, 414; and NAFF,
    378; nowadays, 522; opinion poll
    ratings in 1978, 405; post-1970
    unpopularity, 49; post-war
    change of direction, 25–6;
    replacement of leaders, 12, 411;
    rise in popular support for right
    wing, 284–8; and Scotland, 195,
    196, 501–2; social groups sup-
    porting, 31; and Winter of
    Discontent, 468–9, 474–5
Conservative Research Department
    (CRD), 30, 47, 413, 415
Constable, David, 125–6
consumerism, 418–20, 458
Cooper, Bryan, 190
Coote, Anna, 220, 228, 229, 231
Cormack, Patrick, 287, 288
COUM Transmissions, 287
Courtiour, Roger, 166–8
CP *see* Communist Party of Great
    Britain
CPS *see* Centre for Policy Studies
Craig, William, 99, 116
CRD *see* Conservative Research
    Department
CRE *see* Commission for Racial
    Equality
Crosland, Susan, 173
Crosland, Tony: on changes in
    British society, 173–4; confidence
    and ambitions, 353; and council-
    house sales, 423; and free
    festivals, 249; and Healey's pub-
    lic expenditure cuts, 323; and
    IMF cuts, 350, 352–3;

McWhirter on, 377; and Maplin, 43, 44; in Wilson's sixties governments, 18; and Wilson's 1974 government, 163
Cublington, 37–8
culture: effects of seventies unease, 178–81; move to the right in values, 286–7; nostalgia for seventies popular, 3; publishers and left-wing radicalism, 309
Cunningham, Jack, 324
Curtis, Robert, 106

Dacre, Paul, 301
Daily Mirror, 93, 123
Daily Express, 123
Dalyell, Tam, 44, 202, 502
Daniel Martin (Fowles), 179–80
Davies, Gavyn: and 1976 sterling crisis, 333, 336; and 1979 election, 508; on Callaghan's like of being PM, 460; on Callaghan's postponement of election, 463; on Germany as inspiration, 439; and monetarism, 421–3; on optimism of 1977/8, 404; on Wilson's last term, 162; on Winter of Discontent, 467
Davies, John, 38, 60
de Gaulle, Charles, 88, 90
de Valera, Éamon, 114
De Vries, Margaret Garritsen, 320
Dead Babies (Amis), 180
declinism, 14–18, 176–82, 235; end of, 415–18
defence spending, 407
Defenders of Essex, 42–3
Denmark, 54
Derry *see* Londonderry
Desai, Jayaben, 359–65, 370–2, 383, 388–9, 402–3
Desai, Sunil, 363
Destiny (Edgar), 180
Devlin, Bernadette, 112
Dewar, Colonel Michael, 106

Diggers, 311, 312
disposable income, personal, 404, 518–19
Donoughue, Bernard: and 1974 (Feb) election, 151; and 1979 election, 510, 515; background, 151; and Callaghan, 329; on Callaghan and moral values, 407; and Callaghan's 1976 conference speech, 336; and council-house sales, 422, 423; on government optimism in 1978, 404; and IMF cuts, 355–6; on monetarism, 421; on mood after postponed election, 467; and paranoia, 169; on the social contract, 292; on Wilson, 157–8, 161–2, 163, 165; and Winter of Discontent, 465, 494, 495–6
Doomsday Book, The (Taylor), 234
Doomwatch (TV series), 234
Drabble, Margaret, 127, 179
Dredd, Judge (comic strip character), 287
Drew, Peter, 420
Dromey, Jack: appearance, background and character, 365–6; and Grunwick, 365–7, 372–3, 380, 382–5, 388–9, 391, 401–3; marriage, 366; on NAFF, 382–3; on race discrimination and unions, 368; and Scargill, 388–9
drugs: cannabis and legalization, 327; and free festivals, 245–7, 255
Dwyer, William Ubique 'Ubi', 246–7, 248, 249–50, 251

Eakes, Louis, 211–12
Eastbourne: TGWU Centre, 302–6
Ecologist, The (magazine), 38, 235–9, 241, 242–3
Ecology Party (formerly PEOPLE Party; later Green Party), 240–1, 243–5

Economic Affairs, Department of, 17–18

economic theories: CPS, 278–83; free market, 48, 149, 268–88; Hayek and Austrian School, 268–72, 284; IEA, 48, 149, 271–8, 280, 329; Keynes, 21–2, 317; Macmillan, 22; monetarism, 273, 322–3, 329, 335–57

economy: 1950–1970, 16–18; 1976 crisis and IMF loan, 330–57; Bretton Woods Agreement, 317–19; under Callaghan, 323, 328–57, 404, 406–7; EEC entry's effect on, 95; under Heath, 47–9, 126–30, 150, 276, 281; IMF loans to Britain, 319–21; and North Sea oil, 189, 198–9; Northern Ireland, 98–9; nowadays, 521–2; under Thatcher, 518; and three-day week, 142–3, 145; under Wilson, 163, 171–7, 189, 297, 321–3

Edgar, David, 180

Edgar Broughton Band, 308

education: Callaghan on, 406–7; campus left-wing radicalism, 307–13; Thatcher as secretary, 262, 277

Edward VIII, King, 294

Ehrlich, Paul, 234

elections, general: (1874), 148; (1918), 148; (1924), 148; (1931), 148; (1945), 25; (1959), 195; (1964), 17, 196; (1966), 17, 196; (1970), 9–14, 18, 29, 196, 228; (1974, Feb), 146–54, 157–8, 161, 196, 228, 241, 446; (1974, Oct), 170–1, 196, 241, 446; (1979), 244, 477, 508–17; (1992), 168; Callaghan's postponement from 1978 to 1979, 459–63

Elizabeth II, Queen: and EEC opening gala, 94; and opening of Forties oilfield, 185–6; Silver Jubilee, 407–8; Stirling University student demo, 308

Elms, Robert, 419

emigration, 175, 415

Employment Protection Act (1975), 231

Endurance, HMS, 407

Ennals, David, 470, 473–4, 475–6, 496

Eno, Brian, 218

Environment, Department of the, 33, 38, 136–7

environmental issues: Cublington campaign, 37–8; Defenders of Essex, 42–3; growth of environmentalism, 37–8, 234–44

Equal Opportunities Commission, 231

Equal Pay Act (1970), 230–1

equality, 409–10

Equivalent VIII (Andre), 286

Essex Man, 31

Essex University, 71, 138, 139, 308, 309

Esso, 199

Europe: 1960 Common Market negotiations, 26, 89; 1972 EEC treaty, 40, 90–5; 1975 referendum, 170–1; celebrations of entry, 93–5; entry's effect on economy, 95; and Heath, 22–3, 26, 40, 88–95; history of British attempts to enter, 88–90; and Powell, 92, 149; public attitude to membership, 92–3

Evans, Moss, 435, 486, 491

exports, 16, 95

Ezra, Derek, 64–5

Fall and Rise of Reginald Perrin, The (book and TV series), 181

Fairbairn, Nicholas, 287

Falkland Islands, 407

Family Arsenal, The (Theroux), 179

Fanfare for Europe, 93–4

Fawlty Towers (TV series), 181
Fay, Stephen, 147
Feather, Stuart, 211–20
Feather, Vic, 87
Female Eunuch, The (Greer), 222
Feminine Mystique, The (Friedan), 221
feminism: radical, 232; socialist, 232–3; *see also* women
Ferrier, Louise, 223–4
Festival of Light, 286
festivals, free, 245–59
films *see* cinema
Finch, David, 344
Fisher, Alan, 355, 472, 476
Fisher, Antony, 271, 272
Fitt, Gerry, 505, 506
food: and the EEC, 90, 91, 95
Foot, Michael: Blair on, 1; and fall of Callaghan government, 508; and IMF cuts, 354; and Jones's retirement, 434; and Labour Party 1976 leadership contest, 323; and Scottish devolution, 503; and trade unions, 297; and Winter of Discontent, 495–6
Ford, 464
Ford, Gerald, 328, 342, 349
Forest of Dean, 250–1
Forester, Tom, 176
Forties oilfield, 185–7
Foulness, 36, 38, 39–40
Fowles, John, 179–80
Fox, Dr Richard, 144
France: airports, 40; and Britain's entry into Europe, 88, 90–1; GDP, 16; IMF loans, 344
Franco, General Francisco, 23
Fraser, Michael, 30–1
Free Nation, The (newspaper), 378–9, 395
Friedan, Betty, 221
Friedman, Milton: and Callaghan, 329, 336; on Healey, 323; and Jay (Peter), 338; overview, 283–4;

Sherman on, 280; and Simon, 346
Friends of the Earth: British wing established, 38
FTSE share index performance, 127, 176, 322
Funkhouser, Richard, 197, 202–3

Gaitskell, Hugh, 160, 169
Gandhi, Mahatma, 20
Gardner, Llew, 511
Garnett, Mark, 109
gas: British natural, 187
Gaskell, Jane, 144
Gaskell, T. F., 190
Gatwick airport, 37
Gay Liberation Front (GLF), 210–20, 224–5, 227, 286, 452
Gay News, 219–20, 286
Gay Pride marches, 219
gay rights and politics, 209–20, 224–5, 227, 286; legislation, 211
GB75, 377
GDP *see* gross domestic product
Geary, Roger, 77, 78, 387
geese, Brent, 43
gender issues *see* women
General Theory of Employment, Interest and Money (Keynes), 21–2
Germany: Callaghan seeks loan from, 342; GDP, 16; Heath's visit to Nazi, 23; as inspiration to Callaghan, 439
Gilbert and George, 181
Gilmour, Sir Ian, 442
Gini coefficient, 409
Giscard d'Estaing, Valéry, 479, 481
Gladstone, William, 148
Glastonbury festival, 246
GLF *see* Gay Liberation Front
Goldsmith, Edward 'Teddy', 38, 235–40, 240–1, 242–3
Goldsmith, James, 38, 235, 236, 272

Good Life, The (TV series), 241
Goodlad, Morgan, 203–4, 205
Gormley, Joe: and 1972 miners' strike, 64, 72, 87; and 1974 miners' strike, 145, 147, 148; and 1981 miners' dispute, 519; character, 61; Heath on, 131; lifestyle, 300; and the social contract, 437; and three-day week, 130–1
Gorst, John, 396–7, 401
Gouriet, John: appearance, background and character, 380–2; and Grunwick, 375–6, 386, 388, 393–4, 395–401; and seamen's strike, 378; and Thatcher, 518
Gramsci, Antonio, 179–80, 309
Grant, Duncan, 214
Grantham, Roy, 375
Greece, 223, 308
green issues *see* environmental issues
Green Party *see* Ecology Party
Greer, Germaine, 222
Griffiths, Eldon, 41
Griffiths, Trevor, 180–1
Grimond, Jo, 202
Gristey, Len, 368
gross domestic product (GDP), 16, 127, 172
Grosvenor Square riots, 327
Grundy, Tony, 358
Grunwick strike, 358–403; background, 358–65; breaking of mail boycott, 395–401; mass pickets and policing, 385–94, 403; and NAFF, 375–83, 386, 388, 393–4; Scarman Report, 394, 401
Guadeloupe summit, 479–82
Guinness Book of Records, The, 378

Haines, Joe, 161, 165, 422
Hall, Peter, 425
Hallidie-Smith, Andrew, 140
Hamilton, Jimmy, 507

Hammond, Eric, 492
Hanley, Sir Michael, 168
Harman, Harriet, 366
Harper, Roger, 66, 80–1, 82
Harris, Bob, 144
Harris, Ralph: background, 270–2; and Gouriet, 381; on Heath, 154; and IEA, 273–6; and the McWhirters, 377–8; and NAFF, 379; on public opinion, 284–5; and Thatcher, 278, 283
Harrison, Walter, 498–501, 504, 507–8
Hattersley, Roy, 506
Hayek, Friedrich A.: favourite TV programmes, 477; and Seldon, 273; Sherman on, 280; and Simon, 346; theories and influence, 268–9, 270, 284
Healey, Denis: background and character, 171; Blair on, 1; on Callaghan and trade unions, 438; as Callaghan's chancellor, 331–5, 339–45, 353–4, 356–7, 406; on Conservative Party 1979 manifesto, 513; homes, 298; and IMF crisis, 331–5, 339–45, 353–4, 356–7; and immigration, 442; and Jay (Peter), 339; and 'Labour Isn't Working' campaign, 459; and Labour Party 1976 leadership contest, 323; on North Sea oil, 198–9; on Northern Ireland, 97; at Oxford, 20, 171; and postponement of election from 1978 to 1979, 460–1; rumoured to be PM after Callaghan, 467; Thatcher attack on, 264; on Thatcher becoming Conservative Party leader, 265; and trade unions, 290, 298; on Wilson, 162; as Wilson's chancellor, 171–3, 322–3; and Wilson's 1974 government, 163; and Winter of Discontent, 496

Health and Safety at Work Act, 297
health service *see* hospitals
Heath, Edith, 19
Heath, Ted: and 1970 election,
  9–14, 18, 29; and 1972 miners'
  strike, 79, 87; and 1974 (Feb)
  election, 146–9, 152–4; and 1974
  miners' strike, 145; and 1979
  election, 514; appearance, 28, 29;
  background, 19–20; building
  schemes, 35; and CCU, 481;
  character, 9, 26–7, 92; at
  Colchester Oyster Feast, 138–9,
  142; at Conservative Party 1975
  conference, 411–12; and
  Conservative Party 1975 leadership contest, 260, 263–5, 410;
  early government, 33–5; economic measures and 'U-turn', 48–9,
  126–30, 276, 281; electioneering
  style, 9–10, 149; elections for
  own seat, 12–13; and Europe,
  22–3, 26, 40, 88–95; and feminism, 230; and free festivals, 248;
  and free-market ideas, 278–9;
  funeral, 154–6; homes, 14, 27–8,
  155–6; influences on thinking,
  21–3; interviewed by author,
  27–9, 46, 58, 87, 88, 111, 131,
  154, 189; IRA attack on, 119;
  and Jones, 24–5, 57, 296; and
  Maplin, 40, 44–5, 46; and music,
  20; Nazi Germany visited by, 23;
  and North Sea oil, 189; and
  Northern Ireland, 107, 109–10,
  111–12, 114; at Oxford, 20–1,
  24, 159; plans for government,
  29–32; political career to 1970,
  25–7, 36, 48, 57; political ideas,
  147; political qualities, 26–7;
  popularity, 29–30, 150, 156;
  popularity over Thatcher, 412;
  relations with Neave, 260; rhetoric, 48; and sailing, 27; and
  Scottish devolution, 196; in
  Second World War, 25; at Selsdon
  conference, 30–2, 58; Selsdon's
  effect on reputation, 31–2; and
  Spanish Civil War, 24–5; talks
  with Liberals, 153–4; and
  Thatcher, 27–8, 277, 411–12;
  and three-day week, 130–1, 138,
  143; thyroid problems, 132; and
  trade unions, 57–9, 296; on
  unemployment, 47; and Winter
  of Discontent, 474
Heath, William, 19
Heathrow airport, 36–7
Hell's Angels, 255
Hendrix, Jimi, 213
Hennessy, Peter, 172
Heseltine, Michael, 44
Hickey, John, 358
High Rise (Ballard), 180
Highbury Fields demo, 209–12
Hildyard, Nick, 236, 238, 242,
  243, 244
Hill, Christopher, 311
Hill, Lord, 122
Hiro, Dilip, 367–8
History Man, The (Bradbury), 309
Hitler, Adolf, 23
Hockney, David, 214
Hoggart, Simon, 122
Holdsworth, David, 247
holidays: average paid, 417;
  increase in foreign, 420
Hollingsworth, Mark, 458
homosexuality *see* gay rights and
  politics
Hornsey College of Art, 310
Hoskyns, John, 283, 284, 441–2,
  469, 498, 518
hospitals: strikes, 471–8;
  Westminster, 469–70, 471–8, 479
House of Lords: abolition, 509
houses: council-house sales, 422–3,
  431, 433; prices, 127, 176, 420
Howard, Michael, 155
Howe, Geoffrey: and Conservative

Party 1975 leadership contest, 261, 265; and free-market ideas, 276–7; on length of Wilson–Callaghan government, 414; as Opposition adviser to Thatcher, 283, 284; and Sherman, 279, 284; in Thatcher's government, 518; and Tory Opposition pay policy, 475; and trade unions, 57

Huckfield, Leslie, 68

Hudd, Roy, 462

Huddle, Roger, 448–51, 453

Hull, 484–91, 493, 523

Hurd, Douglas: on 1970 election, 10, 11, 12, 14, 18; on 1972 miners' strike, 86, 130; on Heath and Europe, 88, 90; at Heath's funeral, 155; on Heath's press conferences, 9–10

Hutber, Patrick, 177, 178

Hutton, Graham, 273–4

I'm All Right, Jack (film), 440–1

Ice Age, The (Drabble), 127, 179

IEA *see* Institute of Economic Affairs

IMF *see* International Monetary Fund

immigration *see* race issues

Imperial Typewriters, 369, 370

'In Place of Strife', 56, 295, 327–8

India, 415

Indian Workers' Associations, 369

industrial relations: oil industry, 207–8; *see also* strikes; trade unions

Industrial Relations Act (1971), 58–9, 215

inflation: under Callaghan, 404, 436, 438; and EEC, 90; under Heath, 47, 127, 281; stagflation, 129–30, 172; under Thatcher, 518; under Wilson, 163, 172–3, 322

Ink magazine, 223, 226

Institute of Contemporary Arts, 287

Institute of Economic Affairs (IEA), 48, 149, 154, 271–8, 280, 329

interest rates, 127, 128

International Marxist Group, 71

International Monetary Fund (IMF): creation, 317, 318; loans to Britain, 319–21, 339–57

International Socialists *see* Socialist Workers Party

internment, 109–11

'Into the Eighties', 410

investment, foreign, 175–6

IRA, Official, 104, 105, 114

IRA, Provisional: in eighties, 518; foundation, 104–6; Heath government talks, 114–15; internment, 109–11; late seventies, 454, 456; and Ross McWhirter's death, 378; mainland campaign, 117–20, 124; strategy, 106

Iranian Revolution, 480

Irish National Liberation Army, 509

Isle of Wight festival, 245, 248

Italy, 16, 344

J. H. Richards (company), 78, 85

Japan, 16

Jarman, Derek, 181

Jay, Anthony, 477–8

Jay, Douglas, 337, 338

Jay, Margaret, 337

Jay, Peggy, 337

Jay, Peter: appearance and background, 337; on Callaghan and trade unions, 438; and Callaghan's 1976 Labour Party conference speech, 336, 337, 339; on Callaghan's view of self, 410; family, 337, 523–4; and monetarism, 337–9; on Wilson, 163, 178; on Winter of

Discontent, 474
Jenkin, Patrick, 134–6
Jenkins, Peter, 510
Jenkins, Roy: Blair on, 1; on *Economist* cover, 11–12; and free festivals, 249, 257, 258; and Grunwick, 390; and IMF, 319; and Labour Party 1976 leadership contest, 323; Labour plots to replace Wilson with, 160–1; and Northern Ireland, 123; at Oxford, 20; in Wilson's sixties governments, 18
Jesus College, Oxford, 158
Jimmy Young Programme (radio), 472–3
Johnson, Boris, 46
Johnson, Paul, 287, 288
Jonathan Cape (company), 309
Jones, Bob, 475–6, 518
Jones, Evelyn, 299–300
Jones, Jack: appearance and character, 294–5, 299, 300–1; background, 293–4; Blair on, 1; and Callaghan, 328; and CP, 62; and Grunwick, 402; and Heath, 24–5, 57, 296; and IMF cuts, 355; influence, 297–9, 300–1; lifestyle, 290, 299–300; media and Establishment attitude to, 301; retirement, 434–5; and the social contract, 292–301, 435–8; and Spanish Civil War, 24–5, 294; and TGWU Centre, 302–6
Jones, Michael, 306
Joseph, Keith: background and character, 260–1; and Conservative Party 1975 leadership contest, 260–1, 263; 'eugenics' speech, 261, 281; and free-market ideas, 276, 278, 279, 280–1; in Heath's government, 35; and NAFF, 393; as Opposition adviser to Thatcher, 283; Sherman on, 279; and

speech making, 283; in Thatcher's government, 518
Jubilee (film), 181

Kagan, Joseph, 169
Kaufman, Gerald, 497
Kavanagh, Dennis, 509, 517
Keele University, 308
Kemp, Professor Alex, 192
Kennedy, John F., 415
Keynes, John Maynard, 21–2, 317–19, 322
Khmer Rouge, 242
Kinnock, Neil, 168, 174, 508
Kissinger, Henry, 328, 342
Kitson, Alex, 492
Kneath, D. N., 326
Koestler, Arthur, 17

'Labour Isn't Working' campaign, 458–9
Labour Party: 1976 conference, 333, 335–7, 339–41; 1976 leadership contest, 323–5; 1979 manifesto, 509; changes in traditional Labour movement, 418–19, 420–1; Lib–Lab pact, 408–9, 439; New Labour foreshadowings, 420–1, 509, 517; nowadays, 522; opinion poll ratings in 1978, 405; relations with unions, 288–301; and Scottish devolution, 195, 196, 197–8, 501–2; and trade union vote, 161; and Transport House, 289; TUC–Labour Party Liaison Committee, 289–90, 291, 410; vote in 1979 election, 517
Laker, Freddie, 420
Lally, Jack, 73, 76
Lamb, Larry, 285–6
Lambert, Gavin, 477
Lancaster University, 308
Larkin, Philip, 493
Laura Ashley (company), 241

Law, Andrew Bonar, 97
Law, Roger, 452
Lawson, Nigel, 442
Led Zeppelin, 241
Leicester University, 308
Leigh-on-Sea, 43
leisure, 416–18
Leninism Under Lenin (Liebman), 309
Lennon, John, 120–1, 214, 250
Lerwick, 203, 204
Lessing, Doris, 179
Liberal Democratic Party, 522
Liberal Party: and 1974 (Feb) election, 151–3; and fall of Callaghan government, 505, 507; Heath invites to join government, 153; Lib–Lab pact, 408–9, 439; and Scottish devolution, 501
Liberty and Property Defence League, 269
Liebman, Marcel, 309
Limits to Growth, The, 234
Lindsay, A. D., 20, 21
Linklater, Peter, 207
literature, 179–80
Little Red Struggler, The, 307–8
living standards, 176–7, 404
Lloyd George, David, 114, 148
London: Brent, 359, 366; Brent Cross shopping centre, 420; Brick Lane, 447–8; Brown's hotel, 342–3; Camden Lock, 245; Covent Garden: Middle Earth, 214; docklands regeneration, 420; East End, 38; IRA attacks and sympathizers, 118–20, 123; King's Cross station, 42; Ladbroke Grove, 212–13, 216, 218; Nossiter on habitability, 416; Notting Hill, 216–17, 312–13; Portobello market, 217–18; Smith Square: Transport House, 289, 290; squats, 245; Stoke Newington, 232; Thames

Barrier, 35; Victoria Park, 451–2; Westminster Hospital, 469–70, 471–8, 479; Willesden, 359
London Gay Switchboard, 219
London School of Economics (LSE), 211, 270, 283
London Women's Liberation Workshop, 224, 225
Londonderry, 99, 105; Bloody Sunday, 111–13; Bogside, 100, 111–13; Operation Motorman, 114
lorry drivers *see* road hauliers
Los Angeles, 424–5
LSE *see* London School of Economics
Lumsden, Andrew, 216–17
Lydon, John (Johnny Rotten), 4

McCaffrey, Tom, 482–3
McCartney, Paul, 121
McCusker, Harold, 506
MacDonald, Ramsay, 148
McEwan, Ian, 180
McGahey, Mick, 62, 130, 131
McGrandle, Leith, 207
McGuinness, Martin, 115
McHugh, Peter, 464
McIntosh, Ronald: on North Sea oil production, 192, 194; seventies pessimism, 4–5, 177; on Thatcher becoming Conservative Party leader, 265; on Wilson, 164
MacKeown, Brendon, 187–8
McKie, David, 39
McLaren, Charlie, 59–61, 68, 70, 73, 74–5, 80, 81–2, 83
Macleod, Iain, 31, 47
Macmillan, Harold, 22, 338, 411
McNally, Tom: and 1979 election, 510; Callaghan cautions about bawdy stories, 407; on Callaghan's Barbados visit, 482; and Callaghan's decision to postpone election, 459, 460, 463; and

Callaghan's economic measures, 323, 329, 336; on Guadeloupe summit, 480; on seventies industry, 457; and Winter of Discontent, 482–3, 494

Mac Stíofáin, Seán, 104, 106, 115, 117

McSweeney, Richard, 347–8

McWhirter, Norris, 377–8, 379, 382

McWhirter, Ross, 377–8

Maidstone, 96

Mailer, Norman, 221–2

Major, John, 155

Majority news-sheet, 378

Manchester: Arndale centre, 420

Manifesto for a Sustainable Society, 243

Mansfield Hosiery Mills, 369

Maplin, 35–46

Maplin Movement, 42

Marxism: campus radicalism, 307–13

Mason, Angela (Angie Weir), 219, 225

Mason, Roy, 454

materialism *see* consumerism

maternity leave, 231

Maudling, Reginald: and 1972 miners' strike, 79, 80, 83–4; and Northern Ireland, 107, 112, 117; on picketing law, 68

Measure of Domestic Progress (MDP), 4

media: newspaper coverage of Winter of Discontent, 466–7; newspaper problems, 285; Northern Ireland coverage, 122–3; publishers and left-wing radicalism, 309

Melchett, Lord Peter, 256–8

MI5, 167, 168–9, 301, 376

Middle Class Association, 376, 377

Middle Way, The (Macmillan), 22

Middlemas, Keith, 172, 322

Middlesex Polytechnic, 309–12

Miliband, Ralph, 311

Millar, Ronald, 278

Miller, Henry, 221–2

Millett, Kate, 221–2

Milligan, Stephen, 54, 295

Mills, John Platts, 386

Milton Keynes, 423–33; Heelands, 429–30; Netherfield, 428–9; shopping centre, 432–3

mining and miners: comparative pay, 61; history of, 59–61; *see also* National Union of Mineworkers

Mises, Ludwig von, 270

Miss World contest, 224

Monday Club, 381

Money Programme, The (TV series), 181–2

money supply and monetarism, 273, 322–3, 329, 335–57, 421–2

moral values: Callaghan on, 407

Morgan, Kenneth O., 329, 444, 461

Morris, Jamie, 469–79

Moss, Robert, 413

Mountfield, Peter, 197

Movement for Survival, 239

Moyle, Roland, 470

Murdoch, Rupert, 31, 286, 521

Murray, Len, 402, 476

music, 178

Mussolini, Benito, 23

Nabokov, Vladimir, 271

NAFF *see* National Association for Freedom

Nairn, Tom, 178

National Association for Freedom (NAFF), 375–83, 386, 388, 393–4, 395–401

National Coal Board: and 1972 miners' strike, 63, 87; 1973 negotiations with miners, 130–1; and 1981 miners' dispute, 519; under

Robens, 61

National Economic Development Council: creation, 17–18

National Front (NF), 368, 445–8, 450–2, 517

National Pensioners Convention, 295

National Union of Mineworkers (NUM): 1969 and 1970 strikes (unofficial), 70; 1971 conference, 225; 1972 strike, 63–87; 1974 strike, 145–7, 148, 149, 170; 1981 dispute, 519; and Grunwick, 388–9, 403; Heath on, 58; militancy, 60–3; and three-day week, 130–2; see also Scargill, Arthur

National Union of Public Employees (NUPE), 230, 470–7, 513, 518; see also Fisher, Alan

National Union of Railwaymen, 26, 57

National Union of Seamen, 378

National Women's Liberation Conference, 224, 225, 232

nationalization, 17, 48, 200

Neal, Len, 4–5

Neave, Airey: and Conservative Party 1975 leadership contest, 260–1, 264; death, 509; and free festivals, 253, 256; home, 395; relations with Heath, 260; and trade unions, 376

Nehru, Jawaharlal, 369

Nelson, Elizabeth, 209

Netherlands, 39, 40, 41

New Barons, The (Milligan), 54, 295

New Labour: foreshadowings of, 420–1, 509, 517

New Left Books, 309

New Town programme, 424, 425

New York, 346

New Zealand, 91, 134

newspapers: coverage of Winter of Discontent, 466–7; seventies problems, 285; see also media

Newton, Huey, 214

NF see National Front

Nigg, 192–5

Night Assembles Bill, 248

1922 Committee, 260

Nixon, Richard, 521

Noakes, John, 65–6

Nolan Sisters, 434

NORAID, 112

North Sea, 190

North Sea oil: Benn's attempt to partially nationalize, 200–1; discovery and potential impact, 187–90; effect on Aberdeen, 205–6; extraction technology, 192; Forties oilfield opened, 185–7; industrial relations, 207–8; licences and taxation, 199; oil rig construction, 192–5; oil rig life, 190–2, 206–8; output stats and costs, 198–9; and Scottish independence, 195–8; Sullom Voe terminal, 201–5

Northern Ireland: 1974 strike, 170; annual casualties, 117; author's childhood memories of army in, 95–7; Bloody Sunday, 111–13; British and RUC interrogation techniques, 110–11, 454; British public attitude to Troubles, 116–17, 120–2, 139; Direct Rule, 108–9, 113, 116; economy, 98–9; in eighties, 518; and Heath government, 107–24, 170; Heath government talks with Provisionals, 114–15; history of British involvement, 97, 102–3; internment, 109–11; IRA mainland campaign, 117–20, 124; late seventies, 453–7, 505–6; loyalist organizations, 116; media coverage, 122–3; power-sharing Executive, 170; Troops Out

Movement, 121; Troubles start, 99–100, 103–6; and Wilson government, 170; *see also* IRA
Northern Ireland Civil Rights Association, 98
Norway, 197, 200, 208
Nossiter, Bernard D., 415–18
novels, 179–80
nuclear power, 238, 244
nuclear weapons, 479, 480, 509
NUM *see* National Union of Mineworkers
NUPE *see* National Union of Public Employees

O Lucky Man! (film), 181
O'Connell, David, 118, 120
O'Dwyer, Sir Michael, 369
office heating, 133
oil: 1973 crisis, 45, 128–30, 138; British consumption, 61; *see also* North Sea oil
oil rigs, 190–2, 192–5
On the Buses (TV series), 16
O'Neill, Terence, 99, 100
OPEC *see* Organization of Petroleum Exporting Countries
Open University, 427
Operation Motorman, 114
Orange Order, 120
Organization of Petroleum Exporting Countries (OPEC), 129, 197
Outrage!, 219
Oz magazine, 222, 223

Pankhurst, Christabel, 220
Parker, Stanley, 417–18
Parliamentary Socialism (Miliband), 311
'Part of the Union' (Strawbs), 292–3
pay: under Callaghan, 461; under Heath government, 65; public-sector workers, 471–6; restraint

under Wilson government, 298; and social contract, 434–40; trade unions and wage protection, 177; women's, 141, 221, 230–1; *see also* Winter of Discontent
Peel, John, 144
Pencourt File, The (Penrose and Courtiour), 166–8
Penguin Modern Masters series, 309
Penrose, Barry, 166–8
pensions, 231
PEOPLE Party *see* Ecology Party
Petit, Chris, 181
petrol shortages, 139
Philip, Prince, Duke of Edinburgh, 94, 185–6, 249
pickets: 1969 miners' strike, 70; 1972 miners' strike, 64, 65, 68–9, 70–83; 1974 miners' strike, 148; flying, 70–83; Grunwick, 385–94, 403; legislation, 68, 84; road hauliers' strike, 489, 491, 492, 493
Pimlott, Ben, 168
Pink Floyd, 178
Pinochet, General Augusto, 382, 434
Plaid Cymru, 499, 503, 506, 517
Platt, John, 433
plays, 180
Pliatzky, Sir Leo, 172, 345
Poliakoff, Stephen, 180
police: and 1972 miners' strike, 75–9, 81–3; brutality, 78; and free festivals, 246–8, 249, 254, 255; and Grosvenor Square riots, 327; and Grunwick, 384, 385, 387–90, 391–2; and NF, 447–8; picket tactics, 387–8; Special Patrol Group, 76, 77; TV series about, 287; *see also* Royal Ulster Constabulary
Policy Unit, 162, 163

political trends: Albion Free State, 244–59; environmentalism, 37–8, 234–44; feminism, 220–33; gay rights, 209–20, 224–5, 227, 286; left-wing campus radicalism, 307–13; monetarism, 273, 322–3, 329, 335–57, 421–2; right-wing semi-revolutionary fringe groups, 376–80; right-wing students, 399–400; rise of the right, 268–88

Poltergeist, 254

Pompidou, Georges, 90–1

population, 15, 175

Population Bomb, The (Ehrlich), 234

Porritt, Jonathon, 244

Portugal, 308

Post, Laurens van der, 236

pound *see* sterling

poverty, 16–17, 409–10

Powell, Enoch: and Europe, 92, 149; and free-market ideas, 276; and immigration, 445; and Labour Party, 149, 151; resignation, 149; and Thatcher, 442, 447; trade-union attitude, 367

Power, Lisa, 216

power cuts: 1972 miners' strike, 65–6; *see also* three-day week

Prentice, Reg, 287, 288

Prevention of Terrorism Act (1974), 123

prices: food and the EEC, 90, 91, 95; food subsidies, 297; houses, 127, 176, 420; oil, 128, 129; Resale Price Maintenance abolition, 26, 48; *see also* inflation

Prior, Jim: on 1970 election, 10; and 1974 miners' strike, 148; and Conservative Party 1975 leadership contest, 261, 265; and NAFF, 393; and trade unions, 440; and Winter of Discontent, 474

Private Eye, 168

privatization, 48, 406

productivity: and three-day week, 142–3

Prostitution (COUM), 287

public expenditure: under Callaghan, 332, 344, 349–57, 406, 407; under Heath, 35; Northern Ireland, 97; under Wilson, 172, 323

public-sector workers, 177

publishers: and left-wing radicalism, 309

punk, 178

Pursey, Jimmy, 450–1

Purves, Peter, 65–6

race issues: discrimination legislation, 444–5; immigrants and race relations, 442–53; immigrants and work, 367–70

Race Relations Act (1976), 444–5

Radio On (Petit), 181

Ramelson, Baruch 'Bert', 62

Ramsey, Chris, 207–8

Ranelagh, John, 410, 411–12

Ransome, Dave, 420–1

RAR *see* Rock Against Racism

Rawle, Sid, 250–2, 255, 256, 257, 258, 312

Record Breakers (TV series), 378

Red Mole newspaper, 120

Reece, Gordon, 412, 458

Reed, Laurance, 189

Rees, Merlyn, 451, 497

Rees-Mogg, William, 283

reggae, 178

Reid, Billy, 106

Reid, Jamie, 181

Release, 247–8, 249

Resurgence magazine, 37

Ridley, Nicholas, 376, 397

'Right Approach, The', 413–14

Right Turn, 287–8

Rippon, Geoffrey, 40, 42, 45

Road Haulage Association, 487
road hauliers: strike (1979), 482,
    484–94; working conditions,
    485–6
Road to Serfdom, The (Hayek),
    268–9
Robens, Lord, 61
Roberts, Alfred, 266–7
Roberts, Beatrice, 266
Robinson, Christopher, 306
Robinson, Tom, 451, 452
Rock Against Racism (RAR),
    448–53
Rodgers, Bill: on Callaghan's post-
    ponement of election, 461,
    462–3; and civil service, 497; and
    road hauliers' strike, 487, 491–4;
    on the social contract, 437; and
    trade unions, 298–9
Roe, Nicholas, 490–1, 493
Rolls-Royce, 48, 366
Rose, Sir Clive, 481–2, 492, 496–7
Roskill Commission, 37, 38
Rothschild, Lord, 129
Rotten, Johnny see Lydon, John
Routledge, Paul, 87
Rowbotham, Sheila, 229
Rowe, Marsha, 222–8, 229, 232–3
Royal Ulster Constabulary (RUC),
    99, 110, 454
Rutherford, Andrew, 458
Ryrie, William, 320–1, 356

Saatchi, Maurice, 458
Saatchi and Saatchi, 458–9
Saltley coke depot, 66–9, 71–86
Sampson, Anthony, 19, 29
Samuel, Raphael, 55–6
Saunders, Red, 449, 450
Savareid, Eric, 177–8
Saville inquiry, 112
Saxon, Arthur, 67
Scales, Prunella, 434
Scanlon, Hugh, 297, 301
Scargill, Arthur: and 1972 miners'

strike, 71–4, 78–9, 80–1, 82, 83,
    84; and 1981 miners' dispute,
    519; appearance, 53; background
    and character, 69–70; and
    Grunwick, 388–9, 401; militant
    attitude, 53, 130; and TGWU
    Centre, 305
Scarman, Lord, 394, 401
Schmidt, Helmut, 342, 479
Schumacher, E. F., 241
Scorpio, 253
Scotland: assembly building, 197;
    devolution process, 501–4; inde-
    pendence and North Sea oil,
    195–8
Scott, Norman, 408
Scottish Labour Party, 506–7
Scottish National Party (SNP): and
    1979 election, 517; Edinburgh
    HQ, 197; and fall of Callaghan
    government, 505, 507; founda-
    tion and early history, 195–6;
    and Labour Party, 499; and
    North Sea oil, 196–8
Scunthorpe, 75
SDR see Special Drawing Right
Sea Gem oil rig, 192
Seabrook, Jeremy, 418–19, 420–1
Second Sex, The (de Beauvoir), 221
Seldon, Arthur, 273, 275, 276–7,
    278, 283
Self-Help, 378
Selfridges department store, 383–4
Sellers, Peter, 441
Selsdon conference, 30–2, 58
Sewill, Brendon: and 1972 miners'
    strike, 65; and 1974 (Feb) elec-
    tion, 148; on importance of full
    employment, 47; and plans for
    Heath government, 30; and
    three-day week, 143; on trade-
    union power, 59
Sex Discrimination Act (1975), 231
Sex Pistols, The, 4, 178
Sexual Politics (Millett), 221–2

Sham 69, 450–1
Shanks, Michael, 17
Shell, 199, 207
Sherman, Alfred, 279–83, 284, 379, 413, 424
Shetland islands, 201–5
Shoeburyness, 45
shopping centres, 420, 432–3
Shore, Peter, 351–2
Silent Spring (Carson), 234
Simon, William, 320, 345–9, 355
Singh, Udham, 369
Sivanandan, Ambalavaner, 444
Skytrain, 420
Slater, Jim, 33
Slater Walker, 33–4
Small Is Beautiful (Schumacher), 241
Smith, Adam, 270, 272
Smith, Graham, 379–80, 396–7, 399–400
Smith, John, 506
SNP see Scottish National Party
social contract, 288–301, 434–40
Social Democratic Alliance, 301
social mobility, 409–10
Social Security Pensions Act (1975), 231
social trends: rise of materialism, 418–20; see also political trends
Socialist Workers Party (SWP; formerly International Socialists), 71, 449–50
South Africa, 166–7, 479
South Armagh, 454–7
Southend, 41–2, 43
Soviet Union, 308, 413
Spanish Civil War, 23–5
Spare Rib magazine, 224–30, 232, 372, 512–13
Spark, Muriel, 179
Special Drawing Right (SDR), 319
speed limit, 134
sports centres, 417
Spycatcher (Wright), 168

stagflation see inflation
Stanley, John, 283
Steel, David, 408, 442, 511
Stelzer, Irwin, 521
sterling: 1967 devaluation, 18, 327; 1976 run on, 330–57; pound's value, 17, 128
Stevens, Caroline, 515
Stirling, Colonel David, 376, 377
Stirling University, 308
stock market, 127, 176, 322
Stone, Joe, 164, 165–6
Stone, Richard, 164–6
Stonewall, 219
Stonewall riots, 214
Stowe, Ken, 163, 515
Strauss, Norman, 283, 284
Strawberry Fields (Poliakoff), 180
Strawbs, 292–3
street lighting, 133, 135
strikes: British Asians, 369; dockers (1972), 387; Ford (1978), 464; government emergency machinery, 481; Grunwick, 358–403; legislation, 58–9, 68, 84; miners (1969 and 1970), 70; miners (1972), 63–87; miners (1974), 145–7, 148, 149, 170; Northern Ireland (1974), 170; rise in frequency, 56; road hauliers (1979), 482, 484–94; seamen (1975), 378; students, 311–12; Westminster Hospital, 471–8; Winter of Discontent, 464–96; working days lost to, 404, 441, 465; see also Advisory, Conciliation and Arbitration Service; pickets
Sturdy, Pat, 229–30
Sullom Voe, 201–5
Summer Before the Dark, The (Lessing), 179
Sun, 31, 123, 285–6
Sweden, 54
Sweeney, The (TV series), 287

SWP *see* Socialist Workers Party

Takeover, The (Spark), 179
Tanganyika, 44
Tartan Army, 185
Tatchell, Peter, 219
Tate gallery, 286
taxes, 406
Taylor, Anne, 506
Taylor, Gordon Rattray, 234
Taylor, Robert, 55, 292, 440
Tebbit, Norman, 44, 414
television: evening closedown, 133, 147
Thames Barrier, 35
Thatcher, Carol, 270, 415, 514
Thatcher, Denis, 270, 415, 514
Thatcher, Margaret: on 1970 election, 12; and 1979 election, 508, 509–10, 510–15, 516–17; advantages over Callaghan, 414; advisers in Opposition, 283–4, 412; Amis on, 282–3; appearance, 497; author's verdict, 524; background and character, 261–2, 266–8, 276, 512; on British politics in late 1978, 405; on Callaghan's postponement of election, 463; Cameron on, 1; cartoon owned by Heath, 27–8; and Conservative Party 1975 leadership contest, 261–6, 282, 410; and council-house sales, 422, 423, 433; and fall of Callaghan government, 504; and feminism, 230, 512–13; first visit to US, 329–30; Flood Street home, 282; foreign policy, 413; and free-market ideas, 268–84; and Grunwick, 392–4, 401; and Harris, 271; and Heath, 27–8, 277, 411–12; at Heath's funeral, 155, 156; in Heath's government, 35, 262, 276, 277–8; and IMF loan, 342; and immigration, 442–3, 446–7; and 'Labour Isn't Working' campaign, 459; lack of leisure habits, 418; and Lib–Lab pact, 408–9; on McWhirter (Ross), 378; marriage and family, 270; and Milton Keynes, 433; and miners, 519; and NAFF, 377, 378–9, 393–4; on the Open University, 427; as Opposition leader, 410–15; as PM, 518–20; political and popular appeal, 262, 277–8, 285–8; as product of the seventies, 3; on Saltley, 84; on three-day week, 148; and trade unions, 57, 440–2, 468–9, 472–3, 474, 518; TV performance, 412–13; and Winter of Discontent, 468–9, 472–3, 474
Thatcher, Mark, 270, 415
theatre *see* plays
Theroux, Paul, 179
Thirteen Club, 240
Thomas, Hugh, 287
Thomas Cook (company), 48
Thorneycroft, Peter, 510, 514
Thorpe, Jeremy, 151, 152, 153, 166–7, 408
three-day week: background, 128–32; end, 170; impact, 138–44; productivity during, 142–3; rules, 133–4; was it necessary?, 144–5
Times, The, 92, 93
Tipi Valley, 250
Torrey Canyon, 234
Trade and Industry, Department of, 33, 34, 81
trade figures, 18, 95, 127–8, 150
trade unions: and Callaghan's postponement of election, 463; and equality, 437; and gay rights movement, 215; government relations to 1970, 56–7; and Grunwick, 360–403; and Heath's government, 57–9, 150; history

of British, 54; and IMF cuts, 345, 355; influence in seventies, 64; and Labour government, 288; and Labour vote, 161; and materialism, 419, 435; membership statistics, 437; militancy, 54–6; NAFF campaigns against, 375–8; nowadays, 522–3; organization, 55; public attitude to, 440–1; and race issues, 367–9; shop stewards, 55; and the social contract, 288–301, 434–40; and Thatcher, 57, 440–2, 468–9, 472–3, 474, 518; wage protection, 177; and Wilson's government, 390; and women, 225, 229–30, 231; see also individual unions by name; strikes

Trades Union Congress (TUC): 1978 conference, 461–2; and free festivals, 248; and Grunwick, 394, 402; and the social contract, 436, 437–8, 439; TUC–Labour Party Liaison Committee, 289–90, 291, 410; Valentine's Day concordat, 505; Williams on, 290

Transport and General Workers' Union (TGWU): and 1972 miners' strike, 74; Eastbourne holiday centre, 302–6; and Ford strike, 464; and Grunwick, 366; HQ, 289, 295; membership size and scope, 55, 292, 305; nowadays, 523; and road hauliers' strike, 485, 486, 489–91, 491–3; Rodgers on, 491; and the social contract, 435–6; and Winter of Discontent, 467, 485; see also Jones, Jack

'Treasures from the European Community' (exhibition), 94
TUC see Trades Union Congress
Tuohy, Denis, 511
Twine, Adam, 259

2000AD comic, 287
Twomey, Seamus, 115

Ulster Defence Association (UDA), 116
Ulster Unionist Party, 505–6, 507
Ulster Vanguard, 116
Ulster Workers' Council (UWC), 170
unemployment: before 1970, 16; under Callaghan, 404, 457–9; under Heath, 47, 49; Northern Ireland, 99; seventies overview, 3; under Thatcher, 518; and three-day week, 145; and women, 229
Union of Post Office Workers (UPW), 375, 382, 395, 400–1
Unite, 523
United Nations Continental Shelf Convention, 188
United States: attitude to British economic policy, 320–1, 329–30, 345; and Bretton Woods, 317–19; Callaghan seeks loan from, 342; Callaghan's relations with, 328; cruise-missile deployment in Europe, 479; and IMF, 320; Kennedy and the corporations, 415; mid-seventies economy, 346; New Deal, 35; and North Sea oil, 197; and Northern Ireland, 112
universities: campus left-wing radicalism, 307–13
UPW see Union of Post Office Workers
UWC see Ulster Workers' Council

Valentine's Day concordat, 505
Verney, Stephen, 249, 250, 251
Verso, 309
Victoria Park demo, 451–3
Vietnam War, 308

wages see pay

Walden, Brian, 275, 468–9, 519
Wales, devolution process, 502; *see also* Plaid Cymru
Walker, Derek, 424–6, 429, 430–3
Walker, Martin, 446
Walker, Peter: appearance, 34; background, 33–4; and Conservative Party 1975 leadership contest, 261; and environmental movement, 238–9; and free festivals, 248; and free-market ideas, 279; on Heath's government, 34–5; on Macmillan on Thatcher, 411; and Maplin, 38; at Selsdon conference, 30–1; and Thames Barrier, 35; and three-day week, 132, 137, 143; as trade and industry secretary, 34
Walker, General Sir Walter, 376, 377, 393, 397
Walters, Alan, 44, 281
Wandor, Michelene, 223
Ward, George: background, 358; and Grunwick, 358–65, 373–6, 382, 385–6, 388, 392, 395, 396–7, 402
Warwick University, 308
Wass, Sir Douglas, 335
Watchfield festival, 252–9
Watership Down (Adams), 241
Watters, Frank, 72, 73, 75
Weatherill, Bernard, 501
Weatherstone, Dennis, 330
Webb, Richard, 75, 76, 77, 78, 79, 81
Webster, Roger, 375–6
Weekend World (TV series), 337
Weidenfeld, Sir George, 169
Weir, Angie *see* Mason, Angela
Weir, Stuart, 388, 389
well-being: Britain's best year, 4; late seventies, 416–18
Wells of Mayfair, 347, 348
West Mill Farm, 258–9

whipping: parliamentary, 498–501
White, Harry, 318
White, Michael, 454
Whitehouse, Mary, 286
Whitelaw, Willie: and 1970 election, 14; character, 107; and Conservative Party 1975 leadership contest, 261, 265; favoured to replace Thatcher in seventies, 411; and Northern Ireland, 107–8, 109, 115, 170
Whittome, Alan, 343–5, 349, 354
Widgery, David, 450, 451, 452
Widgery report, 111–12
Wigan, 418
Wilberforce, Lord, 86
Wild, Eric, 254–5
Willesden Friendship League, 368
Williams, Marcia, 161, 167
Williams, Shirley: appearance, 497; Blair on, 1; and Grunwick, 384; public attitude to, 262; and the social contract, 437; and TUC–Labour Party Liaison Committee, 290; on Wilson, 163, 166
Wills, Robert, 397–9
Wilson, Amrit, 372
Wilson, Harold: on 1970 Conservative policies, 31; and 1970 election, 9–14, 18; and 1974 elections, 150–1, 153, 157–8, 161, 170–1; and alcohol, 164–5; appearance, 150; background, 158; and Benn's radical ideas, 174–5; character, 9, 157, 159, 160; and council-house sales, 423; economic measures, 297, 321–3; economic training, 18; on *Economist* cover, 11–12; electioneering style, 149, 160; health, 164–6; and Heath's entry into Europe, 92, 94; and Heath's trade union reform, 58; homes, 298; and Jay (Peter), 337, 338;

Jones on, 295–6; kitchen cabinet, 161; lack of ambition in 1974, 161–3; and North Sea oil, 185–6, 199; and Northern Ireland, 100, 170; at Oxford, 158–9; plots to replace him, 160–1; political career to 1964, 159–60; resignation, 321; and Scottish devolution, 196; and security services, 166–9; sixties governments, 17–18, 56, 89–90, 100, 160–1; on Thatcher becoming Conservative Party leader, 265; and trade unions, 291, 295–6; Walden on, 275; and women's rights, 163, 230–1

Wilson, Herbert, 158

Wilson, Mary, 9, 157

Wilson, Trevor, 391–2

Windsor festival, 246–8, 248–50

Winstanley (film), 312

Winstanley, Gerrard, 312

Winter of Discontent, 464–97; Callaghan's handling, 464–5, 479–84, 494–5; road hauliers' strike, 482 484–94; Westminster Hospital strike, 471–8

Witteveen, Johannes, 319, 349, 354

Wolff, Michael, 147

Wollstonecraft, Mary, 220

women: and 1979 election, 516; Asian women and strikes, 370–2; and Grunwick strike, 385; legislation, 230–1; as MPs, 228; public and media misogyny, 262; radical feminism, 232; rise of feminism, 220–33; socialist feminism, 232–3; Thatcher's non-promotion of, 230, 512–13; and three-day week, 141; Wilson's promotion of, 163, 230–1

Women and Equality Unit, 219

Women's Industrial Union, 229–30

Woodnutt, Mark, 248

Worcester, Robert, 460

Workers' Revolutionary Party, 71

working conditions: hours, 142–3, 417–18; legislation under Wilson, 297; and women, 228–31; *see also* industrial relations; strikes, trade unions

World Bank, 317

World Turned Upside Down, The (Hill), 311

Worthing festival, 246

Wortley Hall, 85

Wright, Peter, 168

Wyatt, Woodrow, 63

Yarwood, Mike, 434

Yeo, Edwin, 349

Yes, Minister (TV series), 477

Yom Kippur War, 128, 129

York, Peter, 29, 178, 285, 415, 419

Young, Hugo, 147

Young, Janet, 514

Zorch, 254

Jones on, 205–6; kitchen table